THE OXFORD INDIA ANTHOLOGY OF BUSINESS HISTORY

'Drawing on a large scholarly literature this magisterial anthology traces the workings of Indian business from its "bazaar" economy, its distinctive "merchant communities", their characteristic family firms, on to the rise of Indian industry, to provide an exemplary guide to its role in India's spectacular economic growth.'

—**Anthony Low**
Emeritus Smuts Professor of Commonwealth History
University of Cambridge

'This innovative and carefully planned collection bridges the past and the present, the traditional and the modern, of Indian business better than any comparable work in the field. The book will prove indispensable for those interested in business history and the interface between business and economic change in modern India.'

—**Tirthankar Roy**
Reader in Economic History
London School of Economics and Political Science

'*The Oxford India Anthology of Business History* is a superb collection of some of the best pieces of writings on Indian business. Individually the essays in this volume explain different aspects of Indian business. Together they provide a valuable perspective for understanding business behaviour in the country. The volume as such holds a great deal of interest for students, teachers, and researchers in history—particularly economic, social, and business history—business management, and economics. For general readers, too, it will be a rewarding reading.'

—**Dwijendra Tripathi**
Former Kasturbhai Lalbhai Professor of Business History
Indian Institute of Management Ahmedabad

THE OXFORD INDIA ANTHOLOGY OF BUSINESS HISTORY

EDITED BY
Medha M. Kudaisya

OXFORD
UNIVERSITY PRESS

OXFORD
UNIVERSITY PRESS

YMCA Library Building, Jai Singh Road, New Delhi 110 001

Oxford University Press is a department of the University of Oxford. It furthers the University's objective of excellence in research, scholarship, and education by publishing worldwide in

Oxford New York
Auckland Cape Town Dar es Salaam Hong Kong Karachi Kuala Lumpur Madrid Melbourne Mexico City Nairobi New Delhi Shanghai Taipei Toronto

With offices in
Argentina Austria Brazil Chile Czech Republic France Greece Guatemala Hungary Italy Japan Poland Portugal Singapore South Korea Switzerland Thailand Turkey Ukraine Vietnam

Oxford is a registered trademark of Oxford University Press in the UK and in certain other countries

Published in India
by Oxford University Press, New Delhi

First published 2011

ISBN-13: 978-0-19-807019-1
ISBN-10: 0-19-807019-5

Typeset in Adobe Jenson Pro 10.5/13
by Sai Graphic Design, New Delhi 110 55
Printed in India at Rakmo Press Pvt. Ltd., New Delhi 110 020
Published by Oxford University Press
YMCA Library Building, Jai Singh Road, New Delhi 110 001

Contents

II MERCANTILE COMMUNITIES

III FAMILY AND FIRM

IV RISE OF INDIAN INDUSTRY

V BUSINESS IN THE POST-REFORMS ERA

Acknowledgements

I have incurred many debts in the preparation of this Anthology. Foremost, I must thank the many scholars who happily agreed to be part of this project and for their encouragement when they were initially approached about this. I must warmly thank Oxford University Press for encouraging me to undertake such a project and for being wonderfully supportive through the long time it has taken to come to fruition. Thanks are due to the editorial team at the Press for being so supportive, for dealing with many administrative and copyright issues, and for patience with delayed submissions. The encouraging comments from two anonymous readers were most valuable. Thanks are also due to three graduate students who provided part-time research assistance—Shabbir Hussain Mustafa, Bittiandra Chand Somaiah, and Mamta Sachan Kumar.

Introduction
Business History in Twentieth-Century India

As the Indian economy stands poised for sustained economic take-off and its businesses look expectantly towards the future, it may be appropriate to look at the evolution and development of business history in twentieth-century India. Although mercantile tellings —in hagiographic fashion—date back to the late nineteenth and early twentieth centuries, business history writings emerged in the inter-war years at the same time when the discipline was establishing itself as a distinct area at the Harvard Business School.[1] Like elsewhere in the world, especially the United States and Europe, Indian business history developed in the shadow of economic history. Economists searching for the reasons for India's economic 'backwardness' also looked at India's business past, its mercantile communities, its 'business leadership', and its organization.[2] Much writing took place in these years which was driven by a search for the causes of underdevelopment and this remained the dominant theme in the field. It was only in the late 1960s and especially in the 1970s that business history came into its own. Inaugurating the 37th meeting of the Indian Historical Records Commission in 1966, C.D. Deshmukh, then Vice-Chancellor of Delhi University and former Union Finance Minister, was heartened that the topic of discussion was the 'sources and problems of business history from 1600–1900'. In the years to come, business history took off as a vibrant area of research and elicited the attention of a number of scholars who showed an interest in many aspects of the business past—individual firms, entrepreneurs and business houses, business culture, family business, relations between state and business, politics of business,

[1] As is well known, even though business history traces its roots to nineteenth-century German and English scholarship, it only emerged as a distinct area in the mid-1920s. For an understanding of current research in business history, see Franco Amatori and Geoffrey Jones (eds), *Business History around the World* (Cambridge, Cambridge University Press, 2003).

[2] See, for instance, D.H. Buchanan, *The Development of Capitalistic Enterprise in India* (New York, Macmillan, first edition 1934).

and the activities of multinationals. This interest has been sustained and further enlivened since India embraced market reforms in the last two decades.

There were, however, two concerns that Deshmukh raised. He asked if there existed the 'necessary materials for a proper study of the subject in our accessible records—public and private? Are there new sources which we could tap and make them accessible to scholars?' He also worried about the institutional support that such new disciplines were achieving, compared to traditional sub-disciplines such as political history. He queried the members of the Commission: 'But are our universities paying the attention that it is necessary to the other aspects of history?'[3] Deshmukh's concerns remain pertinent even today. Unlike Europe, there has been no tradition of companies opening papers to unknown researchers or of them systematically preserving archives. This has meant that researchers have had to depend mostly on what is available in the public domain and it has also meant that company and firm histories have not been written. Further, business history has lacked institutional backing. It has not found a place in educational institutions, surprisingly not even in a sustained manner in the country's premier business schools; there is no association of business history and there is only one journal devoted to its study in the Indian subcontinent. Despite all this, the field has flourished and it can be safely asserted that even though business history in India continues to struggle to find institutional support, its writing is in good shape. This introduction maps how this has come to be.

MERCANTILE TELLINGS

Business history writing in India has mercantile roots, with an active role having been played by merchants and their organizations. This tradition of writing can be traced back to, at least, the nineteenth and early twentieth centuries, and mercantile histories continue to flourish, albeit in a more modern form, even today.

Such writings take the form of merchant family histories and genealogies, *jati* histories, community histories, *abhinandan granths* (commemorative or celebratory texts), *smriti granths* (remembrances and commemorations), and biographical writings. Merchant family histories and genealogies from the nineteenth century gave valuable accounts of merchant lives and business enterprises. By the early twentieth century, there existed the lineage histories of several major mercantile castes. Thus, there came to be published histories of prominent mercantile castes such as the Maheshwaris, the Oswals, and the Agarwals, which vividly recounted their achievements in the field of trading and philanthropy. Such works either looked at the trading activities of the sub-castes as a whole or the kin group in specific regions. They also took the form of hagiographies of individual traders and their business careers.[4] Further, the studies of mercantile communities such as Balchand Modi's *Desh ke Itihas Mein Marwari Jati ka Sthan* put forth detailed histories of

[3] See Deshmukh's speech in C.D. Deshmukh, *Reflections on Finance, Education and Society* (Delhi, Motilal Banarsidass, 1972).

[4] For the history of *jati* lineages see, for instance, Balchand Modi, *Agarwal Itihas Parichay* (Calcutta, n.d) perhaps written in the 1920s; Satyaketua Vidyalankar, *Agarwal Jati ka Pracheen Itihas* (Delhi, 1938); S.R. Bhandari, *Agarwal Jati ka Itihas* (Indore, Bhanpura, 1934); and S.R. Bhandari, *Maheswari Jati ka Itihas* (Bhanupura, Maheshwari History Office, 1940) and his *Oswal Jati ka Itihas* (Indore, Bhanpura, 1934).

Marwari traders settled in different parts of India, their trade associations and activities, alongside short biographical sketches of prominent bazaar traders.[5]

Then, there are *abhinandan granths* or commemorative texts meant to mark special occasions in the lives of business persons, such as the 60th or 70th birthday considered specially significant in the Hindu Vaishnava tradition. Similarly, key milestones in the firm's history also provided occasions for the publication of such works.[6] Such commemorative volumes were produced not only for prominent businessmen such as Raja Sir Annamalai Chettiar, G.D. Birla, and Walchand Hirachand, but also for traders who operated only at the level of the bazaar and were not well known on the all-India scene.[7] For example, the 60th birthday celebrations of the prominent banker Sir Muthiah Chettiar were celebrated with the publication of *Dr Rajah Sir Muthiah Chettiar and Rani Lady Meyyammai Achi, 60th Birthday Commemoration Volume*. The volume typically contained a large number of 'messages and greetings,' : it also looked at Sir Muthiah's trading and banking empire, his Burmese interests, as well as his political inclinations.[8] Such writings tell us much about the individual entrepreneur and the commercial life and customs of the trading community to which he belonged.[9] Likewise, commemorative publications for bazaar-level traders recount trading trajectories and histories of family firms. Thus, *Rashtra-sevi Shri Hanumanbaksh Kanoi Abhinandan Granth* narrates the business career of trader Hanumanbaksh Kanoi, commencing with his family's mercantile antecedents, the larger Marwari interests in the Assam tea plantations, and then goes on to give details of Kanoi's entry into tea and cloth in late nineteenth century, his speculative activities, the intertwining of family and firm, the impact of the great wars and economic depression upon his fortunes, followed by his acquisition of European-owned tea gardens in the late 1940s

[5] Balchand Modi, *Desh ke Itihas Mein Marwari Jati ka Sthan* (Calcutta, Raghunathprasad Simhaniya, 1940). Also see Bhimsen Kedia, *Bharat Mein Marwari Samaj* (Calcutta,National Publications,1947).

[6] For *abhinandan granths*, see Jalan Nandkishore, *Ishwardas Jalan Abhinandan Granth* (Calcutta, Abhinandan Samiti, 1977); *Basantlal Morarka Smriti Granth* (no author, Calcutta, n.d); *Bhagirath Kanoria Smriti Granth* (no author, Calcutta, n.d); *Sitaram Seksaria Smriti Granth* (no name, Calcutta, 1950); Patodia, Rameshwar Prasad, *Anandilal Poddar Smriti Pushpa* (Calcutta, n.d.); V.O. Sharma, *Maheshwari Jan-Jagriti Darshan* (Nagpur, 1956); Singhi Bhawarlal (ed.), *Padma Bhushan Shri Sitaram Seksaria Abhinandan Granth* (no name, Calcutta, 1974); and (No author), *Shradhanjali Swargiya Jugalkishoreji Birla* (Sanskriti Sansthan, Pilani, 1974). Commemorative volumes written in English include C.A. Buch and S.S. Pendse (eds), *Walchand Diamond Jubilee Commemoration Volume* (Bombay, 1942). For birthday commemorations, see Staff of Chettinad Corporation (ed.), *Souvenir to Commemorate the Sixtieth Birthday (Shastiyabdha Poorthi) of Sri SM. SP. Socalingam Chettiar* (Colombo, Staff of Chettinad Corporation, 1957) and B.V.N. Naidu (ed.), *Rajah Sir Annamalai Chettiar Commemoration Volume* (Annamalai Nagar, Annamalai University, 1941). Eighteen volumes have been put together by Rishi Gemini Kaushi Barua, on different Marwari traders. See Rishi Gemini Kaushi Barua, *Main Apni Marwari Samaj ko Pyar Karta Hoon* (Calcutta, Jaimini-Prakashan, 1967).

[7] See, for instance, *Modern India Heritage and Achievement: Shri G.D. Birla 80th Birthday Commemoration Volume* (New Delhi, 1997) and B.D. Sardesai (ed.), *Walchand Diamond Jubilee Commemoration Volume* (Bombay, 1942).

[8] Presented by the Vice-Chancellor, the syndicate, the senate, and the staff of the Annamalai University, *Dr Rajah Sir Muthiah Chettiar and Rani Lady Meyyammai Achi, 60th Birthday Commemoration Volume* (Annamalainagar, Annamalai University, 1965).

[9] See, for instance, Bharati Somosundara, 'The Rajah of Chettinad' and B.V.N. Naidu, 'The Nattukottai Chettiars and Their Banking System', in B.V.N. Naidu (ed.), *Rajah Sir Annamalai Chettiar Commemoration Volume* (Annamalainagar, Annamalai University, 1941).

and his involvement with the Tea Association of India.[10] The contents of the Kanoi volume are, in a sense, typical of the genre of *abhinandan* and *smriti granths*.[11]

Within this mercantile tradition, there have also been studies of entrepreneurship. These have mainly taken the form of biography of individual business leaders, rather than narratives of entrepreneurship in a particular region or sector. Many such works look at the firm and their business leader in the larger cultural, political, and economic setting. Often such works are published privately. A typical example would be Vishambar Prasad Sharma Visharad's *Swargiya Ramkrishnaji Mohta Jiwan Charitra aur Sansmaran*, Rishi Gemini Kaushik Barua's *Shri Surajmal Jalan Madhumangal Shri*, and Radhakrishna Nevatia's, *Shri Ramdev Chokhany*. A concern with similar themes such as the social origins of business leaders, role of culture, relations between family and firm, business 'apprenticeship,' entrepreneurial endeavours, and community life can be found in these writings.[12] Biographical writings were also written in a shorter form within the larger narratives of the community. Thus, Radhakrishna Nevatia's *Bara Bazaar ke Karyakarta* contains biographical profiles of Kolkata's Marwari traders.[13]

This rich tradition of writing in the Indian subcontinent owes much to traders, their community associations, and their caste bodies. They contributed both to maintaining business records, especially community and trade journals, as well as to encouraging scholars from within their ranks. Written in Hindi, Tamil, or old Marwari and subsequently in English, this commemorative tradition continues to flourish.[14] Most often written with the purpose of celebrating and reaffirming shared community values, these writings provide us with insights into merchant families with sufficient details about economic conditions and endeavours, stories of profit- and loss-making, family and lineage (*kul*) histories, and related aspects of mercantile values and conduct.

IN THE SHADOW OF ECONOMIC HISTORY: 1930s–1950s

As distinct from the commemorative form of writings discussed earlier, business history writing in India in its 'modern phase' developed—like many other countries in the world—in the shadow of economic history. Business history came to be subsumed within the rubric of economic history,

[10] See Kanoi Abhinandan Samity, *Rashtrasevi Shri Hanumanbaksh Kanoi Abhinandan Granth* (Kanoi Abhinandan Samity, Dibrugarh, n.d.).

[11] See, for instance, Rameshwar Prasad Patodia, *Anandilal Poddar Smriti Pushpa* (Calcutta, n.d). Then, there are works such as Vishambar Prasad Sharma's *Shradhanjali Swargiya Jugalkishoreji Birla* (Pilani, 1974), which narrates the business career and philanthropic interests of Jugalkishore Birla. Also see *Shri Surajmal Jalan Madhumangal Shri* (Calcutta, n.d.) and R. Nevatia and J. Jaithliya (eds), *Shri Prabhu Dayal Himmatsinghka Abhinandan Granth* (Calcutta, Shri Prabhu Dayal Himmatsinghka Abhinandan Samiti, 1984).

[12] See Vishambar Prasad Sharma Visharad's *Swargiya Ramkrishnaji Mohta Jiwan Charitra aur Sansmaran* (Calcutta, 1941); Rishi Gemini Kaushik Barua's *Shri Surajmal Jalan Madhumangal Shri* (Calcutta, n.d.); and Radhakrishna Nevatia's, *Shri Ramdev Chokhany* (Calcutta, n.d.).

[13] Radhakrishna Nevatia's *Bara Bazaar ke Karyakarta* (Calcutta, Shri Barabazaar Kumarsabha Pustakalya, 1982). Also see Rishi Gemini Kaushi Barua, *Main Apni Marwari Samaj ko Pyar Karta Hoon*.

[14] See, for instance, Ramesh Bhardwaj (ed.), *Sitaram Seksaria Janamshatabdi Granth* (New Delhi, Gandhi Hindustan Sahitya Sabha, 1993) and Vishnu Dayal Jhunjhunwala and K. Bharadwaj, *Marwaris: Business, Culture and Tradition* (New Delhi, Kalpaz Publications, 2002).

as the larger discipline was animated by the broader concerns of economic development in which private enterprise needed to be situated in the context of its past. Many of the studies restricted their focus upon the contextual aspects of business and did not attempt to fully study the firm *per se* as an *active* agent in the economic process. Notwithstanding this limitation, the 1930s and 1940s witnessed a proliferation of writings on Indian economy and industrial development. This was understandable given the times. In the context of an ascendant nationalism, there was growing confidence in the economic future of India.[15] In 1931 India ranked sixth in world trade, with her exports of manufactured goods constituting 23 per cent of total exports. Economic analysis was also greatly influenced by the nationalist critique of colonial rule, based upon an understanding of the economic effects of colonialism. Writings on the economy were a burgeoning field and by the 1930s there were at least 20 universities in India which were engaged in research and publications on economic policy issues and their work extended to undertaking surveys of economic conditions and examining issues in the agricultural and industrial sectors.[16] Research bodies and institutes such as the Indian Economic Association at Allahabad (estb. 1918), the Population Research Institute at Lucknow, the Board of Economic Enquiry at Lahore, the Bombay School of Economics (estb. 1922), the Gokhale Institute of Politics and Economics, Poona (estb. 1930), the Indian Statistical Institute, Calcutta (estb. 1931), and finally the Indian Institute of Economic and Social Research in Delhi (estb. 1940s), all contributed to a growing corpus of studies focused upon Indian economic life. Many of the writings produced in these decades hoped to influence industrial, agricultural, and tariff policies and were often accompanied by specific proposals for reforms, especially in the light of fast-changing political circumstances.[17] Wide-ranging in their coverage, the writings extended to such concerns as the general economic situation, finance and banking, state of agriculture, unemployment, national income, large- and some small-scale industries, handicrafts, labour, industrial organization, and other aspects of economic life.[18]

[15] The interest in economic issues went back to the 1890s, especially to the 1892 lecture by Ranade on 'Indian Political Economy', which is often seen to be the point when economics took off in Indian universities.

[16] On the economists of the time and their contributions see Terence J. Byres, 'The Creation of "the Tribe of Pundits Called Economists": Institutions, Institution-Builders and Debates', in Terence J. Byres (ed.), *The Indian Economy: Major Debates since Independence* (Delhi, Oxford University Press, 1998), pp. 20–73.

[17] There were, of course, many views about the economic trajectories which the subcontinent should take. Yet, most economists believed that industrialization on the Western model, which would occur with the visible hand of the state, was the most appropriate model. Within this, of course, there were debates on the role of agriculture versus industry. It is interesting that despite the strong Fabian socialist leanings of the nationalist rhetoric at the time, there was not much search for alternative models of economic life or much elaboration of socialist economic models. See Max Millikan, 'Economic Thought and Its Application and Methodology in India', *The American Economic Review*, Vol. 46, No. 2, Papers and Proceedings of the Sixty-Eighth Annual Meeting of the American Economic Association, May 1956, pp. 399–407.

[18] Writings of these decades include Radhakamal Mukherjee and H.L. Dey (eds), *Economic Problems of Modern India*, Volumes I and II (Macmillan, 1939 and 1942); Parmathanath Banerjea, *A Study of Indian Economics* (London, Macmillan, 1949); T.N. Maraswamy, *The Economic Problem of India* (Bombay, New Books Company, 1942); H. Venkatsubbiah, *The Structural Basis of Indian Economy* (London, Allen & Unwin, 1940); R. Chaudhuri, *The Evolution of Indian Industries* (Calcutta, Calcutta University, 1939); V.K.R.V. Rao, *The Taxation of Income in India* (New York, Longmans, Green & Co, 1931); Rajani Kanta Das, *Plantation Labor in India* (Calcutta, R. Chatterjee, 1931); and N.M. Joshi, *Urban Handicrafts of the Bombay Deccan* (Pune, Gokhale Institute, 1936). An

Given that economists dabbled in writings about aspects of the business past, in addition to their other preoccupations, unsurprisingly their main concerns still remained themes such as the rise of industry. Writings in the discipline of economics did not treat firms or entrepreneurs as *central* actors in the economic process—the essential hallmark of business history. No doubt, such works undertook more of what could be called 'industrial history' which—as Dwijendra Tripathi has noted—did not 'analyze the industrialization process in the context of entrepreneurial behavior'.[19] Nonetheless, such writings were significant in helping to understand the foundations of industry.

In the economic writings which emanated from the 1930s well into the 1960s, the understanding of business was often located in either a 'culturalist' or 'nationalist' framework.[20] These perspectives were to remain dominant in interpretations of the Indian economy as the chief concern of scholars in these decades was how to make sense of India's 'economic backwardness'. The cultural explanations emphasized the role of cultural values and social mores in shaping and impeding economic development. This view blamed India's economic ills on its dominant social values, especially relating to caste and social stratification. This viewpoint drew inspiration from Max Weber, who was the first to suggest that caste impacted upon entrepreneurial motivations and put forth the argument that it was not compatible with modern capitalism. This viewpoint sometimes went so far as espousing that 'sweeping cultural changes must precede a quickening of the tempo of economic progress'.[21] The 'nationalist' interpretation emphasized the 'glories' of India before the coming of the Europeans, the 'drain' of wealth and 'de-industrialization', and the 'sacrifice for the greater glory of the Empire' which the Indian economy was forced to bear.[22]

Given their preoccupation with issues of economic underdevelopment, an allied research area for economists and economic historians was the process of industrialization. Studies which addressed this theme also looked at the entrepreneur and the firm; however, they viewed them in a secondary role. Amongst the typical writings from this period was the M. Litt thesis of D.R. Gadgil. His work was published as *Industrial Evolution of India in Recent Times,* brought out by Oxford University Press in 1924, with five later editions, the last coming out in 1971.[23] Another noteworthy text was Daniel H. Buchanan's *The Development of Capitalist Enterprise in India* which also looked at

---

impressive account of the Madras Presidency economy is by A. Sarada Raju, *Economic Conditions in the Madras Presidency, 1800–1850* (Madras, Madras University, 1940). On industrial developments in Mysore, see R. Bala Krishna, *Industrial Developments of Mysore* (Bangalore, Bangalore Press, 1940).

[19] See D. Tripathi, 'Occupational Mobility and Industrial Entrepreneurship in India: A Historical Analysis', *Developing Economies*, Vol. 19, No. 1, March 1981.

[20] On this see Tirthankar Roy, *The Economic History of India 1857–1947* (New Delhi, Oxford University Press, 2000), 'Introduction'.

[21] The 'cultural values and economic development' debate has been likened to the 'differing versions of Vishnu', by the anthropologist Richard G. Fox.

[22] Thus Jathar and Beri point out candidly that they could not 'consent to any sacrifice for the greater glory of the Empire of which we are a part, unless we are convinced that the sacrifice asked for is ultimately for the national advantage'. See G.B. Jathar and S.G. Beri, *Indian Economics: A Comprehensive and Critical Survey*, Vols I and II (London, Oxford University Press, 1928).

[23] D.R. Gadgil, *Industrial Evolution of India in Recent Times* (London, Oxford University Press, 1924). Gadgil also examined the 'Rise of Business Communities in India', and charted their fortunes in the seventeenth and eighteenth centuries.

Indian industrial development, and took into account the status of business, 'business leadership,' business organization, and the managing agency system.[24] Similar in scope was the work of the London School of Economics scholar Vera Anstey, which looked at production techniques and their similarities and deviations from those in other industrialized countries. Anstey was concerned with the present state of industry and how economic development may be stimulated. Anxious to emphasize the economic benefits which India secured from colonial rule, Anstey noted that 'India's economic problems were rooted deeply in the everyday life, customs and social organization of the people.' Particularly worrying to her were the 'religious ideas and conventions, and the rigid social stratification and conservatism', which 'pervade every sphere of life and limit economic development at every step'.[25]

Then, there were studies of industry by scholars such as G.B. Jathar and S.G. Beri who published a two-volume *Indian Economics–A Comprehensive and Critical Survey of the Economic Problems of India.* In their detailed study, they looked at 'social and religious institutions' to understand their influence on economic activity, industry, labour, foreign trade, currency and banking, and a host of economic issues, candidly confessing that theirs was 'a study of the present economic position of India from the Indian national point of view'.[26] The same year, Vakil, Bose, and Deolalkar's *Growth and Trade and Industry in Modern India: An Introductory Survey* traced the growth of industry from the 1860s to the 1930s. They examined India's most important industries such as cotton, jute, sugar, tea, wool, silk, coal, cement, matches, and paper.[27] Valuable analyses of many aspects of Indian industry and economy were also put forth in a series entitled *Studies in Indian Economy*, which was edited by C.N. Vakil, then Professor of Economics at Bombay University. One of the titles in this series—D.R. Samant and M.A. Mulky's *Organization and Finance of Industries in India*—examined industrial organization.[28] Another important study of the time was Nabagopal Das' *Industrial Enterprise in India* which followed his earlier *Banking and*

[24] Buchanan, Professor of Economics at Fisk University, had also been at Keigijuku University in Tokyo. He looked at production techniques in India and their similarities to and deviations from other industrialized countries. He used a number of reports of governmental committees such as the Royal Commissions on Indian agriculture and Indian labour and the Indian Statutory Commission, as well as fieldwork. Buchanan studied business organization, profitableness, labour conditions, and the productive efficiency of sectors such as plantation, textile, coal, and ferrous industries. See Daniel H. Buchanan, *The Development of Capitalist Enterprise in India* (New York, Harvard University Bureau of International Research, Macmillan, 1934), esp. chapter VII, pp. 142–75.

[25] Vera Anstey, *The Economic Development of India* (London, Longmans, Green, 1949). Anstey's book was to become highly influential within colonial circles and was even recommended as a textbook in both Britain and in India. Later Anstey also wrote a textbook on economics; see Vera Anstey, *An Introduction to Economics: For Students in India and Pakistan* (London, Allen & Unwin, 1964).

[26] G.B. Jathar and S.G. Beri, *Indian Economics—A Comprehensive and Critical Survey of the Economic Problems of India* (Madras, Oxford University Press, 1931, first published in 1928).

[27] C.N. Vakil, S.C. Bose, and P.V. Deolalkar, *Growth and Trade and Industry in Modern India: An Introductory Survey* (New York, Longmans, Green & Co., 1931).

[28] See D.R. Samant and M.A. Mulky, *Organization and Finance of Industries in India* (Calcutta, Longmans, Green & Co., 1937). Other books in this series include R.D. Tiwari, *Railway Rates in Relation to Trade and Industry* (Bombay, Longmans, Green & Co., 1937) and J.B. Shukla, *Life and Labor in a Gujarat Taluka* (Calcutta, Longmans, Green & Co., 1937).

Industrial Finance in India, both of which also looked at the organization and finance of large-scale industry.[29]

Further, 1929 saw the publication of a fascinating study of indigenous banking by L.C. Jain based upon his University of London doctoral thesis entitled *Indigenous Banking in India*. It threw especially valuable light on the indigenous banker and the moneylender, communities and castes involved with banking, their spread and importance despite the coming of modern banks, the use and methods of the *hundi* network, and the role played by the indigenous banker in the economy.[30]

A pioneering piece of writing on business organization was P.S. Lokanathan's *Industrial Organization in India*, which mainly analysed the reasons behind the rise of the managing agency system that was the dominant form of business organization in the nineteenth and twentieth centuries. He also looked at the ability of the managing agencies to harness financial resources and to manage them effectively.[31] In the 1950s and 1960s a number of studies followed this theme. These included Raj K. Nigam, *Managing Agencies in India*, S.K. Basu, *The Managing Agency System*, and Radhe Shyam Rungta, *The Rise of Business Corporations in India, 1851–1900*.[32]

Even though much of the scholarship in the 1950s and 1960s continued to grapple with the challenge of economic underdevelopment, important contributions were nonetheless made to the study of Indian business. A strand of Western scholarship looked for reasons for economic backwardness in Indian cultural values. This is epitomized by William Kapp's *Hindu Culture, Economic Development and Economic Planning in India*. Kapp considered the Hindu social system to be ill-suited to modernization and took the view that caste rigidity, belief in karma, and the cyclic notion of time, all together hamper individual motivation and result in economic stagnation. He lamented that there were 'no religious or intellectual reformers on the Indian horizon, who may do

29 Nabagopal Das, *Industrial Enterprise in India* (Bombay, Orient Longman, 1956) and his *Banking and Industrial Finance in India* (Calcutta, Modern Publishing Syndicate, 1936). Amongst other works on industrialization published in these decades are R. Chaudhuri, *The Evolution of Indian Industries* (Calcutta, Calcutta University Press, 1939) and P.C. Jain (ed.), *Industrial Problems of India* (Allahabad, Kitabistan, 1942).

30 L.C. Jain, *Indigenous Banking in India* (Macmillan and Co., Limited, London, 1929). There was also a considerable amount of writing on industrial finance and banking such as S.K. Basu, *Industrial Finance in India* (Calcutta, University Press, 1939); S.S. Ali Husain, *Cooperative Land Mortgage Banks in Madras* (Nizamabad, Nizam Governments' Cooperative Department, 1941); B.P. Adarkar, *Indian Fiscal Policy* (Allahabad, Kitabistan, 1941); S. Muranjan, *Modern Banking in India* (Bombay, New Book Co. 1940); and A.I. Quereshi, *State Banks for India* (London, Macmillan, 1939).

31 P.S. Lokanathan, *Industrial Organization in India* (London, George Allen and Unwin, 1935).

32 Raj K. Nigam, *Managing Agencies in India* (New Delhi, Government of India, 1957); S.K. Basu, *The Managing Agency System* (Calcutta, World Press, 1958); and Radhe Shyam Rungta, *The Rise of Business Corporations in India, 1851–1900* (Cambridge, Cambridge University Press, 1969). Other works include Andrew Brimmer, 'The Setting of Entrepreneurship in India', *Quarterly Journal of Economics*, Vol. 119, No. 4, November 1955 and Blair B. Kling, 'The Origins of the Managing Agency System in India', *Journal of Asian Studies*, Vol. 26, No. 1, November 1966.

for India what Luther and Calvin, or Galileo and Newton, did for the modern interpretation of the world in the west'. With such a pessimistic view, Kapp saw the task of Indian economic development as quite hopeless.[33] A similar pessimism marked the writings of Helen Lamb, an MIT economist, who at the peak of the Nehruvian period, pronounced that the business community could not play a dominant part in India's economic development, as it had done in the West.[34] Not surprisingly, these views came to be challenged by a number of scholars, leading to a lively debate, some of it taking place in the Chicago-based journal, *Economic Development and Cultural Change*.[35]

Although the issue of the role of culture in economic development dominated debates, scholarly works nonetheless continued to invigorate the field. Especially useful were sectoral studies and histories of expatriate business, examples of which include S.D. Mehta, *Cotton Mills of India*; N.C. Bhogendranath, *Development of Textile Industry in Madras*; Hilton Brown, *Parrys of Madras: A Story of British Enterprise in India*; and G. Tyson, *The Bengal Chamber of Commerce and Industry: A Centenary Survey*.[36]

[33] William Kapp, *Hindu Culture, Economic Development and Economic Planning in India* (New York, Asia Publishing House, 1963).

[34] Lamb believed that the majority of Indian industrialists, 'some small and some large, who tend to cling to traditional business attitudes—great company secrecy, sole reliance on relatives of fellow castemen for assistance, and emphasis on quick profits'. See Helen Lamb, *Studies on India and Vietnam*, edited by Corliss Lamont and Foreword by Paul M. Sweezy (New York, Monthly Review Press, 1976). Using primarily material which was available in the United States, having not been able to visit India, Lamb concluded that colonial rule was not conducive to economic development and 'viewed with distrust the prospect of India's becoming an industrial nation', until it changed the caste system or abolished the princely states—both of which were, in her view, major obstacles to development.

[35] See Milton Singer, 'Cultural Values in India's Economic Development', *Annals of the American Academy*, May 1958; Ajit Dasgupta, 'India's Cultural Values and Economic Development: A Comment', *Economic Development and Cultural Change*, Vol. 13, No. 1, Part 1 (October 1964), pp. 100–2; Milton Singer, 'Religion and Social Change in India: The Max Weber Thesis, Phase Three', *Economic Development and Cultural Change*, Vol. 14, No. 4 (July 1966), pp. 497–505; John Goheen, M.N. Srinivas, D.G. Karve, and Milton Singer, 'India's Cultural Values and Economic Development: A Discussion', *Economic Development and Cultural Change*, Vol. 7, No. 1, October 1958, pp. 1–12; and Richard G. Fox, 'Avatars of Indians Research', *Comparative Studies in Society and History*, Vol. 12, No. 1, January 1970, pp. 59–72. Also see John Adams, 'Culture and Economic Development in South Asia', *The ANNALS of the American Academy of Political and Social Science*, 573, January 2001, pp. 152–75.

[36] S.D. Mehta, *Cotton Mills of India* (Bombay, Textile Association, 1954) and N.C. Bhogendranath, *Development of Textile Industry in Madras* (Madras, University of Madras,1957). Other sectoral studies include C.A. Eddison, *Case Study of Industrial Development: Growth of the Pulp and Paper Industry in India* (Cambridge, MIT, 1955); J.P. De Souza, *History of the Chemical Industry of India* (Bombay, Allied Publishers, 1961); W.A. Johnson, *The Steel Industry of India* (Cambridge, Mass., Harvard University Press, 1966). Works on expatriate business included G. Harrison, *Bird and Company of Calcutta* (Calcutta, privately published to mark the firm's centenary, 1864–1964, 1964); Hilton Brown, *The Parrys of Madras: A Story of British Enterprise in India* (Madras, privately published by Parrys, 1954); G. Tyson, *The Bengal Chamber of Commerce and Industry: A Centenary Survey* (Calcutta, 1953); Herbert Feldman, *Karachi through a Hundred Years—The Centenary History of the Karachi Chamber of Commerce and Industry, 1860–1960* (Karachi, Oxford University Press, 1960); and F. De Souza, *The House of Binny* (Bombay, Allied Publishers, 1961).

BUSINESS HISTORY COMES OF AGE

Business history was finally able to distinguish itself as a separate field from economic history in the 1970s and 1980s. These decades marked a broadening of the research agenda and an impressive proliferation of writings that engaged with the themes of mainstream business history. Historians were now conscious of the need to examine the Indian context and the 'socio-cultural and politico-economic forces operating in our society' and not merely applying concepts of business history which had developed in the West.[37] The main themes which interested scholars in these decades were mercantile communities, business and politics, state and business, alongside new research on areas which constituted strands within the earlier tradition such as studies of entrepreneurship and business organization.

A number of reasons contributed to the flowering of Indian business history. One was the role of writings by important scholars who were mindful of the centrality of business in processes of historical change. Many of them did not look upon themselves as business historians. Yet their work contributed to the broadening of the field. Examples of such work include C.A. Bayly's writings on commercial groups and the merchant family in the early colonial period, Rajat Kanta Ray on the bazaar, industrialization, and business and politics, Stanley Kochanek on business and politics, Bipan Chandra on business and Nehruvian politics, A.D.D. Gordon on business and politics in Bombay of the 1920s, Claude Markovits on big business and the nationalist leadership in the 1930s, and Omkar Goswami on the Marwaris.[38]

To these broad-ranging writings were added the more specific contributions of business historians. An especially important role was played by Dwijendra Tripathi who through his own research and attempts to bring together scholars concertedly promoted business history as a separate field.[39] In an early seminal piece on 'Indian Entrepreneurship in Historical Perspective:

[37] See Sanjay P. Thakur, 'Business and Politics in India: A Historical Perspective', *Economic and Political Weekly*, Vol. 24, No. 26, 1 July 1989, pp. 1437–9.

[38] C.A. Bayly, *Rulers, Townsmen and Bazaars: North Indian Society in the Age of British Expansion, 1770–1850* (Cambridge, Cambridge University Press, 1983); Rajat Kanta Ray, *Industrialization in India: Growth and Conflict in the Private Corporate Sector, 1914–1947* (Delhi, Oxford University Press, 1979); Stanley Kochanek, *Business and Politics in India* (Berkeley, University of California Press, 1974); Bipan Chandra, 'Jawaharlal Nehru and the Indian Capitalist Class 1936', in his *Nationalism and Colonialism in Modern India* (Delhi, Orient Longman, 1979); A.D.D. Gordon, *Businessmen and Politics: Rising Nationalism and a Modernising Economy in Bombay, 1918–1933* (New Delhi, Manohar, 1978); Claude Markovits, *Indian Business and Nationalist Politics 1931–39: The Indigenous Capitalist Class and the Rise of the Congress Party* (Cambridge, Cambridge University Press, 2002); and Omkar Goswami, 'Then Came the Marwaris: Some Aspects of the Changes in the Pattern of Industrial Control in Eastern India', *Indian Economic Social History Review*, Vol. 1, No. 22, September 1985, pp. 225–49.

[39] Trained at Allahabad in his first degree, Tripathi did a doctorate in 1963 on 'The United States and India: Economic Links 1860–1900' at the University of Wisconsin, Madison under the supervision of Richard N. Current. This was followed by a diploma in International Teachers' Programme specializing in Business Administration History from Harvard University in 1965. Thereafter, he was appointed Assistant Professor at the then newly founded Indian Institute of Management (Ahmedabad) where he later became the Kasturbhai Lalbhai Professor of Business History. In the years after his return from the United States, Tripathi wrote a number of influential articles on a myriad of themes. Some of these had emerged from his doctoral interest and looked at both India and the United States, but there were others which reflect the widening of his research interests. Thus, his publications

A Re-interpretation' published in the *Economic and Political Weekly* in 1971, Tripathi called for 'a new line of inquiry' to understand Indian entrepreneurship and the need to look at varied forces which, he said, 'may consist of an interaction of the ever-changing economic, political, and social environments on one hand and personal influences of caste, family affiliation, nature and level of education, contact with and impact of the activities of others on individual decisions-makers on the other'.[40] Again in April 1987 he urged scholars to not simply apply Alfred Chandler's approach to business history but to examine the Indian context. Tripathi wrote on varied areas such as entrepreneurship, evolution of business communities, business and politics, state and business, technology choices, and histories of banking.

An especially important moment in business history research came with Tripathi's initiative in starting the IIMA (Indian Institute of Management Ahmedabad) Seminar Series on Business History in the early 1980s. Four seminars were held between 1982 and 1989 which were attended by a number of scholars of economic and business history alongside business executives and management experts. The first seminar in March 1982 examined the evolution of business communities and the socio-cultural aspects of business behaviour; the second in 1984 explored the relations between governing structures and economic activities; the third in April 1987 analysed how business practices at the micro level were affected by macro situations; and the fourth session in March 1989 focused on business and politics in India.[41] These resulted in substantial books which gave a much needed fillip for business history to emerge from the shell of economic history and come into its own.[42] Another business historian who wrote at this time was Thomas A. Timberg, who looked at Marwari entrepreneurship, the history of the community, and the nature of the family firm.[43]

---

ranged from issues such as the silver question in India and America, free trade, the effect of the American Civil War on India, the history of Larsen and Toubro, and ways of studying entrepreneurship. For instance, see D. Tripathi, 'The Silver Question, India and America', *Journal of Indian History*, Vol. 44, No. 132; 'Opportunism and Free Trade: Lancashire Cotton Famine and Indian Cotton Cultivation', *Indian Economic and Social History Review*, Vol. 4, No. 3, September; 'Opportunism of Free Trade: Sadasheogarh Harbour Project, 1855–1865', *Indian Economic and Social History Review*, Vol. 5, No. 4, December 1968; 'An Echo beyond the Horizon: The Effect of the American Civil War on India', *Journal of Indian History: Golden Jubilee Volume*, (ed.) T.K. Ravindram (University of Kerala, Trivandrum, 1973); and *Dating the Destiny: History of Larsen and Toubro Limited, 1983–1975* (IIM, Ahmedabad, 1975).

[40] Dwijendra Tripathi, 'Indian Enterprenuership in Historical Perspective: A Re-interpretation', *Indian Economic and Social History Review*, Vol. 6, No. 22, 29 May 1971.

[41] See Sanjay P. Thakur, 'Business and Politics in India: A Historical Perspective', *Economic and Political Weekly*, Vol. 24, No. 26, 1 July 1989, pp. 1437–9.

[42] Dwijendra Tripathi (ed.), *State and Business in India: A Historical Perspective* (New Delhi, Manohar, 1984); (ed.), *Business Communities of India:: A Historical Perspective* (New Delhi, Manohar, 1984); and (ed.), *Business and Politics in India: A Historical Perspective* (New Delhi, Manohar, 1991).

[43] Thomas A. Timberg, *The Marwaris: From Traders to Industrialists* (Delhi, Vikas, 1978); 'A Note on the Arrival of Calcutta's Marwaris', *Bengal Past and Present*, 90, 1971, pp. 75–84; 'A North Indian Firm as Seen through Its Business Records, 1860–1914: Tarachand Ghanshyamdas, A "Great" Marwari Firm', *Indian Economic and Social History Review*, Vol. 8, No. 3, 1971; 'Three Types of the Marwari Firm', *Indian Economic and Social History Review*, Vol. 10, January 1973; and 'Hiatus and Incubator: Indigenous Trade and Traders, 1837–1957', in Asiya Siddiqi (ed.), *Trade and Finance in Colonial India 1750–1860* (Delhi, Oxford University Press, 1995), pp. 250–64.

The flowering of business history saw a proliferation of a number of themes in which impressive scholarship came to be produced. Let us consider some of these themes. Given the fact that certain 'traditional' mercantile communities have historically dominated business activities in the subcontinent, it is not surprising that much work was done on such communities. The communities which have been the focus of attention have been the Parsis, the Chettiars, and the Marwaris.[44] Here the general view has been that mercantile communities possessed certain commercial knowledge, market networks, and access to capital, which encouraged commercial and industrial enterprises. Within these studies, debates have occurred about the role of culture, caste and community solidarities, and the basis of mercantile identities.[45]

Another central research theme that has displayed much vibrancy is the study of entrepreneurship, which has mainly taken the form of biographies and has examined the entrepreneur and the firm together. Often drawing extensively on private archives, these studies have tried to understand the entrepreneur in the social and economic context. The sharp distinction which has marked business history writing in the United States between entrepreneurial history and business history has not occurred within the Indian context.[46] One reason for the sustained

[44] Such writings include James Berner, *Industrial Entrepreneurship in Madras State* (Bombay, Asia Publishing House, 1960); Ray Owens and Ashis Nandy, *The New Vaishyas* (Durham, N.C., 1978); Eckehard Kulke, *The Parsees in India: A Minority as Agent of Social Change* (Delhi, Vikas Publishing House, 1975); Leighton Hazlehurst, *Entrepreneurship and the Merchant Castes in a Punjabi City* (Durham, Program in Comparative Studies on Southern Asia, 1966); E. Wayne Nafziger, *Class, Caste and Entrepreneurship: A Study of Indian Industrialists* (Honolulu, University of Hawaii Press, 1978); Mattison Mines, *Muslim Merchants: The Economic Behavior of an Indian Muslim Community* (New Delhi, Sri Ram Centre, 1972); Raman Mahadevan, 'Immigrant Entrepreneurs in Colonial Burma: An Exploratory Study of the Role of Nattukottai Chettiars of Tamil Nadu, 1880–1930', *The Indian Economic and Social History Review*, Vol. 15, No. 3, 1978, pp. 329–58 and his 'Pattern of Enterprise of Immigrant Entrepreneurs: A Study of Chettiars in Malaya, 1880–1930', *Economic and Political Weekly*, Vol. XIII, Nos 4 and 5; Dwijendra Tripathi (ed.), *Business Communities of India: A Historical Perspective* (New Delhi, Manohar, 1984); and Philippe Cadene and Denis Vidal (eds), *Webs of Trade: Dynamics of Business Communities in Western India* (New Delhi, Manohar, 1997).

[45] Such debates have continued in the 1990s. The anthropologist David Rudner, in a study of the Chettiars, has argued that caste and its values and capitalist enterprise are mutually enforcing; Carol Upadhya has examined caste as social capital; Anne Hardgrove has studied the process of community formation amongst the Marwaris and the role played by social practices and 'performance' in this; and the journalist Harish Damodaran has argued that the social bases of the capitalist class has diversified to include new groups and castes. See David W. Rudner, *Caste and Capitalism in Colonial India: The Nattukottai Chettiars* (Berkeley, University of California Press, 1994); Carol Upadhya, 'Culture, Class and Entrepreneurship: A Case Study of Coastal Andhra Pradesh, India', in Mario Rutten and Carol Upadhya (eds), *Small Business Entrepreneurs in Asia and Europe: Towards a Comparative Perspective* (New Delhi: Sage Publications, 1997); Anne Hardgrove, *Community and Public Culture: The Marwaris in Calcutta* (New Delhi, Oxford University Press, 2004); and Harish Damodaran, *India's New Capitalists: Caste, Business and Industry in a Modern Nation* (Ranikhet, Permanent Black, 2008).

[46] These have taken the form of studies of entrepreneurs of large industries such as R.P. Masani, *Wadia and His Foundation* (1961); K. Nagarajan, *Dr Rajah Sir Muthiah Chettiar: A Biography* (Annamalai University, Annamalainagar, 1989); F.R. Harris, *Jamsetji Nusserwanji Tata: A Chronicle of His Life* (Bombay, Blackie, 1958); K.C. Mahindra, *Sir Rajendra Nath Mookerjee* (Calcutta, 1962); Frank Moraes, *Sir Purshotamdas Thakurdas* (Bombay, 1957); R.N. Jaju, *G.D. Birla: A Biography* (New Delhi, Vikas, 1986); Arun Joshi, *Shri Ram: A Study in Entrepreneurship and Business Management* (Delhi, 1975); G.D. Khanolkar, *Walchand Hirachand: Man, His Times and Achievements* (Bombay, 1969); Blair Kling, *Partner in Enterprise: Dwarkanatha Tagore and the Age of Enterprise in*

engagement of scholars with studies of entrepreneurship is the dominance of family firms in the Indian business landscape. Within this the themes which have been analysed are the nature of the firm, concentration of ownership and how the dominance of the family is maintained, value systems that govern inheritance, marriage and joint family, associates of family firms, foreign collaboration, problems of succession, and the attempts to incorporate managerial expertise.[47]

Business and politics has been a further area of research. Amongst the first to foray into the area was Stanley Kochanek who examined post-Independence business politics, and the development of modern business associations as interest groups. Much work has been done on business and politics in the colonial period by scholars such as A.D.D. Gordon, Bipan Chandra, Rajat Kanta Ray, Claude Markovits, and Aditya Mukherjee.[48] Whilst their scholarship has taken an all-India perspective, some sectoral studies have also looked at the theme of business and politics, such as Leadbeater who examines changing responses in the cotton mill industry to the nationalist movement.[49] Since

---

Eastern India (1976); D. Tripathi, *Dynamics of a Tradition: Kasturbhai Lalbhai and His Entrepreneurship* (New Delhi, Manohar, 1981); S.K. Sen, *The House of Tatas* (Calcutta, 1975); R.M. Lala, *The Creation of Wealth;* C.P. Rao, *Lakshmipat Singhania: His Concept and Creation* (1985); Gita Piramal and M. Herdeck, *India's Industrialists* (1986); Murad Fyzee, *Aircraft and Engine Perfect: The Story of JRD Tata* (1991); Bachi Karkaria, *Dare to Dream the Life of Bahadur Mohan Singh Oberoi* (1992); Minhas Merchant, *Adita Vikram Birla: A Biography* (New Delhi, Viking 1997); F.R. Harris, *Jamsetji Nusserwanji Tata: A Chronicle of His Life* (Bombay, Blackie, 1958); D.R. Mankekar, *Homi Mody, a Many Splendoured Life: A Political Biography* (Bombay, Popular Prakashan, 1968); Chentsal Rao, *BM Birla: His Deeds and Dreams* (New Delhi, 1983); D.D. Shastri, *Ek Bindu, Ek Sindhu* (Mathura, 1948); M.V. Kamath, *The Many-Splendoured Ghanshyam Binani* (Binani Trust, Mumbai, 1999); and more recently Medha M. Kudaisya, *Life and Times of G.D. Birla* (New Delhi, Oxford University Press, 2003). Dwijendra Tripathi and Makrand Mehta have studied debates about entrepreneurship and locate business houses and the entrepreneurial aspects of their development within these. They examine eight families in western India, seven of which have become major business houses—Tata, Khatau, Lalbhai, Amin, Kriloskar, and Walchand Hirachand; one which did not survive—Ranchodlal Chhotalal; and one multinational—Larsen and Toubro. See their *Business Houses in Western India: A Study in Entrepreneurial Response, 1850–1956* (New Delhi, Manohar, 1990).

47 Such writings include R.K. Hazari's work of the 1960s—*The Structure of the Corporate Private Sector: A Study of Concentration, Ownership and Control* (Bombay, Asia Publishing House, 1966), and more recent works such as Sudipt Dutta, *Family Business in India* (New Delhi, Response Books, 1996) and Tarun Khanna and Krishna G. Palepu, 'The Evolution of Concentrated Ownership in India: Broad Patterns and History of the Indian Software Industry', in Randall K. Morck (ed.), *A History of Corporate Governance around the World: Family Business Groups to Professional Managers* (Chicago, University of California Press, 2005), pp. 283–320. Also see ' Family Business: A Symposium on the Role of the Family in Indian Business', *Seminar*, No. 482, October 1999, available at http://www.india-seminar.com/1999/482.htm.

48 See Stanley Kochanek, *Business and Politics in India* (Berkeley, University of California Press, 1974); Bipan Chandra, 'Jawaharlal Nehru and the Indian Capitalist Class'; A.D.D. Gordon, *Businessmen and Politics: Rising Nationalism and a Modernising Economy in Bombay, 1918–1933* (New Delhi, Manohar, 1978); Claude Markovits, *Indian Business and Nationalist Politics 1931–39: The Indigenous Capitalist Class and the Rise of the Congress Party* (Cambridge, Cambridge University Press, 2002); and Aditya Mukherjee, *Imperialism, Nationalism and the Making of the Indian Capitalist Class* (New Delhi, Sage Publications, 2005).

49 S.R.B. Leadbeater, *The Politics of Textiles: The Indian Cotton-Mill Industry and the Legacy of Swadeshi, 1900–1985* (New Delhi, Sage Publications, 1993). This debate was enlivened by a number of scholars in single articles, see, for instance, Antony Low, 'The Forgotten Bania: Merchant Communities and the Indian National Congress', in his *Eclipse of Empire* (Cambridge, Cambridge University Press, 1991).

the 1990s, there has also been interesting work on regional business and politics.[50] The politics of British businesses in India have been analysed by Maria Misra who looks at Calcutta-based managing agencies.[51]

State and business is another theme that has engaged historians. Important research has been carried out on 'business choices and initiatives' in context of the political environment of the time. Businesses have been looked at in different regimes such as the Mughals, the Portuguese, the Marathas, the East India Company, and then under princely regimes and the colonial state.[52]

Though these have been the main areas of study, there has also been important research on other aspects of business such as the bazaar, the rise of industry within which business has been located, and the study of multinationals.[53] At the sectoral level, Indian business historiography has been

[50] See, for instance, Pieter Gorter, 'The Social and Political Aspirations of a New Stratum of Industrialists: Local Politics on a Large Scale Industrial Estate in West India', in Mario Rutten and Carol Upadhya (eds), *Small Business Entrepreneurs in Asia and Europe: Towards a Comparative Perspective* (New Delhi: Sage Publications, 1997); Mario Rutten, *Farms and Factories: Social Profile of Large Farmers and Rural Industrialists in West India* (Delhi, Oxford University Press, 1995); and Sanjaya Baru, 'Enterprise and Development in India—An Interregional Perspective', *India Review*, Vol. 3, No. 4, pp. 385–404 and his 'Economic Policy and the Development of Capitalism in India: The Role of Regional Capitalists and Political Parties', in Francine Frankel et al. (eds), *Transforming India: Social and Political Dynamics of Democracy* (New Delhi, Oxford University Press, 2000), pp. 207–30. For an understanding of policy towards small industry, see Nasir Tyabji, *The Small Industries Policy in India* (Calcutta, Oxford University Press, 1989).

[51] Maria Misra, *Business, Race and Politics in British India, 1850–1960* (Oxford, Clarendon Press, 1999). Also see her 'Politics and Expatriate Enterprise in India: The Inter-War Years', in Dwijendra Tripathi (ed.), *Business and Politics in India: A Historical Perspective* (New Delhi, Manohar, 1991) and 'Business Culture and Entrepreneurship in British India, 1860–1950', *Modern Asian Studies*, Vol. 34, No. 2, 2000, pp. 333–48.

[52] There have also been other important studies on these themes such as the relations between the English, either as officials or private merchants and Indian financiers. See Lakshmi Subramanian, *Indigenous Capital and Imperial Expansion: Bombay, Surat, and the West Coast* (Delhi, Oxford University Press, 1996).

[53] On the bazaar see Rajat Kanta Ray, 'The Bazaar: Changing Structural Characteristics of the Indigenous Section of the Indian Economy before and after the Great Depression', *Indian Economic and Social History Review*, Vol. 25, No. 3, 1988. Also see his 'Pedhis and Mills: The Historical Integration of Formal and Informal Sectors in the Economy of Ahmedabad', *Indian Economic and Social History Review*, Vol. 19, Nos 3 & 4, 1982, pp. 387–96. Anand Yang has also looked at the bazaar in his *Bazaar India: Markets, Society, and the Colonial State in Gangetic Bihar* (Berkeley, University of California Press, 1998). Also see Sudipta Sen, *Empire of Free Trade: The East India Company and the Making of a Colonial Marketplace* (Philadelphia, University of Pennsylvania Press, 1998). Contemporary bazaars have been studied by Akos Ostor; see *Culture and Power: Legend, Ritual, Bazaar and Rebellion in a Bengali Society* (New Delhi, Sage Publications, 1984). On multinationals, see Mira Wilkins' writings such as *American Business Abroad: Ford on Six Continents* (Detroit, Wayne State University Press, 1964) and her edited, *British Overseas Investments, 1907–1948* (New York, Arno Press, 1977) and *The Emergence of Multinational Enterprise: American Business Abroad from the Colonial Era to 1914* (Cambridge, Harvard University Press, 1970). Also see B.R. Tomlinson, 'Colonial Firms and the Decline of Colonialism in Eastern India 1914–47', *Modern Asian Studies*, 15, 1981, pp. 455–86. There are a large number of company histories which have been written of companies established in the eighteenth century such as Binny and Company, Parry and Company, and James Finlay and Company; of those established in the nineteenth century such as Bird and Company, Ralli Brothers, the Sassoon Empire, Greaves Cotton and Company, Grindlays, Shaw Wallace, and Andrew Yule; and of course of twentieth century companies such as Imperial Tobacco. For details on these, see Lionel Carter's compilation which

particularly strong in the study of banking, the jute industry, and cotton.[54] Important works have dealt with other sectors such as iron and steel but have remained isolated. A relatively new area on which there is interesting work is the computer software industry.[55]

Yet there are many gaps which remain. The areas on which there has been little work have been mines and plantations, industry and entrepreneurship in princely India, the public sector, technology choices in business, and business relations with the working classes.[56] Further, there is

---

comprehensively examines this literature: *Chronicles of British Business in Asia 1850–1960: A Bibliography of Printed Company Histories with Short Accounts of the Concerns* (New Delhi, Manohar, 2002), pp. 90–131.

[54] On banking, see, for instance, G.P. Symes Scutt, *The History of the Bank of Bengal: An Epitome of a Hundred Years of Banking in India* (Calcutta, Bank of Bengal Press, 1904); George Findlay Shirras, *Indian Finance and Banking* (London, Macmillan, 1919); Lakshmi Chandra Jain, *Indigenous Banking in India* (London, Macmillan, 1929), and his *The Monetary Problems of India* (London, Macmillan, 1933); Satyashraya Gopal Panandikar, *Banking in India* (Calcutta, Orient Longman, 1956); Sumant K. Muranjan, *Modern Banking in India* (Bombay, Kamala Pub. House, 1952); Prakash Tandon, *Banking Century: A Short History of Banking in India & the Pioneer, Punjab National Bank* (New Delhi, Viking, 1989); R.K. Seshadri, *A Swadeshi Bank from South India: A History of the Indian Bank, 1907–1982* (Madras, Indian Bank, 1982); Amiya Kumar Bagchi, *The Presidency Banks and the Indian Economy* (New Delhi, Oxford University Press, 1989) and his *The Evolution of the State Bank of India* (Bombay, Oxford University Press, 1987); Dwijendra Tripathi and Priti Misra, *Towards a New Frontier: History of the Bank of Baroda, 1908–1983* (New Delhi, Manohar, 1985); and G. Balachandran, *The Reserve Bank of India 1951–1967* (Bombay, Oxford University Press, 1998). On the jute industry, see Goutam K. Sarkar, *Jute in India: An Economic Analysis* (Calcutta, Oxford University Press, 1989); Samita Sen, *Women and Labour in Late Colonial India: The Bengal Jute Industry* (Cambridge, Cambridge University Press, 1999); and Gordon T. Stewart, *Jute and Empire: The Calcutta Jute Wallahs and the Landscapes of Empire* (Manchester, Manchester University Press, 1998). Amongst the writings on cotton are S.D. Mehta, *The Cotton Mills of India, 1854–1954* (Bombay, Textile Association, 1954); N.H. Thakkar, *The Indian Cotton Textile Industry during the Twentieth Century* (Bombay, Vora, 1949); Makrand Mehta, *The Ahmedabad Cotton Textile Industry: Genesis and Growth* (Ahmedabad, New Order Book Co., 1982); Dharma Kumar, S.P. Nag, and L.S. Venkataramanan, *Resource Allocation in the Cotton Textile Industry* (London, Asia Publishing House, 1966); Sung Jae Koh, *Stages of Industrial Development in Asia: A Comparative History of the Cotton Industry in Japan, India, China, and Korea* (Philadelphia, University of Pennsylvania Press, 1966); M.M. Mehta, *Structure of Indian Industries: A Statistical Study in the Size, Location and Integration of Industrial Units in the Seven Selected Industries of India, viz., Cotton, Jute, Sugar, Iron and Steel, Coal, Paper, and Cement* (Bombay, Popular Book Depot, 1955); Kanhaiya Lal Govil, *The Cotton Industry of India: Prospect and Retrospect* (Bombay, Hind Kitabs, 1950); Peter Harnetty, *Imperialism and Free Trade: Lancashire and India in the Mid-nineteenth Century* (Vancouver, University of British Columbia Press, 1972); and S.R.B. Leadbeater, *The Politics of Textiles: The Indian Cotton-Mill Industry and the Legacy of Swadeshi, 1900–1985* (New Delhi, Sage Publications, 1993). Tirthankar Roy's (ed.), *Cloth and Commerce: Textiles in Colonial India* (New Delhi, Sage Publications, 1996) looks at the handloom textile sector between the seventeenth century and the twentieth century and provides a comprehensive analysis of the industry. On cotton trade controversies in the 1920s and 1930s, see Basudev Chatterji, *Trade, Tariffs and Empire: Lancashire and British Policy in India 1919–1939* (New Delhi, Oxford University Press, 1992).

[55] See the Harvard Business School case studies, such as Thomas De Long and Ashish Nanda, *Infosys Technologies*, HBS Case No. 801-445 (Harvard Business School Publishing, 2002). Also see Tarun Khanna and Krishna G. Palepu, 'The Evolution of Concentrated Ownership in India: Broad Patterns a History of the Indian Software Industry', in Randall K. Morck (ed.), *A History of Corporate Governance around the World: Family Business Groups to Professional Managers* (Chicago, University of California Press, 2005), pp. 283–320.

[56] See Tirthankar Roy's *The Economic History of India* (New Delhi, Oxford University Press, 2006), chapter 6, pp. 190–213 on these sectors. On technology choices, see Dwijendra Tripathi, '"Colonial Syndrome" and

limited work on Indian business in a comparative perspective and not enough on small firms and traditional industry even though their role in industrialization is crucial.[57] The role played by the 'artisan–capitalist' in capitalist development is now being recognized with the work of scholars such as Tirthankar Roy and Mattison Mines.[58] Finally, there is no study of business history from the gender perspective.

BUSINESS HISTORY SINCE THE 1991 REFORMS

The liberalization of the economy since 1991 and the country's emergence as a growing economic power has stimulated even greater interest in India's business past. There is a clear recognition that business has played an important historical role in bringing about an unprecedented transformation in India's economic fortunes. Scholars and observers now see the need to understand Indian business as a historical agent, which needs to be understood in its own terms.

A number of new writings have emerged from different disciplines, ranging from business school style case-studies to historical works. Business school style case-studies have concentrated on how firms are responding to the new economic environment. These include studies of family-run multinationals and government enterprises. They focus upon old conglomerates such as Tata, Birla, and Bajaj, as well as comparatively new enterprises such as Infosys and NIIT, together with government-run enterprises such as Life Insurance Corporation and Hindustan Machine Tools Limited.[59] Amongst the new historical writings are the works of Claude Markovits on the Sindhis,

---

Technology Choices in Indian Industry', in Medha M. Kudaisya and Ng Chin-keong (eds), *Chinese and Indian Business: Historical Antecedents* (Brill, Leiden, 2009). Balraj Mehta has looked at technology choices in the fertilizer industry in his 'Foreign Technology Adaptation and Development: The Experience of the Fertilizer Industry', in Amiya Bagchi and Nirmala Banerjee (eds), *Change and Choice in Indian Industry* (Calcutta, K.P. Bagchi and Co, 1980). Important work has been done by Nasir Tyabji; see his *Colonialism, Chemical Technology, and Industry in Southern India* (Delhi, Oxford University Press, 1995). There is limited work on princely India. Amongst the few studies is Raman Mahadevan's analysis of the development of traditional and modern industries and the expansion of entrepreneurship in Travancore, in S. Bhattacharya, Sumit Guha, Raman Mahadevan, S. Padhi, D. Rajasekhar, and G.N. Rao (eds), *The South Indian Economy: Agrarian Change, Industrial Structure and State Policy, 1914–1947* (New Delhi, Oxford University Press, 1991). One of the few studies which looks at business and the working class is Rajnarayan Chandavarkar's *The Origins of Industrial Capitalism in India: Business Strategies and the Working Classes in Bombay, 1900–1940* (Cambridge, Cambridge University Press, 1994). Attitudes of Indian industrialists towards the working class and industrial relations has also been looked at in Nasir Tyabji's *Industrialization and Innovation: The Indian Experience* (New Delhi, Sage Publications, 2000). An important contribution to looking at entrepreneurship in comparative fashion has been Dwijendra Tripathi's *Historical Roots of Industrial Entrepreneurship in India and Japan: A Comparative Interpretation* (New Delhi, Manohar, 1997).

57 Amongst the few studies are E. Wayne Nafziger, *Class, Caste and Entrepreneurship: A Study of Indian Industrialists* (Honolulu, University of Hawaii Press, 1978) and Mario Rutten and Carol Upadhya (eds), *Small Business Entrepreneurs in Asia and Europe: Towards a Comparative Perspective* (New Delhi, Sage Publications, 1997).

58 Tirthankar Roy, 'Capitalism and Community: A Study of the Madurai Sourashtras', *Indian Economic and Social History Review*, Vol. 34, 1997, pp. 437–63; Mines Mattison, *The Warrior Merchants: Textiles, Trade and Territory in South India* (Cambridge, Cambridge University Press, 1984); and Hein Streefkerk, *Industrial Transition in Rural India: Artisans, Traders and Tribals in South Gujarat* (Bombay, 1985).

59 See, for instance, Sumantra Ghoshal, Gita Piramal, and Sudeep Buddhiraja, *World Class in India: A Casebook of Companies in Transformation* (New Delhi, Penguin, 2001) and Nirmalya Kumar with Pradipta K. Mohapatra and

Aditya Mukherjee on business and nationalist politics, Anne Hardgrove on the Marwaris, and Gita Piramal on Indian entrepreneurial leadership.[60] A historical study which brings together much of the research in the field is Dwijendra Tripathi's *The Oxford History of Indian Business*, first published in 2004 and followed by an updated and concise version. This work presents a comprehensive overview of the history of Indian business from 1700 till contemporary times.[61]

LACK OF INSTITUTIONAL FRAMEWORK

From the earlier discussion, it is apparent that business history writing has thrived in India. Yet, institutional support has been lacking and business history has not developed strong roots within Indian academic and research institutions, as compared to the United States, Europe, or Japan.[62] Business history has not found a place in the country's university system as a separate discipline. Even though business schools have flourished in India, they have failed to incorporate a study of the business past within their curriculum. This is ironic because they draw upon the case-study method which is historical, yet there is little appreciation of the need to pursue the deep history of business. Even the country's best regarded business schools do not offer research programmes in business history. The first and perhaps the only prominent Chair in business history was the Kasturbhai Lalbhai Professorship in Business History at the Indian Institute of Management, Ahmedabad.[63] Between the 1960s and the 1990s, considerable efforts were made at the IIMA to promote teaching and research in business history, but it was a solitary attempt and had much to do with the initiative of Dwijendra Tripathi. University departments do not have separate positions for business history and thus it has not institutionalized itself within the social sciences. Further, even business schools do not regard its teaching as critical to a management education and the Indian Institutes of Technology have not integrated the study of the history of business in their curriculum.

Suj Chandrasekhar, *India's Global Powerhouses: How They are Taking On the World* (Boston, Harvard Business Press, 2009).

[60] Claude Markovits, *The Global World of Indian Merchants, 1750–1947: Traders of Sind from Bukhara to Panama* (Cambridge, Cambridge University Press, 2000); Aditya Mukherjee, *Imperialism, Nationalism and the Making of the Indian Capitalist Class, 1920–1947* (New Delhi, Sage Publications, 2002); Gita Piramal, *Business Maharajas* (New Delhi, Penguin, 1997) and her *Business Legends* (New Delhi, Penguin, 1999); and Anne Hardgrove, *Community and Public Culture: The Marwaris in Calcutta* (New Delhi, Oxford University Press, 2004). Also see Medha M. Kudaisya, *The Life and Times of G.D. Birla* (New Delhi, Oxford University Press, 2003); Bhupesh Bhandar, *The Ranbaxy Story: The Rise of an Indian Multinational* (New Delhi, Penguin, 2005); and Harish Damodaran, *India's New Capitalists: Caste, Business, and Industry in a Modern Nation* (Ranikhet, Permanent Black, 2008).

[61] Dwijendra Tripathi, *The Oxford History of Indian Business* (New Delhi, Oxford University Press, 2004) and Dwijendra Tripathi and Jyoti Jumani, *The Concise Oxford History of Indian Business* (New Delhi, Oxford University Press, 2006). Also see P.N. Agarwala, *A Comprehensive History of Business in India: From 3000 BC to 2000 AD* (New Delhi, Tata McGraw Hill, 2001).

[62] The membership of the US Business History Conference is estimated to be about 550 in 2000 and that of the Business History Association in Japan 850. See Franco Amatori and Geoffrey Jones (eds), *Business History around the World* (Cambridge, Cambridge University Press, 2003).

[63] This is now the Kasturbhai Lalbhai Chair in Entrepreneurship, IIMA. See http://www.iimahd.ernet.in/~anilg/.

Thus, business history has not entrenched itself in the Indian university system. Research institutes which support work in this area are few and business archives are a very new phenomenon, still in their infancy. This lack of institutionalization is further highlighted by the fact that there is still no professional organization in the field.[64]

Further, unlike many other countries, the institutional links between business research and business enterprise are almost non-existent. Though some business houses have commissioned histories such as R.M. Lala's work on the house of Tatas and Arun Joshi's study of Lala Shri Ram, there remains much hesitation in opening up business records and Indian companies are not supportive of firm histories.

In conclusion, though research in Indian business history is thriving, there are huge challenges to the field. It lacks an institutional framework; teaching business history has not taken off in universities and management institutes; business archives are disorganized and inaccessible; and firms do not encourage researchers.[65] Yet, there is no denying the importance of business as a historical agent in India's ongoing economic and social transformation. If this transformation is to be understood in its complexity, a study of business history has to be part of that larger understanding. It is hoped that this Anthology would make a small contribution towards this effort.

* * *

The intention of this Anthology is to portray a composite picture of some important aspects of Indian business life in the nineteenth and twentieth centuries through the writings of scholars, observers, and business persons themselves. The choice of themes is a reflection of the writings which have dominated the field of Indian business history. The Anthology is divided into five sections—the bazaar, mercantile communities, family and firm, rise of Indian industry, and business in the post-reforms era. Each section opens with a theme essay which sets the scene by placing the overall theme in historical context. This is followed by chapters, which consist of essays and extracts, from the writings of scholars, government officials, traders and observers, all in their original forms. The theme essays and chapters are preceded by a short introduction by the editor which places the piece in historical context. The overall intention is to put together both secondary and primary material for general readers and scholars to gain a flavour of the times they portray.

[64] There is one journal devoted to the field—*Journal of Entrepreneurship*, published by Sage Publications, India and brought out by the Entrepreneurship Development Institute of India at Ahmedabad.

[65] There are some exceptions such as the 123-year-old Tata Group which launched the Tata Central Archives, which contains the Group's records, in February 1990 and the 100-year-old Godrej Group which has opened up private papers, speeches, annual reports, and so on, to researchers. In addition, in September 2006 the Godrej Group has started a lecture series, 'Reinterpreting Indian Business History'. The setting up of these business archives has been noted by other groups and there have recently been reports that the Murugappa Group is also thinking along the same lines.

THE BAZAAR

SECTION I

1

Bazaar

'Pulsating Heart' of the Indian Economy

*Rajat Kanta Ray***

Flourishing bazaars have historically been pivotal to the successful functioning of the Indian economy. In colonial India, the bazaar played a vital role in both propelling the local economy as well as connecting it to the capitalist world economy. The dependence of colonial systems on the bazaar was multi-pronged: the bazaar facilitated the commerce of peasant farmers and landlords who then paid tax in cash; the bazaar network ensured the flow of goods and credit through the subcontinent; it hosted the merchants who facilitated European penetration into the local economy; the bazaar helped sell European produce; and, finally, it was the site where colonial authorities hoped to find early evidence of any revolts. In contemporary India too, the bazaar remains the site where retail and wholesale businesses thrive, where urban 'rajas' are created and where important industrial groups continue to take root.

This essay by the noted historian Rajat Kanta Ray serves as an introduction to the bazaar in nineteenth and twentieth century South Asia. It understands the bazaar not only as a venue of petty trade but also as a whole gamut of financial and commercial transactions that encompassed the entire subcontinent and often transcended it. Ray makes a powerful case against notions of the bazaar as a fragmented, sidelined sector that was marginalized by the capitalist world economy. By documenting the bazaar's structural characteristics, nature, size, hierarchies, the ways in which it integrated indigenous capital, and its penetration into modern business, Ray elaborates how the bazaar was integral to the economy of South Asia and the world.*

* Also see Rajat Kanta Ray, 1995, 'Asian Capital in the Age of European Domination: The Rise of the Bazaar, 1880–1914', *Modern Asian Studies*, Vol. 29, No. 3, 1995, pp. 449–554. A different point of view is put forth by Anand Yang in a fascinating study of Bihar. Yang examines rural markets as places of exchange and as political

As Ray shows, the bazaar played an invaluable role in facilitating the outward flows of agricultural produce, the inflow of manufactured goods, and the cross-flows of money and credit that kept the entire economy functioning. A trans-Indian bazaar network operated through the indigenous financial nexus of commission agents (*arhat*), while the use of indigenous credit instruments (*hundi*) enabled the flow of goods and credit throughout the subcontinent. And when colonial rule made inroads, the bazaar not only survived but even flourished. It now provided a bridge between the colonial hold on industry and external trade, and the indigenous economy. Ray highlights the bazaar's advent in modern arenas of business, even as it continued to play a part in ensuring seasonal flows of goods and credit. He employs the unforgettable extended metaphor of the 'pulsating heart' to depict the importance of the bazaar in India's economic organism.

An integrated and dense web of credit and exchange, which had come to link two separate and yet inter-related tiers of the business world in late Victorian India, came under the strain of conflicting developments during and after the First World War. At the upper tier of this pre-war exchange economy, European managing agencies, international export-import firms and London-based exchange banks had grown big on the profits of the external trade, large-scale industry and corporate business since the opening of the Suez Canal. On the eve of the First World War, these activities formed a separate and predominantly white sphere that had expanded without interruption since the rupee-sterling exchange problems of the 1890s were brought to an end by the establishment of the gold exchange standard around 1900. Below this tier lay the sphere of bazaar bankers and merchants working at inland exchanges which formed an altogether different world. Operating through an older indigenous financial nexus of commission agencies (*arhat*) and bills of exchange (*hundi*), they enabled inland produce and credit transactions before and after the war to take place increasingly on an all-India basis. The linking up of wide-apart inland exchanges by means of traditional business devices, now successfully geared to the railways and the telegraph, slowly produced an integrated indigenous exchange system. Finally, the integrated bazaar network broke across the colonial division of spheres confining the bazaar bankers and merchants to the financing of crop movements and the marketing of goods, and the white business preserves indicated above could no longer be maintained as a monopoly.

The beginnings of the national economy that emerged in free India in 1947 can be detected none too obscurely in the conflict growing out of this invasion during and after the First World War, and through the troubled events of the 1930s and the Second World War. These years have emerged from recent historical writings as the period when the nascent Indian capitalist class created wider commercial, financial and

---

forums in the 1920s and 1930s. He commences his analysis of markets in Bihar with Patna and its hinterland, which is seen as the central place, then he looks at the intermediate market or the *qasba* (town or large market village) as the next rung, then the standard market, and finally the *haat* or the periodic market—and he emphasizes their overlaps. See Anand Yang, *Bazaar India: Markets, Society, and the Colonial State in Gangetic Bihar* (Berkeley, University of California Press, 1998). For an interesting study of contemporary bazaars in Bengal, see Akos Ostor, *Culture and Power: Legend, Ritual, Bazaar and Rebellion in a Bengali Society* (New Delhi, Sage Publications, 1984).

industrial networks spanning the subcontinent, a process backed by the closer integration of the indigenous produce and credit markets across the land. Indian bankers and merchants, from whose ranks many of the new industrialists emerged, added a corporate industrial and business component to their earlier investments, carrying on at the same time their involvement in the tightly intermeshed inland exchanges they had meanwhile concentrated in their hands. By a common historical consensus explaining these developments, the First World War, the Great Depression and the Second World War have been identified as successive shocks that profoundly shook the colonial business structure.[1] By the end of the Second World War, the Indian capitalists, an articulate class speaking through the Federation of Indian Chambers of Commerce and Industry, were well entrenched in modern business, large-scale industry and external trade, besides retaining their tightened control over the credit flows sustaining the inland trade and the operations of countless country traders, moneylenders, artisans and peasants.

These developments have attracted intensive study by historians of the Indian economy, for it is well known that the modern Indian business class, which controls large-scale industry today, sprang from the merchant communities involved in bazaar trade and banking.[2] The subject first attracted in-depth research between the two world wars, when critical changes in the commodity and credit markets stimulated several contemporaneous economic studies.[3] More recently, the interest has acquired a wider historical dimension ranging from the pre-colonial systems of banking and commercial credit[4] to the processes by which these were subordinated to the colonial forms of Indian trade and finance[5] and the subsequent structural tensions and changes releasing the Indian mercantile formation from these superimposed bonds.[6]

The antiquity and complexity of *hundi* operations, as established by these researchers, have revealed the truly continental scope of monetary flows in pre-colonial India, with the great Mughal money market of Surat stretching out one arm across the subcontinent to Dacca and the other arm over the Persian Gulf and the Red Sea to Mokha.[7] It has also been established that when the crisis of the eighteenth century contracted the volume of trade, the bankers found alternative employment of their funds by financing the growth of the regional powers, and more especially the expansion of the English East India Company, a process that brought the bankers of Banaras into the limelight as the principal element in the Indian money market at the close of the century.[8] The consolidation and reorganization of the British empire in the 1830s, however, enabled the English East India Company to clip the wings of their native financiers, and to create a colonial monetary and commercial order whose function, as ongoing work suggests strongly, was to segregate the native bankers and merchants, and to push them into a subordinate sphere of the exchange economy.[9] As Surat and Banaras receded from their financial prominence and Calcutta and Bombay emerged as the centres of the money market, an export economy backed by cash crop farming was stimulated by railways, steamships, canals and various other colonial inputs, creating burgeoning inland produce and credit markets in which the Indian merchant communities found an expanding field of investment as a subordinate class of 'marketeers'.[10] As long as the expanding inland and overseas traffic in the prosperous decades following the opening of the Suez Canal brought matching gains to the top corporations and the intermediate marketeers, the friction inherent in their give-and-take was kept in check. But when this era of easy commercial prosperity came to an end with the First World War, the tension exploded and, as recent findings indicate, mutual aggressions across demarcated spheres (which had so long been respected in a well-adjusted colonial economy) worked to the ultimate advantage of the Indian intermediaries who had, in a manner unsuspected, got a grip over the supply lines of their European principals.[11]

In view of the wider links laid bare by these explorations, it is now appropriate to view the indigenous system of credit transfers and commodity exchange in the context of the entire country. This essay seeks to bring into focus the integrated indigenous marketing and credit nexus of the 1920s and 1930s with the help of material from the reports of the various banking enquiry committees before and during the Great Depression and the marketing surveys of the Agricultural Marketing Adviser carried out after the depression. This material helps to address certain questions relating to the land as a whole. How was the bazaar, which supplied the basis of capital accumulation by India's industrial capitalists, situated within the wider economy? What was its relation to the dominant European complex of business and industry, and to the local rural economy of pedlars, peasants and artisans? How was the bazaar organised, and what were its instruments of operation and devices of control? What changes in the bazaar and the wider economy enabled the merchant communities to break into modern business and industry? What operations were the bazaar bankers and commission agents handling during the critical years when their penetration of the European preserve got under way? These are questions of long-term significance: during the period under study and well beyond it, Indian industrialists continued to be heavily involved in bazaar finance and speculation, a factor that explains not merely the origins of the class but many of its characteristics to this day.

The basic argument here is that even before this class established itself in the sphere of the central money market which controlled India's international economy, its progenitors had concentrated in their hands a largely autonomous indigenous money market that had already incorporated distant parts of the land in their credit operations.[12] The bazaar bankers and commission agents had woven a seamless web of credit and exchange by means of older indigenous devices (such as the *hundi* and the *arhat*), a nexus through which money moved rapidly and regularly across the length and breadth of India. Before the Great Depression, for instance, the Multani bankers were sending money from Shikarpur in Sind to Madurai in the deep south, or to take another example, the Marwari bankers were remitting funds from the desert towns of Bikaner and Shekhawati to the Brahmaputra valley.[13] This financial and marketing network, tied at two ends to Bombay and Calcutta, emerged from the Great Depression more closely intermeshed than ever, consisting of 12 money exchanges and 1,718 produce markets, all linked to each other by daily transactions operating at telegraphic speed and each pulling into its orbit the local rural economies of its hinterland, linking them by its wide ranging *hundi* and *arhat* operations to the European banks and firms at the ports.

It must not be thought, however, that the most important function of the *hundi* and *arhat* operations was to feed the requirements of the import-export business managed and financed by modern European enterprise. While the bazaar bankers and commission agents devoted a part of their business to serving the modern banks, managing agencies and import-export firms controlling India's international economy, their operations consisted principally in inland movements of credit and produce. Organised European-style business and industry was a narrow segment of the economy even in the flourishing 1920s when the exchange banks and agency houses reaped handsome profits. Far greater in size at this time was the sector which the Controller of Currency in his annual reports on rates of money designated by the term bazaar.

The bankers (*shroffs*) and commission agents (*arhatiyas*) who constituted this sector used the term in a specific technical sense, meaning the market for indigenous credit they drew upon to sustain domestic traffic in produce, manufactures and bullion. Thus the bazaar rates recorded by the Controller of Currency meant the rates at which inland bills of exchange (*hundis*) were discounted by the *shroffs*.[14] The term also embraced the trade itself that this indigenous money market financed by cash and credit. The *hundi* bazaar run by the *shroffs* sustained the grain and seeds bazaar, the raw cotton bazaar, the piecegoods bazaar, the gold and silver bazaar, the *futka* bazaar (futures trading), to name only a few of the most important spot and forward trade transactions of the *arhatiyas*. In other words, the bazaar in its wider sense meant the system of banking and trade that ensured, through long-tried and tested indigenous methods, the massive flows of money, credit, crops, manufactured goods and precious metals within the domestic commercial economy of India. It was distinct, on the one hand, from the European-dominated organised business and industry above, and, on the other hand, from the small peasant and artisan economy below. The bazaar appeared to be 'unorganised' by the Western standards of organisation which prevailed in exchange banking, foreign trade and factory industry, but it commanded its own complex and sophisticated form of organisation finely adjusted over centuries to the monsoon economy and rural production organisation of India.

THE MARKET: NATURE, SIZE AND HIERARCHY

The vast and growing population of India could not have sustained its gradual increase through the nineteenth and early twentieth centuries but for the extensive and integrated services provided by the bazaar, which expanded in response to the slow increase of the population—some three hundred million on the eve of the First World War, and growing much faster after the peace. The massive poverty of the enormous population and the seasonal cycle of the dispersed production system were the two dominating factors shaping market conditions in India. In their reports to the US government, American trade consuls in India stressed these factors, the vastness of the country, its diversity, and its teeming population. While assessing its commercial opportunities, they stressed above all the uncertainties which prevented the growth of a uniform, centrally-controlled market in India. A poor wheat crop, they saw, might put the Punjab peasant into deeper debt; while Bengal jute would fetch the highest prices. Tea in Assam might be depressed, while hides and skins from the Central Provinces would get unprecedented offers from foreign buyers. The lack of two inches of rain in a given region might bring the great mass of peasants to the abyss of famine, yet other and larger masses of population would be unaffected elsewhere. Market conditions, they stressed, were altogether different from those in the West. The expectation of a large uniform market was frustrated by the nature of the production organisation, which hinged on low paid human labour, and which could be harnessed to the rearing and marketing of crops only with the aid of the indigenous trading and credit hierarchy. Dependence on it was unavoidable for outsiders, given the vast number of small units of production and the extreme variability of conditions in which these worked across the country and through the seasons.[15]

On account of the low purchasing capacity of the people, profit margins on goods sold were small, and large profits could only be made by mass selling at low profit margins: something that required patient effort and, as the US trade consuls never tired of telling American businessmen—'channels'. These channels lay, of course, through the bazaar; there was no means of bypassing it, much as foreign exporters and importers would have liked to do so. The US trade consuls distinguished from this mass market (where the main consideration in selling goods was not how good but how cheap) a small market for high-class goods, catering to about one million people whose incomes and living styles were substantially higher—the European population of merchants, missionaries, civil administrators, and officers and soldiers of the British army, the Indian princes, large landowners and Westernised merchants, and the Parsee community of Bombay and the Anglo-Indian population, with Western tastes. The department stores and shops which they patronised—and where the same quality of goods were sold as in Europe and America—lay outside the sphere of the bazaar. Selling goods to the mass of the people was a radically different proposition from catering to the limited market for high-class goods. The problem, as one American Trade Consul put it succinctly, was:

> to sell goods suitable not only for the comparatively small upper and middle classes, but goods cheap enough and simple enough to be within the reach of over 300,000,000 people who belong to the poor and illiterate classes of society. In doing business with the upper classes and middle classes it is possible to secure a rather wide margin of profit, but the sales must be comparatively small. In doing business with the great masses of the people the margin of profit must be extremely small; however, the sales and collective profits may be enormous.[16]

The extremely low profit margins at which the bazaar people—even the biggest of the *arhatiyas*—were willing to work, depending on a very large turnover at huge risks among so poor a people, would have been unacceptable to large western corporations, which perforce had to accept the *shroffs* and the *arhatiyas* as their commission agents and guarantors for sales and purchases.

The cost of efficiency of peasant agriculture and several important branches of artisan manufacture, which had been established beyond doubt by the beginning of the twentieth century, implied that colonial interests could not take over these areas of the inland economy. The white plantations being unable to survive on the plains, and the mills being able to command only a part of the crops for processing, the corporate sector was necessarily smaller in size; and the greater part of the Indian work force—the millions of peasants and artisans who by the very nature of their dispersed operations could not be pressed into larger units—remained beyond direct production control by the European business class, which had no alternative but to obtain crops and distribute goods through the indigenous marketing and financing hierarchy that had naturally grown out of the rural production organisation. Hence India could be subordinated to the world capitalist economy only by the concession of a large economic space to the bazaar.

At the beginning of the twentieth century, not a single crop on the vast plains of India was a genuine plantation crop. Even indigo, the crop which white planters in Champaran continued to force the peasants to grow, was produced within the small farm framework. Jute, the great colonial crop that the British developed after the collapse of indigo in Bengal, remained uncompromisingly a peasant crop. Genuine plantation crops, tea and coffee (but even coffee was mainly a peasant crop and only partially a plantation crop), grew mainly on the hills. Tea was about the only crop in India which was exclusively produced on plantations, and which the British managing agencies could control right from its cultivation through its dispatch by rail to its shipment for final sale in London. But leaving aside Darjeeling and the Assam hills, where intensive peasant agriculture had not been previously established and where conditions were favourable for capital-intensive tea plantation, nowhere else could planters compete with peasants in terms of costs. New capital inputs were proportionately small in Indian agriculture, labour and cattle inputs massive and cheap. Systematic efforts by Western machinery manufacturers to sell tractors and other unsuitable machinery to Indian peasants ran quickly aground,[17] and one possible means of remote control of Indian agriculture through agricultural machinery supply was denied to colonial manufacturing interests. Furthermore, peasants not merely barred the way for potential planters; they were also artisans in their spare time, and employers of artisans in agricultural work in peak seasons. Peasants who were part-time artisans and artisans who were part-time peasants were a frustrating combination for the mills, the reason why neither Manchester, nor Bombay, could accomplish their long desired objective, namely monopoly of the immense market for piecegoods in India. Except towards the very end of our period, handloom production kept pace uniformly with mill production.[18]

The predominance of small peasant agriculture and cottage industries in the total Indian output was a factor of vital importance in the development of Indian capitalist enterprise. Compared to many other colonial countries where plantation agriculture was fully established, India was able to develop a larger capitalist class, in fact the largest in the decolonised third world. Why? Because here the colonial sector could not replace agriculture with plantations, nor even cottage industries with mills, and to assemble the produce from so many peasants and so many artisans, it had to leave a substantial part of the economy to the bazaar, which provided a firm basis for the growth of an indigenous capitalist class out of the merchant communities which dominated the bazaar. Only the bazaar could 'deliver' the goods from the bottom to the top by virtue of complex financial arrangements that interlocked its own numerous successive layers. These arrangements generated the essential flows of credit without which the economy would grind to a halt. In an economy characterised by high credit risks at the base, the bazaar represented the perfection of financial methods adjusted to the stark poverty of the population and the uncertain seasonal agricultural conditions. Necessarily, the British had to fit India into the world capitalist economy, not through the direct control of the labour process by mills and plantations financed by banks, but through the operations of numerous *shroffs* and *arhatiyas* gathering in and financing the produce of countless farms and cottages.

Hence the size of bazaar operations still exceeded, between the two world wars, that of modern banking, export-import trade and factory industry. It was the bazaar, through its twin instruments of the *hundi* and the *arhat*, which assembled, distributed and financed the produce of close on 36 million small, dispersed agricultural households with tiny surpluses destined for the market.[19] As the exchange banks were confined to financing the external trade, and the joint stock banks had little capital to spare for the interior, the financing of the massive movements of crops and goods within the country remained the preserve of the *shroffs* and *arhatiyas*, assisted by some crucial seasonal help from the Imperial Bank of India. Before the onset of the Great Depression, the railways carried 85 million tons of goods from the inland centres to the ports, and between the inland centres.[20] This, in view of the still marginal volume of road traffic in India, may be taken to be not far short of the total volume of long distance domestic trade in India.[21] Out of this huge volume of goods moving within the country, the overseas ships took to and from the ports of India just about 9 million tons of goods.[22] These figures would set the volume of railway-borne inland traffic at almost ten times the volume of ship-borne overseas traffic. During the Great Depression, imports and exports became even more marginal in the total production and distribution of agricultural produce in India (see Table 1). In view of the fact that the banks had few branches in the interior, the *shroffs* and *arhatiyas* financed all but a small part of this great inland traffic.

It was these indigenous financiers again who kept the country's production process going by their advances and loans to countless small peasants, artisans, rural traders and moneylenders. Since agricultural produce was the main part of the output, and as large-scale industry was outweighed by small-scale and cottage industries[23] right up to the outbreak of the Second World War, the banks played a lesser role in financing the economy than the *shroffs* and *mahajans*. The indigenous money market financed much of the production of the country except for the sector of mines, mills and plantations served by the central money market, revealingly described by an indigenous banker as the 'English bazaar'.[24] No wonder, then, that the Bombay Shroff Association affirmed that the total turnover of cash during a working day in their Bombay exchange far exceeded the corresponding figures of all local banks taken together.[25]

The export-import figures of Indian trade, and the allied volume of exchange bank operations, would, therefore, reveal only the tip of the iceberg. From the tip downwards, Indian trade and finance broadened at each successive level. To take figures for 1928–29, there were, at the peak, 9 million tons of imports and exports, mainly through eight ports—Karachi, Bombay, Cochin, Tuticorin, Madras, Vizagapatam, Calcutta and Chittagong. At the second level, there were these 9 million tons moving along the railway lines from and to the ports, and in

Table 1 Production and Trade in Three Crops (in tons), Mid-1930s

	Rice (1937/37)	Wheat (Average 1925/26– 1934/35)	Linseed (1936–37)
Total production	28,380,000	9,300,000	4,75,000
Marketed surplus	11,500,000	5,100,000	3,80,000
Exports & imports	2,000,000	25,000	3,00,000

Source: *Report on the Marketing of Rice in India and Burma* (Delhi, 1941), pp. 104, 492; *Report on the Marketing of Wheat in India* (Delhi, 1937), pp. 13–14, 16, 40, 44; *Report on the Marketing of Linseed in India* (Delhi, 1938), pp. 13, 21, 25, 40.

addition something like 76 million tons of goods moving along the railway lines without ever reaching the docks, but moving simply between market towns. Finally, at the base of this trading system was the movement of these 85 million tons of goods on carts along roads running to the railheads, *plus* the indeterminate volume of goods marketed within the locality away from the railheads, perhaps an additional 50 million tons.[26] Thus at the three successive levels of the market, the tonnage of traded goods increased from 9 million to 85 million to 135 million.

Taken together, these levels defined a three-tier marketing hierarchy—the financial and commercial centres, the market towns and the rural periodical markets—which served to structure India's domestic economy and to connect it with the world markets. At the top of the pyramid were the great cities and towns—Bombay and Calcutta towering over the rest—through which the country as a whole was kept in touch with the international economy of the post-Suez era. The two great colonial port cities, the lesser ports such as Madras and Karachi, and the burgeoning inland centres of import-export trade (for instance, Delhi and Cawnpore), were at one and the same time the bases of the banks and corporations which controlled India's international economy, and the headquarters of the indigenous banking and commission agency firms which operated the integrated inland economy of the country. These big towns and cities were the financial centres for both the Western and indigenous money markets, one serving the external trade and the other the long distance inland trade. Around these financial and commercial nodal points were arranged numerous market towns or *mandis*, such as Lyallpur, the cotton and wheat mart of the Chenab canal colony of the Punjab; Hapur, the granary of the canal tracts of western UP; Khamgaon, the cotton assembling centre of the black soil tract of Berar; and Guntur, the rice assembling and milling centre of the canal irrigated Krishna valley. The *mandis* were the points at which primary produce was assembled for dispatch to the main distributing or exporting centres; they were also the points at which goods were sent up from the main importing or distributing centres for inland wholesaling and retail distribution. Below this urban network of financial centres and country towns was the vast rural hinterland, served by seasonal fairs and weekly or bi-weekly markets dispersed over the countryside. The fairs were annual or seasonal gatherings, one of the most critical functions of which was to enable the peasants to buy cattle from the stock breeders and livestock traders. The more regular rural markets, known as shandies in Madras, *painths* in northern India and *haats* in Bihar and Bengal, assembled once or twice a week for retail transactions in agricultural produce and urban manufactures. The typical shandy, which unlike the urban retail market had no permanent market structure, was held on the roadside or in the grove, where the producer brought his produce to sell in small quantities to the shopkeeper or pedlar, and purchased with the cash thus obtained a wide range of articles imported from towns for household use, such as cloth, salt and brass vessels.[27]

Nothing brings out more clearly the distinction between the successive levels of the marketing hierarchy than the respective amounts of produce handled in the shandies, the market towns and the colonial port cities; and the whole amount handled in this manner, and its proportion to the unmarketed produce are indicators of the extent to which the market had penetrated country life. Keeping in mind the diversity of the land, the amounts and proportions would no doubt have varied considerably from one part to another. For a typically poor area pulled into the orbit of world markets by imperial communications, Bihar would be a good example. A backward and famine prone rice producing area, it had developed sugar, lac, oilseeds and other commercial crops exported by the railways to distant destinations.

Aided by a numerous body of exploited agricultural labourers, 22 million Bihari peasants produced Rs. 47 crore worth of rice before the Great Depression set in. They consumed, without any marketing at all, 60 per cent of the rice, eating the major part of it themselves, storing a part for seed and paying out on the threshing floor a portion as grain wage to labourers and village artisans. The non-peasant rural population, numbering 10.5 million, purchased another 29 per cent of the rice for their own consumption, which they bought at the village shandy. A shandy was to be found every six miles in Bihar. The produce was assembled there by village pedlars (*beparis*) and by the peasants themselves, mostly for local sales which never reached the *mandi*, a large mart for storing grain found every fifteen miles, at main road junctions, district headquarters and railway centres. Only Rs. 5.5 crore worth of rice reached the 500 *mandis* of Bihar, as against Rs. 27 crores worth of rice which was never traded, and Rs. 14.5 crore worth of rice which reached the 2,500 shandies and no further. The other crops were more intensively commercialised. Taking the total agricultural produce of Bihar, Rs. 40 crore worth of crops was handled in the market towns, and Rs. 75 crore worth of crops was consumed or exchanged within the country, either through the shandies or through non-cash crop sharing transactions. Exports out of Bihar, not all of it to foreign countries, were less than half the value of the goods traded in the *mandis*, the principal items of foreign export being oilseeds, jute and lac. The surplus sugar sent out of Bihar was for distribution in other parts of India, and formed another important component in the business of the bazaar.[28]

Certain facts stand out clearly from the available figures. While foreign imports and exports never formed a considerable portion of the country produce, the amounts passing into the market towns were many times more, and the produce traded in the country fairs and markets at least one-third more than that handled by the *mandi*-based bazaar. The proportion of the total produce of the country that never reached the market was well below half, and that leaching the higher commercial world of the bazaar was somewhat over a third. Even the portion of the crop retained by the country entered into a well-established nexus of exchange and credit, comprising both market transactions by cash or barter through the shandies, and important non-market transactions such as crop sharing (*batai*) between peasant, labourer and landlord, and ritualised exchanges (*jajmani*) between peasant and artisan regulated by hereditary custom and conducted on an annual basis. The spirit of exchange had undoubtedly penetrated the country deeply, and the marketing hierarchy was arranged in three distinct layers—rural periodical markets, market towns and the financial and commercial centres.

There was a clear distinction between the three levels of the hierarchy in terms of transport systems, credit structure and market personnel and organisation.[29] The shandies were connected to the *mandis* by *kutcha* roads, on which peasants and pedlars took their produce on bullock-drawn carts and pack animals to sell through commission agents based on market towns. At the rural level of marketing, *hundis* were not in use. Peasants and pedlars settled their transactions in exchange of produce or in hard cash. They obtained hard cash from

Table 2 Marketing of Produce in Bihar (1929)

Name of crop	Total value of produce (Rs. crore)	Traded in 2500 *haats* (Rs. crore)	Traded in 500 *mandis* (Rs. crore)	Exported out of Bihar (Rs. crore)
Rice	47	20	5.5	1
Gram & pulses	22	15	8	2
Other food grains	12	6	3	1
Oilseeds	13	8	7	3.5
Sugar	4.5	0	6	4
Jute	4	3	3	3
Tobacco	2	2	2	1.5
Other crops	7	5	3	1
Lac	2.5	2.5	2.5	2.5
	114	61.5	40	19.5

Source: *Report of the Bihar and Orissa Provincial Banking Enquiry Committee 1929–30*, Vol. I (Patna 1930), pp. 12, 160, 102.

the *arhatiyas* of the market towns in payment for their produce. Once the produce entered the market towns and reached the hands of the *arhatiyas*, it entered a different world. The *arhatiyas* sent the produce on metalled roads to the railheads for transportation to the port towns and the inland centres, using the *hundi* network serviced by the *shroffs* (often the biggest *arhatiyas* being themselves *shroffs* under the interlocking system of indigenous banking and commission agency). A fraction of the produce moving on the railways reached the hands of the agents of the international firms, either based on port towns or posted upcountry. At this level the produce entered a third and higher world, leaving the ambit of the bazaar. It was processed in mills or presses, and shipped through the ports with the credits, exchange facilities and telegraphic transfers arranged by the exchange banks. The financial structure of each sector was so different that credit did not flow from one sector to the other except through bottlenecks: the banks gave credit for domestic trade through listed *shroffs* with definite borrowing limits, while the *shroffs* in their turn funnelled funds to the rural producers through known *beparis* (shopkeepers) and *mahajans* (moneylenders).

The rates at which money could be obtained at each tier of the marketing hierarchy were different, and there was no single money rate. The bank rate, which determined the rate at which credit was obtained by the corporations for import-export trade, and the *hundi* rate, which determined the cost of credit for inland merchants and commission agents, fluctuated from season to season, but the seasonal fluctuations of the bank rate and the *hundi* rate diverged markedly from each other. By contrast, the rates of loans to peasants and artisans did not vary, like bank or *hundi* rates, from season to season, but remained at a uniformly high level through the year on account of the risk involved in such loans. In the UP towns, for instance, the *arhatiyas* and *shroffs* charged on average 9 per cent on *hundi* loans, while in the countryside the most common rate of advances to peasants by Banias and *mahajans* was 24 per cent.[30] Here was a clear break in the continuum of credit from the market town to the village. Though there was large downward flow of credit, the credit assumed an altogether different form and meaning at the bottom. It functioned at far higher interest and on practically no security, and was able to function only because of the close personal connection between creditor and debtor. Rural moneylending was a form of high risk lending which no respectable *shroff* would touch. *Arhatiyas* and *shroffs* could venture to channel funds from the bazaar to the indigent peasant economy only through village traders and rural creditors who knew how to assess credit risks in the village.

The weakness of the link between the rural credit system and the bazaar was responsible for a paradox. During the monsoon there was a slack in the urban money market while the country experienced stringency. From May to August rural creditors needed more funds to make advances to the cultivators for sowing the kharif. The funds lying idle in the bazaar at the end of the grain trading season in June could not find congenial employment in the mofussil precisely when there was stringency there. The reason for this is clear: the whole rural economy lay outside the sphere of the *hundi* money market. As is clear from the evidence of the banking reports and marketing surveys, *hundis* did not circulate through the rural economy, and a money market can be said to exist only when negotiable instruments are in use. In the absence of rural *hundis*, the bazaar money could not be efficiently employed in the country during the sowing season. It moved to the country through the clumsy device of book credits, which prevented the expansion of mobile credit—the sort of credit which could have eased the seasonal stringency in the country. The fault did not lie with the bazaar. It lay in the very nature of the rural economy—a chronically deficit and insecure economy in which mobile credit simply could not develop.

Here was a cleavage within the indigenous system of trade and finance. The distinction was clearly perceived by a British official who said in his evidence to the Indian Currency Committee of 1898: 'There are two sorts of loan transactions upcountry. There is the loan by the bunneah or village money-lender who deals with his own money and there is the loan by the mahajan or banker, who deals with other people's money as well as his own.'[31] The distinction here lay between a rural finance system in which the lender's own funds were used, and the bazaar which in addition to lending money mobilised new credit resources by drawing, discounting and rediscounting *hundis*. The two types of loan transactions had separate spheres. The *hundi* money, consisting of trade bills, was invested in the movement and marketing of produce. The rural loanable money, consisting of advances to peasants and artisans, was invested in the cycle of production and upkeep of producers (especially after food stocks ran out).

The sphere of the bazaar is thus clear: it operated at the tier of the marketing hierarchy where *hundis* were in circulation. This excluded at one end the village shandies which had no sources of mobile credit, and at the other end the international ports-of-call which possessed the higher but entirely alien financial instruments of the exchange banks. Its critical function was to generate the indigenous flows of mobile credit without which the market economy could not have functioned, and which in turn generated the opposite flows of produce, manufactured goods, bullion, currency and revenue, adjusting these two-way flows between town and country to the highly uncertain seasons and their extremely taxing credit demands. Shipments of agricultural produce, which were intimately connected with the country's crop calendar, determined the timing of currency and bullion inflows and revenue outflows. The exchange banks and import-export corporations which financed and made these shipments had neither the information nor the infrastructure to generate the credit movements necessary to guarantee the timely flows of produce, currency, bullion and revenue. The crop seasons dictated the interior demand for currency, credit and bullion, and accordingly there were marked seasonal fluctuations in bullion trade, currency absorption and loan business.[32] The colonial banking and business sector did not possess the necessary sensitivity to seasonal variations—it was the bazaar which had its ear to the ground, gathering information and reacting instantly to daily changes in widely dispersed markets.[33]

The two main crops—the monsoon crop (kharif) and the winter crop (rabi)—provided the time-table for bazaar operations, the agricultural year being divided into two parts, one of rearing and harvesting the successive monsoon and winter crops (July-December) and the other of selling one after the other (January-June). Prevailing conditions in the indigenous money market differed drastically through the seasons, a fact reflected in the fluctuating bazaar rates at its twin centres, Bombay and Calcutta. The rates were high from January to June, a busy season of intensive crop sales when money was tight. They were low from July to December, a slack season when the rain and winter crops were being successively sown and gathered and when there was plenty of money lying idle.

The busy season for trading in grain started around January. It did not, it should be noted, begin at once after the kharif harvest around September–December. The peasant stocked most of the grain for his food and for sale in small lots for periodical purchase of necessities—a stock which ran out only towards the end of January. Heavy trading in grain by means of *hundi* financing began in January, reached a climax with the rabi harvest in March, and sustained itself through June. There were extremely heavy shipments of agricultural products through these months. The vast peasant population used the proceeds of their sales to purchase a massive quantity of gold and silver from January to May, partly on account of the marriage season in May and partly as a means of carrying over the proceeds of a successful harvest until funds were required to purchase seed for planting the kharif on the eve of monsoon.[34] During the same months, January to March, and also through April, the flow of currency into the country reached its peak. There was great demand for small coins among traders and peasants after the wheat and late rice harvest. The great indigenous money markets of Bombay and Calcutta faced such stringency at this time that they drew on *hundi* finance from the upcountry homes of the *shroffs*—on Multani funds in Shikarpur and Marwari funds in Rajputana. From December to March money flowed from the Marwari *shroffs'* branches in the native states of Rajputana to Calcutta and Bombay for more profitable employment. Delhi, the third great indigenous banking centre, relied on its own funds to send in April (immediately after the rabi harvest) a great quantity of silver coins to upcountry grain *mandis* like Hapur for the purchase of wheat from peasants.

From the next month the pumping of funds from the banking centres to the upcountry *mandis* ceased. The onset of the monsoon brought on the slack season in the mofussil money market. This was a time of intense agricultural activity associated with the sowing of the kharif crop (May-June). The kharif seed, however, was cheap at this time. The cultivator had already stocked his grain and there was little need to borrow till mid-September. He used his funds to pay the revenue instalments, which were so heavy from May to July that the flow of silver coins was now reversed. In June, July and August there was large return of silver from the interior. No profit was to be obtained from the employment of funds in the mofussil and in August Hapur traders who had borrowed silver coins from Delhi would return the money through *hundis*. Funds were invested in the big urban markets during the slack season to pay for imported goods. The bullion import through Bombay, however, was sluggish, for the cultivator had large expenses to meet in connection with planting and watering his crops. Even after the kharif harvest, he could not afford to buy ornaments, for the rabi crop was planted at this time and he had to take advances for that in October. Such advances for planting had no connection with the *hundi* market which was sluggish.[35]

This was clear evidence of the distinction between rural credit and urban finance referred to earlier. The involvement of the big merchants and bankers in the cycle of agricultural loans was, as already mentioned, indirect. They seldom found it feasible to finance the peasants directly as the credit risks were too great. The village *mahajan*, who was in closer touch with his peasant client, could risk loans which the *shroff* could not. He could draw if necessary on the town *sowcar*, who, in turn, being of greater credit, received accommodation from the big *hundiwal* when he ran short of funds. The total sum which was thus invested by *mahajans*, *sowcars* and *shroffs* in agricultural advances around 1930 was estimated by the Central Banking Enquiry Committee at roughly Rs. 900 crore, of which at least Rs. 400 crore was short-term seasonal loans for seed, cattle, and so on.[36] The kharif advance was taken from June onwards and was repaid after harvest in December or January. The rabi advance was taken in October and repaid after marketing in April.[37] This entire agricultural credit was extended through book entries, and not by means of *hundis*.

THE BAZAAR AND THE COLONIAL TRADE

If the sphere of the *hundi* did not penetrate downwards to the cycle of agricultural operations, it did not extend upwards to the marketing of agricultural produce abroad either. The trade of the colonial ports, with its lines running through the Suez Canal to England, Europe and America and eastwards to China and Japan, was under the regime of the Western money market. Indian finance and trade were dominated in the upper reaches by the City of London, and by 18 foreign exchange banks formed into an association under the leadership of the Chartered Bank of India, Australia and China.

The close connection with London meant that there was no uncertainty regarding values, since the Government of India maintained a fixed basis for converting silver rupees into gold sovereign. Its financial and monetary policies offered excellent security to international trading corporations operating through the sterling exchange, a strong inducement for American and Continental firms to move into India through the London money market. The US trade consuls in India, in fact, warned American exporters against trying to sell direct to unreliable native houses, and recommended that the task be left to London indentors.[38] A long chain of intermediaries arose in the import trade on account of the low credit of native merchants: exchange banks, indent firms, guarantee brokers, and so on.

Of the 18 exchange banks operating in India, eight were British, the rest—which had their operations mainly outside India—were American, Japanese, Dutch, French and Portuguese. The Chartered Bank of India, Australia and China, with its head office in London, operated mainly on the London-India-Straits Settlements-China run. The National Bank of India, also London-based, concentrated on the London-Aden-East Africa-India run. The Eastern Bank, another London-based British exchange bank, operated on the London-Mesopotamia-India line. The Hongkong and Shanghai Banking Corporation, a Hongkong based British exchange. bank, was concerned with the China-India-London line. Among the non-British banks, the National City Bank of New York concerned itself with foreign exchange transactions between America-London-India; the Yokohama Specie Bank was concerned with Japan-India-London; the Netherlands Trading Society with Holland, Belgium, Germany, London and India. The Tata Industrial Bank, which operated for some time in foreign exchange transactions, was soon forced out of existence. All these exchange banks had access to the vast resources and connections of the London money market, which enabled them to offer important assistance to the foreign manufacturing corporations, and to European managing agencies, export-import houses and indent firms.[39]

The role of the exchange banks in the import trade expanded perceptibly in the 1920s as their number increased from 10 in 1918, with Indian deposits worth £46,392,000 to 18 in 1922, with Indian deposits worth £55,038,000. This was accompanied by a considerable expansion of inland activity by the exchange banks, as 6 new upcountry branches were opened by Chartered, Lloyds and Mercantile Bank after the First World War in addition to the 13 upcountry branches already in existence before the war. Their activities no longer stopped at the ports but extended to the principal inland centres for the distribution of imported goods. In Delhi, for instance, Chartered, National, Mercantile and Lloyds each had a branch and were engaged in financing the import of piecegoods, bullion, metals and machinery, negotiating the foreign shippers' drafts on native importers in Delhi.[40] When the goods arrived in port, the banks cleared the goods from the port and charged the Delhi merchants 10 per cent for the clearing service. On arrival of the goods in Delhi, the four banks made advances to the importing merchants by opening loan accounts against hypothecation of goods stored in their godown. The total margin of the invoice value of the goods consumed by the big four was estimated at 40 per cent in 1930, including clearing charges and customs duties.[41] The role of the exchange banks was critical in the import trade because, in the absence of a regular machinery of open credit ratings as in Wall Street, American and other foreign manufacturers were reliant on the British exchange banks for information regarding the credit of Indian importers. There was a general feeling in the bazaar that the British banks gave poor references to foreign manufacturers regarding the credit of Indian merchants, undermining the whole position of the latter in foreign trade.[42]

Because of the uncertain financial standing of Indian importing merchants, a peculiar type of business organisation—the indent firm—had sprung into existence. The indent firm was an international mercantile house which brought Indian buyers in touch with foreign manufacturers by receiving indents from Indian merchants, passing them on to foreign manufacturers, and charging a commission on the transaction. But it was more than a mere international broker between buyer and seller. The smaller bazaar dealers who distributed the imported goods had no credit, and upon arrival of goods they would sometimes refuse to take all the packages, though willing to take a part which they needed immediately. The indent firms would in such cases clear through customs the goods they had already sold on commission, place them in warehouses and release them in small lots, thus minimising the credit risk of the foreign manufacturers in dealing with the bazaar dealers. The indent firms were thus a dominant factor in the import trade: they would take indents from small dealers, land the imported goods, store them in their own godowns, charge 9 per cent in interest and godown rent after 30 days of landing the goods, and release the goods to the dealers in small lots as and when demanded. The indent firms were mostly non-Indian (ordinarily British) export-import houses engaged in trading on their own account as well.[43]

The importing houses used another device to minimise the credit risk in import trade: the 'guarantee broker' of Bombay and the Banian of Calcutta. A native merchant of standing, the guarantee broker or Banian brought in orders and financed and guaranteed the bills. For about 1.5 per cent commission be undertook to guarantee that the bazaar merchant would pay in full the bill for the order which the broker had brought in and financed.

'When business is done through a strong guarantee broker', the US Trade Consul advised American businessmen, 'there is little danger to the seller, as the former pays the bill if the buyer does not'.[44]

Some of the Banians or guarantee brokers were big merchants of national standing. The big Marwari banking firm of Calcutta, Tarachand Ghanshyamdas, were Banians to Shaw Wallace, guaranteeing their oil and fertiliser imports everywhere in India. Ramdutt Ramkissendas, the big Goenka firm of Calcutta, were Banians to the house of Ralli in jute supply and piecegoods distribution, besides being jute balers and traders on their own account. The European importing houses, financed by the exchange banks, dealt—through guarantee brokers—with big bazaar merchants who bought the goods on commission at the port, using *hundis* and other indigenous credit; the bigger merchants in turn passed the goods on directly to mofussil shopkeepers or through the intermediary of a wholesale bazaar dealer.[45]

While the financing of the import trade was done entirely by exchange banks by means of discounting of sterling import bills, the financing of the export trade was shared by the exchange banks with the London money market. The exchange banks provided the cash for the purchase of goods for export until the sterling export bills were received in London and discounted there, from which point onwards the funds were furnished by the London market. The foreign bills of exchange—invariably sterling bills for both imports and exports—were of the two kinds: (*a*) D/A drafts, which provided credit on acceptance of the draft by the importer, and (*b*) D/P drafts, which meant delivery only on payment and no credit. If an Indian importer dealt with a foreign manufacturer on a D/A basis, he would obtain possession of the bill of lading as soon as he 'accepted' the draft drawn on him by the foreign party through an exchange bank. As such drafts did not become due until 30, 60, or 70 days after the date on which they were accepted by the purchaser, the Indian purchaser would obtain possession of the goods on arrival by producing the bill of lading, and would get time to sell the goods and pay the accepted draft out of the proceeds of sale. This was acceptance credit and it was usually given only to 'first class' Indian parties with which a foreign manufacturer had long dealings. In the D/P contract, on the other hand, the Indian purchaser would have to pay in order to get possession of the bill of lading, without which the steamship company would not deliver the goods to the consignee.[46]

The low credit ratings which the exchange banks generally gave to Indian merchants undermined their position in this entire bills of exchange business, which came to be so structured as to force the Indian merchants to participate in import-export trade on systematically adverse terms. R.G. Saraiya, a Bombay businessman with a large stake in the cotton trade, gave a critical but balanced analysis of these terms in his evidence to the Central Banking Enquiry Committee. When the Bombay cotton merchant shipped raw cotton to London, he gave credit to the London buyer for three months. In the meanwhile, he took an advance from the exchange bank against the shipment at the rate of three months' sight bills. His bill was a D/A draft payable by the London buyer only after three months from the time of shipment, and the Bombay shipper did not make the London buyer directly responsible for payment, but released the bill of lading to the buyer's bank simply on the basis of the buyer's bank accepting the bill. But when the Bombay merchant imported merchandise from London he did not get the same acceptance credit for three months. The bill which he had to pay was a D/P draft, which meant that he would get the bill of lading only when he paid up to the exchange bank which presented the bill. The bank stipulated as a matter of practice that the draft would be on the Bombay merchant and not on the bank itself. Furthermore, he would have to pay interest at 6 per cent from the time when the London exporter sent the draft to Bombay to the time when the remittance reached the hands of the London exporter. In short, as Saraiya pointed out, interest was paid by the Indian merchant both ways, whether he was buying or selling.[47]

Further, the risk of fluctuations in the rupee-pound exchange rates fell on him while the merchandise or money was in transit either way, and to cover himself against the risk he had to pay for exchange risk and brokerage to the exchange bank, something which would not have been necessary if the bills had been rupee bills instead of sterling bills. The big international trading corporations buying and selling in India through London in sterling did not have to pay these foreign exchange charges. Trading in sterling value, they set off the values of exports against imports, while their puny Indian rivals lost something both in exports and imports by way of commission in exchange. Again, the international trading firms were invariably accommodated by the exchange banks both when they made purchases and shipments from India and when they accepted bills for their imports into India—an accommodation not so easily given to Indian traders. The Andhra Chamber of Commerce, stressing these disadvantages for Indian merchants, stated:

> In the Andhra districts, the whole of the foreign export business in groundnuts, cotton, oilseeds, etc., is done by Messrs Volkart, Rally (*sic*) and Gordon and Woodroff, who have established their agencies in all the centres of production. As these rich foreign firms are backed up by the exchange banks in India and supported by their business relations and banking connections in foreign countries, no Indian can undertake the export and import business unless he had equally good facilities as mentioned above which he had not got now.[48]

It is not surprising, then, that large international trading concerns—like Ralli, Volkart, Shaw Wallace, Sassoons and Mitsui Bushen Kaisha—dominated the exports of India's agricultural produce and her imports of piecegoods, kerosene oil, sugar and other manufactured goods. Among these international firms, two giants stood out from the rest: the Greek firm of Ralli Bros. and the Swiss firm of Volkart Bros., both operating through the London money market. Both maintained the most extensive purchasing organisations in the main assembling centres of agricultural produce, but while Volkart Bros. operated in the Bombay Presidency, Madras Presidency, Central Provinces, and Punjab and Sind, Ralli operated in these places as well as the Gangetic valley. In buying wheat, grains, seeds and cotton, Ralli and Volkart were close competitors in southern, central, western and north-western India, but Ralli was in addition the biggest exporter of raw jute and jute fabrics from eastern India, a considerable exporter of shellac and hides and skins from the Indo-Gangetic valley, and the greatest importer of cotton piecegoods in the country as a whole. Together these two overshadowed the rest. Ralli's major operations were through Calcutta port, through which it imported piecegoods and yarns, and exported raw jute, jute fabrics, lac, hides and skins, wheat and oilseeds. Volkart Bros., which had its headquarters in Winterthur in Switzerland, was another great international firm with branches in London, Bombay, Karachi, Calcutta, Madras, Cochin, Tellichery, Tuticorin, Colombo, Singapore, Shanghai and Osaka. Its main imports into India were steel, iron bars, and sheets and its exports were all kinds of Indian manufactured goods and produce, with cotton and cotton goods as a speciality. It owned cotton gins and cotton presses throughout the interior for export through Bombay, Karachi and Madras. Along with Ralli it figured as the main buyer in practically every major upcountry cotton assembling *mandi*.[49]

Naturally, Indian merchants who banked on the lucrative business of purchasing and railing of export produce to the ports as the commission agents of the international exporters regarded the setting up of the upcountry buying organisations by Ralli, Volkart and others as an economic invasion of the interior. The method of direct purchases from the *mandis* to reduce the *arhat* or commission of the *arhatiyas* was initiated as a systematic policy by Ralli and Volkart before the First World War, and they carried on the policy after the war by pushing still further into the interior during the 1920s. They set up a number of agencies at key points for the purchase of grains, seeds and cotton, which in turn supervised the buying operations of a large number of sub-agencies staffed with the exporter's own personnel. Whereas Ralli Bros. staffed its agencies with its extremely numerous Greek personnel, Volkart Bros., in addition to its German (Swiss) personnel, also appointed trusted Indian agents at key points. English, Japanese and various other foreign firms followed similar methods. These firms set up smaller versions of the purchase machinery maintained by the big two in the buying of cotton from upcountry centres such as Nandyal, Guntur, Tuticorin and Coimbatore in rural Madras.[50] Native commission agents, who, with the credit supplied by Marwari, Multani and Natukottai Chettiar bankers, had long played a key role in the Kongunad cotton market in Madras, would no doubt have perceived the posting of a Greek agent by Ralli in Coimbatore in 1919 as an intrusion in their customary sphere of operations. Of course such intrusions took place only in the more lucrative spheres of inland buying and selling, and not always even there. To take the instance of rural Madras again, Natukottai Chettiar bankers had an assured hold over the financing of the heavy shipments of rice exported by the *mirasdars* of the Kaveri valley to inland Coimbatore and to Ceylon. But significantly big international firms (like Ralli and Volkart) maintained elaborate purchasing machineries in the Arcot plains, which enabled them to monopolise the highly lucrative export market in groundnuts from rural Madras.[51]

The Great Depression hit at the foundations of these widespread upcountry buying organisations of the international export houses. As exports fell, costs had to be reduced. Consequently much of the upcountry buying organisations folded up. An alternative method of purchase, which had been less in vogue in the pre-war and early post-war years, gained ground in the 1930s. This was the system of using *arhatiyas* based on upcountry *mandis* as 'guarantee brokers'. These commission agents guaranteed at a pre-arranged rate of commission the due fulfilment of all contracts for supply to the export houses brought in by them from the *mandi* merchants. The big *arhatiyas* were keen enough to win the valuable position of 'guarantee brokers' by putting in a security deposit of substantial cash with the great export houses. After 1930 the export houses closed down a large number of sub-agencies as uneconomic: direct sub-agency buying in small lots from producers who were represented by smaller commission agents (*kutcha arhatiyas*) was no longer profitable. The volume of direct small-unit purchases, which had formed a large portion of the total purchases in the 1920s, fell to insignificant proportions in the 1930s and were practically replaced by 'port pass contracts' with big commission agents (*pucca arhatiyas*) acting as guarantee brokers. Under the port pass contract the inland *arhatiya* received an advance of 80 to 90 per cent of the value of the consignment railed by him to the shipper. In return he undertook to accept without question the shippers' analysis and weighing of the produce at the port of loading. After analysing the quality of the produce and weighing it with his own weights the shipper paid the balance of the value of the consignment with such deduction as he thought fit. Wheat exports were practically eliminated after 1930 and such exports as still continued were consigned, to the extent of not less than three-fourths of the total, under the popular port pass contracts entered into by the guarantee brokers with their principals.[52]

THE INTEGRATION OF INDIGENOUS CAPITAL

As the whole grain business turned inwards, the colonial relationship between the international trading corporations and their guarantee brokers ceased to be the key economic relationship. This is not to say that while the foreign corporations lost out, the Indian marketeers profited at their expense. Indian grain merchants suffered, too, as the total volume of domestic trade in wheat declined perceptibly in the 1930s. But they were willing to continue trading within the contracting domestic market at far lower profit margins than the giant export houses would work on in their reduced international operations. Furthermore, Indian merchants had the means of reducing their losses by greater industrial investment at a time when the domestic prices of industrial products were holding up better. It should be stressed that the financial and commercial infrastructure for a rapid domestic integration of the Indian economy already existed. Also the nodal points of this domestic integration were the very port cities, Bombay and Calcutta, which had played the key role in integrating India into the international economy.

It is not adequately appreciated that on the eve of the Great Depression, Bombay and Calcutta were already controlling an enormous volume of financial transactions which had nothing to do with export-import trade. At one time, presumably, indigenous financial and banking for trade between any two *mandis* must have been provided mostly locally, i.e., by bankers on the spot. But this was no longer so. A large part of the inland trade between different upcountry *mandis* which never touched the ports at all was now financed by Bombay and Calcutta. Such inland inter-*mandi* commercial transactions had always, of course, formed the overwhelming proportion of Indian trade. What was new by 1929 was that Bombay and Calcutta had moved into key position as *hundi* bankers to this trade.

The point may be illustrated by a striking instance which the Bihar and Orissa Provincial Banking Enquiry Committee recorded in 1930. Coconuts were grown extensively in Puri district, which exported annually about 30,000 maunds, almost entirely to confectioners in the Central Provinces. Four coconut dealers at the railhead, one Marwari and three Oriyas, bought up the coconuts from local Brahman agriculturists who collected the produce of other ryots and moved the nuts by road to the railhead. The four coconut dealers financed one quarter of the nuts by advances which carried no stipulation of exclusive right of purchase and they paid cash down for the other three-quarters. When the *mandi* merchant at the railhead filled an order from a CP confectioner by railing the ordered coconuts, he telegraphed the buyer, who wired back that he should draw a *hundi* on a particular merchant in Bombay or Calcutta. The coconut merchant drew a *hundi* accordingly and sold it locally in Puri to a merchant willing to remit money to either Calcutta or Bombay. He usually got a premium for a *hundi* drawn on Calcutta, to which plenty of merchants wished to remit. By contrast, he had to sell *hundis* at a discount in Bombay where fewer merchants wanted to remit money. 'This,' observed the Bihar and Orissa Banking Enquiry Committee, 'seems to us to be a fairly typical account of business carried on in a local product for which there is a distant sale, and there must be a great many similar enterprises going on throughout the province in other commodities .... Remittance is put through by means of the indigenous system of *hundis*, and no use whatever is made of banks of a western type.'[53]

Thus the indigenous money markets of Bombay and Calcutta and the inland railway network had already created the infrastructure of a national economy in which the bazaar occupied the key position. As the great export houses began to withdraw their agencies from the interior, and the inland trading in grains came to represent practically the entire grain trade of India, the bazaar established an independent command over the Indian economy in the Great Depression. Not only did it occupy the void created by the withdrawal of Ralli and Volkart to the ports, it also penetrated deeper into the country to compensate for the falling profits of the grain trade. A series of investigations by the Punjab Board of Economic Enquiry in the marketing of wheat in nine markets of Lyallpur, Ferozepore and Attock showed that the grain *arhatiyas* in the *mandis* were now buying between 66 to 77 per cent of their wheat purchases direct from the peasants. Direct dealings between the peasants and the commission agents had been pushed up by the Great Depression, which had all but eliminated the pedlar who had hitherto mediated between the *mandi* and the peasant homestead. At the same time the organised modern business sector had been compelled to effect a partial withdrawal from the *mandis*. In the nine *mandis* surveyed, *arhatiyas* numbered 438, European firms 25 and flour mills 12.[54]

When the Indian economy emerged from the Great Depression and commercial activity once again entered into the upswing merging with the speculative boom of the Second World War, the market network in India had achieved a fuller articulation, exhibiting in clear outlines the shape of a pyramid. The knitting together of financial and commercial transactions at the higher levels of the network had created a national market in which indigenous capital was the integrating factor. At the base of the pyramid were the weekly or biweekly markets and seasonal fairs dispersed over the countryside and serving the peasant population. There were in all 1,733 main fairs, about half of which assembled annually along a strip of plain stretching from central Punjab to north Bengal along the Gangetic valley and 22,080 shandies, *haats* and *painths*, which dotted the countryside at intervals of six miles or so from one another. At the middle tier of the structure, there were 1,718 *mandis*, among which closer relations had been established by constant movements of goods and credit. These regularised interchanges, that were made possible by the *hundi* facilities provided by Bombay, Calcutta and ten other exchanges on the coast and inland, had integrated the commercial economy of

Table 3 Number of Produce and Cattle Fairs and Markets in India, 1943

	Fairs	Shandies	*Mandis*	Foreign trade centres and money markets
India	1,733 (809 cattle fairs, 712 produce fairs, 212 cattle and produce fairs)	22,080	1,718	12
Main Provinces				
Assam	4	1,213	4	
Bengal	61	5,862	174	Calcutta, Chittagong
Bihar	348	2,535	4	
Bombay	36	961	198	Bombay, Ahmedabad
CP & Berar	13	2,307	64	
Madras	113	906	237	Madras, Cochin, Tuticorin
Orissa	533	533	30	
NWFP	—	7	14	
Punjab	127	23	157	Lahore, Amritsar, Delhi
Sind	7	—	25	Karachi
UP	190	5,376	471	Cawnpore

Source: *Report on Fairs, Markets and Produce Exchanges in India* (Delhi, 1943), Appendix Tables I, V & VII, pp. 110, 119, 121–22; *Handbook of Commercial Information for India* (3rd edn, Delhi, 1937), pp. 62–113. Minor fairs not included.

the country. The growth in the number of the foreign exchange and *hundi* transactions of the 12 money markets headed by Calcutta and Bombay had gradually lifted them to the top of the structure. In 1929 they provided the nodal points of an all-India economic system (see Table 3).[55]

Among these 12 centres of monetary and financial transactions, Bombay and Calcutta stood out from the rest, forming the axis of the entire system. They were the twin financial and commercial capitals of the country, capitals not merely of the colonial enclave but also of the indigenous sector of banking and commerce. There had emerged in addition 10 more financial centres dependent on the Bombay and Calcutta exchanges and giving clearer definition to the system—Madras, Karachi, Delhi, Cawnpore, Amritsar, Lahore, Ahmedabad, Cochin, Tuticorin and Chittagong. There were, of course, other large and important towns, but long distance financial and exchange facilities were overwhelmingly concentrated in these 12 nodal points of the Indian commercial system in the late 1930s. Excluding Ahmedabad, the other 11 towns and cities were the centres of exchange banking in India, and hence also the centres of import-export trade. Naturally most of these were port towns. However, Delhi, Cawnpore and Amritsar were upcountry centres for the distribution of imports (especially piecegoods) and the assemblage of exports. Together with Ahmedabad, these three inland emporia were also important centres of the indigenous money market, with the largest volume of *hundi* transactions outside Bombay and Calcutta, and possessing solid financial connections with the *hundi* exchanges of these two cities. Thus 12 towns and cities in India had come to represent by the 1930s not merely the points of concentration of the import-export trade and exchange banking, but also the critical financial centres for the indigenous money market and the long distance inland trade.

The bazaar thus emerged from the Great Depression as an integrated system of inland business transactions between distant market towns moving through the key financial exchanges. The network of 1,718 *mandis* with its 12 nodal points was connected visibly by the railways and the telegraph, and invisibly by the dense web of *hundi* and *arhat* arrangements. All-India surveys of a wide variety of crops—rice, wheat, gram, barley, potatoes, linseed, groundnut, coconut, cashewnut, castor seed, rapeseed, mustard, lac, hides and skins, and tobacco—showed that a new concentration of the marketing and financing of agricultural produce had been effected through the *arhatiyas* and *shroffs* based on the *mandis*.[56] It may be argued that the financial integration of the inland produce trade was still not complete. The instance of the coconut trade between the coconut merchants of Puri and the Central Provinces confectioners which we have cited may be taken to indicate that the bill market in *hundis* between upcountry centres had been insufficiently developed, so that remittances between the Central Provinces and Orissa had to move through Calcutta and Bombay. But imperfect as this financial integration was, it was a step further from long distance peddling and itinerant trading between Orissa and CP which would have been the only means of trade between the two regions had there been no mediation by the *hundi* markets of Calcutta and Bombay. The instruments through which the bazaar operated in order to achieve this imperfect degree of integration were basically four: *goladari* (storage), *badni ka satta* and *teji mandi* (futures trading and speculation), *arhat* (commission) and *hundi* (inland bill of exchange). It is time now to survey these four instruments of the bazaar in some depth.

BAZAAR DEVICES—STORAGE AND SPECULATION

Goladari, which meant the business of storing and trading in grain, was the basic factor which distinguished the bazaar from the pedlars and the peasants. Facilities for storage existed of course in both the country and the bazaar and differed in degree rather than in kind. The market *khatti* was an underground pit like the villagers', only larger. The *kotha* or market warehouse was simply a large enclosed space in which grain was stocked in bags or sacks, which replaced the peasant's earthen pots or bins made of matting, mud and wickerwork. Contrary to general notions, peasants and pedlars did hold on to crops by means of the primitive facilities available in the village, and substantial villagers, such as the *mirasdars* of Madras and the *jotedars* of Bengal, made a regular business of storing grain by such means. But for the mass of ordinary peasants, caution bred by generations of experience was a pressing indicator to dispose of their crops in the *mandi* as quickly as possible, for prices were as liable to fall as to rise. Investigations by the Indian Central Cotton Committee into the finance and marketing of cultivator's cotton in eight widely dispersed cotton tracts in India (Berar, Khandesh, north Gujarat, middle Gujarat, Sind, Punjab and the northern and western areas of Madras) showed that villagers sold off early as much for fear of a falling market as on account of financial pressures. When pedlars or richer peasants wanted to store grain for commercial purposes, they would as often as not use the professional services of a *goladar* or *arhatiya*, storing with him for short periods against advances. Price fluctuations were a complex and dangerous game and those who did not have proper sources of information ran a high risk of being altogether finished in it.[57]

Only the big merchant could play the game effectively and he was, not unexpectedly, contemptuous of smaller fry in these unpredictable operations. O. Krishnamurti Rao Garu, a big cotton merchant of Adoni in the Madras Presidency, had this to say of smaller village dealers who traded with the market towns:

> Most of these petty dealers who bring a large number of carts to the principal markets are being financed either by the big landholders of the village or by the *dalals* of the principal markets. They do business headlong and in most cases do not watch the trend of the market and consequently wind up their business themselves being in debt either to the prominent moneylender of the village or *dalal* and leave the place for good.[58]

The real man who benefited from storage through the rapid fluctuations of the agricultural cycle was neither the village Bania nor even the small commission agent (*kutcha arhatiya*) in the *mandi*, but the wholesale dealer in big markets like Delhi, Bhagalpur or Lyallpur. In fairness to him, it should be said that he was not profiting much, if at all, in the 1920s, and he suffered much in the 1930s. With a harvest price of Rs. 4 a month, it was estimated by the British Cotton Grower's Association in the Punjab that it would not pay to hold wheat over the monsoon (in view of the cost of storage), unless the price rose to Rs. 4-6-0. Only in two years (between October 1924 and March 1929) did it pay, in these terms, to hold cotton and wheat for any length of time in Lyallpur. According to a graph prepared by the Punjab Provincial Banking Enquiry Committee showing the seasonal fluctuations in the wholesale prices of wheat and cotton, the net result upon wholesale dealers over the period was a loss, though occasionally, as with wheat in 1928, large profits were made. A similar enquiry for Bihar and Orissa showed that no fortunes could have been made in Patna, Bhagalpur, Muzaffarpur, Ranchi and Cuttack from fluctuations of grain prices in the 1920s. Indeed, in 1929, a dealer who bought an equal quantity of paddy in January at all five centres and held for sale either in June or August would not only have made no profit, he would have lost his interest as well as his warehouse charges.[59]

Goladari was thus a risky business which required the special skills and facilities of the bazaar. The business was of ancient standing, and Buchanan Hamilton had noted and commented upon it in Bihar in 1811.[60] Substantially the same structure was revealed by the Bihar Banking Enquiry of 1930. The function of the *goladar* or grain merchant and warehouse-keeper was three-fold: (*a*) to store grain for his client (who could be a pedlar, a peasant, a *mandi* merchant, or zamindar) or on his own account, (*b*) to sell grain on commission basis (*arhat*) for his client, and (*c*) to make advances against the grain entrusted to his warehouse to the extent of 85 and sometimes even 100 per cent until the goods were sold off. The warehouse charge was minimal and the main profit came from his acting as commission agent in exports to the ports or the big distributing centres. The advances were made at an interest of about 9 per cent, which was low compared to rates prevailing in the country.

The Bihar *goladars* financed their exports by drawing *hundis* on the port consignees or commission agents in Calcutta, the *hundis* being negotiated through Barabazar. As the *goladars* were also large importers of cloth and other goods, ordinarily from the same commission agents and *hundi* bankers of Barabazar, most of their transactions were settled by contra account. *Goladari* was commonly combined not merely with cloth business but, in the case of the biggest *goladars* and cloth merchants, with *hundi* banking. In Bhagalpur town the grain and seeds business was worth 4 to 5 crore rupees and piecegoods import was worth one crore. There were ten big *goladari* firms which stored grain and oilseeds, and all their warehouses were located in one street, which served as the grain wholesale market where samples were displayed and sales were arranged. The same firms were involved in the cloth business and had a stake in urban banking and rural money-lending too. Khaliram Kedarnath, one such leading *goladari* firm which held at the same time an agency of Esso for selling kerosene oil, bought grain through agents who operated in different parts of Bhagalpur district. The owner, Seth Kedar Nath, employed 30 servants to collect grain for him. Normally he waited three or four months after purchase to sell off the grain bought on his own account. He also stored grain for his clients, to whom he advanced money to a limit even of 100 per cent depending upon the credit of the borrowing party. He charged 8.5 per cent on these advances, and sold the grain of his clients at a commission of 12 annas per cent. He refused to accept grain for storage when he had no more money to lend against the grain, but there were other *goladars* in Bhagalpur who borrowed money to oblige customers when their own loanable capital ran out. Seth Kedar Nath charged no warehouse rent if the period of commission storage did not exceed a month and a half, after which he charged a nominal rent of one rupee per month 100 bags (each bag containing two and a half maunds of grain).[61]

In the more flourishing grain trading centres, grain storage was used as a means of raising credit. Having stocked his *khatti* (grain pit) or *kotha* (grain warehouse) with grain purchased on his own account or taken on commission from clients, the grain merchant would pledge the goods to a financier and formally transfer possession of the godown to him. If the financier was a bazaar banker he would simply content himself with the key of the godown, but a bank would put on its own lock and signboard. The banker would make the advance to the grain merchant, not so much on the security of the grain in the godown, as on the borrower's reputation for personal integrity, for he could not be certain that the goods shown in the invoice (*beejak*) were the same as the actual contents of the godown. A *kotha* or *khatti* could be sold along with the invoice several times before it was finally emptied and its contents sold for consumption or export; and if on opening the store a discrepancy was discovered between the actual weight and quality of the grain and that described in the invoice, the responsibility for making good the difference fell on the original warehouse keeper.[62]

As may be imagined from the fact that a *khatti* could change hands as many as twelve times during a season, grain storage was used not merely for raising credit, but for speculation as well. This brings us to an important feature of the bazaar which distinguished it from the rural economy—i.e., the presence of produce exchanges. The produce exchanges in the port towns and the big grain marts of the Punjab and western UP were mainly for speculative transactions, as distinct from spot and forward transactions. Two basic types of speculative transactions had been traditionally known in India: (*a*) futures transactions known as *badni ka satta*, and (*b*) options known *as teji ka satta* (put option), *mandi ka satta* (call option) and *teji-mandi* or *nazarana* (double option). A futures contract, like a forward contract, carried a stipulation for delivery at a future date, but was distinguished by the fact that it could be liquidated by payment of differences at any time during the currency of the contract. In the produce exchanges in India, very few transactions were genuine spot or delivery transactions. Purchases and sales were cancelled against each other before the actual date of maturity—and on most exchanges throughout the months of futures trading only an insignificant number of transactions remained to be settled by means of actual delivery. In addition to futures trading, an enormous volume of *teji-mandi* gambling went on in the produce exchanges. *Mandi* or call option was an option to sell a certain commodity at a specified future date and price. *Teji* or put option was in converse—a right to buy at a given future date and price—while *teji-mandi* combined the right to buy and sell on the same terms. A report on the produce exchanges during the Second World War described the operation in detail:

> The buyer of an option has to pay some money to secure an option to buy or sell during a specified period a specified quantity of produce at the current rate. The money is commonly known as *nazarana* or premium. The party which takes the premium is known as the 'eater' (*khanewala* or *khanar*) and the party which pays the premium is known as the 'supplier' (*laganewala* or *lagandar*). The buyer of a *teji* option is a 'bull' i.e., he believes that the prices are likely to rise. If he finds that the price has not risen, he does not demand delivery of the produce purchased by him and forgoes the consideration money paid by him. The buyer of a *mandi* option, on the other hand, is a 'bear,' i.e., a person who expects the price to fall. If he finds that the prices have not gone down, he keeps quite and allows the premium paid by him to be forfeited. The buyer of a *teji-mandi* option secures the option to buy or sell as it suits him. The buyer of a double option is both a 'bull' and a 'bear'. In other words he expects the market to fluctuate appreciably.[63]

The volume of the speculative transactions can be estimated from the fact that wheat was traded in futures to the extent of 70 million tons, though 10 million tons were produced in India. An enormous amount of futures trading and *teji-mandi* gambling went on in India in the inter-war period. Such speculative transactions had long been a part of the Indian commercial scene, but their volume had been far less before the First World War. Law court records showed that *teji-mandi* gambling had been in vogue for a very long time; so were futures.[64] But formerly their volume had been kept down by the fact that till a few years after the First World War, the greater proportion of the export trade in grains and oilseeds and a considerable part of cotton and jute export trade had been in the hands of a few international trading houses, especially Ralli and Volkart. These two firms maintained direct contact with the producing areas through their upcountry buying organisations and quickly gathered in the saleable surpluses for quick export out of India. They needed price stability to sustain these large international operations and their impact was to stabilise or at least coordinate prices in different markets. During the First World War, the normal channels of trade were disrupted. The war-time uncertainty produced a wave of speculation in the bazaar which spilled over into the post-war years. Extensive gambling in wheat, seeds, cotton and gunnies in Barabazar to the detriment of 'legitimate business' so alarmed the organised European business and industry that the Bengal Chamber of Commerce contemplated ways and means to check it. But to no effect.[65] Even before this, futures trading in cotton and some other agricultural commodities had taken a kind of organised form in Bombay, where indigenous traders had indulged in it before the First World War. But now this widening activity was threatening to disrupt the supply lines of the dominant European business in Calcutta too.

Soon the activity extended beyond Bombay and Calcutta. The first step towards organised upcountry futures trading was taken in 1920 with the formation of the Sugar and Grain Merchants Association of Amritsar, which was later converted into the Indian Exchange Ltd. During the Great Depression, as European control over the trade in agricultural commodities collapsed, bazaar speculation in the upcountry *mandis* galloped. During 1932 and 1933 more than 60 speculative produce exchanges were formed in the Punjab alone. Their main business was trading in wheat futures, with some marginal speculation in gram, barley and rapeseed. By 1934 many of these badly organised produce exchanges collapsed. The better organised exchanges in Bombay and Calcutta, though fewer in number, showed greater tenacity. In Calcutta a small jute futures trading association had been formed in 1912. The authorities suppressed it on charges of pure gambling in 1927, and two more such associations in the next two years. In 1927 the Birlas took the lead in organising the much bigger East India Jute Association, which gradually secured control of the jute futures market in India. In Bombay, where the indigenous business element had always been much stronger than elsewhere, there had been several cotton produce exchanges before the First World War. These were replaced in 1922 by the more organised East India Cotton Association established by statutory authority. A few years afterwards a smaller and more 'indigenous' cotton produce exchange, the Shree Mahajan Association, sprang up, operating a smaller unit of transaction and giving formal recognition to *teji-mandi* gambling, which gave rise to great discord between organised business and the bazaar in the Bombay cotton trade.[66]

It was not merely the supply lines of the international trading firms and the industrial managing agencies that the bazaar threatened by its rampant speculation. In active trade seasons or times of political uncertainty, violent fluctuations were produced in the market by *badni ka satta* and *teji-mandi*. Such fluctuations, besides involving the speculators in losses, forced many consumers and shippers to withdraw from the market, so that peasants found their markets narrowing at such times. However, in normal times such speculative transactions had a more positive effect. They were controlled by a particular group among the grain traders who specialised in undertaking commercial risks and who were aware of the seasonal and world movement of prices. Their business tended to make the daily market prices correspond to the movements in supply and demand as they varied from season to season. Not unexpectedly, the *badni ka sattas* in upcountry markets, such as Hapur, Meerut, Muzaffarnagar, Hathras and Agra were concentrated in the hands of that important group among the grain dealers which controlled the warehouses—*pucca arhatiyas*.[67]

ARHAT—AN IMPORTANT BAZAAR DEVICE

This takes us to *arhat*, a central lever in the mechanism of the bazaar. In various forms the root word occurs in many Indian languages: *arhat* in Hindi and Maithili, *arat* in Bengali, Gujarati and Sindhi, and *adat* in Marathi; whence *arhatiya* (Hindi), *aratdar* (Bengali), *adatya* (Marathi), *adathi* (Tamil), *arti* (Punjabi), and so on.[68] The word was presumably of an indigenous origin, unlike the Arabic *sarraf* (money-changer) from which the Anglicised form *shroff* (indigenous banker) derives. The word was well in use in commercial parlance during Buchanan Hamilton's survey of the Bengal and Bihar districts, and he gives instances of the various inter-related uses of the term in his account of Patna:

> Here are several merchants called Aratiyas, who receive goods from merchants at a distance, and dispose of them by commission, taking upon themselves the responsibility for the purchaser, on which account they are men of property or credit. They also purchase on commission, and transact business at the custom house for merchants at a distance . . . [There were also] Aratiyas, who keep commission warehouses; they receive various kinds of goods, according to their different inclinations, and dispose of these on commission.[69]

In the sense used here, *arhatiya* is synonymous with the *goladar*, the warehouse owner and stockist of grain, who was destined later on to take to wheat 'futures' (*badni ka satta*) trading in western UP and the Punjab. Finally, Buchanan Hamilton also mentions bankers known as *aratiyas* in smaller towns like Gaya and Daudnagar, who granted *hundis* for cash on Patna and Banaras, obviously acting here in the capacity of correspondents to the *kothiwals* (bigger banking and trading houses) of the major centres of the money market. Three separate roles are mentioned here by Buchanan Hamilton; (*i*) commission agent for sales and purchases on behalf of others, (*ii*) warehouse keeper dealing in stocking and commission sales of grain, and (*iii*) correspondent of the Banaras and Patna bankers on whom they could grant *hundis* (obviously because they were selling grain to them on commission and were realising the dues in this manner—taking cash from local merchants who had to send remittances to Patna and Banaras). These three roles were inter-related, and one business may have arisen from the other. There were other possible uses of the term: in the Madras Presidency in the 1920s there were *adathis* who were brokers in *hundis* to and from Burma[70]—bill brokers as distinguished from banking correspondents and commission agents in *hundis* for other bankers. But whatever the specific contextual sense of the term, all traders were agreed on the root meaning of *arhat*: it meant 'commission,'[71] and by derivation, the warehouse where goods were stored on commission.

In Bikaner, in Punjab, in UP, in Bihar, in Bengal, in CP and Berar, in the Bombay Presidency—in practically every province of Northern and Western India surveyed by provincial or native state banking enquiry committees in 1929–30, the *arhatiyas* formed the crucial link in the marketing chain from the producer in the village to the exporting firm in the port. In the deep south, where the *arhatiya* did not figure in agricultural marketing, his place was taken by the *dalal*. The enquiries of the Central Cotton Committee into the marketing of cotton in eight different tracts in Berar, Khandesh, Gujarat, Sind, Punjab and Madras during 1925–28 revealed the same dominance of *adatyas*, *arhatiyas*, *artis*, *dalals* or *dalalidars* as they were known in different cotton tracts.[72] The Bengal Jute Enquiry Committee reports in the 1930s showed the importance of the *aratdars* in the supply of jute to Calcutta for milling and export. Finally, a marketing series issued by the Agricultural Marketing Adviser to the Government of India in the period 1937–45 showed that the marketing and export of practically every agricultural commodity in India would have collapsed but for the crucial link supplied by the *arhatiya* in the assembling and distribution of crops within the country.

The *arhatiya* figured mainly as a *mandi*-based commission agent through whom the pedlar or the producer from the country sold his crops, or conversely as a commission agent through whom Manchester, Bombay or other manufacturing centres sold its piecegoods to millions of retailers. The cultivators' crop passed through four middlemen according to a survey made by Malcolm Darling in the Punjab in 1929. The village shopkeeper or a pedlar, variously known as *bepari*, *faria* or *dalal*, brought it to the *mandi* and sold it through a broker (*dalal*) and a commission agent (*arhatiya*) to a *mandi* merchant, a port buyer or a mill. The *arhatiya* was the critical link in the chain. In the 408 shops surveyed by Darling, there were 231 *kutcha arhatiyas* and 40 *pucca arhatiyas*. Darling distinguished the two categories in terms of size and function: 'The agent with limited resources usually acts as an agent for the seller and does not buy on his own account, and does little, if any, storage. But the agent with ample resources acts as an agent for the buyer, often buys for himself, and stores freely.' Most of the *arhatiyas* in the surveyed *mandis* belonged to the merchant communities.[73] Before the Great Depression, they faced tough competition from agents of European, Japanese, Karachi, Bombay and Calcutta firms posted in the bigger Punjabi *mandis*. The onset of the depression, however, left the *arhatiyas* in possession of the field.

In the princely state of Bikaner, the system of marketing revealed by a banking enquiry committee appointed by the Maharaja corresponded to the system found in the Punjab by Darling, except for the fact that the place of the Karachi, Bombay, Calcutta and European and Japanese firms was taken here by the big Bikaner whole-sale merchant and banker with a wide network of branches in the main trade centres of the Indian empire. Here, too, the grain dealers in the villages, who were also the moneylenders to the peasants, sold the produce through *dalals* or brokers to *kutcha arhatiyas* in the *mandis* who usually financed the village Banias and enabled them to make advances to the peasants. Having bought the produce by cash payments either on his account or—as was more usual—on account of another merchant, the *kutcha arhatiya* transported the grain or cotton to the *pucca arhatiya* in other Indian cities. When the *kutcha arhatiya* sent his goods to the *pucca arhatiya* in another city, he drew 75 to 90 per cent of the face value of the produce through *hundis* on the *pucca arhatiya*, who in turn discounted his bills either with exchange or joint stock banks in the ports or with shippers like Ralli Bros., E.D. Sasoon & Co. and Andrew Yule & Co., till the goods reached the foreign markets.[74]

E.A.H. Blunt's enquiries in UP in connection with the provincial banking enquiry committee of 1929–30 showed that while the *kutcha arhatiya* operated in small as well as big markets, the *pucca arhatiya* was to be found usually in the bigger and organised markets, such as Hapur, Ghaziabad, Meerut, Muzaffarnagar, Deoband, Shamli, Secunderabad, Dankaur, Hathras and Agra, where the volume of trade was large enough to stimulate the development of grain futures markets. The *kutcha arhatiya* was basically an intermediary, whose function was to introduce the *bepari* to a purchaser, and to arrange a bargain, usually with the help of the purchaser's *dalal* or directly with the purchaser. He did not buy on his own account; he was merely the commission agent of the village dealer, and his aim was to secure the custom of as many village dealers as possible by making them advances for produce. The *pucca arhatiya*, on the other hand, was a true commission agent, who bought on behalf of some wholesale firm in another city. Thus the purchaser to whom the *kutcha arhatiya* introduced the *bepari* was usually a *pucca arhatiya*. In the bigger *mandis* of the prosperous canal tracts of Western UP, valuable crops were produced in large quantities, communications were good, *mandis* were small in number and well organised, and the traders were rich. The *pucca arhatiya* predominated here: a financier who made advances to village dealers to make sure of his produce, a commission agent of buyers in ports and flour mill centres, a grain stockist and a speculator and trader in 'futures'.

> The *pakka arhatiyas* at such a market as Hapur are in close touch with the foreign markets through their head offices at the ports; and thus the movements of world prices govern the Hapur prices, which in turn govern the prices of the small market and the village. But the *arhatiyas'* sales are not only to the export and wholesale trade, but to the retail trade too. He is the primary distributor of agricultural produce, and so stands at the apex of the structure of Indian marketing, with the *kachcha arhatiya* and the dealer in the small mandi in the middle and the village *bania*, beopari and cartman at its base.[75]

In Bihar the same system of commission agency prevailed in the marketing of grain and oilseeds; and the system also operated, as we have seen, in reverse gear, because the *arhatiyas* who dispatched rice and seeds to Calcutta were also the commission agents for piece-goods sent from Calcutta for distribution in the Bihar countryside. The *arhatiyas* supplied on commission to the distributing merchants in the town and country. A Patna *munsif* gave a neat description of the reverse operation of the *arhatiya* to the provincial banking enquiry committee:

> Even a big merchant arranges to get goods from big trade centres through the local *aratias* or brokers. The merchant deposits some cash with the brokers and brokers who are also bankers discount their customers' *hundis* or grant them credits in their books, purchase goods from the wholesale dealers of their towns and consign them to their customers. The *aratias* generally make a good profit out of their business for they charge brokerage as well as interest on book credits allowed or discount on the *hundis* discounted and in addition receive trade discount from the wholesale dealers on the goods purchased for their customers. The brokers generally employ their own funds in the business but in busy seasons they have to raise money by endorsing their customers' *hundis* and rediscounting them with the joint stock banks.[76]

It must not be thought that the *arhatiyas* as a class consumed high profit margins as intermediaries or made their living by fleecing the cultivators. In the Punjab, where dealings between *arhatiyas* and peasants were becoming increasingly direct in the 1930s, the *arhatiya* generally acted in the interest of the cultivator as the volume of his business with the peasant sellers depended on his reputation. The same group of peasants would employ him year after year, showing their confidence in him, though of course there were individual cases of complaint that the *arhatiya* was cheating the cultivator.[77] But this was not a structural characteristic of the commission agency system, for the system earned its commission not on high margins but on large turnovers. The rate of commission (*arhat*) in Delhi and Punjab after deducting expenses, was no more than 1 per cent.[78] That he still earned a large profit was due to the great volume of his business—a volume which could be sustained only by low rates of commission. The business was highly competitive and depended on the terms offered by the *arhatiyas* to the country folk. In Delhi alone—the largest grain mart between Amritsar and Cawnpore—the *arhatiyas* numbered 200 in 1935; and in the Punjab—the granary of India—not less than 4,000.[79] Their average annual earnings from commission business were estimated by Darling to range between Rs. 1,100 at Toba Tek Singh to Rs. 2,165 at Gojra (see Table 4).

The *arhatiyas* employed several market personnel—*dalals* (brokers), *tolas* (weighmen), *hammals* and *palledars* (market labourers, usually dependent, who attended to cleaning and handling produce), sweepers, water carriers, *munims* (salaried employees of the *arhatiyas*) and *shagirds* (*arhatiyas*' apprentices). Besides his own commission, therefore, the *arhatiya* made other charges for the market services provided by him. The various market charges were (*a*) *arhat* (commission), (*b*) *dalali* (brokerage), (*c*) *palledari* (handling charge), (*d*) *tulai* (weighment charge), (*e*) charges for other market services, (*f*) *dharmada, gaoshala*, etc. (charities), (*g*) *karda* (quality deduction) and *dhalta* (weight deduction), and (*h*) miscellaneous.[80] The unique item among these were the charity charges which, as Darling observed, were 'characteristic of the way religion and business in India often join hands'. The rates for *dharma* and *gaoshala* were fixed by the *arhatiyas*' market panchayat, but the income was spent at the discretion of the individual *arhatiya*, who was not accountable to any one. Some *arhatiyas* devoted the amount to schools, orphanages and other charitable institutions, but others—the majority—spent it

Table 4 The Structure of the Commission Agency Business in the Punjab

Market	Number of *arhatiyas*	Volume of produce (*maunds*)	Value of produce (Rupees)	Annual income from commission business (Rupees)	Annual income per commission agent
Chichawatni	50	589,000	61,00,000	82,356	2,165
Okara	67	668,000	1,01,00,000	1,11,248	1,100
Gojra	106	1,567,000	1,81,00,000	2,29,189	1,325
Toba Tek Singh	6	818,000	55,00,000	69,000	1,647

Source: Report of the Punjab Provincial Banking Enquiry Committee 1929–30, Vol. I (Lahore 1930), pp. 201–207.

on religious ceremonies, feasting of Brahmans, pilgrimages to Hardwar and Banaras, bathing in the sacred waters of the Ganges, the upkeep of temples, and the maintenance of alm houses for old and infirm cattle.[81] The merchant communities of India were deeply religious; and in these *mandi* charges levied by them on millions of peasants (including, indiscriminately, the Muslim peasants), and their own substantial contributions, lay the financial basis of the pervasive rural religious culture of India and the enormous infrastructure of Hinduism—its priesthood, its temples, its pilgrimage centres, its festivals and ceremonies, and its enormous and debased cattle population.

The form of commercial organization in India, the *arhat* or indigenous commission agency system, was peculiar to the country, and it took the place of wholesale trading. Firms operating on the scale of wholesale trade were almost invariably commission agency firms which bought and sold not so much on their own account as on behalf of other buyers and sellers, whom they financed to the extent of three-quarters or more of the goods and produce which they handled on their behalf. Under the commission agency system, losses in transit would never fall on the commission agent, but would be borne by the consignee. On the other hand, bad debts would fall on the commission agent.[82] Funds had to be pumped into a chronically deficit economy which could give no guarantee of repayment of loans. The only safe form of credit was an advance against a crop, or against goods in transit. The Indian merchant, who was at the same time a *mahajan*, *sowcar* or *shroff*, was in a position to locate exactly the produce which could be used to secure a loan. Yet, while trading in the located and financed amount of produce, the wholesale merchant might run into an unpredictable monsoon fluctuation. The risk had to be shared with the producer, and this implied that the producer had to be given a share in ownership of the produce. Thus wholesaling was substituted by commission agency, a far safer form of business.

The producer or the village dealer retained under the system ownership of the crop entrusted to the *arhatiya*. While the crop was being held in the *arhatiya's khatti*, the producer took the risk that it might not fetch a higher price even after three months. Of course the *arhatiya* whose storage space was taken up by the produce faced the same risk, but he could share it with the *bepari* or the *kisan* customer who had carted the produce to his *khatti*. Once the goods were sold to a *pucca arhatiya* who was consigning it to a wholesale firm in another town, the consignee at the other end bore the risk of transit, not the *arhatiya*. The commission agency system was a system of distributing and sharing risks and it extended from the top to the bottom of India's monsoon economy.

The intermeshing system of commission agencies through which the commercial centres of India were linked to one another was a complete system of market intelligence. This indigenous system of commercial intelligence integrated the vast economy of the subcontinent and linked it to the world markets. The telegraph in the nineteenth century, and the wireless in the twentieth, quickened the flow of information on prices through the invisible wires of the commission agency system. Intelligence moved through these wires with speed and accuracy. The older rulers of India had always relied on this market network for the passing of strategic intelligence. News of the Maratha debacle at Panipat in cryptic language, for instance, had apparently been conveyed in 1761 through the commercial network. The British government similarly found it necessary to rely on the commission agency system for the market intelligence essential to economic administration, especially during war-time. E.A.H. Blunt, when he was serving as Director of Civil Supplies in 1918–19, was kept regularly informed of prices in all the principal grain markets of Upper India by some Cawnpore wholesale grain dealers, who obtained the information by wire from their *arhatiyas* in those markets. The more enterprising commission agents were by now making systematic use of the wireless to carry out their operations, and Darling recorded the case of an *arhatiya* in Okara who had set up a wireless at his house to obtain market quotations from Bombay. The *arhatiya*, in his capacity as a banker, served as a correspondent to other bankers who had no branch in a particular city. Rates of money were regularly telegraphed from one money market to another by the *arhatiyas*. They thus facilitated flows of money to take advantage of differences in *hundi* rates.[83] *Arhat* and *hundi* were the two crucial binding factors in the vast Indian market.

HUNDI—THE CENTRAL DEVICE OF THE BAZAAR

This brings us to what C.N. Cooke identified in the mid-nineteenth century as 'the most perfect portion of the Indian commercial system,' namely the circulation of *hundis*. Like Tavernier, Cooke, too, was impressed by a system in which, 'although millions were invested, the loss by bad debts, arising out of the dishonour of the instruments at maturity, was a most insignificant fraction per cent.'[84] The system, found by Tavernier in full articulation in the seventeenth century, seems to have been older than the establishment of Muslim rule in India. The word *hundi* is used in every modern Indian language, and is derived from the Sanskrit word *hundika*.[85] The UP Banking Enquiry Committee refers to current stories of the use of *hundis* as early as the twelfth century, without naming the sources; the reference is possibly to a legendary story recorded by L.C. Jain that the architect of the Dilwara temples, which on epigraphic evidence was built by two Jain bankers of Gujarat between 1197 and 1247, drew a *hundi* of 10 crore on the Nagar Seth of Ahmedabad for his operations.[86]

Jain uncritically repeats Cooke's unfounded speculation that the word *hundi* was a corruption of the word Hindi or Hindu.[87] The word is undoubtedly a derivative of the Sanskrit *hundika*, and is derived from the root verb '*hund*,' i.e., 'to collect'. Professor Vaman Shivaram Apte in his Sanskrit-English dictionary gave the meaning of *hundika* alternatively as a bill of exchange and as an assignment (for the maintenance of soldiers).[88] The word is used in the latter sense in the *Rajatarangini*, a history of the *Hindu* kings of Kashmir composed by Kalhana between 1148–50. A group of infantry called the Tantrin had formed a league in Kashmir which, like the Praetorian guards, made and unmade its kings.

> In that realm whose kings had occupied Kanauj and other territories the livelihood of kings depended upon the delivery of hundikas to the Tantrin .... That man became acceptable to the ministers who by selling the subjects in that plight was in a position to honour the payments due on the hundikas to the Tantrin .... In Pausa of the same year having failed to pay, through lack of funds, the sum due on the hundikas to the Tantrin he [i.e., King Chakravarman of Kashmir] fled in fear and tribulation. (*Rajatarangini*, verses 266, 275, 302).[89]

The reference by Kalhana is apparently to assignments which were used as negotiable instruments falling due at specified dates.

The system, which must have worked through bankers, continued to be in use in the Delhi Sultanate. In the reign of Firuz Tughlaq (1351–88) soldiers at Delhi were paid by cash orders (*itlaq*) on outlying places which were locally discounted by financiers in Delhi who made a regular business of it and earned a good income.[90] The oldest surviving firms in Bikaner and Sekhawati had traditions of having been hereditary treasurers and ration suppliers to Mughal troops. The soldiers of the Mughal army were paid by cash orders on different treasuries of the empire which were realised through the Marwari bankers attached to the regiments.[91] *Hundis* thus seem to have originated from the discounting of revenue assignments for the army by bankers. The discounted assignments had fully developed as trade bills used for remittance and accommodation in the heyday of Surat in the seventeenth century. By that time *hundis* were also serving in foreign exchange operations as import and export bills, and such bills of exchange could be bought and sold—and moneys transferred—between any two ports of the Indian Ocean where Gujarati Bania *Shroffs* were firmly established.[92] While the great Gujarati houses of Surat developed *hundis* to finance India's overseas trade, and also serviced an inland market of trade bills extending to Dacca at the other end of India, the house of Jagat Seth increasingly centralised the business of remitting the revenues of the Mughal empire through *hundis* between Delhi, Patna and Murshidabad.

By the end of the eighteenth century these great controllers of the *hundi* market—the Surat Banias and the Jagat Seths of Patna, Murshidabad and Delhi—were in irreversible decline. The great banking houses of Banaras led by Gopaldas Manohardas came to provide a centre for the *hundi* market in the late eighteenth and early nineteenth centuries.[93] The regular postal services of the British in the 1820's led to an increase in speculative transfers of money through *hundis* on account of the greater facility of obtaining knowledge of the state of the money market in all the principal commercial cities.[94] Telegraph and railways still further swelled the volume of *hundi* traffic in the later nineteenth century, and Bombay and Calcutta replaced the declining Banaras as the centre of the *hundi* market. At the same time the use of *hundis* in overseas trade declined and their circulation was restricted to the inland trade. Although the Natukottai Chettiars extended *hundis* to South-East Asia in the last quarter of the nineteenth century, they did not build this business as an independent exchange business, but operated through the Presidency Banks and the Chartered Bank for effecting the *hundi* transfers between India, Burma and the Malay Peninsula.[95]

The *hundi*, according to a short definition given by the Bengal Provincial Banking Enquiry Committee, was an inland bill of exchange and was in effect an order signed by the drawer addressed to the drawee to pay to the person named in the *hundi* a sum of money either at sight or at a certain period after presentation. The sight bill or *darshani hundi* was usually drawn by a seller of goods on the purchaser requesting him to pay on sight the banker or the merchant through whom the bill was negotiated. Used sometimes as accommodation bills to raise short-term credit, such *darshani hundis* might pass through many hands during their currency. The *muddati hundi* or usance bill was used more specifically to borrow funds. The period of usance was normally three months, and for longer term credit it might be renewed at the end of the period, sometimes more than once. The *muddati hundi* was thus an important instrument of credit in the hands of the *shroffs*. A *hundi* was employed for three distinct purposes: (*a*) to make remittances, (*b*) to raise a loan (i.e., a finance bill), and (*c*) to finance movement of goods (i.e., a trade bill, but not necessarily accompanied by documents of title, since *hundis* were given purely on personal credit).[96]

The holders of *hundis* raised money from the bazaar by discounting it in the market with their own endorsement, and a *hundi* might come to bear many such successive endorsements. There was brisk buying and selling of *hundis*, aided by brokers or *dalals* who brought the buyers and sellers of *hundis* in touch with each other. All *arhatiyas* drew *hundis*, and discounted their bills with other merchants and bankers; but those among them who specialised in discounting *hundis* might set themselves up as *shroffs*. As evidence from grain and cloth merchants and bankers before the Bihar Provincial Banking Enquiry Committee makes clear, the bigger Marwari houses throughout the Gangetic valley combined *goladari* and cloth selling with the discounting of *hundis* and money-lending and would shift their funds to buying *hundis* whenever they found it more profitable than investing in cloth or grain. The highest group among these traders and financiers were known in the Upper Gangetic Valley as *kothiwals*, an honorific title to which every prosperous merchant or financier aspired. He operated through a network of branches of *kothis* (literally warehouses) in different centres, and almost invariably though not always specialised in *hundi* business—buying *hundis*, meeting *arhatiyas'* bills and writing *hundis* on himself to raise money in the bazaar. The smaller financier who dealt in bullion and ornaments and discounted *hundis* was known in the Upper Gangetic Valley as *sarraf* (whence *shroff*). When the holder of a *hundi* was a *kothiwal* he would often send the *hundi* for sale or discount to a branch where it would fetch the best price. Smaller *shroffs* who had no branches would take advantage of the same facilities through *arhatiyas* or correspondents, to whom they would pay a small commission for selling the *hundis* sent by them.[97]

Despite such movements of money, the *hundi* bazaar was a fragmented market. Important differences in rates prevailed between Bombay, Calcutta and the various inland centres, which would have been flattened out had the flows been sufficiently great in volume. The main indigenous money markets—Bombay, Calcutta, Delhi, Madras, Rangoon, Cawnpore, Amritsar, Ahmadabad, Shikarpur, Ajmer, Bikaner, and the Shekhavati towns (to name some of the most important in terms of flows)—formed no single bazaar. Furthermore, at each main centre there might be several markets with different rates of money, in Bombay, the Gujarati, Multani and Marwari bazaars; in the towns of the Madras Presidency, the Natukottai Chettiar, Marwari and Multani bazaars; in Rangoon, the Natukottai Chettiar and Multani bazaars; and so on. The evidence of Multani, Chettiar and Marwari bankers before the various provincial banking enquiry committees suggests that the greater part of the flows of money from one centre to another passed through the Multani, Chettiar and Marwari networks of branches, partnerships and correspondents. Thus in addition to regional money markets, there were inter-regional community markets. While the inter-regional Multani, Marwari and Chettiar bazaars played an important role in linking up the different regional bazaars, they obviously hindered integration within each centre.

Small panchayats of leading merchants and bankers existed in many of the towns of India—Sarrafa Panchayat in Agra, the Gyarah Panch in Indore, the Naupatti Mahajan in Banaras—but the influence of these traditional institutions on market practices was small, confined usually to certifying the dishonour of a *hundi*, acting as insolvency courts and dealing with liquidation.[98] A few modern associations of *shroffs* had made their appearance as well: the Bombay Shroffs' Association (an association of Gujarati *shroffs* formed in Bombay city in 1910), the Multani Shroffs Association in Bombay (of uncertain date, supplemented by the Shikarpur Shroffs' Association formed in 1929 to give evidence to the Bombay Provincial Banking Enquiry Committee), the Marwari Chamber of Commerce in Bombay, the Ahmedabad Shroffs' Association, and the Nattukottai Nagarathars' Association. There was once an association of *shroffs* in Calcutta but this body—which seems to have been principally an organ of Barabazar Marwaris—ceased to exist by the 1920s. The Multani Shroffs' Association was more active. B. Ramachandra Rau refers to it in 1922 as a body of 200 to 250 members with a small committee of five seniormost bankers who regulated the *hundi* rate. The rate fixed by the committee, however, did not operate outside the Multani bazaar. The Ahmedabad Shroffs' Association was perhaps the only body which had succeeded in completely integrating the local money market under its centralised control. The Ahmedabad *shroffs* met regularly in the Manikchowk bazaar which served as a clearing house. They had an excellent system of clearing house among themselves without any charge, dating back to the time before the English clearing system was introduced in India. Barring such exceptions, however, the *shroffs* and *kothiwals* acted alone, did not meet together, and came into contact with each other and with the bazaar only through *hundi dalals* who went round from house to house collecting information about the day's financial requirement and communicating this intelligence to the financiers.[99]

The rates thus determined through the informal mechanisms of the bazaar bore—for the greater part of the year—no relation to the rates in the modern money market. Only in the busy season was there a perceptible, but by no means pronounced, sympathy in the movement of rates. The link between modern banks and the indigenous bankers was through the endorsement of *hundis* by *shroffs* which were discounted by banks. A trader who drew a *hundi* to avail himself of bank funds had to get a *shroff's* signature on his paper for the bank to discount it. The endorsing *shroff* had to be on the bank's approved list of *shroffs*, and each *shroff* on the secret list had borrowing limits beyond which the bank would not accept paper endorsed by him. This was the only connection between the banks and the bazaar and it was tenuous. In the off season the *shroffs* did not go to the banks at all, and might even underquote them by as much as 2 per cent if money was easy. But in the height of the busy season for jute and the season when oilseeds and other winter crops were exported, money in the bazaar became tight and the bazaar rates climbed well over the bank rates. Unable to meet all the *hundis* drawn on them, the listed *shroffs* resorted to their defined borrowing limits with the banks. They borrowed at bank rates and lent out on higher *hundi* rates, deriving their profit from the difference. But if the bank rate rose much above 8 per cent they stopped borrowing. During the busy season, the banks might influence the bazaar rates to some extent, but not during the rest of the year. The difference between the bank rate and the *hundi* rate was inevitable in view of the fact that the *shroffs* controlled in the aggregate a greater volume of mobile credit which was channelled into the internal and not the export trade.[100]

THE PENETRATION OF THE BAZAAR INTO MODERN BUSINESS

Beyond the operations of the bazaar lay the sphere of high international finance and trade, the structure of which was completely different. Since the First World War a movement of penetration from the bazaar into this sphere had begun but it was still European at the highest level. This level accommodated twelve international giants, including three international produce exporting firms[101] and nine exchange banks (see Table 5). The exchange banks played the key role in the import of bullion, distribution of foreign piecegoods, and financing of produce exports. In addition to mobilising deposits in India to finance the exports, they obtained further sums from re-discounting their bills with the Imperial Bank of India, by sale of sterling drafts on London, and by importing sovereign and bullion. The international export houses provided themselves with funds in India by

Table 5 International Giants on the Indian Business Scene in the Inter-War Period

	Name	Headquarters	Branches
1.	Ralli Brothers	London	Manchester, Liverpool, Dundee. Calcutta, Bombay, Madras, Karachi, Shanghai, Egypt, Sudan, Uganda and upcountry branches all over India
2.	Volkart Brothers	Winterthur, Switzerland	London, Karachi, Bombay, Madras. Calcutta, Cochin, Tellicherry, Tuticorin, Colombo, Singapore, Shanghai, Osaka, and upcountry branches all over Southern, Western and North Western India
3.	David Sassoon & Company	London	Bombay, Calcutta, Karachi, Hongkong, Shanghai, Hankow, Bagdad, Basra and Manchester
4.	Chartered Bank of India Australia and China	London	Calcutta, Bombay, Madras, Rangoon, Karachi, Amritsar, Delhi and Cawnpore
5.	National Bank of India	London	Calcutta, Bombay, Madras, Rangoon, Karachi, Lahore, Amritsar, Delhi, Cawnpur, Chittagong, Mandalay, Tuticorin, Cochin and Aden
6.	Mercantile Bank of India	London	Calcutta, Howrah, Madras, Rangoon. Karachi, Simla and Delhi
7.	Eastern Bank	London	Calcutta, Bombay, Karachi, Madras and Bagdad
8.	P & O Banking Corporation (a Chartered subsidiary)	London	Calcutta, Bombay, Madras
9.	Lloyds Bank	London	A British bank with Indian branches in Bombay, Calcutta, Karachi, Rangoon, Delhi, New Delhi, Simla, Lahore, Amritsar, Rawalpindi, Muree, Srinagar and Gulmarg
10.	Hongkong and Shanghai Banking Corporation	Hongkong	Indian branches in Bombay, Calcutta and Rangoon
11.	Yokohama Specie Bank	Yokohama	Indian branches in Calcutta, Bombay, Karachi and Rangoon
12.	National City Bank of New York	New York	Indian branches in Calcutta, Bombay and Rangoon

Source: *Thacker's Indian Directory 1926* (Calcutta, 1926), passim; *Handbook of Commercial Information* (Delhi, 1937), p. 114.

selling sterling bills of exchange and telegraphic transfers to the exchange banks, and also used the proceeds of the sale of imported commodities to finance their exports. Their upcountry buying agencies were financed in two ways—by sale locally of *hundis* drawn on port headquarters or by telegraphic transfers through exchange banks. In some cases local *shroffs* and *arhatiyas* were authorised to finance the upcountry agencies, and they were reimbursed by drafts or cheques.[102]

Clearly, the financial structure of this sector was so different as to make it difficult for Indian houses based on the bazaar to penetrate the export-import trade. A description of the widespread and interlocking operations of Ralli will make it clear why Indian houses had such a small share in this overseas business. But equally, the contraction and alteration of Ralli business at the end of the period under review will afford an insight into those structural changes in the Indian economy during the 30s and the 40s which enabled Indian houses rising from the bazaar to seize important sections of business, industry and foreign trade. It should be noted, in parenthesis, that Ralli Brothers was in some respects not so different from the *kothiwals* of the Indian bazaar: it was a Greek family partnership which trained up virtually all its personnel from the teens, filled in the managerial level with family members, relations and friends trained in this manner, dealt purely in agricultural commodities and piecegoods on an international scale and appeared to distrust anything industrial. However, this international house started working from the nerve centre of the British empire, London, with all the connections, facilities and resources available in the world's leading money market which possessed at the same time a crucial political dominance over India.

The firm started between 1818 and 1826 as a partnership between five Ralli brothers located in London, Marseilles, Constantinople and Odessa trading in grain and silk and dealing in Manchester piecegoods. It entered India in 1855 by setting up an office in Calcutta, which was followed in 1865 by two branches in Bombay and Karachi. It became in the course of time the leading importer of piecegoods in India. But even more impressively, as the largest exporter of cash crops, it built up an unparallelled upcountry organisation for buying raw produce. Large quantities of wheat and other grains from the Punjab and groundnuts, linseed and other oilseeds from western, southern and eastern India formed its principal item of business, the destination being the ports of England and the Continent. Second in importance was the cotton it purchased from Punjab, Sind, the Central Provinces and the Madras Presidency. It prepared the cotton at its own ginning and pressing factories in Sind, CP, Madras Presidency and Bengal for export through Karachi, Bombay, Madras, Tuticorin and Calcutta. The cotton exports went in different directions. The bulk arrived in Liverpool, where Ralli had an office for landing and supervision of all deliveries to Lancashire and a Sample Room where a staff of expert selectors examined and graded the cottons for re-exports to the Continent. Some of the cottons took the other way to the Far East, especially to Japan where, before the Second World War, the Ralli subsidiary, Showa Menka Kabushiki Kaisha, figured among the principal importers of Indian cottons in Japan. The third most important item of Ralli export was jute through Calcutta and Chittagong, for which it had built up, since 1872, a wide organisation in Bengal with five principal *pucca* building premises in the principal jute marts of Bengal. Ralli had an office, two warehouses and a showroom in Dundee to attend to jute sales to the Scottish mills, and extensive arrangements for marketing jute and jute goods in America and the Continent. It pioneered the export of shellac through Calcutta, took a large part in the export of raw hides and skins collected in Cawnpore, Lahore, Karachi, Bombay, Madras and Calcutta, and handled consignments of Indian, Central Asian and Afghanistan wool to the Liverpool auctions on behalf of Indian merchants. It had arrangements and connections in New York which developed into Ralli Brothers New York Inc., for large exports of jute, gunnies, cotton and shellac. Finally, it balanced these exports by importing Java sugar through Calcutta and other ports.

This extensive international export-import business was controlled by the Ralli head office in London, which chartered vessels on the Baltic Exchange, arranged marine insurance through its subsidiary Orion Insurance Company (first started in 1931) with Lloyds' underwriters, and controlled the costing of all its operations. These world-wide operations consisted of (i) buying, collecting and taking delivery in certain world centres of production—Lancashire, India and Java; (ii) processing of Indian crops by ginning, grading, cleaning, bagging and baling according to manufacturer's or consumer's requirements and packaging according to transport requirements; (iii) arranging movement of goods by rail, road or inland waterway to port of shipment; (iv) insurance of goods on land and sea and booking of sea freight; (v) arrangements for delivery to overseas buyers, for weighing, invoicing and settlement of quality problems and for collection of payment; and (vi) making advances to suppliers and giving credit to buyers, arranged through a series of forward purchases and sales. From start to finish these operations had to fit into the ever increasing complexities of international trade and finance and called for careful disposition of financial and foreign exchange dispositions, which no Indian house could carry out on a competitive basis for lack of international connections and access to the London market.

The Ralli empire reached its climax in 1920 when its turnover reached the record figure of £63 million. Though prices were then high, the tonnage was greater than anything handled in later times. With the fall in prices in the 1930s, the annual monetary turnover came down from about £40 million to the region of £25 million. After the Second World War it again rose to £30 million but the tonnage was irreversibly lower. The composition and direction of trade also underwent matching changes. Depressed international prices reduced Ralli exports of grain to negligible proportions and increased internal consumption ruled out a resumption of exports at the end of the Great Depression. In Punjab and Sind, Ralli had to abandon the vast shipments of wheat and concentrate on exports of the spreading long staple cottons. But in the part of the country which came to form the Indian Republic, massive increases in mill consumption of cotton reduced the quantities available for shipment. The logic of the same process reduced the Ralli import of cotton piecegoods into India. To sustain its declining business in raw cottons and piecegoods, Ralli entered Africa in 1933 where it resorted to large scale purchases of Uganda, Sudan and Egyptian cotton. In 1947 it formed Dehns (Africa) Limited in order to augment, by means of cotton piecegood exports to East Africa, the activity of its now oversized Manchester office and packing establishment. Already, however, the war with Japan had led to the loss of its Japanese subsidiary, and its

Table 6 Percentage Share of Indians in the Bills through Exchange Banks 1925–29

Export bills				Centre and nature of banks	Import bills			
Indian		Non-Indian			Indian		Non-Indian	
1925	1929	1925	1929		1925	1929	1925	1929
				Calcutta				
19	35	81	65	British	70	69	30	31
42	56	58	44	Non-British	54	78	46	22
				Bombay				
25	29	75	71	British	70	76	30	24
28	40	72	60	Non-British	73	77	27	23
				Madras				
44	43	56	57	British	76	77	24	23
				Karachi				
13	17	87	83	British	67	78	33	22
–	–	100	100	Non-British	31	13	69	87
				Delhi				
100	100	–	–	British	95	95	5	5
				Cawnpore				
95	95	5	5	British	95	95	5	5
				Amritsar				
84	80	16	20	British	100	100	–	–

Source: *The Indian Central Banking Enquiry Committee 1931*, Volume II, Evidence (written), (Calcutta, 1931), pp. 858–59.
Note: The table does not indicate the size of the total non-Indian share in the foreign trade of India, since some import and export bills of major international houses were adjusted against each other and did not move through the exchange banks.

large raw cotton shipments to Japan. Within India, Ralli took a rearguard action: as exports of oilseeds practically ceased due to increased oil milling, it entered this new line of business by acquiring several oil mills with a crushing capacity of 100,000 tons. Its imports of Java sugar had wholly stopped with the rapid growth of sugar milling in India in the 1930s. Instead of importing such consumption goods as yarns, piecegoods and sugar, Ralli turned to importing increased quantities of agricultural machinery and diesel engines for the growing needs of Indian agriculture. But despite these adjustments, its business in India after the Second World War was but a fraction of its former turnover.[103]

Bazaar-based Indian houses steadily advanced into foreign trade as the international trading houses declined. While Ralli and Volkart were dwarfed towards the end of our period, the Sassoons pulled out of India altogether in the late 30s. In the meanwhile, according to figures supplied by the Exchange Banks' Association to the Central Banking Enquiry Committee, the percentage share of Indian merchants in the import and export bills negotiated through the exchange banks increased perceptibly between 1925 and 1929 at all the major centres of foreign trade: Calcutta, Bombay, Madras, Karachi, Delhi, Cawnpore and Amritsar (see Table 6).

Many of the new Indian houses which began to push into the sphere of overseas trade rose from the bazaar. There was a connection between the earlier migrations of merchant communities and their later participation in the trade through the ports.

Two examples will make this clear, both arising from long distance migrations to Calcutta and extensions of community financial and commercial networks from inland to the port city. One was a Marwari Maheshwari family migration from Bikaner down the Gangetic valley to Calcutta. The other was an Iranian Muslim merchant family migration to Madras and then to Calcutta. The first movement gave rise to the house of Birla, closely connected to Gandhi and destined to play a large role in the economy of independent India. The second movement gave rise to the house of Ispahani, closely connected to Jinnah and poised to play a key part in the economy of Pakistan. The Birla family, which came from Pilani in Bikaner, rose to a commanding position in Calcutta during the First World War by speculative activities which formed the base of commercial and industrial expansion. The Ispahani family, which started trading in indigo in Madras around 1867, set up a permanent office in Calcutta in 1900 and soon emerged as one of the leading Muslim merchant families in Calcutta.

By 1927, as *Thacker's Directory* indicates, Birla Brothers and M.M. Ispahani & Sons were already firmly established in the bazaar as well as in the sphere of external trade. In 1917 Birla Brothers started jute shipments to Europe and its expanding produce trade was carried on through its correspondent in Europe, East India Produce Company. The firm was organised into five main departments, each of which conducted a principal component of its multifarious business: Produce Department, Jute and Gunny Department, Piecegoods and Import Department, Cotton Mills and Insurance Department and Jute Mills Department. It was also involved, as a member of the Bombay Bullion Exchange, in importing large quantities of bullion through Bombay. It figured as an exporter of jute, oilseeds, tea, rice, shellac, hemp, myrobalans, mica and gunnies and as an importer of piecegoods, precious metals, hardware, automobiles and sugar. It was the managing agent of several cotton and jute mills and in addition it owned the Govind Rice Mills. The firm acted as jute supply agents, jute and gunny brokers and cotton agents. M.M. Ispahani & Sons, with headquarters in Calcutta, had branches in Madras, Bombay, Rangoon, London and Tehran and agencies in Ispahan, Ahwaz and other towns of Persia. It exported tea, indigo, hides and skins, shellac and oils, imported Burma rice and coral, and dealt in Persian products. It was a large factor in the rice trade of eastern India, and it exported from Madras hides and skins to Europe, Japan and America. It also purchased large quantities of tea in the Calcutta auctions, and was reckoned as the third largest tea exporting firm of Calcutta.[104]

The transformation of the Indian bazaar was well on the way. The intersectoral relations within the Indian economy must be understood in terms of these structural changes in the bazaar, and its changing relationship to the rural economy, on the one hand, and the modern capitalist sector, on the other. High risk and low profit margins—these were the twin conditions of Indian finance and trade, bred by the rural production organisation. These conditions impeded the deeper penetration of foreign capital and enabled the bazaar to survive by using its indispensable connection with the country to finance, assemble and distribute the enormous quantities of goods required to feed, clothe, house and entertain a huge and growing population. The total volume of mobile money invested in these trading and financing operations expanded with the increasing population and achieved greater mobility over time through a better concentration and organisation. Its circulation at the higher levels of the economy had been inhibited by the domination of foreign capital in international trade and large-scale industry, but the narrow channels of contact between the bazaar and the central money market enabled the bazaar to conserve and augment its strength within its own isolated but vast sphere until it could seek to broaden these channels of contact on its own, and better terms at the end of the period under review.

SUMMARY AND CONCLUSIONS

To summarise briefly the main developments of the period, the bazaar underwent major structural changes between 1914—47 as a result of the three dominating events of the age—the First World War, the Great Depression and the Second World War. The First World War slackened the grip of the British capital on the economy, and gave rise to extensive speculation in grain, seeds, jute and cotton in the bazaar. Speculation by Indian traders was sufficiently intense to threaten the supply lines of the mills and the exporting firms. The organised sector—both European and Indian—took counter action to ensure supply lines in export and milling.[105] A systematic attempt was made in the 1920s to bypass the bazaar. Export firms vastly extended their buying organisation in the interior, the mills sought through combination and government legislation to control the raw material markets, the Imperial Bank and the exchange banks opened a large number of branches in the interior. The attempt by the European-dominated organised sector to reach the upcountry economy received a serious check with the onset of the Great Depression. The export and import firms had to fold up much of their upcountry buying and selling organisation as it was found too costly. They reverted once more to the system of relying on Indian commission agents for obtaining produce from the interior and for distributing goods upcountry. Inland trade, like overseas trade, suffered greatly from the depression, but the reversal of the bullion flow shored up inland markets to some extent.[106] Indian merchants and bankers also steadily increased their participation in mill industry and export-import trade during the inter-war period. The process quickened during the Second World War, at the end of which the organised sector was itself substantially composed of men who had risen from the bazaar.

Certain general conclusions may be drawn from the material presented in the foregoing. The economy of India in the late colonial period was not a dual economy, cleaved between a capitalist international enclave on the one hand, and a primitive, pre-capitalist, peddling sector on the other. If we take the different prevailing rates of money as an indicator of the true divisions within the economy, then three distinct conglomerations would emerge: (i) the predominantly white enclave of corporations, banks, managing agencies, mines and plantations, governed by the bank rate; (ii) the indigenous network of commission agencies linked by mobile *hundi* credit and governed by the fluctuating bazaar rates; and (iii) the subsistence economy of peasants, artisans and pedlars, governed by the high and inflexible rates of moneylenders. In other words, it will not do to dismiss the indigenous part of the economy as a subsistence sector in which all trade was of a peddling variety and where mobile bankers' credit had not developed. The colonial enclave was not the only 'organised' sector in the economy. On the contrary, it secured export produce and distributed imported goods through a network of *hundi* bankers and commission agents who had achieved an integrated organisation over the subcontinent and whose business was only partially directed to serving the white import-export sector, being concerned mainly with the much larger movements of raw produce, manufactured goods, precious metals, money and credit within the country.

The growing awareness of the importance and sophistication of their functions has resulted in several in-depth explorations with reference to Bombay, Tamil Nadu and Hindustan. I have sought to emphasise the wider dimension of these regional studies by bringing into focus the integrated credit-and-agency nexus in operation between the distant parts of the country. Using traditional devices, such as *satta, teji-mandi, goladari, arhat* and *hundi*, Indian bankers, speculators and merchants generated increasing commodity and credit flows along the lines of a long distance network between 1,718 market towns with 12 nodal points, the whole nexus being centred on the twin headquarters of Bombay and Calcutta. The purpose of this essay has been to bring this trans-Indian bazaar network into focus, because it forms the necessary background to the rise of the modern Indian capitalist class.

Before the indigenous bazaar nexus penetrated the white preserves of industry and external trade, it was engaged in facilitating along the long lines of its distant connections the essential flows of India's monsoon economy: the outflow of agricultural produce, the inflow of manufactured goods, and precious metals and hard cash, the reverse flow of revenue, and the circular flow of money and credit which kept the whole system functioning. After it penetrated the more modern spheres of business, the bazaar still continued to assist the seasonal flows, pumping in and pumping out the commodities and the credits as the seasons dictated. The bazaar thus remained at the pulsing heart of the country's economy, each throb and each pause marked by the alternating cycle of the 'busy' season and the 'slack' season. The flows generated by the pumpings of the bazaar reached the distant corners of the country's economic organism, and over time the ever widening operations of the bankers, speculators and commission agents created a more sophisticated and integrated nerve system, until an all-India capitalist class, sprung from and strongly linked to the bazaar, worked its way into the heart of the economy.

Originally published as Rajat Kanta Ray, 'The Bazaar: Changing Structural Characteristics of the Indigenous Section of the Indian Economy before and after the Great Depression', in *The Indian Economic and Social History Review*, Vol. 25, No. 3, 1988, pp. 263–318.

NOTES

** I am deeply indebted to Dr Lakshmi Subramanian who collected much of the material and supplied many of the ideas of the essay, and to Professor Dharma Kumar who went through the earlier drafts several times and helped reshape it.

1. Amiya Kumar Bagchi, *Private Investment in India 1900–1939* (Cambridge, 1972); Rajat K. Ray, *Industrialization in India: Growth and Conflict in the*

Private Corporate Sector 1914–1947 (New Delhi, 1979); B.R. Tomlinson, *The Political Economy of the Raj 1914–1947* (London, 1979); Claude Markovitz, *Indian Business and Nationalist Politics 1931–39: The Indigenous Capitalist and the Rise of the Congress Party* (Cambridge, 1985); and Bipan Chandra, *Imperialism and Nationalism in India* (Delhi, 1979).

2. D.R. Gadgil, *Origins of the Modern Indian Business Class* (New York, 1957); Dwijendra Tripathi (ed.), *Business Communities in India: A Historical Perspective* (New Delhi, 1984).

3. L.C. Jain, *Indigenous Banking in India* (London, 1929); Bimal C. Ghose, *A Study of the Indian Money Market: With Special Reference to the Calcutta Money Market* (Calcutta, 1943); S.A. Husain, *Agricultural Marketing in Northern India* (London, 1937); J.C. Bahl, *The Oilseeds Trade of India* (Bombay, 1938); and M.L. Dantwala. *Marketing of Raw Cotton in India* (Bombay, 1939). For an early example of historical treatment, see Brij Kishore Bhargava, *Indigenous Banking in Ancient and Medieval India* (Bombay, 1934).

4. Irfan Habib, 'Banking in Mughal India', in Tapan Raychaudhuri (ed.), *Contributions to Indian Economic History I* (Calcutta, 1960); J.C. Heesterman, 'Was There an Indian Reaction? Western Expansion in Indian Perspective', in H. Wessling, *Expansion and Reaction* (Leiden. 1978); B.R. Grover, 'An Integrated Pattern of Commercial Life in the Rural Society of North India during the 17th and 18th Centuries', in *Proceedings of the Indian Historical Records Commission*, Vol. 37 (1966); Frank Perlin, 'Money Use in Late Pre-Colonial India and the International Trade in Currency Media', Mughal Monetary Conference, Dukes University, June 1981; H.W. Van Santen, 'De Verenigde Ost-Indische in Gujarat en Hindustan 1660–1662', Ph.D. Dissertation (Leiden, 1982), referred to in Om Prakash, 'Trade and Commercial Organization in India in the 17th and the 18th Century', Indian Institute of Management Seminar, Ahmedabad, 1987.

5. N.K. Sinha, *The Economic History of Bengal* (Calcutta, 1961–70); Asiya Siddiqi, 'The Business World of Jamsetjee Jeejeebhoy', *Indian Economic and Social History Review*, Vol. 19, Nos 3–4 (1982); Thomas A. Timberg, 'A North Indian Firm as Seen through Its Business Records 1860–1914: Tarachand Ghanashyamdas. A "Great" Marwari Firm', *Indian Economic and Social History Review*, Vol. 8 (1971).

6. B.R. Tomlinson, 'Colonial Firms and the Decline of Colonialism in Eastern India 1914–47', *Modern Asian Studies*, Vol. 15, No. 3 (1981); Omkar Goswami, 'Sahibs, Babus and Banias: Changes in Industrial Control in Eastern India 1918–1960', IIM Seminar, Ahmedabad, 1987.

7. Ashin Dasgupta, *Indian Merchants and the Decline of Surat c. 1700–1750* (Wiesbaden, 1979).

8. C.A. Bayly, 'Political and Economic Networks in Eighteenth Century India', paper prepared for the panel on '250 Years of Agrarian Regimes in India' at the American Association of Asian Studies Meetings, San Francisco, March 1983; Lakshmi Subramanian, 'Banias and the British: Role of Indigenous Credit in the Process of Imperial Expansion in Western India in the Second Half of the Eighteenth Century', *Modern Asian Studies*, Vol. 21, No. 3 (1987); Karen Leonard, 'Banking Firms in Nineteenth Century Hyderabad Politics', *Modern Asian Studies*, Vol. 15, No. 2 (1981); C.A. Bayly, *Rulers, Townsmen and Bazaars: North Indian Society in the Age of British Expansion 1770–1870* (Cambridge, 1983); Moti Chandra, *Kashi Ka Itihas* (Bombay, 1962).

9. Amiya Kumar Bagchi, *The Evolution of the State Bank of India: The Roots 1806–1876*, 2 parts, (Bombay, 1987): *idem*, 'Merchants and Colonialism,' Occasional Paper No. 38; Centre for Studies in Social Sciences, Calcutta, 1981; *idem*, 'Money and Credit as Areas of Conflict in Colonial India', Occasional Paper No. 51, Centre for Studies in Social Sciences, Calcutta, 1982.

10. A.D.D. Gordon, *Business and Politics: Rising Nationalism and Modernizing Economy in Bombay 1918–1933* (New Delhi, 1978); Thomas A. Timberg, *The Marwaris: From Traders to Industrialists* (Delhi, 1978); Christopher John Baker, *An Indian Rural Economy 1880–1955: The Tamilnad Countryside* (New Delhi, 1984).

11. Omkar Goswami, 'Then Came the Marwaris: Some Aspects of the Changes in the Pattern of Industrial Control in Eastern India', *Indian Economic and Social History Review*, Vol. 22, No. 3 (1985).

12. The distinction between the 'Western' or 'Central' money market and the indigenous money market is set out in John Maynard Keynes, *Indian Currency and Finance* (London, 1913), pp. 195–6; *Indian Central Banking Enquiry Committee 1931*, Vol. 1, Part I, *Majority Report* (hereafter *Central Banking)*, pp. 401, 587.

13. Rajat Kanta Ray, 'The Bazaar: Indigenous Sector of the Indian Economy', in Tripathi, *Business Communities*, pp. 254, 256–8.

14. *Report of the Controller of Currency for the Year 1927–28*, p. 17.

15. US Department of Commerce, Bureau of Domestic and Foreign Commerce, Emmett A. Chapman, *India as a Market for American Goods*, (1925), p. 1.

16. US Department of Commerce, Bureau of Domestic and Foreign Commerce, Henry D. Baker, *British India with Notes on Ceylon, Afghanistan and Tibet* (Special Consular Report No. 72), (hereafter *British India*), pp. 9, 17.

17. US Department of Commerce, Bureau of Domestic and Foreign Commerce, *Trade Conditions in India* (Trade Promotion Series, Washington, 1935), pp. 23–4.

18. S. Sivasubramanian, 'Income from the Secondary Sector in India 1900–1947', *Indian Economic and Social History Review*, No. 4, 1977.

19. *Central Banking*, p. 721.

20. Figure for 1928–29 in *Statistical Abstract of British India* from 1922–23 to 1931–32, p. 542.

21. According to the Grady Mission of 1942, the railways still carried 90 per cent of the land-borne traffic of India. Report of the American Technical Mission to India, August 1942, unpublished (hereafter *Grady Report*), p. 7.

22. *Statistical Abstract*, pp. 714–15.

23. Sivasubramanian, *op. cit.*

24. *Bombay Provincial Banking Enquiry Committee 1920–30* (Calcutta, 1930), (hereafter *Bombay Banking*), Vol. 3, p. 155.

25. *Ibid.*, p. 494. The Indian Chamber of Commerce reported from Bengal that out of a total finance of Rs. 46 crore available for inland trade, the merchants themselves supplied Rs. 22 crore, the shroffs Rs. 22 crore and the Imperial Bank of India Rs. 2 crore. *Report of the Bengal Provincial Banking Enquiry Committee 1929–30* (Calcutta, 1930), (hereafter *Bengal Banking*), Vol. 1, p. 186.

26. This figure is based on assuming roughly a ratio of 1:2 between goods never carried to market towns and goods brought there for shipment by rail. That is the ratio given in *Report of the Bihar and Orissa Provincial Banking Enquiry Committee 1929–30* (1930), (hereafter Bihar and Orissa Banking).

27. For a description of fairs and markets, see *Agricultural Marketing in India: Marketing Series no. 45, Report on Fairs, Markets and Produce Exchanges in India* (Delhi, 1943), passim.

28. *Bihar and Orissa Banking*, Vol. 1, pp. 59–61.

29. For a clear picture of these differences, see *Fairs, Markets and Produce Exchanges*, passim.

30. *Report of the United Provinces Provincial Banking Enquiry Committee 1929–30* (Allahabad, 1930), (hereafter *UP Banking*), Vol. 1, p. 280; see also *Bombay Banking*, Vol. 1, p. 20.

31. Quoted in *Bengal Banking*, Vol. 1, p. 50.

32. The annual *Report of the Controller of Currency* made every year an analysis of the year's fluctuations and flows, which showed how the economy achieved equilibrium during the year through bazaar operations.

33. *UP Banking*, Vol. 1, p. 60n.

34. Don C. Bliss, *The Bombay Bullion Market* (US Department of Commerce, 1927), p. 7.

35. This account of seasonal flows is based on numerous scattered references in *UP Banking*, Vol. 1; *Bihar and Orissa Banking*, Vols 2 and 3; *Madras Provincial Banking Enquiry Committee 1929–30* (hereafter *Madras Banking*), Vol. 1 (Madras, 1930); *Report of the Banking Enquiry Committee for Centrally Administered Areas 1929–30* (hereafter *Central Areas Banking*), Vols 1, 3 and 4; *Report of the Controller of Currency* (various years); and Bliss, *Bombay Bullion Market.*

36. *Central Banking*, Vol. 1, Part I, p. 70.

37. Report of the *Central Provinces Provincial Banking Enquiry Committee 1929–30* (hereafter *CP Banking*), Vol. 1 (Nagpur, 1930), p. 114.

38. Baker, *British India*, p. 160.

39. Central Banking, Vol. 1, pp. 21, 29, 310–11; Vol. 1, Part II, pp. 175, 194; Vol. 2, pp. 410, 729.

40. *Central Banking*, Vol. 1, pp. 29, 323–33; Vol. 2, p. 53.

41. *Central Areas Banking*, Vol. 1, pp. 274–5; Vol. 4, 279–81.

42. Charles K. Moser, *The United States in India's Commerce* (US Consular Report, 1939), passim; S.A. Palekar, *Trade of India* (Bombay, 1939), pp. 106–8.

43. Palekar, *Trade of India*, pp. 206–7; E.A. Chapman, *India as a Market for American Goods* (US Consular Report, 1925), pp. 8–9; *Madras Banking*, Vol. 4, pp. 57–68.

44. Chapman, *India as a Market*, p. 8.

45. *Shaw Wallace & Co. 1886–1947*, compiled by Sir Harry Townsend (Calcutta, 1965), p. 117; Tinberg, *Marwaris*, p. 154; *Thacker's Indian Directory 1926* (Calcutta, 1926), p. 75 of Calcutta Section; *Bengal Banking*, Vol. 2 Part I, pp. 765–6.

46. *Central Banking*, Vol. 2, p. 743; Chapman, *India as a Market*, pp. 9–11.

47. *Central Banking*, Vol. 2, pp. 373–4.

48. *Central Banking*, Vol. 2, pp. 469–70.

49. Thacker's Indian Directory 1926, passim; *Report on the Marketing of Hides in India and Burma* (Delhi, 1943), pp. 243–6; *Indian Cotton Committee 1919* (Calcutta, 1920), Vol. 5, Part II, passim.

50. *Report on the Marketing of Wheat in India* (Delhi, 1937), p. 254; *Indian Cotton Committee*, Vol. 5, Part II, pp. 1–79, 130.

51. Baker, *An Indian Rural Economy*, passim.

52. *Marketing of Wheat*, pp. 187, 254.

53. *Bihar and Orissa Banking*, Vol. 1, pp. 67–8, Vol. 3, pp. 69–70.

54. F.A. Shah and L.R. Dawar, *Finance and Marketing of Cultivators' Wheat in the Punjab* (Lahore, 1934), pp. 50–4.

55. These 12 nodal points of the Indian trading and credit systems have been identified after a close reading of *Handbook of Commercial Information* (1937), and the voluminous evidence of the Central and Provincial Banking Enquiry Committees of 1929–31. Criteria for selection are: (i) centres of exchange banking (and therefore of external trade); (ii) the big *hundi* markets with inter-provincial connections; (iii) the great inland emporia.

56. See the series headed *Agricultural Marketing in India. Marketing Series*, published by the Agricultural Marketing Adviser to the Government of India. The series came to contain as many as 60 reports on different crops by 1947, for a list of which see Marketing Series no. 60. *Agricultural Marketing in India. Report on the Production and Marketing of Cardamoms in India* (Delhi, 1947). I have seen all these reports, which convey in their totality an unmistakable sense of the market integration of India through *hundi* and *arhat* operations. See especially *Report on the Marketing of Rice in India and Burma* (Delhi, 1941); *Report on the Marketing of Wheat in India* (Delhi, 1937); *Report on the Marketing of Barley in India* (Delhi, 1945); *Report on the Marketing of Linseed in India* (Delhi, 1938); *Report on the Marketing of Tobacco in India and Burma* (Delhi, 1939).

57. Indian Central Cotton Committee, *General Report on Eight Investigations into the Finance and Marketing of Cultivators' Cotton 1925–1928* (Bombay, n.d.), pp. 32–3; *Central Areas Banking*, Vol. 1, pp. 262–3; *CP Banking*, Vol. 1, p. 200.

58. *Madras Banking*, Vol. 2, pp. 298–9.

59. *Bihar and Orissa Banking*, Vol. 1, p. 63; *Central Areas Banking*, Vol. 1, pp. 262–3: *Report of the Punjab Provincial Banking Enquiry Committee 1929–30* (hereafter *Punjab Banking*), p. 58.

60. Buchanan Hamilton, *An Account of the Districts of Bihar and Patna in 1811–1812* (Patna, n.d.), passim.

61. *Bihar and Orissa Banking*, Vol. 1, p. 77; Vol. 3, pp. 146–8, 150, 151, 158.

62. *UP Banking*, Vol. 1, pp. 157–8.

63. *Fairs, Markets and Produce Exchange*, p. 79.

64. *Ibid.*, pp. 78–9.

65. Bengal Chamber of Commerce Committee, Minutes of Proceedings Commencing from 7 August 1919 (manuscript minute book preserved in the committee room of the Chamber).

66. *Fairs, Markets and Produce Exchange*, p. 67.

67. *Ibid.*, p. 67; *UP Banking*, Vol. 1, pp. 62, 157–8.

68. Haricharan Bandyopadhyay, *Bangiya Shabdakosha*, Vol. 1 (Calcutta B.S. 1341), S.V. *Arat*; also evidence volumes of the Banking Enquiry Committees 1929–30.

69. Buchanan Hamilton, *An Account of Bihar and Patna*, pp. 683 ff.

70. *Madras Banking*, Vol. 4, pp. 244–7.

71. *UP Banking*, Vol. 1, p. 59.

72. *Finance and Marketing of Cultivators' Cotton*, pp. 40–41.

73. *Punjab Banking*, Vol. 1, p. 200.

74. *Report of the Bikaner Banking Enquiry Committee* (Bikaner, 1930), pp. 53, 66, 75–6.

75. *UP Banking*, Vol. 1, pp. 60, 152, 155, 159.

76. *Bihar and Orissa Banking*, Vol. 2, pp. 246–7.

77. *Marketing Cultivators' Wheat in the Punjab*, p. 62.

78. *Punjab Banking*, Vol. 1, p. 206; *Central Areas Banking*, Vol. 1, p. 276.

79. *Marketing of Wheat*, p. 133.

80. *Fairs, Markets and Produce Exchanges*, pp. 53, 59, 60.

81. *Punjab Banking*, Vol. 1, pp. 206, 276.

82. *Ibid.*, p. 214.

83. *UP Banking*, Vol. 1, pp. 60, 266; *Punjab Banking*, Vol. 1, p. 205; *Bombay Banking*, Vol. 1, p. 34; *Central Areas Banking*, Vol. 1, p. 336.

84. C.N. Cooke, *Rise, Progress and Present Condition of Banking in India* (Calcutta, 1863), p. 83.

85. Haricharan Bandyopadhyay, *Bangiya Shabdakosha*, S.V. *hundi.*

86. *UP Banking*, Vol. 1, p. 262; L.C. Jain, *Indigenous Banking*, pp. 10, 70–1.

87. L.C. Jain, *Ibid.*, p. 70. Irfan Habib traced the word *hundi* to the dictionary of Nawal Kishore, *Bahar-i-Ajam* (1739–40), which identifies it as a Hindi word, with *safta* as its Persian equivalent. Irfan Habib, 'The System of Bills of Exchange (*Hundis*) in the Mughal Empire', in *Indian History Congress: Proceedings of the Thirty-Third Session* (Muzaffarpur, 1972), p. 301. Nawal Kishore, CM. Cooke, L.C. Jain and Irfan Habib have missed the Sanskrit origin of the word.

88. Vaman Shivaram Apte, *The Practical Sanskrit-English Dictionary*; s.v. *hund*, s.v. *hundika*.

89. Ranjit Sitaram Pandit (trans.), *Rajatarangini* (New Delhi, 1977), pp. 208, 209, 211.

90. L.C. Jain, *Indigenous Banking*, p. 10; Tapan Raychaudhuri and Irfan Habib (eds), *Cambridge Economic History of India* (New Delhi, 1984), p. 86.

91. *Bikaner Banking*, p. 97.

92. Ashin Dasgupta, *Indian Merchants and the Decline of Surat c. 1700–1750* (Wiesbaden, 1979), p. 86.

93. C.A. Bayly, *Rulers, Townsmen, Bazaars*, passim.

94. Quoted in *CP Banking*, Vol. 1, p. 334.

95. *Madras Banking*, Vol. 4, pp. 157–67, 244–7; Compton Mackenzie, *Realms of Silver: One Hundred Years of Banking in the East* (London, 1954), pp. 112–13.

96. *Bengal Banking*, Vol. l, pp. 188–9; *UP Banking*, Vol. 1, pp. 260–70; *Fairs, Markets and Produce Exchanges*, p. 52.

97. *UP Banking*, Vol. 1, pp. 63–4, 263–4, 269–71; *Bihar and Orissa Banking*, Vol. 3, pp. 158, 190–1.

98. *UP Banking*, Vol. 1, p. 266; L.C. Jain, *Indigenous Banking*, p. 40.

99. *Handbook of Commercial Information*, passim; *Bengal Banking*, Vol. 2, Part I, pp. 421–5; B. Ramachandra Rau, *Present Day Banking in India* (Calcutta, 1925), pp. 135–6; *Bombay Banking*, Vol. 3, pp. 408–16.

100. M.M.S. Gubbay, *Indigenous Indian Banking*, pp. 13–15; G. Findlay Shirras, *Indian Finance and Banking*, p. 342.

101. Ralli Bros, Volkart Bros and David Sassoon & Company. These were the biggest in the Indian produce trade.

102. M.M.S. Gubbay, *op. cit.*, pp. 114–15; *Fairs, Markets and Produce Exchanges*, p. 51.

103. In Pakistan, however, Ralli continued for some time to have a flourishing cotton baling and export business. *Ralli Brothers Limited, 1951* (author and place of publication not mentioned, 1951), passim.

104. *Thackers' Indian Directory 1926*, passim; Somerset Playne, *Bengal and Assam, Behar and Orissa* (London, 1917), p. 670.

105. Committee of the Bengal Chamber of Commerce. Minutes of Proceedings commencing from 7 August 1919 (manuscript), proceedings dated 25 November 1919.

106. *The Conditions and Prospects of United Kingdom Trade in India*, Report by Sir Thomas M. Ainscough (London, 1934), p. 22.

2

The Bazaar from a European Traveller's Perspective

Maria Graham

The bazaar occupies an important place in the European imagining of the Orient. This excerpt, from the memoirs of British author and traveller Maria Graham, provides an illustration of such imagining.* Eloquently and lucidly, Graham recounts the sights she witnessed during a trip to a Bombay bazaar in 1808. She describes the sweetmeats, grains, condiments, cotton, fruit and vegetables, betel leaves, perfumes, measurements and monies, and the processions the market played host to. She observes the special position occupied by the barber and his '*gup* shop', the site of market gossip. Noting the bazaar's cosmopolitan nature, where holidays of Hindus, Muslims, Jews, Armenians, Portuguese, and English were celebrated, Graham likens it to an 'Arabian night's entertainment'.

Graham's description of the bazaar typifies European travel writing on India, grounded as it was in ideas of a subject race, a heathen culture steeped in superstition, and the native town as both exotic and troublesome. The imagery used to recreate the bazaar is replete with narrow lanes, incessant noise and activity, buyers and sellers working on principles not in keeping with 'Western' economic rationality. In many ways, the bazaar epitomized the disparity between the East and Europe. It was thus 'not a coincidence that for over a century visitors saw glimpses of the Arabian tales and biblical stories in India.'† Bazaars often blurred the lines between classes, ethnic groups and races,

* Maria Graham (1785–1842) was visiting her father, a Scottish Navy Commissioner, when he was posted to India. For details on Maria Graham, see Jennifer Speake (ed.), *Literature of Travel and Exploration: An Encyclopedia* (London, Fitzroy Dearborn, 2003), Vol. II, pp. 497–9.

† See Swati Chattopadhyay, *Representing Calcutta: Modernity, Nationalism and the Colonial Uncanny* (London, Routledge, 2005), especially chapter 1. Also see Gautam Chakravarty, *The Indian Mutiny and the British Imagination* (Cambridge, Cambridge University Press, 2005), p. 172 and Emily A. Haddad, 'Better than the Reality: The

and travellers noted the cosmopolitan nature of the populace here. Not surprisingly, the bazaar worried the colonial administration which viewed the coming together of casual economy and culture in the bazaar as a potential threat to public order. As the historian Dipesh Chakraborty points out, 'The bazaar was seen as a den of lies and rumours, *bazaar gup* through which the ignorant, superstitious and credulous Indian masses communicated their dark feelings about the doings of an alien *sarkar*.'‡

[...] On opening one of their bales, I was surprised to find at least half of its contents of British manufacture, and such articles were much cheaper than those of equal fineness from Bengal and Madras. Excepting a particular kind of Chintz made at Poonah, and painted with gold and silver, there are no fine cotton-cloths made on this side of the peninsula; yet still it seems strange, that cotton carried to England, manufactured, and returned to this country, should undersell the fabrics of India, where labour is so cheap. But I believe this is owing partly to the uncertainty and difficulty of carriage here, although the use of machinery at home must be the main cause. The shawls are brought here direct from Cashmeer, by the native merchants of that country, so that we sometimes get them cheap and beautiful. The Banyans ought to be Hindoos, though I have known Mussulmans adopt the name, with the profession; their distinguishing turban is so formed as to present the shape of a rhinoceros' horn in front, and it is generally red.

The *Borahs* are an inferior set of travelling-merchants. The inside of a *Borah's* box is like that of an English country shop, spelling-books, prayer-books, lavender-water, eau de luce, soap, tapes, scissors, knives, needles, and thread, make but a small part of the variety it contains. These people are Mussulmans, very poor, and reputed thieves. The profits on their trade must be very small; but the Banyans are often rich, and most of them keep a shop in the bazar, leaving one partner to attend it, while the other goes his rounds, attended by two or three koolis, with their loads on their heads.

It reminds one of the Arabian Nights Entertainments, to go through the bazar of an evening. The whole fronts of the shops are taken down and converted into benches, on which the goods are disposed, and each shop is lighted with at least two lamps. Here you see grain of every description heaped up in earthen jars; there, sweetmeats of all sorts and shapes, disposed in piles on benches, or hung in festoons about the top and sides of the shop, which is commonly lined with chintz or dyed cotton. Farther on, fruits and vegetables are laid out to the best advantage; then you come to the *paung*, or betel leaf, nut, and chunam, ready for

---

Egyptian Market in Nineteenth Century Travel Writing', in Diane Long Hoveler and Jeffrey Cass (eds), *Interrogating Orientalism: Contextual Approaches and Pedagogical Practices* (Columbus, Ohio State University Press, 2006), pp. 72–89.

‡ Dipesh Chakraborty, *Habitations of Modernity: Essays in the Wake of Subaltern Studies* (Chicago, University of Chicago Press, 2002), p. 76. The bazaar was thus viewed as a 'place against which one needs protection' and 'which harbours qualities that threaten one's well being'. Colonial authorities were keen to turn the bazaar into 'benign regulated places, clean and healthy, incapable of producing either disease or disorder.' See Dipesh Chakraborty, 'Open Space/Public Place: Garbage, Modernity and India,' *South Asia*, XIV(1), 1991, pp. 15–31.

chewing, or the separate materials; beyond are shops for perfumes, linens, oils, toys, brass, and earthen ware, all set out in order, and the owner sitting bolt upright in the middle of his sweetmeats or grain, waiting for custom. The shops of the *schroffs*, or bankers; are numerous in the bazar; you see the master sitting in the middle of his money-table, surrounded by piles of copper and silver money, with scales for weighing the rupees and other coins presented for change. But it is the barber's shop that is always most crowded, being, particularly at night, the great resort for gossip and news, on which account the natives call it *gup shop*; the barbers themselves seem to enjoy a prescriptive right to be lively, witty, and good story-tellers. I have seen some excellent buffoons among them, and a slap given to a bald new-shaven pate, in the proper part of a story, has set half a bazar in a roar. The barbers keep every body's holidays,—Hindoos, Jews, Mussulmans, Armenians, Portuguese, and English,—and reap a good harvest at each by their comic way of begging.

On first coming here, one would imagine that none of the people ever slept at night; for, besides, that the coppersmiths and blacksmiths generally work all night, and sleep all day, on account of the heat, there are processions going about from sunset till sunrise, with *tom-toms*, (small drums,) kettle-drums, citarrs, vnis, pipes, and a kind of large brazen trumpet, which requires two people to carry it, making altogether the most horrible din I ever heard. These processions, with the picturesque dresses of the natives, and their graceful attitudes, the torches carried by children, and the little double pipe blown by boys, whose wildness might make them pass for satyrs, put one strongly in mind of the ancient Bacchanals. It is usually on account of marriages that these nocturnal feasts are held. When they are in honour of a god they take place in the day, when the deity is carried on a litter in triumph, with banners before and behind, and priests carrying flowers, and milk and rice, While hardly any one joins the procession without an offering. All this looks very well at a distance, but, on coming near, one is shocked at the meanness and inelegance of the god, and at the filth and wretchedness of his votaries.

With one procession, however, I was much pleased; it took place a month ago, on the breaking up of the monsoon, when the sea became open for navigation. It is called the coco-nut feast, and is, I believe, peculiar to this coast. About an hour before sunset, an immense concourse of people assembled on the esplanade, where booths were erected, with all kinds of commodities for sale. All the rich natives appeared in their carriages, and the display of pearls and jewels was astonishing. At sunset, one of the chief Bramins advanced towards the sea, and going out a little way upon a ledge of rock, he launched a gilt coco-nut, in token that the sea was now become navigable; immediately thousands of coco-nuts were seen swimming in the bay; for every priest and every master of a family was eager to make his offering. The evening closed, as usual, with music, dancing, and exhibitions of tumblers, jugglers, and tame snakes.

Originally published as Maria Graham, *Journal of a Residence in India* (Edinburgh, Archibald Constable and Company; London, Longman, Hurst, Rees, Orme, and Brown, 1813),
pp. 33–5.

3

Indigenous Credit Instruments and Systems

L.C. Jain

In the nineteenth century and a large part of the twentieth century, the bazaar economy formed a crucial interface between foreign trade, European firms, and the world economy, on the one hand, and the agrarian subsistence economy of artisans, moneylenders, and peasants, on the other. The bazaar constituted an intermediate level, with the Westernized economy above it and the subsistence economy below.* The bazaar was an urban market which connected the subcontinent through a number of devices, such as the *hundi* (indigenous credit instrument). The *hundi* allowed bazaar firms to form sophisticated networks that covered the entire subcontinent and expanded beyond into Southeast Asia, especially Burma and the Straits Settlement and even to China, the Middle East, and East Africa.

It was this network that facilitated much of the movement of inland produce and credit transactions within the subcontinent. *Hundis* were mercantile instruments of credit and remittance, and though devoid of legal standing in formal courts of law, they were widely recognized as legitimate credit instruments. Recent research suggests that the *hundi* served as a letter of credit, a promissory note, as well as a remittance note. Such was its importance that the *hundi* 'embodied economic and cultural sanctions' and was acknowledged to have 'enhanced merchant reputations'.† Even the advent of the

* It was different from rural markets where petty traders and moneylenders operated, dealing mainly in agricultural produce.

† Marina Martin, '*Hundi/Hawala*: The Problem of Definition', *Modern Asian Studies*, doi: 10.1017/S0026749X07003459, published online by Cambridge University Press, 18 June 2008. On the role of the *hundi* in raising credit and transmitting money during the rule of the Mughals, see Irfan Habib, 'Banking in Mughal India', in Tapan Raychaudhuri (ed.), *Contributions to Indian Economic History I* (Calcutta, K. L. Mukhopadhyay, 1960) and

railways, cable, and telegraph could not subordinate the *hundi*, which remained in use well into the mid-twentieth century.[‡]

This excerpt from the writings of the noted economist L.C. Jain illustrates some of the hundis prevalent in the 1920s and examines the characteristics and customs of their use.

No statistics are available and it is difficult to estimate the amount of total deposits received by the bankers in the whole country, or even in any one province, just as it is almost impossible to arrive at any accurate or reliable estimate of the total amount of capital invested in indigenous banking in India. Personal inquiries have met with no better results. The following remarks of Prof. Burnett-Hurst in regard to the difficulty of ascertaining the income of the bankers reveal the truth and would apply to the estimation of their capital or deposits as well.

> Most persons of the middle and upper classes will hesitate to disclose their income for fear of increased taxation. It is true that some may be prepared to make statements, but it will be to their interest to minimise their receipts. It is very doubtful whether it will be possible to ascertain the income of money lenders, money changers, etc., in large villages and towns. If compulsory powers are employed, the statements made would probably be purely fictitious.[1]

The bankers in India mostly invest their own capital. They do not make it a regular business to attract large sums of money in deposits, and lend them at higher rates of interest than what they have to pay on the deposits, thereby earning the difference for the risk and labour.

HUNDIS

The system of drawing *hundis*[2] has been in vogue from 'very remote times'.[3] A *hundi* is perhaps the oldest surviving form of a credit instrument. There is a legendary story that Vastupal Tejpal drew a *hundi* of ten crores[4] on the *Nagar Seth* ('City Banker') of Ahmadabad, and that the temples of Dilwara[5] were built with the money. Another legend of the times of Lord Krishna has it that Narsimha Mehta of Junagarh drew a *hundi* on Seth Samalsah of Dwarka about 2500 years ago. Again, it is said that Atmaram Bukhan of Surat, in the times of Sivaji, had extensive banking business, his *hundis* being honoured far and wide. His credit stood so high that a story is told about it. Once a person ran short of money while passing through a forest, but he happened to have with him the *hundis* of Atmaram Bukhan. He tied one of them to the branches of a tree. A merchant was passing that way, saw that it was the *hundi* of a great banker and cashed it then and there. In old days, when travelling with cash was even more risky than it is now, people kept with them the *hundis* of well-known bankers.

Lakshmi Subramanian, 'Banias and the British: The Role of Indigenous Credit in the Process of Imperial Expansion in Western India in the Second Half of the Eighteenth Century', *Modern Asian Studies*, Vol. 21, No. 3, 3 July 1987.

‡ A number of different *hundis* were in use in the subcontinent's bazaars. Some common ones were the *Sahjog hundi* which required no endorsement and thus attested to the credit of the bearer; the *Roznama hundi* which required payment on the day of presentation; and the *Darshini hundi* which entailed payment on sight. The broker of the instrument was called the *hundiwalla*. He was often a general commission agent involved in a number of trading activities. In most cases, the *hundi* had to be repaid within a few days at high rates of interest. According to Marina Martin, the *hundi* network 'ensured overall liquidity and easy access to capital' and borrowing and lending within the community was common. See Martin 2008.

Definition. Although a *hundi* has existed from very early times, there is no legal definition of the term available. Section 5 of the Indian Negotiable Instruments Act of 1881 contains the definition of a 'bill of exchange' which is applicable to bills, promissory notes and cheques. The *hundis*, as a rule, are deemed to lie outside the provisions of the Act. A *hundi* is governed by the time-honoured custom and usages of the various localities. It is only where no specific customs obtain that a *hundi* is treated as a 'bill of exchange' within the meaning of the Act.

In simple words, a *hundi* may be defined as a written order—usually unconditional—made by one person on another for the payment, on demand or after a specified time, of a certain sum of money to a person named therein. This definition, it may be pointed out, differs from that of an English bill of exchange in one important respect. While an English bill *must* be an unconditional order, a *hundi may* not be so, *e.g.*, a *jokhami hundi*.

Functions. Again, it may be explained that a *hundi* is not quite an inland Indian 'bill of exchange' which the existing text-books often make it out to be. One of its main functions is to enable one to get advances. A merchant who needs money may draw a *hundi* on his agent or firm or some one with whom arrangement is made beforehand. It is also a convenient form of remittance of money from one place to another. But in the financing of the trade of the country a *hundi* does not occupy the same position as a bill of exchange does in England. Under the English practice, a bill is drawn by an exporter upon a certain bank which, acting under instructions from the importer's bank, accepts such bills, provided they are drawn in accordance with the terms of the credit. Such bills invariably bear on them the evidence that they are drawn against actual goods duly dispatched from one trade centre to another and therefore afford a perfectly sound means of investment. Such a method of finance does not exist in the system of indigenous banking. The *hundis*, it may be emphasised, cannot, as a rule, command ready acceptance by a joint-stock bank, because there is nothing to show that they are drawn against commercial goods. The banks usually insist upon the endorsement of well-known bankers before dealing in small traders' *hundis*. In actual practice, it may be pointed out, the *hundis* approximate more to cheques than to bills, although in legal phraseology they fall in the category of bills.

Darshani and Muddati Hundis. The *hundis* are of two kinds, *Darshani* (sight or demand bills) and *Muddati*, sometimes called *Miadi* (deferred or usance bills), *i.e.*, bills payable after a stipulated period of time mentioned in the *hundi* and reckoned from the date of drawing.

Illustrations. The drawing of a *hundi* is a simple affair. It will be clear from the specimens given on p. 55.

Comparison and Contrast with an English Bill of Exchange. In its essentials a *hundi* is similar to an English 'bill of exchange. A *hundi*, like a 'bill,' has a drawer called *likhaiwala dhani*, a drawee called *uparwala dhani*, and a payee called *rakhyaiwala dhani*. Again, as in a ' bill,' so in a *hundi*, an amount certain in money is mentioned and it is payable either at sight or on a determinable future date. Furthermore, both instruments of credit are subject to stamp duty.

But points of difference arise in the forms of the two. To begin with, a 'bill' is a briefly-worded document written in a perfectly business-like style, but a *hundi* is in the form of a letter, with salutations and words invoking divine blessings. These words, of course, vary with the religious sects to which the drawers belong. Again, in a 'bill,' the name of the drawer is given at the right-hand bottom corner, and in a *hundi* it is written in the actual body of the instrument. Then, in a 'bill,' the name and address of the drawee are placed at the left-hand bottom corner, but in a *hundi* the name is given in the body and the name and address on the reverse. Furthermore, the amount, in a 'bill,' is mentioned twice, once in figures at the top corner of the left-hand side and once in words in the body. The amount in a *hundi* occurs five times. First, at the beginning of the body it is given both in figures and words and then elucidated by stating 'the twice of R......' Then at the back the amount is again given in figures within a small square, and below it the same is explained by the words 'one-fourth of the amount (is) ......'

Sub-divisions. The *darshani* and *muddati hundis* are again sub-divided as follows:

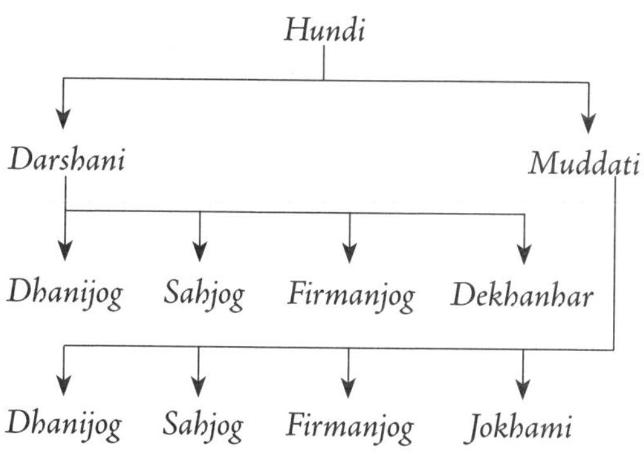

The *dhanijog hundi* is one which is payable to a *dhani,* or a person, as distinguished from the *sahjog hundi* which is payable to a *sah,* or a respectable person. The word *dhani* or *sah* is written, as the case may be, in the body of the *hundi.* The banker who cashes a *sahjog hundi* is responsible to see that the presenter is the proper person to get the payment, but no such liability attaches in the case of the *dhanijog hundis.* Nowadays the *sahjog hundis* are the more common.

A Darshani Hundi [Translation]

No.........
Presentation Date.
Shri.
To pleasant and prosperous town Bombay, the abode of merit therein to *Bhai* (brother) .... written from Amraoti by Singhai Moti Lal Khub Chand whose greetings you be pleased to accept. Further a *hundi* is drawn for R ....in words Rupees .... twice of R .... the double of which, in favour of *Bhai* (brother) ....
....
Immediately on the presentation of this *hundi,* you will (please) pay the amount thereof in current coin to the presenter, after ascertaining his respectability, title and address.
Samvata .... Date (Indian) ....
Date (English) ....
Signature ....

A Muddati Hundi [Translation]

Stamp.

No. ....
To the pleasant and prosperous town Bombay the abode of merit (therein to) *Bhai* (brother) Manna Lal Karodi Mal written from Bombay by Ram Prasad Uttam Chand whose greetings you may be pleased to read. Further a *hundi* for R. 500, in words five hundred, twice of rupees two hundred and fifty, is drawn upon you in favour of Mool Chand Kesari Mal on *Chait Sudi* 12. Sixty-one days after date you will (please) pay the amount thereof in current coin to the presenter after ascertaining his respectability, title and address.
Hundi written on *Chait Sudi* 12, *Samvat* 1983.
On the Reverse Side.
Rupees ....
One fourth of the amount (is) ....
of (this) four times pay ....
Full amount.

The *firmanjog* hundi is one which is made payable to order, the word *firman,* which is written, meaning 'order'.

The *jokhami hundi,* which is drawn against goods dispatched, resembles an English 'documentary bill of exchange' and contains certain conditions, in accordance with which, if the goods are lost or destroyed in transit, the drawer or the holder of the *hundi* has to suffer the loss. The interests of the drawee of a *jokhami hundi* are thus carefully safeguarded, the risk of the loss of value in the transport of goods being transferred from him to the drawer, or the holder of the *hundi,* who buys it with full knowledge of the risk. The buyer of such *hundis,* therefore, acts as an insurance agent.

The *dekhanhar hundi* is one which is payable to the presenter or bearer. In it the word *dekhanhar* and sometimes even the English word 'bearer' is written in the vernacular.

All these kinds of *hundis* except the *dekhanhar* are of ancient origin. The *dekhanhar,* however, was introduced about the beginning of this century. The credit of its introduction belongs, to a great extent, to the *Shroffs'* Association of Bombay. All these *hundis* are current at the present time, but the *jokhami hundi* has fallen into disuse, in consequence of the establishment of insurance companies.

Advice of a Hundi. At the same time that a banker or merchant draws a *hundi* on a correspondent in another centre, he sends him an advice which is called *nakal.*

In the *nakal* are clearly set out the name of the drawer, the amount payable, the name of the payee and the period of usance. Unless such advice be received and it tally in these essentials with the *hundi,* the *hundi* is not discounted by the drawee, but is kept in suspense, called *khadi,* for three days, within which instructions are obtained from the drawer by telegram.

Nakal [Translation]

Shri.
To pleasant and prosperous town Bombay, the abode of merit (therein to) *Bhai* (brother) .... written from Amraoti by Singhai Moti Lal Khub Chand whose greetings you be pleased to accept. Further a *hundi* payable on demand is drawn for
R. ....in favour of *Bhai* (brother) .... on ....So on its presentation please make due payment thereof. Please write to us, if we can be of any service to you.
Dated........................

Amount. The *hundis* may be drawn for any sums according to the requirements of the parties concerned. It is, however, striking that usually *hundis* are drawn for amounts like R. 200, 400, 800, 1000, 1200, 1600, and so on.

Usance. There is no fixed period of time for which a *muddati* (usance) *hundi* may be drawn, except that it rarely exceeds one year. In older times the usance was fixed for bills on different centres, according to the time taken in transit from one centre to another. Nowadays it all depends upon the convenience of the parties, although custom is still a governing factor in many places. The *muddati hundis* are sometimes classified according to the days for which they are drawn from 11, 21, 41, 51, 61, or even more or less days, up to 361 days. They are more largely used in central India, the Central Provinces, Bombay and Bengal than elsewhere. In the Central Provinces there are three accepted varieties, viz. (*a*) *iksathdini,* or of 61 days, (*b*) *eksovisdini,* or of 120 days, and (*c*) *baramasi,* or of one year. In central India, the *muddati hundis* drawn are usually of 45 or 61 days, in Bombay 41 days, in the Punjab 121 days, in the United Provinces 61 or 91 days, and in Bengal 61 days.

Days of Grace. Three days of grace are allowed in the case of English bills of exchange, but with the *hundis* they vary with the usance. No days of grace, or *gilas* to use the indigenous term, are reckoned, if the *hundis* are of less than 11 days' maturity. For *hundis* of 11 to 20 days' usance the days of grace permitted are 3, and for those of longer than 20 days' maturity they are 5.

Endorsement and Discount of Hundis. After drawing the *hundi* in its proper form, it may be sold at the current rate of discount called *hundiyana* or *hundiyavana*. The *hundi* can be discounted and re-discounted any number of times and may be sent to distant places in the country, by means of endorsements at the

Stamp Duties. The stamp duties on *hundis* are as under:

			R.	A.
1.	*Darshani hundis* for amounts exceeding R. 20		0	1
2.	*Muddati hundis.* (Up to 1 yr. usance.)			
	For amounts up to R. 200		0	3
	Exceeding R. 200 but not exceeding R. 1,600.			
	For every complete R. 200, and any fractional part of R. 200..		0	3
	Exceeding R. 1,600 but not exceeding R. 2,500		2	4
	Exceeding R. 2,500 but not exceeding R. 10,000.			
	For every complete R. 2,500, and any fractional part of R. 2,500..		2	4
	Exceeding R. 10,000 but not exceeding R. 30,000.			
	For every complete R. 5,000, and any fractional part of R. 5,000		4	8
	Exceeding R. 30,000.			
	For every complete R. 10,000 and any fractional part of R. 10,000		9	0
3.	*Muddati hundis.*			
	(Exceeding 1 yr. usance.)			
	For amounts exceeding R. 10..................................		0	2
	" " " R. 10 but not exceeding	R. 50 -	0	4
	" " " R. 50 " "	R. 100 -	0	8
	Exceeding R. 100 but not exceeding R. 1,000.			
	For every complete R. 100, and any fractional part of R. 100..		0	8
	Exceeding R. 1,000.			
	For every complete R. 500 and any fractional part of R. 500		2	8

back, before it is finally collected on due date. The discounting of a *hundi* is called *sakarana.* Every endorser of a *hundi* is liable to the holder for its payment, but he can make a special endorsement called *sira* to the effect that, if the *hundi* is not cashed by the drawee, it may be presented for payment to a specified person. Such special endorsement enables its author to escape from liability, unless the payment is refused both by the drawee and the person intended to take the drawee's place. In the event of the double refusal, the special endorser has the same position as an ordinary endorser. Such an especially endorsed *hundi* is called a *jikri chiththi.*

Dishonour of Hundis. The dishonouring of *hundis* is 'an event of rare occurrence'.[6] If they are not honoured on due dates, the drawers are considered bankrupt. The drawee of the *hundi* may, however, refuse to accept it, if he does not hold any deposit for the drawer or no arrangement has been made for the acceptance beforehand. When a *hundi* is so invalidated, it is sent to an indigenous bankers' association at a centre such as Calcutta, Bombay, Madras, or Cawnpor—which puts its seal on it. The *hundi* is then returned to the drawer and he has to pay special charges called *nikrai sikrai* at one rupee per *hundi,* irrespective of the amount for which it is drawn. The drawer is also liable to this penalty, if the *hundi* is returned to him for some irregularity in its drawing.

Additional Copies. If the original *hundi* called *khoka* is lost, a second copy called *paith* is issued; if even the second is lost, a third called *parpaith* is given; and in the event of all the three being lost, a fourth called *maijar,* or *panchyati,* is provided. The last is so called because it is drawn by the *Pancha* (five leaders of the bankers) of the place of issue. A bill of exchange, on the other hand, is sometimes drawn in a set of three, called the 'First of Exchange,' the 'Second of Exchange' and the 'Third of Exchange.' The examples of the indigenous 'Second, Third and Fourth of Exchange' are given on pp. 59–60.

Hundis—the Best Form of Investment. The *hundis* afford an excellent source of investment to the indigenous bankers. Some of them do not draw *hundis* but purchase them. The *Multani* bankers of Bombay who specialise in this kind of business purchase the *hundis* drawn for two or three months. These are discounted at the rate of anything from 6 to 9 per cent. and are re-discounted with the Imperial Bank of India. The difference between the *Multani* banker's rate of discount and that of the Imperial Bank is the profit which he earns. The *hundis* are discounted both with the Imperial Bank and the Indian joint-stock banks, but not with the Exchange banks, which have nothing to do with this kind of business.

METHODS OF ACCOUNTING

A few words may be said about the system of indigenous accounting, which is reputed not only for its antiquity, but also for its simplicity and efficiency. A town money-lender or banker keeps several account books called *bahis,* viz., a *rokad bahi* ('cash book'), a *nakal bahi* ('journal'), containing credit transactions, and a *khata bahi* ('ledger'). A village money-lender maintains the *khata bahi* and one *roznamcha* ('day book'), in place of the two *rokad* and *nakal bahis.*

In the *roznamcha* or the *rokad bahi,* on the left side, are entered the credit entries and, on the right side, the debit entries. At the end of each day both the sides are totaled and the cash compared. From these day books the names of the customers are carried on to the *khata bahi.* The pages and dates of the *roznamcha* or the *rokad bahi* are noted in the *khata bahi*. An index of the names is given at the beginning of the *khata bahi*, and on reference the account of any customer can be easily found and inspected.

In the *khata bahi* ('ledger') there are various accounts which are called *khatas*. There are two kinds of accounts: personal, called *dhaniwar-khata*, and other called *shri-khata*. Some money-lenders keep these two kinds of *khatas* in two separate *bahis*.
In the personal 'ledger' are entered the personal accounts and in the general 'ledger' other transactions such as sale and purchase of commodities undertaken by the money-lenders on behalf of their customers.

Calculation of Interest. Some money-lenders keep a separate book for calculating interest called *sood bahi* or *vyaj bahi*, which may be translated as an 'interest book.' Interest is usually calculated on what is called the *katmiti* system. Receipts and advances are regularly entered in the account books and interest is charged on the daily balances.

Banking Scripts. The accounts are kept in different languages, scripts and numerals which vary not only from province to province, but sometimes, in the same province, nay, in the same town, from money-lenders to money-lenders. It is said that as many as fifteen thousand sets of numerals are prevalent in the Punjab alone. But the *mahajani* numerals

Paith [Translation]

To the pleasant and prosperous town Bombay Port—the abode of merit—(therein to) *Bhai* (brother) Manohar Lal Hira Lalji written from Lalitpur by Mansukh Das Virdhi Chand whose greetings you be pleased to read. Further a *hundi* for R. 500, in words five hundred, twice of rupees two hundred and fifty, was drawn upon you by us in favour of Ram Chand Beni Ram on *Chait Sudi*, 14, to be paid on demand in current coin with due regard to (the qualifications) respectability, title, address of the payee. Now the aforesaid payee informs us that the *hundi* has been lost. Therefore this second document is being drawn upon you. Of these we shall be responsible for the amount of one. You will (please) consult your cash book, day book, and other account books, before making payment. If the *hundi* has been paid, the *paith* becomes cancelled, if the *paith* is paid, the *hundi* is to be regarded as void. This *paith* is drawn up on *Vaisakh Badi* 1, *Samvat*, 1983.

Parpaith [Translation]

To pleasant and prosperous town Bombay Port, the abode of merit (therein to) *Bhai* (brother) Manohar Lal Hira Lalji written from Lalitpur by Mansukh Das Virdhi Chandji whose greetings you be pleased to read. Further a *hundi* for R. 500, rupees five hundred, twice of rupees two hundred and fifty, the double of which was drawn upon you by us in favour of Ram Chand Beni Ram on *Chait Sudi* 14, to be paid on demand in current coin with due regard to (the qualifications) the respectability, title and address of the payee. And a *paith* was also drawn on *Vaisakh Badi* 1. Now the payee of the *hundi* informs us that the *paith* is also lost. [Therefore this third document is being drawn upon you. Of these we shall be responsible for the payment of one only. You will (please) consult your cash book, day book, and other account books, before making payment. If the *hundi* has been paid, then the *paith* and the *parpaith* are to be regarded as cancelled, if the *paith* is paid the *hundi* and the *parpaith* are to be taken as void. This *parpaith* is drawn on *Jeth Badi* 2, *Samvat*, 1983.

Maijar [Translation]

To pleasant and prosperous town Bombay Port, the abode of merit, (therein to) the *Pancha* (five leaders of the bankers) written from Lalitpur. by the *Pancha* (the five leaders of the bankers). Further a *hundi* for R. 500, rupees five hundred, was drawn here by Mansukh Das Virdhi Chandji on *Bhai* (brother) Manohar Lal Hira Lalji in favour of Ram Chand Beni Ram on *Chait Sudi* 14, to be paid on demand in current coin with the due regard to (the qualifications) the respectability, title and address of the payee. And a *paith* was drawn on *Vaisakh Badi* I and a *parpaith* on *Jeth Badi* 2. Now the payee of the *hundi* informs us that the *hundi*, its *paith* and *parpaith*—all the three are lost. Therefore if the *hundi*, the *paith* and *parpaith* are all lost, please consult the drawee's day book, ledger, cash and credit books, and then have this fourth document paid. If the *hundi*, or *paith*, or *parpaith* has been paid, then this *maijar* is to be regarded as cancelled and to be returned after perusal. This fourth document is drawn on the aforesaid drawee and we hold ourselves responsible for only one of the four documents.

(Signed)	1.	
	2.	
Dated *Jeth Sudi* 1,	3.	The Pancha.
Samvata, 1983	4.	
	5.	

are most widely used throughout the country, except Madras. The *mahajani* numerals are distinguished for their simple forms for vulgar fractions such as quarter-rupee, half-anna, quarter-anna, which are used in accounts.

Indigenous Banking Year. It may be stated here that the *mahajani* year, or the indigenous banking year, closes on the *Indian* date *Kartika Badi* 15 which falls in the month of October or November. In 1926, for example, the *Kartika Badi Amawasya* was 5th November, and in 1927, 26th October, when the last banking year closed. This last day of the banking year is a great Hindu festival called *Dipawali* or *Diwali*, meaning 'a row of lamps,' which is celebrated with great rejoicings. All the houses are washed and cleaned, they are lit in the evening with innumerable lights, the old *bahis* are posted up to date and worship is offered to the Goddess of Wealth, Lakshmi.[7] The following day of the *Dipawali, i.e. Kartika Sudi 1*, is the New Year's Day, when the indigenous banking year commences. On that day it is considered inauspicious to read or write. So the indigenous bankers, students and authors have it as a general holiday.

TRADE SIGNS, SECRETS AND SUPERSTITIONS

Signs and Secrets. Like most traders the indigenous bankers have their own signs and secrets. They vary from place to place, every group of bankers having a separate code. For instance, in Kathiawar, the following is in vogue:

Kits = one,	*Goth* = four,
Dhar = two,	*Mul* = five,
Udhan = three,	and so on.

Another example of the special words for numerals is the following, used by a class of small traders and bankers in the Central Provinces:

Sang – 1	*Swan* – 2	*Ekwai* – 3	*Fouk* – 4
Budh – 5	*Dhink* – 6	*Pank* – 7	*Rakh* – 8
Nung – 9	*Mindhi* – 10	etc. etc.	

Furthermore, some bankers decide among themselves that the number spoken must be deducted from a certain fixed figure, say 100, to get the figure really meant, this secret being carefully kept. So that if 97 is said, it may actually mean (100–97) or 3, and so on.

I noticed a curious system among the cotton traders of Indore who are also bankers. They keep with them a piece of cloth, and whenever a trader wishes to transact some business with another, he spreads this cloth over his hands and brings the other party's hands also under the same cloth. Then the two proceed to talk in a quaint language, the actual offer of a transaction is made under the secrecy of the cloth, while the rejection or acceptance is made verbally. So that even if any one is hearing the conversation near by, he can have no idea as to the size or price of the bargain.

Superstitions. Like other traders again, the bankers and money-lenders are not free from superstitions. For instance, to utter the number seven in *Telegu* (*Yedu*) is regarded as unlucky, because it means weeping. So even an educated banker will, in place of seven, say 'six and one.' Then again, the *Hindus*, when counting, always begin with the Sanskrit word *Labha*, which means profit, instead of saying 'one'.[8] Similarly the Mahomedans start with *Bismillah* or *Barkat*,[9] as words invoking divine blessing.

Originally published as L.C. Jain, *Indigenous Banking in India* (London, Macmillan and Co., Limited, 1929), pp. 70–92. Reproduced with permission of Palgrave Macmillan.

NOTES

1. *Note of Dissent*, by Professor A. R. Burnett-Hurst (*Report of the Indian Economic Enquiry Committee*, 1925, p. 116).
2. *Hundi*, or *hoondee*, or *hoondy*, as C. N. Cooke writes, seems to be a corruption from the word *Hindi* or *Hindu*.
3. C. N. Cooke, *op. cit.*, p. 21.
4. Ten crores = 100,000,000.
5. These are the famous Jaina temples on Mt. Abu, in Rajputana, noted for their wonderfully fine carving work.
6. Cooke, *op cit.*, p. 15; also Shirras, *op. cit.*, p. 341.
7. '... the worship of the precious metals in some form is indispensable, as this is believed to be productive of wealth and prosperity throughout the coming year. The account books of the family or the firm are also brought out and worshipped, and many people open new account-books from this date' (*Hindu Fasts and Feasts*, by A. C. Mukerji, 1916, p. 141).
8. The Oriya merchants say *Labo* instead of 'one'.
9. In Garhwal, they say *Bargad*.

4

The *Gaddi*—An Indigenous Firm

D.K. Taknet

The indigenous firm in the context of the bazaar is known as the *gaddi*. Literally, the word '*gaddi*' means a seat but in the context of business it is an allegory for a conventional firm. A *gaddi* would typically consist of substantial *gadda*s (cushions) upholstered in shiny white cloth, with the largest back-rest reserved for the *seth* (trader) and smaller ones for his *munims* (clerks) and *gomashtas* (sub-clerks), each of whom was assigned a separate ledger. The main business apparatus were the cash boxes and red- and yellow-coloured ledgers.

This excerpt, translated from the Hindi writings of historian D.K. Taknet, recreates the activity at a *gaddi* in Kaligodam, Bara Bazaar, the Marwari cosmos of Calcutta in the early twentieth century.* The *gaddi* was the site of much commercial and social activity from 7 AM when business commenced with the *seth*'s arrival till almost midnight. At night, tired traders often used it for accommodation. The day, as recreated in this excerpt, is representative of bazaars across the subcontinent in the nineteenth and twentieth centuries.

In contemporary India, smaller traders and wholesalers still function from their *gaddis* in the bazaar. A study conducted in the seventies in Vishnupur in Bengal notes a similar rhythm to the one Taknet recreates for the early twentieth century. It notes: 'Trade is brisk in the morning ... By noon the pace becomes calmer ... Some trading takes place in the late afternoon and evening. But the evening is the time for serious or light discussions among bazaar men, friends, relatives, or just passers by ... drinking tea, chewing *paan*, and smoking, the men discuss everything from business to theatre to rituals, American

* Also see D.K. Taknet, *Industrial Entrepreneurship of Sheikhawati Marwaris* (Jaipur, Kumar Prakashan, 1986).

hippies, politics, conditions of life elsewhere in the region or abroad. Newspapers are read and exchanged, radio news broadcasts are heard and interpreted.'[†]

GADDI CULTURE

Calcutta's Bara Bazaar was home and the world to the Marwaris—the site of their places of residence, on one side, and of the pursuit of Lakshmi (wealth), on the other, with the numerous small *gaddi*s being their places of worship. There were many such *gaddi*s in Kaligodam on Malik Street. The Birlas too had set up their *gaddi* here under the name Baldevdas Jugalkishore. The famous Tarachand Ghanshyamdas firm also had its *gaddi* here. In every *gaddi* there would be a huge mattress covered with a white cloth (*chandni*). Decked in his *pagri, kamri, angrakha, dhoti* and *dupatta*, the Seth*ji* parked himself on the mattress after the daily morning prayers (*puja*). His *munims*, experts in book-keeping and usury, sat beside him. The ups and downs of the commercial stampede that began at seven in the morning went on unabated till midnight. In fact, in the cloth trade, sometimes orders were placed and payments made even an hour or two after midnight. So many coins were received in payments that the hands ached counting them. The money bags received from reputed commercial firms would be kept in the treasury without the money being counted. In those days transactions in cash were given more importance than those involving credit.

There were skilled *munims* and *gumastas* (accountants or agents) at the *gaddi*s of the Marwari traders and they were good at everything ... They would keep in mind the rise and fall of prices in the market on a given day while placing orders for commodities and selling them. They got the merchandise loaded carefully, prepared the invoice and paid the taxes. It was also their task to recover loans, manage *hundi*s and do futures trading. In the night they would update the account books and count the coins. In the big firms they would also have to prepare reports of transactions between branches and of imports and exports, and despatch them to the office. In those days the Marwari traders used to make their experienced and trustworthy *munims* their partners and allowed them to carry on the business independently. In the case of Tarachand Ghanshyamdas, the most important firm in Calcutta, the business was always taken care of by the *munims*. The *munim* was the authority here, whose word was never disregarded even by the owner of the firm. One such influential *munim* of this firm was Jainarain Poddar. Let alone the others, even the owners of the firm, Janaki Prasad and Srinivas Poddar, would sit at their allotted places in a row facing Jainarain*ji* to show him due respect. Those were times when *munims* and *gumastas* were highly regarded. It was common for a *munim* to become a millionaire through his partnership with the owner of the firm. There are several such instances in Marwari society.

[†] Akos Ostor, *Culture and Power. Legend, Ritual, Bazaar and Rebellion in a Bengali Society* (New Delhi, Sage Publications, 1984), pp. 95–6. On life in contemporary Bara Bazaar, see Martin Beattie, 'Hybrid Bazaar Space: Colonization, Globalization and Traditional Space in Barabazaar, Calcutta, India', *Journal of Architectural Education*, Vol. 61, No. 3, 2008, pp. 45–55.

These small *gaddis*, where transactions worth crores used to take place, were in this way the ancestral heritage of today's Marwari industrialists. *Seths* and *munims* used to sleep on the *gaddis* at night. Such was the volume of the trade that many *munims* and *gumastas* were unable to leave the *gaddis* for even five days at a stretch. 'Not a thread on his body, he's come to loot Calcutta!' This was said of the Marwaris, but they went on to make remarkable commercial progress. The former President Giani Jail Singh once said that first industry came to Calcutta, and naturally the Marwari brethren followed and added their bit to the city's splendour. The number of affluent Marwaris in Calcutta kept growing and, with that, more and more Marwari *pagris* began to be seen in Bara Bazaar's Sutapatti, Tulapatti, Harisen Road, Opium Chaurasta, Bartalla, Kaligodam and Banstalla areas. With their wealth they started buying the *kothis* (bungalows) of the *munshis* and *naibs* of the Bengali zamindars. And, after this, new buildings belonging to Marwaris started coming up one after the other. Electric bulbs replaced oil lamps to brighten up the homes of the Bara Bazaar traders. And motor cars started replacing the *tam-tams* and other horse-driven carriages that used to run on the unmetalled road in Bara Bazaar.

This is a translation of an extract originally published in Hindi as D.K. Taknet, *Marwari Samaj* (Jaipur, Kumar Prakashan, 1989), pp. 52–3.

5

Leadership in the Bazaar

D.K. Taknet

In colonial India, a hierarchy existed within the subcontinent's markets. Often, the prominent merchants were based in port cities and up-country trade centres, operating on a large geographical scale in an array of commodities and enjoying immense power and prestige. At a lower level were those operating on a smaller scale in interior markets, and at the lowest were traders whose commercial activities were restricted to local markets at the village level.

This selection, translated from the Hindi writings of historian D.K. Taknet, examines the major players in Bara Bazaar, Calcutta, in the late nineteenth and early twentieth centuries. These players had earned their fortunes in trade and speculation in commodities such as tea, opium, jute, silver, and cotton. The most affluent were popularly christened 'kings' of the trades they specialized in. Thus, there was a 'tea king', a 'cotton king', a 'jute king', a 'silver king', and a 'shares king'. The 'king' was respected in the community and often called upon for financial advice, resolution of family/commercial disputes, and settlement of community matters and community representation before official authorities.

HIGH PROFITS FROM SPECULATION

By 1860 the Marwari traders had made a fortune by speculating in opium, jute, cotton, silver and grain, besides acting as brokers. In fact, they had a monopoly over the speculation in opium and jute. Rampratap Chamaria had made crores as the main speculator in opium in Calcutta. But, on the other hand, heavy losses in speculation wiped out many other firms. It was the Marwari traders who developed the Calcutta market for speculation in opium and jute. Their numbers gradually increased and by 1905 they made up one-fourth of the speculators. Over time, the Marwaris established their monopoly over speculation in opium and jute. Ramdayal

Nevatia and Gujraj Singhania of Fatehpur, Jokhoram Ruia and Nathuram Poddar of Ramgarh, Surajmal Nagarmal and Panaychand Singhi of Bikaner made a special place for themselves in the speculation market by acquiring a lot of wealth. Harduttrai Chamaria, Swaroopchand Hukumchand, Jugalkishore Birla, Nirmal Lohia, Swaroopchand Prithviraj Rungta and Chaturbhuj Piramal were the major Marwari speculators. Shivnarain Birla had started his career in commerce with opium-trading in Calcutta. The *fatka* trade was behind the expansion of Baldeodas Birla's business. Ramrikhdas Parasrampuria, Govindram Sekhsaria and Anandilal Poddar of Nawalgarh had by 1930 become famous as speculators in cotton and silver. The *Bombay Gazetteer* (1909) mentioned that the Marwaris had become prominent in the speculation in opium, cotton, silver and gold. Harduttrai Chamaria started the first speculative market in silver in Calcutta and Swaroopchand Hukumchand earned two crore rupees from speculation in opium after 1909. Jwalaprasad Bhartiya and Sohanlal Dugad did not dabble in any trade other than the one in *fatka*. Prosperous speculators used to appoint their own men as brokers or got Modi's firms established and used them to carry out transactions. The major speculators kept several things in mind while speculating in order to minimise losses. After the First World War, several Marwaris tried their luck at the Calcutta speculation market and made lakhs of rupees. Prominent among these were Baldevdas Dudavewala, Keshoram Poddar and Bishweshwarlal Halwasia. They used the wealth acquired in this way in the national movement, social welfare and trade.

DOMINATING TRADE

After making money as Banias and speculators, the Marwari traders turned towards trade once again. Soon they achieved remarkable progress in various businesses and, therefore, began to be called 'kings' of those particular businesses. Ramgopal Mohta of Karachi was the 'iron king'. Hanumanbaksh Kanoi was famous as the 'tea king', Banshidhar Jalan as the 'jute king', Motiram Jhunjhunwala as the 'silver king', Ramnarain Ruia as the 'cotton king', and Baldevdas Dudavewala as the 'share king'. ...

This is a translation of an extract originally published as D.K. Taknet, *Marwari Samaj* (Jaipur, Kumar Prakashan, 1989), pp. 56–7.

6

Organization and Structure of Governance

Radhakrishna Nevatia

Within the bazaar milieu, mercantile organizations played a critical role of helping the trading communities govern themselves. These organizations were of different persuasions and denominations; they could be *jati*-level bodies, wider caste-based organizations, community-based organizations, associations founded purely on the basis of commercial interests by fellow traders, as well as conglomerations of leading merchant families cutting across caste lines.*

These organizations helped trading communities by adjudicating over disputes between traders and families according to mercantile custom, discouraging merchants from taking recourse to formal (and expensive) law courts, regulating speculative activity, settling rates of interest and commission, certifying *hundi* transactions, and dealing with cases of liquidity and insolvency. They also represented traders' interests vis-à-vis European firms, colonial authorities, as well as the larger political arena.

This translation from Hindi is authored by Marwari chronicler Radhakrishna Nevatia, from a book he dedicated to Ramdev Chokhany, cotton trader and 'reformer' within the Marwari trading community in early twentieth century Calcutta.† It examines the organizations prominent in regulating trading activities in the bazaar at that time.

* See, Chris Bayly, *Rulers, Townsmen and Bazaars: North Indian Society in the Age of British Expansion, 1770–1870* (Cambridge, Cambridge University Press, 1983), pp. 175–8.

† Ramdev Chokhany came to Calcutta from Mandava in Rajputana. Alongside his trading activities, he was active in a large number of community organizations in Calcutta, such as the Shri Vishudanand Saraswati Vidyalaya, Shri Vishudanand Marwari Hospital, and the Marwari Association. For details on Chokhany, see Radhakrishna Nevatia, *Bara Bazaar ke Karyakarta* (Calcutta, Shri Barabazaar Kumarsabha Pustakalya, 1982), p. 18.

Opium Chaurasta's Panchayat: Opium Chaurasta in Bara Bazaar was a major centre of trade and its name was known far and wide. It had its own Panchayat, and the following were the members (*panch*)—1. Shri Binjrajji Chaudhuri, 2. Shri Hardutt Raiji Chamaria, 3. Shri Vishweshwarlalji Chitlanjia, 4. Shri Chunnilalji Binnani, and 5. Shri Shivnandraiji Tiwari.

Marwari Association: This institution was founded in 1898.

Marwari Chamber of Commerce: An event that occurred around 1895 gave rise to this institution. Cloth from Manchester used to be brought in through Graham and Railey Brothers. The terms and conditions relating to this were made somewhat stricter, leading to discontent among the traders. As a result, the cloth traders assembled at No. 46 Khengrapatti to hold a meeting. My father was also among them. Everybody opposed the new terms. The assembly was initially called 'Marwari Association's Cloth-Branch Assembly' and this went on to become the 'Marwari Chamber of Commerce', which is today the 'Bharat Chamber of Commerce'.

This is a translation of an extract originally published in Hindi as Radhakrishna Nevatia (ed.), *Shri Ramdev Chokhany* (Calcutta, 'Shri Ramdev Chokhany' Aayojan Samiti, Akhil Bharatvarshiya Marwari Sammelan, 1950), p. 46.

7

Mercantile Codes of Status

Jawaharilal Jain

Interactions among merchants were influenced by conceptions of status and honour. Creditworthiness and business integrity were closely interwoven; trust (*sakh*) and honour were crucial indices of a merchant's economic standing.* *Sakh* meant much more than financial liquidity; it incorporated a moral dimension and indicated 'honourable' stature within mercantile public opinion. Moral stature could be acquired by maintaining an unblemished personal record, adhering to market obligations, extending patronage to religious and community activities, and extending generosity to philanthropic work valued by the community.†

In a commemorative volume for cotton trader Ramvilas Poddar, trader and author Jawaharilal Jain recounts how Poddar started out simply as a *dalal* (broker) in the raw cotton trade but soon reached an eminent position in the bazaar by gradually consolidating his reputation and acquiring *sakh* within the community. This community capital helped Poddar set up an independent brokerage within the short period of two years. His 'honesty', 'high conduct', and 'reputation' encouraged several older and more established firms to entrust the novice Poddar with their brokerage.

* On the role of trust, see David Rudner, 'Bankers Trust and the Culture of Banking among the Nattukottai Chettiars of Colonial South India', *Modern Asian Studies*, Vol. 23, No. 3, 1989, pp. 417–58 and his *Caste and Capitalism in Colonial India: The Nattukottai Chettiars* (Berkeley, University of California Press, 1994). For an interesting analysis of the role of 'trust' in trading communities, see Avner Greif's work on Maghribi traders in the eleventh century Mediterranean. Greif shows how Mediterranean traders were able to conduct overseas trade and deal with contractual problems by building up a reputation mechanism based on observed 'trust'. See Avner Greif, 'Reputation and Coalitions in Medieval Trade: Evidence on the Maghribi Traders,' *Journal of Economic History*, Vol. 49, No. 4, 1989, pp. 857–82 and 'Contract Enforcement and Institutions among the Maghribi Traders: Refuting Edwards and Ogilvie', available online at http://ideas.repec.org/p/ces/ceswps/_2350.html, last accessed on 14 January 2010.

† See Chris Bayly, *Rulers, Townsmen and Bazaars: North Indian Society in the Age of British Expansion, 1770–1870* (Cambridge, Cambridge University Press, 1983), p. 180.

Seth Sahib came to Bombay and started business as a broker in the cotton trade. Praise for his honesty and truthful behaviour reached the ears of Seth Keelachand, the owner of the famous cotton firm 'Keelachand Devchand', who asked him to act as broker in cotton and grain for the firm. His diligence and intelligence bore fruit. In the second year he went to Nawalgarh and happily organised the wedding ceremony of his younger brother. He christened his dealer firm 'Anandilal Ishwardas'. His partners in this firm were Seth Anandilalji Kulwal, Seth Durgaduttji Jalan and Seth Ishwardasji Poddar. The business ran for years under this name. Seth Sahib made regular progress and his reputation kept growing. He acted as a broker for Seth Keelachand Devchand for two decades. The firm made crores in profit and he earned in lakhs. He and Seth Keelachand*ji* were very fond of each other. Seth Keelachand*ji* was dependent on his advice, and he in turn used to regard Seth Keelachand like he would his own father. Seth Sahib's goodness and foresightedness got so well-established and fortune favoured him so much that he was fully successful in everything he tried to do. In addition to Seth 'Keelachand Devchand', he became a broker for Messrs. 'E. D. Sassoon', a firm well-known throughout the country, and earned prestige there as well for his honest behaviour and high reputation. Gradually he started his own trade alongside acting as a broker, and was soon being counted among the major cotton and grain traders in Bombay.

In the world of commerce his life was particularly notable. Very courageous in trading, he was also very concerned with ethics, which is considered among the best qualities in trade. He was ever concerned with the interests of traders and, especially, brokers. Whenever uncertainty and chaos gripped the cotton and grain trade, he played a major role in finding the solutions, giving ample evidence of his own powerful personality.

This is a translation of an extract originally published as Jawaharilal Jain, *Ramvilas Poddar: Jiwan Rekha aur Smritiyan* (n.p., 1936), pp. 5–6.

8

Bazaar Fortunes
World War

Balchand Modi

The tumultuous periods of the World Wars were turning points in the fortunes of several bazaar merchants. Spectacular profits were accumulated via speculation, via increased opportunities for local manufacturing due to the disruption of imports (with wartime demands on shipping) and via India's emergence as a centre for the wartime production of important commodities such as jute, coal, and steel. These profits enabled enterprising bazaar firms to make the daring move to industry, a sector dominated by European interests.

Though both the Wars witnessed the entry of bazaar groups into the world of modern large-scale industry, the breakthroughs following World War I were more dramatic since the barriers to entry were higher, considering that the industrial sector was then almost completely monopolized by foreign businesses. Among those that emerged after World War I as industrial pioneers were the Birlas who entered the cotton and jute sectors, Sarupchand Hukumchand who set up three cotton mills in Indore and a jute mill in Calcutta, Hargovind Dalmia who acquired Mathudas Mills (Calcutta), the Singhanias who established a mill in Kanpur, and Anandilal Poddar who set up the Toy-Poddar Cotton Mills in collaboration with a Japanese firm.* After World War II, bazaar groups such as the Bangurs (traders and share brokers) entered cotton and cement as did others such as the famous Raja Sir Group of Annamalai and Muthiah Chetty who entered textiles.†

* On the impact of World War I on Indian business, see Dwijendra Tripathi, *The Oxford History of Indian Business* (New Delhi, Oxford University Press, 2004), pp. 166–70.

† On this, see Tripathi, *The Oxford History of Indian Business*, pp. 237–8.

In this excerpt, Balchand Modi, chronicler of the Marwari community, reminisces about the years of World War I.‡ In this translation from Hindi, Modi recalls the 'flood of prosperity' that trading firms experienced and the 'wealth pouring into Bara Bazaar'.

When the German Great War began and its impact was felt the world over, the situation began to change once again. The war had a major impact on India. The world of commerce changed more than it had ever before. The import of English goods was much reduced and their prices quadrupled; the prices of raw materials that were exported from India went up because of increased demand. The war continued for about four years. There were major economic changes. For once, Indian traders gained immensely from this. The Marwari traders too made tremendous profits. It was a flood of wealth that gushed in. The greater the volume of a trader's trade, the higher was the profit he made. It began to rain wealth in Calcutta's Bara Bazaar. …

This is a translation of an extract originally published as Balchand Modi, 'Kalkatta ke Bade Bazaar main Dhan Barasne Laga', *Desh ke Itihas Mein Marwari Jati ka Sthan* (Calcutta, Raghunathprasad Singhania, 1930), pp. 541–2.

‡ Balchand Modi from Churu was based in Calcutta. He wrote a number of books with the objective of community publicity and encomium, such as *Desh ke Itihas Mein Marwari Jati ka Sthan* (Samvat, 1986) and *Agarwal Jati ka Itihas* (Samvat, 2006). On Modi, see Radhakrishna Nevatia, *Bara Bzaaar ke Karyakarta* (Calcutta, Shri Barabazzar Kumarsabha Pustakalya, 1982), p. 17.

9

Speculative Profits during War Times

Ramkrishna Dalmia

In this further elaboration of the extraordinary opportunities which World War I heralded for bazaar traders and speculators, well-known industrialist Ramkrishna Dalmia recalls his personal experiences.* A young, adventurous trader, Dalmia had then recently defaulted on payments and been declared insolvent by the bazaar community. In a moment of desperation, he turned to speculation in silver. He had received confidential information from an agent in London that the price of silver would rise. When he tried to pass on this information to the market, the 'unreliable' Dalmia was dismissed by fellow traders. He then approached a rich astrologer who agreed to make a purchase; but he later backtracked, fearing manipulation by Dalmia. However, Dalmia had entered the deal by then. As it passed, the price of silver fell initially but ultimately rose and rose immensely. Making a handsome profit due to quick thinking, adroit action, and supposed divine intervention, Dalmia learnt about business sense, income, wealth, riches, commodities, conditions of everyday life, and more.

* Ramkrishna Dalmia (1893–1978) was a Bania from Rohtak district, Punjab. He belonged to a family of traders and started his career with trading and speculating. The profits made from speculative activity during the years of the Depression enabled Dalmia to break into industry in the 1930s. He had interests in cement, sugar, paper, and chemicals. He also controlled *The Times of India*. For details on Dalmia, see his *Some Notes and Reminiscences* (Bombay: Times of India Press, 1948) and *A Short Sketch of the Beginnings of My Life and a Guide to Bliss* (New Delhi: Published by R.K. Dalmia, 1962).

All of a sudden one fine day, I received a cable from one of my agents in London, informing me that silver would go up. With that cable I went to the market and entreated some businessmen to do some business on my behalf or at least to utilize the information in any case, even for themselves. But who could attach any importance to the statement of a "persona non-grata," as I was, in the business world? Nobody paid any heed to me.

Strange is the irony of fate! Today I find people anxious for my advice regarding any business, merely because, I am now considered to be a successful and rich businessman. But who is really a rich person? Not one who has a large bank balance, nor one who controls big business or large property. Richness, in reality does not reside there. It resides in a large heart, a heart which is full of the milk of human kindness, found in greater measure in the poor than the rich who, keeping faith in wealth more than in God, forget, in their vanity, the virtues of piety, generosity and charity.

To revert to my story. Distressed, though not fully disheartened, I again went to my friend—the wealthy astrologer, who had been extremely courteous and gentle towards me. Showing him the cable, I told him that if I did my own business and there was a loss, which I could not then bear, I would lose Rs. 50 p.m., that I used to get as commission—my only source of income, with which I had been supporting my family. He agreed to purchase silver worth £7,500. I told him that I would be getting about Rs. 100 as commission. As I had no resources, on my request he also paid me Rs. 10 for sending a cable to London. Not in a position to hire a tonga I boarded a tram, hurried to the General Post Office at Calcutta and despatched the cablegram. The incident is about thirty years old, but even now, whenever I am reminded of that night, the whole incident is unrolled like a film on the canvas of my mind with all its details and vividness.

But misfortune seldom comes alone. I used to take a dip daily in the Ganges, early in the morning. The following day, while going for my bath, I met a messenger sent by the astrologer, who conveyed to me the message that Panditji would not like any business to be done on his behalf. This message from Panditji stunned me.

So, forgetting my bath, I immediately ran to the astrologer and with pathetic entreaties wept so bitterly before him that tears trickled down to my chest. But the Pandit was adamant. Inscrutable are the ways of Destiny! The astrologer who had predicted such a bright future for me was unable to believe himself.

Though generous and sympathetic towards me, Panditji had been convinced by some of his friends, that being resourceless, I was playing a trick by taking advantage of Panditji's trust in me and that I would not purchase any silver whatsoever but would keep him under the impression that I had done so; and if the market went up, I would not give any profit to him, while in the event of a fall in prices, he would have to pay. Under the circumstances, it was not unnatural for Panditji to believe this story. Reluctantly assuring him that he would not be held responsible for that transaction, I left him in despair and went straight to the Ganges. I used to perform my 'Sandhya' and 'Gayatri Japa'—the most famous and powerful of the Hindu Mantras (prayers)—standing in the Ganges water. That day I performed Gayatri Japa with greater earnestness and for double the time. On my return home, I received a cable informing me that the transaction had been completed; but, contrary to expectations, the following day there was a fall in the market and there was a loss of Rs. 3,000. Being unable to pay this sum, I did not square up the business and waited on God's mercy.

There is a silver lining behind every dark cloud and, observed with a correct foresight, it becomes clear that whatever God does, is for the best. All this may sound fatalistic rubbish to many but I believe that since God is all goodness and purity, no evil can emanate from Him; although we the mortals, with blurred visions and limited faculties, are not in a position to comprehend all this. Life moves according to certain preordained laws. After two days, the trend of the market became favourable and had I squared up the business then, I would have got about Rs. 4,000 as profit.

Human memory is very short, particularly about adversity. Forgetting my past very quickly I became ambitious for more and more. I stealthily took out the only ornament left with my wife, Durga Devi, and without her knowledge mortgaged the same for Rs. 200. As a devoted wife, she would never have objected to it, yet I had not the courage to ask her, because, though a young girl of seventeen, she had always bravely and calmly shared with me my distress and adversity, and for this act I consider myself morally guilty of a kind of theft.

This money all the more stimulated my ambition and I at once sent a cable to another Agent at London to purchase silver worth £10,000 and, a few days later, my profit rose to Rs. 20,000. On the strength of this estimated profit, I again purchased silver from the third agent and then again from the first one and then from the second and so on. By this process my profit went on increasing.

I was in a peculiar mood in those days. In my saner moments I likened myself to a rubber balloon, which goes on inflating when more and more air is pumped into it, till at last it bursts. A young lad, with no sympathisers as I was, I could not find any one before whom I could open my heart. At last, I could not check myself and divulged my secret to my mother, in the presence of my wife, but only partially. My mother, a noble and wise lady, advised me to be contented with only that amount and cautioned me always to bear in my mind the saintliness of my father, and asked me to square up my business. She has throughout my life advised me not to jump into difficulties, nor to crave for more money. She assured me that I could live with peace and comfort on Rs. 50 p.m., the interest I could get on investing the estimated profit of Rs. 10,000. When I told her that my profit would be Rs. 20,000 she observed that money earned, only with honest and earnest labour, afforded the greatest satisfaction. By her frequent and timely advice she has all along been restraining me from falling a prey to avarice, discontent and selfishness. Such pious and noble souls are very rare.

Now my estimated profit had risen to about Rs. 75,000. While musing over it again and again, I suddenly became apprehensive of an unfavourable trend in the market, and went to the office of my uncle, whose father and my grandfather were real brothers. I still remember that period vividly. My uncle's office was hardly 5' by 5' yet at that time he was considered to be a well-to-do person with a flourishing business. Keeping some margin in hand, I told him that I had done some business in which my profit would be Rs. 50,000. He did not believe me but still told me that even ten thousand could make a person live comfortably for his whole life and advised me not to crave for more. Quite unlike the present times, commodities were very cheap then and one could live comfortably on a small income. At one time he had refused a five rupees loan to me!

A comparison, between the present high soaring prices and those prevalent in medieval India, clearly indicates that people were very prosperous and happy then, even though not possessing wealth as reckoned today; because the commodities of daily use were very cheap and any man could live comfortably on a meagre earning. Butter which is not easily available at Rs. 4 a lb. these days, was sold at 20 seers or 40 lbs. per rupee for centuries before the advent of the British in India. This shows a 160 fold increase in prices, while wheat and other foodstuffs at present indicate a fortyfold rise. Then the village folk considered it improper and sinful to sell milk which was freely served to the guests, strangers and beggars alike, because the cow was considered sacred and never slaughtered. The present enormously disproportionate rise in the prices of commodities has hit the middle classes very hard, specially the literate service class which is feeling pinched and squeezed in narrow circumstances.

Though, as one associated with business from my early childhood, I had handled quite big amounts but all belonging to others, and never my own, to spend as I liked. So I wanted to have at least a glimpse of my own money cash in hand. Being ambitious and precocious, I did not like to square up the business but took a peculiar course. I instructed one of my agents to sell some silver and square up the business outstanding with him and asked another one to purchase the same quantity of silver on my behalf. In this process I had only to pay the extra commission.

Destiny was smiling at me; but people were entirely ignorant of all this. To them, I was still the same, unreliable defaulter. As fate would have it, my cable got mutilated in transmission and my agent asked for fresh instructions and did not sell my silver. But the other agent purchased silver on my behalf as directed. Without any effort on my part, my commitments for the purchase of silver increased. The market went up still further and my profits rose to over a lakh and a half. Being too young and inexperienced, I directed all my agents to square up my business in full. I did not then imagine that selling such a large quantity at a time may considerably reduce my large profits in the event of the market going down. But as the Hindi couplet says—

"Whomever the Lord protects, none can dare harm,
Not a hair can be bent, let the world arm."

During the first world war there was a great demand for silver in London and my whole stock was very soon absorbed in the market, leaving me a profit beyond my expectations—to the extent of Rs. 1,56,000.

In my narrow circumstances, I could never dream of possessing even a thousand rupees at one time. But fate had thrust, so to say, this enormous fortune on me. I had struck the iron while it was still hot for a delay of even two or three days would have reduced my profits by one half.

Originally published as Ramkrishna Dalmia, *Some Notes and Reminiscences* (Bombay, Times of India Press, 1948), pp. 11–17.

10

Historical Continuity and the Present-Day Bazaar

Bunny Gupta and Jaya Chaliha

For much of the nineteenth and twentieth centuries, the bazaar was an intermediary between the European-dominated industrial sector and the local subsistence economy. It was an important site for both modern and traditional traders. It was where fortunes were built and important industrial houses emerged from active trading firms.*

Though much has changed in contemporary India and the colonial division between the modern industrial sector and the subsistence economy no longer applies, the rhythm of life in the bazaar is still much the same. Though more affluent traders have moved out to avoid its noise and congestion, the bazaar remains the site for wholesale and much of retail business. High-rise buildings have replaced old structures and modern-style businesses such as travel agencies have emerged alongside old-style retail and wholesale trades, yet interactions continue to be largely based on trust, and despite the accelerated flows of people, commodities and information due to globalization, many elements of the 'traditional marketplace' have persisted.†

This excerpt outlines the continuities as well as the changes in Calcutta's Bara Bazaar, one of the oldest bazaars in the subcontinent and one that has been a major centre of indigenous banking and commerce since at least the eighteenth century.‡ The history of Bara Bazaar from the pre-British era, 300 years ago, through to contemporary times is recounted from its origins as a biweekly *haat* to its emergence as an enduring

* On this, see Dwijendra Tripathi, *The Oxford History of Indian Business* (New Delhi, Oxford University Press, 2004), pp. 237–9.

† See Martin Beattie, 'Hybrid Bazaar Space: Colonization, Globalization and Traditional Space in Barabazaar, Calcutta, India', *Journal of Architectural Education*, Vol. 61, No. 3, 2008, pp. 45–55.

‡ On Bara Bazaar, also see Meera Guha, 1964, 'Concentration of Communities in Burra Bazaar, Calcutta', *Man in India*, Vol. 44, October–December, 1964, pp. 289–97.

wholesale market. The diversity of goods in the humongous marts of Bara Bazaar has hardly changed over the centuries. More than half the wealth of Calcutta's Marwaris is estimated to be here. Though street names have changed and trucks have replaced bullock carts, the character of the trade is still the same. Even today, Bara Bazaar continues to be a hub of private markets where lives are still run according to rural traditions with a hint of the impermanence characteristic of all bazaars. The authors commemorate contemporary Bara Bazaar as a place pulsating with considerable profits and magnanimous energies.

The 'Great Bazaar' or strictly 'Buro Bazaar' (from 'Buro', the fond appellation of Lord Shiva) existed before the British arrived 300 years ago. Sutanuti Hat, the thread and yarn market, gave its name to the riparian village on the Bhagirathi river (later named the Hugli) and spread over a quarter of its 1,692 bighas. By 1707, 80 per cent of the market area was crowded with houses and shops, though these were only of mud and thatch: it was always the most populous part of the young city. No wonder its new-comer English neighbours to the south named it the 'Bara' or Great Bazaar. The rest of Sutanuti consisted chiefly of jungle, swamp, and ricefields. On a few bighas were planted cotton, tobacco and bananas.

The Sheths, Basaks, Sheels and Dattas, pioneers of trade and the banians of Bengal, moved in from Hugli town and settled in Gobindapur when the port of Saptagram or Satgaon on the western bank, the commercial centre of old Bengal, went into decline. They conducted their business in Sutanuti Hat, which had grown in importance as the Portuguese power declined: shipping was diverted there from Betore on the opposite bank. Thursdays and Sundays were market days. Sellers of iron and silver, rice and lentils, fish and meat, bananas, sugar-cane and vegetables, all assembled at what was basically the cotton market. Stevedoring began to flourish, as sailing ships from the West called for re-victualling and other necessities. There was good reason why Job Charnock chose the neighbourhood of Sutanuti for an important factory on the eastern bank of the river.

In 1727, a Mayor and aldermen constituted a court, on today's Old Court House Street, to administer British law to British subjects. Civil, fiscal and judicial powers over 'natives' were vested in the White Zamindar, the official who formally held Zamindari rights over Calcutta on the Company's behalf. A part of the municipal revenue was collected, on the Mughal pattern, from the eighteen bazaars, big and small. The markets were auctioned to the highest bidder. The ground rent he paid the Company was Rs 3 per bigha in 1745. In return, he could levy a 9 per cent tax on all consumer items. Craftsmen making fireworks, vermilion, chests etc. paid more, to protect their monopolies.

The loot from the Battle of Palashi (1757) funded the new Fort William in Gobindapur. The displaced Sheths and Basaks were compensated with more land in Sutanuti, and the bi-weekly *hat* grew into a *bara bazaar*, a permanent residential wholesale market.

Like some lodestone, Barabazar attracted traders from near and far. The Armenians, the Jews and the Chinese even brought their countrywomen with them and settled on the edge of the great Asian bazaar. The Greeks came too, and the Portuguese were already well ensconced. Colesworthy Grant in 1850 described a 'diversified group' of 'oriental heads' hailing from Turkey to the China Sea, bearing spices, incense and drugs; silks and brocades; furs, fruits and gems; shawls and calicoes, Murshidabad and Benares silks; muslins from Dhaka and broadcloth from England.

Most crucial, however, was the arrival of the frugal Rajasthani or 'Marwari' with his proverbial 'brass pot and blanket': the brass soon turned to gold at the Midas touch of Barabazar. The influx increased with the rail link in the 1860s, and the newcomers outnumbered the already domiciled Khatris. They remained, and changed the face of Barabazar.

The fortunes of the original settlers declined with the change in the Company's policy for the procurement of goods. Rajasthanis replaced the Bengali merchants or *banias* in economic power: the latter henceforth confined themselves to the roles of landlord, civil servant, lawyer, doctor, poet and politician. Some remained owners of prime property in the area, but these assets were eroded by fragmentation and litigation. The Marwaris, meanwhile, evolved a distinctive economic system, only tenuously linked to orthodox models of political economy. Floating, small-time operators joined hands with the large monopolists to take over the distribution of many commodities, above all of basic consumer goods. In this century, the wealthiest Marwaris inevitably turned to industry. With this change of outlook there gradually came a change of life-style: they moved to more spacious quarters in Alipur and Baliganj, once the suburbs of the city.

Though most Marwaris still live in Barabazar, the area basically continues to be a conglomerate of private markets, huddled within the compass of a single square mile. The weekday population is nearly 8 lakh, including business travellers and commuters. Lives are still based on rural traditions, with the element of transience common to all bazaars. Yet despite its squalor, there is no real poverty in Barabazar. Violent crime is at its lowest in this part of the city. The evident underworld is confined to pickpockets and petty thieves who find easy victims in the crowds and quick escape among the maze of lanes. But ticking away among the lanes is a 'parallel economy' that defies quantification and indeed description. This is vividly symbolized by a thirteen-storey market building: unauthorized and much litigated, it is without water and electricity, but a huge and flourishing trade carries on by lamplight.

The centuries have scarcely changed the variety of merchandise in the gigantic marts of Barabazar. Porters with baskets dodge the overloaded Tata trucks along the same cobbled roads where bullock carts once carried bales of cotton. Labyrinthine lanes lead off into *pattis* or wholesale marts. Pagayapatti offers blankets by the score, cloth by the *than* (roll) and cut pieces by the kilogram. Khangrapatti's *khangras* or broomsticks have themselves been swept into a corner by canvas and tarpaulin. Cloth and readymade garments have similarly usurped Sutapatti, yarn market and direct descendant of Sutanuti Hat. A commerce graduate from St. Xavier's College sits here at his ancestral *gaddi*, his telephone perched on hanks of yarn. He estimates his annual turnover at about Rs 100 crore. It is said that 60 per cent of the total wealth of Calcutta's Marwaris is here in Barabazar.

In Darmahata (now Maharshi Debendranath Road, the impermanent *darma* (reed matting) has been replaced by bricks and bags of cement. The hardware shops of old now stock sophisticated building materials. That the river flowed by the western edge of the market is remembered in Mirbahar Street, where the Harbour Master or *mirbahar* was stationed in Mughal times.

We pass through more alleyways to the *postas* (warehouses) of Gopal Mallik and Gobardhan Das, the wholesale potato and onion markets. Dust from the gunny bags mingles with spices: coughs and sneezes punctuate the way to the Raja of Bardhaman's chowk, Raja Katra. Here a sea of green betel leaves, betel-nuts both whole and chopped, little bricks of brown *katha* (catechu) and all the flavourings for a good *khilli* of *pan* are skilfully sorted into heaps of muted colours and musky smells. Stepping out again, the eye blinks at the sudden light, through which the span of Haora Bridge gleams like a permanent silver bow.

Sonapatti, the gold-traders' mart, paves Manohar Das Street metaphorically with gold. *Dashakarma bhandars* store the thousand and one items needed for pujas and other ceremonies. Hole-in-the-wall shops sell bulky account-books bound in red *shalu* (cotton gauze). A Bhatia merchant holds up strings of pearls quoted in linear measure. 'American diamond' ear-rings and nose-pins glint in the roadside showcase, while the real stuff is locked away in a Chubb safe in the depths of the long narrow shop. The thoroughfare changes its name after a while to Nalini Sheth Street; in the old bazaar this was Mairadanga, where confectioners *(mairas)* sat stirring casein for *sandesh*.

A mobile community, the Subarnabaniks represented the quintessence of Bengali *baniadom* in the late eighteenth and early nineteenth centuries. The Chandra and Sheel families still carry on the bullion business and goldsmith's craft in what was once the only place where gold could be bought in Bengal. Others like the Malliks and Lahas became urban rajas. Away from inquisitive eyes, bare-bodied men sit in Sonapatti stirring cauldrons of molten gold and silver brought by customers for sale or refashioning. During the wedding season, part of Manohar Das Chowk is strung with threads of pure gold for bridal clothes. Kalakar Street deals in baser metals: here salesmen conduct a brisk business in stainless steel ware. Conversation is rudimentary and bargaining hard.

The noise reaches a defeaning crescendo as trams rumble along Mahatma Gandhi (earlier Harrison) Road; a flowing human mass out-jostles motor vehicles on this, the city's busiest thoroughfare. Traffic disruption is an everyday feature here: so much so that the local police station often resorts to leg-power when responding to emergencies. After the completion of Harrison Road, connecting Haora and Shealdah Stations, in 1892, land on either side was rapidly bought up by Marwaris for residential houses with shops on the ground and first floors. The buildings present an unbroken façade, a grotesque mixture of showy stucco at one level with corrugated iron sheets, wood and *darma* above it.

The air in Tulapatti is filled with fluff from the twanging bow-strings of the *dhunari* (cotton-teaser) as we make our way to *Aphing Chourasta* or Opium Crossing, where the river hugged the shoulder of the bazaar, and sailing-boats would load and unload their precious chests of opium. Only the name remains. But even today, somewhere close by, a little door can lead into a damp mossy courtyard where a wizened old man exchanges the proffered two-rupee note for a *chhillum* and a brick. A deep draw, and the head comes to rest on the brick for a half-hour of oblivion. Armenian Street is given over to more respectable addictives, tobacco and biri leaves, their scent hanging in the air.

On a Sunday, Barabazar relaxes. The numerous food shops are conspicuously open, but there are no crowds except around the street entertainers, on pavements whose true width is apparent at last. Busloads of businessmen and their families set off on picnics. Pickle and preserve shops dole out dollops of mango *achar* and *gulkhand* in the plastic bags that have replaced the earlier leaves or jars. The ubiquitous betel-seller sells the famous Barabazar *pan*. Busy cobblers sit in a row mending slippers and polishing shoes. And even on a Sunday, carpenters and plumbers hang around waiting for work, advertising themselves by the tools of their trade.

From British times, there existed a plan to beautify north Calcutta; but 'alas the exigencies of commercial activity defeated those early schemes...' Hence Satyanarayan Park is the Bazar's only lung. Here, controversially but no doubt beneficially, Calcutta has set up its first underground market clad in marble and aluminium—350 shops over a 2-bigha area, still capped by the restored park. Around its well-laid garden are the Satyanarayan and Swetambar Jain Temples, the latter 175 years old. On the main road stands the seven-storeyed Gurdwara Bara Sikh Sangat. Gobindaji, the tutelary deity of the Sheths, was installed at Banshtala in the *thakurbari* built by Jagabandhu Sheth in the early eighteenth century. Worship is still carried on there. Similarly, behind the Old Mint, the bells of the Jagannath Temple of the Basaks have rung in 1990.

When the rest of Calcutta lies submerged during the monsoons, Barabazar sits high above the floods. Perhaps this is symbolic. Money makes the Bazar go round. There is almost a creative energy pulsating in every lane and *patti* of this teeming, squalid, raucous yet mysterious wonderland of wealth.

Originally published as Bunny Gupta and Jaya Chaliha, 'Barabazar', in Sukanta Chaudhuri (ed.), *Calcutta: The Living City*, Vol. II: The Present and Future (Calcutta, Oxford University Press, 1990), pp. 113–16.

11

Contemporary Informal Credit Markets and Systems

Thomas A. Timberg and C.V. Aiyar[#]

Modern banking evolved in India in the last quarter of the eighteenth century but could become pervasive only in the mid-twentieth century. Till then, organized banking was restricted in terms of the range of services and the number of banks and clients they served. In such a situation, the principal sources of commercial and industrial finance were the community, clan, and family networks. Indigenous bankers (*shroffs*, *sahukars*) were responsible for providing much of the required finance, and mercantile interests dominated industrial finance well into the mid-twentieth century. Despite the extensive availability of modern banking and finance in contemporary India, indigenous bankers and informal credit continue to play an important role in both urban and rural credit markets even today.

This article by noted economists Thomas Timberg and C.V. Aiyar (of the Reserve Bank of India) examines urban, commercial, and legal informal credit markets in the India of the seventies.* It reveals both continuities as well as changes in the markets, banking instruments, and roles of indigenous bankers. While informal credit provides up to 20 per cent of commercial credit in certain markets and many of the traditional

* Thomas Timberg's earlier work was on the Marwaris; see *The Marwaris: From Traders to Industrialists* (New Delhi, Vikas, 1978); 'A North Indian Firm seen through Its Business Records, 1860–1914: Tarachand Ghanshyamdas, A "Great" Marwari Firm', *Indian Economic and Social History Review*, Vol. 8, No. 3, 1971, pp. 264–83; and 'Hiatus and Incubator: Indigenous Trade and Traders, 1837–1857', in Asiya Siddiqi (ed.), *Trade and Finance in Colonial India* (Delhi, Oxford University Press, 1995), pp. 250–64.

trading communities such as Shikarpuri financiers, Gujaratis, Marwaris, and Chettiars continue to be key players, several changes have occurred too.†

A marked difference from traditional informal finance, according to the authors, is that the more meaningful differentiations are now functional rather than ethnic, and new players have emerged. Three important functional categories are of full-service indigenous bankers who take deposits and give loans; commercial financiers who lend on their own credit; and brokers who link borrowers with lenders. Timberg and Aiyar examine how contemporary informal credit markets function, their rates of interest, instruments for borrowing, transaction costs, and criteria for credit. They appreciate these markets for the role they continue to play in the urban economy in providing credit to wholesale trade and small-scale industry, which modern banks do not serve adequately.

Informal financial markets, those which are not regulated or monitored by the banking authorities, account for much of business credit in developing countries.[1] These unregulated, informal credit markets (ICM) are important both in their own right, as part of each country's financial system, and because of their reciprocal relations with growing enterprises and the regulated financial sector. In order to study the operations of some of these markets in detail, in urban commercial settings, we conducted an extended survey of some of the informal credit markets of India.[2] Based, in some cases, on centuries of operation, these markets proved to be important in the functioning of the contemporary economy. "Indigenous-style bankers," belonging to particular ethnic communities and castes, formerly provided the full range of banking services to their clients.[3] With the rise of modern, Western-style banking the indigenous bankers either have transformed themselves to serve sectors, such as wholesale trade, not well served by the modern sector or provide services which the modern bankers cannot provide. Though any estimate is very approximate, it seems that informal credit markets account for as much as 20% of commercial credit outstanding in the various markets surveyed.

We began by surveying the Gujeratis, some of whom still practice their traditional form of full-service banking in their homeland of Gujerat and adjoining Bombay, the Shikarpuris or Multanis (originally full-service bankers in Sind, who now provide commercial credit in various other centers), the Chettiars in South

† Also see Government of India, *Report of the Study Group on Indigenous Bankers* (Bombay, Banking Commission, Government of India, 1971). Indigenous banking instruments continue to persist and fulfil an important role in remittance systems, especially used by migrant workers. See Marina Martin, 'Hundi/Hawala: The Problem of Definition', *Modern Asian Studies*, Vol. 43, 2009, pp. 909–37, doi: 10.1017/S0026749X07003459. Also see Roger Ballard, 'A Background Report on the Operation of Informal Value Transfer Systems (HAWALA)', Centre for Applied South Asian Studies, University of Manchester, 2003, available online at http://www.arts.manchester.ac.uk/casas/papers/pdfpapers/hawala.pdf, last accessed on 14 January 2010, and 'Hawala Transformed: Remittance-driven Transnational Networks in the Post-imperial Economic Order', Centre for Applied South Asian Studies, University of Manchester, 2004, available online at http://www.arts.manchester.ac.uk/casas/papers/pdfpapers/transformed.pdf, last accessed on 14 January 2010.

India, the Rastogis in Uttar Pradesh, and the Marwaris, especially in Eastern India.[4] But our surveys revealed that a wide range of ethnic groups were now involved in informal credit markets, and the more meaningful differentiations were now functional rather than ethnic. There were three important functional categories: full-service indigenous bankers who took deposits and made loans; commercial financiers who lent primarily their own resources; and brokers who connected potential lenders and borrowers. All of these sometimes existed in particular markets, but one or the other was usually dominant. Outside Gujerat, indigenous bankers of the traditional sort were rare. In Gujerat and Bombay, such bankers provided deposit, remittance, and other banking services to a large number of firms, primarily in wholesale trade. New "finance companies" (unincorporated commercial deposit and lending institutions), which resembled the old-style indigenous banker in many ways, were flourishing. Commercial financiers were present everywhere, but especially in the older Shikarpuri markets in the port cities. Brokers were even more common and seemed the dominant financial intermediary in the wholesale and small industrial markets we surveyed. Brokers secured their funds both from commercial financiers like the Shikarpuris and from an increasingly diverse investing public.

Since this study is one of the first of urban informal financial markets, any theory must be tentative, but three salient characteristics of the intermediaries in this market seem to lead to lower transactions costs: (1) the intermediaries' intimate knowledge of their clients, which reduces their information costs compared to those of commercial banks; (2) the absence of government control on lending and borrowing rates governing the intermediaries, which enables them to adjust more fully to market forces than regulated intermediaries; and (3) the absence of charges on the informal intermediaries in the form of idle or low-interest reserves, which are imposed on regulated intermediaries. The second and third characteristics clearly result from the lack of regulation of the informal markets. As John Gurley says, "If there is anything different about commercial banks . . . it is because they are controlled; they are not controlled because they are different."[5] The lower transactions costs lead to a higher level of intermediation for the economy overall and an increase in savings and productive investment.

But the small scale of ICM agencies and markets also has negative results. They function in small, localized markets, do not necessarily distribute funds to the best potential users, and may possess a large degree of monopoly power. None of these negative characteristics seemed marked in the Indian cases we studied.

We should emphasize that our survey concerns only urban (not rural), commercial (not consumer), and legal (not "black money") credit markets. All of the other forms of credit market are important in India but were not the focus of our study. The intermediaries we studied appeared to be involved only peripherally, if at all, in these other markets.

MODUS OPERANDI

The borrowers in the informal market are "known" parties—under continuous surveillance in the closely packed lanes of the urban wholesale markets. Each bale of cloth that goes in and out is observed by neighbors, the finance brokers and bankers among them; an expensive night on the town is reported and judged the next morning in market gossip. In contrast to the relatively anonymous world of Western businessmen, even in the larger metropolitan centers Indian businessmen live their lives in a narrow social ambit. Most of the intermediaries interviewed seemed incredulous at the suggestion that they would have to ask formal questions of borrowers in whose shops they visited every day and with whose business confrères they were in continuous contact. Still, one Shikarpuri financier in Bombay said he asked to see borrower income tax returns in about 10% of his transactions, and one in Madras indicated that he, too, occasionally asked for income and wealth tax forms. These requirements are common, and some Shikarpuris in Bombay and elsewhere will only lend to income tax assessees. But the Shikarpuris deal with a more varied clientele than the typical informal market lender—a fact reflected in their higher than average interest rates.

In fact, the people in the market not only have a 24-hour relationship, they typically have one that extends over generations. We asked one finance broker how he evaluated "new borrowers"—he answered that he never took them. All his clients were children and grandchildren of businessmen with whom he and his father and grandfather had done business.

Informal financial intermediaries, by and large, concern themselves with the overall credit standing of the borrowing party rather than the specific enterprise or project for which credit is taken. They thus do not do any close check of the specific use of their funds but are generally content with monitoring borrowers' overall activity. In bankers' jargon, they lend on the basis of "cash flow" rather than asset protection. And they consider the borrower's total financial situation. The brokers in the informal market watch closely the level of business activity not only in their borrower's main establishment but in any others he may have. They watch his personal expenditure. They talk with his competitors and especially his employees. They then judge what sort of margin he is operating on and how likely he is to pay them. Most especially, they watch his payments record to see if he may be faltering on any of his market obligations.

CRITERIA FOR CREDIT

It was difficult to get informal market lenders and brokers to specify their criteria for lending. They resisted using banker's language and most of the standard banking ratios. For them the key elements were the overall prosperity, wealth, and cash position of the borrower and an evaluation of his commercial integrity. Most important seemed to be a reputation for punctiliousness in meeting debts. One elderly cloth market finance broker stated the principle, "Payment! Payment! Payment!" Borrowers, potential and actual, felt that to qualify for a loan they had to have a reputation for meeting their obligations promptly.

One explicit criterion for lending which seemed common was some target relationship between total borrowing and net worth. Two Shikarpuris (one each in Bombay and Madras) and one Rastogi in Kanpur mentioned 25% of net worth as their normal limit. A third Shikarpuri in Bombay set 33%—though he clearly had a relatively adventurous financing posture. In Amritsar, there seemed to be an informal rule—one-third from banks, one-third from the informal market, and one-third from own resources—at least for large borrowers. On the other hand, an informant who audits the books of larger trading firms in Calcutta said most of them try to limit their own equity to 25% of the gross capital employed, though only a portion of the remainder would be borrowed on the informal market. The Gujerati firms in particular seemed reluctant to commit themselves to any net worth figure, perhaps because their concerns are more focused on the cash and stock position of their clients than on their net worth.

In general, urban informal intermediaries try to avoid coming under the restrictive state moneylending acts and thus do not usually lend in amounts of less than Rs 3,000, nor do they lend to agriculturists, who are normally protected under these acts. They usually provide working capital accommodation to prosperous enterprises in well-known markets. Their major risk is either of a wave which sweeps under all firms in their market or of the bad faith nonpayment of their dues, which they reduce by lending only to those with strong roots in the community. As one financier said, "I guess they could run away, but where would they go? They would have to do business with their friends and relatives and I would find them."

Many lenders also have informal limits on their maximum lending to any one party. Shikarpuris usually limit their exposure to one party to Rs 25,000, though by selling Rs 5–25,000 notes on a single borrower to many Shikarpuris the brokers can put together loans of many hundreds of thousands of rupees. Two of the larger non-Shikarpuri firms surveyed—one a Gujerati indigenous-style banker and the other an Amritsar broker—had several much larger debtors. Except for the Shikarpuris, most lenders and brokers were too specialized in one or another commodity or product market to limit their exposure in it.

PURPOSES OF LENDING—WHERE THE MONEY GOES

The bulk of informal lending goes to finance trade and industry, mostly the former as shown in table 1. *Badla* financing of stock market speculation is a large and important exception which flows through specialized channels. Essentially, *badla* finance involves short-term lending at rates about 14% plus 1.2%–2.4% brokerage on the security of shares with no margin requirement.

Gujerati credit goes almost entirely to funding trade, especially wholesale trade in agriculture and in craft work commodities. The Shikarpuris lend to a wide variety of small and occasionally large enterprises, as do "finance companies." Rastogis and Chettiars finance smaller traders and artisans.

Table 1 Destination of Informal Credit Market Funds in Percentage of Loans Outstanding

Source	Trade	Exports	Small-scale industry	Large-scale industry	Other
Shikarpuri financiers	32	20	16	7	25
Gujerati bankers	60	10	5	10	15
Chettiar financiers (in Tamil Nadu)	45	10	5	10	20
Rastogi bankers (in Uttar Pradesh)	55	12	...	...	23
Chettiar pawnbrokers (in Tamil Nadu)	22	...	5	...	73
Finance companies (in Trichy and Karur)	40	...	8	...	52

Source: Data gathered by C. V. Aiyar, 1979.
Note: In December 1976, according to the *Statistical Tables relating to Banks in India* (Bombay: Reserve Bank of India, 1976), fig. 7, 10.27% of commercial bank advances were to trade, 7%–8% to exporters, roughly 10% to small-scale industry, 44% to large-scale industry, and 19% to other commercial borrowers.

The credit provided by brokers in wholesale markets for cloth and grain is obviously solely credit to wholesale traders. Obviously brokers who provide money to industrial firms in the form of deposits, call money, or promissory note lending serve industry. Special demands on the informal financial market come from exporters who need quick money and from builders and restaurant owners who have no physical security to give. Certain industries—tanneries in Madras, *zari* cloth manufacturers in Surat, silk weavers in Benares, and *biri* (indigenous-style tobacco) merchants in Gujerat—have needs which banks are unable to meet and informal credit markets can accommodate.

None of the groups of informal intermediaries is involved to any notable extent with agricultural financing or speculative activities. Films, a high-risk proposition, are normally financed by a separate set of lenders, mostly in "black" money on which income tax has not been paid. Informal money is, in fact, generally only available for working capital purposes, precisely because new ventures are seen as too risky.

Much of the routine wholesale and export trade, and even many industrial firms on a sporadic basis, turn to the informal market for flexibility and accommodation that cannot be obtained from the commercial banks, in financing working capital.

While it is clear that the bulk of informal finance is provided directly to trading enterprises and very little is provided directly to very small units (under $14,000 capitalization), the borrowers are not the ultimate beneficiaries of the credit. The working capital needs that are financed are typically for advances to trading partners and actual manufacturers, large and small, who demand cash payment. The advances also fund the 30–90 days of credit on which the smaller retail shops subsist. Thus the entire economy is indirectly dependent on informal market advances.

ADVANTAGES—AND WHY THE BORROWER CHOOSES

At times the advantage of the informal financial sector for the borrower is the rapidity with which it can provide money or the cheapness of the money provided, though neither of these is the norm. Generally, informal money is slower to arrange and more expensive for the borrower than money from the organized sector would be if it were available. In several markets, informal market rates are even quoted in terms of a 1%–3% premium on bank rates. The exceptions to this slowness and expensiveness are found primarily in the large metropolitan markets, where indigenous-style bankers and commercial financiers provide money far more quickly than the banks and brokers in markets like the cloth market or the intercorporate call money market provide financing more cheaply than do the banks.

The informal money market has some other advantages from the borrower's point of view. Informal lending generally is unsecured. Borrowers do not have to tie up their stocks as collateral. Restaurant owners, exporters, and construction contractors often borrow on the informal market because their business does not generate acceptable collateral. Even where collateral is available, the restrictions on the use of collateral and the procedures for checking it often prove onerous. Indian bank credit to small-scale industry is almost always secured—and the procedures for checking and conserving the collateral often appreciably increase the real cost of the loan. On the other hand, there are forms of secured credit in the informal market. Firms that buy up Bombay textile mills' accounts receivable extend secured credit.

Informal finance generally is provided without having to fill out forms or spend much time in the intermediary's office—and is not tied into all sorts of formal requirements like compliance with municipal land use regulations, of which small-scale units are often in tolerated violation. In these respects, the cost to the borrower is not higher than face interest cost, unlike most formal bank lending. Small businessmen complain that they are foreclosed from loans for lack of official clearances and the burden of the connected paperwork. In fact, in many informal credit markets the broker visits the client's place of business and does all the preparatory work for the loan as part of his service. That is, the broker does what the borrower has to do when dealing with a commercial bank.

On the other hand, there are some negative aspects to informal sector borrowing. Much informal credit is "call" money and in any case may have to be paid on some precise due date, whereas "bank" credit is more flexible and it is easier to delay payment. Informal credit is also less reputable than bank credit, and informal market transactions are more likely to be challenged by income tax authorities. Almost half the units we surveyed, even in markets in which informal finance is important, denied using it—often because they were either too rich or too poor to be accommodated. Some of them, however, may have simply been reluctant to admit involvement on prestige grounds.

VOLUME AND TERMS OF CREDIT AND DEPOSITS

Rough estimates of the volume and rates charged for credit in various ICMs are found in tables 2 and 3.[6] In general, brokers and indigenous bankers provide money at an annual equivalent of 18%–24% to larger established traders, with 18% the norm, and to smaller artisans and traders in a range sometimes as high as 24%–36% annual equivalent. Checks and bills are discounted at 18%–24%. Call money loans in urban areas are sometimes provided at rates as low as 12%. Black money, on which income tax has not been paid, is normally available at slightly cheaper rates—12%–15% annual equivalent in Bombay and 24% in Madras. In general, South India has higher informal rates, and a wider variety of recently started informal institutions (*nidhis*, finance companies, and *chit* funds), possibly reflecting a greater capital shortage there. Shikarpuri bankers' rates also seem higher than those of other lenders, though more so in Bombay and Madras, where they are adjusting to a decline in bank finance, than in the smaller towns.

Table 4 sets forth data on commercial lending in India for the purpose of comparison. Normal bank lending rates in June 1978 were 13%–16% per annum. Total bank credit at that date was Rs 160 billion; outstanding credit to wholesale trade, excluding three large public sector corporations, was Rs 10 billion. Most informal market clients might well pay the higher rates, if they could get any credit. The modal informal rate is thus only 2%–8% higher than the bank rate and probably less if we take into account the actual transactions costs to the borrower. The All-India Debt and Investment Survey, 1971–72, reported that 75% of households (accounting for 85% of borrowing) in rural areas borrowed at rates under 25%.[7] The comparable bank rate is 9%–11%, charged on agricultural loans. The gap is roughly comparable to that in urban areas.

Many of these interest rates are fixed in competitive markets. In some cases there is some price leadership or institutional fixation,

Table 2 Indigenous Credit Systems and the Credit They Extend

Type of firm	Number of firms	Credit extended (millions of Rs)	Rates (% per annum)
Shikarpuri financiers:			
Members of local assns.	550	600	21–37
Nonmembers	650	650	21–120
Brokers	550	1,250	20–120
Shikarpuri submarkets:			
Bombay members	238	240	Max. 30
Bombay nonmembers	350	330	N.A.
Madras members	126	150	Max. 37
Madras nonmembers	200	160	N.A.
Madurai members	20	30	21–25
Madurai nonmembers	10	N.A.	N.A.
Trichy members	30	8	21–25
Trichy nonmembers	12	N.A.	N.A.
Tanjore	4	6	21–25
Salem	40	50	21–25
Calicut	20	10	27
Coimbatore members	20	30	21–25
Coimbatore nonmembers	35	40	N.A.
Bangalore members	N.A.	45	N.A.
Bangalore nonmembers	N.A.	55	N.A.
Hyderabad members	N.A.	30	N.A.
Hyderabad nonmembers	N.A.	45	N.A.
Vijayawada	N.A.	10	N.A.
Marwaris in Madras doing similar work	100	104	N.A.
Gujerati indigenous-style bankers:			
Pure bankers	2,000	7,460	18
Bankers and commission agents	N.A.	N.A.	18
Chettiars bankers:			
Chettiar bankers	2,500	3,800	18–30
Chettiar pawnbrokers	25,000	12,500	18–30 +
Rastogi bankers	500	1,000	18–24 up to 36

Source: Data gathered by C. V. Aiyar, 1979.
Note: All rates are approximate: the interest rates and number of firms figures more solid than the estimates of credit extended. Shikarpuris receive Rs 30–Rs 60 million in bank refinance and have Rs 75 million in deposits. Chettiars have perhaps Rs 2,500 million in deposits. Rastogis have approximately Rs 550 million in deposits.

Table 3 Finance Companies and Brokers and Their Rates

		Rates (%)
1.	Intramarket and intermarket lending through brokers:	
	Lending to cloth commission agents in Amritsar	9–18
	Lending to cloth commission agents in Delhi	15
	Lending to cloth commission agents in Kanpur	13–16
	Yarn traders advances to powerlooms, Kanpur	18
	Yarn traders advances to powerlooms, Amritsar	14–22
	Bombay:	
	Lending to Bombay rice and gram traders	15
	Lending to Bombay dried fruit traders	18
	Lending to Bombay jute traders	18
	Lending to Bombay iron and steel traders	18
	Lending to Bombay share traders *(badla)*	15–16
	Calcutta:	
	Lending to Calcutta cloth commission agents	16.2
	Lending to Calcutta yarn traders	15
	Lending to Calcutta grain traders	15.2
	Lending to Calcutta oil seeds dealers	15–18
	Lending to Calcutta gunny dealers	18
	Deposits with small Pharmaceuticals firms	14.5–15
2.	Finance companies:	
	There are 60 in Trichy, 40 in Kothamangalam, and 100 in Karur. Twenty firms in Trichy had assets of Rs 440 million. They pay 7%–15% on deposits and charge 21%–24%.	

Source: Data gathered by C. V. Aiyar and Thomas A. Timberg, 1978–79.

and in others the degree of association between lenders must lead to some coordination. The rates clearly move in some sympathy with bank lending rates, as is documented in some unpublished work by V. V. Bhatt and T. R. Venkatachalam.[8] The differences in interest rates from city to city are substantial and reflect the largely local and even sub-local nature of the markets surveyed. Even the Gujerati bankers who moved back and forth between Bombay and Gujerat report money a percentage point or so cheaper in Bombay. Some of this difference may reflect the greater availability of bank credit in Bombay or the greater liquidity of Bombay as a financial center. The difference clearly does not reflect arbitrage costs which are less than 0.2%, or 0.3% if one assumes a need to cover double the remittance costs. The differences between Madras and Bombay Shikarpuris are equally hard to explain because the firms are related, though money is not freely transferred from place to place. Perhaps the perceived risk level is higher in Madras, or the lower Bombay figure may reflect the inelasticity of demand in the Madras market within the ranges the Shikarpuris charge (i.e., they could not place more of their Bombay funds in Madras at lower rates, since the demand for their funds is interest inelastic).

As to the persisting difference between the intermarket credit rates offered by brokers and Gujerati indigenous bankers, and those charged

Table 4 Comparative Data on Commercial Banks

A. Advances to Small-Scale Industry by State by Commercial Banks (in billions of Rs)

State	1976	1977
All India	14.2	17.02
Maharashtra (including Bombay)	2.9	3.3
Gujerat	1.3	1.5
Uttar Pradesh	1.07	1.4
Tamil Nadu	1.5	1.8

B. Outstanding Credit of Scheduled Commercial Banks (As of the last Friday of December 1977; amounts in millions of Rs)

District	Total credit	Of which for trade
Bombay	21,297.7	5,360.8
Kaira (Gujerat)	485.7	34.9
Kanpur	1,071.3	123.2
Amritsar	662.3	79.2

Sources: Information in part A was obtained from *Statistical Tables Relating to Banks in India, 1977* (Bombay: Reserve Bank of India, 1978), p. 56. Part B is from a communication from the Credit Planning Cell, Reserve Bank of India, Bombay, April 15, 1980.

by Shikarpuris and finance companies, we must assume that the Shikarpuris and finance companies deal with people who do not have access to sufficient lower-priced finance from either informal sources or the banks, and that seems largely the case.

Normal brokerage is less than 0.5% of the loan principal (on an annual basis), but Shikarpuri brokers charge, as we noted, 2%. In no case that we know of does the broker guarantee the loan, but his continuance in business is obviously based on his track record in finding good borrowers who repay on schedule.

Along with lending rates, tables 2 and 3 include some estimates of the size of the informal markets we surveyed. Short of an economic census, it is impossible to determine what percentage of total capital employed in trade and industry is accounted for by informal lending and what relation informal capital employed has to that provided by the commercial banks who are the other prime urban credit source. Urban cooperatives are relatively small and weak; development finance is available elsewhere but usually not for working capital purposes (from state finance corporations, industrial development corporations, and small-scale industry corporations).

Some of the urban markets surveyed generated some indicative estimates. As much as 50% of the working capital employed in the wholesale cloth trade in Calcutta and 20% of that in the grain trade may have come from the informal market. The percentages in Kanpur and Amritsar in the cloth wholesale market were probably lower. These are markets in which little if any bank finance is available. Small industrial units in the Amritsar powerloom industry get

5%–10% of their capital in peak season from the informal market. The Gujerat *biri* tobacco trade receives 15%–30% of its working capital as advances from Gujerati indigenous-style bankers.

The Banking Commission of 1981 reported that indigenous-style bankers provided one-twelfth to one-half of all credit to various different categories of industrial units.[9] The amount ranged from an average of Rs 300, or 20%, of borrowings for units of under Rs 25,000 capitalization and increased to Rs 35,000, or 7% of capitalization for those with over Rs 750,000 capitalization.

Table 2 also deals with the volume of deposits with indigenous-style bankers and the rates paid on them. Rastogis and Chettiars, but especially Gujerati bankers, had significant public deposits, while "finance companies" were entirely dependent on such deposits.

INSTRUMENTS

The instruments for borrowing in the informal market vary. One of the most common is the demand note, often "informally" endorsed for a term and rate on the back. As a demand bill the instrument avoids the stamp tax on term bills such as those traditionally used by Shikarpuri commercial financiers. The Shikarpuris clearly feel that even with the added cost the stamp gives their notes greater authority, and in any case only stamped notes can be discounted with the banks. As bank discount has declined, they have largely abandoned this term note. In the smaller centers in the south where bank finance is unavailable, the bulk of Shikarpuri advances are done on demand notes. Shikarpuris have, in any case, been moving away from 90-day promissory notes toward installment credit, which now accounts for about half their advances in the south. The installment notes, especially in the south, are commonly supported by postdated checks, one for each installment payment.

Thirty to forty percent of Gujerati banker finance is done by direct cash advance and 60%–70% through the issue of checklike bills. The Chettiars obtain both promissory notes and securities from their clients, or hire purchase agreements when appropriate. Intermarket lending is most usually done on promissory notes. Finance companies often lend on a term bill. Deposits are often given on the strength of a simple receipt, which now is needed for income tax purposes; traditional deposit receipts simply bore a name and date. Much lending is done by discounting demand notes, trucking bills, and especially postdated checks.

TRANSACTIONS COSTS I: THE COSTS OF ADMINISTRATION

Transactions costs in those markets where brokers are the only intermediary may be as little as 1.2% on annual average outstandings, though they may go as high as 1.2% of turnover, or 4.8% of average outstandings. Shikarpuri brokers charge 2% per annum on each transaction, usually a 3-month loan. Indigenous bankers and commercial financiers typically have higher costs. All of these costs are summarized in tables 5 and 7.

There are several reasons for informal intermediaries' relatively low costs. The employees, if any, in informal credit agencies are typically less well paid and educated, the establishment less elaborate, and the paperwork less complex than in commercial banks. Operations are smaller and typically under the personal supervision of the owner, so numerous cross-checks against fraud are not needed. Not surprisingly, costs are usually somewhat lower

Table 5 Data on Different Informal Credit Market Agencies

	Expense ratios		Spreads between borrowers and lenders			
Type of agency	% Wages and salaries to total expenses	% Rental to total expenses	Cost of lendable funds in % per annum (as % of working funds)	Charge to borrower in % per annum	Margin	Deposit cost in % per annum
Shikarpuris	25	20	20/20.5	31.5	11.5	15
Gujeratis (Bombay)	45	20	11	20	9	8
Chettiars	55	15	14	24.5	10.5	9
Rastogis	35	25	14	20.5	6.5	9
Finance companies	...	...	15	26.5	11.5	10

Source: Data gathered by C. V. Aiyar, 1979.

Table 6 Transactions Costs of Commercial Banks as Percentage of Outstanding Loans and Advances (1975)

Bank	Administration	Default loss	Total
Syndicate bank	2.24	.52	2.76
Other small enterprise (nonindustrial, small business loans)	2.75	1.00	3.75
Large metropolitan bank	1.70	.70	2.40

Source: V. V. Bhatt and Alan R. Roe, "Capital Market Imperfections and Economic Development," World Bank Staff Working Paper no. 338 (Washington, D. C.: World Bank, July 1979), p. 42.

than those reported by the Indian commercial banks, as shown in table 6.

The intermediaries in the informal market have a limited span of lenders and borrowers. The largest brokers surveyed in Kanpur and Amritsar dealt with 15–30 firms each, on both the lending and borrowing side. The Shikarpuri brokers in Bombay deal with a clientele that changes but may be no larger at any given time. Shikarpuri market borrowers are usually expected to deal with only one broker, but lenders may deal with many and thus they constitute the market. Gujerati indigenous-style bankers rarely have more than 200 clients in a single branch.

By contrast, commercial banks deal with larger and more rapidly changing clienteles, who are far more varied in terms of the markets in which they deal. While this gives them a flexibility in adjusting to market fluctuations, they lose in the detailed knowledge of their clients, and thus they have increased information costs.

TRANSACTIONS COSTS II: BAD DEBTS AND RESERVES

Besides administrative costs, a major transaction cost is typically represented by bad debts (see tables 6 and 7). Bad debt figures, as reported,

Table 7 Transactions Costs as Percentage of Working Funds of Informal Credit Systems

Type	Administration	Default loss	Total
Shikarpuri	4.5	1.0	5.5
Gujerati (Bombay)	2.5	0.5	3.0
Chettiars	3.1	1.5	4.6
Rastogi	3.5	1.5	5.0

Source: Data gathered by C. V. Aiyar, 1979.

are particularly questionable because of the obvious opportunities they present to "whiten" money that has been kept off the account books. The 5%–10% of profits reported as bad debt may thus be an underestimate, since it is understood that income tax authorities will rarely allow more.

Informal intermediaries avoid legal proceedings. They find them too costly and the resulting judgments hard to collect. For some, the fact that bad debts can be used to "whiten" money on which income tax has not been paid is also a reason not to pursue them. In any case, bad debts are usually compromised or rescheduled.

Whatever the precise figures, it is clear that bad debts are few and relatively easy to accommodate. In fact, they are roughly comparable to or slightly higher than those reported for small-scale enterprise lending by the commercial banks. But it is generally understood that the commercial banks seriously understate their losses on these small-scale enterprise loans.

One cost advantage of the informal agencies is their exemption from the large idle reserve requirements imposed on the organized sector—over 30% of total deposits. The larger proportion of their own capital that they use, however, achieves a somewhat similar anti-inflationary effect.

SUMMARY

Legal, informal financial market intermediaries finance much trade in certain commodities and 10%–30% of the capital needs of small-scale producers like powerloom owners and pharmaceutical manufacturers. Despite the rapidly increasing bank credit for small-scale industrial units, most of these units find it necessary to go into the informal market, at least during their busy season. The rates in the informal financial markets are generally 2%–4% higher than the bank lending rates, but there is great variety in rates and forms of lending. Very small enterprises when served by these markets directly may pay nominal rates as much as 10% higher than normal bank rates, but usually this sort of unit is financed through trade credit refinanced through the informal market and increasingly by discount facilities. In southern Gujerat, a parallel system of indigenous-style bankers successfully serves much of the urban economy. Elsewhere informal markets are dominated by commercial financiers like the Shikarpuris or by brokers.

This informal market provides funds for purposes like wholesale trade, which the banks do not finance sufficiently, more rapidly than the banks can for those who require speed like exporters, and without security for those including restaurant owners and building contractors for whom security is difficult to produce.

The operating margins—the transaction costs and bad debt experience of these markets—are by and large superior to the banks' and their normal lending rates are 2%–4% higher. They benefit from lower information search, overhead, and reserve maintenance costs.

The Shikarpuri financiers of Bombay and South India might be presumed to be an exception since their margins and rates are higher than the banks by a considerable margin, but some of this is due to the limited funds in their market due to the banks' cutting off funds since 1970 and the resulting pressures of demand. One also might consider that their borrowers represent relatively high risks, and perhaps increasingly so as the banks accommodate their safer clients.

The result of the existence of these markets is that more credit is provided to activities such as wholesale trade and smaller-scale industry than otherwise, and their activities can be correspondingly expanded. The resulting pattern of economic activity will be a closer approximation to the pattern dictated by the market than would otherwise be the case.

Originally published as Thomas A. Timberg and C. V. Aiyar, 'Informal Credit Markets in India', *Economic Development and Cultural Change*, Vol. 33, No. 1, 1984, pp. 43–59.

NOTES

[#] This paper emerges from a broader study sponsored by the IBRD (World Bank), the results of which are available in a monograph by Thomas A. Timberg and C. V. Aiyar, *Informal Credit Markets in India*, Domestic Finance Studies 62 (Washington, D.C.: IBRD, 1980). Some of the theoretical schema used here is contained in V. V. Bhatt and Alan R. Roe, "Capital Market Imperfections and Economic Development," World Bank Staff Working Paper no. 338 (Washington, D.C.: World Bank, July 1979), pp. 78–82. We wish to thank the numerous commentators on that study and monograph, including R. Krishnan, T. N. Srinivasan, U Tun Wai, V. V. Bhatt, S. Yusuf, Promodh Malhotra, B. S. Minhas, Avishay Braverman, Michael Lipton, Dale Adams, and Raymond Goldsmith. Needless to say, the resulting product is our own and in no sense reflects the position of the commentators or of the World Bank. These data were collected in 1978–79, and much has changed since then. In particular, a whole set of regulatory initiatives have been proposed which limit the scope of the markets surveyed.

1. Earlier treatments include J. A. Bottomley, "The Cost of Administering Private Loans in Underdeveloped Rural Areas," *Oxford Economic Papers*, N.S. 15 (July 1963): 154–63; U Tun Wai, "Interest Rates Outside the Money Markets of Underdeveloped Countries," *IMF Staff Papers* 6 (November 1957): 80–142; J. A. Bottomley, "Interest Rate Determination in Underdeveloped Rural Areas," *American Journal of Agricultural Economics* 57 (2d quarter 1975): 279–91, "Monopoly Profit as a Determinant of Interest Rates in Underdeveloped Rural Areas," *Oxford Economic Papers* 16 (November 1964): 431–37, and "The Premium for Risk as a Determinant of Interest Rates in Underdeveloped Rural Areas," *Journal of Economics* 77 (November 1963): 637–47. U Tun Wai updates his work in "A Revisit to Interest Rates Outside the Organized Money Markets of Underdeveloped Countries," *Banca Nazionale de Lavoro Review* 122 (September 1977): 291–312. Some specific studies include Yung Chul Park, *The Unorganized Financial Sector in Korea, 1945–75*, Studies in Domestic Finance 28 (Washington, D.C.: World Bank, Public Finance Division, 1976); Richard E. Benedick, "The Money Market in Iran," *Pakistan Development Review 2* (1962): 406–21.

2. The data for this article come from a series of selected interviews with lenders, borrowers, intermediaries, and trade associations involved with informal credit markets. Over the course of the study almost 1,000 people were interviewed (not always singly) by three investigators, and these interviews represent the data base for the article. More complete details on the survey are available in Aiyar and Timberg, *Informal Credit Markets in India.*

3. These Indian markets have been extensively studied both in monographic literature and by various

government commissions of inquiry. Most recently, see, e.g., the *Report of the Banking Commission* (Bombay: Government of India, 1972), 413–68. The standard work is still L. C. Jain, *Indigenous Banking in India* (London: Macmillan Co., 1929). They are treated in passing in Raymond W. Goldsmith, *The Financial Development of India, 1860–1977* (New Haven, Conn.: Yale University Press, 1983).

4. See n. 3 above and Thomas A. Timberg, *The Marwaris* (New Delhi: Vikas, 1978); and Raman Mahadevan, "Immigrant Entrepreneurs in Colonial Burma—an Exploratory Study of the Role of Nattukottai Chettiars of Tamil Nadu, 1880–1930," *Indian Economic and Social History Review* 15 (1978): 329–58; "Pattern of Enterprise of Immigrant Entrepreneurs: A Study of Chettiars in Malaya, 1880–1930," *Economic and Political Weekly* 15 (1978): 146–52; and "The Development of Modern Entrepreneurship in the Chettiar Community of Tamil Nadu, 1900–1930" (paper presented at the Indian History Conference, n.d.).

5. John G. Gurley, "Financial Institutions in the Savings Investment Process, I," in *Readings in Financial Institutions*, ed. Leon T. Ketchum and Marshall D. Kendall (Boston: Houghton Mifflin, 1966), p. 14.

6. Normally interest is paid when the note is paid off, or on current account for credits from Gujerati bankers. In that case it is collected when the account is brought into balance. Shikarpuris and some other lenders take their interest in advance, and we have taken that into account in reporting their rates on a basis comparable to others. In each case, there may be some incidental fees—brokerage, charity, *shigriti* (speed money), and stamp taxes—but we consolidate these in our reported rates.

7. *Indebtedness of Rural Households and Availability of Institutional Finance* (Bombay: Reserve Bank of India, 1977), p. 146.

8. See also S. Ghatak, *Rural Money Markets in India* (Delhi: Macmillan Co., 1976), pp. 98–101.

9. *Report of the Banking Commission 1972*, pp. 144–46; and *Economic and Political Weekly* 15 (March 8, 1980): 490.

MERCANTILE COMMUNITIES

SECTION II

12

Merchant Communities
Identities and Solidarities

C.A. Bayly

Commercial activity in India has historically been dominated by merchant banking communities. These include Banias, Marwaris, Khattris, Bhatias, Khojas, and Parachas in the north Indian hinterland; Gujarati Banias, Parsis, and Muslim traders in the western Indian economy and the maritime trade between the Gujarat coast and Persian Gulf, Arabia and Africa; Sindhis (especially from the *bhaiband* segment) in northwestern parts; and Chettiars and Komatis in South India.

Thus, it is important to ascertain the basis of commercial solidarities and mercantile identities before commencing any discussion of merchant groups.* Needless to say, this has been debated extensively. Some scholars have emphasized the importance of religion, ethnicity, and language in fostering solidarities and structuring mercantile identities. Strong cases have also been made for the role of regional identities and common localities. In some studies, especially relating to the Chettiars, caste has been regarded as a corporate element critical in structuring mercantile communities. In an influential work, anthropologist David Rudner regards caste membership as a

* There has been much discussion on merchant groups since D.R. Gadgil's (with staff of Gokhale Institute of Politics and Economics, Pune) *Notes on the Rise of Business Communities in India* (New York, Institute of Pacific Affairs, 1951) and his *Origins of the Modern Indian Business Class: An Interim Report* (New York, Institute of Pacific Affairs, 1959). See, for instance, Helen Lamb, 'The Indian Business Communities and the Evolution of an Industrial Class', *Pacific Affairs*, Vol. 18, No. 2, June 1955; Andrew E. Brimmer, 'The Setting of Entrepreneurship in India', *Quarterly Journal of Economics*, Vol. 119, No. 4, December 1955; Dwijendra Tripathi (ed.), *Business Communities of India: A Historical Perspective* (Delhi, Manohar, 1984); and Philippe Cadene and Denis Vidal (eds), *Webs of Trade: Dynamics of Business Communities in Western India* (Delhi, Manohar, 1997).

social investment yielding 'symbolic capital' which could be invested in corporate and quasi-corporate groups.†

In this article, noted historian Chris Bayly analyses the basis of merchant solidarities. Scrutinizing historical data on the cultural prestige, *entrepot* position, and prosperity of Benares of the late eighteenth and early nineteenth centuries, Bayly concludes that while caste may have been significant, it cannot be considered the primary basis of merchant organization. Caste may have played a role in the organization of trading diasporas at the level of geographically-extended kin groups, may even have been important to the socio-economic organization of artisan groups and may have held implications for general mercantile status in terms of *varna*, but it was not the prime parameter of mercantile organization. Instead, a wide array of principles operated to organize commercial solidarities and networks, beyond and across caste ties. According to Bayly, 'Forms of arbitration, market control, brokerage, neighborhood communities and, above all, conceptions of mercantile honor and credit breached caste boundaries, however construed, and imposed wider solidarities on merchant people.' Thus, while Bayly does not discount that caste played a commercial role, he forcefully argues that the complex system of trade could not be explained in terms of caste alone.

The 'pre-modern' Indian merchant has achieved considerable theoretical importance in several fields of study. Historical accounts of the expansion of European private merchants into the Indian interior have suggested that groups of Indian traders played a significant part in providing finance for their enterprises.[1] Politically, the great trader-bankers are known to have been prominent in the factional conflicts in Bengal and Benares which culminated in these provinces' loss of effective sovereignty to the East India Company.[2] In economic historiography the stress has varied widely. For recent Indian commentators, the late Moghul merchant, benefiting from a widely monetized and commercialized cash-crop economy and a sophisticated system of *hundi*-brokerage,[3] was the prototype for an indigenous Indian bourgeoisie whose development was frustrated by the impact of colonialism. For western historians of economic development, the traditional merchant, based on a small family firm, hoarding resources, and tramelled by market poverty, lack of investment opportunities, and arbitrary political power has been the shadowy standard by

† David Rudner argues that caste was central to the success of the Chettiars as a commercial community and was itself constituted by the nature of their economic enterprise. It played the role of a corporate financial institution, allowing the community to take advantage of economic opportunities. He argues that caste organization must not be seen as an artifact of colonial politics but that commercial considerations shaped caste and it functioned as a corporate group in the accumulation and distribution of capital. Rudner also shows how economically 'irrational' activity and ritual was important to commercial activity and points out that non-tangible forms of capital such as reputation, prestige, and religious and social relations were important in commercial activity and capital accumulation. See David W. Rudner, *Caste and Capitalism in Colonial India: The Nattukottai Chettiars* (Berkeley, University of California Press, 1994). The picture is somewhat complicated in the case of the Chettiars because there was also complete congruence between caste and locality for the Chettiars as they all originated from 78 villages in Paddukottai state.

which movements towards a more modern entrepreneurial class are judged.[4] Speculation about the pre-modern merchant has been most fecund in sociological literature where interest in social restraints and encouragements to the development of the entrepreneurial spirit has derived from Weber's theses in *The Religion of India.* Recent work in this area has emphasized the fragmentation and bitter internal conflicts of the merchant class which is held to have been generally divided along the lines of 'caste', religion, and town neighbourhood.[5] Following Gideon Sjoberg,[6] the low, even outcaste, status of the merchant has been emphasized, and the town he inhabits has been described in terms of an Indian derivation of the 'pre-industrial city', the Moghul court-camp settlement which was characteristically dominated by the land-controlling aristocrats.

The volume of theoretical speculation about the pre-modern merchant is almost in inverse proportion to what is known about him. In historical literature, the Jagat Seths have served as the single, recurring example of the early commercial collaborating elite. Indian historians of the Moghul period have provided valuable information about commodities and flows of trade. But they have only lightly touched on the social and economic organization of the merchant classes and their analyses are generally confined to the 'high' Moghul period. Sociologists have relied to an alarming extent on several important introductory articles, in particular D. R. Gadgil's *Origins of the Modern Indian Business Class.*[7] Two particular phrases in this work, to the effect that outside Gujarat, 'trade organizations embracing more than one caste appear to have been uncommon in the Eighteenth Century', and that in this period, 'social and economic functions were merged into and managed by the caste',[8] have been adduced as historical evidence to support sociological theories. Yet Gadgil's own evidence is limited to secondary sources and the whole drive of his argument is to emphasize that remarkably little is known about the organization of trade in the eighteenth century. What has happened is that in the absence of historical data a consensus has been built up on the basis of random insights which treats the pre-modern Indian merchant and the traditional city as single, undifferentiated types. This in turn has led historians such as Kenneth Gillion to discount as special cases their own solidly-based research findings because they do not fit with the prevailing sociological constructs of the past. In fact, Gillion's description of Ahmedabad with its 'corporate tradition and spirit, an hereditary bourgeois elite, and a history of indigenous financial, commercial and industrial activity'[9] has much evidence to recommend it as a type of some classes of larger cities, or sectors within cities, in pre-industrial India and deserves to be set alongside the palace-market model. This essay suggests that Benares in the early colonial period (1780 to 1820) was another such unified city inhabited by a high status commercial community whose economic organizations and 'moral community' breached caste and neighbourhood boundaries in many important aspects. My aim is not to discount the value of the sociological theories as types, or to present a general description of the economic and social structure of Benares city. It is merely to suggest that a 'burgher' city could exist in late eighteenth-century north Indian conditions and to establish a rough scheme for the classification of merchants in a pre-modern setting. It may then be easier to go on and ask at what points in their social universe concepts such as caste, Nawabi ideas of status, and arbitrary pre-modern government, which figure prominently in the general theories, became practically relevant to merchants.

SOURCES

Benares is relatively rich in historical materials for the eighteenth and early nineteenth centuries. Its sanctity preserved it from destruction at the hands of the insurgent Jats and Mahrattas, and the 1857 Rebellion left it untouched. The most useful sources remain the local and regional records of the East India Company because of their sheer variety and volume. The evaluations of the Residents and Agents to the Governor-General must be treated with circumspection but 'impersonal' records such as those of the Benares Customs House (India Office Library Range 97)[10] which include translations of depositions by Indian merchants can be relied on to give a partial picture of trading types. The inflexibility of the internal transit duties system introduced under the Regulations of 1795 meant that small traders and hawkers as well as large merchants were involved in summary customs tribunals. The Proceedings of the Resident (1787–95), the Duncan Records, and the Benares commissioners' and collectors' records, which are held in the Regional Records Office, Allahabad, contain a mass of administrative correspondence, plaints and petitions, and reports of Indian subordinates to the Residency on points of custom and practice.[11] Most valuable are the full proceedings of about sixty-two cases held in the Benares Town Court (Adalat) which were appealed to the Resident and were written up into proceedings. The Town Adalat with its head magistrate was established by Warren Hastings in 1783 as a lineal successor to the tribunal of the town *kotwal* (an appointee of the Moghul Emperor), who added the police jurisdiction of the Faujdar's Office to his own civil and criminal powers during the period of the Benares Raj and continued to exist as a subordinate magistrate after 1783.[12] For the rural areas, the Raja's 'Mulky Court' continued to function, subject to increasing interference by the Resident. The cases in the proceedings record the pleadings of the lawyers of commercial people and landlords in a court where no Europeans were present and where judgments were ostensibly made according to 'custom', 'the custom of the caste', 'the Shasters', and 'Mahomedan Law'. They give an unusual insight into the attitudes of eighteenth-century Indians, subject to the caveat that only certain types of litigant were able to prosecute their cases to the highest court and that it is often difficult to be sure what eighteenth-century English terms such as 'respectability', 'calling', 'profession', etc., are supposed to represent in the Persian originals which no longer exist.[13]

Private records of various sorts are also available. For the period after 1840, several families, especially in the *mohullas* of Chaukhambha and Shivala[14] preserved bankers' books or *bahi khatas* which include daily household expenses as well as commercial transactions. In one case a correspondence book of a banker for the period 1829–45, containing *mahajani* notes and Persian letters to clients, officers of government, and the Raja, has been preserved.[15] But generally the existing pre-1830 private papers appear to be *firmans*, property deeds, records of court cases, and stray *hundis* or promissory notes. Nevertheless, these can be used in conjunction with interview materials and direct examinations of the *havelis* of the old city to build up a picture of residential patterns and traditional social connections. Family history material is available in private manuscript forms and also in compilations of the 1920s and 1930s such as the *Agrawal Jati ka Itihas*,[16] *Oswal Jati ka Itihas*,[17] *Vanshwali Sipahi Nagar*

Kashi Niwasi,[18] etc. These must, however, be used with great circumspection and provide only a very shaky base for statistical studies of social mobility or demographic growth. Important families are omitted because they were extinct before the later compilations were made or because they refused to cooperate with the authors of the survey. Most seriously, genealogies and histories are often idealized. There was a historical stereotype for a prestigious commercial family. Ancestors were great *mahajans* who lent to the Moghuls and were ruined by them; they were driven from Delhi by Nadir Shah; they aided Warren Hastings against Cheyt Singh, and so on. One aspect of the rising status of lower commercial people in the nineteenth century was that their family histories came more and more to resemble those of the great merchant princes.

LEVELS OF TRADING AND COMMERCIAL ACTIVITY

Following, for convenience, Irfan Habib's classification, we can distinguish three levels of trading activity around Benares during this period. First there was an upper stratum of credit-worthy, affluent, and politically powerful trader-bankers who maintained inter-regional luxury trades and provided credit note facilities for regional authorities remitting land-revenue or tribute. This type of business involved large capital, high risks, and relatively large profits. It was closely dependent on the safety of the long-distance trade routes and on the affluence of the landed and service classes which congregated in the town centres. The gathering of many powerful families of immigrant trading people reflected the periodic decay and revitalization of the long-distance trade routes. As trades declined, families which had been dependent on them moved to intensive moneylending in the town and its environs. The sequence of dominant commercial people in Benares went something like this:

(a) Seventeenth-century trades through Surat-Agra-Benares-Murshidabad in fine cloth and silks left in Benares 'residual' communities of Gujarati Vaishyas which provided the oldest and most prestigious members of the city's commercial oligarchy.[19] Some Purbiya ('Eastern') Khattri families which moved into Hindustan from the Punjab at an early date, appear to have reached Benares in this period, probably moving down the thriving Multan-Agra-Benares-Bengal trade route, along which they exported Kashmiri shawls, hill fruits, and horses;[20]

(b) The mid-eighteenth century saw the rise of the Deccan Bundelkhand-Benares trade, serviced particularly by Gosains and Maharashtrian 'Kallea' firms which benefited from the growing wealth of the Mahratta military aristocracy. A seasonal flow of credit notes from Bengal and the Deccan brought by pilgrims to Benares consolidated links of credit and trade through the city to the east and south west.[21] A series of powerful Pacchaina ('Western') Khattri families, mostly cloth trading Mehras from central Punjab by origin, and Deccan or Agra-based Oswal Jains, also diversified into the provinces of Oudh, Benares, and Bengal during this period. The relative decay of Multan, Delhi, and Lahore and the re-emergence of the shawl trade through the more secure mountainous route of Kashmir-Bilaspur-Moradabad facilitated the eastward migration. The 'new' Khattri merchants were sometimes associated as government treasurers with the Nawabs and Rajas of the sub-Moghul courts and displayed a partially Islamicized life-style. In Benares the most important families of this sort were those of Lala Kashmiri Mull and of Gokal Chand.[22] Though their political power and association with the revenue-farms atrophied under British rule, they continued to remit Benares silk goods to the Sikh states before and after the annexation of the Punjab;[23]

(c) The late eighteenth and early nineteenth century saw the height and decline of the luxury Bundelkhand trade route.[24] The Gosain groups of Benares and Mirzapur either declined absolutely or moved into moneylending, property ownership,[25] or the cotton trade.[26] The emergence of a massive trade in this staple through Agra, Mirzapur, and Bengal to the British or China markets was the most profound innovation in the long-distance trade patterns which accompanied the early stages of colonial rule.[27] The social effects on Agra, Kalpi, and Mirzapur were considerable, but while Benares merchants were involved in financing and import for local consumption, it is difficult to find examples of fast social mobility resulting from wealth acquired through cotton trading in the city. More obviously, newcomers were families moving into banking on the basis of government service and connections with the British authorities. These included the Rai Patnimal,[28] Fateh Chand Sahu,[29] and Sipahi Nagar families which opted for the British as Mahratta and Oudh influence in Hindustan weakened. Inter-regional trades in *lac*-dye, salt, opium, indigo, and sugar continued important for these families as occasional 'speculations', but the return on moneylending to the landed aristocracy of Benares province appears to have become the most important guarantee of their income. Besides the great trade and banking families, long-distance trade also provided the livelihood for large numbers of *arethias* or commodity brokers who stored and released to the market the foreign merchants' commodities. *Banjaras*, nomadic grain merchants moving over great distances with herds of pack animals, also survived into the British period. But the establishment of a regular Commissariat Department gradually restricted this type of trade to the medium or local levels.

Medium level trade and its associated webs of services and credit provision had a range of about fifty or a hundred miles from Benares and was likely to be associated with weekly or bi-weekly commodity markets in large villages and with small towns such as Azamgarh, Jaunpur, Phulpur, and Kantit. The most characteristic figures in medium level trade were the wholesale dealers of the commodity and foodgrain marts on the periphery of the city and the larger dealers of cloth, or *bazazas*, in the central markets. They were connected with another class of small town trader who might be called a 'commercial *malik*'. Typically, these commercial *maliks* worked from the base of a rural *golah* or grain market but held *dukans* in a series of villages around. There is some evidence to suggest that this class was important in buying up the revenue farmers' share of the harvest when land-revenue was still paid in kind. In the few cases where a record of the property of such 'commercial *maliks*' has survived as a result of inheritance cases,[30] one can observe that they owned large quantities of draft animals and agricultural implements and had small-holdings farmed for them by dependants. They were evidently more substantial men than the village *bania*. A similar case can be made out for middle-range entrepreneurs dealing in commodities such as liquor and tobacco. The Kalwar distillers based on the lineage centre of Kantit, for instance, appear to have built up capital and then 'invaded' the town of Mirzapur, establishing political power with the police and local magistracy.[31] Other medium-distance trades which converged on Benares included sugar from Ghazipur, chewing and smoking tobacco from Jaunpur, and trade in livestock and bullocks. These were handled by middling merchants in the small towns and wholesalers in Benares. Some articles (such as chewing tobacco) were partly re-exported to other parts of India, reminding one that the medium and long-distance trade networks were often linked. In the Benares region, 'commercial *maliks*' and intermediate *arethias* were drawn from a wide spectrum of castes, including Rajputs, Brahmins, Bhumihars, Telis, and Kalwars as well as local and immigrant Vaishya castes.

On the finance side, groups of moneylenders congregated around the exiled or immigrant town notables of Benares, and serviced a different level of political power from the major trader-bankers. Typical was the group of predominantly Agarwal bankers dependent on the exiled Delhi and Lucknow Moghul notables of the Shivala *Mohulla*.[32] Smaller Kallea and Nagar Brahmin moneylenders served the needs of the estimated 8,000 Mahratta chiefs and noblemen who resided in and around Benares at the close of the eighteenth century.[33] Immigrant Sikh chieftains and Punjabi Ḍiwans swelled this class of financier with their dependants after the fall of the Sikh state.[34]

Parochial commerce in the villages was, of course, centred around the *bania* grain merchant, the rich peasant who lent money and grain, and the petty *banjara* or nomadic peddler trading with ten or a score head of cattle. In addition the customs records reveal a type of trader working an itinerant cyclical trade between periodic *haths* or periodic markets usually on a barter system. Tobacco, sugar, indigo seed, ghee, and vegetables were the staples of this cyclical trade.[35] Also in this local category of trade falls regular interaction between centres of cloth production outside Benares, but within a few hours' journey, and the city itself. Apart from the weavers of the city *mohulla* of Madanpura, Benares citizens appear to have acquired much of their ordinary cloth from the two entrepot and weaving villages of Baragaon[36] (one and a half miles north-west of the city) and Sheopore (two miles west).[37] Individual weavers or merchants of Baragaon and Sheopore brought their goods to city retailers. This sort of relationship between an external productive or entrepot unit and a nearby town was typical of the north Indian city in the period before village products began to feel the pressure of European imports.

The division of trade into three levels is primarily a descriptive convenience, and could no doubt be employed for any trading system. But in the Indian case some structural features did underlie it. Firstly, as far as long-distance trade was concerned, the nature of demand and the prosperity of the consumer market was peculiarly dependent on the affluence of ruling aristocracies and land-controlling elites gathered near the main centres of government. One of the most persistent of the long-distance trades, that in Rajasthan 'Sambher' and Punjabi rock salt, was entirely directed towards the consumption of 'the higher class of people'. Kashmiri shawls (which cost up to Rs 200 a piece) and other woollen goods were luxuries which might remain unsold for several seasons until an aristocratic buyer could be found.[38] The most extended trade routes of all were connected with diamonds and other precious stones which were brought from as far afield as Herat, Kandahar, and Hyderabad along the routes of the Multani traders.[39] The dependence of this level of trade on the upper land-controlling elite was demonstrated by the marked decline of the shawl and luxury piece goods trade in the early years of British rule.

> The late Nawaub Assafful-Dowlah kept up a large establishment of troops throughout these provinces and had a numerous description of natives of high rank employed under his government, whose wants in the luxuries of life increased with their opulence

> which of course was a considerable encouragement to the consumption of spices and the finer articles of the produce and manufactures of Bengal which demand at present does not exist from the reduced state of that description of people . . .[40]

On the other hand, the emergence of long-distance cotton, indigo, and opium trades, directly responsive to the demands of the international market imposed a new network of *kothis* and commercial facilities from Bundelkhand and the Doab along the great rivers to Bengal. In turn, the growth of more local centres associated with some particular land-controlling magnate and the revival of population growth in the cities after 1800 benefited the medium and parochial trades.

Secondly, in the north Indian case, the long-distance level of trade also attained a peculiar degree of definition over both local and medium trade because of the possibilities of rapid and relatively inexpensive riverine carriage. The volume of trade along the Ganges, Jumna, and Goghra Rivers was very large. Related webs of specialization grew up around riverine entrepots which provided storage warehouses, bulking facilities (cotton screws, for instance), insurance firms, and boat serving depots.

Thirdly, all levels of the trading system were closely intermeshed with levels of political authority derived from the control of the land, and these relationships tended to fix and maintain the system of trade itself. A regular return on moneylending to *zamindars* was important to traders who required large capital for long distance trading. The land-controlling elements needed cash to convert, as it were, the seasonal return from the produce of the villages into a permanently available capability for military, marriage, and status expenditure. At the highest level, the big trader-bankers provided *dakhillas*, or advances on the land-revenue, to the Raja of Benares and the revenue farmers.[41] At the lowest level, the rudimentary police system impinged on the trade of hawkers and small market stallholders, and in Benares much of the benefits of this trade was reaped by the *kotwal* and his officers. They in turn provided protection and support for the petty trader.[42]

SOLIDARITIES AND ORGANIZATIONS INSIDE AND OUTSIDE THE CITY

The maintenance of links between traders, especially in long-distance trades, depended on a complex series of relationships which would have been impossible in a trading system characterized exclusively by tight caste groupings or by absolute competition mediated only by dominant political authorities. Extended linkages of kinship and marriage, perceived by contemporary Indians and later commentators as 'caste', played a significant role in reinforcing the community of trust and mercantile intelligence which was essential to long-distance trading. The 'diaspora' of trading groups was accomplished by the hiving-off of younger sons to centres where commercial openings appeared to exist. Links between the firms were maintained because the complex divisions into *gotras*, and within *gotras* into status groups, meant that few suitable matches were available among newly-settled trading people, and they would generally look back to their ancestral area for brides. Bankers' books from later in the century suggest that among the major Khattri and Agarwal families' related branches in different cities provided an important minority of regular correspondents in *hundi* remittance—but it was only a minority, and the *hundi* business was inevitably carried on largely outside the boundaries of kin and caste.[43]

Even in tightly organized family firms some of the most basic relationships of trust were conducted outside the immediate commensal community. Many Benares firms had hereditary families of *munims* or *gomastahs* who were not of the same 'caste'. In the 1780s the great Surat firm Arjunji Nathji Tiwari employed an up-country Brahmin, Mulchand Dube, as their Calcutta *gomastah* and the Benares firm Manohar Das (Agarwal) retained one Harak Ram Tiwari, a Brahmin.[44] The Azmatgarh Agarwal family of Azamgarh and Benares had hereditary Gujarati *munims*;[45] Khattris in Benares were often associated with Brahmin *gomastahs* though some of those were Punjabi Saraswat Brahmins with whom the Khattris were ritually related.[46] Now this is not to deny that considerations of caste status in a wider sense did not to some extent influence the type of mercantile alliances made outside the ritual group. Clearly, there was a preference for the use of Brahmins as commercial agents by the big traders. But this is a very different point from writing that commercial organization was 'merged into' and 'managed by' the 'caste' unit, however caste is defined.

Other solidarities, particularly those based on regional associations, were of importance also. Active trading groups were described in terms of their area of origin, though they themselves might have been acutely aware of caste distinctions. When dealing with the authorities, in particular, they maintained a cohesion based on the regionality of their trades. Thus the 'Sundry merchants of Kabul, Panjab, Multaun etc.'[47] who approached the Resident in 1787 included Khattris, Aroras, Gosains, Moghul, Afghan, and other Muslim merchants, and they had a recognized head. We also come across the 'merchants of the Ducin [Deccan]',[48] and the 'merchants residing in Benares', the 'merchants of Bundelcund', and so on. None of these was a caste-defined group, though certain caste groups may have been prominent within them. Regional origins remained important, as we shall suggest, in living areas,[49] and in domestic language. 'Western' Khattris in Benares in the 1790s still used Punjabi,[50] while Gujarati was used until recently as a domestic language by Vaishya and Brahmin immigrants from that region. The importance of regional attributions, a characteristic of the eighteenth century, has been preserved in the attitude which Indian traders held towards 'Marwaris' in more recent times. Though sometimes applied specifically to the Maheshwari group, the term was often taken to include Oswals and Marwari Agarwals as well.

This 'regionality' of organization was reinforced by the circumstance that merchants trading from a particular area would need to establish relations with particular groups of brokers or *arethias* who themselves dealt with commodities, not with castes. The *arethia* was the crucial link between the merchant and his market. In the case of long-distance luxury trades the merchant was often unable to dispose of his shawls or silks in a single season and the *arethia* was responsible for releasing them to the market when demand appeared. *Arethias* also obtained customs passes for goods and dealt with the authorities on behalf of the merchants. The importance of their role was illustrated by a case in 1811 when a total interruption of the cloth trade was attributed to 'a contention between the Mirzapore Aurotheas [*sic*] and those of Bundelcund, who should monopolise the commission accruing from the agency of the merchants'.[51] A full description of an incident in the Benares jewel trade associated with the case Bowanny Das *v*. Chehta Mull[52] also illustrates the pivotal role of the broker (here called a *dalal*). Khattri merchants had brought jewellery from Kandahar, but the moment when it passed into the hands of the broker was the moment it passed out of the ambit of a caste-defined trade. In fact, the emphasis on brokerage, custodianship, and agency in a sharply seasonal, long-distance trading economy was bound to work against the maintenance of commercial organizations based on ritual distinctions. Only where a group of related families had happened to gain a complete monopoly of a particular trade might caste sentiment and organization act to reinforce monopoly and price-fixing.[53] But in complex and competitive trades this was likely to be the exception rather than the rule.

As far as the organization of commerce was concerned, cities were points where merchants working at different levels of trade were brought into close proximity with each other and with the regional political and legal structures. In both social and economic life the organizations which resulted were characterized by elective or hereditary councils (often called *panchayats*) and by heads, either elective or hereditary, called *chaudhries*. At least four different types of *chaudhries* existed in the Benares urban communities and it is sometimes difficult to separate their roles:[54]

(a) Bazaar *chaudhries*. These acted as intermediaries between the merchants of particular markets and the local authorities, in particular the *kotwal*. They were responsible for local collection of town duties and the maintenance of the standards of weights and measures within the bazaar. They were either appointees of the local authorities or were selected through the offices of private individuals such as relations of the Raja or major trader-bankers who had established marts and were entitled to a share in their produce;

(b) *Chaudhries* of individual trades or crafts who were not also *chaudhries* of caste groups. Their duties were to maintain trade standards, to represent the opinion of the tradesmen to the authorities, and to deal with demands for supply from government officers and notables. In the case of the cloth, grain, and other major trades, the jurisdiction of the *chaudhri* necessarily embraced several communities and the *chaudhri* himself was not always of the 'traditional' commercial castes. In Mirzapur, for instance the *chaudhri* of the cloth merchants in the 1820s was a Dube Brahmin;[55]

(c) *Chaudhries* of individual ritual units who, though they might be tradesmen, were not *chaudhries* of trades. In Benares these were naturally the heads of commensal groups which would be able to exercise ritual sanctions in cases of moral or ritual turpitude. For instance, the 'Eastern' and 'Western' Khattris had separate *chaudhries*, as did various regionally based groups among the Agarwals which did not inter-marry;

(d) *Chaudhries* (or other descriptions of head) who exercised authority over both the economic and ritual life of trades where the 'guild' and caste (*jati* level) were coterminous. This was most likely to be the case among lower artisan groups such as oil-pressers, distillers, and weavers.

Some towns apparently had general councils of trading people with elected heads who arbitrated disputes between various different types of traders. In Benares the Naupatti Sarrafa was the organization which most nearly approximated to this, though strictly it was the society of the major trader-bankers. The Naupatti *mahajans* controlled rates of *hundis*, arbitrated many of the mercantile disputes within the city, and maintained a list of credit-worthy individuals. The organization derived initially from the requirements of the regional authorities.

The Nouputtee mahajans so-called—the Nabob Shujaa oo Dowlah in the plenitude of his power when he determined to raise a forced loan . . . from the Benares bankers, nine of them

[nau] undertook the charge (hissa [share] called puttee).[56]

The descendants of the nine great burghers who saved the city carried the name Naupatti as a hereditary title. They included two Gujarati Vaishya families (one of which provided the hereditary *chaudhri* of the Naupatti), three Agarwals, two Brahmins, and a Khattri. In the course of the nineteenth century, the decline of the Gujaratis left the great Shah family (Agarwal) as effective leaders of the banking community. But, although the state was instrumental in the foundation and perpetuation of the privileges of the Naupatti, the credit-control of the major bankers had by the mid-eighteenth century put them covertly in a position where they could, to use Duncan's own words, 'command the state'.[57] By withholding the issue of advances on the revenue they had a powerful hold over a regional kingdom such as the Raj of Benares. Moreover the revenue farmers remained entirely dependent on the credit they could raise from the bankers. If pressed to extremes, the state could always resort to distraint or coercion, but accommodation was the safest course. Since the great bankers were the channel whereby the grievances of smaller commercial people were brought to the notice of the rulers, the covert influence of the mercantile sector in the eighteenth century state system was substantial.

One of the most important functions discharged by the Naupatti *mahajans* and other 'respectable' bankers was the arbitration of disputes between commercial people. In the majority of the thirty-two cases in the Resident's Proceedings where arbitrations of this sort are set out, parties appointed at least one of their arbitrators from among merchants 'not of the caste'. In a small number of cases arbitrators were appointed from caste-fellows and issues of 'caste custom' were adduced in the pleading. These were concerned with matters of inheritance and the division of property. In the two cases of this sort which actually deal with mercantile disputes between traders of the same caste, strong ritual elements were involved. One, for instance, an 'arbitration of Khuttrees and Sarswat Brahmans' was held as a result of the claim by Sukhoo on Pindee Mull.[58] The claim concerned an ornament which was allegedly deposited with the defendant during a cremation ceremony of the Mehra subcaste at the *ghats;* the other concerned the bearing of the outcaste status of an individual on the discharge of mercantile debts. Clearly there were good reasons why a caste arbitration took place in these cases. But there is no evidence that caste *panchayats* would ordinarily take cognizance of disputes of a mercantile nature, even when they occurred between members of the same caste. Material for the Agarwals from a later period reinforces the distinction between ritual and commercial arbitration.[59] Lalas Fatteh Chand, Harrakh Chand, and Gopal Chand, successively *chaudhries* of the 'Western' Agarwals, often adjudicated mercantile disputes in their role as Naupatti *mahajans,* and some of these were between Agarwals, but in their role as *chaudhries* they dealt specifically with ritual matters.

What is most striking in the caste cases preserved in the records is the apparent amorphousness of *panchayats* and caste custom even in cases of inheritance, adoption, consanguinity, and other matters of a ritual nature. Pleaders are able to throw doubt on the nature of important aspects of ritual procedure; no one has a clear idea of the jurisdiction of a *panchayat* or of the nature of caste custom. These bodies are fraught with faction and show a strong tendency towards differences of wealth and status. In the Pindee Mull case, for instance, it was deposed that 'It is not the fashion of my caste to mention at arbitration others who are poor brethren.'[60] In another case, 'my client says that the arbitrators of her caste will by no means give a decision for her as she is a poor woman'.[61] By any standard the organizations revealed in these cases are not the tightly-bound caste corporations held by Gadgil to have been the only bodies which survived the collapse of regional and state-level power in the late Moghul period.[62] However important caste status may have been for individuals, 'caste custom' was only one of the normative codes to which they might appeal. There were said to be only forty families of the Rastogi caste group in Benares in the 1780s,[63] for instance. Here one may have expected to encounter a close-knit community. But a case of division of profits among heirs revealed a fairly typical pattern. Arbitration by 'custom of the caste' was only one of the several methods of arbitration suggested by the parties and their *vakils*. Others were 'the Shaster', immediate appeal to the city magistrate on the merits of the case, or arbitration by 'creditable shroffs not of the caste'. Caste authority was not necessarily binding, but individuals might opt for it in preference to other tribunals if it was to their advantage to do so. The defendant in this case, a powerful man among the Rastogis, was content to leave the matter with his peers and 'was by no means willing to have the cause decided by Hindoo Law'.[64]

One argument produced by the complainants' *vakil* suggests why caste arbitrations might have been avoided even in cases concerning marriage and property relations:

> ... altercations will ensue; some are related to my constituents, some to Bowanny Das and an arbitration of those of their caste or an enquiry into their customs will create differences and nothing will be done.[65]

One piece of evidence in the Pindee Mull case suggests that it was the first general arbitration of Khattris and their Brahmins within four years.[66] The evident difficulty of assembling more than fifty, and possibly as many as two hundred, men of great dignity to agree on a common pronouncement suggests how cumbersome and ineffective caste arbitration might be in an urban context.

In lower occupational or entrepreneurial groups, there was a much greater congruence between caste and 'guild' types of organization and much more of an individual's life was directed by authorities whose sanctions derived from hereditary positions exercised within ritually-defined groups. Richard Heitler has shown how the caste-councils of weavers, boatmen, bearers, and other artisan groups played an important part in organizing the great strike of 1809. Even here, however, it would be difficult to decide whether the caste units had absorbed and 'managed' commercial organization or whether commercial organization had subsumed and strengthened caste solidarity. Sjoberg notes that in most pre-industrial cities the 'localization of particular crafts and merchant activities in segregated quarters or streets is intimately linked to the society's technological base'.[67] The rudimentary transport system dictates that buyers, middlemen, and sellers must all be concentrated together, and this is likely to increase the strength of community among artisans. In Benares administrative arrangements also contributed to physical concentration and social control.

> The oil merchants reside chiefly together in the suburbs of the city and they erect their dwellings in the neighbourhood of the customs chokeys [posts] in a position which whilst it facilitates their smuggling interpreses [*sic*] during the dark of the night renders it extremely embarrassing to the collector of customs to decide whether the oil when seized was seized within the prescribed limits or not. These people are all under the influence of one man who they look

upon as their chowdree. If therefore an arrangement can be made with this man, the beoparies [merchants] would have no further inducement to smuggle.[68]

In the case of the weavers of Madanpura their status as a Muslim 'subcaste', the centralized organization required for controlling price levels, and their relations with the authorities all tended to reinforce the identification of the quasi-guild with caste. The Magistrate noted in 1815,

This class of people who subsist by daily labour, are becoming so formidable that not an individual case occurs in which a weaver is involved but hundreds immediately assemble. Every summary proceeding is laid before the Magistrate and whatever costs they may incurr by the suit they are ready to pay.[69]

In both these cases a continuity between the administration and the social unit is apparent. Anthropologists have tended to assume a model of the progressive decay, during the nineteenth century, of organic caste *panchayats* fortified with generally accepted bodies of custom dispensed by hereditary heads. Owen Lynch, for instance, presents a fascinating picture of the displacement (after 1900) among the Jatavs in Agra of traditional caste leaders by 'big men' of the political broker type.[70] But it is, of course, possible that the traditional leaders of 1900 were descendants of 'big men' of an earlier period when fast administrative and economic change had impinged on the Jatavs. In the Benares region in the 1830s, for instance, the boatmen of Benares and Mirzapur were subject to unusually heavy demands for boat supply from the Commissariat Department and the local authorities. A dispute arose among the Ghat Manjis, the several families which claimed the right to head the boatmen.

The result of this feud has been incessant applications from a variety of individuals for the appointment of Ghaut Manjee, some claiming it as an hereditary right, others from their election by *panchayat*, a third by perwannas [charters] from Government and Mr. J. Duncan, and four or five others as belonging to them individually as chowdrie of separate ghauts.[71]

It may be acceptable at this stage of our knowledge to suggest that for upper and middling merchants, caste (in the *jati* sense) was not, and could not practically have been, the prime parameter of the organization of trade. Political, economic, and ritual factors, however, tended to make guild-type organizations congruent with caste in the sense of Bailey's 'caste status groups'[72] among artisan and inferior traders. Even here, however, we must beware suggesting too great a discontinuity between the state and economic organization, on the one hand, and 'caste bodies', on the other.

CATEGORIES OF STATUS

Transcending regional, caste, and occupational identifications, we glimpse in the town court proceedings a series of categories of status among Benares mercantile people, which provided an ideal pattern for social mobility. Reading down the columns from highest to lowest status, the hierarchy went something like this:

MERCHANTS	MONEY-DEALERS
Naupatti Mahajan	*Naupatti Mahajan*
Kothiwal (principal of a business house)	*Kothiwal*
Mahajan (merchant)	*Mahajan*
WHOLESALERS	
RETAILERS	
Beopari (tradesman)	*Sarraf* (money-dealer)
Bakkal ('grocer')	
Paikar ('chandler')	
Faria ('huckster')	
Bisatta (pedlar)	*Khurdea* (petty, wandering money-changer)

These categories were imprecise and were often used loosely both by Indians and Europeans. Again, most merchants were also money-dealers, while occupational attributions which cut through these divisions of status were often used (e.g., *bazaza* was applied to large cloth wholesalers as well as small retailers). Buchanan in his complex discussion of the dignity of contemporary commercial people in Patna[73] implies the existence of at least four criteria of status. Firstly, the extent of dealings was a factor. Theoretically, a *paikar* did not deal with goods under the value of one or two annas, while a *faria* did. Secondly, the extent of capital was significant. A *faria* was supposed to have a capital of under Rs 50. Thirdly, it was important whether a merchant worked face-to-face with his clients. The most elevated merchants, *mahajans* and *kothiwals*, were wholesalers who used agents to run any retail trade they might conduct. Finally, Buchanan implies that a trader's origin, caste, and the ritual acceptability of his trade might influence aspects of status. Thus a *bakkal* was a rural trader of 'low origin', while some really big merchants remained *mahajans* rather than *kothiwals* because they dealt in degrading articles such as shoes.

What comes out clearly from the Benares material is the importance of 'credit' in the eyes of one's peers and status in legal arenas. The *bakkal* and the *sarraf* held higher status than the *faria* or *khurdea* respectively due to their possession of a shop, a location, and somewhere where they could be 'dunned' or subject to mercantile coercion if necessary. The feature of a *mahajan* in the town context was to use standard bankers' books (*bahi khatas*) and to have his credit notes accepted without investigation in the bazaar. A high commercial status in Benares arose, in fact, from participation in what has been called the 'moral community' of the merchants. This was demonstrated in acceptance of word-of-mouth agreements unsupported with bonds, and access to interest-free or low-interest loans from peers in cases of mercantile embarrassment.

Purely verbal agreements based on trust of a man's respectability were common among high status merchants dealing even in articles of great value such as pearls. Among brokers, poorer merchants, and foreigners, however, man-to-man agreements were not always the rule, and instead we find cases where mediators such as religious mendicants or *atits* were used to give an external religious sanction to the bargain.[74] The 'moral community' of the 'professed *mahajans*' was clearly reinforced by certain common religious assumptions. This can be seen in the cases of mercantile coercion through *dharna* or 'dunning' with the aid of religious sanctions, which the British tried to prohibit in Benares. The creditor sitting before the house of the debtor would threaten to impair his own caste or ritual status, or to do himself, or cause hired Brahmins to do themselves, physical injury.[75] This would by implication detract from the religious merit of the debtor. Obviously, such sanctions could only be effective in a tightly-knit face-to-face society; and they were not universally applicable even among high-status merchant groups. But they were not negligible. When financial embarrassment put intolerable strains on a 'respectable' individual, he might choose suicide rather than dishonour, or flight back to the ancestral village. The number of suicides by defaulters in Benares astonished Jonathan Duncan who remarked on 'the particular propensity which the natives of this country seem to have towards taking poison upon slight pretences'.[76]

The upper merchants' moral community was not a consequence of their relationship with political authorities or the legal structure, but prior to it. The production of a recognized *mahajan*'s books before the *kotwal*'s tribunal or later before the city court was considered evidence of greater value than even the oral deposition of respectable people. This in turn required that the system of book-keeping should be regular, and in the course of time, keeping proper books itself became the chief characteristic of the *mahajan*.[77] These assumptions about the veracity of account books were taken a stage further by the Naupatti *mahajans* who claimed that, for them, it was sufficient merely to have their agents affirm in open court that a particular entry was in their books, and the enforced production of books in court became itself a source of discredit to them.

Legal status, credit-worthiness, and mercantile status, then, were closely interlinked. The accumulation of wealth alone did not guarantee acceptance as a *mahajan*. Some examples will help make clear the distinction. The father and grandfather of Ghoreeb Das of Mirzapur, for instance, had sold slippers 'in distressed circumstances'. Their family house had to be mortgaged, but the two sons continued to run the business. Ghoreeb Das says,

> I hired a shop and lived for fifteen years as the gomastah of Chehra Sah and Govind Dauss. Thereafter I quitted their employ having acquired some money and supported myself by acting as a shroff and trading in cotton. Fortune became auspicious and I came to be considered as a mehajin.[78]

Ram Narayan and Kanhaiya Lal, trading in Benares and Kanpur in cloth and grain, were of doubtful status, according to the official delegated to report on them; they were 'believed to have realised large sums during the late wars [with the Mahrattas] in the grain department and have since been called shroffs'. Doubts about them were related to their lavish house-building and their reputation as 'expensive people', which reflected badly on their mercantile credit.

In Benares the highest status among the merchant people was that of Naupatti *mahajan*. This was, as we have seen, an hereditary title, and though families might drop out of the category through demographic extinction, it could not be entered. Significantly, Wilson's *Glossary* referred to the Naupatti as 'the highest caste of Bankers of Benares',[79] an indication of the manner in which any closed social group came to be regarded as a 'caste' by the early administrators. But other 'respectable *mahajans*' who had business dealings with the court and were exceptionally credit-worthy came to share many of the privileges and much of the status of the Naupatti. Entitlement to attend of right the Maharaja's levees was complemented by exemption from attendance at British courts. The authorities also allowed them to maintain guards and distributed plaques which became a symbol of prestige for the bankers.[80]

We have indicated that merchant society in Benares cannot be described in terms of a series of tight-knit, caste-defined groups. Instead merchant people perceived social distance and patterns of status in terms of credit worth and mercantile honour and this classification was not necessarily congruent with ritual status. People from all the 'twice-born' castes down to the level of the lower Vaishyas (Umar, Keserwani, and Agrehi) could be considered *mahajans* and call upon the services of the Naupatti in arbitrations. The evidence from Benares suggests, however, that a line of differentiation roughly equivalent to the Shudra/Vaishya distinction separated merchants of this sort from members of castes which were technically of much lower ritual status, such as *kalwars, sonars* and *telis*. These castes used each other in arbitrations but do not generally appear to call on the services of Naupatti *mahajans* or merchants from the higher status group. Yet even here low ritual status does not seem to have been an inflexible bar to participation in the community of the merchants.[81] Rich *barhais* and *kalwars*[82] attained great 'respectability' and were mobile in terms of their occupation in Benares and Mirzapur. Moreover it is evident that the political influence of such groups, or of Muslim merchants, in local society was never impaired by their ritual standing. This was unlikely in an area where the police and the magistracy were still dominated by Muslims.

RESIDENTIAL PATTERNS

The residential patterns of commercial people in Benares reflected aspects of their social organization. The traditional unit for analysis of the north Indian city has been the 'caste-*mohulla*', the quarter inhabited either by a single commensal caste group or by a small number of caste groups with some kind of ritual link. In Benares such tightly defined caste *mohullas* were characteristic of some areas inhabited by artisan groups such as weavers, dyers, and low-caste servants. But as far as superior commercial and service people were concerned, the city could be described in terms of spatial communities which were both larger and smaller than the caste-*mohulla* and which were themselves not necessarily congruent with ritual distinctions.[83]

(i) *The Haveli* (lit. great house, palace): This type of dwelling, characteristic of some of the older Hindustani commercial cities, was a large three-or four-storey house which housed several related families (usually parents and the families of their sons).[84] Domestic and ritual servants would be housed within the building, while poorer relatives and clients might inhabit verandahs or makeshift external arcades, paying ground rent to the owner. The *haveli* was an ideal structure for preserving both commercial security and domestic inviolability. Robbers and prying intruders could easily get lost in the maze of keeping-rooms and small courtyards. In the case of the *havelis* of great magnates established on the outskirts of the city, such as the dwellings of the Bhumihar Babus of Ausanganj, Babu Deokinandan, or the Shahzadahs (imperial royal family) of Shivala, the magnate *haveli* became the centre of its own web of service communities.

(ii) *The Neighbourhood Community*: The most obvious physical unit in Benares greater than the *haveli* was the closed street or gated area (*phatakbundy*) to which the word *mohulla* was sometimes applied in official documents.[85] Neighbours were involved in the management and funding of an unofficial security system which provided watchmen and maintained heavy wooden gates at the end of *cul-de-sac* streets. Common veneration of neighbourhood shrines such as the great Vallabhacharya temple, Gopal Mandir, or maintenance of bathing *ghats* could also create community of neighbourhood interest. Attitudes to property, the construction of shrines or the building of *chabutras* in a locality were regulated in theory by meticulous codes of 'neighbourliness'. In particular, neighbours could invoke what is described in the British records as the 'right of vicinity'.[86] That is to say they could claim the right of preemption of property to be sold within a particular gated area. Attestation of property rights or sales before the traditional registration officer, the *kazi*, was also often accomplished by men of the gated area or *mohulla*. Since kin or caste relations regularly did not encompass all the ties within a gated area or *mohulla*, the concept of neighbourhood took on a particular importance. The quality of a man's neighbours affected his credit.

(iii) Wider than the gated area, several weaker ties of community can be seen in operation. Certain areas of the city seem to have been settled in the same historical period by families who were linked by association with some of the patterns of trade and service which we have noted. Regional communities in various degrees of definition are apparent. Bengali Tola and the Madanpura area had become a regional residential area before British rule, and Bengalis of all the upper castes resorted to the Kedareshwar Ghat for prayer.[87] Lahori Tola, rising behind the Manakarnika Ghat, was the residence of many families of Khattris, Aroras, Saraswat Brahmins, and Kayasths who were associated with the Punjabi trades of 1780–1820. The Chaukhambha Bazaar area seems pre-eminently the residence of the great commercial families of the Naupatti who rose during the days of Cheyt Singh and the early British period. The impression is that the oldest commercial areas stretched from around the Aurangzeb Mosque (originally a riverside Hindu temple), north through Gai Ghat and out towards Raj Ghat which was once the main grain depot and an ancient strong-point. The older Mahratta Kallea, 'Sipahi' Nagar, and Gujarati families appear to have lived in the lanes between the Gopal Mandir and Aurangzeb Mosque. Purbiya or 'Eastern' Khattris who emigrated from the Punjab at an early stage also lived away from their Lahori brethren in the Gai Ghat area. Families in these localities were aware of each other's historical associations and often maintained ancient credit relationships with them. These residual regional affiliations were shadowy in Benares, but in Mirzapur they can be seen in much greater definition in the 'Deccani' and 'Bundelkhandi' *mohullas* which were originally settled by the merchant people engaged in trade to those areas.

(iv) At the widest level, people at Benares made a traditional distinction between the *Pacca Mahal* and the *Kacha Mahal*. The former, the 'City Proper', was the central area more or less coterminous with the Police Station (Kotwali) Ward.[88] It was the oldest and holiest part of the city, the residence of the bankers of Benares, unified not only by the complex patterns of intermarriage exhibited by the great Agarwal families, but also by close knowledge of each other's credit and mercantile standing. By contrast, the *Kacha Mahal* was a lower status area, inhabited by travellers, dancing girls, Muslims, and also by the Raja, his collaterals, and the intrusive landholding lineages of the wold Benares Province and western Bihar. In cases of social tension, the chief *mahajans* of the *Pacca Mahal* were consulted on an equal footing with the Bhumihar and Rajput notables of the *Kacha Mahal*.[89] At the same time, they exercised an important role as spokesmen for their poorer clients and the artisan guilds. Though the links between the landed and commercial notables of Benares became blurred in the later nineteenth century, the status of the great traders did not initially derive from their landed associations.

The relationship of these patterns to the traditional caste-*mohulla* unit is difficult to reconstruct. But house deeds and oral evidence suggest the existence of a much more fluid pattern, with members of the higher castes living mixed up together within the gated areas. It is important to note that ritual exclusiveness often appears to be working only at the level of the individual family group inhabiting a single *haveli* or group of two or three *havelis*, and not at the level of community *mohullas* inhabited by five hundred people or more. Contiguous *havelis* were therefore regularly inhabited by members of different caste groups. It is true that when asked about the residential patterns of castes, older men of the city will readily point to areas where 'Khattris', 'Agarwals', or 'Gujarati Vaish' are said to have their ancestral places, and this may superficially resemble the community-*mohulla* model. But on investigation the historically prior unit often appears to have been the single *haveli*. What seems to have happened is that wealthier immigrants to Benares in the late eighteenth or early nineteenth century would purchase a single *haveli* which would serve the needs of the family group until it grew too large. Later nearby *havelis* would, if possible, be purchased or built. Over two or three generations the original single family settlement might grow into a largish area of housing inhabited by distantly related caste-fellows. What dictated the pace of this development was not only a general preference to live with one's ritual group among immigrants, but also the rate of demographic growth of the family, and the state of the local property market which determined whether it was feasible for younger branches to continue to live contiguously. Families of the Assarpurwal Gujarati Vaish, for instance, lived in a gated area near the Gopal Mandir temple.[90] They derived from one family, associated with the firm 'Madhusudhan Das' which inhabited one single *haveli*. In the mid-nineteenth century, as daughters came to marriageable age, members of the sub-caste from outside Benares had to be attracted since the community in Benares was unable to provide matches who were not over-closely related to the brides. Young men were attracted with offers of a house, an amount of money, and some gold. Whether they settled in the vicinity of the parent *haveli* depended on the availability of housing. But since several 'secondary' family groups came to be located in the Gopal Mandir area, the appearance of a 'Gujarati Vaish *mohulla*' was established. On the other hand, in the case of the family of Munshi Bishun Singh, head of a group of Kohli Khattris from Delhi and Muttra, the single *haveli* purchased in 1815 remained the family residence throughout the century, and members of other castes lived contiguously to it in the Sakshi Binayak quarter. A community-*mohulla* failed to develop here because sons and daughters of the family moved out of the city, and few Kohlis immigrated to Benares.[91]

It has been necessary to allude to this rather complex question because the nature of the pre-industrial city in India, and of the classification of merchants within it, has been closely linked to the concept of the community-*mohulla*. Richard Fox, for instance, writes of the characteristic 'segmentation into ethnic or caste divisions' which exist as 'self-contained, non-cooperative, and sometimes hostile neighbourhoods' in these cities.[92] But in Benares at least, various communities wider than the (*jati* level) caste group transcended these neighbourhoods. To emphasize the *haveli* rather than the *mohulla* as a unit is also suggestive in the context of problems of the historical development of the north Indian city. For the great cities of the Moghul period, there is evidence that the basic unit of settlement was the quarter which developed around the magnate *haveli* of the Moghul prince or official.[93] There is an obvious difficulty in relating this pattern of cross-caste dwelling patterns with the caste-*mohulla* pattern which is usually proposed for the nineteenth century. If, however, the *haveli* is taken as the basic unit in both cases, it is possible to see how changed economic and political circumstances might dictate the evolution of one into the other. Such a process can perhaps be seen in miniature in the case of the Benares suburban *mohulla* of Shivala. This was originally a village located about a mile from the boundaries of the city proper. It grew up around the palace of Raja Cheyt Singh and later the exiled members of the Royal Family of Delhi who had settled there in the 1780s after the flight from the capital of the Moghul prince Jahandar Shah. Two or three Agarwal families from Delhi and Lucknow which were associated with the service and supply of the Royal Family also settled there. Subsequently, minute subdivision and dissipation of the property and pensions of the 'core' Muslim family, and the growth in numbers of the commercial families, shifted economic and political power within the *mohulla*.[94] By the later nineteenth century, the Agarwals, as creditors of the impoverished nobility, were in regular receipt of their pensions, and dominated the *mohulla* as a high status commercial group.[95]

CONCLUSION

It should be evident that this essay has not sought to simplify or dismiss the role of caste in eighteenth-century Indian commercial society. We need to know more about trading methods at various levels in the urban and rural economies and test this evidence against the sophisticated categories which anthropologists have used to analyse the various phenomena grouped under the heading 'caste'. The Benares material suggests some preliminary observations. Caste at the level of geographically extended kin groups had an important role in the organization of trading diasporas; at the level of the commensal *jati* group it was relevant to the social and economic organization of artisan groups; at the level of *varna* it had some implications for general mercantile status. Nevertheless, it is difficult to see how caste in any sense could have been the prime parameter of mercantile organization in complex cities. Forms of arbitration, market control, brokerage, neighbourhood communities, and above all conceptions of mercantile honour and credit breached caste boundaries, however construed, and imposed wider solidarities on merchant people. The cultural prestige, entrepot position, and prosperity of Benares during this period probably make it a polar example. But there is no doubt that some of these features were present in most Hindustani cities. In Mirzapur, a 'Durnam Pancham' or 'general body of the trading people of Mirzapore' arbitrated disputes between people of all castes running to thousands of rupees.[96] In Agra the Merchants Guild (*Sarrafa*) included a Rajput moneylending family as well as rich members of the leatherworker caste.[97] In Lucknow, Farrukhabad, Delhi, and other cities there are references to *chaudhries* of tradesmen and merchants who are separate from caste heads.

Originally published as C.A. Bayly, 'Indian Merchants in a "Traditional" Setting: Benaras, 1780–1830', in Clive Dewey and A. Hopkins (eds), *The Imperial Impact: Studies in the Economic History of Africa and India* (London, The Athlone Press, University of London, 1978), pp. 171–93.

ABBREVIATIONS

BRP	Benares Resident's Proceedings
CCPR(C)	Conquered and Ceded Provinces Revenue Proceedings (Customs)
IESHR	*Indian Economic and Social History Review*
IOL	India Office Library
NAI	National Archives of India
UPR	Regional Records Room, Allahabad

NOTES

(The research of which this paper is the first result has been generously funded by a grant from the United Kingdom Social Science Research Council)

1. Holden Furber, *John Company at Work* (Cambridge Mass, 1951); see also the forthcoming work of P.J. Marshall, King's College, London.

2. K.P. Mishra, 'The Administration and Economy of the Benares Region, 1738–95' (unpublished PhD

thesis, University of London, 1970); J. Nichol, 'British Expansion into Bengal, 1757–64' (cyclostyled seminar paper, Centre for South Asian Studies, University of Cambridge, 1972); B.S. Cohn, 'Political Systems in Eighteenth Century India', *Journal of American Anthropological Society*, lxxxii (1962), pp. 312–20; P.B. Calkins, 'The Formation of a Regionally Orientated Ruling Group in Bengal, 1700–1740', *Journal of Asian Studies*, xxix (1970), pp. 797–81.

3. Irfan Habib, *The Agrarian System of Mughal India* (London, 1963), passim. Cf. his paper on 'Banking in Mughal India', presented to the Indian History Congress, 1972; H.Q. Naqvi, *Urbanisation and Urban Centres under the Great Moghuls: An Essay in Interpretation* (Simla, 1972).

4. E.g., V. Anstey, *The Economic Development of India* (London, 1957).

5. R.G. Fox, *From Zamindar to Ballot Box* (Ithaca, NY, 1969); see also his later gloss 'Pariah Capitalism and Traditional Indian Merchants, Past and Present', in Milton Singer (ed.), *Entrepreneurship and the Modernisation of Occupational Cultures in South Asia* (Duke University, 1973), pp. 16–43.

6. Gideon Sjoberg, *The Presindustrial City* (New York, 1970), ch. VII, passim.

7. D.R. Gadgil, *Origins of the Modern Indian Business Class: An Interim Report* (New York, 1957); another influential article has been Helen Lamb, 'The Indian Merchant', in Milton Singer (ed.), *Traditional India: Structure and Change* (Philadelphia, 1959), pp. 25–34.

8. Gadgil, op. cit., pp. 24–6.

9. Cf., K. Gillion, *Ahmedabad: A Study in Indian Urban History* (Berkeley, 1968).

10. Besides the material which reached the provincial revenue (customs) proceedings, no local customs records appear to exist for Benares. But the detailed correspondence of the Agra customs houses (c. 1807–33) deposited in the Regional Records Room, Allahabad (hereafter UPR), throw light on long-distance trade from and to the east. For a somewhat polemical view of the institutional background, see J.G. Borpujari, "The Impact of the Transit Duty System in British India', *Indian Economic and Social History Review* (hereafter *IESHR*), x (1973), pp. 218–43.

11. The internal customs system was dismantled after 1835, but material of a similar sort on trade and trade practices is available in the weekly 'Zilla Court Decisions, North-West Provinces', *c.* 1840–60, in the Judges' Library, Allahabad High Court.

12. For the background before 1783 see William Bolts, *Considerations on Indian Affairs . . .*, 3 vols (London, 1776), III, Appendix C, pp. 300ff.

13. Miss M. Vicziany has also pointed out that the absence of the sanction of prosecution for perjury makes extreme care in the use of such records necessary. I have assumed a fact only when the prosecution, defence, and judgment agree on it. Even plausible untruths, however, may throw light on 'attitudes'.

14. The most useful collections have proved to be those of the Agarwal Chaudhri family in Chaukambha; of the Hanuman Das, Bisheshwar Das branch of the Shah family (filmed extracts of these are in the author's possession); of Sri Ram Krishna in Shivala. Sri Devi Narayan of Sakshi Binayak possesses copies of documents from about 1800 relating to the Jangamabari Math in Madanpura and papers on the Gosain firm 'Iccha Puri' (films also in the author's possession).

15. In possession of Dr Giresh Chandra, Chaukambha (films in the auhor's possession).

16. Agarwal History Office (Bhanpura, Indore, 1938).

17. S. S. Bhandari (ed.), *Oswal Jati ka Itihas* (Bhanpura, Indore, 1934).

18. Mehta Baldeo Das Vithal Das Vyasa, *Vanshawali Vadnagara Sipahi Nagar Kashi Niwasi* (Nagar Union, Benares, 1938).

19. Gowal Das Sahu, Gujarati, was said to have been *chaudhri* of the Benares bankers in the early eighteenth century; his miniature portrait exists in the Bharat Kala Bhawan, Benares; interview with Sri Govind Das Kathiwal, Gopal Mandir Gulli, Benares, March 1974.

20. For Khattris see M. A. Sherring, *Hindu Tribes and Castes as Represented in Benares* (London, 1872); interview with Diwan Ram Chand and Diwan Gokal Chand, Lahori Tola, Benares, December 1973; case of Sukhoo *v.* Pindee Mull, Benares Resident's Proceedings (hereafter BRP) 16 May 1789, UPR.

21. R. Jenkins, *Report on the Territories of the Rajah of Nagpore* (Calcutta, 1827), p. 99.

22. Dwarka Das *v.* Golab Chaube, BRP, 29 January 1789, UPR.

23. Interview with Diwan Ram Chand and Diwan Gokal Chand, Lahori Tola, Benares, January 1974.

24. Jenkins, op. cit., pp. 92–3.

25. See the court paper book of the Jangambari Math (cited in note 14). The 'Nagpuri' Gosain Math in Sakshi Binayak, the related firm 'Iccha Puri', and the Udasi *fakhirs* of Shivala and Assi appear to have begun to invest in government paper and property before 1840.

26. E.g., the prominent Gosain traders of Mirzapur, *mahants* Syd Giri and Persram Giri, Magistrate Mirzapur to Commissioner, 23 July 1834, Collector of Mirzapur (Judicial Series vol. 83), UPR.

27. See C. A. Bayly, 'Town Building in North India, 1780–1820', paper presented to Conference on 'Society in War: India 1794–1808', School of Oriental and African Studies, London, July 1974.

28. Family history available with Dr Anand Krishna, Benares Hindu University.

29. Printed family history in the author's possession.

30. E.g., BRP 30 April 1789; BRP 7 March 1790; BRP 7 November 1790; BRP 23 August 1790; BRP 8 January 1793, case of Balchand '. . . a man of large property in Ghazipore', UPR.

31. BRP 7 March 1790, UPR.

32. For this credit relationship see Benares Agency Files (Persian), UPR, especially Basta 3, Files 20; 12, 22; 18, 18.

33. Agent to the Governor-General, Benares, to Secretary to Government, Calcutta, 4 July 1817, Benares Agency Records volume 54, UPR.

34. Interview with Diwan Ram Chand and Gokal Chand, Lahori Tola, Benares.

35. E.g., representation of Ujoodheea, proceedings, 31 October 1815, Conquered and Ceded Provinces Revenue (Customs) (hereafter CCPR(C)), vol. 56, range 97, UPR.

36. Deputy Collector Government Customs, Benares, to Collector Government Customs, Mirzapur, 6 July 1815, CCPR(C), vol. 55, range 97, India Office Library (hereafter IOL).

37. Deputy Collector Government Customs Benares to Collector Government Customs Mirzapur, 27 August 1816, Bihar and Benares Revenue (Customs), vol. 38, Range 97, IOL.

38. E.g., Board to Governor-General, 4 July 1817, CCPR(C), vol. 61, range 97, IOL.

39. Umer Das *v.* Chehta Mull, BRP 27 February 1789, IOL.

40. Collector Government Customs, Cawnpore, to Board, 27 October 1789, 28, 97, IOL.

41. See Mishra, op. cit.

42. BRP 18 February 1792, UPR.

43. This generalization is based on a preliminary survey of the *rokarh khatas* of the Shah family, the Agarwal Chaudhri family of Chaukambha, Manohar Das Kandheya Lal of Allahabad, Chunna Mai Saligram of Delhi, etc., for the period 1870–90.

44. From Arjunji Nathji, 5 November 1794, *Calendar of Persian Correspondence X, 1794–5* National Archives of India, New Delhi (hereafter NAI), 1969, p. 184; from Harak Ram Tewari, 14 March 1795, ibid., p. 193.

45. Interview with Sri Jyoti Bhushan Gupta, Benares, April 1974.

46. Interview with Sri Devi Narayan, *vakil*, Benares, January 1974; cf. examination of Oogurnarain Misser, 22 August 1815, CCPC(C), vol. 56, range 97, IOL.

47. BRP 4 December 1787, UPR; cf., Duncan Records, vol. XI, UPR, proceedings of the same date. Other Punjabi Khattris are closely associated with Brahmins, while 'tribes' such as Iraqis and Gosains did act separately.

48. BRP 18 January, 4 December 1788, UPR.

49. For African parallels, see Abner Cohen 'Cultural Strategies in the Organisation of Trading Diasporas', in Claude Meillassoux (ed.), *The Development of Indigenous Trade and Markets in West Africa* (London, 1971).

50. Reply of Gunga Bhye's *vakil* in Gunga Bhye *v.* the mother of Jwala Nath, BRP 3 August 1792, UPR.

51. CCPR(C) 26 May 1812, vol. 21, range 97, IOL.

52. Umer Das *v.* Chehta Mull, BPR 27 February 1789, UPR.

53. Gautam Bhadra, 'Some Aspects of the Social Position and Functions of the Merchants at Murshidabad, 1763–93', paper presented to the Indian History Congress, Chandigarh, 1973.

54. Report on the *chaudhries* of Benares by Ibrahim Ali Khan, BRP 18 December 1788, UPR. Note that he specifically distinguishes between 'tribes' (i.e. *jati*) and 'bodies of traders' both of which have *chaudhries.* British officers were also aware of the distinction, but their tendency to emphasize the caste category at the expense of all others caused them to 'fudge' the issue, e.g., J. Prinsep, '... the Hindoos are divided by the circumstances of their castes, and of such trades and professions as are of a similar exclusive character ...', 'Census of Population of the City of Benares',

Asiatic Researches, xvii (Calcutta, 1832), p. 476. Cf., 'Chaudhries of the Respective Classes', Magistrate, Benares, quoted by R. Heitler, 'The Varanasi House Tax Hartal of 1809', *IESHR* ix (1972), p. 251.

55. Magistrate Mirzapur to Lieutenant Edwards, 18th North India Horse, Jubbulpore, 28 October 1830, Collector of Mirzapur (Judicial Series vol. 81), UPR.

56. 'A Short Account of the Nouputtee mahajans of Benares', Foreign Department Miscellaneous, serial 12, part i, National Archives of India, New Delhi.

57. E.g., the case of the *amildari* balances of Kutb Ali Beg, BRP 17 August 1788.

58. BRP 16 May 1789, 21 September 1789, UPR.

59. Hindi proceedings of the Agarwal *panchayat* Benares, 1862–63(?), 1884–88, Chaukambha, in possession of Sri Kumud Chandra, Benares (films of extracts in the author's possession).

60. BRP 31 July 1790, UPR.

61. Shyam Kuar *v.* Kewalram, BRP 3 September 1793, UPR.

62. Gadgil, op. cit., p. 14.

63. Bowanny Das *v.* Sader Kuar, BRP 29 October 1790, UPR.

64. *Arzie* of Bowanny Das, idem.

65. *Arzie* of Sader Kuar, idem.

66. Of course it is possible that the impression of confusion in caste arbitrations was accentuated by the erosion of caste authority by European influences, first the power of the head of the Company's factory at Benares, later by the formalized system introduced by Warren Hastings. But these influences were limited before 1790 and there is no evidence to suggest that caste bodies had been a more important part of the local judicial system in the period of the Benares Raj.

67. Sjoberg, op. cit., p. 101.

68. Acting Deputy Collector Government Customs, Benares, to Collector Government Customs, Mirzapur, 1 May 1816, Proceedings, 23 May 1816, Behar and Benares Revenue, vol. 68, r.III, IOL.

69. Report of Deputy Collector Government Customs, Benares, to Board, 23 July 1813, CCPR(C), vol. 56, range 97.

70. O.M. Lynch, 'Rural Cities in India; Continuities and Discontinuities', in P. Mason (ed.), *India and Ceylon: Unity and Diversity* (London, 1967), pp. 142–58.

71. Collector to Commissioner, Benares, 24 September 1829, Benares Commissioner's Records, Judicial, vol. 9, UPR.

72. F.G. Bailey, 'Closed Social Stratification in India', *Archives Europèennes de Sociologie*, iv (1963), pp. 107–24.

73. F. Buchanan, *An Account of the Districts of Bihar and Patna in 1811–12*, 2 vols (Patna, 1937), II, pp. 683–95.

74. Examination of the *Khurdea*, BRP 27 January 1792, UPR.

75. Sir J. Shore, 'On Some Extraordinary Facts, Customs and Practices of the Hindoos', *Asiatick Researches*, iv (Calcutta, 1795), p. 331; BRP 7 March 1788, UPR.

76. Regulations on *dhama*, BRP 24 October 1794, UPR.

77. Pandit's judgment in the case of Habib Khan, '...the Law directs that the books of merchants being considered as more to be depended on than the evidence of witnesses...', Duncan Records, vol. 52, p. 67, UPR.

78. BRP 5 January 1791, UPR.

79, H.H. Wilson, *Glossary of Judicial and Revenue Terms*, 2nd edition (Delhi, 1968) p. 371.

80. Reference of Lala Harakh Chand, Chaukhambha, 23 November 1843, 'Memory Book' of Harakh Chand (film in author's possession).

81. E.g., some famous firms of *zarda* tobacco and *pan* dealers.

82. Communication of Rai Krishna Dasji, Benares, March 1974.

83. One of the difficulties is to ascertain to which unit precisely the word *mohulla* refers. I take it that the list of '*mohullas* with *phatakhs* and watchmen paid for by the citizens', pp. 154–7, vol. 8 (1809), Collector of Benares Miscellaneous Series, UPR, is the same unit referred to by Heitler, op. cit., p. 257, where he suggests that '...in this period, the population of each *mahalla* was primarily made up of one caste'. My impression from property documents and enquiries is that this cannot be the case for many of the *mohullas* in the collector's list. In the first entry on the list, for instance, *mohulla* Lahori Tola, I found that Western Khattris, Agarwals, and Bhojpuri-area Brahmins lived in adjoining ancestral *havelis*; in *mohulla* Sakshi Binayak, a house sale deed of 1815 in possession of Sri Devi Narayan, *vakil*, reveals Kohli Khattris, Kayasths, Aroras, and Gosains living in contiguous residences; in the Chaukambha area, Rastogis, Agarwals, Halwais, Bengalis lived close together in the Gopal Das Sahu *mohulla*, and so on.

84. The *haveli* is described by J. Prinsep, op. cit., p. 475.

85. Policing arrangements and list of *mohullas* (actually *phatak* areas), Collector of Benares, Miscellaneous Series, vol. 8, UPR.

86. BPR 5 December 1790, UPR.

87. H.R. Nevill, *District Gazetteers of the United Provinces of Agra and Oudh*, XIX (Allahabad, 1906), p. 242.

88. Nevill, op. cit., pp. 239, 254; see J. Prinsep's map of Benares, IOL; communication from Rai Krishna Dasji.

89. Heitler, op. cit.; the role of the *mahajans* in social control is brought out clearly in Magistrate, Benares to Superintendant of Police, 7 August 1852, *Uttar Pradesh State Records Series, Selection from the English Records, Banaras Affairs* (Allahabad, 1957), II, pp. 168–9.

90. Interview with Sri Govind Das Kothiwal, Gopal Mandir Gulli, March 1974.

91. Interview with Sri Devi Narayan, Sakshi Binayak, May 1972, January 1974 and estate documents 1815, in author's possession.

92. Fox, op. cit., ch. 14.

93. E.g. the case of Shahjehanpur, 'Report on the Police of the City of Shahjehanpore', *Selections from the Records of Government, North-Western Provinces* (Agra, 1865), XXV, article 48, p. 96; or the case of magnate based *mohullas* in late Moghul Delhi in the Aligarh translation of a contemporary tract entitled in Hindi, *Mohomed Shah ki Rangil ki Dilli.* The patronal rather than caste origin of *mohullas* or gated areas in Benares is also suggested ky their names e.g., Phatak Rangil Das, Gopal Das Sahu Tola, Gowal Das Sahu Tola, etc.

94. See Benares Agency Records (Persian) and the collection of Sri Ram Krishna, Shivala (photographs in author's possession). (See also note 14.)

95. North Western Provinces Proceedings, February 1899, pp. 131–6, IOL.

96. BRP 3 April 1971, UPR.

97. 'Working Book of the Merchants of Agra' (Hindi, c. 1878?) (film in author's possession); interview with Rai Sahib Khandelwal, Agra, March 1974.

13

The Parsis
Entrepreneurial Success

Ashok V. Desai

Behind the debate over the basis of commercial solidarities lies a quest to understand the phenomenal success of certain mercantile communities. One such highly entrepreneurial community is the minority community of the Parsis. Immigrants into India from Persia in the eighth century, the Parsis played a pioneering role in developing industry in western India from the nineteenth century. Initially, the Parsis were primarily engaged in agricultural interests and agriculture-related trades in the Surat–Navasari area. Later, with the emergence of Bombay as a leading port city and a hub of commerce and finance, several Parsis moved there to become brokers and middlemen to European traders. Somewhat more open to Western influences and values than other trading groups, the Parsis developed a special rapport with the European traders. They also took to ship building and independent trade, getting especially active in the opium trade with China.* When they lost prominence in the China trade, they diversified into other areas such as cotton and, by the late nineteenth century, became pioneers of the cotton mill industry. Thereafter, they spearheaded diverse industrial and trading activities.†

* In 1756, H. J. Readymoney was the first Parsi to settle in China. By the 1840s, the Parsis owned the largest block of shipping tonnage in India, second only to the British East India Company. It is well known that in the 1730s the Wadias, who were shipbuilders, came from Surat to Bombay to lay the foundations of the Bombay dockyard. See R.A. Wadia, *The Bombay Dockyard and the Wadia Master Builders* (Bombay, published by R.A. Wadia, 1957).

† Also see R.P. Paymaster, *Early History of the Parsees in India* (Lucknow, University of Lucknow, 1954); Ashok Guha, 'Parsi Seths as Entrepreneurs, 1750–1850', *Economic and Political Weekly*, Vol. 5, No. 35, 1970, pp. 107–15; Asiya Siddiqui, 'The Business World of Jamsetji Jeejebhoy', in Asiya Siddiqui (ed.), *Trade and Finance in Colonial India* (Delhi, Oxford University Press, 1995); D.F. Karaka, *The History of the Parsees* (London, Macmillan,

Seeking to unravel the secrets of Parsi achievements, this article by economist and business journalist Ashok V. Desai attributes their success to their unique historical context. Countering the view that Parsis were inherently more entrepreneurial due to socio-cultural factors, Desai examines the historical conjectures from which they benefited. He asserts that the Parsis unlocked the door to entrepreneurship due to the fact that they were not limited to internal trade, not imprisoned by hierarchies of authorities like the Hindu trader, and not disaffected like Muslim traders by the East India Company's colonization of the seas in the eighteenth century. The author lavishes praise on the Bombay Parsis for their role in industrial upsurge while simultaneously crediting the connection between their achievement to their British auspices and the dramatic fluxes in political power and trade flows of the eighteenth and nineteenth centuries.

The Parsis played an outstanding role in the growth of Indian industry in the nineteenth century. They pioneered the cotton textile industry in western India; and in all types of industrial and trading activity in the Bombay Presidency their participation was quite out of proportion to their numbers.

The Parsis' success has invited a number of explanations.[1] It has been attributed to their spirit of enterprise, their lack of caste, their foreign origin, etc. Some evidence can be found for these explanations; but their significance cannot be assessed unless various contributory factors are considered together. Further, such explanations do not take into account the historical character of the Parsi achievement. The Parsis played a smaller and diminishing role in the industrial development in this century, but that cannot be attributed to their becoming less enterprising, or their developing a caste system. Many of the old Parsi concerns, founded in the nineteenth century, continue to exist; but their growth in recent decades has been less rapid than the overall growth of industry in the country.

Thus, it is necessary to put Parsi enterprise in its historical context. Fortunately the documentary basis for doing so is fairly firm. With their strong sense of community, the Parsis have written a great deal about themselves.[2] Community news was reported extensively in their newspapers.[3] Hence the record is quite complete for most of the nineteenth century; fragmentary information is also available for the two previous centuries. The object of this paper is to review the evidence

---

1884); R.E. Kennedy, 'The Protestant Ethic and the Parsis', in N.J. Smelser (ed.), *Readings in Economic Sociology* (Englewood, Prentice Hall, 1965); H.E. Kulke, *The Parsees in India—A Minority as an Agent of Social Change* (New Delhi, Vikas, 1993); Christine Dobbin, *Urban Leadership in Western India—Politics and Communities in Bombay City 1840–1885* (Oxford, Oxford University Press, 1972); H. D. Darukhanawala, *Parsi Luster on Indian Soil* (Bombay, G. Clearidge, 1939); and Amalendu Guha, 'Parsi Seths as Entrepreneurs, 1750–1850', *Economic and Political Weekly*, Vol. 5, No. 48, 28 November, 1970, and his 'More about the Parsi Seths: Their Roots, Entrepreneurship and Comprador Role, 1650–1918', in D. Tripathi (ed.), *Business Communities of India: A Historical Perspective* (New Delhi, Manohar, 1984). For a fascinating anthropological study of the contemporary community which argues that the Parsis are adapting to a new political reality in the post-colonial world, see T.M. Luhrman, *The Good Parsi: The Fate of a Colonial Elite in a Postcolonial Society* (Cambridge, Harvard University Press, 1996).

and explore the origin of the entrepreneurial activities of the Parsis.

The Parsis came to Gujarat in the year 697 A.D. to escape persecution by Mohammedans in Persia. Nineteen years later they moved to Sanjan, which was then a port in the Gulf of Cambay. Nothing is heard of them in the following 700 years, and it is likely that they were substantially assimilated in the indigenous population and took up the native occupation of farming. Right up to the nineteenth century the Parsis showed the great influence of Hindu ways and manners. Some of them had Hindu names; and their rituals at birth, marriage, etc. also incorporated Hindu customs.

Sanjan was overrun by the Muslims in 1315, and apparently the Parsis were uprooted. They are next found settled in the Surat-Navsari area in the fifteenth century; by then they were no longer confined to agriculture, but had extended their activities to tax farming, shipbuilding, shipping and trading.[4] The growth of occupational and economic differentiation was probably behind the theological controversies that began to arise in the fifteenth century. We hear of leading Parsis getting worried about the adulteration of their religion and exchanging notes with the Parsis in Persia regarding correct procedures.

In the seventeenth and eighteenth centuries there were some famous shipbuilders among the Parsis of Surat. There is a reference in East India Company records to a Parsi shipbuilder in Surat, Cursett, who built warships around 1672.[5] When the East India Company wanted a ship in 1735, its agent was sent to Surat, and he placed an order with one Dhunjibhoy. Later, Lowjee Nusserwanji, a Parsi foreman of Dhunjibhoy, was engaged by the Company to set up a shipyard in Bombay.[6] He set up the Mazagaon Dock which built over 350 ships in the next century and a half.[7]

Besides building ships, the Parsis were also engaged in foreign trade and in textile manufacture. They were particularly active in the trade with the Persian and Arabian Gulfs;[8] they also exported opium to China.[9]

The major export of Surat was cotton and silk textiles; and the Parsis were actively engaged in their manufacture. Some Parsi families were famous for their silks, and at least one of them—the Chhois—continued to manufacture into the twentieth century.[10] By the eighteenth century, the Parsis were almost entirely urban residents; only a few of them were engaged in farming. But some of them were rewarded with *Jagirs* (estates) by Mogul Kings. Thus, Meherji Rana, a priest who educated Akbar in Zoroastrianism, was given a heritable estate of eighty acres by him; his son was given a further forty acres.[11] The Dordi family also received a Jagir from Jehangir, the son of Akbar. A Parsi named Sorabji Kavasji (1697–1760) repaired a clock belonging to the Mogul Emperor in 1744; in return he was given the title of Nek Sant Khan, as well as a number of Jagirs in Surat District and the right to farm the customs of Surat. His sons, who were awarded titles of Beheremandkhan and Talyarkhan, took up trade in cotton piece-goods and silk, besides their inherited activities.[12] Beginning with Changa Asa in 1419, many Parsis became tax farmers.[13]

Thus, the Parsis in the eighteenth century engaged in manufacture, shipbuilding, exports, imports and revenue collection. They were therefore in a very favourable position for capital accumulation.

Yet the Parsis were not the only people who had opportunities for capital accumulation. The Moguls systematically farmed out taxes in their entire empire, and created hundreds of Jagirdars. The same practice was followed by other kings also. And trade and handicrafts were not the monopoly of Parsis. In the Surat region itself we know of some extremely rich Hindu and Muslim merchants.[14]

The reason for the later success of the Parsis and the failure of other rich people must be looked for in the Parsis' close contacts with the British East India Company. The East India Companies from the sixteenth to the early eighteenth century were not traders in the same sense as the 'country' traders of Surat. The traders of that time were a combination of merchants and tramp shippers: the ships which they owned travelled between a number of ports, picked up the specialities of the ports and unloaded them where they were valued most. The English, French and Dutch East India Companies that traded in India at that time did a very different kind of business: they were interested primarily in taking a small range of commodities, especially textiles, to Europe, where they fetched very high prices. The range of European goods they could sell at a profit in India was limited, and they paid for the wares in bullion mainly. Thus, they were interested only to a limited extent in building up a marketing organization in India; and since they earned a handsome profit just by transporting goods from India to Europe, they were interested only to a limited extent in manufacturing and buying goods cheaply in India. This lack of interest, as well as, perhaps, unfamiliarity with languages and customs, led the Companies to rely on locally-based brokers, agents, and shippers, both Indian and European, in each port.[15] On the other hand, local traders came to rely on the Companies for protection on the sea. By 1750 Parsi traders were entirely dependent on the British and the Dutch for protection on the seas.[16]

The Parsis in Surat also acted as agents for the Companies.[17] The ancestors of the Frenchman family acted as agents for French and Dutch traders.[18] The Modis (literally, grocers) were originally priests, and got their new surname when one of them became the house steward and general agent of the East India Factory at Surat.[19] Another Parsi, Rustam Manak Seth (1635–1721), was broker, banker and money-changer to the East India Company, and travelled to Delhi in 1660 to make representations for the Company against the Nawab of Surat.[20]

Hence when the East India Company got political power, the Parsis came to share in it. Before Bombay was ceded to the British in 1668, it was ruled by the Portuguese. They employed Dorabji Nanabhai as their broker. The British, on coming into possession of the island, continued to use his services. They imposed a poll tax on the population, and entrusted Dorabji with its collection. Thus he became the first Patel (tax farmer) of Bombay. His son Rustomji (1667–1763) raised a force to defend Bombay against the Sidis of Janjira in 1692. Rustomji's son Kavasji became Patel of Thana and Bassein, Portuguese outposts near Bombay, when the British took them in 1774. He was also a shipper; and his son Hirji had an extensive China trade. His brother Dorabji supplied cotton, timber, saltpetre, etc. to the Company government.[21] In Surat, in the early nineteenth century, two brothers who were descendants of Beheremandkhan entered the service of the Company, and one of them, Ardeshir Dhanjishaw Kotwal Bahadur, was made the warden (*Sadar Amin*) of Surat castle and town while the other, Pherozsha, became a political agent of the East India Government in various districts of Gujarat.[22]

When the Maratha empire succumbed to the Company in 1802, the latter was as unprepared to administer the new territory as in Bengal and the North-west Provinces earlier; as in those areas therefore the Company farmed out the tax revenues of the empire. Two Parsi trader brothers, Pestonji and Vikaji Merji, were made farmers of the land and sea customs of Konkan and the land customs of Poona, Ahmednagar and part of Khandesh. They doubled the revenues in seven years. They also engaged in the collection of cotton for export, and later extended their cotton trading to the state of Hyderabad. They made advances to the Nizam in return for privileges of tax farming and currency issue. Ultimately their firm failed in 1851 owing to the refusal of the Nizam to repay certain loans.[23]

Traders, brokers, shippers, shipbuilders, financiers, industrialists, tax farmers—which of these people went into industry? Curiously, the pioneers in the Bombay textile industry came almost entirely from among the Parsi traders, shippers and financiers of Bombay. Cowasji Nanabhoy Daver, the founder of the Bombay Spinning and Weaving Company, the first cotton textile mill in India, was the son of a rich merchant who had agencies of a number of English firms. Cowasji himself was active in cotton export and in finance. He started three banks (Commercial Bank in 1845, Mercantile Bank in 1853, and Broker's Loan, Discount and Banking Company in 1861), and installed the first hydraulic press in Bombay in 1853.[24] Jeejeebhoy Dadabhoy (1786–1849), the father of Byramjee Jeejeebhoy who started a weaving mill at Kurla, a suburb of Bombay, was a broker, director of banks, shipowner and financier of plantations in Malabar, Ceylon and Java, and traded with Europe, Egypt and the East.[25] Mancherji Nowrojee Banaji (1837–90), founder of the city of Bombay Mill in 1885, was the descendant of a merchant who migrated to Bombay in 1690,[26] and was himself engaged in trade, shipping, real estate and company promotion.[27]

Three families were the most active in the textile industry—Wadia, Petit and Tata. The Wadias were descended from Lowjee Wadia, the master builder of Mazagaon Dock, and made fortunes in shipping, trade and finance.[28] Of them, Nowrojee Nusserwanji Wadia was the owner of the Textile Mills, Bombay Dyeing, and Century Mills and built over ten other mills.[29] Manakji Petit, the founder of Oriental Spinning and Weaving Mills, was a merchant; and his son Dinsha, who was the chief shareholder of six mills and the richest Parsi of his time, traded with China.[30] Nusserwanji Rattanji Tata, founder of Central India Mills at Nagpur, was a shipper and China trader; he exported cotton and opium, and imported tea, silk goods, camphor, cinnamon, copper, brass and gold. He made large profits on contracts with the Commissariat during the occupation of Bushire in 1857 and on export of cotton during the American Civil War.[31] Later his son Jamshedji started three textile mills as well as the steel plant in Jamshedpur.[32]

The direct investments in the textile industry were not the only Parsi contribution; Parsis were often secretaries, managing agents or managers of mills started by non-Parsis. Muncherji Nowrojee Banaji, mentioned above, was secretary to the Great Eastern Spinning and Weaving Mills;[33] Dorabji Framji Panday (1828–90), who began exporting cotton during the American Civil War, later became the agent of Dharamsi and Coorla Mills.[34] The Parsi contribution to the management of the textile industry in the nineteenth century was perhaps as great as its contribution to investment.

While the Parsi contribution to the foundation of textile mills is outstanding, they were pioneers in many other fields. Nowrojee Wadia started a paper factory around 1870, but had to close it down for lack of capital.[35] Jeejeebhoy Dadabhoy introduced steam navigation to India in 1841, and set up a highly profitable coastal shipping concern.[36] Jamsetji

Dorabji Naegaumwalla (1804–82), who began as a shipwright in the Wadia dockyard, was the first Indian railway builder, and constructed nearly 80 miles of railways around Bombay in the 1850s. Earlier, he also constructed saltworks for Dadabhoy Wadia.[37]

Among the pioneers in other fields mentioned above were a Wadia and another connected with the Wadias. Wherever we look among pioneers, they are found to come from or be related to a small circle of shippers, shipbuilders, traders and financiers in Bombay; the landlords and manufacturers of Surat-Navsari do not figure among them. This phenomenon calls for an explanation.

The roots of this phenomenon are in the eighteenth century. The British obtained Bombay in 1668. In the entire eighteenth century, Bombay was the major British possession in western India; and since it was in their possession, they were keen on developing it into a port. That was why they took Lowjee Wadia to set up a dockyard. At the same time, the Mogul empire had declined, and the Surat-Navsari area was in the intermittent control of the Mogul representatives and the Marathas. It was therefore subject to political uncertainty and occasional raids; it was a bad place for men of means. Among them, however, those whose wealth depended on trade with the interior stuck on; those whose dealings were mainly abroad moved gradually to Bombay, and Parsi shipper-traders were heavily represented among them. The latter had not only more to gain from the move, they also had a community of interests with the British who were also maritime traders.

Three radical changes occurred in the nineteenth century. First, the British achieved a technological breakthrough in cotton textiles. Second, they pioneered revolutionary improvements in land and sea transport. Third, as a result of technological and military supremacy, the British began to force their way into Asian markets.

The Bombay Parsis were the first in India to feel and to share in these changes. They caught each British fashion as it came up: they went in for women's education, for racing, and finally for baronetcy-bound philanthropy.

When the British forced their way into Western India and China, the Parsis went with them. We have described how Vikaji and Pestonji became tax farmers in Maharashtra and promoted cotton export. Parsis were involved in the export of opium to China in the eighteenth century; they greatly expanded their business, and benefited when the British opened up China with the opium war.[38] Many Parsi merchants were imprisoned by the Chinese government during the opium war, including Jamshedji Rustomji Irani, Dadabhai Rustomji Banaji, Hirjibhai Rustomji Patel, Nusserwanji Bomanji Mody, Ardeshir Furdoonji Panday, etc.—representatives of many of the Parsi families which were later involved in textiles.[39]

Thus, the Parsis, owing to their tradition of maritime trading and their close connections with the British, shared in the profits of international trade. In the early nineteenth century these profits grew enormously because they were based on the extensive exploitation of large international markets; they rose far above the profits from intensive exploitation of courts and upper-class markets. This change in relative profits also led to the rise of Bombay Parsis in relation to Parsis and other merchants of Surat.

Further, their position earned the Bombay Parsis a lion's share in the export of cotton to Britain and the import of British textiles; and they were among the first to realize the profits that would result from manufacturing cotton textiles in Bombay. A place in western India was obviously a far more economical location than Lancashire for spinning and weaving Indian cotton for the Indian market, and once the import of textiles from Lancashire was well established, it was only a matter of time before import substitution would take place.

The lucrative opportunities of import substitution were realized early by the British also, who carried the trade in cotton and textiles between Britain and India, and they invested heavily in the Bombay cotton textile industry between 1850 and 1880. They continued to play an important technical and managerial role right up to the First World War.[40] But they could not trade and manufacture without intermediaries because of their linguistic disability; their Parsi agents and brokers filled this intermediary role.

The early dominance of the British and the Parsis disappeared with time. Cotton was an agricultural commodity liable to wide price fluctuation; hence merchants and their capital were attracted from all over western India into cotton trading. Gradually this trading filtered into textile manufacture, and non-Parsi Indians increased their participation in the industry: the profit rates fell, and investment became unattractive.

At the same time, the Parsi ran short of investment opportunities. In the late nineteenth century, the momentum of foreign trade shifted to eastern India, where plantations of tea and indigo were developed and manganese and mica mines were opened. In western India, opium exports gradually declined, as did the exports of cotton which were increasingly absorbed by home consumption.

With the stagnation of trade, the demand for ships also fell off. Shipbuilding, which was virtually a Parsi monopoly in India in the eighteenth century, died a slow death. The size of sailing ships increased in the eighteenth and nineteenth centuries, and the shallow port of Surat went out of use for shipbuilding. The Wadias continued to build ships in Bombay; but the British closed down the shipbuilding activities of Mazagaon Dock in 1885, just when the steamship revolution was beginning.[41] Indian shipbuilding never recovered from the decline.

In a country without an independent capital-goods industry, two kinds of industries are at a disadvantage relative to their foreign competitors: capital intensive industries whose costs are raised by the high import cost of equipment, and industries producing high value commodities which incur very low transport costs. Hence India was bound to develop industries with low capital intensity, such as oil milling, rice milling and sugar, and industries with bulky products such as bricks and cement. These were also industries in which material and transport costs were predominant. Hence they would grow up close to centres of material supply or markets. In fact they were dispersed all over India so as to minimize transport requirements. Cotton textiles were an exception; while their capital costs were low their transport costs were also low. Hence, while their production in India rose, it was neither dispersed all over the country nor concentrated in cotton-growing areas of the country.

The Parsis, who were concentrated in Surat, Navsari and Bombay had many advantages in the setting up of the cotton textile industry. But their very concentration prevented them from entering the other industries in which India had an advantage and which grew rapidly after 1900. Parsi capital did not enter any new industry except cement. Perhaps there was also a hiatus of scale: after going into cotton textiles, the Parsis would not have thought of going into, say, oil milling, whose capital requirements were tiny compared to textiles.

To conclude, the origins of Parsi enterprise of the nineteenth century are not to be found in their social or psychological characteristics. Being a Parsi helped in emergence as an entrepreneur; but only because a Parsi trader was neither confined to internal trade nor suffered from the depredations of authorities like the Hindu trader, and because he did not have to share the defeat of the Muslim trader by the British East India company in the eighteenth century struggle for the mastery of the seas. Nor was it enough to be a Parsi; the rich Parsis of Surat declined together with their Hindu and Muslim neighbours. It was the Bombay Parsis that were responsible for the industrial upsurge, and their achievement cannot be divorced from their British auspices and the drastic changes in political power and trade flows in the eighteenth and nineteenth centuries.

Originally published as Ashok V. Desai, 'The Origins of Parsi Enterprise', in Rajat Kanta Ray (ed.), *Entrepreneurship and Industry in India, 1800–1947* (Delhi, Oxford University Press, 1992), pp. 99–108.

NOTES

1. According to Sir John Malcolm, 'There is no body of natives so remarkable in their intelligence and enterprise as the Parsis' (Dosabhoy Framji Karaka, *History of the Parsis, including their Manners, Customs, Religion and Present Position*, London, 1884, Vol. 1, p. 116). For more recent views in the same vein cf. Vera Anstey, *The Economic Development of India*, London, 4th edn, 1952, p. 232; Daniel Houston Buchanan, *The Development of Capitalist Enterprise in India*, New York, 1934, p. 144.

2. D.F. Karaka, op. cit., Vols 1 and 2; Khan Bahadur Bomanji Byramji Patel, *Parsi Prakash* (in Gujarati), Bombay; Ratanji Framji Wachha, *Mumbaino Bahar*, (in Gujarati), Bombay 1874; H.D. Darukhanawala, *Parsi Lustre on Indian Soil*, Bombay, 1939.

3. *Bombay Samachar* and *Jam-e-Jamshed* in Bombay, and *Gujrat Mitra* in Surat were the best known ones; besides there were dozens of magazines and pamphlets.

4. D.F. Karaka, op. cit., Vol. 1, pp. 1–30.

5. Rottonjee Ardeshir Wadia, *The Bombay Dockyard and the Wadia Master Builders*, Bombay, 1955, p. 106.

6. Ibid., pp. 124–7.

7. Ibid., pp. 329–60 where a list is given.

8. Holden Furber, *John Company at Work*, Cambridge (Mass.), 1951, pp. 21, 66.

9. D.F. Karaka, op. cit., Vol. 1, p. 45.

10. H.D. Darukhanawala, op. cit., pp. 382–3.

11. D.F. Karaka, op. cit., Vol. 2, p. 374.

12. Ibid., pp. 21–3.

13. Ibid., pp. 4–7.

14. H. Furber, op. cit., pp. 167–8; W.H. Moreland, *From Akbar to Aurangzeb*, Cambridge, 1929, pp. 153–5.

15. For an excellent account of the state of the companies' trade, see H. Furber and W.H. Moreland, op. cit.

16. Holden Furber, *Bombay Presidency in the Mid-Eighteenth Century*, Bombay, 1965, p. 64.

17. D.F. Karaka, op. cit., Vol. 2, p. 322.

18. H.D. Darukhanawala, op. cit., p. 322.

19. Ibid., pp. 368–9.

20. D.F. Karaka, op. cit., Vol. 2, pp. 9–16.

21. H.D. Darukhanawala, op. cit., p. 497.

22. D.F. Karaka, op. cit., pp. 49–54.

23. Ibid., Vol. 2, pp. 124–9.

24. R.F. Wachha, op. cit., Vol. 1, pp. 328–9.

25. D.F. Karaka, op. cit., Vol. 2, p. 133.

26. Ibid., Vol. 2, p. 54.

27. *Bombay Gazette*, 27 October 1890.

28. R.A. Wadia, op. cit., pp. 1–72.

29. Mancherji Hoshangji Jagosh, *Seth Nowrosji Nusserwanji Wahadia* (in Gujarati), Bombay, 1901, pp. 34–8.

30. D.F. Karaka, op cit., Vol. 2, pp. 134–6; H.D. Darukhanawala, op. cit., p. 423.

31. Bahamanji Behramji Patel, *Parsi Martyuk* (in Gujarati), Bombay, 1915, Part 3, pp. 142–3.

32. F. R. Harris, *Jamshedji Nusserwanji Tata. A Chronicle of His Life*, Bombay, 1958, pp. 5–7.

33. *Bombay Gazette*, 27 October 1890.

34. *Jam-e-Jamshed*, 4 June 1890.

35 *The Times of India*, 21 December 1899.

36. D.F. Karaka, op. cit., Vol. 2, pp. 132–3; H.D. Darukhanawala, op. cit., pp. 340–1.

37. B.B. Patel, op. cit., Part 3, pp. 33–7.

38. While the East India Company had a monopoly in the export of opium from Eastern India, this only

meant that 'a favoured few of the company's servants arranged opium contracts to their best advantage' (Holden Furber, *John Company at Work*, p. 165). The export of opium from the Native States of Malwa developed independently through Bombay and Daman; the East India Company charged a duty on exports that passed through British territory but which had no monopoly of them.

39. H.D. Darukhanawala, op. cit., p. 209.

40. S.D. Mehta, *The Indian Cotton Textile Industry. An Economic Analysis*, Bombay, 1953, pp. 2, 57.

41. H.D. Darukhanawala, op. cit., pp. 494–5.

14

Sindh Merchants and Their Reputation

T. Postans

The Sindhi community has been another highly successful mercantile community. The Sindhis are currently located in over 100 countries, ranging from the small Mediterranean island of Malta, the Canary Islands, Hong Kong, Singapore, Philippines, and the United Kingdom to India, especially Mumbai. Predominantly concerned with business, this community has migrated for trade purposes since at least the mid-nineteenth century, with a spike in migration occurring after India's Partition in 1947, which caused the Sindhi homeland to become part of the newly-formed Pakistan. In the early nineteenth century, apart from trading, Sindhis performed an important role as tax farmers, moneylenders, and financiers, both in Sindh and Central Asia, and were critical to the success of the caravan trade between north India and Central Asia.* Two major networks emerged from the Sindhi traders: the Shikarpuris and the Sindworkies. The Shikarpuris were prominent in Central Asia during the Durrani domination of 1747–1823 and thereafter as a result of their financial control over large areas stemming from their role as middlemen and their ability to transfer large amounts of finances through the *hundi* network.† Even the collapses of empires did not impact the commercial activities of the Sindhis.‡ Their main commercial network encompassed most of Central Asia, while another extended from Karachi to southern India up to Southeast Asia,

* For recent work on the Sindhis, see Mark-Anthony Falzon, *Cosmopolitan Connections: The Sindhi Diaspora, 1860–2000* (Leiden, Brill, 2004) and Claude Markovits, *The Global World of Indian Merchants, 1750–1947: Traders of Sind from Bukhara to Panama* (Cambridge, Cambridge University Press, 2000). Also see Anita Raina Thapan, *Sindhi Diaspora in Manila, Hong Kong, and Jakarta* (Quezon, Ateneo de Manila University Press, 2002).

† On the *hundi* network, see excerpts in Section I: 'The Bazaar', this volume.

‡ On this see Markovits, *The Global World of Indian Merchants*.

particularly Burma. The Sindworkies, by contrast, established themselves along major maritime trade routes from Cairo and Alexandra to the Mediterranean islands, Africa, Latin America, Singapore, Malaysia, the Philippines, China, Hong Kong, and Japan. They carved out their niche in the curios and textiles trades, while ensuring that their networks were centralized in Hyderabad.

This selection, from an official report written in 1843 by T. Postans, Captain of the Bombay Army and former assistant to the Political Agent in Sindh and Baluchistan, recounts the trading activities of Hindu Sindhi traders in the mid-nineteenth century. In his *Personal Observations on Sindh: The Manners and Customs of Its Inhabitants and Its Productive Capabilities*, Postans admires Hindu merchants who (he notes) commanded respect due to their commercial acumen, despite facing prejudices. For instance, they were compelled to keep beards and don turbans, to pass off as Muslims, just to be tolerated in a predominantly Islamic society. Their 'good faith and integrity' in mercantile transactions inspired Postans to comment that 'it is proverbial and a great proof of the honour of the Sindhian Sooucars that their bills are always considered as cash in every part... and are recognized as such all over India.'

The Hindús in Sindh bear evident traces of emigration to that country from Múltan, Amritsir, and other parts to the north; locating themselves on the banks of the Indus, as in Central Asia, they have become here, as elsewhere, a highly valuable portion of the community, commanding by their commercial activity, habits of business, and energy, a certain respect despite the most unmeasured bigotry. They are still but a tolerated class, however, and nothing short of extreme cunning and perseverance could enable them to exist in such a country as Sindh, where their wealth is the constant object of Mahommedan rapacity, and where they are only considered as dogs in the eyes of the true believers; they are divided into two great classes, *Lohanas*, and *Bhatias*. The whole of the trade of Sindh, from the extensive mercantile and banking transactions of Shikarpúr, to the smallest supplier of the ordinary wants of life, are in the hands of the Hindús. Their command of ready money gives them also a certain power over the rulers, who, looking only to the revenue of the country as a means of present gratification, are too happy to farm its resources to these Soucars (as the Hindú traders are called) for any sum which may be immediately commanded. In these transactions the Hindú always runs the greatest risk of being called upon to disgorge any profits he may amass, and he knows that his bonds and contracts with Mahommedan chiefs are so much waste paper; but he makes his calculations accordingly, and, despite power and despotism, never fails to accumulate wealth at the expence of the profligacy of the rulers.

Hindús, from their intelligence and habits of business, are also employed by the government throughout Sindh as revenue servants of every description, but all such are obliged to wear the beard and turban, adopting in their exterior so completely the Mahommedan garb and demeanour, that they are no longer recognizable. In Sindh and the countries north-west of the Indus generally, the Hindú is not particular as to caste or religion, and his constant neglect of both would indeed horrify the stricter brother of the same faith in India, but in such situations it is in vain to attempt to preserve purity, and the trial would only induce additional persecution. The few Brahmins or Gúrús in this country are of the Sarsat caste and occasionally a temple to Mahadiú is to be seen, but only at Shikarpúr are the Hindús allowed to celebrate their festivals or religious rites: during the Mohurrum and other Mahommedan fasts or feasts, they are obliged to shut up their shops all over the country. The ass is used by the Hindús in Sindh for carriage and travelling; in India the animal cannot be touched without defilement. It is curious to observe that in the neighbouring country of the Punjaub, the Mussulman is as much degraded, and treated with the same intolerance by a Hindú heresy, as the Hindú is by the Moslem in Sindh.

Hindús are dispersed over the whole of Sindh: in the wildest fastnesses of the Bilúchi mountains, in the deserts and smallest collection of huts in the jungles of the plains, a Hindú and his shop of tobacco, spices, groceries, or cloths, is sure to be found; but their principal localities are in Northern Sindh at Shikarpúr, and in Southern at the port of Karrachi. The former has at all times held a prominent influence over the trade of the countries from the sea to the Caspian. The Hindú merchants or bankers have agents in the most remote parts of Central Asia, and could negotiate bills upon Candahar, Kilat, Cabul, Khiva, Hírat, Bokhara, or any other of the marts in that direction. These agents, in the pursuit of their calling, leave Sindh for many years, quitting their families to locate themselves amongst the most savage and intolerant tribes, yet so essentially necessary are they to the wild Túrkoman, rude Affghan, or blood-thirsty Bilúchi, that they are, with trifling exceptions, generally protected. The smallest bargain even is never struck between two natives of these countries, without the intervention of the Hindú *Dillal* or broker; covering his hand with a large cloth, he runs backwards and forwards between the parties, grasping alternately the hand of each. The cloth is used to cover certain signs which are conveyed as to the amount offered by squeezing the joints of the fingers, which stand for units, tens, or hundreds, as the case may be: thus the bystanders are kept in the dark as to the price at which an article is sold, and irritation avoided at offering before others a lower sum than is expected would be taken.

At Karrachi, the principal port of Sindh, and therefore of the Indus and countries beyond it, the Hindús are very numerous and influential: here and at Shikarpúr they enjoy greater protection than in any other part of the Sindhian dominions; for short-sighted and covetous though the Amirs were, they could yet estimate the value to the revenues of protecting, to a certain extent, those on whom all such as are derivable from trade, were entirely dependent; indeed many of the principal Hindú merchants who traded very extensively, could command abatement in tariffs, only granted to them with the obvious inducement to continue their transactions.

The Hindús in Sindh are of very fair complexion: a few of the wealthier live in comfortable style in the cities, but the poorer traders are a mean race, filthy in the extreme, having much of the abject shuffling manner of the Jew, as seen in countries where he is despised and oppressed: the costume differs little from that of the same class in India; the turban is occasionally large, after the Múltan fashion: all however studiously hide their wealth with the garb of poverty. The Hindú women in Sindh are considered as having some claims to regularity of features, but all are, if possible, dirtier in their persons and dwellings than the Mahommedans: the dress differs in nothing from that of the Mahommedan women.

The Hindú in Sindh is not the same orderly and respectable individual outwardly as his brother of the same faith in India: living in a state of society where he is only tolerated in proportion to his acceding to the customs of those about him, he has become half a Mahommedan in his habits and practices, as well as dirty and slovenly in his person, totally neglecting those rules of caste and religion, which have in India the peculiar merit of raising the Hindú above the debauched Moslem. In one point, however, in Sindh does this otherwise degraded class stand pre-eminent above those about him, and that is in the good faith and integrity shown in his mercantile and money transactions, when met with confidence by his employer. In dealing with the chiefs and government of Sindh, he is obliged to defeat indirect oppression by duplicity and double-dealing as his only chance of success or safeguard against violence; but this is by no means a fair criterion of his claims to a higher character for business under different situations. It is proverbial and a great proof of the honour of the Sindhian Soucars that their bills are always considered as cash in every part of the vast countries to the north-west, and are recognized as such all over India. This is the class in Sindh whom it will be our policy to foster and protect. The country, if it ever becomes of commercial importance, must be so through the Hindús: they have long striven against disadvantages which can only be understood by a comparison to the state of the Jews in England during certain periods of our history; but despite obstacles which would appear to be insurmountable, they have maintained their footing, and carried on the whole of the great and important trade between the Lower Indus and the countries beyond the Affghan passes as far as Hírat and Bokhara. They have all the speculative energy adapted for extending commerce, and protection will alone be required to bring it forward.

The population of Sindh has been estimated in round numbers at about a million; but judging from those portions where actual inquiry has enabled us to test the correctness of former calculations, it would appear to be overrated at the above. In a country like Sindh, however, where there are comparatively few towns, one part of the population leading a wandering life, whilst another is dispersed over its river, it is difficult to arrive at any accurate conclusion with respect to numbers; but that Sindh is for its whole extent very thinly populated is obvious to the most superficial observation. The capital, Hyderabad, does not contain more than thirty-five thousand, whilst Shikarpúr, the next in size, formerly rated at thirty-five, was found to yield only twenty-two thousand. The numbers in most of the modern maps as annexed to the various places appear to be exaggerated, from the absence of correct information. In the large trading towns the Hindús bear a proportion of about one fourth to the Mahommedan, but in other parts of the country much less.

Originally published as T. Postans, *Personal Observations on Sindh: The Manners and Customs of Its Inhabitants and Its Productive Capabilities* (London, Longman, Brown, Green, and Longmans, 1843), pp. 63–9.

15

Marwaris
From 'Community' to 'Class'

Dwijendra Tripathi

A business community from which entrepreneurs continue to emerge even in twenty-first century India is the Marwari community. Hailing from Rajasthan, these merchants have a long history of migration, going back to the fifteenth century at least. With the establishment of the British ascendancy, the community started exploiting new commercial opportunities that arose in the mid-nineteenth century in the metropolises of Calcutta, Bombay, and Madras. Marwari traders played crucial roles in the new economic order as brokers, *banias*, sub-contractors, and agents to European business, making themselves indispensable to trade and commerce. They also had interests in speculative markets and engaged in futures trading in opium, spices, hessian, and jute. With the outbreak of World War I and the resultant emergence of extraordinary economic opportunities, Marwari traders were propelled into the manufacturing sector. Thereafter, while they kept up their interest in trading, moneylending, and speculative markets, increasing numbers of Marwari trading houses also adapted to changes in the colonial economy and emerged as major industrial houses.*

* On the Marwaris, also see Thomas Timberg, *The Marwaris: From Traders to Industrialists* (New Delhi, Vikas, 1978) and his 'A Note on the Arrival of Calcutta's Marwaris', *Bengal Past and Present*, 90, 1971, pp. 75–84, 'A North Indian Firm as Seen through Its Business Records, 1860–1914: Tarachand Ghanshyamdas, A Great Marwari Firm', *Indian Economic and Social History Review*, Vol. 8, No. 3, 1971; and 'Three Types of the Marwari Firm', *Indian Economic and Social History Review*, Vol. 10, January 1973; D.K. Taknet, *Industrial Enterprenuership among Shekhawati Marwaris* (Jaipur, Manohar, 1986) and his *Marwari Samaj* (Jaipur, 1989); G.D. Sharma, 'The Marwaris: Economic Foundations of an Indian Capitalist Class', in Dwijendra Tripathi (ed.), *Business Communities of India: A Historical Perspective* (New Delhi, Manohar, 1984); K.L. Sharma, 'Aspects of Merchants, Markets, Moneylending and Migration: Reflections based on Field Notes from a Village in Rajasthan', in Philippe Cadene and Denis Vidal

In this chapter, pioneering business historian Dwijendra Tripathi debunks the view that capitalist development in India was brought to the fore by a number of discrete business communities rather than a composite business class. Tripathi clarifies the deceptively naturalistic connotations of the term 'business community'. He questions the use of the term 'community', preferring to use 'mini-business class' instead. Tripathi's research is driven by this question: How did the designation 'Marwari' come to be identified with a particular group of Indian businessmen? He addresses the question by analysing the history of migration from the Marwar region to the rest of India, but specifically to Bengal. He elucidates how the Marwaris constituted a culturally and religiously heterogeneous group consisting of Oswal Jains and Hindu Bania castes such as Agrawals, Porwals, and Maheshwaris. He uncovers the mixed connotations of the appellation 'Marwari' and its pragmatic acceptance by the labeled outsiders, as a suitable umbrella description of themselves which outwardly kept secret their in-group diversities for reasons of maintaining a sense of identity and a front of unified solidarity. In proclaiming the Marwaris as part of the emergence of a national bourgeoisie, Tripathi takes the reader on a journey in understanding themes of assimilation and integration associated with Marwari migration, in appreciating their chosen fields of trade and moneylending, of witnessing the birth of the Marwari Chamber of Commerce, and the agency of the Marwaris within conflicting Indian and European interests.

Lack of empirical research has resulted in the persistence of some folklores about Indian business behaviour. One of these, perhaps the most pervasive, was popularised by the celebrated German sociologist, Max Weber, about three quarters of a century ago who held that the Indian religio-cultural ethos and social system were inherently subversive of material aspirations and economic progress. Based though it was on a faulty understanding of Indian values and occupational organisation, the thesis received an uncritical acceptance not only in the West but also among Indian scholars who ought to have had better insights into the behavioural dynamics of their own people. Critical evaluation regarding actual experience of Indian business has, however, rubbed the glitter off the Weberian postulates in recent years.[1] And yet they continue to pervert our understanding of Indian business and its various ramifications. Such is the aura of authenticity Western enunciations about us ring in our ears.

A case in point is the widespread belief that the capitalist development in India brought to the fore a number of discrete business communities rather than a composite business class. Propounded by the late D.R. Gadgil, the thesis implies that this phenomenon differed markedly from the development in other countries where capitalist enterprise flourished.[2] The proponents of this view have never cared to explain the implication of the phrase '*business community*' with any degree of precision, but the context of its use seems to suggest that

(eds), *Webs of Trade: Dynamics of Business Communities in Western India* (Delhi, Manohar, 1997), pp. 174–94; and Anne Hardgrove, *Community and Public Culture: The Marwaris in Calcutta, 1897–1997* (New York, University of Columbia Press, 2002).

it denotes a group of businessmen who, in addition to a common occupational affiliation, share certain socio-cultural characteristics inherited from birth and, thanks to this accident, the business interests pursued and strategies adopted by one community are clearly distinguishable from those of the others.

This thesis appears to be a direct corollary of the Weberian postulates. The fact, however, is that viewed in a proper historical context the so-called business communities would appear to be mini-business classes emerging in various parts of India before the country achieved political and economic integration. As India until the British conquest was politically fragmented and communication between one part and the other none too easy, businessmen in one region could not have made common cause with their counterparts elsewhere.

But within their own region, they represented a variety of distinctive socio-cultural groups which became even more varied as the traditional barriers to occupational choices began to crumble. More importantly, distinctiveness in their socio-cultural backgrounds did not prevent them from joining hands to safeguard their purely business interest while going their own separate ways in their religious-cultural spheres. In other words, what bound them together despite cultural diversities was the economic concern which is the basic characteristic of a class.

As the country became more unified and internal communication more efficient, the regional boundaries became blurred and businessmen in various parts of the country drew increasingly closer, paving the ground for the absorption of region-specific collectivities in an all-India pressure group. Seen in this fashion, the so-called business communities represented an intermediate stage in the formation of the Indian business class. This was not very different from the process through which business classes emerged in other capitalistic societies. The American business class for instance comprises a number of clearly identifiable socio-cultural groups but nobody calls them business communities.

A study of the evolution of each of the Indian business communities will support these general remarks but the Marwari perhaps offers the best example. For one thing, the term 'Marwari' has a distinctly business connotation while all other communities—Gujarati, Punjabi, Parsi, or Chettier—represent both a business group and a regional, linguistic, racial or cultural collectively. True, in Rajasthan itself, a Marwari is one who belongs to the Marwar region of the state whatever his occupation. But in the rest of the country the term is used for all and only such Rajasthanis who are engaged in some kind of business outside Rajasthan. How did this appellation come to stick to a specific group of Indian businessmen? To answer this question we have to go far back into the history of migration from the Marwar region.

Comprising a vast area of awesome sandy rocky monotony with infertile soil, and inhospitable climate the region bears the most appropriate name which means desertland. Colonel James Tod, a 19th century British officer quite familiar with the region referred to it as 'the region of death.[3] The children of the soil perhaps would have felt less oppressed than was the British observer by the rigours of elements but movement of people out of Marwar has been a continuing phenomenon throughout its history. Merchants and traders constituted a large majority of the Marwari diaspora because a thinly populated region, as Marwar was, could have provided but limited business opportunities.

Well until the first quarter of the 19th century most of the Marwari migrants except a few daring spirits moved either to more prosperous parts of Rajasthan or other neighbouring regions. As the means of communications improved and internal movement became much safer, the Marwari merchants began to cast their eyes far and wide in search of more lucrative business locations. They moved in all directions and to most of the major trading centres in India, but Bengal held a special attraction for them.[4] This was because of two reasons.

First, a few Marwari merchants had been operating there for the last several decades; some of them like the house of Jagat Seths had even amassed great wealth and financial powers. Since these early adventurers had never severed their links with their original homeland, they formed a sort of resource group for others who decided to follow suit. In many cases, the newcomers started as employees of those who had already settled down in the province.

Secondly, as the first region to fall to the British might, Bengal was emerging as the most attractive theatre of business in the land. The number of these immigrants had grown sufficiently large to warrant the formation of a Marwari *panchayat* in Calcutta by 1828 and by 1860 some of the firms set up by them had become prestigious enough to deserve listing in the commercial directories of the city.[5]

Culturally or religiously, the emigrants did not form a homogeneous group. Admittedly, a large majority consisted of Oswal Jains (who trace their origin from Osian near Jodhpur) and Hindu *bania* castes such as Agrawals, Porwal, Maheshwari etc. This is understandable. Material impediments to occupational mobility, including limited opportunities for commercial success in the desertland, had left the caste basis of professional choice more or less intact, and propensity to migrate was most pronounced among those already engaged in mercantile pursuits. And yet there were some among the emigrants who belonged to the non-business castes. As early as 1829, John Malcolm, a British traveller, discovered some Jodhpuri Brahmans among their ranks and Thomas A. Timberg in the course of his research recently found the presence of several *non-banias* in Calcutta business whose ancestors had migrated from the desertland.[6] In due course of time, their regional cohesiveness also suffered a dent by the entry of people from other parts of Rajasthan who were lured to Bengal by the success of the earlier groups of immigrants with whom they were connected through kinship, friendship, or other social ties.

These fine distinctions, however, were unnoticed by the native Bengali who called the entire Rajasthanis diaspora by the generic title of Marwari after the name of the region from where the earlier bands of settlers had come. In view of the fact that all immigrant businessmen from Rajasthan shared a common lifestyle, spoke the same language, wore similar kind of dresses, and specialised primarily in trading and moneylending, this was not unjustified. Also since most of them maintained their links with their original homeland and their distinctive cultural and linguistic characteristics prevented their integration with the native Bengali population, they remained a discrete class by themselves.

To an extent the appellation Marwari seems to have been born in contempt and jealousy. Contempt for the immigrant's frugality which was interpreted as stinginess, for his commercial preoccupation which seemed to symbolise lack of interest in socio-cultural concerns, for his dress and food habits which evoked nothing but amusement, and for his clannish interdependence which made him appear as an incorrigible outsider. And jealousy because more often than not the immigrant seemed to leave his Bengali counterpart far behind in the race for business success. Whatever its origin, the immigrants did not unduly resent this appellation; they in fact adopted it as a convenient description of themselves which seemed to conceal their diversities. A minority group operating in a somewhat hostile milieu often needs this kind of a prop to sustain a sense of identity.[7]

It is significant that the generic title of Marwaris for the immigrant Rajasthani merchants was used only in those areas where they failed to achieve a measure of socio-cultural integration with the native population. In the cities of Uttar Pradesh, Madhya Pradesh, Bihar and Punjab, where their number was relatively small and linguistic and cultural barriers to integration less formidable, they identified themselves completely with the local mercantile communities. Likewise the term Marwari was never applied to the Jain businessmen in Gujarat although the ancestors of a large majority of them (all Oswal Jains of Gujarat claim their descent from Osian near Jodhpur) came from Marwar. Did anybody ever call Kasturbhai Lalbhai a Marwari even though his ancestors had migrated to Ahmedabad about four centuries ago from the same region which was the original home of the Jagat Seth family, once the most leading Marwari house in Calcutta?[8] This is so because the Marwari immigrants in Gujarat found it easier to merge themselves with the local population, linguistic and cultural constraints to integration being far less pronounced than in the case of migrants to the remote east.

As an identifiable business community, thus, the Marwaris for a long time were confined to eastern India, primarily Bengal, where their number and business presence continued to rise throughout the 19th century, particularly after 1860. The period witnessed the gradual withdrawal of the native Bengalis from business scene although they had responded very creatively to the emerging business opportunities in the first half of the century.[9] This is not the occasion to discuss the cause of the Bengali failure and Marwari success but it was not due to the choice of business lines or operational strategies of the two respective groups as has been suggested by some writers. Both were competing in the same field—trade, moneylending, import—export business and as brokers and agents to European firms. But whereas the Marwaris could depend on an extensive network of their kinsmen scattered in small pockets throughout the country, the Bengalis had no such advantage. The result was that the Marwaris rose from strength to strength. The establishment of their own chamber of commerce in 1900 headquartered in Calcutta, symbolised the growing consciousness on their part of their power and identity.

The Marwari Chamber of Commerce proved to be a non-starter. But it was a sign of a widening gulf between the native and European business interests in Indian markets. Almost up to the end of the 19th century, their relations were marked by a remarkable degree of cordiality and interdependence, occasional irritants notwithstanding. As the native bourgeoisie gained in strength, ironically because of the forces of change generated by the British ruling presence, it was no more willing to play a second fiddle to the European business interest or to put up meekly with racial discrimination and prejudice. The rift between the two groups became even more pronounced in the wake of rising tide of nationalism beginning with the early years of the present century. The growing number of indigenous trade organisations, as distinct from those promoted by the British in which the Indians were poor partners, was only one of the many manifestations of this trend. The first of such native pressure groups had come into being as early as 1885—the year which saw the birth of the Indian National Congress. Others to follow were the Bengal National Chamber of Commerce (1887) and the Indian Merchants Chamber in Bombay (1907). Realising the meaning of such ominous developments, the Europeans tried to frustrate the Indian moves wherever they could. The premature eclipse of the Marwari chamber was largely due to their machinations.[10]

The Marwaris in the meantime had accumulated sufficient capital resource and business experience to move into manufacturing which they had all along shunned during the age of Indian-European cordiality. Dislocation of imports and rising internal demand consequent upon the outbreak of the First World War came as godsend, pointing to rich returns on investment in industrial ventures. G.D. Birla, whose family had moved from Shekhawati first to Bombay and then to Calcutta in the latter half of the 19th century, led the way by setting up a jute mill in Calcutta. Starting as a broker Birla had grown to be the wealthiest Marwari in Calcutta. With a first-hand experience of racial discrimination perpetrated by English merchants, he had developed a great deal of antipathy towards the foreigner which continued to influence his behaviour all through his life. Inspired by his example, some of his fellow Marwaris in Calcutta also went into jute manufacturing and coal mining. A little later Birla built a cotton mill in Delhi and another at Gwalior. This was a signal, as it were, for the Marwari merchants in other cities of north India to launch manufacturing ventures. By the beginning of the 1920s, thus, the signs of the Marwaris shifting from commercial pursuits to industrial enterprises were clearly noticeable.[11]

Also noticeable was the growing conflict between the Indian and European interests. The Marwari played a very active role in this drama. As if their attempt to storm the exclusive British preserves such as jute and coal industries was not reprehensible enough, they began to acquire shares in the British controlled companies through stock market operations and force their entry into their boards.[12] This was bound to create scare among the European business community whose leaders expressed their resentment in no uncertain terms. They lambasted not only the Marwari 'pirates' for the 'dirty work' but also the government of the day which in their eyes seemed to pamper the Indian interests. The confrontation between the European and Indian business was reaching the point of no return when the Associated Chambers of Commerce (Assocham), an all-India organisation ostensibly representing the entire Indian business but functioning under a tight European control, passed a resolution in 1923, in the teeth of bitter Indian protest, opposing the grant of protection to Indian steel industry. This was the last nail in the coffin of the facade of unity.

G.D. Birla once again led the way. By this time he had already become an all-India figure with whom business leaders all over the country were in intimate contact. He had also emerged as the undisputed spokesman of the Marwaris. Realising that an insular mentality would no more serve the interest of his community and lack of a common platform was detrimental to Indian business as a whole, he immediately initiated the move for the formation of a rival body. Practically all prominent business leaders in India, representing various regions and communities—Purshotam Thakurdas, Lala Shri Ram, Dinshaw Petit, Kasturbhai Lalbhai, M.C.T. Muthia Chettier, M. Jamal Mohamed Sahib, Walchand Hirachand, D.P. Khaitan, A.C. Banerjee and a host of less famous luminaries—supported his initiative. The result was the formation of the Federation of Indian Chambers of Commerce and Industry (FICCI) in 1927.[13]

The formation of FICCI was not the cause but the effect of a growing sense of interdependence among the businessmen all over India. The political unification of the country providing for unhindered movement of goods and people, discriminating—often humiliating—treatment meted out to Indian business interest by the expatriates, and rising nationalism were some of the major factors that forced the region-specific industrial-commercial groups to realise that a community of interest bound them together despite their socio-cultural diversities. What can be a better example of this development than the changing attitude of the Marwaris, perhaps the most insular of them, who had developed a remarkable sense of forbearance and patience thanks to their long interaction with a none-too-friendly environment?

Once this realisation dawned on them, the so-called business communities outgrew their regional affiliation. Not only did they expand their operations in new lines—such as sugar, cement, and chemicals—and out of their respective regions, but also their functional strategies and managerial structures lost much of their distinctiveness. The advent of freedom, opening up an entire new vista of profitable opportunities, reinforced this trend still further, completing the process of the emergence of a national bourgeoisie of which the Marwaris, as other regional collectivities, are an integral part. To view their place in Indian business today in any other manner is to indulge in a fruitless pastime of drawing needless circles around us.

Originally published as Dwijendra Tripathi, 'From Community to Class: The Marwari in a Historical Perspective', in B.L. Bhadani and Dwijendra Tripathi (eds), *Facets of a Marwar Historian* (Jaipur, Publication Scheme, 1996), pp. 189–96.

NOTES

1. Max Weber, *The Protestant Ethic and Spirit of Capitalism* (New York, 1958); Weber, 'India: The Brahman and the Caste', in *From Max Weber: Essays in Sociology*, ed. by H.H. Gerth and C. Wright Mills (New York, 1958). Some of the studies pursuing Weberian line directly or indirectly include P.B. Medhora, 'Entrepreneurship in India', *Political Science Quarterly*, Vol. 80, No. 46 (December 1965); H.B. Lamb, 'Indian Business Communities and the Evolution of an Industrial Class', *Pacific Affairs*, Vol. 18, No. 2 (June 1955); K.W. Kapp, *Hindu Culture, Economic Development and Economic Planning in India* (New York, 1963); V.K. Agarwala, *Initiative, Enterprise and Economic Choices in India* (New Delhi, 1975). For critique of Weberian approach, see D.P. Pandit, 'Creative Response in Indian Economy: A Regional Study', *Economic Weekly*, Vol. 9, Nos. 8 and 9 (23 February and 2 March 1957); M.D. Morris, 'Values as an Obstacle to Economic Growth in South Asia', *Journal of Economic History*, Vol. 27, No. 4 (December 1967); Dwijendra Tripathi, 'Indian Entrepreneurship in Historical Perspective', *Economic and Political Weekly*, Vol. 6, No. 22 (29 May 1971).
2. D.R. Gadgil, *Business Communities in India* (Mimeo, Institute of Pacific Affairs, New York, 1951); for a critique see, Dwijendra Tripathi, 'Class Character of the Gujarati Business Community', in Dwijendra Tripathi (ed.), *Business Communities of India* (New Delhi, 1984).
3. James Tod, *Annals and Antiquities of Rajasthan* (Delhi, 1971 reprint), II p. 929.
4. T.A. Timberg, *The Marwaris: From Traders to Industrialists* (New Delhi, 1978), pp. 43–56; G.D. Sharma, 'The Marwaris: Economic Foundations of an Indian Capitalist Class', in Dwijendra Tripathi (ed.), *Business Communities of India*, pp. 185–207.
5. Balchand Modi, *Desh ke Itihas me Marwari Jati ka Sthan* (in Hindi) (Calcutta, 1940), pp. 610–20; also D.K. Taknet, *Marwari Samaj* (in Hindi) (Jaipur, 1989), pp. 1–70.
6. John Malcolm, *A Memoir of Central India and Malwa* (London, 1824), p. 159; Timberg, *The Marwaris*, pp. 10–11.

7. A good example is that of 'muckrakers'—a group of young reformers in the United States in the first decade of this century, who through their writings laid bare various ills of the society. President Theodore Roosevelt contemptuously called them 'muckrakers'. They accepted it as a convenient collective appellation for themselves.

8. For details see Dwijendra Tripathi, *The Dynamics of A Tradition: Kasturbhai Lalbhai and His Entrepreneurship* (New Delhi, 1987), pp. 9–39.

9. See N.K. Sinha, 'Indian Business Enterprise: Its Failure in Calcutta (1800–1848)', *Bengal Past and Present*, Diamond Jubilee Number (July–December 1967), pp. 112–23 for failure of Bengali business.

10. Dwijendra Tripathi, 'The Congress and the Industrial Question (1919–1935)', in B.N. Pande and R. Kumar (eds), *A Centenary History of the Indian National Congress*, (New Delhi, 1985), pp. 493–523.

11. R.N. Jaju, *G.D. Birla: A Biography* (New Delhi, 1985); Timberg, *The Marwaris*, pp. 42–58.

12. Omkar Goswami, 'Then Came the Marwaris: Some Aspects of the Changes in the Pattern of Industrial Control in Eastern India', *Indian Economic and Social History Review*, Vol. 22, No. 3 (Oct. 1985), pp. 225–49.

13. Stanley Kochanek, *Business and Politics in India* (Berkeley, 1974), pp. 108–30.

16

Nattukottai Chettiars
Caste and Business Organization

Christine Dobbin

While Parsis carved out niches in western India in the nineteenth century and Marwaris found their forte in the north Indian hinterland, the Nattukottai Chettiars of Ramnad district in the Pudukottai region were well ensconced as traders and moneylenders within the south Indian economy from at least the seventeenth century and in Southeast Asia from the mid-nineteenth century. Though there were many eminent mercantile communities in southern India such as the Komatis of Andhra, the Nadars of Tamil Nadu, and the Syrian Christians of Kerala, the Chettiars have gained the most eminence because their trading activities extended far beyond their home base in Chettinad and flourished well into the twentieth century.*

Evolving from their origins as salt traders in the seventeenth century, the Chettiars adapted to the colonial economy and became a major merchant capitalist caste of south

*On the Chettiars, also see David W. Rudner, *Caste and Capitalism in Colonial India: The Nattukottai Chettiars* (Berkeley, University of California Press, 1994); Raman Mahadevan, 'Immigrant Entrepreneurs in Colonial Burma—An Exploratory Study of the Role of Nattukottai Chettiars of Tamil Nadu, 1880–1930', *Indian Economic and Social History Review*, Vol. 15, 1978, pp. 329–58 and his 'Pattern of Enterprise of Immigrant Entrepreneurs: A Study of the Chettiars in Malaya, 1880–1930,' *Economic and Political Weekly*, Vol. 15, 1978, pp. 146–52; Ramdas Menon, 'Banking and Trading Castes in the Colonial Period: The Case of the Nattukottai Chettiars of Tamil Nadu', *South Asia Bulletin*, Vol. V, No. 2, Spring 1985, pp. 19–26; Shoji Ito, 'A Note on the Business Combine in India with Special Reference to Nattukottai Chettiars', *Developing Economies*, Vol. 6, No. 3, September 1966; and Rajeswary Ampalavanar Brown, *Capital and Entrepreneurship in South-East Asia* (Hampshire, Macmillan Press, 1994), pp. 173–89. On the community in Singapore, see Hans-Dieter Evers, Jayarani Pavadarayan, and Heiko Schrader, 'The Chettiar Moneylenders in Singapore', in Hans-Dieter Evers and Heiko Schrader (eds), *The Moral Economy of Trade: Ethnicity and Developing Markets* (New York, Routledge, 1994), pp. 198–212.

India. From the 1830s, responding to changes in the world economy and the emergence of a proto-capitalist global system, they began to migrate in waves to Malaya, Burma, and the Straits Settlement and subsequently to Siam, Java, Indo-China, northern Sumatra, and Thailand. And gradually, they became indispensable as financiers of commercial production of primary products, as senders of remittances, as intermediaries of Western capital, and as providers of agricultural credit so critical to the emergence of the plantation economy in Sri Lanka, the opening up of the Burmese rice frontier, and the setting up of tin and rubber plantations in Malaya.[†]

In this piece, historian Christine Dobbin traces the reasons for their entrepreneurial success by analysing their role as a 'middleman minority' in the period of European commercial dominance in Asia, the nature of their firms, their religious beliefs, their interests in commerce, and their entrance into industry. Dobbin sees Asian merchant minorities, who maintained independent commercial roles throughout the period of European domination over Asia, as key players in the evolution of the world economy. Dobbin ascertains that it is in their dual identity—as a business community that stresses the importance of a strictly ascetic business life and as a community with an affinity for a spiritual life of a populist nature—where the spirit of this community's economic creativity must be sought. Employing a Weberian model and related ideas about 'the spirit of capitalism', Dobbin assesses this Asian entrepreneurial minority.

From the time of their conquest of Lower Burma in 1852 the British were aware of the great potential of the fertile Irrawaddy Delta region as a source of foodstuffs and raw materials and a possible market outlet for British manufactured goods. So far, throughout the eighteenth century, the Delta had been poorly developed, sparsely populated and a mere backwater of the last Burmese kingdom.[1] Indian commercial ties to the region were long-standing, but they were now given substance by the British conquest. The earliest British endeavours to develop the region were based on attempts to settle Indian agriculturalists on land by a programme of land grants begun in 1874. Between 1876 and 1878 more than 15,000 Indians came to the Delta to claim government land as free cultivators, but the type of agriculture was unfamiliar to them and these efforts were generally regarded as unsuccessful. An equal failure was an attempt to make large grants to Indian capitalists on attractive conditions, and although about 9,500 Indians were brought to work on these estates, this too did not succeed.[2]

Instead, Indian settlement in Lower Burma proceeded very similarly to that of Chinese settlement in the early days of Manila and Batavia. In 1862 the four provinces of Pegu, Martaban, Arakan and Tenasserim became

† Interestingly, the Chettiars, though prominent as moneylenders and traders till the 1930s, did not take to manufacturing and large-scale industry in a large way. After they were eased out of their niche areas of moneylending and trading during the 1930s due to extant political conditions and economic depression in their territories (like Burma), they were unable to make the transition to industry. On this, see Medha Kudaisya, 'Marwari and Chettiar Merchants, 1850–1950s: Comparative Trajectories', in Medha Kudaisya and Ng Chin-keong (eds), *Chinese and Indian Business: Historical Antecedents* (Leiden, Brill, 2009), pp. 85–119.

consolidated as the Province of British Burma, directed from the port city of Rangoon. While Indian land settlement schemes had failed, Rangoon acted as a magnet for Indians from across the Bay of Bengal in Madras Presidency. The entire character of the city was Indian; where there were only nineteen Indians in Rangoon in 1838, by 1881 there were approximately 65,000. By 1891 the Indian population of Rangoon outnumbered the Burmese, a trend that continued until 1931. In that year Indians were 54 per cent of the population and Burmese 32 per cent.[3] The majority of the Indian immigrants were labourers coming to work on the docks, but Indians of all castes and classes made their way from Madras to the new frontier city. Among these were members of a small Tamil caste, the Nattukottai Chettiars, first recorded in Rangoon in the early 1850s, who arrived in the train of the early Indian expeditionary forces and found among them the possibility of engaging in their developing occupation of moneylending, an opportunity which expanded when they discovered they were able to collaborate with arriving British exchange banks to open up the Delta frontier.[4]

THE MADRAS PREADAPTATION

The term Chettiar is etymologically allied to the Sanskrit term *sreshti*, the literal meaning of which is 'banker' or 'big merchant'. The prevalence of the term *shetia* in Bombay has already been discussed. In the nineteenth century the homes of the most important part of the caste were the districts of Ramnad and Trichinopoly in the Presidency of Madras in Southern India. The Nattukottai Chettiars had their business headquarters in an area popularly known as 'Chettinad', comprising the eastern part of Ramnad district and a part of Trichinopoly.[5] They were a tiny caste, numbering 7,851 in 1891, and divided into exogamous subdivisions or 'clans' named after nine temples in Chettinad.[6] Their homeland was in close touch across the Bay of Bengal with developments in the Delta and their long centuries of evolution as a commercial community, culminating in involvement with European commerce, prepared them to work with Western banks and joint-stock companies such as the Imperial Bank of India and the Indian Overseas Bank, which provided them with sources of working capital not readily available to Burmese brokers and moneylenders.[7]

Chettiars espoused a unique blend of religion and commerce dating from at least the eleventh century. The economic function of the South Indian temple is well known. Temples in the Tamil cultural area functioned as institutions of capital investment, accumulation and distribution, initially receiving endowments from local rulers and notables and from trading guilds. This income not only covered temple capital and operating expenses, but was used as loan money for irrigation, animal breeding and long-distance trade. Temple assets were generally located in regional market towns and managed by assemblies representative of the towns' chief merchants.[8] David Rudner has carefully explained the role of temples and temple-gifting in the economic development of the Nattukottai Chettiar caste, a phenomenon which led the caste from the interior of Tamilnad to economic relations with Europeans on the coast. Their gradual involvement in the economic life of the temple preadapted the caste to take advantage of the new opportunities presented by the encroaching world-economy from the seventeenth century.

Rudner focuses on the seventeenth-century commercial expansion of the Nattukottai

Chettiar caste in terms of its rituals of religious gifting to temples. In that period, Nattukottai Chettiars were primarily employed as salt traders in a small area of ninety-six villages in the northern part of present-day Ramnad district. Salt in various forms was produced in coastal districts and traded inland. By this time Nattukottai Chettiar lineages had already established links with temples in their residential villages throughout their Chettinad homeland, exerting control over the markets, fairs and economic activities associated with their own temples.[9] But in order for itinerant trading activities to be successful outside their own residential limits, it was necessary for further ties to be forged by individual Nattukottai Chettiar traders by involvement in religious gifting in the locality to which they addressed their commercial endeavours.

Rudner uses the example of Nattukottai Chettiar salt traders in the pilgrimage town of Palani, about 80 kilometres west of Chettinad. A manuscript beginning in 1600 recounts the story of a Nattukottai Chettiar trader who came to Palani from Chettinad to investigate the prospects for expanding his salt business. Much more than merely selling in the market, he was required to establish a relationship with the temple deity of Palani, mediated through the deity's priest, by giving a tithe on his profit. Other salt traders gradually joined him and, at periods of pilgrimage, Nattukottai Chettiars established religious endowments at the temple. These acts of religious gifting and collective worship were 'integrative temple rituals'[10] which made it possible for new traders to enter market towns. The gifts were functional and were thought of, in part, as licence fees and financial investments. By worshipping in temples that lay outside their residential homeland, small groups of Nattukottai Chettiars established themselves over a broad geographical area, while at the same time retaining their ability to draw on the financial resources of other members of the caste.

Rudner's salt trader ultimately became Endowment Manager of the temple in Palani; he was judged by his trustworthiness and, in return for his transactions with both the deity and other members of the temple community, he received a certain share of the endowment he managed which was available for reinvestment in his business. This, in turn, led to further endowments to the temple and further Nattukottai Chettiar involvement in the Palani economy. Trustworthiness provided the moral basis of credit on which all mercantile activities were based. Rudner concludes that religious gifts performed not only religious and political functions but also important economic functions, including the acquisition and reinvestment of funds in mercantile enterprises. The Nattukottai Chettiars were able to engage in trade by worshipping the deities of their customers and, gaining positions of trust in the temple, were able to expand the market for their salt.[11]

The Nattukottai Chettiars were now ready to take advantage of new opportunities. With the coming of the European companies and the expansion of commerce the Nattukottai Chettiar caste, already specialized around activities of capital accumulation and investment, was preadapted for economic success. Their inland location initially placed them at a disadvantage compared to the coastal castes which were the Europeans' first collaborators, but their ritual techniques for entering new markets, pooling capital and transferring money enabled them to compete very rapidly.[12]

Capital was, of course, a European requirement on the coast. Francis Day chose the site of Madras city in 1639 for the English

East India Company's settlement because the region was known for its superior weavers and dyers who produced cloth more cheaply than that which European rivals were buying elsewhere.[13] Within a very short time merchants of some substance were attracted to set up residence in Madras and to engage in a whole range of wholesale and retail trading in a variety of merchandise. Several Chettiar castes came, including Nattukottai Chettiars.[14] From the mid-eighteenth century an increasingly large European private trade led to additional opportunities for Indian middlemen, and a small circle of elite merchants came to exercise a dominant role in the organization and financing of Anglo-Indian trade. South Indian society became 'credit hungry', as local chiefs engaged in military forays and European trading companies depended on forward advances of credit provided by local moneylenders.[15]

The Nattukottai Chettiars were prepared to adapt their traditional practices to these new circumstances. Their chief seventeenth-century occupation, salt-trading, did not recover from a development that took place towards the end of the eighteenth century, when a severe drought reduced commerce between the inland salt-consuming and the coastal salt-producing regions. By 1805 the major salt renters had become so weak that the East India Company was able to do away with them as middlemen in the salt trade and take on something like monopolistic control over salt production. Nattukottai Chettiars responded by slowly extending their commercial operations as far south as the pearl, rice, cloth and arak trade of Ceylon and as far north as the rice and wheat trade of Calcutta. By the end of the eighteenth century they had gained control of the pearl fisheries in the Ceylon Straits, and from at least 1820 they also dominated the major coastal trade in arak and in coconut products from Ceylon to Madras. Contemporaries claimed they had cornered the Ceylon rice market, controlling all imports not only of Tanjore rice but of Bengal rice too. As early as 1820 they had also established firms in Calcutta, exchanging salt for Bengal grains.[16]

Nattukottai Chettiar financial transactions formed the heart of these commercial enterprises. In a process that is still unclear, they developed a sophisticated financial apparatus which included provisions for making forward loans, for extending short-term and long-term loans to political and military collaborators, and for transmitting bills of exchange among themselves and their clients. By obscure and not so obscure means they evolved into a long-distance, merchant-banking caste. Rudner states that there remains scope for considerable research into the precise nature of Nattukottai Chettiar credit networks and the various commodities' markets with which they were involved. What is clear is that late eighteenth-century and early nineteenth-century Nattukottai Chettiar commodities trading was tied to some kind of exchange banking system, the Chettiars combining their trade undertakings with the purely financial transactions of moneylending, remittance of funds between geographically distant locations and to government authorities, and the supply of credit to the new landlord class of Madras Presidency.[17]

The final alteration in the Madras business climate before large-scale Nattukottai Chettiar investment in the Burma rice Delta comprised a series of changes which made further profit in the Madras Presidency difficult to acquire. The credit needs of the cotton traders of Coimbatore, once a Nattukottai Chettiar preserve, were taken out of their hands. Beginning in 1843 with the founding of the Presidency Bank of Madras, Europeans established their own banks, thereby excluding Nattukottai Chettiars and other indigenous moneylenders from the market in mercantile finance and currency exchange for private European firms. An alternative was sought in investing in or converting bad debts into land ownership, and Rudner estimates that between 1850 and 1900 perhaps 200 Nattukottai Chettiars were able to obtain minor landlord titles but these, using a population basis of 10,000, could have represented at most one-fifth and more likely one-tenth or even one-twentieth of joint family units. For the remainder, the failure of opportunities for financial investment in India, coupled with caste techniques of capital penetration, provided a stimulus to search for new ways of putting money to use.[18]

THE NATTUKOTTAI CHETTIAR FIRM IN BURMA

Displaced from the credit markets of Madras, displaced from exchange markets throughout the greater part of British India, Nattukottai Chettiars found a new niche in servicing the credit needs of indigenous Southeast Asians who were being drawn into the production of agrarian commodities for the world market. Involved in both Ceylon and Malaya, the leading economic frontier in which they became enmeshed was the Lower Burma Delta. Their first offices were opened in Rangoon in 1852, not for agricultural lending but to advance money to contractors who brought over coolies and also to invest in the rising import-export business carried on between India and Burma. Some also invested money in businesses unconnected with agriculture, such as the sale of wholesale oil and the operation of saw mills.[19] British policy, however, gradually opened the Delta area to a mass of Burmese peasant proprietors, sucked into the region by new opportunities for profitable rice-growing for a European market brought closer by the opening of the Suez Canal. In terms of subsequent Chettiar involvement, one of the most important British changes introduced after 1852 was the introduction of a new system of land tenure. The loose, noncontractual rights which had been common in the previous period were replaced by a land tenure system modelled on that of South India. This had as its major goal the concentration of ownership in the hands of individual cultivator-landholders. The implication of this system was that agriculturalists would be able to mortgage their holdings as security for loans granted by moneylenders and others. Further, the village system was reorganized in a new, decentralized manner whereby self-government no longer existed over any unit larger than the village; such villages were internally weakened and ripe for moneylenders' activities.[20]

As peasant contractors were drawn into the Delta, paddy acreage began to expand. Whereas in 1845 annual exports totalled only 74,000 tons, this had slowly increased to 160,000 tons by 1861. In 1864–65 exports amounted to 470,000 tons until, after some decline, the 1872–73 figure rose rapidly to 720,000 tons. After that figures were much higher. In the decade 1889–99 the annual average tonnage was about 1,370,000 and by 1911–14 that figure had increased sixfold.[21] There was a concomitant huge expansion in the area under rice cultivation, and a population increase of from approximately 1 million in 1852 to over 4 million in 1901.[22] Lower Burma was now fully integrated into the world-economy. With the disruptions of the American Civil War, Burma became a major rice supplier for London, Liverpool and continental milling centres like Hamburg and Bremen. 'The expansion of the Delta rice industry in the last half of the nineteenth century', writes Michael Adas, 'represents one of the most impressive examples of sustained economic growth under the aegis of a European colonial regime.'[23] But the British government and private British firms never had the money or the administrative apparatus to undertake so vast an enterprise as the development of the Delta. This would have been impossible without Nattukottai Chettiar capital.[24]

Migrants from Upper Burma or migrants from more populous areas of the Delta normally possessed little or no capital when they arrived on the rice frontier. They rarely succeeded in bringing waste land under cultivation without borrowing. Although there is no record in the settlement reports of the 1880s of cultivators taking loans from Nattukottai Chettiars, it is likely that agriculturalists who lived in the neighbourhood of Rangoon and other large towns did so. In some regions Chettiars financed agricultural production indirectly through loans to Burmese moneylenders, who in turn lent to cultivators at higher rates. In 1881 only 587 professional moneylenders were recorded in Lower Burma, while by 1901 nearly 3,200 bankers and moneylenders were enumerated: From the 1880s agents of Nattukottai Chettiars began to penetrate the Delta area beyond Rangoon and other urban areas. They established branches in the larger villages and also in towns along the railway line. In this way Rangoon-based millers gained control of the rice crop; once the agriculturalist began borrowing Chettiar capital, his indebtedness forced him to sell his crop at the miller's prices in order to meet his obligations. These rice-millers were largely Europeans, who developed a symbiotic relationship with the Nattukottai Chettiars' commercial activities. The opening of the Suez Canal in 1869 enabled them to supply large quantities of higher-priced husked and even white rice to European markets, leading to a considerable growth in the rice industry from which both Chettiars and European rice millers profited. Rice mills multiplied, from 52 in 1890 to 613 in 1930. Rangoon became a great modern port through which the world's largest rice exports flowed.[25]

Because there never developed any significant alternatives to Chettiar agricultural credit in either the private or public sector of Burma's economy, nor did there develop any alternative to Chettiar land alienation when debts could not be met. Large-scale transference of land out of Burmese ownership was a key aspect of Nattukottai Chettiar activities in Lower Burma, becoming noticeable as early as 1872.[26] The indications are that the Chettiars did not generally want land; in most areas they took over debtors' lands only as a last resort in order to prevent further monetary losses. By the end of the first phase of development, about 1905, the incidence of land alienation to non-agriculturalists was highest in the frontier districts of the tidal Delta and in the districts near Rangoon where rice production was particularly market-oriented and agricultural credit most readily available. Where Chettiars were forced to take over rice lands for unpaid debts, they normally tried to resell them as soon as possible; only if this was unsuccessful would they become landlords, with tenants working for them.[27]

Whatever their aims, the world-economy in which they were enmeshed disrupted totally their preferred commercial pattern. Quite some time before the Great Depression, the Delta rice frontier was experiencing serious agrarian problems. In the years after the First World War the export market upon which the Delta economy had grown dependent began to deteriorate, with new competitors and new market demands for higher quality.

Debtors became unable to repay loans and by the early 1930s there was a great acceleration of land alienation.[28] The amount of the total occupied area in Lower Burma held by non-agriculturalists rose from 31 per cent in 1929–30 to nearly 50 per cent by 1934–35. The proportion of land held by Nattukottai Chettiar moneylenders greatly increased. In 1930 they were listed as the owners of only 6 per cent of the total land occupied in the Delta and 19 per cent of the area held by non-agriculturalists; by 1937 they controlled 25 per cent of the cropped area in Lower Burma, and 50 per cent of that held by non-agriculturalists.[29] The regular functioning of Chettiar moneylending depended on the maintenance of a balance between their liquid assets and investment in immovable property. The new conditions placed a considerable strain on their moneylending system and many small Chettiar firms and a few large ones collapsed.[30]

Up to this point the history of the main Nattukottai Chettiar moneylending firms had been one of considerable economic success. The magnitude of the Chettiars' investment in Burma's rice production is indicated by the fact that by the late 1920s there were over 1,650 Chettiar firms in the main rice-growing districts of the colony: These firms advanced an estimated 450–500 million rupees a year in both crop and long-term loans to cultivators or to middlemen who lent it to cultivators. The government's role in credit provision remained marginal.[31] Of the 1,650 businesses mentioned, 360 or above one-fifth were in Rangoon while about 1,443 or seven-eighths of the total were in Lower Burma including Rangoon. Chettiar businesses were carried on in 217 towns and villages, and throughout every well-populated part of Lower Burma there was a Chettiar within a day's journey of every cultivator.[32]

Nattukottai Chettiar firms in Burma operated under an agency system very similar to that of the Ismailis in East Africa. At the age of about 18 a young man would be sent away from Chettinad for a tour of duty under older members of his clan, lasting approximately three years. 'Prior to this, from quite a young age the caste member would have undergone instruction in the arts of banking and moneylending. Scholars have stressed certain individualistic aspects of the young apprentice's family life as helping to provide an explanation for Nattukottai Chettiars' particular success. From at least the late nineteenth century family members, while living in the same compound, were constituted an independent unit on marriage and required to purchase, cook and eat their food separately. The married couple formed a separate unit of accounting and were obliged to exist as a discretionary and self-reliant entity.

Brought up in this system, children learned to practise thrift. Males were usually presented at birth with a small sum of money which was left to earn interest until it was needed for education or investment. Then at the age of 12 or so the boys were apprenticed to their fathers or to other members of the clan.[33] The milieu in which they lived, stressing the importance of bearing one's own financial burden, has been argued to have made young Chettiars self-reliant, ambitious and anxious to make their own fortunes. This strong emphasis on personal accountability, individual achievement, separate private consumption together with joint ownership of resources could then be the basis for successful long-distance commercial migration. The strict accountability of small units made it possible for Nattukottai Chettiars to send representatives abroad with small amounts of money which would not be rapidly exhausted in consumption.[34]

The Nattukottai Chettiar banker at home in Tamilnad began his career early. The age of 12–15 being the age of apprenticeship, about nine years were spent in this position or in a subordinate position in the banking business. At 22–25 years of age promotion occurred to a principal position. In the early years payment was generally in the form of board and lodging supplemented by bonuses. Those young Chettiars who were sent abroad could often be entrusted with sums as large as 100,000 rupees. The frugality and responsibility learnt at home were now rewarded, since each employee was normally allowed a percentage from the profits of any successful enterprise he was involved in. He was encouraged to save such allowances and use them, together with his salary, for further investments. After home leave and further training, his second tour saw him granted increased responsibility with the possibility of acting independently in ways such as lending money on his own initiative. Renewed success led to even more independence on his third tour, and increasing sums to supervise.[35]

Generally every place at which a firm carried on business had a separate agency. There were also outstations opened in villages at a reasonable distance from the main town, although usually not more than one for one business.[36] An agent, who was usually in his fifteenth or later year of employment, generally had an establishment of five to six, the main individuals being the assistant, the cashier and the accountant. The Burma Banking Inquiry noted:

Great care is taken in selecting agents and other members of the establishment. Owing in part to this and to the family connections often existing between them and the principals, there are practically no cases of dishonesty ... in addition to the salary every employee, including the agent, receives free board and lodging and has all his reasonable wants in other directions satisfied, so that he has no need to use any money of his own.[37]

No member of the establishment, not even the agent, was permitted to bring his wife with him.[38]

The individualistic manner in which the joint family treated its members did not mean that the family was not the key economic unit in Burma. Most Nattukottai Chettiar firms there were owned by individual families, generally consisting of two or more individuals in partnership, with the bulk of the capital provided from within the family. The Banking Inquiry looked at this closely:

Each Chettiar business is owned by a partnership of closely related persons and managed by an agent. The partners are commonly related to each other through their wives, people who are related directly being more likely to set up separate firms because of certain rules of a Hindu joint family as to ownership of property. When a partner has grown-up sons willing and able to take part in managing a business, he usually breaks off and sets up a new partnership consisting of himself and his sons; when the father dies the sons generally separate before long to form independent firms. Agents who have done well are sometimes taken into partnership. Under these conditions there are fairly frequent dissolutions of partnerships and formations of new firms ... Another result is that by the relationships of partners a firm is often closely connected with other firms, which accordingly, in case it gets into difficulties, can have reliable knowledge of its affairs and are often more willing therefore to help it over its difficulty than other firms would be.[39]

Whatever its other activities, each Nattukottai Chettiar firm operated as a commercial bank, taking money on deposit or drafting bills or other financial instruments for use in the transfer of loanable capital to branch offices and to other banks. All firms, largely headquartered in Chettinad, were in practice tied together to form a unified banking system employing sophisticated accounting techniques and possessing an efficient organization for collective decision-making. Each firm maintained contact with the 'clearing house' of Chettiar activity in Burma, the community temple in Mogul Street in Rangoon.[40] It was in this street that all Chettiar firms in Rangoon were concentrated. Six rooms in the temple were used by firms to do business with their clients. The Banking Inquiry pointed to the solidarity generated by this form of business existence:

> A few other buildings in Mogul Street, within a hundred yards from the temple up and down the street, have ground floors divided into similar rooms, making altogether (including the six-rooms) 23 such rooms. About 14 or 15 of the very largest firms have separate flats including either one or two business rooms, usually on the first floor of a building, and all situated in the same short piece of Mogul Street; most of the 14 or 15 firms have a desk also in one or other of the 23 rooms. In the 23 rooms and the flats and the temple itself all the Chettiar business is conducted. All the managers and their staff live close by, mostly in the rooms above the business-rooms; some sleep in the 23 rooms themselves to act as guardians. All meet one another frequently, not only in business and in attendance at the temple and at communal meetings, but also on the casual occasions of everyday life, such as the morning toilet, and in the casual attendances at the six-rooms in the morning to hear the gossip.[41]

In the towns and villages Nattukottai Chettiars occupied brick houses for security reasons. Anywhere between two to eight firms could occupy the same building, and where there was more than one Chettiar building in a town the other would unfailingly be close by. Disputes were settled out of court, with community elders conciliating. Apart from lending money these firms, whether in Rangoon or in the towns or villages, offered a range of financial services; they accepted deposits, honoured cheques, discounted bills of exchange, changed money, accepted documents and valuables for safe deposit and even dealt in gold.[42]

A further institution promoting caste solidarity was the *vituti* or community-supported lodging house located in the same building as or adjacent to a Nattukottai Chettiar-supported temple. These *uitutis* provided services for travelling caste members which greatly facilitated their commercial operations; they were able to obtain accommodation and meals, use mailing facilities, find assistance with travel arrangements and baggage clearance and even arrange for absentee prayers at local temples. Nattukottai Chettiars built *uitutis* whenever they had permanent business interests, commercial information could be readily exchanged and the reputations of individual houses investigated.[43]

Of course there was a wide difference between the scope of the activities of the largest and smallest firms. The largest firms belonged to *adathis*—important men—who controlled wealthy 'parent banks' and business enterprises[44] throughout South and Southeast Asia. In 1929 a new form of association appeared with the registration in Madras as a private company of the Bank of Chettinad, consisting of members of one family who had previously constituted two partnerships working in Burma, Ceylon, Malaya and Cochin China. The bank had a paid-up capital of 30 million rupees and its head office was established in the Ramnad district in Chettinad. All agencies of the two partnerships were converted into branch offices of the bank.[45] This bank, and other major Nattukottai Chettiar firms, were able to maintain excellent connections with European banks in both Madras and Rangoon; from these they occasionally borrowed money during periods of seasonal shortages. Relations were often so good that the Chettiars could acquire loans merely on promissory notes without collateral.[46] An *adathi* has been called a 'merchant-prince and banker';[47] while all Nattukottai Chettiar firms acted like commercial banks, making loans and taking deposits, *adathis* acted like reserve banks for the Nattukottai Chettiar banking system as a whole. David Rudner calculates their number in Burma in 1953 as twelve, based on the size of their land-holdings; they held political office and served on boards or acted as trustees of temples and charitable institutions. Like the Parsi and Ismaili *shetias*, they were an elite group with interlocking connections,[48] and, as disparities of wealth and economic differentiation became a marked feature of the community, internal solidarity became less firm. Community concern about this development was publicly uttered in Rangoon in the early 1920s, when attempts were made to regain the cohesiveness of the community and revive a sense of unity in the face of severe internal competition for resources and government favour.[49]

THE NATTUKOTTAI CHETTIAR RELIGIOUS IDENTITY

The Nattukottai Chettiars are Saivaite Hindus, worshippers of Siva. Siva is one of the major gods of the later Hindu pantheon, forming with Brahma and Vishnu the great triad of Hindu deities. Most of the Chettiar temples were dedicated to Siva's son, and this deity was sometimes regarded as the chairman of the temple committee.[50] The role of 'temple gifting' in the Nattukottai Chettiars' preadaptative period has already been noted. The temple's role in business in the later period in Burma has also been seen to be important; the main Chettiar temple in Mogul Street was called the 'Chettiar exchange' where regularly current interest rates were determined, business disputes settled and commercial information exchanged.[51] Hans-Dieter Evers and Jayarani Pavadarayan have shown for the Singapore Chettiar temple at a later period that religious significance was attached to borrowing from temple deposits, which were accumulated from a percentage contribution from the profits of firms. Capital drawn from temple funds and lent to traditional firms was felt to have special religious significance, as it drew the major deity of the temple into direct participation in business. The god was treated as a divine witness and dishonesty and default invoked religious sanctions.[52]

But of course there was a spiritual side to the Nattukottai Chettiars' religious existence, and Evers and Pavadarayan have pointed out that this leads to a curious dual identity in the community, where business life was conducted on principles of strict asceticism and yet much spiritual life was in the form of more popular, ecstatic religion.[53] The earliest indication of this is in the particular school of Saivaism which Nattukottai Chettiars followed. This was the Saiva Siddhanta, which placed great emphasis on *bhakti*, 'attachment' or fervent devotion to god. *Bhakti* seems to have had its origin in the Dravidian South as part of a great medieval spiritual revival, stressing the need for a personal relationship with god and a deeply emotional worship of him. A series of Tamil saints spread the gospel that salvation could only be won by a total self-surrender to Siva and the hymns of these saints remained vital among overseas Tamils. All *bhakti* sects were characterized by self-abandonment to a personal god, carried out with considerable emotion.[54] This is not to say that emotion and religious ecstasy were ungoverned and uncontrollable. The path of devotion, as Milton Singer points out, could also be one of discipline, subject to well-understood rules in which the devotee finds a model for his attitude of devotion to the deity and disciplines his emotions and actions in accordance with the requirements of the model he wishes to follow.[55]

Nevertheless; *bhakti* is one aspect of the 'ecstasy' that has been noted in Nattukottai Chettiar religion. The other, described by Evers and Pavadarayan for contemporary Singapore but without doubt having much earlier roots, is their association with popular Tamil temple festivals and participation in the ecstatic rituals connected with these.[56] In the late nineteenth century Nattukottai Chettiars spent large sums on restoring several of the famous Saivaite shrines in the Madras Presidency, notably those at Chidambaram, Madura and Tiruvannamalai. Associated with this was extensive spending on ceremonies and festivals, some newly established after years of neglect, coupled with a particular attention to the repair and restoration of those shrines that were hymned by the great poet-saints.[57]

We do not know the details of the rituals that took place at these festivals, but Evers and Pavadarayan have described these for the Thaipusam festival in Singapore, of which the Nattukottai Chettiars were the main organizers and participants. The ecstasy involved in these religious manifestations included elements such as entering into a trance, dancing while in a trance, frantic utterances and bodily mutilation, although the ecstatic manifestations of the Nattukottai Chettiars were somewhat restrained and regulated. Further, the religious verses sung by Nattukottai Chettiars contained references to the caste as a separate cultural and religious entity, pledged to lead a life of sobriety and refraining from indulgence in the ways of the world.[58] Evers finds this a strange contrast of both asceticism and ecstasy[59] but, looked at within the framework of the dual nature of a minority business community, perhaps the combination is somewhat more explicable.

Evers himself notes that one might assume that tremendous internal stress and strain arise from leading a highly inner-worldly ascetic life in which frugality, self-discipline and self-control are emphasized. The response might then be a restrained and controlled type of religious ecstasy, coupled with extensive involvement in charitable works, which often involved paying for religious festivals.[60] In this respect there is a clear line of connection with the medieval period, when an emphasis on *bhakti* and the construction of temples went together.[61] There is a connection, too, with Milton Singer's group of Madras industrialists—which included Chettiars—who, he found, downgraded ritual observance generally and concurrently moved to adherence to *bhakti* as a path suited to their entrepreneurial existence.[62]

FROM COMMERCE TO INDUSTRY

It is hardly surprising that the Nattukottai Chettiars followed the pattern of all other communities dealt with so far and responded to opportunities for industrial ventures. In Burma they began by exporting considerable quantities of timber to India and hence becoming involved in the saw-milling industry. Ties between Rangoon and Madras were strong. An important figure in the Madras timber business was P.A. Chockalingam Chetty, who inherited a family timber concern and came to notice about 1902 for the huge quantities of timber he imported weekly from Burma. Among his customers were the government of Madras and private contractors as far afield as Hyderabad and Mysore. Other firms also imported huge quantities of timber.[63] Not surprisingly, considering the direction of their lending activities, Nattukottai Chettiars also either established or acquired a number of rice mills, some being set up by Burmese with

Chettiar capital. Among important Chettiar rice mills by 1915 was the M.M.P.L. Palaniappa Rice Mill at Akyab, with further Burmese branches at Dedaye and Rangoon. Its registered headquarters was in Ramnad district in Madras and it also had branches spread over India and Ceylon. The Chettiars who engaged in rice-milling, many of whom had come to Burma from Calcutta, were formidable rivals for the European rice-millers, whether they milled in Rangoon or Madras. The Depression and the concomitant loan foreclosures meant that considerable sums were converted from liquid to fixed assets such as mills.[64]

It was in South India itself, however, that the change from traditional moneylending to modern enterprises took place, the pace accelerating in the period after the Depression. Here individual Nattukottai Chettiars were among the first Tamil businessmen to divert their assets from banking and trade to capital-intensive industry.[65] Their chief success was in the cotton textile industry, centred around Coimbatore in Madras Presidency. By the 1950s this was by far the most important factory industry in Madras state, dominated by Coimbatore spinning ventures but with some money also put into factories in Chettinad itself.[66] Chettiar groups such as the Raja Sir Annamalai Chettiar Group and the A.M.M. Murugappa Chettiar Group were established, the capital involved being accumulated by joint families. Collaborative arrangements with foreign capital also played their part in the rise of Nattukottai Chettiar business combines.[67]

Milton Singer collected material in 1954–64 on nineteen industrial leaders in Madras, most originating in banking and trade. Four of the nineteen were Chettiars, although it is not specified whether they were Nattukottai Chettiars.[68] One of the Chettiar industrial leaders owed the origin of his financial stability to his grandfather, who had gone into overseas banking at the age of 14 and made a vast fortune through this and the purchase of rice land in Burma and elsewhere. He brought his three sons into the business during the First World War while they were still in their teens. Before the outbreak of the next war they anticipated difficulties ahead in Southeast Asia, transferred their banking operations to Madras City, and started a small manufacturing industry in 1938. By 1949 they were able to negotiate conjoint agreements with British and American firms to manufacture bicycle tyre tubes, cycle saddles, chains, dynamo sets, lamps and other bicycle parts. Three of the grandsons were sent to England for technical training in the collaborating British plants.[69] It was in this period, if just a little later, that the founders of the great Chinese conglomerates on Java were beginning their collaboration with foreign firms,[70] repeating a pattern originating in the days of the East India Companies. In both cases, and in others we have mentioned, the importance of the joint-family system was paramount, making individual families' unique characteristics deserving of the closest attention. It was never an entire community which developed specific areas of economic activity, but only a small number of families from within that community; no matter, as Singer says, how much members of a particular community are predisposed to enter a particular line of economic activity, only a small and localized fraction of the community may be so predisposed by special experience, abilities, opportunities and other circumstances to lead and to succeed.[71]

REPRISE

The Nattukottai Chettiars' dual identity as a business community has been explained in terms of the tension between the need to carry on a strictly ascetic business life and the affinity for a spiritual life of a more populist, ecstatic kind. It is in this duality that must be sought the spirit of Nattukottai Chettiar economic creativity. At the same time, as we have noted in earlier chapters, the joint family and then the community, rather than the individual, was at the centre of business existence.

As David Rudner has now shown, under the heading 'A Collectivist Spirit of Capitalism'; Nattukottai Chettiars belonged to a range of social groups: joint families, lineages, village clans, business associations operating out of specific localities and the caste as a whole. Like the peranakan of Java, 'these groups were marked by common and collective forms of worship in cults of specific deities, and these collective ritual practices were central to the way business was carried out in the wider society'.[72] Their ethic was marked, 'from a Weberian viewpoint, by a paradoxical amalgam of rationality and collectivism, rather than by rational individualism'.[73]

Weber, as we have already noted, insists that he was only investigating a series of conditions necessary for the emergence of modern capitalism, not for its subsequent adoption elsewhere. However, Weber did deny the existence of collectivist or supra-individual actors, and committed himself to a distinctive ethical approach to the individual.[74] What we have seen so far in our communities, however, is that in them the spirit of capitalism rests on the spirit of business confidence and economic creativity. This emotional climate can flow from numerous spiritual sources, and in particular from the creativity brought into being by the florescence of certain types of identity. But it is economic creativity in the collective sense, with the family at the core of the collectivity. In this collectivity, 'the sacred is seen as group life and a moral individual as one who grows as a social person'.[75]

Originally published as Christine Dobbin, 'From Madras to Burma: The Nattukottai Chettiars and Development 1852–1939', in Christine Dobbin, *Asian Entrepreneurial Minorities: Conjoint Communities in the Making of the World Economy 1570–1940* (Surrey, Curzon Press, 1996), pp. 131–55.

NOTES

1. M. Adas, 'Immigrant Asians and the Economic Impact of European Imperialism: The Role of the South Indian Chettiars in British Burma', *Journal of Asian Studies*, Vol. 33, No. 3 (1974), p. 387.
2. P. Siegelman, 'Colonial Development and the Chettyar: A Study in the Ecology of Modern Burma, 1850–1941', Ph.D., University of Minnesota, 1962, pp. 18, 88–90.
3. Ibid., pp. 86 ftn. 13, 267.
4. D.W. Rudner, 'Caste and Commerce in Indian Society: A Case Study of Nattukottai Chettiars, 1600–1930', Ph.D. University of Pennsylvania, 1985, pp. 89–91.
5. L.C. Jain, *Indigenous Banking in India*, London, Macmillan, 1929, pp. 37–38; E. Thurston, *Castes and Tribes of Southern India*, Vol. 5, Madras, Government Press, 1909, pp. 249–50; Siegelman, 'Colonial Development and the Chettyar', pp. 122–3.
6. H.D. Evers, 'Chettiar Moneylenders in Southeast Asia', in Lombard and Aubin, *Marchands et hommes d'affaires*, pp. 202–3.
7. M. Adas, *The Burma Delta. Economic Development and Social Change on an Asian Rice Frontier, 1852–1941*, Madison, The University of Wisconsin Press, 1974, p. 114.
8. For the classic formulation see B. Stein, 'The Economic Function of a Medieval South Indian Temple', *Journal of Asian Studies*, Vol. 19, 1959–60, pp. 163–170; D.W. Rudner, 'Religious Gifting and Inland Commerce in Seventeenth-Century South India', *Journal of Asian Studies*, Vol. 46, No. 2 (1987), p. 362.
9. Rudner, 'Religious Gifting', pp. 361, 363–5.
10. Ibid., p. 369; see also pp. 365–8.
11. Ibid., pp. 365, 375–7.
12. Ibid., p. 377.
13. M. Singer, *When a Great Tradition Modernizes.*

An Anthropological Approach to Indian Civilization, London, Pall Mall Press, 1972, p. 307.

14. S. Arasaratnam, *Merchants, Companies and Commerce on the Coromandel 1650–1740*, Delhi, Oxford University Press, 1986, p. 217; S. Arasaratnam, 'Society, Power, Factionalism and Corruption in Early Madras 1640–1746', *Indica*, Vol. 23, 1986, pp. 115–16.

15. Rudner, 'Caste and Commerce', pp. 41–2, 92–5.

16. Ibid., pp. 92–5, 98–101.

17. Ibid., pp. 96–7, 101–6, 194–9.

18. Ibid., pp. 108–10, 116–17; R. Mahadevan. 'Immigrant Entrepreneurs in Colonial Burma—An Exploratory Study of the Role of Nattukottai Chettiars of Tamil Nadu, 1880–1930', *Indian Economic and Social History Review*, Vol. 15, No. 3, 1978, p. 331.

19. Siegelman, 'Colonial Development and the Chettyar', pp. 132–3.

20. Ibid., pp. 61–3, 88, 90; Adas, *Burma Delta*, p. 28; Adas, 'Immigrant Asians', p. 387.

21. Siegelman, 'Colonial Development and the Chettyar', pp. 101–2, 106–8.

22. Adas, *Burma Delta*, p. 58.

23. Ibid., p. 58; see also pp. 30–31.

24. Adas, 'Immigrant Asians', p. 390; Siegelman, 'Colonial Development and the Chettyar', p. 182.

25. Adas, *Burma Delta*, pp. 62–3, 66–7, 109–10; Adas, 'Immigrant Asians', p. 390; Siegelman, 'Development and the Chettyar', pp. 108–17.

26. Siegelman, 'Colonial Development and the Chettyar', pp. 171, 224.

27. Adas, *Burma Delta*, pp. 71, 119, 172–3.

28. Ibid., pp. 128, 185–7.

29. Ibid., p. 188.

30. Mahadevan, 'Immigrant Entrepreneurs', pp. 356–7.

31. Adas, *Burma Delta*, pp. 136, 138.

32. *Burma. Report of the Burma Provincial Banking Inquiry Committee, 1929–30*, Vol. 1, Rangoon, Superintendent of Government Printing, 1930, p. 203.

33. Rudner, 'Caste and Commerce', pp. 173–5, 180; Jain, *Indigenous Banking*, pp. 31–2, 37; Thurston, *Castes and Tribes* 5, pp. 250, 258; Adas, *Burma Delta*, p. 115.

34. Jain, *Indigenous Banking*, p. 37; S. Ito, 'A Note on the "Business Combine" in India—with Special Reference to the Nattukottai Chettiars', *Developing Economies*, Vol. 4, 1966, p. 370; H.D. Evers and J. Pavadarayan, *Asceticism and Ecstasy: The Chettiars of Singapore*, University of Bielefeld, Sociology of Development Research Centre Working Paper No. 79, 1986, p. 5.

35. *Burma Banking Inquiry* 2, pp. 135–6; Siegelman, 'Colonial Development and the Chettyar', pp. 126–7.

36. *Burma Banking Inquiry* 1, pp. 205–6.

37. Ibid., p. 207.

38. Ibid., p. 208.

39. Ibid., p. 204.

40. Rudner, 'Caste and Commerce', pp. 159, 244ff.; Siegelman, 'Colonial Development and the Chettyar', p. 142.

41. *Burma Banking Inquiry* 1, p. 195.

42. Ibid., pp. 194, 196–197; Thurston, *Castes and Tribes* 5, p. 263.

43. Rudner, 'Caste and Commerce', pp. 201–5; an institution of this type was important for commercial castes: the Marwaris had their *basa* or collective messes as described in T.A. Timberg, *The Marwaris. From Traders to Industrialists*, New Delhi, Vikas, 1978, pp. 5–6.

44. *Burma Banking Inquiry* 1, pp. 196–7; Rudner, 'Caste and Commerce', pp. 180–2.

45. *Burma Banking Inquiry* 1, p. 205.

46. Ibid., 2, p. 134; Siegelman, 'Colonial Development and the Chettyar', p. 238.

47. Markovits, *Indian Business*, p. 121.

48. Rudner, 'Caste and Commerce', pp. 180–8.

49. Mahadevan, 'Immigrant Entrepreneurs', pp. 347–8.

50. Evers, 'Chettiar Moneylenders', p. 204.

51. Jain, *Indigenous Banking*, p. 37; Thurston, *Castes and Tribes* 5, pp. 262–3; Adas, *Burma Delta*, p. 117.

52. H.D. Evers and J. Pavadarayan, 'Religious Fervour and Economic Success. The Chettiars of Singapore', in K.S. Sandhu and A. Mani (eds), *Indian Communities in Southeast Asia*, Singapore, Institute of Southeast Asian Studies, 1993, p. 856; see also Rudner's view, 'Caste and Commerce', pp. 263–4.

53. Evers and Pavadarayan, *Asceticism and Ecstasy*, pp. 18–21.

54. P. Jash, *History of Saivism*, Calcutta, Roy and Chaudhury, 1974, p. 18; R.C. Zaehner, *Hinduism*, London, Oxford University Press, 1962, pp. 164–7, 171, 182; Thurston, *Castes and Tribes* 5, p. 254.

55. Singer, *A Great Tradition Modernizes*, p. 233.

56. Evers and Pavadarayan, *Asceticism and Ecstasy*, pp. 13–17; Evers and Pavadarayan, 'Religious Fervour', pp. 857–60.

57. Thurston, *Castes and Tribes* 5, pp. 251, 254; see also Rudner, 'Caste and Commerce', p. 257.

58. Evers and Pavadarayan, *Asceticism and Ecstasy*, pp. 13, 15–17.

59. Ibid., p. 20; Evers and Pavadarayan, 'Religious Fervour', pp. 860–1.

60. Evers and Pavadarayan, *Asceticism and Ecstasy*, p. 20; Evers and Pavadarayan, 'Religious Fervour', p. 862.

61. Jash, *Saivism*, pp. 18–26.

62. Singer, *A Great Tradition Modernizes*, p. 336.

63. *Burma Banking Inquiry* 1, pp. 197–8; Mahadevan, 'Immigrant Entrepreneurs', p. 351.

64. Mahadevan, 'Immigrant Entrepreneurs', pp. 349–50; Siegelman, 'Colonial Development and the Chettyar', pp. 259–60.

65. Evers, 'Chettiar Moneylenders', pp. 212–13; Rudner, 'Caste and Commerce', p. 38.

66. J.J. Berna, *Industrial Entrepreneurship in Madras State*, Bombay, Asia Publishing House, 1960, pp. 22–3, 44; Singer, *A Great Tradition Modernizes*, pp. 309, 359; Lamb, 'Indian Business Communities', p. 105; Government of Tamil Nadu, *Tamil Nadu District Gazetteers. Ramanathapuram*, Madras, Director of Stationery and Printing, 1972, p. 339.

67. Ito, '"Business Combine" in India', pp. 371–2, 374; Mahadevan. 'Immigrant Entrepreneurs', p. 330; Rudner, 'Caste and Commerce', pp. 160–6.

68. Singer, *A Great Tradition Modernizes*, pp. 283–4, 301, 346.

69. Ibid., p. 305.

70. Robison, *The Rise of Capital*, pp. 277–305.

71. Singer, *A Great Tradition Modernizes*, p. 310.

72. D.W. Rudner, *Caste and Capitalism in Colonial India. The Nattukottai Chettiars*, Berkeley and Los Angeles, University of California Press, 1994, p. 105.

73. Ibid.

74. For a discussion, see Abercrombie et al., *Sovereign Individuals*, p. 16.

75. Ibid., p. 129.

17

The Bohras Today
Characteristics of Business Enterprise

Asghar Ali Engineer

The highly entrepreneurial Daudi Bohras, of Ismaili Shia descent, have been mercantile traders throughout their history and became especially prominent during colonial rule. Surat, the community's hub for almost a century, was an important commercial port from the mid-sixteenth century onwards and its establishment as a trading port of the East India Company facilitated several trade advantages to the community.* In the early nineteenth century, the community moved to Bombay and took to commercial activities and contracts for English traders, much like other Gujarati trading communities. Most Daudi Bohras owned shops and small businesses, while some also entered the banking and industrial sectors.†

The Bohras have stayed a community of traders and businessmen. A survey conducted by anthropologist Joanna Blank in the 1990s showed that three-quarters of Bohras surveyed listed their occupation as business, an increase from 73.1 per cent of the

* Several important entrepreneurial groups have emerged from the Surat region of Gujarat, such as Parsis, Sunni Memons, Ismaili Khojas, Jain Banias, and Daudi Bohras. One reason for this may have been that Gujarat has long been the scene of commercial activity and its coast is dotted with important ports such as Surat which, from at least the mid-sixteenth century, was the centre of much commercial activity. See Ashin Das Gupta, 'The Merchants of Surat, c1700–1750', in Uma Das Gupta (compiled), *The World of the Indian Ocean Merchant, 1500–1800: Collected Essays of Ashin Das Gupta* (New Delhi, Oxford University Press, 2001). The most famous Bohra of the eighteenth century was, of course, Virji Vora who dominated the city's trade, owned the pepper monopoly for the region, had commercial interests from Ahmedabad to Golconda, and had agents in Southeast Asia, the Red Sea, and the Persian Gulf.

† See Joanna Blank, *Mullahs on the Mainframe: Islam and Modernity among the Daudi Bohras* (Chicago, University of Chicago Press, 2001), pp. 46–8.

earlier generation of the same households. Among their favoured trades were hardware, glassware, metals, electrical supplies, cutlery, printing, cloth, foodstuffs, and cosmetics. Today, though younger generations have taken to diverse professional activities, the Bohras are an influential business community in Gujarat and Bombay.[‡]

This excerpt from the writings of scholar–activist Asghar Ali Engineer details the contemporary commercial activities of the Daudi Bohras, their involvement in varied businesses, and their inclination towards commerce.[§] After citing population patterns of Daudi Bohras within India and elsewhere, Engineer traces complex social, cultural, historical, and religious reasons to understand why most Daudis are engaged in businesses such as petty shopkeeping instead of industrial enterprises.

More than 50 per cent of the Daudis live in Gujarat. Maharashtra comes next. The highest population of Daudis is in Bombay there being 60,000 of them in this *urbs prima*. Outside India the highest number of Bohras is found in Karachi where there are around 25,000 of them. In India there are found in Madhya Pradesh (170 towns), Gujarat (164 towns), Maharashtra (101 towns), Rajasthan (53 towns), Kerala (5 towns), Tamil Nadu (4 towns), Uttar Pradesh (4 towns), Mysore (3 towns), Andhra Pradesh (3 towns), Bihar (2 towns), Orissa (2 towns), Goa (l town), and West Bengal (1 town).[1] In India the major centres of Bohra population after Bombay are: Dohad, Gujarat (11,200), Udaipur, Rajasthan (10,000), Indore, M.P. (7,750), Ujjain, M.P. (7,143), Surat, Gujarat (7,601), Ahmedabad, Gujarat (7,803), Siddhpur, Gujarat (6,675), Calcutta, West Bengal (5,400), Godhra, Gujarat (5,200), Jamnagar, Gujarat (4,833), Poona, Maharashtra (4,127), and Madras, Tamil Nadu (2,757).

Outside India the Daudis are found in 31 countries. The Daudi population abroad is around 75,000. The foreign countries where the Bohras have settled are Pakistan (30,000), Tanzania (7,500), Madagascar (6,500), Ceylon (2,500), Kuwait (2,500), Kenya (5,800), U.K. (2,000), Uganda (1,500), Yaman (2,500), Singapore (550), Malaysia (500), Hongkong (200), Thailand (900), Japan (15), Comores (200), Dubai (750), Indonesia (800), Burma (150), Bahrain(500), Bangla Desh (750), Aden (950) Iraq (125), Ethopia (350), America (875), France (100), Muscat (100), Maldive (5), Mauritius (5), Saudi Arabia (550), and Sweden (90).[2]

As pointed out earlier, most of the Daudis are engaged in business. But nowhere in the world do they control big business or industries, not even in India. The overwhelming majority is engaged in petty shopkeeping and only a few can be said to be doing business on even a middle scale. Several factors are responsible for lack of industrial entrepreneurship among Bohras. Traditionally they have been doing petty business and it was not easy for them to accumulate the capital needed for industrial enterprises. They were a persecuted community and often in the past the rich had to part with their wealth to save their faith or honour. Religious leadership discouraged Western

‡ Ibid., p. 13.

§ Engineer has written extensively on the Bohras. See his *Muslim Communities of Gujarat: An Exploratory Study of Bohars, Khojas and Memons* (Delhi, Ajanta, 1989).

learning as well as institutions like banking etc., due to religious inhibitions. The Daudis, therefore, could not realize the importance of developing industrial enterprises. Moreover, it was difficult for them to compete with other non-Muslim industrial giants. However, in Pakistan a few families like the Walikas succeeded in developing big industry. But it is an exception rather than a rule. Again, it being a petty-shopkeepers' community, the percentage of education too is not very high and for this reason we find relatively few academicians, university teachers, doctors, lawyers, management experts, etc. And there are practically no renowned scientists, poets, novelists, painters, etc. If a comparison be made with the Parsis, the Daudis will emerge in a poor light.

The Parsis are certainly not as numerous as the Daudis and yet we see that they have produced many world renowned scientists, artists, legal luminaries as well as big industrialists. The percentage of education among them would be far higher than that among the Daudi Bohras especially among the women. The Daudis too, being primarily a business community, had better resources at their disposal to promote a higher degree of education. However, the priestly class, as we shall see while discussing the reform movement in the community, became a great obstacle in that direction and always sought to discourage the spread of modern education. It was only lately that they realized the importance of education; but again what followed was mere relaxation and not a vigorous step to promote education. The spread of education certainly undermines the priestly authority. Even the Sulaimani Bohras, who are very few in number compared to the Daudis and do not suffer from the strict priestly control have produced more world renowned personalities than the Daudis. We will discuss this in greater detail in the next chapter.

According to the compilers of *Gulshan-i-M'alūmāt* the total number of shops among the Daudi Bohras is around 18,321 of which 3,090 are of hardware followed by *kirana* (provision) shops numbering around 2,088. Cutlery and cloth shops come next being around 1,290 and 1,027 respectively. The other business activities include tin-works, glass-frames, shoe selling, timber, general merchandizing, paper electric goods, watch-repairing, perfumeries, aerated drinks, plumbing, medicines, sweet-meats, book-binding, hosiery, floor-mills, rope and coir, book-selling, gold and jewellery, etc. And at the bottom of the list come the fire-work shops, these being no more than 25 in number. It will be seen that in the above list wine-vending, tobacco, narcotics, etc, are conspicuous by their absence. Drinking and smoking is strictly prohibited among the Bohras although tobacco chewing is not uncommon. Although under modern influences many people drink and even smoke, still they refrain from dealing in these commodities.

Being petty shopkeepers, as the above data shows, the Bohras have a rather narrow *Weltanschauung*. They are more concerned, even in the big cities like Bombay, with maintaining their traditions and past practices, such tendencies being much more pronounced among the ladies. The ladies, having nearly no intercourse with their counterparts in other communities, tend to become more conservative and exercise a restraining influence on their husbands who meet a variety of people. The percentage of the educated among Daudi ladies is comparatively much less. The priesthood encourages this narrow-mindedness and lack of higher education among the ladies, as given these conditions they become the bulwark of priestly dominance.

The Daudi Bohras generally do not like to serve; at least it was so until a few decades ago. Most of them preferred to take up petty hawking rather than serve elsewhere, while many of them were forced to do so for lack of education. Also, being a petty business community, it was against their values to work for others. However, with the spread of modern education and rapid industrialization, the situation is fast changing. Although it still remains a predominantly petty-business community, many of the Bohras are taking to various professions like law, medicine, teaching, engineering, etc. Quite a few are now doing various government and semi-government jobs as well. In 1920 Mulla Abdul Husain wrote: "Except the inhabitants of a few villages in Dholka and in the north of Gujarat, who are peasants and some who have risen high in government services, like Abde ali Qaziji, High Court judge. Abdulla Esufali, Commr. in U.P. service, and a few in provincial and medical services, almost all Dawoodi Bohras live by trade, some are merchants having large dealings with Arabia, China, Siam and Zanzibar. One Aniq, son of Shaikh Mohammad Ali Aniq, has an export business in London and was last year Worshipful Master of the London Masonic Lodge. Bohras are mostly local traders in hardware, silk, hides, horns, and live-cattle but most of them are town and village shopkeepers selling hardware, cloth, stationery, books, groceries and spices, and a few in Ahmedabad. Baroda, Surat and Bombay are confectioners and hotel keepers."[3]

Originally published as Asghar Ali Engineer, *The Bohras* (Delhi, Vikas Publishing House, 1980), pp. 145–7.

NOTES

1. S.K. Rayaq, *Gulshan-i-M'alumāt*, Kalim Kutub Khana, Kamari Marg, Ujjain M.P., 1975, p. 350.

2. The figures in brackets indicate population in the respective countries. These figures are based on *Gulshan-i-M'alumāt*, op. cit. As these figures were collected from 1970 to 1974, as per the instructions of the compilers they have been increased by about 20 per cent to 40,000 to make them up-to-date. There are different estimates about the Daudi population in Yaman, some sources putting the figure as high as 30,000. It is also reported that during the civil war in Yaman in the sixties the partisans of Zaidi Imam massacred some 10,000 Daudis. However, it is difficult to check the veracity of these reports. It is also said that many Daudis fled from the Hamadan region and that many from Harrad region embraced the Nizari faith. Another independent source from Yaman puts the population of Daudis there as 6,000.

3. Mian Bhai Mullah Abdul Husain, *A Short Note on Daudi Bohras*, (Gulzare-Daudi) Progressive Publication, Surat, 1920, p. 75.

18

Entrepreneurs in Present-Day India
Beyond Caste and Community

Pieter Gorter

The long-held dominance of business activities by 'traditional' merchant banking communities has been slowly eroded, since the late colonial period, especially after Independence. Business has ceased to be the preserve of certain communities, and entrepreneurial groups have increasingly emerged from a heterogeneous variety of backgrounds—Brahmins, lower castes, agricultural castes, professionals, and technocrats—indicating flux in the landscape of commercial enterprise in India.*

* A recent book that examines the same phenomenon is Harish Damodaran, *India's New Capitalists: Caste, Business and Industry in a Modern Nation* (Ranikhet, Permanent Black, 2008). Damodaran argues that the social base of the capitalist class has diversified since Independence to include dominant agricultural castes, agro-commercial groups, and upper- and lower-caste groups. New entrants include Kamas, Naidus, Reddys, Rajus, Gounders, Nadars, Ezhavas, Patidars, Marathas, and Ramgarhas. However, he makes the point that this 'inclusive capitalism' has been more a feature of southern and western India and not the north where business continues to be dominated by traditional mercantile communities. Further, the lowest rungs of the social ladder have not been part of this change which, notes Damodaran, is apparent from the fact that not a single major entrepreneur has emerged from the Dalits. A similar trend has been highlighted in a study of the Indian software industry by Tarun Khanna and Krishna G. Palepu who note the emergence of entrepreneurs from middle-class backgrounds trained in engineering colleges. See Tarun Khanna and Krishna G. Palepu, 'The Evolution of Concentrated Ownership in India: Broad Patterns and a History of the Indian Software Industry', in Randall Morck (ed.), *The History of Corporate Governance around the World: Family Business Groups to Professional Managers* (Chicago, University of Chicago Press, 2005) and Ashoka Mody, 'Comment', in Randall K. Morck (ed.), *A History of Corporate Governance around the World: Family Business Groups to Professional Managers* (Chicago, University of Chicago Press, 2005), pp. 283–324. Also see Carol Upadhya, 'Social and Cultural Strategies of Class Formation in Coastal Andhra Pradesh', *Contributions to Indian Sociology*, Vol. 31, No. 2, 1997, pp. 169–93.

Tracing this phenomenon, this excerpt looks at the ascent to industrial prominence by small- and medium-sized enterprises in the south Gujarat industrial township of Vapi, since the 1970s. Till the 1970s, notes Gorter, Vapi's development was dominated by industrialists from traditional trading groups and castes and established industrial families. He then introduces reasons that attracted heterogeneous entrepreneurs to Vapi in the second phase, 1975–85. In this phase, entrepreneurs gained prominence because of new subsidy schemes, easy availability of credit, protection for the small-scale sector, and the economic emergence of south Gujarat. Though these entrepreneurs differed in terms of social background and, most notably, caste, yet many of them were connected to the original group of entrepreneurs; they had either been neighbours or caste fellows or belonged to the same ancestral place or knew each other from the Bombay Juhu Rotary Club. The 'Juhu group' was especially important according to the author, since they maintained strong socio-economic links. In terms of entrepreneurship, Gorter discerns rent seekers, workshop owners, and technocrats.

Gorter makes a point similar to that made by Chris Bayly in the first excerpt in this chapter when he points out that a variety of collectivities came together in the making of Vapi's business community—from caste to regionality to even club membership.

NEWCOMERS, ENTREPRENEURSHIP AND SOCIAL STATUS

The first phase of Vapi's development was dominated by industrialists from established industrial families. In line with a general trend in India's history of industrialization they belonged mainly to the trading castes, who invested trading capital in manufacturing during the inter-war period. In their wake a group of first generation industrialists came who, for a long time at least, were dependent on them for capital, business, facilities and bureaucratic contacts. The overall expansion of the estate in these first years was slow, however.

The years between 1975 and 1985 represent the period of fastest growth in the Vapi GIDC. The entrepreneurs who flocked to Vapi in the second phase were attracted by the introduction of generous subsidy schemes, easy credit, increasing protection for the small-scale sector on the one hand and the growing economic development of South Gujarat on the other. These new entrepreneurs are far from homogeneous. They differ in terms of social background, entrepreneurship, and in their position *vis-à-vis* large industry. They no longer include mainly Banias, but also Brahmans, Suthars and members of the lower castes. Many are first generation industrialists with professional backgrounds as diverse as agriculture, civil service and trading. In terms of entrepreneurship, rentseekers, workshop owners, and technocrats can be roughly distinguished. The first category includes those who have set up a unit to benefit solely from government regulations. They focus on reserved items and keep investment as low as possible. Their technical expertise is fairly low. We can find this type of entrepreneurs mainly in the production of chemicals and plastics.

The second category consists of the owners of small engineering workshops. They usually hail from lower castes and rely, for their business, on local firms. Some are dependent on sub-contracting arrangements with large engineering firms on the estate.

The third category of technocrat industrialists is found in all lines of production. They are first generation industrialists with a high degree of formal, technical training. Among these, high caste Brahman entrepreneurs and members of artisan castes are most prominent. The former tend to come from families where civil service or the medical and judicial professions are traditionally preferred and education is therefore highly valued. They are new in the field of industry and use technology to compensate for a lack of commercial contacts. At least as important, however, are status considerations. Industry and commerce are traditionally eyed with suspicion in their social circles and the stress on quality and technology is an attempt to rid especially small-scale industry of its tainted image. This category of entrepreneurs appears to be fairly new in the small-scale sector which is dominated by members of merchant castes on the one hand and artisan castes on the other. In 1962 a UNESCO funded research programme on small-scale industries still concluded that

> It is not usual for persons with education and higher caste origins to enter entrepreneurship in small industry. ... Few young men of the so-called bourgeois class, ..., will be eager to start their career as a worker-entrepreneur. (1962: 36)

Artisan castes have a longer tradition in the small-scale sector. In the case of Gujarat Streefkerk (1985) traces the entrepreneurial history of the Suthars back to the 1920s. For the Suthars and other artisan castes active in Vapi the stress on technology is a legacy of their caste background. But for them too social ambitions play an important role. The stress on technology and quality is a strategy to become socially accepted.

The importance of status considerations for the entrepreneurship displayed by both high caste Brahman entrepreneurs and artisan castes, forces a reconsideration of the relevance of values for the study of small industrialists in India. Ever since Marxist models replaced the modernization theory, values disappeared as a variable in the study of entrepreneurship. But the mistake of the modernization theorists of the 1960s was not that they included values as such in their evaluation of Indian entrepreneurship. What was wrong was their Eurocentric stress on this factor based on a misguided, Parsonian interpretation of Weber's *Protestant Ethic and the Spirit of Capitalism*. For Weber the protestant ethos was an important variable in the western European trajectory to capitalism. But he never claimed that such an ethos was indispensable for capitalism to develop elsewhere.

There is no reason to assume that the importance of technocrat entrepreneurs, be they high caste or artisans, is confined to Vapi. Panini (1978), for example, mentions a category of 'executive' entrepreneurs active in Faridabad. They held managerial positions in large-scale industries before they set up their own firms. As far as their social background is concerned he remarks that they

> belonged to upper class families. The fathers of most of these entrepreneurs had been engaged in one of the urban professions. They had educated their sons well. All the executives except one are graduates. (Ibid.: 98)

Of course, they resemble Holmström's technicians, at least the ones who come from the upper social strata.

> Technicians (apart from the old-style craftsmen) include graduate engineers and chemists. These 'technocrats'... are generally from professional or landowning families, with a high proportion of Brahmans. (1984: 89)

In a more recent study of small-scale enterprises in Kheda and Vadodara Districts in Central Gujarat, Hashim (1988: 267–8) concludes that

> The small scale industry sector does encourage first generation entrepreneurs, *particularly those who have special training or an artisan background.* ...These industrial units have access to wider markets, and use the well-established market channels. Marketing and finance do not appear to be significant problems. (author's emphasis)

All these newcomers, technocrats as well as rent-seekers, could not, as their predecessors, rely on contacts in Ahmedabad but had to rely on local Vapi bureaucrats. In view of the importance of government support for large sections of these new industrialists, it is not surprising that they would look for avenues into bureaucratic favour. They recognised such an avenue in the Vapi Industries Association. But in spite of their numbers, the new groups of entrepreneurs faced a business association dominated by the established industrialists.

Originally published as Pieter Gorter, *Small Industrialists, Big Ambitions: Economic and Political Networks on a Large Industrial Estate in West India* (Delhi, Oxford University Press, 1996), pp. 92–5.

REFERENCES

Hashim, S.R. (1988) 'Nature of Small Scale Industry and Its Developmental Role' in K.B. Suri (ed.) *Small Scale Enterprises in Industrial Development: The Indian Experience*, pp. 256–68. New Delhi: Sage.

Holmström, Mark (1984) *Industry and Inequality. The Social Anthropology of Indian Labour.* Cambridge: Cambridge University Press.

Panini, M.N. (1978) 'Networks and Styles: Industrial Entrepreneurs in Faridabad', in Saberwal (ed.) *Process and Institution in Urban India*. New Delhi: Vikas.

Streefkerk, Hein C. (1985) *Industrial Transition in Rural India. Artisans, Traders and Tribals in South Gujarat*. Bombay: Popular Prakashan.

UNESCO (1962) *Social Research on Small Industries in India*. Delhi: UNESCO Research Centre on Social and Economic Development in Southern Asia.

SECTION III

FAMILY AND FIRM

19

The Family Firm
A Microcosm

C.A. Bayly

Family businesses have dominated business organization in India, even though the corporate structure of the firm had developed in the mid-nineteenth century with the managing agency system.*

This excerpt from the writings of historian Chris Bayly constitutes the theme essay for the selections on 'Family and Firm'. Bayly examines the distinctive styles of life and business in family firms in the context of north Indian merchant families in the transition period from Mughal to British India. Though the excerpt studies family firms in eighteenth century India, many of the themes it highlights remain pertinent in contemporary India. These include the inseparableness of family and firm, the rootedness of the firm in culture and local community, the significance of 'status' within commercial circles (symbolic capital), the importance of social relations in commercial practices, and the necessity of comprehending the family firm in the totality of its relationships. Many of these themes also resonate in the excerpts that follow.

In the context of eighteenth century India, Bayly notes that merchants considered three factors to be the bases of mercantile society: the family 'firm', its creditworthiness (*sakh*), and the totality of its relations with gods and men, with creditors and debtors. The 'firm' could not be separated from family, and could not be divorced from credit. Community consisting of families was the basis of business organization. The socio-economic status

* On the managing agency system, see Radhe Shyam Rungta, *Rise of Business Corporations in India 1851–1900* (Cambridge, Cambridge University Press, 1970). For a discussion on the larger literature on family firms, see Andrea Colli and Mary Rose, 'Family Business', in Geoffrey Jones and Jonathan Zeitlin (eds), *The Oxford Handbook of Business History* (Oxford, Oxford University Press, 2007), pp. 194–218.

of merchant families was dependent on their practice and behaviour; to be successful, merchant families had to be perceived as 'respectable' and 'trustworthy'. Merchants often invested in charity, community causes, and religious ritual to enhance their social capital among peers. The merchant household had, in Bayly's view, a dual role as a profit-making enterprise and as a constellation of relationships through which honour was acquired and conferred. As such, merchants often had to straddle two boundaries—the expected inward, frugal life of the merchant, and the kingly manner of constant giving and receiving.

THE MERCHANT FAMILY AND ITS CREDIT

From the perspective of the merchants themselves, the basis of mercantile society was the family 'firm', its credit (*sakh*) and the totality of its relations with gods and men, creditors and debtors. The 'firm' was not seen as something separate from the family; there was no commonly used word for firm as a concept, only as a location (*dukan* or *kothi*). And credit or reputation was not simply a residual category of financial benefit like 'goodwill' in a modern European firm. Without 'credit', a family could not trade or call on merchant arbitration at all. Merchant corporations kept lists of creditable merchants whose credit notes could expect rapid discount in the bazaar (*sahajog hundis*).[1] Even small dealers knew whose *hundis* were 'current' in the market and whose were not. In traditional commercial centres, the corporations imposed heavy penalties for breaches of trust in the same way that caste councils punished immorality. Sharp practice and unorthodox behaviour reflected both on the social and economic status of the group since merchant families had to be respectable marriage partners as well as trustworthy traders.

Even the word 'business' is a simplification of the term *mamle* ('concerns') which eighteenth-century merchants often used. For merchants concerns included the management of their temples, *ghats* and the ritual organisation of the bazaars which all impinged on the life of the family. Like the peasant 'family farm', the merchant family business was a 'special kind of economic enterprise' and one in which mercantile decisions were constantly taken with a view to their wider implications for the life of the family as a social group. In most firms, cash accounts and annual profit and loss accounts were meticulously kept, but the profitability of the business was almost impossible to calculate because many of its goals were incalculable social benefits. As in the peasant family, for instance, family members, servants and agents were rarely paid a cash wage; instead they had rights and obligations within the family economy. Many of the great houses provided accommodation and commercial space for poorer relatives and caste fellows within their own premises, and these were assessed as *prajawat* (a lordship due) which was generally customary. Like the classic peasant family, the whole household was also able to expand or restrict consumption in relation to the success of the trading season. Some families observed a rule of thumb that only ten or twenty per cent of their annual income should be expended, but during years when the family was anticipating a prestigious alliance, massive expenditures on charity, feasting and ritual were contemplated.[2] Orthodox economic reasoning might see this as 'conspicuous consumption', but from the point of view of the family it could equally be seen as 'investment' in social relationships which might have definite financial advantages in bad seasons, or at times when the family had to fall back on the resources of its peers to raise cash speedily.[3] There are problems with this, however. We should not assume that certain types of 'uneconomic' behaviour on the part of merchant families can always be explained in terms of an underlying rationality based upon the hope of future profits. In some cases, the profit-making part of a family's concerns was simply kept moving slowly in order to provide modest resources on which it could base its strategy for acquiring higher status through marriage alliance or royal office. It is common for economic historians to report that luxurious firms engaging in unwise expenditure were ousted by shrewd new men who turned their capital over more rapidly and avoided aristocractic connections. However, from the point of view of many high-status merchant families among the Khattris or Agarwals, notoriously high rates of profit were a positive mark of discredit. These new men may have achieved success in the bazaar, but the proper area of entrepreneurship was society as a whole, and it was the cautious, pious and creditworthy who succeeded here.

This dual role of the merchant household as a profit-making enterprise and as a constellation of relationships through which honour was acquired and conferred was vividly illustrated in the standard form of account books (*bahi khatas*) which all significant families kept. Besides the daily cash book (*rokad khata*) and individual's account books (*lekha khata*), there often existed separate books dealing with a family's bullion and jewellery, urban and rural property, and daily expenses. In theory, all deposits or expenditures made by any member of the household in any domain of life could be traced here. Most books begin with salutations to various deities, lists of temple accoutrements and accounts of offerings to religious preceptors. The daily expense account (*kharach khata*) recorded constant expenditures on worship, bathing in the Ganges and gifts to Brahmins.[4] As in other highly orthodox communities, gods were considered to be integral, living members of the family, so that elaborate provisions were made in wills and trusts to see that they were clothed, fed and fanned during the hot weather. Besides the worship of family deities, most merchant families paid regular *puja* (worship) to Lakshmi, goddess of wealth, especially at Diwali and Holi festivals which were the beginning and end of the busiest part of the trading year respectively. Brahmins were also closely involved in the daily life of the business family. Many firms employed Brahmins as their agents or debt collectors, thus acquiring spiritual merit and an added religious sanction over their debtors. Among the Benares and Patna Khattris it was even common for their Saraswat Brahmin domestic priests to enter into business partnerships in the Punjab shawl and horse trades.[5]

Merchant books also reveal how different family members operated within the total economy. In one firm where the business was undivided and carried on by three brothers, their mother (always *Maji* in the accounts) appears to have been the linchpin in the purchasing of jewellery and provisions.[6] In general, access to family resources was determined by status within the family. In one case it was said that the elder brother was a spendthrift, but his sober younger brother was unable to 'say anything' because of his junior status. In undivided joint families where a senior partner had died, it was quite common for the uncle of the man's heirs to take over effective running of the business because of his greater experience.

More important even than these family relationships, however, was the relationship between the proprietors and their business clerks or *munims*, for it was often in their hands that the continuity and credit of the family were entrusted. Sometimes *munims* used their reputation to establish their own firms on the basis of the credit of their original employer. But *munims* often seemed to have passed on their employment to their heirs, so that an hereditary relationship grew up between the families of the principals and their clerks. *Munims* were not always of the same caste as their employers but nevertheless became an essential part of the extended household.[7] In the epidemic-ridden conditions of nineteenth-century Indian cities, it was common when adult male members of the family died to leave a *munim* as effective manager directing the business of female and minor members. Trusted retainers were necessary for the continuity of the family, and many didactic tales were in circulation to illustrate the honourable role of the *munim* in the family's credit.[8] One such has the spendthrift sons dismissing the aged *munim* on the death of their father. The business then goes from bad to worse. Finally, one evening a massive credit note for payment on sight (*darshani hundi*) arrives, running to lakhs of Rupees, which must be paid before the gun on the fortress signals nightfall if credit is to be retained. In a panic the young men beg the *munim* to return to the firm. At length he comes to the shop and mobilises his dead employer's friends among the merchants to provide cash to pay the *hundi*.

Finally, the books reveal the family acting as a system of ritualized occupational relationships within the city and its environs. For instance, dyers (*rangil*) appeared frequently in the expense books of the Agarwal firms.[9] This was because the colour of the saris of female members of these families was governed by peculiarly rigid conventions. Family priests, barbers, gold and silver workers and all sorts of artisans appear as borrowers, depositors and lenders. The hierarchy of relationships was not confined to humans either. In many of the more orthodox merchant households, cows occupied the bottom storey of the house. Their preservation and feeding was an act of religious devotion which also provided the family with milk and butter, and echoed the Vaishya scriptural occupation as cattle keepers. Men honoured the gods and the sacred animals, but a reputation for piety no doubt redounded to their commercial credit. One story has the great merchant prince Kashmiri Mull visiting his rival, the austere and orthodox Manohar Das as the latter mucks out his cow sheds. 'Watch out for your shoes' cries Kashmiri Mull; 'Watch out for your accounts!' responds the other, implying a relationship between piety, frugality and mercantile success.

The merchant account books indicate how inextricably linked were the commercial and social goals of merchant families. But there was a sense in which the books themselves were a symbolic affirmation of the unity, continuity and credit of the family. Some of the older Delhi firms actually staged an annual ritual at which the old account books were worshipped as a virtual representation of the dutiful lives of the ancestors who founded the 'firm'. The idea of the long continuity of the family's substance and credit over time was reflected in other ways. In one firm, the sum total of capital passed over from one year's books to the next was entered in the name of the founder of the firm three generations before;[10] elsewhere account books which were no longer current were religiously returned year by year to the ancestral village of a family which had left it eight to ten generations before. The most crucial span of generations for the passage of credit, however, was three. According to the Shastric texts, a man was responsible for the debts of his forefathers to this extent.[11] The payment of such debts was a prior duty even to the fathering of an heir, though it was only a male heir who could guarantee his own translation to the status of an honoured ancestor after death, and to ultimate salvation, through the rites of *shraddha*. Thus, the names of firms often joined together grandfather and grandsons in a three-generation span, and the evidence suggests that such relationships of credit and debt did persist over very long periods as late as the eighteenth century. When the British tried to introduce the idea of individual competence in law and temporal limitation of liability in the Bengal Regulations of 1793, there was an immediate outcry:

> In bankers' concerns it is the old established rule that the descendants are responsible for and must pay the debts of four generations, whether they have inherited of a grandfather's wealth and possessions or may have been left nothing in consequence of their poverty. . . . The purport of the order in the existing regulations is that if a son shall not have inherited the wealth of his father that son shall not be responsible for his father's debts. Honourable Sir, the concerns of the bankers are decreased and their incomes ruined.[12]

Liability for debts was thus conceived to be coterminous with the ritual unit which was directly involved in the oblation rite of *pitraprajna* or *shraddha*. But the consequence of failure to repay, which was deemed a sin, should also fall on the debtor's family as a whole.

> In former times when any person became bancrupt [sic] and was absconding, he absconded with all his family from apprehension of his creditors, and we who were in search of him obtained intelligence of his place of residence in consequence of his family being along with him. And then indeed being embarrassed and distressed from his being accompanied by his family, he informed us that our money should be paid.[13]

But as a result of the Regulations, the petition went on, a debtor could 'sit quietly at his home with comfort and satisfaction to his women and children, with ornaments and numerous attendants'. Here again the slow introduction of elements of British commercial law had cut into areas of customary practice which derived from an almost physical notion of the passage of credit within a family.

This helps to explain the extreme reluctance to show books to outsiders which characterised the old-style firm. Their opening is always attended by a feeling of ceremony. When a man agrees to show 'my books' (never 'the firm's books') he is, as it were, discovering the credit of his ancestors. The most reluctant of all to do this were the Jains who maintained strong sanctions against the release of any information about ancestry, commercial or sexual practices, even to Brahmin families which had been associated with them for generations. When merchants claimed that their credit would suffer by showing their books in the ruler's court, they were not simply making a statement about commercial morality, but about the honour of the family. Hence it followed that the production of books in open court was considered superior evidence in a suit even to oaths made on Ganges water. The witness was making a solemn statement equivalent to a Muslim oath over the tombs of ancestors. For merchants of prestige even to be called upon to produce books in court was, therefore, a source of discredit:

> in consequence of their books being there produced [in court] our concerns appear to foreign bankers to be unimportant and embarrassed.[14]

One of the features of merchant society before the middle of the nineteenth century was the devastating consequences of loss of credit. A trader who could no longer buy and sell in the market might be reduced to penury more speedily even than a peasant who lost his land. The peasant at least retained the hope of being employed as a field labourer by the new owner. But there were cases in the Benares of Jonathan Duncan where great merchants who had participated in the business of state lost their credit and died of starvation.[15]

Interpretations of the behaviour of the peasant farmer in an uncertain world have stressed that his first concern was always to guarantee subsistence. Many of the seemingly irrational procedures for working land, 'hoarding' and investment seem explicable in these terms. The political and social priorities of cultivators seem to reflect what has been called the 'subsistence ethic'. The behaviour and ideals of the merchant family firm were also directed to survival first and foremost, but survival here meant above all the continuity of family credit within the wider merchant community. There is nothing to suggest that the old-style Indian merchant did not wish to make money, but questions of profit and loss had always to be set in the context of the future of the family as a whole. Like modern western business enterprises, they split up their trading operations into 'portfolios' which could be manipulated in order to avoid risks. Yet at the same time decisions in the sphere of money-making had to be adjusted to the goals of social survival and enhancement in the uncertain world of caste politics and marriage alliance.[16]

Business credit was a commodity which could slowly disappear if a family allowed its substance to be degraded by suspect behaviour or by unworthy marriage alliances. Marriage for all Indian families has been a most tricky and complicated aspect of life. The higher the caste, the higher the status and fewer the options. For Indian merchants marriage posed even greater difficulties because of their commitment to a highly orthodox and Brahminical style of life. A number of suggestions have been made as to why this was so. Some commentators have argued that the 'Brahminising' behaviour of merchant people was a reaction to their somewhat ambiguous position in caste society: that they were trying to throw off the taint of inferior, Shudra status. Others have detected an instrumental relationship between the need to preserve mercantile credit or security and rigid social mores. But whatever the origin of their style of life, aspirations to higher caste status imposed severe restraints on the more prestigious merchant families. Khattris, for instance, were divided into a number of overlapping 'clans', regional 'factions' and marriage groups.[17] These distinctions severely limited the number of families who could consider marriage alliances with each other. In relatively recent times, the most prestigious Khattri clans of the most prestigious subdivisions (Bahri Khattris of the Mehra, Khanna, Kapur and Seth exogamous clans) developed a further set of rules which limited even further the number of subdivisions with which they could marry. Thus the 'purest' were called the Dhaighar—'those who could only marry with two and a half houses'.[18] These families exclude as marriage partners 'not only the father's clan but also such families of the mother's clan as are closely connected with her; and thus reduce the clans available for intermarriage to two and a half'. Elaborate exogamy to keep the clan 'pure' was characteristic of many other prestigious mercantile clans also, so that 'most Banias prohibit intermarriage, at any rate nominally, up to five degrees'. During the nineteenth century, boundaries of this sort seem to have become stronger. As the urban population grew, families developed stable sets of marriage patterns within their own localities. For instance, after 1780, more exclusive marriage patterns became evident among the Benares Agarwals who had at one time drawn their brides from a much wider geographical area, and probably from a much larger number of subdivisions.[19] Involution as a social group went hand in hand with their metamorphosis from an open group of traders to a closed group of landowners and zamindari moneylenders.

Success as an 'entrepreneur' in marriage and social relations therefore implied a gradual narrowing of marriage circles and a gradual elimination of all practices and relationships which might endanger the purity of the family group. This tactic of withdrawal fitted well with the frugal and cautious mentality of the village or small town moneylender. But it created profound cultural tensions for those families who sought wider fields of action. Previous chapters have shown that connection with military contracting and political power offered the most rapid social advancement in north India into the colonial period. Against the background of a slow-moving, low-demand rural economy, it was state finance and revenue management which held forth the opportunities for real wealth. The conditions of the wider political economy forced merchant families to steer between the twin perils of failure in the marriage market and extinction in the commercial market. But one can recover enough of the merchant mentality from stories and random judgements of value to appreciate that failure in either sphere was a constant nightmare for them.

Two pictures of merchant behaviour can be seen in stories and legends. These might be called the 'frugal merchant' and the 'great *sahu*'. The frugal merchant avoids expense and luxury, inhabits a modest house and uses his adequate wealth to establish relations with learned men and priests; at the age of fifty or thereabouts, he is likely to leave his business to sober heirs and become a religious mendicant. This was a professional rather than a caste model of behaviour. We hear of such and such behaviour as not being suitable for a 'professed *mahajan*' or not creditable for a 'money dealer' (*sarraf*). By contrast, the 'great *sahu*' character is both admired and disapproved of. There is a pull towards establishing oneself as a magnate or little king; but it is also realised that this behaviour is ultimately destructive of mercantile credit. The 'great *sahu*' is free spending; he lives in a great palace rather than a modest mud-brick house; often he has Muslim concubines. The 'great *sahu*' has an ancient tradition. He appears for instance in Banarsi Das's poetic autobiography of the early seventeenth century, the *Ardha-Kathanak*. Here Banarsi, a middling Jain merchant of Agra, writes of the tycoon Sehbal Singh:

> He [Banarsi] went to Sahu for several days, but he [Sahu] had no time for accounts. Sahu was intoxicated with prosperity. The singers sang; the *pakhvaj* was sounded constantly in his court, and it resembled that of princes. He gave in charity incessantly, and poets and bards sang his praises ... Banarsi did not know how the accounts could be settled. He attended on the Sahu for several months but the latter had no time to spend on business or the dispute. Whenever he spoke of the accounts to Sahu, he promised to settle them in the morning. But for one engrossed in carnal pleasures the Sun neither rises nor sets.[20]

In anecdotes regarding the Benares of the late eighteenth century, the figure of the 'great *sahu*' is represented by Kashmiri Mull, head of the Pacchaina Khattris. His humiliation and ouster by the Agarwal family of Gopal Das is attributed to the Khattris' magnificent life-style which is contrasted with the Agarwal's piety and frugality. In one story, Kashmiri Mull, who apes

Persian manners and lives in a great Mughal-style palace, is discovered by his father smoking a *hookah* and is forced to throw it out of the window. The frugal merchant stands somewhere between the 'great *sahu*' and the despised miser figure who has no money even for Brahmins and charity. In one case, considerations of profit were allowed to override the religious objects which were part of the *mahajan*'s function; in the other, the 'great *sahu*' ignored the need for profit and honour, thus undermining his credit. The aim of merchant *dharma* was to steer a middle course between these two extremes.

The one thing which could be guaranteed to draw a merchant into an uncontrollable web of demeaning social relationships was an attempt to manage land. Yet all the changes in the eighteenth- and early nineteenth-century political economy pointed in this direction. Somehow a method of indirect, covert management had to be found which did not reflect adversely on mercantile credit. Kashmiri Mull was asked by the Raja of Benares to hold the revenue-farm of Ghazipur District in 1786.

> On this I replied that my business was that of a mehajin or banker and that partnership in land management was not my business, in consequence of which the Raja taking the Ganga or Ganges and the deity Beeshesher between us declared that the secret should not be revealed to anyone.[21]

The banker persuaded the Raja to keep the revenue-farm publicly in the name of one of the royal princes, so that the credit of his business house should not suffer. Throughout, the attitude of business houses to estate management remained ambiguous. In the nineteenth century, they were prepared to accept the enhanced status that being a landlord gave them in local society and the district office. But they rarely took an active part in running their zamindaris, preferring instead to leave this to an agent. The notorious inadequacies of 'moneylenders' as landlords derived in part from their reluctance to become entangled in the duties and rights which were appropriate to a 'little king'.

How did merchant families seek to avoid these grave social risks and still carry on their businesses? It was perhaps among the Jains that the code of conduct was most elaborate and rigid. According to Jain teaching, business provided the sustenance for members of the family who 'cannot afford to renounce the World at once'.[22] A balance must be held between legitimate pleasures and comforts which result from honest business, and over-indulgence which would result in lust, greed and dishonest business. There is 'always a kind of fear while enjoying or using money earned dishonestly'.[23] For the Jains, then, there were certain danger spots in a man's life when the householder, rather than holding himself in balance for future spiritual progress, could actually degenerate into a lower moral (and material) being. He is at risk from intoxication, lust, meat-eating, boisterous and unseemly behaviour; but also from the conspicuous creation or consumption of wealth which might give rise to these vices. In particular, a man should not keep a large number of vehicles, accumulate even necessary possessions in large numbers, express envy at the prosperity of others, overload his pack-animals or in anyway take part in business which risks the destruction of life.

There emerges a code of piety and restraint in which spiritual risks can be balanced out by acts of pilgrimage, meditation and vows to limit worldly possessions (called *parigraha-parinama*), 'once having fixed the measure of one's worldly possessions, grain, cash and the like'. Banarsi Das's *Ardha-Kathanak* shows how this higher teaching might actually impinge on the life of men in the bazaar. Almost all the incidents in this poetic autobiography relate to business and moral risks. The first can be overcome by knowledge of the market, restraint and listening to the advice of mercantile elders.[24] Moral degeneration can be avoided by pilgrimage, vows and meditation. To all intents and purposes, the distinction between bad moral and bad economic conduct disappears altogether. The wise merchant like Kharagsen makes a vow of restraint from the building of another house. The foolish and profligate merchant like Sehbal Singh damages his accounts, his reputation and his moral being by lust and bad management.

The ideal life-style of the Jain merchant householder was, of course, modified in practice. The famous Jagat Seth himself declared that he would be unmoved if the whole tribe of Brahmins immolated itself at his door. But participation in the moral community of the Jain merchants entailed at least an outward reverence for religious values. Moral peril and economic unreliability were seen to be closely connected. When spies were sent out to ascertain the credit of firms which had applied for the farm of government monopolies, the most damning report was that they were 'expensive people', indulging in much building and retaining many servants. Family histories and stories told in merchant schools also explain the economic fortunes of different groups largely in terms of the moral conduct of family members or the rapacity of rulers. We often hear of the young men of the family pushing expenditure beyond the 10 per cent of the annual income which is considered safe. Degenerate Muslim or European ways are acquired. The family credit collapses, there is a run on the firm, and starvation looms. The cycle begins once again when a younger son refounds the business on the basis of piety and moderation.

Similar codes of conduct were current among Hindu merchants who often found themselves in close social communion with the Jains. Once again, physical and moral 'substance' must not be endangered by contact with pollution lest marriage alliance and the continuity of the family be endangered.[25] There was constant pressure to withdraw from relationships or trades which might be considered harmful. Wisely perhaps, the Hindu lawgivers regarded money itself as a neutral medium, but commerce in polluting substances was avoided. Buchanan-Hamilton, for instance, noted that in Patna, wealthy and high caste traders in leather shoes were regarded as of low status.[26] Once they had acquired wealth oil-pressers, liquor distillers and traders in base metals generally tried to abandon their original staples and cut themselves off from those members of their castes who continued to trade in them. But insecurity was enhanced by the travel abroad, which was an essential part of merchants' lives and tended to make them suspect in the eyes of the most orthodox. Hindu merchants tried to avoid the public Mughal *sarais* and lodged with relatives and caste fellows. But beyond a point, travel took merchants into areas where the basic rites de passage of orthdox life could no longer be guaranteed. *Prayaschita*, the rites of purification which Hindus were supposed to undergo on return from travel before they could be received back into caste, originated as a system of security against social risks. It was an attempt to guarantee the continuance of trade, not as it later came to be seen, as a means of restricting contact between India and the rest of the world. Returning merchants were considered to be actually purged of foreign and impure substances by imbibing the products of the cow. That travel beyond the seas (the *kala pani*) necessitated purification is widely known. What is less well known is that the River Attock in the west Punjab formed the northern barrier of the 'safe' cultural area.[27] Khattri merchants moving up into Central Asia and the towns of

Balk and Astrakhan where they had substantial colonies were considered to have lost caste in the same way as sea-voyagers. Even the Himalayan Terai to the north-east appears to have been regarded as a barrier in the late eighteenth century. Caste Hindus were said to regard the area with suspicion so Gosain traders who were considered 'dead to the world' dominated the trade route at this time.[28]

The area of the greatest and most pervasive social risk, however, was for Hindus, like Jains, the boundary between the inward, frugal life of the merchant and the kingly manner which involved constant giving and receiving. Merchant families might find themselves trapped in the limbo between these two styles of life, unable to command the power and respect of the ruler yet 'expensive' enough to forfeit credit in the mercantile sphere. For merchants necessarily became involved with political power. They needed to have a hand in the organisation of mints. They were forced to take leases and control market sites in order to guarantee the sale and passage of their goods without harassment. Since they were dealing with landowners and Muslim judicial officials, they needed some entrée into the Persian courtly culture. The service or succour of kings which was enjoined in the law books was constantly reiterated as a goal in merchant family histories.[29] It involved the giving and getting of political honour and tied them yet more closely into darbars. The ideal balance between merchant, king, priest and labourer could not be maintained in practice. Money was coming into a commanding place in the economy, reducing the importance of other forms of redistribution of food, land or followers through the king.

Confusion of life-styles and ideals was deepened. How, for instance, was a community like the Khattris to be ranked within the Hindu system? Under the Mughal rulers of the Punjab they had achieved political power and influence, and many 'western' Khattris had assumed a life-style which was at least externally Islamic.[30] Even the four basic sub-caste divisions into which all Khattris were grouped had supposedly come about as the result of an intervention in the community's marriage practice by early Muslim rulers. Khattri family histories also display a similar ambiguity. On the one hand, they take pride in close association with the great Muslim dynasties. On the other hand, family migration is often attributed to lust by Muslim rulers for Khattri women. The dispute as to whether Khattris were of princely (Kshatriya) or mercantile (Vaishya) stock was of consuming importance, and it rumbled on throughout the nineteenth century until it was spurred into frenzy by the British Census commissioners in 1911.[31]

Merchant people adopted various stratagems which served to reduce the danger of being caught between two conflicting models of behaviour. First, they sought anonymity, avoiding publicity when they became involved in the management of land or men. Secondly, they maintained a sharper distinction between their inward and outward styles of life. For instance, amongst the Khattris of Benares in the late eighteenth century, 'Punjabi' dialect was used in the home,[32] Persian outside; Persian court dress was exchanged for the *dhoti* at home; the outward magnificence of the *haveli* palace contrasted with the severity of the inner rooms; 'Khattri' jewellery was kept separate from 'Mughal' jewellery.[33] In the nineteenth century, one often finds that the very same family which built huge Mughal-style palaces on the outskirts of cities continued to inhabit small mud-walled quarters in the old central city area.

The tension between the ascetic and self-denying and the lavish and outgoing appears also in the religious practice of merchant people. For some, indeed, lavish religious activity appears as an attempt safely to resolve this inner conflict. For, paradoxically, wealthy merchants who were noted for their restrained style of life were generally devotees of the Vaishnavite rather than of the more austere Shaivite cult.

> the Vaishnava cultus, partly from the opportunities it affords for magnificent display, partly from the absence of blood-offerings, which commends it to a class deeply influenced by the Buddhistic [sic] reverence for the sanctity of life, is more popular among the rich merchants of the towns.[34]

This love of devotional display was particularly strong among some branches of the Vallabhacharya sect which was influential in Gujerat and in Hindustani towns where there had been an early Gujerati influence. Vallabhacharya had preached that fasting and asceticism had no particular merit in themselves. He exalted the service (*sewa*) of the deity and complete surrender which included the 'giving up of the body, mind and worldly belongings of the devotee'.[35] But in time, the luxury and display of the spiritual heads of the sect (the Goswamis or Maharajs) caused a reaction in favour of a simpler and more austere form of religion. The first of these movements of reform was associated with Charan Das, a Delhi teacher of the 1730s, who attracted a large following among the merchants of the commercial towns.[36] In Bombay in the 1850s, a similar internal movement of reform to purify the practices of the Maharajs merged with the zeal of the first generation of 'social reformers' and gave rise to one of the most notorious court cases of Victorian India.[37] Among the Jains also there was a similar tension between austerity and religious display. On the one hand, there were the austerities of the priestly class and the moderation of the laity; on the other hand, the dazzling images and lavish shrine building. One need only think of the crores of Rupees spent on embellishing Mount Abu or Delhi by the great Jain families of the eighteenth century.[38]

In the individual's mind, the lavish expenditure no doubt reflected simple devotion to the god or teacher. But this is not incompatible with the notion that it also fulfilled a social function. Lavishness—costly, regal display in worship—was enhanced precisely because the merchant life-style discouraged other forms of conspicuous expenditure. Religious donation exalted the merchant as a substantial and pious man capable of fulfilling his role in society. It was at the same time safe, since the feeding of gods and Brahmins could only redound to his spiritual credit. In Allahabad, a merchant of the early nineteenth century was in the habit of distributing fifteen *maunds* of split peas (*dal*) daily in the bazaar and feeding many hundreds of cattle.[39] This was a similar act to the redistribution practised by rajas, and yet it was devoid of the element of risk because it was conceived of as meritorious charity, having first been given to the gods. The merchant was able to become a king by proxy.

Merchant families in many societies have been associated with particular, sectarian forms of religious practice. But the relationship between mercantile credit and exclusive forms of worship has remained obscure despite constant debate. India provides no exception here. Quite apart from the obvious examples of Jainism and Parsi Zoroastrianism, merchants were well represented among sectarian groups which grew more directly out of the Vaishnavite Hindu tradition, such as the Vallabhacharyas, Satnamis and Radhavallabs. To what extent are we justified in regarding sectarian attachment of this sort as a tactic in the maintenance of family credit? Certainly, devotion to a *guru* or a set of precepts which attracted a group of devotees from several different castes fulfilled the requirement that involuted social relations had to subsist with wider business contacts. In the late eighteenth century, for instance, the Jains were still increasing in numbers by incorporating Hindus of the merchant castes. The peculiar inwardness of Jain religious and social life might actually increase the credit of families which still had to work partly within a Hindu context. There was a great emphasis on secrecy. No doubt the austere nature of Jain domestic life also had its advantages during a century when rulers were always on the lookout for opulent merchants to mulct. In areas such as Malwa where Jains dominated commercial life, a shift across sectarian boundaries was not unusual. Malcolm recorded:

> The Soucars, Shroffs and Bunnias in Malwa are either of the Jain or Vishnu faith, but by far the greatest numbers are of the former, and their prevailing influence and wealth attracts many converts. Almost all the Vaisya and Sudra agents and servants they employ, if not before Jains, conform to the tenets of that sect.[40]

Other sects also gained adherents as a result of close commercial relations. For instance, Vallabhacharyas and Nanakshahi Sikhs continued to increase their numbers in the Gangetic cities during the eighteenth century. However, slow adaptation to a prevailing culture could also work in the other direction. In Bengal, the great Jagat Seth family which had once been among the chief donors of Jain temples throughout India, gradually abandoned their Jain practices and drifted back into the Vaishnavite business and landowning community which surrounded them. In the same way, 'western' Khattri merchants from the Punjab who moved down into the plains of Hindustan often came to place less emphasis on the Islamic and Punjabi part of their cultural inheritance as they were drawn into more intimate communion with the orthodox life of the banks of the Ganges.

While 'changes' of religious affiliation of this sort cannot be regarded as simple utilitarian acts, they certainly enhanced the social, and hence commercial security, of trading families isolated in a new environment. Viewed from the inside of merchant family life, these were, perhaps, not dramatic events. The family was in continuous communion with a whole range of business associates, gods and men. All that happened was that a portion of family resources and worship was redirected to deities which were honoured by neighbours and business associates. Earlier religious practices usually continued alongside the new. So among Jains in Bihar in the early nineteenth century, Brahmins and Hindu deities were venerated without embarrassment.[41] Similarly, in the case of the Nanakshahi Khattris, Hindu forms of worship were not felt to be incompatible with accepting the holiness of the Guru Granth Sahib (the Sikh holy book).[42]

Before moving on from the question of the 'credit' of the merchant family, it is worth considering it in the context of the political response of the commercial community. As we have seen, genealogies exult in connections with famous rulers both Hindu and Muslim, but over-close association with rulers might lead a family into expense and depravity. In the same way, fear of the predatory ruler was a constant refrain in the demonology of merchant people. Mughal rulers and nawabs were popularly remembered for their benevolence, but their lieutenants were accused of meddling in commercial custom. In 1813–15, unease in the bazaars of Benares and Mirzapur was heightened by the comparisons which were being made between an unpopular British judge and Todar Mull, the famous Mughal financial minister.

. . . the townsmen consider him to be a sort of mostaufee, which means one who takes all—some such officer as Torur Mull was under Akber—how popular their likening him to Torur Mull proves him to be may be judged by the well known quatrain which gives the date of that financier's death—'when Torur Mull whose oppressions had overspread the World went towards hell, a whole world of people were rejoiced, 998 Hijree'.[43]

The Todar Mull legend was very general. He is supposed to have enforced the standard form of account books which was used throughout India in the eighteenth and nineteenth centuries and to have been responsible for many interventions in the business of the commercial corporations.

Many other stories related to the levy by impoverished or avaricious rulers of forced loans which were never repaid. But it is important to catch the nuances of these legends. Family histories often seemed to take pride in succouring a great king with no hope of repayment, yet still remaining rich and creditable people. The great Gurwala banking family of Delhi, for instance, claimed to have lent up to ten lakhs of Rupees to the Mughals during the early nineteenth century on an interest-free loan which was never repaid.[44] Such stories were probably exaggerated, but the mentality underlying them may help further to correct some of our notions of the anarchy of the eighteenth century and the meaning of the 'Pax Britannica'. Under indigenous regimes 'plunder' (*zulum*) was expected, and could partly be insured against. Forced loans could be seen in the light of 'protection rent'. Indeed the Hindu law books themselves sanctioned the seizure of up to one quarter of the total assets of merchants during times of famine or danger. In that pregnant metaphor, the merchants were the ruler's cattle, to be milked by him if the necessity arose.[45] 'Plunder', then, was built into the theory and practice of Indian states and their mercantile subjects. It could carry connotations of an exceptional levy or of equitable redistribution rather than the criminality and breakdown implied in the English word. In some regimes, 'plunder' took the form of a periodic readjustment in the context of a low fixed land-revenue and minimal customs charge. British observers noted with bewilderment that townsmen and peasants seemed to remain in contentment and that Hindu merchants could adjust to the direst forms of what they took to be oppression. Among the unwilling suppliants at the darbar of the ruler of Kandahar in the 1820s:

there were invariably from fifty to one hundred Hindus, some of them doubtless men of respectability and wealth, and all merchants and traders who had been seized in their houses and shops and dragged before the Durbar for the purposes of extorting money. This was not an occasional or monthly but a daily occurrence. . . . I have seen on an occasion of a festival the Hindus of this city assembled in gardens without their walls and displaying every sign of ease and wealth in their apparel and trinkets; nor were they the less grateful than they would have been in a Hindu kingdom. The gains of these men must be enormous, or they would never provide to the exactions of their governors, and without such profit operating as an offset never would submit to the indignities they are compelled to suffer.[46]

But plunder, even social indignity, could be tolerated by a cohesive merchant group fortified by its own internal perceptions of credit. Merchants could only be forced to flee if the ruler appeared to push them below the margin of subsistence during a bad period, or if their credit which was the basis of their livelihood was threatened in any novel or discriminatory manner. It is against this background that we should place the many stories claiming that merchant families migrated from a particular city because its ruler had designs on their womenfolk or was forcing upon them some practice which was obnoxious to their religious feeling. Here it was the credit, continuity, even bodily substance of the individual family which was in jeopardy, and the danger was greater than from any forced loan which could be absorbed and discounted by the community as a whole.

These notions also provide a key to the issues which brought merchants and townsmen into conflict with early colonial rulers. Almost always there was some perceived threat to the moral economy of the merchant family. The British attempted to introduce conceptions of individual legal responsibility limited to one lifetime. Earlier, debt had been a matter of family credit over several generations. As a Persian newsletter of 1837 commented,

> the chain which bound the soucars [bankers] together in their trading relations is broken ... Previously in cases of bancruptcy the whole body of the soucars would get together and award equitable reparations, but now a son could declare himself bankrupt in a civil court when his father was still in possession of lakhs.[47]

The reorganisation of tolls, bazaar duties and urban taxation by the colonial authorities posed another subtle threat to merchant status because it overturned local indemnities and privileges. The sphere of mercantile custom was invaded in many minor but irritating forays. At one time or another, the colonial authorities demanded the production of bankers' books in court; they tried to suppress the 'plunder' of a failed merchant's stock or they attempted to make registers of bullion dealers which violated the basic tenets of mercantile secrecy. Finally, they blundered once or twice into policies which offended the religious interests of the commercial population. It is notable that the only times when Hindustan's bazaars closed down altogether during our period were when cattle, Brahmins and the purity of the River Ganges seemed under threat.

Originally published as C.A. Bayly, *Rulers, Townsmen and Bazaars: North Indian Society in the Age of British Expansion 1770–1870* (Cambridge, Cambridge University Press, 1983), pp. 375–93.

NOTES

1. S. Roy, *Customs and Customary Law in British India* (Calcutta, 1911), ch. XIV ('Trade Customs'), esp. p. 536; for an earlier exposition, 46 of 1853, Kanpur, 15 Aug. 1854, *ZC*; one type of *hundi* required endorsement, the other made out to 'bearer' often included the words 'Make sure you pay a respectable man, for you pay to any other at your own risk'. The intrusion of subjective notions of 'respectability' into *hundi* transactions enhanced the security consciousness of the old-style firms.
2. *Panchayats* for the arbitration of separations in joint families took into account matters such as the imminence of a daughter's marriage. In one case 20% of the firm's assets are set aside for this purpose, see 199 of 1847, Saharanpur, June 1848, *ZC*; one branch of the Benares Shah family opened a special *khata* for the expenses of a daughter's marriage, beginning under date *Aghun Sudi*, 10, *Sambat*, 1911 (1854 A.D.), Shah Khatas (film in author's possession).
3. Communication from Prof. Alan Heston to participants in the conference on 'Risk and Uncertainty', University of Pennsylvania, 1977.
4. See, for example, the Shah *kothi*'s expense and daily books, *Sambat*, 1929–33.
5. Interviews, Sri Devi Narayan; family histories, Benares, 1973.
6. Shah *kothi* expense books, *Sambat*, 1929–33.
7. Thus the families of the connection of Sir Motichand Gupta in Benares traditionally had Gujerati *munims*, while the 'Calcuttawallah' Gujerati firm had north Indian Agarwal *munims*, interview, Sri Jyotibhushan Gupta, Feb. 1974; similar cross-caste relationships of trust bound firms' principals to *gomashtas* and *arethias*; there are cases where Hindu firms retained Muslim *arethias*, particularly in the shawl trade.
8. Sri Ram Krishna and Sri Mathura Das of Benares provided many of these stories, interviews, 1972–4.
9. Daily cash books of the family firm of Bhartendu Harish Chandra, *Sambat*, 1942–3, in possession of Dr Kumud Chandra, Chaukambha.

10. Books of Gappoo Mall Kandheya Lal, Ranimandi, Allahabad.

11. Raghunandan, cit. H. T. Colebrooke, *A Digest of Hindu Law on Contracts and Succession. Translated from the Original Sanscrit* (Calcutta, 1797), pp. 1, 6.

12. Representation of the Principal Bankers of Benares, 13 Jan. 1795, PR. 13 Ibid.

14. Representation of Bankers, 15 Sept. 1790, PR.

15. Case of Manohar Das Rora, 26 Aug. 1788, 30 Jan. 1790, PR; governments might actually precipitate bankruptcy by declaring a firm insolvent, e.g., Mughal *shuqqa* declaring a Delhi bankruptcy, *CPC*, v, 19 Oct. 1780.

16. I am indebted to members of the SSRC Conference on 'Risk and Uncertainty', University of Pennsylvania, 1977, for discussion of these notions.

17. Kashi Nath, 'Khattris', *IA*, ii (1873), 27; Harnan Das Varma, *An Account of the Khattris as a Race of Ancient Kshatriyas* (Lahore, 1901), pp. 23–4.

18. D. Ibbetson, *Panjab Castes* (Lahore, 1916), p. 250.

19. *Agrawal Jati*, II, *passim*; Benares Agarwal family histories in author's possession; communication from Dr Anand Krishna, Rai Kishen Das, Jan. 1974; cf. R. V. Russell and Rai Bahadur Hira Lal, *Tribes and Castes of the Central Provinces* (London, 1916), II, 115.

20. Banarsi Das, *Ardha-Kathanak*, ed. R. S. Sharma, *Indica*, vii (1970), 2, 114.

21. Reply of Kashmiri Mull, 13 June 1788, PR.

22. Sri Samanta Bhadra Acharya, *Ratna Karanda Sravakachara*, tr. C. R. Jain (Arrah, 1917), p. 30.

23. H. Warren, *Jainism* (Arrah, 1912), pp. 77–8.

24. *Ardha-Kathanak, Indica*, vii (1970), 65; Ibid., p. 114; cf. Warren, *Jainism*, p. 30.

25. Cf. McKim Marriott, 'Hindu Transaction: Diversity without Dualism', in B. Kapferer (ed.), *Transaction and Meaning* (Philadelphia, 1976); this model is useful for understanding the attitudes of north Indian merchants who are cognisant of the 'religious' way of life; it seems doubtful whether it could be extended to the 'South Asian mind' in general as the article intends.

26. Martin, *Eastern India*, 1, 369.

27. Forster, *Journey*, 11, 292.

28. E.g., Representation of Geean Gir, 7 Sept. 1791, PR.

29. See, e.g., P. N. Mullick, *History of the Vaishyas of Bengal* (Calcutta, 1902), pp. 31–3.

30. E.g., the 'Western' Khattri families of Chipiwara, Delhi, esp. that of Munshi Raghunath Singh which appears to have had a particularly 'Islamicised' life-style, being creditor to the Mughal nobility of the area, interview, family documents, Dec. 1973.

31. H. D. Varma, *An Account of the Khattris*.

32. *Gunga Bye* v. *the Mother of Jwalanath*, 3 Aug. 1792, PR.

33. Ibid.

34. Crooke, *North Western Provinces*, p. 247.

35. N. A. Thoothi, *The Vaishnavas of Gujerat* (London, 1935), pp. 92–7.

36. H. H. Wilson, 'The Religious Sects of the Hindoos', *AR*, xvii (1832), pp. 181ff.

37. C. Dobbin, *Urban Leadership in Western India* (London, 1972), pp. 65–70.

38. Sayyid Ahmed Khan, *Asar-us Sanadid*, tr. Tassy, 'Description des Monuments de Delhi', *Journal Asiatique*, 5e série, xv (1869), 4.

39. *Agrawal Jati*, II, 15, Lala Har Bilas.

40. Malcolm, *Central India*, 11, 160.

41. Vaishnavite and Jain Agarwal families in Benares also regularly intermarried.

42. *Bedamo* v. *Bowanny Singh*, Benares Adalat, 6 Jan. 1792, PR.

43. Second Judge Benares to Magt., 12 Jan. 1813, BCJ, 12 July 1816, 132/43, IOL.

44. Gurwala family history, copy in author's possession; but see *Ramji Das and Narain Das* v. *Agent to the King of Delhi*, 91 of 1852, Delhi, June 1852, *ZC*.

45. P. V. Kane, *History of Dharmasastra (Ancient and Medieval Religious and Civil Law)* (Poona, 1941), II, i, 41; cf. Hocart, *Caste*, p. 39.

46. G. W. Forrest, *Selections from Journals*, p. 110.

47. 'Dishonest Sowkars', Extracts from Persian *Akhbar*, *Delhi Gazette*, 29 Mar. 1837.

20

Family Values
The Birlas

Medha M. Kudaisya

This excerpt is a case study that reconstructs how family was enmeshed with firm in the 1930s in the case of the Birla family, one of the most eminent business groups in India.* It examines how the extended family of the four Birla brothers functioned as a social group and how carefully the family 'tradition' was defined and perpetuated.

The four Birla brothers assumed well-demarcated roles in the family and the firm. Thus, care-giving functions including education and upbringing of all the children of the four Birla brothers were handed over to the youngest brother, Braj Mohan, and his wife. As with other Marwari families, girls were expected to play minimal roles in family business and did not inherit immovable properties. Sons, on the other hand, were expected to shoulder the responsibilities of managing the family business. Deep regard for tradition and respect for the framework of the joint family was conscientiously inculcated in the children. They had to follow a strict regimen of traditional Hindu rituals and were exposed to important holy texts from a young age. The children were also encouraged to subdue individuality and value the importance of the family as a social unit. No deviation from family tradition was tolerated, especially in areas such as marriage since compatible partners had to be found in order to build networks and enhance the family honour within the larger Marwari community.

An essential element of family tradition was the grooming of sons to manage the family business. Sons were initiated into business at an early age through financial and

* On the story of the Birlas in these years also see Ram Nivas Jaju, *G.D. Birla: A Biography* (New Delhi, Vikas, 1985); Alan Ross, *The Emissary: G.D. Birla, Gandhi and Independence* (London, Collins Harvill, 1986); and D.K. Taknet, *B.M. Birla: A Great Visionary* (New Delhi, Indus, 1996).

accounting matters until they were single-handedly able to prepare an entire cash book, balance receipts and payments, and meticulously account for every *paisa*. They were initiated into the family's code of business and were taught to value the dignity and status of the family and firm.† Upon the completion of their apprenticeship, the members of the younger generation were placed in charge of industrial units, though their progress was monitored. Such strict training ensured that the next generation closely followed the overall ground rules laid down by the elders.

Birla could play his new public role only because of the strong support network which he enjoyed from within the larger family, especially from his brothers Rameshwardas and Braj Mohan. Birla's most active years in public life were also the most momentous for the family. The children were at a crucial age—all in their early teens when they needed attention. However, between 1930 and 1943 all of Birla's children were married and the boys were inducted into different branches of the family business. After 1926, following Mahadevi's demise, the children were placed under the charge of different branches of the family in Bombay and Calcutta. Birla tried hard to keep track of how they were doing. However, as his public life increasingly grew more hectic and his business commitments multiplied, he was required to spend long periods travelling within the country and to the UK. In view of these circumstances Birla increasingly realized that he could not provide the care which his young children needed and had to depend upon the help of his brothers and their wives.

Responsibility for the children came to be shared by Rameshwardas and Braj Mohan. Rameshwardas lived at Birla House on Mount Pleasant Road in Bombay while Braj Mohan was based at Birla Park, the family's Calcutta home. Birla, as we have noted earlier, had moved to Delhi in 1929 along with Jugalkishore. There were five running establishments which the family maintained by the late 1920s—in Banaras, Delhi, Bombay, Calcutta and Pilani to which periodic visits were made. Yet, the geographical distance was not allowed to upset the family's cohesion and solidarity. Over the years, the brothers had assumed well demarcated roles within the family. After Baldeodas' retirement, Jugalkishore donned the mantle of the patriarch and his views were considered binding on all. While keeping a sharp eye on what he saw as important family and religious matters, Jugalkishore, however, remained uninvolved with the daily concerns of caretaking and upbringing. Birla could take an interest in the children only when critical decisions were to be made. Rameshwardas and Braj Mohan looked after day-to-day socialization, education and apprenticeship. Birla could leave all these matters to them because of the manner in which the family functioned.

FAMILY AS A SOCIAL GROUP

The family functioned as a social group and sustained the children through their growing-up

† Certain fundamental rules had to be followed, namely the need to control finances by monitoring daily financial performance through the *parta* system and the need to exact complete loyalty from senior employees who would be rewarded with agency and distribution rights.

years. Close contact was maintained among the different households. All important decisions were taken by the elders, and the younger generation—which consisted of Birla's own six children, six of Rameshwardas' and two of Braj Mohan'—moved easily between Calcutta and Bombay. Relations among the cousins were intimate. Because of a fortuitous set of circumstances, all the children of the Birla brothers had, by the late 1920s, come to live together. When Rameshwardas' first wife expired in 1923 he sent his sons to be cared for by Braj Mohan and his wife in Calcutta, while his daughters remained with him. Although he later remarried, this arrangement continued. Then, when Mahadevi expired in 1926, Birla too made similar arrangements for the care of his children. The sons were put under the charge of Braj Mohan and his daughters under Rameshwardas. Thus, all six sons of the three Birla brothers came to live together in Calcutta. Their education and upbringing became the responsibility of Braj Mohan and his wife. The seven daughters of Rameshwardas and Birla came under the care of Rameshwardas and his second wife in Bombay. The family met once a year during the holidays which were spent either in Calcutta or Bombay, or in one of the family houses in the hills.

Whilst their relation with their uncles was an intimate one, the relation of the children with Birla was somewhat aloof and formal. Meeting him sometimes after long intervals the children grew to be intimidated by their father. Most often these meetings were short—while he was on a business visit to Bombay or Calcutta and he barely had time to spend with them. Overall the atmosphere was of deep respect mingled with fear for elders. The youngsters felt deserted and yearned to be with him. Even when he was at home, their formal relation made it difficult for them to express their emotions frankly. So much did they fear him that they almost never had the courage to question his long absences.[1] It was only many years later, when their father was well into his eighties, that the children dared to confess what they had dearly missed him. As Shanti, his daughter, told Birla: 'I wish you could always have loved us as much as you do now. When we went to Delhi or you came to Bombay, we only knew of your arrival and departure; you could seldom spare us any time.'[2]

However, it seemed to Birla that arrangements for their care could not be better under the circumstances. Keeping them close to him and Jugalkishore in Delhi in the absence of a matriarchal figure made little sense.[3] He felt inadequate to care for the young children on his own. Moreover, the Delhi home was more like an official residence while Bombay and Calcutta remained family homes where they lived amidst the extended family and community networks.

However, in the early 1930s, the experiment of keeping the children with him in Delhi was made. Both Krishna Kumar and Basant Kumar along with Ganga Prasad (Braj Mohan's son) and Madhav Prasad (Rameshwardas' elder son) were called to stay in Delhi. Lakshmi Niwas, already in his twenties, was based in Delhi and was involved in the family business. The younger two—Krishna Kumar and Basant Kumar were admitted into the prestigious Modern School. However, the arrangements did not work. The boys were both forcibly admitted to the school hostel, Krishna Kumar came down with pneumonia and the children missed the warmth of the Calcutta family home. What made matters worse was Birla's hectic schedule. Finally, the boys, to the relief of all, were sent back to Calcutta.[4] Circumstances thus conspired so that in their crucial growing-up years the children could not enjoy a satisfying relationship with their father. He grew to know his sons only after they joined the family business, and while grooming them, developed an appreciation of their abilities, strengths and weaknesses. His relation towards his daughters remained formal. This had much to do with the way the girl-child was perceived by the elders. In an orthodox family such as theirs the status of a girl was markedly different from that of a boy. Though as children they all enjoyed an equally affectionate relationship with their elders and shared in the family's prosperity, the girls were brought up on the premise that the family's responsibility did not extend beyond giving them primary education and finding suitable grooms for them. Like other Marwari families, it was taken for granted that the girls would not play any role in business nor inherit immovable properties.[5] The family's responsibility was to nurture them in an affectionate environment, impart to them 'some education' and find a 'good husband'.

Through these early years, the values which the family elders hoped to instil in the daughters were of service, restraint and renunciation. The position of a daughter is perhaps best captured by a conversation which Shanti, Birla's youngest daughter had with her father. He told her: 'The first lesson in the *Gita* is to do your duty at all costs. Spinning, reading, domestic chores—all these are your work and duty... The greatest duty is to serve your household and make it a happy home.'[6] The girls thus came to appreciate that their primary loyalty lay with their husband's family. They were to become their 'husband's associate and protector of his righteousness.'[7] Daughters who resisted early marriage or expressed ambitions for higher education were counselled. When Shanti expressed a desire to complete her High School examination before her marriage Birla told her that mere degrees would not take her far. 'Real examinations are held in everyday life and success or failure are assessed there', he said.

Sons were, however, given a different treatment. The expectation from them was that they would train to take up the responsibility of the family business and demonstrate qualities of leadership. They were expected to complete their school education although higher education was not encouraged. Hands-on training in business was considered more valuable than a formal college degree. Among Birla's sons and nephews only Ganga Prasad, Braj Mohan's son, became a graduate. Although Birla's younger sons Krishna Kumar and Basant Kumar too spent some time in college they soon left to join business.

DEFINING THE FAMILY 'TRADITION'

A great deal of emphasis was placed in inculcating a sense of tradition among the children. This was typical of a Marwari business family. The joint-family structure and its hierarchies were paramount. The children were taught to respect the framework of the joint family and not allowed to differentiate among the elders. They thus called Jugalkishore *Bade Baboji* or elder father even though he had no children of his own. Rameshwardas was addressed as *Baboji* or father, Birla as *Kakoji* which meant elder uncle, and Braj Mohan was called *Chachoji* or uncle. Likewise, their wives were also addressed similarly by the new generation. Jugalkishore's and Rameshwardas' wives were called *Badi-Ma* or elder mother in keeping with their exalted status and Braj Mohan's wife was addressed as *Kakiji* or aunt by all the children of the family.

A strict regime of traditional Hindu rituals was inculcated in the daily lives of the youngsters. Jugalkishore ensured that the family strictly followed religious practices prescribed by the Sanatan Dharma tradition of Hinduism. Astrologers were consulted before all important occasions. Jugalkishore kept the horoscopes of the entire family in his charge and regularly organized prayers and religious ceremonies, to 'ward off suspected obstacles and neutralise evil influences.'[8] From a young age, the children were exposed to important holy texts and made to 'memorise good quatrains from the *Ramayana* and also verses from the *Gita*.'[9] Jugalkishore instructed the younger generation to 'carry on with *bhajans*, *kirtans* and *havans*' and to strictly observe the chanting of prayers.[10]

Another essential element of the family tradition was the shunning of individuality. The importance of the family as a social unit rather than the individual was emphasized to the Birla children. Individualistic behaviour was discouraged and they were expected to respect decisions made by elders. In social life a strict 'code of restraint' was practised at home. This meant an austere lifestyle which emphasized control over individual expenditure. 'Never utilise wealth only for fun and frolic', Birla told Basant Kumar. He compared expenditure of wealth on 'worldly pleasures' to the demon-like conduct of Ravana in the epic *Ramayana*.[11] A frugal lifestyle was emphasized to the children who were instructed to 'spend the bare minimum on yourself'. Birla regarded over-spending as 'committing sin' which would 'destroy our business'.[12] This code translated into a control over consumption. To 'waste money on worldly pleasures' was derided. The youngsters were discouraged from taking to enjoyments such as the theatre. On learning that his elder daughter, Chandrakala, had developed some interest in theatre, Birla immediately took her to task. He derided her interest in theatre, declaring that it was purely for entertainment, not for instruction. 'Girls should pay more attention to holy thoughts and sinless conduct.'[13] All pleasures should be shunned, he told her. During vacations, which were sometimes spent in hill stations, the children were discouraged from mixing with 'Anglicized ladies and gentlemen'.[14]

In keeping with Sanatani practices, the entire family followed a strict vegetarian diet and even the consumption of onions and garlic was disallowed.[15] 'Those who eat food only for taste die prematurely', Birla warned Basant Kumar and asked him to 'take food as you would take medicines'. Sweets, cakes, pastries were regarded as European and were also taboo to the children for fear of encouraging spendthrift tendencies.[16] Consumption of *paan*, betel-nuts and tobacco was discouraged and children who dared indulge, were reprimanded. Consumption of alcohol was regarded no less than a sin.

Signs of opposition or revolt against the austere lifestyle invited censure and punishment. The case of Gajanan, Rameshwardas' son provided a living example of how unbecoming conduct was dealt with. When Gajanan showed a 'fondness for high living, for gourmet style food, ... for song and dance, and for smoking' he was severely taken to task.[17] Birla was given the responsibility of disciplining the youngster. Birla advised his 25-year-old nephew to give up his bad habits and to follow the family's traditions. When his discussions and warnings to Gajanan failed to have the desired effect, severe measures were taken. He was ostracized by the family elders. An unrelenting Gajanan, however, found it difficult to follow the beaten path. He had, in 1929, been married against his wishes. Although he had two children, his marriage was not successful. He was unable to mend his ways. Then the family discovered that he had developed another relationship and wanted to separate from his wife. This proved to be the last straw for the family elders. Birla and Rameshwardas worked out a legal settlement in 1935 which severed Gajanan's ties with the family. Under its terms he was disinherited and given an allowance of Rs 1000 every month. His wife and her two children were taken under the family's charge while he was forced out of Birla Park, his home. The family elders continued to give the respect and privileges due to his wife as a daughter-in-law.

This served as an example to all the youngsters. They understood that no deviations from the family tradition would be tolerated and acquiesced in all important individual decisions made by the family patriarchs, including marriage alliances. Such alliances were seen to be critical in continuing the family's traditions. Considerations of compatibility in terms of status within the community were paramount. Marriages were seen to be important for building networks and enhancing the family honour and prestige within the larger Maheshwari community. Brides were chosen from families which were seen to have superior status within the community. It was hoped that alliances would bring contacts and valuable advice on business matters. The *kutumb*—or in-laws—were invaluable for forging community links. Thus Birla's eldest son, Lakshmi Niwas, was married in 1927 to the daughter of Shyamsundarlal Loiwal, who held the important position of Diwan in the princely state of Kishangarh in Rajputana.[18] So well connected was the family that the Maharaja of Kishangarh himself attended the wedding. It was perceived by the elders to have 'elevated the prestige of the Birla family in the Maheshwari community' after the setback to its reputation over the unfortunate Kolwar controversy. The other boys were also married into prominent families—Krishna Kumar married into the prominent Taparia family.[19] Perhaps the most prestigious was the match for Basant Kumar in 1942 with Sarala, the daughter of Brijlal Biyani, who had been president of the All India Maheshwari Mahasabha and a prominent leader from the Central Provinces known among political circles as Berar Kesari.

Marriages of the daughters was less complex. While considerations of ritual status were important, the prominence of the family was not an important consideration. Since he was based in Calcutta where community networks existed, it often became the responsibility of Braj Mohan to find marriage alliances. Chandrakala was married in August 1931 to Bansi Dhar who came from the Daga family which had businesses in Jalpaiguri. The family had a flourishing business in tea, textiles and insurance. Chandrakala was then only 14 years old. After the marriage ceremonies which took place at Birla Park in Calcutta, Birla gave her the following advice for her married life:

> You must remember, you now have to cement relations in your new home. You must do your duty unflinchingly. Do not lose patience. I gave you some education and found you a good husband... What else can I do for you now? May God give you moral strength... Never neglect your duty. Service, restraint and renunciation... You must love your life-partner, which you must already do, I am sure... Remain happy and do not neglect your daily prayers.[20]

In 1941 the family was able to find suitable matches for the younger daughters, Anusuiya and Shanti. Anusuiya was married to Narendra Singh Taparia, a scion of a Calcutta Maheshwari family. Shanti was married to Krishnagopal Maheshwari.[21] The following year when the marriage of Basant Kumar and Sarala was celebrated Birla had the satisfaction of seeing all his children settled. He developed a close relationship with his daughters-in-law. With Sarala he developed a special bond as Gandhi, who knew the Biyani family well, had played a role in encouraging the match. Although he had warned Sarala that 'the Birla family is used to traditional methods. There won't be much freedom for you', he had been delighted at this alliance and the engagement had taken place in his ashram at Wardha.[22] This made the youngest daughter-in-law special in Birla's eyes. In later years he looked upon her as the lady of the house.

BUSINESS GROOMING

An essential element of the family tradition was the initiation and apprenticeship of sons into family business and their grooming for future leadership. Sons were initiated into the business once they finished schooling. Birla and Braj Mohan took active interest in their apprenticeship.

The new apprentice typically underwent initial training for approximately a year. In this period he was put under the charge of a trusted senior manager who regularly reported progress to Braj Mohan and Birla. Having lived with Braj Mohan through their childhood years, the boys found it easier to work with him and felt intimidated if they had to deal with Birla at the work-place. Thus Lakshmi Niwas started his apprenticeship in the jute trade with Braj Mohan. Krishna Kumar was initiated into the sugar mills in the late 1930s. Basant Kumar initially began with stock operations and then joined the Kesoram Cotton Mill. Birla's nephews Ganga Prasad and Madho Prasad started out with shipping and jute respectively.[23] Senior managers played a critical role during the apprenticeship years. Basant Kumar, for example, was placed under the charge of Sitaram Khemka, a trusted kinsman and employee. An essential component of the training was in learning financial and accounting matters. 'Keeping accounts, maintaining cash books, ledgers, vouchers, bills and outstanding accounts, reconciling bank records' were part of this preliminary training which also included preparation of 'daily reports, parta, monthly and annual income and expenditure accounts, sales procedures'. Such training continued for as long as it took them to single-handedly prepare the 'entire cash book, balance the receipts and payments, meticulously account for every paisa'. This could sometimes even take up to a year. Thereafter they were attached to other departments such as sales and manufacturing.

Perhaps more significant than learning these skills was the inculcation of the family's code of business in the young initiates. This was not difficult to imbibe as it was merely an extension of the code of restraint which they had been taught at home. They were taught that the dignity and status of the family within the community and in the industrial world were the most important. They were repeatedly reminded that the family name must not be dishonoured. 'It didn't matter', Birla told the younger generation as they took their first steps in the world of business, 'if we should expand slowly, but we should proceed with abundant caution'. The reputation of the family was most important since the 'community had reposed full faith on us. Even if a single enterprise failed, the blame would fall ... on the entire Birla family'.[24]

There were certain fundamental rules which were always to be followed. Foremost was the need to keep a tight control on the finances by monitoring daily financial performance achieved through the parta system which was followed in all Birla enterprises. This entailed the calculation of cost, output and profit on a daily basis. Their training emphasized an almost obsessive concern with financial performance and control which characterized the Birla business philosophy. 'Major effort' was to go 'into financial and commercial matters.' Each parta statement was looked at on a daily basis and sometimes up to ten to twelve days of each month were spent in examining the accounts of the previous month. Birla himself insisted that daily parta statements from each of the mills under his charge be sent to him each day wherever he might be.

Other principles which were passed on to the next generation related to the extended family. Complete loyalty was expected from senior employees. They were considered to be a part of the extended joint-family staff. Senior employees inevitably came from the Marwari community preferably from the Maheshwari subcaste. Many of them also had a Pilani connection and had spent long years with the business. They were often indebted for help rendered in personal affairs. A prime example was Durga Prasad Mandelia—called *Chachoji* by the younger generation. He had started his career with Birla at the age of 14 and had risen to become a key business associate. The new generation was similarly encouraged to select a team of their own and were encouraged to recruit sons of senior employees. This ensured stability and loyalty which was sometimes rewarded by giving away of agency and distribution rights. Thus from within the community satellite groups were created which strengthened the business network, provided managerial talent and enhanced trust.

Once their apprenticeship was completed and real business responsibilities started the younger generation were given charge of the units where they had been trained. By 1940 Birla's three sons and nephews had completed their initial training and taken over individual charge of different factories. Thus Lakshmi Niwas was looking after the New Asiatic Insurance Company and had opened a starch unit in Rangoon. Madhav Prasad had taken charge of the Birla Jute Mill. Basant Kumar had been elevated to become the chairman of the Kesoram Cotton. Krishna Kumar had a number of sugar mills under his control. Ganga Prasad too had begun to take responsibility. It was only Gajanan who had been left out of these business endeavours.[25]

While the new generation had taken charge of different units, Birla and Braj Mohan continued to keep a watchful eye on their progress. They had to be consulted before any major investment decisions were made. As Basant Kumar recalls his early days in the family business: 'I did have to approach Kakoji for permission whenever I wanted to raise fresh capital. Without his advice and clearance, I did not raise even Rs 50 lakhs from the market.'[26] Diversification plans were discussed carefully with the elders and had to be approved by them. Certain areas of business were considered taboo such as the hotel business because it involved 'drinking and dancing' which was not in keeping with the austere tradition of the family.

As they expanded their horizons, the younger generation knew that the family tradition had to be adhered to. For example, in 1938, Basant Kumar started a new company, Kumar Chemical and Pharmaceutical Works Ltd., for the manufacture of pharmaceuticals. He made a substantial investment of over rupees two and a half lakhs and hired a foreign expert from Hungary to help set up the new enterprise. When his plans were well advanced, Jugalkishore was horrified to learn that the manufacturing process would involve the use of animal glands to produce hormone-based medicines.[27] Uncle and nephew argued over the issue for over two months. However, Jugalkishore remained adamant and Basant Kumar ultimately had to give in and abandon the project.[28]

By the early 1940s the Birla brothers had the satisfaction of seeing the next generation take up business responsibilities. Except for Gajanan, all other sons earmarked for them in the business empire. This was well timed as the business was poised for unprecedented growth thanks to the economic opportunities thrown up by the outbreak of World War II in 1939.

Originally published as M. Kudaisya, *Life and Times of G.D. Birla* (New Delhi, Oxford University Press, 2003), pp. 188–96.

NOTES

1. Basant Kumar Birla, *A Rare Legacy*, p. 20.
2. R.N. Jaju, *G.D. Birla: A Biography*, p. 172.
3. Jugalkishore's wife had expired in 1927.
4. Ibid., pp. 18–19.
5. For a valuable study of how family businesses function see Sudipt Dutta, *Family Business in India* (New Delhi, 1997).
6. Ibid., p. 151.
7. Birla to Chandrakala, in Jaju, *G.D. Birla: A Biography*, pp. 99–100.
8. Basant Kumar Birla, *A Rare Legacy*, p. 283.
9. Birla to Shanti, in R.N. Jaju, *G.D. Birla: A Biography*, p. 131.
10. See Basant Kumar Birla, *A Rare Legacy*, p. 281.
11. Ibid., pp. 350–1.
12. Ibid., pp. 350–1.
13. R.N. Jaju, *G.D. Birla: A Biography*, p. 110
14. Basant Kumar Birla, *A Rare Legacy*, p. 23.
15. Ibid., p. 280.
16. Ibid., pp. 350–1.
17. Ibid., pp. 310–13.
18. Loiwal had been an important figure in the Maheshwari community. He was instrumental in the establishment of the Maheshwari Mahasabha in 1890 and had inaugurated the first session of the Maheshwari Mahasabha which had been attended by Maheshwaris from all over the country.
19. Gajanan married the daughter of Jamnadas Malpani of Jabalpur, in 1929. The Malpanis were 'considered then to be one of the finest in the Marwari community' and Madhav Prasad's bride was from the Mohta family, a prominent Maheshwari family from Sirsa.
20. R.N. Jaju, *G.D. Birla: A Biography*, pp. 99–100.
21. Ibid., p. 131.
22. Basant Kumar Birla, *A Rare Legacy*, p. 36.
23. Ibid., pp. 25–6.
24. Ibid., p. 80.
25. Ibid., pp. 310–13.
26. Ibid., p. 80.
27. Ibid., pp. 31–2
28. Basant Kumar's first independent venture was thus stopped in its tracks by Jugalkishore. The Hungarian consultant was stupefied by what appeared clearly to be a completely irrational decision, involving large financial losses.

21

'Family and Firm'
Commercial Concerns and Social Mores

Basant Kumar Birla

This excerpt elaborates how family came to be enmeshed with firm in the case of the Birla group. Basant Kumar Birla, industrialist and third son of G.D. Birla, recalls his initial initiation into the business in 1934 at the age of 13 and his early training in business and accountancy as an apprentice in the family firm. At the young age of age 19, Basant Kumar was entrusted with independent charge of a firm. Yet the opinion of elders remained critical. Thus, in 1938, an enthusiastic Basant Kumar's plans for a new company, Kumar Chemicals and Pharmaceuticals Works Ltd., for the manufacture of pharmaceuticals were shot down by family elders horrified to learn that the manufacturing process would involve the use of animal glands to produce hormone-based medicines. With a keen sense of his heritage, the author recollects his early ventures, the tutelage of the family elders, the fallouts for those in his generation who did not follow the family's rules, and the business choices he made in these years.

I made my entry into business in 1934. I was then 13 years old. In a piece titled 'My Best Friend Gangadasji Jhawar' I have given an account of this experience:

ENTERING THE SHARE MARKET

In 1934, when I was 13 years old, Chachoji suggested that we should not depend upon the family for pocket-money—we should start buying and selling shares and meet our expenses from our earnings. I was a bit surprised—and worried, too—at least, in the beginning. What was the thing called the 'share market', how was I going to earn, how could I possibly fend for myself?

Gangadasji Jhawar was associated with the share market. We invited him, explained everything, sought his advice and received encouragement from him. That is how I began dealing in shares. The shares of Indian Iron, Howrah Jute and two or three other Companies were very popular in those days. I remember that, during the initial stage, I used to deal in one hundred shares at a time. The brokerage then was one anna per share. For every 100 shares, Gangadasji earned six rupees and four annas as brokerage, and my loss or gain amounted to 40 or 50 rupees. Mornings and evenings, and during lunch breaks in school, I would phone up Gangadasji and do the buying and selling. Gangadasji was pleased that I followed his advice. If I profited, he derived as much pleasure as I did from the achievement. Fifty rupees in those days was a large sum for me. Six rupees and four annas for Gangadasji was no big deal. Anyway, this mix of friendship and business continued. It pleased me that, at my young age, I had the friendship of a good man and I started doing business under his advice. By God's grace, during the first year, my earning was between 3,500 to 4,000 rupees. Gangadasji's joy exceeded mine. I informed Chachoji, who was delighted and said, "Gango, he is simple and straight. You can trust him completely." The income that I earned had to be declared in the Income Tax returns at the end of the year. I had no idea what 'income tax' was, and why tax had to be paid to the Government. It was weird—a 14 year old boy being taxed by the Government on whatever little he earned. Gradually I grew up, the friendship strengthened, the share business increased and the ups and downs multiplied. Sometimes I accepted Gangadasji's advice, sometimes I did not. How he chided me—with what deep sorrow—if I lost in a share deal undertaken against his advice! And if I happened to make a profit in such a transaction, not only did he not admit defeat, he positively chortled, as if he himself had won the victory!

You will see that from 1934 I became self-supporting. I got the feel of business—it was the beginning of a self-educative career.

FIRST DAY IN OFFICE

18th March, 1936. A momentous date for me. My diary entry tells me that I went to the office for the first time in my life on this day—at 3.00 p.m. My business training began. That day I spent some time in the offices of Birla Jute and Kesoram Mills till 5.45 p.m., and started picking up the nitty-gritty of accounting. My diary records a prayer on that day: "I ask God to spread His blessings upon me as a good business man."

FIRST VISIT TO FACTORY

19th March, 1936. This morning I paid my first visit to Kesoram Mills. There are two points that I would like to mention about this event. I have already written that my last day of school was 17th March, 1936. From 18th March, I began attending office and, from 19th March, I started going to the mills: I did not take even a day's holiday. The second point is that I expressed my faith in God at the young age of 15. When I think of these two minor details today, I feel a deep sense of satisfaction and mental peace.

I attended Birla Jute for not more than a couple of days. It was decided that I was going to learn about business in Kesoram. Simultaneously, Chachoji instructed me to join the Sales Department of Bharat Sugar Mill, under the supervision of Juharmalji Jalan.

KUMAR CHEMICAL—MY FIRST BUSINESS VENTURE

15th July, 1936. On the advice of Shantimalji Mehta, I started the Kumar Chemical Works, for manufacture of perfumery, hair oils, cosmetics and allied items. It was a small venture but it gave me excellent experience. This was the factory where I prepared my first parta or complete costing. My brother Krishna's letter of 30th January, 1937, shows how pleased he was over this development:

As regards your Kumar Chemical, I give you a guarantee that, from February 15th, I will give you a sale of Rs. 1500/- p.m. As a matter of fact, I am canvassing hard for you.

I moreover want your shares. You promised to take me as a Director of your Company. Please let me know if you will be able to give me 30% or 40% of your total shares and retain 60% for yourself. I can tell you that I am taking great interest and pains with your work.

The support of my brother inspired me with confidence. And so, from June, 1936 onwards, I attended classes in college and, at the same time, got training in the mill and office of Kesoram, sold Bharat Sugar products and ran the Kumar Chemical Works. I was only fifteen-and-a-half years old then.

Kumar Chemical Works did not prove to be smooth sailing. Later on, it was taken over by the Kumar Chemical and Pharmaceutical Co. Ltd., which I established. In this way, from March, 1936, to January, 1938, my training stumbled along, because I also had to attend college.

HORMONE-MEDICINES AND MR PERCS

One day, towards the end of 1937, Kakoji out of the blue told me, "Basanta, your college career will end in March, 1938. You will have to give your full time to business after that. I have arranged for you to enter into medicine manufacture. I have engaged a foreigner, Mr. Percs, for this scheme. He is a specialist in hormone-medicines. He will be in Calcutta in March or April, 1938. I will arrange a meeting with him. I have specially selected this project for you. It's a new field, you will have to work hard." That was all; and then he changed the topic! It was done so casually that I felt a little nervous.

I had no idea what hormones were, how much investment would be required to set up the factory, what the sales possibilities were, from where I would get a manager, and so on. My mind was in a whirl. After all, I was just seventeen and a college student. One more thing to keep in mind—a seventeen year-old Birla boy of today is altogether different from a seventeen year-old Birla boy of those days. Television, computers, comics, foreign travel and schooling from the age of two onwards—make today's children mature much faster than they did in those days.

A few days later, when I wanted to discuss this new scheme with Kakoji, the reply I got was, "We will talk about it when Percs comes."

KUMAR CHEMICAL AND PHARMACEUTICAL WORKS LTD.

I entrusted the task of incorporating this Company to Bibhuti Bhusan Mukherjee, who worked in our Law Department and to Prabhu Dayalji Himmatsingka. Kumar Chemical and Pharmaceutical Works Ltd. was born on 15th November, 1938. The first Directors of the Company were we three brothers: Madhav, Krishna and myself. The first shareholders were, we three, Gangadhar Makharia, Hariram Sultania, Suraj Bhaiji Mohta and Kissanlalji Thirani. I will give more details of this enterprise later.

TRAINING PROGRAMME

My studies ended in January, 1938. Foreign travel followed, and in the beginning of March was Bhai Madhav's wedding in Pilani. After the wedding we came to Calcutta. Kakoji drew up a training programme. Three days a week, three to four hours each morning, I would go to Kesoram Cotton Mills. The Manager of the Mill was Madan Lalji Dalmia. He was having difficulty in running the factory—in fact, it was showing a loss. This greatly worried Kakoji. He called Sitaramji Khemka, who was the General Manager of the Gwalior Mill, and an acknowledged expert in his field. I began my training under him. He taught me the intricacies of technology with loving care. In addition, a programme was drawn up for my education in financial and commercial fields. Keeping accounts, maintaining cash books, ledgers, vouchers, bills and outstanding accounts, reconciling bank records—these comprised the preliminary training. Then came daily reports, parta, monthly and annual income and expenditure accounts, sales procedures etc. Kakoji drew up this programme with great personal interest and advised me to follow it diligently and intelligently. He reckoned that I would need a full year to pick up all these details. But he emphasized strongly that there was no harm in taking a couple of months more, because any task taken up should be accomplished to perfection.

The Financial Manager of the Kesoram Head Office was Damodardasji Dalmia; under him was Shantimalji Mehta. Damodardasji was not even a matriculate but he was a wizard in accounts. Shantimalji was what you might describe as "modern" or "progressive" and was quite proficient in accounts. I remember that Pujya Kakoji gave them elaborate instructions on how to train me. The direct responsibility was Shantimalji's, and Damodardasji was told to check up on my progress, at intervals of two or three weeks.

And so I started my business learning with the cash book of Kesoram. It took me six or seven days to pick up what I thought were the ins and outs. Shantimalji tested me; I passed, but scored only between 50 to 60 marks in different questions. Shantimalji advised me not to proceed any further, but to spend a few more days in the same section. This irritated me. I was rather upset. Why was he dragging me through all this? Why was he wasting my time? But I had no choice. However, after a few more days of application, I realized that Shantimalji's advice was correct. The day I prepared by myself the entire cash book, balanced the receipts and payments, meticulously accounted for every single paisa, and succeeded in answering correctly all questions put to me—I was promoted to the "next class".

Arithmetic fascinated me from early childhood. Not only was I good in dealing with numbers and calculation, I derived positive pleasure in figuring out sums and problems. So I went on working, went on learning, while promotions kept coming my way. Thus I progressed quite fast and my confidence grew. Shantimalji and I often had friendly arguments. Damodardasji was pleased with me and sent satisfactory reports of my progress to Kakoji. It took me about a year to get a good grip on accountancy and bookkeeping. It was indeed a profitable year for me and it laid the firm foundation of my future career.

RELATIONSHIP WITH COLLEAGUES

For one full year I sat and worked at the same level as the other members of staff of the Company. I discussed matters with them. I ate what they ate. I knew almost all of them by their names. It was a cordial relationship. I felt for them and with them and, in turn, I think I received their love and goodwill. I was the son of the Chairman and, in course of time, perhaps I would become the Chairman. Notwithstanding this background, we mixed freely, and I truly felt as one of them. Three or four members of staff of those times continued to be with Kesoram even until some years ago. Whenever I meet them, I am delighted. The old memories return. I enquire about their health and welfare, their joys and sorrows and, if necessary, I also help them. Sometimes I think: This gentleman was with Kesoram half a century ago. At that time his salary must have been about Rs. 30 a month. Fifty years later, he is still in the same Department, earning perhaps Rs. 1600 a month or, at the most, Rs. 1800. But prices have spiralled. Come to think of it, how has his situation improved? Here he is standing before me, speaking to me politely, but with a little fear also. What must he have passed through in these fifty years, what delights and despairs, what problems he must have faced, and what is going to happen to him when he retires? How will he make ends meet, how will he survive? All these thoughts come to me, and I become pensive and anxious. But these are passing perplexities. After some time I forget everything and I am caught up again in the whirligig of life. Are these thoughts all false, are they illusory? If they are real, why do I forget them so quickly? I really have no answer to all this.

DISTURBED TRAINING

My training at the Mills was somewhat disturbed because Sitaramji fell ill. Murlidharji Dalmia was called to help out. He was working in the Delhi mill. Murlidharji was an extraordinary man. He had a clear, brilliant, analytical mind. A flawless Manager, he had a genius for explaining things. On the advice of Kakoji, he prepared a week-by-week production programme for the mill—and he achieved the targets. He taught me all aspects of mill management with great diligence, but ill health forced him also to return to Delhi. Brijmohan Bagri was the next Manager, but I did not receive training under him. To complete my business education, in 1940 I went to Delhi, to be with Murlidharji Dalmia, and to Gwalior, for a month, to be with Sitaramji Khemka, who again welcomed and taught me very affectionately.

I think my technical training did go off smoothly. I learnt a lot. I even learnt how to operate machines. The financial details of business also came well within my grasp. I applied myself to my assignment with zeal. I believed in hard work and rigorous application and picked up the workings of each Department by actually attending to every nitty-gritty detail. I refused to proceed ahead until I had a thorough knowledge of how each Section functioned. For this I give the credit to Shantimalji Mehta, who trained me with such loving care. Credit for enlightening me on the technical side of industry I give to Murlidharji and Sitaramji.

GREATER RESPONSIBILITIES

The workings of Kesoram were in Kakoji's hands and Bhaiji worked directly under him. During the period of my training itself, after a few months, Pujya Kakoji handed over the Hosiery Department of Kesoram to me. In those days, this was the biggest factory of its kind in India. I think I managed my job responsibly. This plant made good progress.

The Manager of this Department at that time was Chotan Lal, a thoroughly dependable man. He gave me his full support. From the middle of 1939, Kakoji started giving me more and more responsibilities for running the mill. In the beginning I was put in charge of the Accounts Section, then came Sales, and finally the factory. I think I was entrusted with the entire charge of the mill within a period of no more than one year. But, of course, Kakoji kept himself fully in touch with all that went on. He personally discussed matters with the Managers, inviting me to attend these meetings. The final decision was always his.

The Company was in a bad state in 1938–39. Losses amounting to 3 or 4 lakhs of rupees were being incurred each year. We had to think twice before spending even a hundred rupees. At the end of each month, Kakoji examined the accounts in detail. The Managers quaked. Kakoji laid down production targets—every day he would check them, and he personally supervised the Sales Department. I had begun controlling the Accounts, but he would constantly cross-examine me and often showed his displeasure.

KAKOJI'S NOBLE GESTURE

I remember an occasion when he was furious over an accounting detail. I was firm, too, and insisted that he was in the wrong, not I. There was a ding-dong argument. Finally, I said, "If you don't even try to understand what I am saying, I won't even attempt to explain things to you. I will follow what you say blindly and mutely." Kakoji immediately quietened down and replied, "Very well, go on, explain to me, I will try to understand," which indeed he did, and acknowledged that I was right. The gesture was typically noble of him. That was a period when Kakoji used to flare up, and I stuck to my guns. There were occasions when heated exchanges took place between us every eight or ten days. And then, in less than five minutes, Kakoji would put aside all differences and talk to me with perfect ease and calm, as if nothing had happened. He kept no bitterness in his heart.

In September, 1939, World War II commenced. War meant more Government purchases which, in turn, meant good times ahead for India's industries. The Government went in for large-scale purchases of textiles. This resulted in rise in cloth prices, and larger profits for textile Companies.

CHAIRMAN OF KESORAM

The War benefited me considerably. In the beginning of 1940, Kakoji handed over the charge of Kesoram to me in large measure. On the auspicious day of 23 August, 1940, I was made the Chairman of the Company. Bhaiji and Kakoji stopped discussions with the Managers of the Company towards the end of 1940. They consulted me instead. In practical terms, this meant that the entire function of running the affairs of Kesoram was placed in my hands when I was nineteen-and-a-half years old. God's grace and Pujya Kakoji's blessings gave me this great responsibility, and I think I discharged it conscientiously and satisfactorily.

STORY OF KUMAR CHEMICAL'S WINDING UP

Now I will relate in detail the story of Kumar Chemical. Mr. Percs came to India on 4th April, 1938. I was seventeen years old at that time. Pujya Kakoji introduced me to him, saying, "Please talk things over with Basant and, with his advice, let the work start." The entire meeting lasted no more than 8, may be 10, minutes. Mr. Percs was visibly astonished. He must have been puzzled by the fact that I was just seventeen years old. How could a stripling like me run such a complex operation? On top of that, there was the fact that he would have to work under me! He asked me point-blank what my plans were. I told him the simple truth that our family had no experience in pharmaceuticals. So I suggested that he scout around and find out which medicines and drugs needed to be produced. He was embarrassed, perhaps he felt that he should not have come to India at all. Here was a callow youth of seventeen acting the role of big boss and, that too, with no experience at all in the field of medicine manufacture! But he was a good and honest man, and conscious of his responsibilities. I engaged an assistant named Gadia—a good sort, but lackadaisical and unsuitable for the work entrusted to him; not very good at accounts, either. I kept searching for a competent candidate. I consulted Shantimalji; but all in vain.

I was in a fix, close to panic. I had no experience at all of business. Even today, drug and medicine manufacture is a tricky business at best, but in those days, in 1938, competition was so cutthroat that success was very doubtful.

Kakoji didn't come forward with any advice. All he did was to invite Mr. Percs over from Hungary and appoint me captain of the ship. Mr. Percs alone was paid six or seven thousand rupees a month. Once or twice I tried to explain to Kakoji my deep concern about the viability of such a venture. All I got from him was, "Keep on trying—gain experience—there will be problems in the beginning—yet you will succeed in the end."

After a couple of months of field survey of the market, Mr. Percs advised on the feasibility of producing hormone-based pharmaceuticals. Sales would be slow to start with, but would gradually pick up. Hormones? What were hormones? I was told that production of hormones would involve the use of animal glands—of cows, goats and sheep. A depressing truth. The very mention of animal gland caused revulsion. Nowadays we are used to the idea of taking drugs made out of animal gland secretions, but those days were different. I felt nauseated. But there was no way out. I told Percs to prepare a full-fledged scheme. We were then running at a monthly loss of around Rs. 12,000. Today this seems to be a small sum, but it was a lot of money then—especially for me, because this was my very first business endeavour. The headaches this gave me! Sleepless night after night. I could see failure facing me. Taking Gadia with him, Percs went to the slaughterhouses. Would we get good quality glands and other animal matter regularly in the required quantities? The final report was optimistic: we could. We asked father—no objection from him.

But when revered Bade Baboji heard about the scheme, a veritable tempest broke loose. Glands? Intestines? Of animals? Of cows! God forbid! Baboji was adamant. He expressed his total disapproval to me and Kakoji. What a mess! Over two months passed, the argument went on and all work came to a standstill. The upshot was that we would have to find a different avenue for our business skills. Percs was disappointed, hurt and angry. He just could not understand the rationale behind the scuttling of this scheme.

So, we searched for a new project, but with no success. In the meantime, World War II had broken out. This upset Percs. He was a Hungarian, and Hungarians, I have noticed, tend to be impulsive and temperamental. Percs was no exception. He withdrew from all activities. Day and night he brooded on the fate of his country. Suddenly, he made up his mind to return to his homeland. Gadia and I tried our best to persuade him to get some programme going before leaving, or else all our efforts and investments would go down the drain. At our insistence he stayed on a little longer, but only a little—he was determined now to leave as soon as he could. He was afraid that, if hostilities flared into an all-out conflict, he would be stranded in India for good. Finally, he left India in the beginning of 1940. Our venture grounded to a halt. We suffered a large financial loss. The accounts were clumsily kept. On Chachoji's suggestion, Kishenduttji Goenka proceeded to sort out the mess. A loss of two and half lakhs of rupees was discovered; he also stated that the accounts were unmethodical and defective. Chachoji summoned me. I was chastised. I can understand the loss, he said, but why are the accounts not properly kept? I had already informed Kakoji about what had happened. He did not admonish me; he merely said that Percs was a good man, and that if he had stayed on, the scheme would have succeeded. Whatever the reason, my first attempt at business was unsuccessful. Two years wasted! "Failure" and "shame" haunted my days and nights. Kumar Chemical was closed. For sentimental reasons I have preserved some important documents relating to this Company. I was branded a failure at the age of nineteen! I was very sad. The fact of the matter, though, is that I was a fish out of water for this kind of work. Had Percs stayed on, I fear there would have been further losses of three or four lakhs. Even today, fifty years later, I don't dare enter the pharmaceuticals field. At that early age, and in the context of those times, how could I have ever expected to succeed? My next meeting with Percs—when and where and how—I will describe later.

In 1938 I bought a resin and turpentine factory and established its operations at Lilooah near Calcutta. This factory did very well for a decade. Then shortage of raw materials forced me to close it down.

Kesoram's hosiery and cloth manufacture went on swimmingly. After the outbreak of World War II it prospered by leaps and bounds. The sweet taste of success exhilarated me. I think I was able to improve the system of accounting in that Company, and also revitalize, in some measure, the factory organization.

Originally published as Basant Kumar Birla, *A Rare Legacy: Memoirs of B.K. Birla* (Bombay, Image Incorporated, 1994), pp. 25–32.

22

Decision-Making within Family Firms

R.K. Hazari

This excerpt is from the writings of well-known industrial economist and bureaucrat R.K. Hazari, who chaired the Committee on Industrial Planning and Licensing Policy in 1967. Hazari's findings showed that, at the dawn of Independence, Indian business was in the hands of 18 Indian families and two British houses. This excerpt looks at decision-making within the family business groups.

Hazari defined a group as the 'area over which a decision-making authority holds sway'. This decision-making authority was almost always a family, though it could be a close-knit ethnic community as well. The area of control in effect was almost always a very diversified range of businesses. A corporate group thus, in Hazari's view, consists of units that are subject to a major source of authority that exercises wide-ranging control or influence over the decision-making processes. Such an authority usually presides over prices and profits, investments, production, purchases and sales, and employment and labour, as well as responding to economic and political developments. An ultimate authority only decides on major investment decisions, relying on periodical reports from sub-units and functionaries. The fanning out of group interests usually assumes a variety of forms such as mere management or a sleeping partner's financial interests, and full participation in financial as well as managerial control. Some groups have clusters of companies that act as sub-groups, where the management of these clusters is often autonomous and the ownership of shares is often not closely inter-connected with the rest of the group although their operations tend to appear as part of the group's activities. Groups that contain sub-groups include companies owned or superficially controlled by nominees who are usually relatives or executives or hangers-on who derive social security for lending their names to the owners.

The group, according to Hazari, is more of a concentric circle, rather than a closed one. The innermost circle often consists of the decision-making authority that exercises control over other bodies that have varying degrees of public participation. The inner circle often refers to sole control and majority companies. The influence of the group extends to the outer circles in which the group has 50:50 or minority participation, although it does not have the controlling voice. For the sake of convenience, the outer circle data is often presented as a whole, without further distinctions of the extent and form of interest. This does not affect the conclusions significantly as the concentration of economic power is often measured from the size of the inner circles and the problem of indirect minority interests is often confined to a few companies.

Since the 1950s, much has changed in family businesses. Dwijendra Tripathi has noted three major developments that have caused tensions within these firms—the opportunities which have arisen because of the government's decision to develop industrial infrastructure, the setting up of financial institutions by both central and state sector to provide finance to the private sector and, finally, the appearance of tensions in joint family structures with urbanization and Westernization. These have impacted on family firms, of which many have faced divisions.* Despite this, even in twenty-first century India, as many as 461 out of 500 of the most valuable companies remain under family control.

DEFINITION OF CORPORATE GROUP

A corporate group may be defined as consisting of units which are subject to the decision-making power of a common authority. There may be a wide range of variation in the degree of control or influence which the decision-making authority exercises over the different units. This authority may delegate some functions to subordinates and specify their separate duties, but there should be no doubt about the source from which those who are placed in charge of the units or who are entrusted with various functions derive their authority.

The decisions made by this authority generally cover, besides prices and profits, investment, production, purchases and sales, employment and labour. The responses to particular economic and political developments are also derived from the same source and so are the measures to advance the interests of the group, and a host of other matters that crop up from time to time. The implementation of policies and the working out of their details may be delegated to subordinate authorities, but the extent of delegation and the allocation of functions at various levels are themselves matters of policy. The ultimate authority may make only the major investment decisions and rest content with periodical reports from units and functionaries. The group functions as a single organisation, nevertheless, though each of the corporate units under its control is a separate legal entity.

A company the decision-making power of which is shared between two or more

* See Dwijendra Tripathi, 'Change and Continuity', *Seminar*; 'Family Business, A Symposium on the Role of the Family in Indian Business', October 1999, available at http://www.india-seminar.com/1999/482/482%20tripathi.htm.

authorities can be said to be a 'majority', '50–50' or 'minority' company, as the case may be.

The above definition of the group explicitly provides for a frequent contingency in the business world: the need for or the expediency of entering into collaboration with other groups for the furtherance of common objectives, or a situation in which one group is burrowing its way into another. Collaboration may be needed in order to secure foreign exchange and know-how or to combine and face a market situation, or because one group may be in the process of acquiring another wholly or partially through acquisition of equity in its principal company or in one or more of its controlled companies. A group may also extend financial assistance to enterprises floated by other groups or independent businessmen.

These contingencies are illustrated in a number of joint enterprises. Tata joined the Associated Cement Companies in the 1930's, along with Killick, F. E. Dinshaw (now a Shapoorji company) and Khatau to face the depression in the cement market. After Independence, the Tata group gradually took over Forbes, Forbes & Campbell and acquired the minority interest in MacNeill and Barry. The need for foreign collaboration in the manufacture of a new product induced the group to form Indian Tube and Tata Fison in partnership with Stewart Lloyd and Fison, respectively. The Tata-controlled Investment Corporation of India has acquired a minority interest in a number of companies in the course of its investment banking operations.

The Mafatlal group has a large financial interest in several Ahmedabad mills, which are not under its management, as well as in Scindia Steam. Walchand has the largest single equity block in Scindia Steam, which is under the management of the Narottam Morarjee family. In the mid-forties, Walchand invited Kilachand and Khatau to join as partners in setting up and managing Premier Automobiles. Bangur recently took over Bengal Paper with the help of Dhanuka. Shapoorji has a minority interest in Associated Cement and the Nowrosjee Wadia group. Thapar's Greaves Cotton is a partner with foreign interests in several ventures.

The fanning out of group interests may (and actually does) take a variety of forms ranging from mere management or a sleeping partner's financial interest, on the one hand, to full participation in financial as well as managerial control, on the other. Martin Burn and Seshasayee manage several companies in which their equity interest is practically *nil*. Andrew Yule manages Bengal Nagpur Coal though the majority of the share capital of this company is held by Thapar. For some time, Andrew Yule continued to manage the three jute mill companies which were cornered by Dalmia Sahu Jain in the late forties, till it was voted out of the managing agency. On the other hand, Bangur, Mafatlal and Walchand have substantial financial interests in several concerns which are not under their management. Tata Steel holds the minority block in Bird Heilger's Bisra Stone Lime and Kumardhubi Fireclay without, it is believed, taking an active part in their management.

A partner is a partner, nevertheless, whether he is an active or a sleeping partner, and whether he is liked by the other partners or not.

Some groups, moreover, have clusters of companies which function as *sub-groups* in the sense that the management of the clusters is more or less autonomous and the ownership of shares is not always closely inter-connected with the rest of the group, but their operations generally appear to form part of the group's activities. Somani, for instance, constitutes a sub-group within Bangur. The Birla group includes within its fold the Kanorias, Thiranis,

Kotharis, Mantris, Newars, Kejriwals, Himatsingkas, Nevatias, Rajgarhias, Somanys, etc. (All persons with these surnames do not belong to the Birla group). The phenomenon of sub-groups is akin to the former native states which enjoyed a kind of internal autonomy but their subjects were British protected subjects and, except in the technical sense, no different from British subjects.

The groups which contain sub-groups also generally include some companies owned and superficially controlled by nominees. Such persons are connected with these groups either as relatives or executives in some capacity or as hangers-on who may, among other things, derive some social security benefits as *quid pro quo* for lending their names to the property of the beneficial owners.[1]

INNER AND OUTER CIRCLES

The group is, therefore, not always a closed circle. Rather, it may be compared to a series of concentric circles.

The innermost circle may be said to consist of the decision-making authority (whether it can be detected straightaway or not) which exercises control and influence in varying degrees, through investments made by it or on its behalf over the series of circles. More tangibly, it is made up of a hard core of bodies which are in general but not always, largely or wholly owned by, and are under the sole control of, the decision-making authority.

Also within the inner circle are other bodies (including companies in sub-groups and those superficially controlled by nominees) which are under the sole control of this authority but have varying degrees of public participation, which brings in share capital from external sources but leaves the power of control essentially intact in the hands of the decision-making authority.

There is, next, a circle formed by the majority companies in which one or more interests outside the group have a share in the control, but the majority vote is retained with the group.

Defined in terms of controlling power, the group proper ends at this stage. For the sake of convenience, sole control and majority companies may be collectively called the Inner Circle.

The influence of the group extends also to the outer circles, in which the group has fifty-fifty or minority participation or, merely looks after the management with only a nominal participation in share capital. These companies may be referred to in general as the Outer Circle, in which the group (or rather its decision-making authority) has a voice and a material influence, but not *the* controlling voice. The group's financial interest in them may range from 49 per cent to a negligible proportion (see para. 7 below).

The two Circles together can be referred to as the Complex.

CONTROLLING INTEREST

Since the group has been defined as the area over which a decision-making authority holds sway, it is necessary to complement it with a definition of the controlling interest.

In the abstract, the controlling interest may be defined as that interest which has sufficient voting power, exercised directly or indirectly, to get formal sanction or approval from shareholders for decisions which it has always made for and on behalf of the company concerned. The controlling interest need not hold the majority of equity capital except, when the ownership of shares is very narrowly distributed or, when the group has entered into partnership with other groups and desires to retain the majority block of shares or, as a matter of deliberate policy.

In fact, if the shareholding is widely dispersed, even a fractional holding of equity can suffice to ensure control over the company. For instance, the Tatas seem to hold only about 5 per cent of the equity of Tata Steel, while the total controlling block (most of it held by a trust) in Indian Iron equity is only 17 per cent. The actual proportion of controlling blocks in these two leading companies might be larger, owing to the registration of some part of the controlling blocks in the names of banks.[2] Even if allowance is made for under-estimation, the fact, nevertheless, remains that the control of Tata and Martin Burn over Tata Steel and Indian Iron, respectively, is unquestioned though Birla has acquired substantial equity interest in Tata Steel, the Life Insurance Corporation owns about 6 per cent of the equity of Tata Steel and more than 7 per cent of Indian Iron; Bangur also holds a substantial part of Indian Iron equity.

One need not, however, generalise too far on the basis of Tata Steel and Indian Iron since their controlling interests can, in the event of a contingency, count upon the support of the large body of uncommitted shareholders, as well as Government backing.[3] Other groups are, in general, not so well placed, nor is the size of their companies so large that they must, of necessity, rely upon wide public participation for their requirements of share capital. Barring Seshasayee, whose holding in its companies is extremely small and whose group is kept together more by means of common management than control of equity, most controlling interests tend to have fairly substantial equity holdings in their companies. The fear that speculators might corner the equity of their companies has also led some groups, e.g. Andrew Yule and Bird Heilger, to hold in recent years a larger equity than they might, perhaps, have held otherwise. Some controlling interests, moreover, do not like to dilute their holdings. In most Mafatlal, Shri Ram and Walchand companies, for example, the controlling interests generally have a very substantial equity holding though the shares of these companies are quite popular with investors.

A controlling interest must have sufficient voting power (it need not be any fixed percentage in the company, whether controlled singly or jointly) to get formal approval and/or sanction for its decisions, *and* must also have control, explicit or implied, over the management of the company.

The possession of voting power alone is not always sufficient to enable an interest to control a company or bring it within the Complex, unless more than 50 per cent (like, for example, the Birla holding in Hukumchand Jute, which is managed by Goenka) or a comparable proportion of its equity is held by or on behalf of a particular interest. In the case of companies like Bisra Stone Lime and Kumardhubi Fireclay of the Bird Heilger group, it can, for example, be safely assumed that no major investment and price decisions can be taken without the express consent of the minority partner, namely, Tata Steel, which absorbs a large part of their production, but does not interfere in their routine management.

CLASSIFICATION OF JOINT VENTURES

The distinction of sole control, majority, 50–50, minority and 'under management' companies from one another has to rely essentially on the application of arithmetic, tempered with an element of discrimination, to the list of shareholders. This distinction cannot be made mechanically in all cases on the basis of fixed percentages.

Generally, one can classify a *narrowly owned* company, whether public or private, as under sole control if the relevant controlling interest holds roughly about 80 per cent or more of its equity. In some cases, however, the remaining 20 per cent or an even smaller proportion may be held by a major group (e.g. Tata, Birla, Bangur or J.K.), the significance of whose participation cannot be ignored, in which case it is justifiable to label the company as 'majority' rather than 'sole control' for the first group and as a 'minority' company for the second group. Otherwise, it is generally not difficult to distinguish majority, 50–50 and minority companies on the basis of arithmetical ratios.

'Under management' companies form the fringe of the Outer Circle. These are companies in which the group concerned has no or practically no equity interest but retains the power of management through a managing agency agreement. For instance, in 1958, Seshasayee held the managing agency of three government companies in Kerala but had practically no equity interest in them. In the same year, Forbes Forbes & Campbell remained as the managing agent of Simplex Mills without holding any significant part of its equity, most of which was held by Damani who, later, took over the management as well. Among other companies, attention may be drawn to West Bokaro, which is wholly owned by Tata Steel but was managed by Anderson Wright (a Kedia firm) till 1960, and Tinplate of India, which is jointly owned by Burmah Oil and Tata Steel but is managed by Shaw Wallace. West Bokaro and Tinplate would be 'under management' companies for Kedia and Shaw Wallace, respectively.

The real difficulty arises in the case of *widely owned* public companies. The large number of small investors in these companies can be safely ignored, but how does one treat the holdings of the large investors? Among the large investors are banks, L.I.C., state governments and some private financiers.

A significant part of the share capital of many big public companies is registered in the names of banks, mainly in their capacity as pledgees, trustees, nominees and executors, not as beneficial owners. It is seldom possible in such cases to discern the identity of the actual shareholders. The holdings of banks, even if substantial, have, therefore, to be generally ignored.

The Life Insurance Corporation has acquired a dominant position in the private capital market and holds a significant part of the share capital of large companies. Much of this holding, however, is in the form of preference shares which do not, in general, carry voting rights. Besides, the L.I.C. explicitly refrains from intervention in the management of companies in which it is a large shareholder—though there have been a few exceptions to this rule in certain extraordinary cases. The L.I.C. holding can also, therefore, be ignored.

Several state governments have inherited large blocks of equity in certain companies from the former princely states. In addition, the central as well as the state governments have made fresh investments also. Such investments give the government an 'interest' in the companies concerned when they are quantitatively significant in relation to those of the controlling interest. Correspondingly, such investments can be treated as mere investments without conferring an 'interest' if they are insignificant in terms of total share capital or the investment by the controlling interest.

This brings us to the rather intricate and broader question of distinguishing, in general, a minority interest from a mere investment. Basically, the distinction rests upon the motives of the large investors and the formal or informal understanding between the controlling interest, on the one hand, and the large outside investors, on the other. Since these motives and understandings are a closed book to the disinterested observer, he has to fall back upon the facts, documented and other, available to him.

In general, the classification of a widely owned public company can be based upon the relative size of the total holdings of large investors alone, by applying roughly the same ratios as in the case of narrowly owned companies. This method does not work always, as is evident from the examples of Tata Steel, Indian Iron and some Seshasayee and Kirloskar companies. The varying nature and degree of foreign collaboration also cause complications in some companies. In a few companies (e.g. some companies under the management of Andrew Yule), a further difficulty is introduced by the retention of the managing agency by one group and acquisition of substantial equity by another. Such difficulties have to be resolved by deductive judgement.

To add another twist to the complications, how does one treat the fairly common case in which a company, that has been classified as a minority company in relation to a particular group, in turn, holds an interest in other companies?

What is, for instance, the position of the subsidiaries of Scindia Steam in relation to Walchand? Obviously, since Walchand has a minority interest in Scindia Steam, it can be deemed to have a minority interest in the subsidiaries of Scindia Steam as well. The problem becomes more complicated in the case of Scindia Steam's minority interests, e.g. Hindustan Shipyard. Because of the well known close association of the Walchand group with the shipyard, this company can also be classified as a Walchand minority company, though the minority interest is indirect, i.e. of a second order.

On a comparable basis, the minority interest of A.C.C. in Asbestos Cement gives Shapoorji, Tata and Khatau also a joint minority interest in Asbestos Cement.

Similarly, Tata has a minority interest in all companies in the MacNeill & Barry-Kilburn group, except those companies in which these two managing agencies are mere managing agents and hold no equity. Jenson and Nicholson (a subsidiary of a British company) is, for example, treated in this study as a Tata minority company, since MacNeill & Barry is not only its managing agent but also holds nearly one-third of its equity. In 1951, MacNeill & Barry held 50 per cent of the equity of Kettlewell Bullen (later wholly acquired by Bangur); the companies controlled by Kettlewell Bullen are included in the Tata Outer Circle in 1951. On the other hand, the Tata Outer Circle in 1951 excludes Rameshwara Jute, which was merely managed by MacNeill & Barry without the latter having any stake in Rameshwara Jute equity. On the same ground, the Tata Outer Circle in 1951 excludes some companies which were merely managed by Forbes Forbes & Campbell, then a Tata minority company; such companies, e.g. Goodlass Nerolac Paints, became 'under management' companies in 1958, by which year Forbes came fully under Tata control.

This chain-of-holdings-carrying-interest has to end somewhere for, beyond a point, the indirect investments cease to be meaningful in terms of some degree of control over the management of companies in which these investments are made. The final line of demarcation of the Complex in this study is drawn at minority companies of the second order, i.e. if A has a minority interest in B, which in turn has a minority interest in C, which in turn has an interest, majority or minority in D, etc. the Complex is terminated at C, and the subsequent links, if any, in the chain are disregarded.

For the sake of convenience, however, the Outer Circle data are presented as a whole without further distinctions of the extent and form of interest.[4] This does not affect the conclusions significantly, first, because the concentration of economic power is measured primarily from the size of the Inner Circles, and, second, because this problem of indirect minority interests is practically confined to the Tata, Walchand, Shapoorji and Khatau Complexes.

Originally published as R.K. Hazari, *The Structure of the Corporate Private Sector: A Study of Concentration, Ownership and Control* (Bombay, Asia Publishing House, 1966), pp. 5–11.

NOTES

1. The problem of finding out who is a nominee and when, is extremely difficult. It is further complicated by the fact that some nominees have their own trading interests, of which they are the beneficial owners. It is justifiable to presume, nevertheless, that, by and large, all the activities of nominees are subject to the *control* of their principals, whether the latter are beneficial owners or not in the sense of getting dividends, etc.

The status of a nominee, in other words, has a much wider connotation in this study as compared with common and legal usage. It includes individuals and what have been described above as sub-groups who may be the beneficial owners of their properties but who are under the protective umbrella of some higher authority. The treatment of certain individuals and sub-groups as nominees in this sense is not meant to cast aspersions or to attribute ulterior motives to them and their principals.

2. The actual proportion in Tata Steel is said to be about 11 per cent, a little more than one-half of which is registered in the names of banks.

3. Since 1951, a change in the managing agency of a company requires prior Government approval.

4. Except in Chapter 8 (para. 5 and Table 8.3) where minority interests of the second order are distinguished from those of the first order.

23

Family Firms in Present-Day India

Sudipt Dutta

This excerpt ties the story of family firms in with the contemporary times.* Sudipt Dutta, business journalist, looks at family businesses in contemporary India and emphasizes their strong traditional bases, which ensure that they do not engage in open conflicts. He shows how family and strong community links continue to help in networking and capital mobilization thus enabling firms to reduce transaction costs.

Yet, despite having similar value systems and external environments, no two Indian companies are financially alike. Although there are many types of businesses, the quoted family companies are mostly controlled by family groups. In India, there is a tendency to focus investments in smaller portfolios, where management control is critical. Different communities, says Dutta, have different attitudes towards preserving wealth and attracting public investment. While Parsis and Tamilians tend to push for higher share prices, Marwaris and Punjabis do the opposite. These strategies reflect the public demand for shares in the successful companies. The companies also often operate on both the bull and bear phases of the market, making them highly traded stock. Reputations of family businesses are appended to their performance and market capitalization, which in tandem determine their attractiveness to banks, financial institutions, and the investing public. Hostile takeovers are avoided as they threaten the business network and draw unwelcome attention to the business community. Dutta looks at financial management in these firms, how they deal with tax concerns, and their attitudes towards investors.

* Also see Dwijendra Tripathi, 'Family Business: A Symposium on the Role of the Family in Indian Business', Seminar, October 1999, available online at http://www.india-seminar.com/1999/482.htm, last accessed on 17 December 2009 and D. Sampath, *Inheriting the Mantle: Management of Succession and Transition in Indian Family Business* (Thousand Oaks, Response Books, 2001).

Dutta's research shows that family businesses are a vital part of the business landscape in contemporary India. Such evidence disputes the view that family businesses are merely a stage in the shift from traditional to corporate capitalism.[†]

In the ultimate analysis, the sources and uses of finance are the key to differentiating one enterprise from another. Despite a similarity in value systems and an identical external environment, no two Indian companies are alike in finances. There are, first, differences of size. There are businesses with capitalisation of less than Rs 1,000 and others with capitalisation running into thousands of crores of rupees. Then, there are types of family businesses. In the first category, there are the unincorporated firms, which can be sole proprietorships or partnerships; the latter constitute the vast majority of firms but are largely irrelevant in the context of this book. The tax and inheritance laws of India since 1950 have forced sizeable partnership firms to ultimately incorporate themselves to avoid eroding their net worth on account of taxes. However, the recent scaling down of income tax may help bring the partnership back into vogue. The tax system and its effects are discussed in greater detail later in this chapter.

The second category are the closely held private limited companies. The larger of these are closely held deemed public companies. These attract the provisions of the Companies Act reserved for public companies. Yet, these companies remain unquoted and intransparent. The draft 1993 amendments to the Companies Act have tried to do away with this differentiation of the large closely held private company, an artificial form of public company. The amendments were sent back for deliberation by the committee and have not yet been accepted. These companies are important to this book because they are the 'milch cows', or high surplus generators, for groups and their public limited companies.

The most important category are the quoted public companies, most of which are controlled by family groups (Chapter One). The method of this control becomes apparent when the shareholding patterns are studied (Figure 1).[1] Corporate bodies hold an average of 24 per cent of shares in 488 companies. In contrast, directors, friends and associates average only 3.21 per cent of equity. Individuals hold more than 30 per cent of the shares only in 35 companies out of 380 companies. This has significance because the tax laws inhibit individuals from holding large amounts of equity.

There are two other major categories of shareholders, namely, government financial institutions, which hold an average of 25 per cent of equity, or about the same as corporate bodies, and financial institutions, where holdings are less than 10 per cent in 208 companies and more than 50 per cent in just 25 companies out of the 519 companies studied. Public shareholding is more than 40 per cent in just 123 companies out of 519 companies. This establishes that groups control through equity held by the other corporate bodies they control and that such control is the largest bloc in these companies.

† See Andrea Colli and Mary Rose, 'Family Business', in Geoffrey Jones and Jonathan Zeitlin (eds), *The Oxford Handbook of Business History* (Oxford, Oxford University Press, 2007), pp. 194–218.

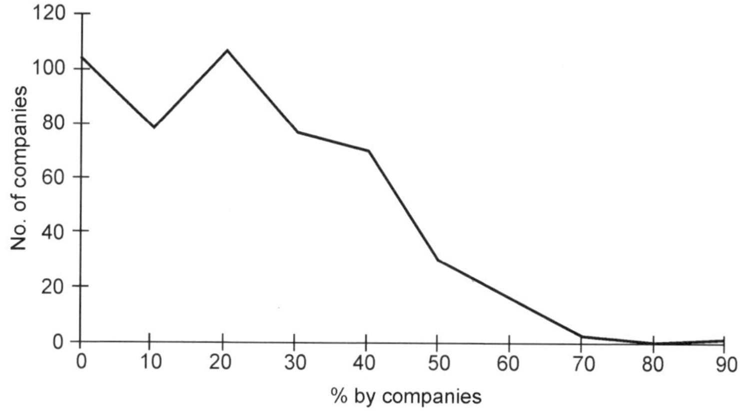

Figure 1 Companies, seemingly unconnected with family business groups, own vast number of shares in large public companies. N = 225.

Data: *The Economic Times*, 20 June 1991.

This data should be compared with Figure 2,[2] which shows the frequency distribution of holdings of the largest businessmen in India. There are some significant differences in these holding patterns. There is a large gap in the number of shares claimed to be held by these promoters and the number of shares held by corporate bodies. Undoubtedly, some of these shares are held by unconnected companies as part of their treasury operations. However, such operations are unlikely to be able to account for such a large proportion of shares. This portion is, in all likelihood, held in non-group investment and trading companies, which are critical to the investment and control in the bigger family group businesses to avoid attracting the provisions of the old MRTP and the Companies Act.

These non-group investment and trading companies are, in effect, the hidden reserves of family business in India. Edward Herman[3] says that the second largest investing category

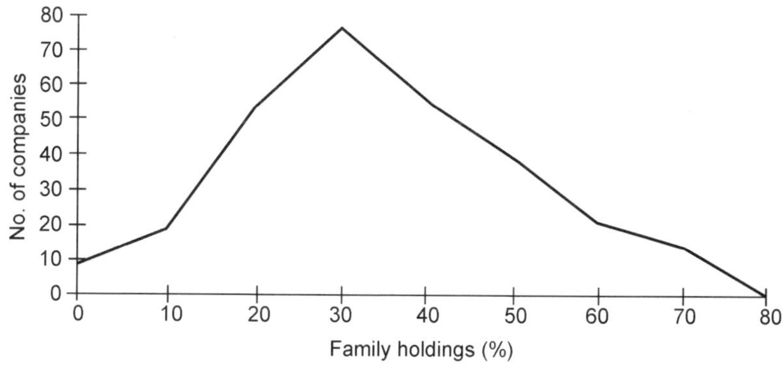

Figure 2 Business family holdings in group companies are evenly distributed. N = 292.

Data: *E-Square*, November–December 1994.

in the US is the 'personal trust fund'. However, such funds tend to diversify their portfolio at the cost of managerial control. There has been a movement in the US towards a clear differentiation between management and ownership since the great Railroad Magnates of the 1880s. Estate planning to minimise the effect of US laws has dissipated wealth through the creation of tax-free foundations. Most of these foundations, originally created to retain family control over large blocs of stock, have now moved into professional hands, leading to a decline in family control. As a result, less than 8.5 per cent of the 200 biggest companies in the US have directors who control more than 20 per cent of the stock. In fact, the 20 biggest owners of stock in the 122 largest companies in the US, mainly institutional investors, held a total of 18 per cent of stock between them. The frequency of corporate takeovers in the US is on account of this weak holding pattern.

In India there is a tendency to concentrate one's investments in a smaller portfolio, where management control becomes critical. Another critical difference is that the Indian family business retains control through chains of holdings, where the wealth of the family remains under control but never gets appropriated to the family or the individual.

There are some interesting variations when shareholdings (Figure 3) of some of the richest businessmen are compared by community. These, when compared with the variation in share prices (Figure 4) by community, reflect the attitudes of the communities towards holding wealth and attracting public investment. The Marwari and Punjabi communities have lower declared shareholding and lower share prices in their companies as compared to the more conservative Tamilian and Parsi communities. The Parsis and Tamilians try to push for higher share prices because this adds to the value of their holdings. It also reflects public demand for shares in the successful companies of these communities. It appears that the Marwari and Punjabi communities are confident that they can hold on with lower shareholdings. This confidence possibly derives from their undeclared holdings in community investment and trading companies. These companies also regularly operate on both the bull and the bear phases of the market, making them highly traded stock. Stock market experts allege that these stock movements could be based on inside information. The degree of truth in this is difficult to determine because the holding structures are so complicated that they are impossible to unravel without inside information (Table 1).

Quoted family companies are more sensitive to stakeholders and are difficult to control. Family businesses stake their reputations on the performance and market capitalisation of these companies, which determine the track

Table 1 Biggest Indian Family Business Groups (1994–5)

Business group	*Gross block (Rs crore)*
1. Tatas	15,771
2. B.K.-A.V. Birla	8,821
3. Ambanis (Reliance)	5,659
4. Ruias (Essar)	4,793
5. R.P. Goenka (RPG)	3,793
6. M.A. Chidambaram (Spic)	2,278
7. K.K. Birla	1,754
8. H.S. Singhania (JK)	1,584
9. L.M. Thapar	1,566
10. Rahul Bajaj	1,512
11. K.S. Raju (Nagarjuna)	1,277
12. S.K. Birla	1,212
13. Arvind Mafatlal	1,071
14. O.P. Jindal	1,026

Source: *The Economic Times*, 23 October 1995.

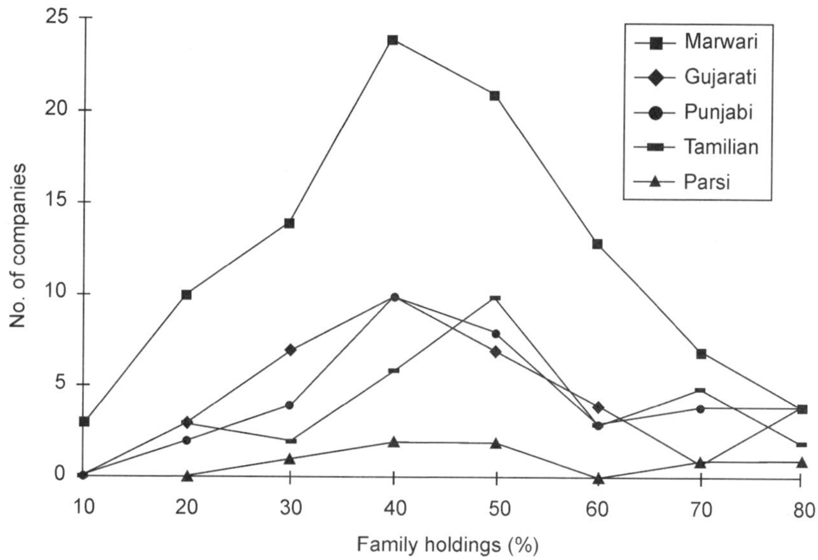

Figure 3 Tamilian and Parsi family businesses are more conservative in their holdings. N = 205.

Data: *E-Square*, November–December 1994.

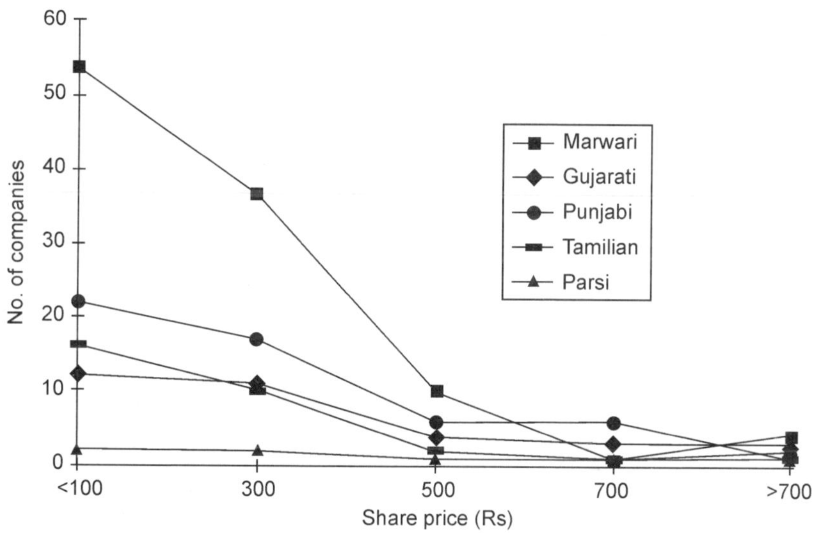

Figure 4 Parsi, Gujarati and Tamilian family business shares tend to be higher priced. N = 292.

Data: *E-Square*, November–December 1994.

record of the group and their attractiveness to banks, financial institutions and the investing public. All family businesses retain management control, though financial institutions, foreign collaborators and general shareholders often have sizeable holdings. Only in a very few does the public investor have critical control, and such shareholders are rarely united. However, the family has to make concessions to small shareholders in order to continue being an attractive investment for them.

The financial institution stake is another matter. Development banks and mutual funds are emerging as major players in corporate control. Although direct intervention by these institutions in the management of the company is still very rare, managements are being forced to pay some attention to them. Largely unobtrusive bystanders, the possibility of the financial institutions throwing out family-controlled managements is hovering on the horizon (Box 1).

A comparatively new entrant on the investor scene in India is the mutual fund. Mutual funds have been buying sizeable stakes in family businesses, which are therefore under pressure to report continuous growth of net asset values (NAV). As is common in the West, they may, in the near future, be tempted to throw in their lot with a hostile bidder promising better results.

Another new player on the scene are foreign institutional investors (FII), which evaluate companies quarterly and have no compunctions about dumping their holdings in the market if the share is not performing to plan. They are less sensitive to the business environment and are liable to sell their stake to a hostile bidder. Foreign institutional investors openly recommend buy and sell advice to their clients in faxed updates. However, their holdings are still low and have not threatened the balance in any company and hostile takeovers have not occurred. Family businesses till now use mutual fund and foreign institutional investment interest in the company to market their company with the small investor. The interest shown by these investor institutions is presented as a sign of positive professional appraisal of the family management of the company. In truth, however, the lack of good scrips in the market

Box 1 Financial Institution Muscle

In early 1983 there was a landmark battle between the family business and the financial institutions. London-based Swraj Paul tried to take control of the Delhi-based Escorts Limited. Escorts is the flagship of H.P. Nanda. Paul began to mop up shares from the market to take control over the company. Nanda began to fight him off. The trouble was that the institutions held 52 per cent of Escorts as against Nanda's 15 per cent.

Paul began to use a strong politician lobby to get the institutions to back him. and remove the Nanda management. The latter went to court. A series of legal battles ended with the courts ruling that the institutions had to back the existing management unless it could give clear reasons for withdrawing such support.

This settled the stability of the promoter. In 1993, Tata Steel chairman Russi Mody fell out with the Tata empire head Ratan Tata over his continuing in the company. Mody took the battle to the public. The ageing J.R.D. Tata visited Delhi to convince the government that it could not back Mody. His view prevailed and Mody had to quit the company because the financial institutions did not agree to back him.

The financial institutions similarly refused to back up the professional management led by S.P. Acharya when he resisted the takeover by Manu Chhabria. The financial institutions led by ICICI have been campaigning for the removal of Kashinath Tapuriah from the management of Indian Cables (Incab).* The company has been going downhill. The financial institutions and bankers are working together to have him removed. They want to hand over the company to any taker who is willing to revive the company and have justified their action by saying that they are protecting their investment. The financial institutions have been similarly

* Madhumita Bose, 'In Search of a White Knight', *Business India*, 11 April 1994.

ambivalent in the attempted takeover of Larsen and Toubro, the country's largest professional engineering firm by the Ambanis of Reliance. However, the adverse publicity surrounding their case has led to a withdrawal by all parties.

has forced the mutual funds to accept large portfolios with wide variation in returns. In time, they will begin to pressure managements to turn in attractive quarterly performances if they want to stay in control. This will upset the current structure because family businesses play for long-term returns.

Family businesses have been relaxed about their shareholdings. Percentage holdings of equity have never been an issue because the Indian business community culture avoids hostile takeovers. Such takeovers threaten the network and also draw unwelcome attention to the business community. For example, stock market circles know that for decades past and till last year, the Birlas held a greater stake in Tata Iron and Steel Company than the Tatas themselves. However, the price to be paid for a hostile takeover is so high in terms of goodwill and money that no serious bid has ever been made.

FINANCIAL STRUCTURES

Financial structures have changed over the years, but there is a clear continuity. C.P. Mall[4] has analysed the changes in the capital structure of medium and large limited companies between 1960 and 1983. The trend continued through 1990 and 1993 (Figure 5). He finds that these companies rely more on short-term debt than on long-term debt. A possible explanation is that the procedure and regulations required to take on long-term debt discouraged the growth of such debt. He also finds that companies tended to rely more on retained earnings till

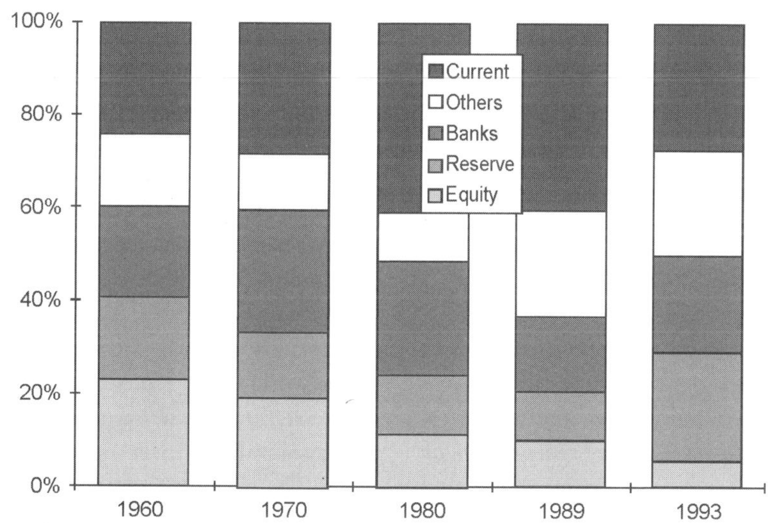

Figure 5 The increasing role of internal resource generation is evident from the capital structure of the private sector between 1960 and 1993.

Data: Statistical Outline of India 1994–95, Tata Services Limited; C.P. Mall, 'Trends in Capital Structure of Medium and Large Private Limited Companies', *Chartered Accountant*, December 1987.

1983 rather than on fresh infusions of paid-up capital, which has increased since then.

Till 1991 because of MRTP companies found it difficult to increase their capital base because of government regulations. Since companies were tightly held, there was little need to disburse profits as dividend. After 1991, with the stock markets vibrant, companies have largely gone in, for equity capital issues on a rights basis with premiums which swell the reserves and surplus. Also, in an effort to look better with the public, many companies have been revaluing their assets. This revaluation reserve fund also swells the shareholder fund. Mall's[5] study also shows that companies go into debt with financial institutions rather than with the market. The market itself plays a minor role, and the businessman's strength lies in his ability to make deals with financial institutions. It is cheaper to work out something with the government and financial institutions than mop up funds from the small securities markets. Till 1991, when the MRTP Act was severely curtailed, there were severe restrictions on growth of the private sector and most of the companies could not leverage their net worth into fast growth. The restrictions imposed by the industrial licensing regime had made the entry of private companies into new businesses and the expansion of existing businesses daunting. Mall[6] finds that till 1960–61 companies rarely reached the permitted debt-equity ratio of 2:1, and averages in 1960–61 ranged from 0.5 in the primary sector to 1.16 in the case of consumer goods. Equity was growing then. However, the subsequent lack of growth in equity and the increasing role of the public sector financial institutions are revealed in the 1982–83 statistics. The debt-equity ratio in the primary sector rose to 3.7:1, while in consumer goods it rose to 2.2 and was just 1.5 in the capital goods industries. The study further reveals that the areas where growth was highest showed the lowest coverage ratio. This is explained by the skewed distribution of funds by financial institutions, which were forced by government policy to give predetermined percentages of their investible funds to sectors, regions and projects prioritised by the Planning Commission, even when they were commercially illogical. The low debt-equity ratios are particularly significant when compared to the Korean *chaebol*, which were encouraged by the government to take debt-equity ratios of as much as 9:1 to grow new lines of business, especially in capital goods and consumer product industries.[7]

Things began to change around 1980 with the entry of Dhirubhai Ambani and his Reliance group, which took the equity culture to the middle-class home. The change was complete by 1992.[8] The equity culture had caught on and companies were not wary about increasing paid-up capital stocks. However, equity as a percentage of funding for companies did not change very much, since the premium charged for these shares was reflected in the reserves of the company and not in paid-up capital (Figure 5 shows the increase in such reserves).

If the bigger Indian players have been responsive to changes in the financial market environment, the smaller entrepreneur continues to depend on his network to raise funds for new ventures. Although there is little opportunity for small entrepreneurs anywhere in the world to tap equity markets for finance, there are, however, strong start-up bank finance packages and debt markets, which are lacking in India. The strength of the network, therefore, is very critical in starting small enterprises. Murthy, Chandrashekhar and Rao's[9] study of 334 small entrepreneurs in Anakapalle and Gudivara in Andhra Pradesh reveals that the network's role in these enterprises is very large and the majority of funds are raised through it. In South Africa, organised finance is available for Whites but is relatively lacking for Blacks and Indians. Gillian Godsell's[10] analysis of South African entrepreneurship reveals that while the Blacks have not been able to organise community networks, the Indian community has managed to grow through strong networking for raising finance. The trends among Indians in South Africa compare favourably with the Indian situation (Figure 6).

SOURCES OF EQUITY

Larger projects, however, are the focus. Smaller projects usually have very high promoter stakes, but larger projects have only between 20 and 40 per cent of their cost borne directly by promoters' investment syndicates. This equity is raised from personal funds, by the individual or family promoting the project, or from subscription by companies under their control, or through the network of relatives and friends who have the money to invest in the new venture. An irrevocable power of attorney may be sought from these investors by the promoters to set up the project. Often word of mouth is sufficient. The social prestige of being known within the community as an unavaracious but astute businessman is key to not upsetting the free hand a promoter has in the running of the company.

Even if the investor feels that the promoter is not performing, he can rarely justify

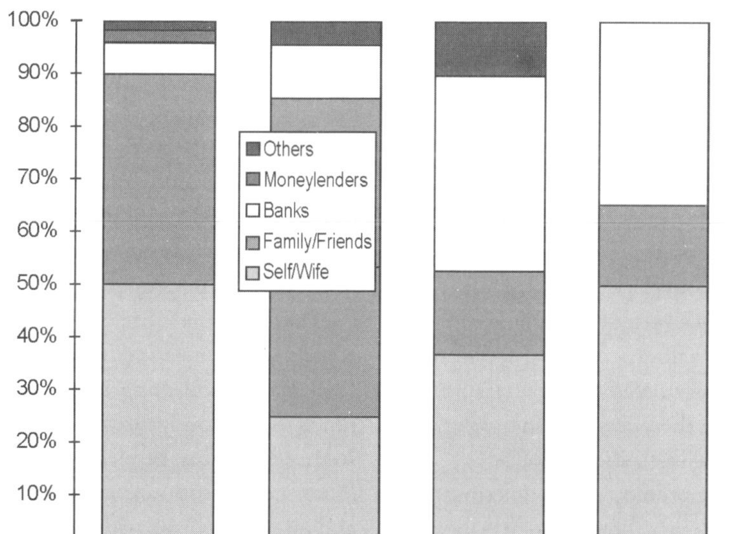

Figure 6 The community network plays a major role in funding new enterprise in Indian communities here in India (N = 192) and in South Africa (N = 40).

Data: Gillian Godsell, 'Entrepreneurs Embattled: Barriers to Entrepreneurship in South Africa', in Brigitte Berger (ed.), *Culture of Entrepreneurship*, Tata McGraw Hill, 1992; Bevvn Murthy, M. Chandrashekhar Rao and M. Gangadhara Rao, 'Entrepreneurial Process and Promises', in Narendra S. Bisht, Ramesh C. Misra and Anil K. Srivastava (eds), *Entrepreneurship: Reflections and Investigations*, Chugh Publications, 1989.

intervention in his business. The promoter's reputation in the network, however, gets tarnished and he finds it difficult to find backers for his next project. Investors may pressure him to restructure the firm and bring in advisers and executives from major shareholding groups. Sometimes, complicated lease and renting arrangements are worked out so that the backers can minimise losses.

The second source of equity and finance is the financial institutions that lend funds after evaluating the project on its merits. Working out loans and equity placements with financial institutions is a formal and tedious process, and promoters need specialised and expensive consultants and advisers to push it through. Here again, the business community network makes the search for such advisers and consultants easier. Generally, the security and collateral arrangements make the exercise self-defeating. Bankers in India, like elsewhere in the world, want their investment covered and then some. Therefore, funds are rarely available for new entrepreneurs unless they can line up guarantors or back their application with a portfolio of assets. This then means that an entrepreneur from the networked business community stands a better chance at getting such finance than a non-networked applicant. This problem is aggravated by the widespread corruption among those involved in project finance in financial institutions. Political connections of the promoter can sometimes swing an arrangement. Often, money loaned to the company is converted into equity and the debt retired. These are discretionary powers of the government-owned financial institutions and are open to abuse by politicians.

Financial institutions and foreign partners usually insist that about 30 per cent of the equity be placed with small investors through public offerings. This entails additional cost. Pradeep Kapasi[11] says the rule of thumb is that cost in a public offering is 10 per cent of the amount collected. The break-up is: underwriting commission at 3 per cent, brokerage at 1.25 per cent, brokerage fee management at 0.5 per cent, stationery, printing of prospectus, application forms and cost of transportation at 1.25 per cent, postage at 0.25 per cent, advertisement and road shows at 2.25 per cent, and registrar and other charges at 1.5 per cent. For a well-established business group these do not present any problem, but they can be daunting for a start-up venture in a cash squeeze. Big companies include the collection cost in the project cost and finance it from the market offering.

In a market looking for a good scrip, it makes sense to pass on a maximum of shares to the market. However, it has to be balanced so that control remains with the family. The family puts up funds to invest in the equity of its new projects. Having taken control of the equity, the family uses these funds to plan the project, acquire the land and start civil construction. This ordinarily accounts for about 30 per cent of the cost of the project.

These funds are used to place orders and pay advances to domestic equipment manufacturers. Financial institutions are approached to release funds for the foreign exchange component so that orders can be placed for equipment. Financial institution experts appraise the project and offer term loans with optional convertibility into equity at interest rates varying between 14 and 18 per cent. Ideally, six months before commercial production can begin, the project is marketed to the public, where 30 per cent or more of the project cost is recovered. Good shares routinely open at multiples of the face value. In time, shedding just 10 per cent of holdings of the promoter can make the family control free. Having recovered his initial investment, the promoter then continues to run the company to maximise profits and growth. He may then reinvest his profits from the equity in the expansion of the project or in setting up another one.

This leveraging is the strength of the business community, which can put funds upfront. It has also developed a vast knowledge and experience base related to resolving the numerous details with the various ministries of the government, the Reserve Bank of India, financial institutions, stock markets etc., to get to the public subscription stage. The large amounts of time and effort and money invested in procedure has made taking companies public a highly regarded expertise. Some of them have emerged as fly-by-night operators who have bilked public investors in non-existent projects. However, most of the progressive businessmen realise that using the stock exchanges is not a one-time affair. The majority of investors look closely at the performance of previous public ventures and only short-sighted businessmen try such fly-by-night operations.

There are variations to the 'formula' for floating a successful public company. Throughout the 1980s there was a shortage of scrips from the successful family businesses. High-performance promoters tied equity share offerings to fully or partially convertible debentures. Public offering rules demanded that the applicants be given a minimum of 100 Rs 10 shares irrespective of how many shares were sought. A stratified lottery was conducted, with the strata dependent on the number of shares applied for. The issues were oversubscribed many times over. There was no system of proportional allotment, and since there were fewer applications for larger amounts, these stood a better chance at being allotted the 100 shares, the smallest marketable lot.

Debenture-linked issues thrived in these circumstances because the debentures were for larger amounts and had clearly allotted quotas attached. This, in turn, meant that the company could place cheap debt with investors looking for high-growth equity shares. There were market-friendly add-ons with these offers, worked out with the larger financial institutions. The small investor sold the inconvertible portion of his debenture, called khoka (literally, son in Bengali), to designated bankers at a discounted price. For the investor, appreciation on the stock exchange over the offer price almost immediately compensated the loss on the sale of the khoka debenture. The high opening price was just the beginning of capital appreciation for the investor. This created a large army of shareholders, each holding just minimum marketable lots. Companies would also often tie up the shareholding further by issuing bonus shares in odd ratios so that an investor with 100 shares was allotted, say, 40 shares on a bonus issue of 2:5. The small shareholding of 140 shares was not marketable since shares are sold in lots of 100. This tempted him to hold on to the complete 140 instead of selling 100 at market price and retaining or selling 40 at the highly discounted price for odd lots. The investor held on to the shares if performing adequately so that with future bonus issues he could build up a marketable lot. The shareholding of the individual was therefore kept under control as long as he received a fair return on his investment.

Promoters have also found that shareholdings can be split further for the stability of their control. Companies offer non-resident Indians a preferential quota for investing in unrepatriable rupee-value equity shares as part of government's efforts to increase the inflow of foreign exchange. The non-resident investor is not likely to participate in a takeover and is therefore a stable and quiet investor who demands attractive returns. Also, Indian industrialists have been smuggling black money abroad for years through 'hawala' (colloquial term for illegally transferring funds abroad) channels. Simplistically, hawala operators network Indians and others abroad who want to remit money to India. They offer them a premium on the official exchange rate and deliver cash to their nominee in India and collect the foreign exchange from the remitter, which is then offered at black market rates to industrialists wanting to smuggle funds abroad. Some of this money remains abroad; often, however, industrialists then create dummy entities in tax havens to reinvest the money in their companies as legitimate non-taxable non-resident investment.

India has been safe from the depredation of corporate raiders also because of the absence of leverage finance strategies and the junk bond phenomenon. Junk bonds are high-interest unsecured instruments issued by takeover tycoons abroad to fund acquisitions, while leverage buy outs are when banks finance an acquisition against the future value of the assets to be acquired from the target company. The nearest example of such a phenomenon is the entry of non-resident Indians. In the 1980s, Shaw Wallace chairman Manu Chhabria and former Britannia chairman Rajan Pillai acquired control by buying over foreign shareholdings in Indian companies with funds borrowed from banks abroad against their extensive holdings there. Caparo chairman Swraj Paul tried to mop up shares of DCM and Escorts in the domestic market, but withdrew when the strategy fell through. Chhabria is now in trouble because yields from these companies are lower than envisaged due to the depreciation of the rupee relative to the dollar borrowings. Pillai similarly fell out with his foreign partners and lost control over Britannia. Others, like Purnendu Chatterjee, who is affiliated to the George Soros international investment fund, are now entering the Indian market. Chatterjee earned his reputation in the US as an investor who made a company perk up or face liquidation so that sale of company assets could return profits on the investment on the so-called break-up value. However, inflexibility in restructuring Indian companies or liquidating them has made such possibilities remain merely academic till now.

Another factor that has worked against hostile takeovers is the greenmailer. While family businesses say that they have gained by their presence, greenmailers have no interest in taking over the management of the company because they tend to concentrate on the stock market. They also realise that they will have to find a buyer from within the community if they want to offload their positions. However, most industrialists are disinclined to make a hostile bid because that acts as a brake on the growth of greenmailers. Greenmailers, on the other hand, watch stock activity closely and push up prices, making any attempted takeover so much more expensive.

Originally published as Sudipt Dutta, *Family Business in India* (New Delhi, Response Books, 1997), pp. 124–37.

NOTES

1. Pattern of Ownership of Equity Shares', *The Economic Times*, Calcutta edition, *Midweek Review*, 20 June 1991.

2. Binoy Thomas, 'India's Billionaires', cover story, *E-Square*, November 1994 and December 1994.

3. Edward S. Herman, Corporate Control, Corporate Power, Cambrdige University Press, 1981. Also see, A.A. Berle Jr. and Gardiner C. Means, *The Modern Corporation and Private Property*, Macmillan, 1932.

4. C.P. Mall, 'Trends in Capital Structure of Medium and Large Private Limited Companies, *Chartered Accountant*, December 1987, Vol. XXXVI, No. 6.

5. Ibid.

6. Ibid.

7. Survey on Korea, *The Economist*, 3 June 1995.

8. News item, *The Economic Times*, Calcutta edition, 21 November 1994.

9. Bevvn Murthy, M. Chandrashekhar and M.G. Rao, 'Entrepreneurial Process and Promise' in N.S. Bisht, R.C. Misra and A.K. Srivastava (eds), *Entrpreneurship: Reflections and Investigations*, Chugh Publications, Allahabad, 1989.

10. Gillian Godsell, 'Entrepreneurs Embattled: Barriers to Entrpreneurship in South Africa' in Brigitte Berger (ed.), *Culture of Entrepreneurship*, Tata McGraw-Hill, 1992.

11. Pradeep Kapasi, 'Management of Public Issue—Going Public', *Chartered Accountant*, February 1985, Vol. XXXIII, No. 8.

RISE OF INDIAN INDUSTRY

SECTION IV

24

Milestones in the Rise of Indian Industry

Tirthankar Roy

This excerpt from the writings of noted economic historian Tirthankar Roy serves as an introduction to the saga of the rise of Indian industry. Roy identifies five broad chronological milestones in the rise of industry from the nineteenth century till Indian Independence in 1947.* The mid-nineteenth century, which witnessed the emergence of cotton and jute spinning in keeping with increased global demand, is regarded by Roy as the take-off point of large-scale industry. Cotton spinning and weaving were concentrated in Bombay and Ahmedabad while the jute industry was located in Calcutta, making Bombay and Calcutta the key nodes of industrialization.† The second milestone, which was especially important in the emergence of Indian-owned industrial enterprises, was the onset of World War I. Roy points out that as worldwide shortages increased and imports were disrupted due to the wartime engagement of British shipping, the demand for goods manufactured in India rose. Despite wartime shortages of machinery and raw materials, industrial production expanded and conditions were conducive for

* A very useful text for understanding India's economic history from the mid-nineteenth century is B.R. Tomlinson's *The Economy of Modern India, 1860–1970* (Cambridge, Cambridge University Press,1993), part of the *New Cambridge History of India Series*. Tomlinson argues that there was some growth in commercial agriculture, manufacturing, and capital accumulation under the colonial regime. On the other hand, there was little improvement in productivity, decline in food consumption, and minimal improvement in per capita income and the standard of living. For a general economic history, see Dietmar Rothermund, *An Economic History of India* (London, Routledge, 1993). For a study of the industrial sector, see Rajat Ray, *Industrialisation in India: Growth and Conflict in the Private Corporate Sector, 1914–1947* (New Delhi, Oxford University Press, 1979) and R.S. Rungta, *Rise of Business Corporations in India, 1850–1900* (Cambridge, Cambridge University press, 1970). On the impact of the Great Depression, see Dietmar Rothermund, *India in the Great Depression, 1929–1939* (New Delhi, Manohar Publications, 1992).

† For the story of Calcutta and Bombay, see Chapter 8, this volume.

the emergence of new players. In such circumstances, many traditional bazaar firms took the leap into industry.‡ The inter-war years provided the third landmark with enhanced protection for Indian manufacturers and a resultant expansion of large-scale industry. Older sectors like cotton and jute expanded capacity, new sectors such as sugar, iron and steel, chemicals, cement, matches, paper, and woollens developed, and Indian merchants actively bought up shares of British companies in jute and coal and challenged the European monopoly over these sectors.§ This was also a time when industrialization spread from its earlier confines in western and eastern India to other regions. This development was, however, somewhat offset in the 1930s by competition from Japanese products and the impact of the Great Depression, which marks the fourth phase in Roy's periodization. Yet, though export-driven industries were hit hard, the Depression had minimum impact on industrial development in overall terms. The years of World War II mark the fifth stage when conditions for industrial expansion were 'qualitatively' similar to those during World War I. Yet, by this stage, Indian industry was at an advantage given that it was much more diversified and could deal easily with the decline in global supplies of capital goods. Apart from charting out the larger picture of the rise of industry, Roy also looks at large-scale industry across India's princely states and notes trends that were similar to British India.¶

In the 100-odd year history that Roy recounts, the Indian economy transformed itself significantly, producing 'both segments of growth and segments of decline'. Roy shows in his work that throughout the colonial period, there is no evidence of large-scale decline but of the growth in real incomes. Sectors such as large-scale manufacturing, mines, plantations, and financial services (banks and insurance) witnessed growth. By contrast, small-scale industry experienced slow growth while traditional services declined. Agriculture expanded and flourished when commercialization was accompanied by investment.** By 1947, India emerged as the most industrialized country in Asia, after Japan.†† Yet, industrialization had only touched the fringes of the economy and vast regional disparities still persisted and firms continued to depend on imports. India at Independence was, in the words of Dwijendra Tripathi, 'still a proto-industrial society'.

‡ See Chapter 25, also see Section I: Bazaar, this volume.

§ See Chapter 29, this volume.

¶ On industrialization in Travancore and Hyderabad, see Raman Mahadevan, 'Industrial Transformation in Princely Travancore, 1930–1947' and C.V. Subbarao's article in Sabyasachi Bhattacharya et al. (eds), *The South Indian Economy: Agrarian Change, Industrial Structure, and State Policy, 1914–1947* (Delhi, Oxford University Press, 1991).

** See Tirthankar Roy, *The Economic History of India 1857–1947* (New Delhi: Oxford University Press, 2000), especially 'Conclusion', pp. 304–8. There has been much debate on the economic impact of colonial rule. The Left-nationalist view is that the economy experienced widespread decline, mainly due to colonial policies. See Bipan Chandra, 'The Colonial Legacy', in Bimal Jalan (ed.), *The Indian Economy: Problems and Prospects* (New Delhi, Viking, 1992); Aditya Mukherjee and Mridula Mukherjee, 'Imperialism and Growth of Indian Capitalism in Twentieth Century', *Economic and Political Weekly*, Vol. XXII, No. 11, 12 March, 1988, pp. 531–46; and Bipan Chandra et al., *India's Struggle for Independence, 1857–1947* (New Delhi, Viking, 1988).

†† By 1947, foreign enterprise controlled only 25 per cent of the total gross output of Indian industry with 12.5 per cent of the total output for export. This figure, when added to the net imports, suggests that foreign capital only controlled 28 per cent of the Indian domestic market, allowing indigenous firms to fill in the gap of 72 per cent. See Chapter 30, this volume.

STAGES OF INDUSTRIALIZATION[1]

The growth of large-scale industry in India went through certain stages. For historians, the issues are somewhat different in each stage. A convenient time division is the following: (1) 1850s to 1914, or the pre-war period, (2) World War I, (3) the War and shifts in policy, (4) 1920–39, or the interwar period, with special reference to the Great Depression of 1929–30, and (5) World War II.

The Pre-war Period

The growth of large-scale industry took off from the middle of the nineteenth century. Where did the invested capital come from? Why did investments begin from the middle of the century? The capital came partly from foreign investments and partly from internal accumulation in the wake of the first wave of commercialization in India. The growth of India's trade with China after the East India Company's monopoly in China trade ended (1834–5) was a significant episode. Bombay and Calcutta benefitted from the exceptional growth of foreign trade in the next twenty years. These were the cities where large-scale industry first appeared. It built on trading profits and the enterprise of the communities who dominated foreign trade.

In a general way, the nineteenth century saw the rise of large-scale industry the world over and especially in parts of Europe and North America. India was a resource-rich colony of the 'first industrial nation' and was a potential candidate for industrialization by 1850. Given Britain's own stage of industrial maturity, the 1850s were a decade when the prevailing mood was to look for profitable business opportunities abroad. The steam ships and the telegraph brought the continents closer than before. The Suez Canal was the climax of this infrastructural leap. A key episode in the transition from trade to industry was the American Civil War (1861–5), which cut off supplies of American cotton to Britain's textile industry. Indian cotton was suddenly in great demand. The resultant boom in cotton prices created the profits that, once the boom ended, found its way to a cotton-mill industry in western India. A tea mania of a similar nature occurred about the same time in Calcutta. And a gold mania took place in Madras. These too ended in a crash that finished off many small companies. But all three booms left a permanent impact. The companies that had been quickly formed had stimulated the local stock exchanges and popularized the notion of joint-stock companies. Partly as a cause and partly as an effect of these first steps into large-scale industry, company laws were being legislated about this time.

The most important large-scale industries in this period were cotton spinning and weaving, and jute spinning and weaving. The one group was based in Bombay and Ahmedabad and the other in Calcutta. The history of these cities, therefore, dominates any discussion of large-scale industry in the pre-war period. And conversely, pre-war industrialization tells us a great deal about the history of these cities. Another important theme of the pre-war period is the growth of infrastructure and institutions. To these themes, we shall return.

World War I

The war diverted the resources of the belligerent nations into producing war supplies. India was not directly at war, but Britain was. In India's case, Britain's engagement in war had two contradictory effects. On the one hand, demand for goods made in India and now in worldwide shortage increased. But on the other hand, machinery, raw materials, spares, and chemicals earlier imported by Indian industry either from Britain or from her enemy Germany stopped coming in. Thus, while there was excess demand for Indian goods, there were also constraints on their supply. Some industries on the whole suffered a setback from this situation. Some others on the whole gained. An example of industries that were badly affected by supply constraints is handloom weaving, which relied on English yarn. Examples of industries that gained are steel, jute, and cotton mills. By the third or fourth year of the war, there was a massive shortage-induced inflation. The inflation benefitted existing producers. The supply constraints eased somewhat as the war went on.

By the end of the war, industrial production had expanded and conditions were ripe for the start of new industries and the making of new types of products by old industries. The war, together with growing nationalist discontent, had also induced a change in government policy. Until the war, the government followed a policy of non-intervention in the promotion of industries. Thus purchase of industrial goods for defence, railways, or administrative use was earlier heavily dependent on Britain. This dependence created sudden shortages of these goods in India during the war. It also justified the criticism that the government was indifferent, even hostile, to Indian entrepreneurship. Such a view was being voiced every year since 1905 in a forum called the Indian Industrial Conference.

The Inter-War Period

After the war, the government began to look towards local sources and talked about promoting such sources. The result of the new outlook was the Fiscal Autonomy Convention (1919), which formally accepted India's right to pursue an independent tariff policy, finally ending an era that had seen Lancashire exercising a lot of influence on India's trade policy. Fiscal autonomy was effectively respected in that the inter-war period saw fewer active interventions by the secretaries of state in Indian economic affairs. Nevertheless, fiscal autonomy was also diluted somewhat by the desire to protect British goods against non-British goods in the Indian market, a desire that shaped the Imperial Preference policy. Three further events that represented this shift in attitude were the establishment of the Indian Munitions Board (1918), the Indian Industrial Commission (1916–8), and the Indian Fiscal Commission (1921–2). The Fiscal Commission sanctioned the use of protective tariffs for industrial promotion, provided the protected industry had natural advantages that made it capable of eventually competing with foreign goods without protection.

Between 1923 and 1939, 51 enquiries were made about the suitability of the demand for protective tariffs. In 11 of these cases, tariffs were raised. These included salt, heavy chemicals, magnesium chloride, sericulture, plywood chests, gold thread, iron and steel, cotton textiles, sugar, paper and paper pulp, and matches. The Industrial Commission stressed the government's responsibility in matters of technical and scientific advancement. It listed the industries that the government could promote directly or indirectly. These possibilities were partly realized in the next twenty years, though the financial capacity of the government was a severe constraint on what it could do directly in the matter of industrial promotion. After 1921, the main responsibility for industrial development passed on to the ministers in the provinces, and the provinces were even more financially constrained.

The first half of the 1920s and the second half of the 1930s were a relatively good time for industry and trade worldwide. In India, large-scale industry expanded and diversified in this period. Industries such as sugar, iron and steel, cement, matches, paper, and woollens were established and expanded. In this process of growth and diversification, tariff protection to some industries was crucial. Much of this growth occurred in cities other than Bombay or Calcutta. In the latter cities, the labour movement had become stronger. Further, infrastructure such as the railways and electricity had extended into the interior. This made it possible for industries to locate at points of supply of raw material. New factories thus came up in or near cities such as Coimbatore, Kanpur, Madras, and Jamshedpur.

Within older industries such as cotton and jute mills, the inter-war period saw both the start of new firms in new locations and crises in old firms in the old locations. Competition in textiles and steel was keener in this period than before. In textiles, competition came from Japan and from the many new mills that were started in small towns away from Bombay. In steel, worldwide capacity-building progressed faster than new demand. In jute, the Indian capacity grew faster than the world demand. The result in each case was low or fluctuating profits that combined with adverse factors specific to these industries. The demand for tariff protection arose largely from this crisis. But tariffs alone could not solve this problem. Some of the industries had to make innovations in technology and management.

Between 1925 and 1935, the world in general was in mild or deep depression. Capacity in some industries worldwide had expanded too fast. This included steel, paper, sugar, and cement. Competition from Japan was keen in all textiles. Indian industries faced both cheap imports and falling world prices. The Indian nationalists convincingly argued that the rupee was an overvalued currency in these years, which would have made competitive imports cheaper than they ought to have been. The competition from Japan's textiles, especially, was keen and possibly aided by the exchange-rate policy. An overvalued exchange, however, is likely to have had contradictory effects. If the rupee was indeed overvalued, it made the import of machinery that much cheaper and may have been a stimulus for investment. The Great Depression (1929–30) hurt the industries that were mainly selling abroad, such as jute. Other key Indian industries affected by excess capacity in the world were saved by tariff protection in the 1920s.

If we look not at specific industries but at industry overall, the Depression did not have a deep impact. The real income from industry hardly changed in the depression years. Trends in wages in these years suggest that money-wages in India were quite flexible. Thus, one reason behind the severity of the Depression—one on which Keynes built his theory of short-term fluctuation: the downward rigidity of money-wages—did not hold for Indian industry by and large. The Depression did have a deep impact on financial markets in India. As prices fell, debtors experienced an increased real burden of debt. This situation saw a great deal of transfer of mortgaged assets and sale of assets that otherwise would not have come to the market. In a general way, banking seems to have benefited from such transfers, and made credit flows to large-scale industry easier.

World War II

Qualitatively, the effects of World War II were similar to those of World War I. Again, excess demand developed and prices soared. Again, supply constraints developed. But Indian industry in 1939 was much more diversified and better equipped to diversify than in 1914. Thus, the real growth of industrial incomes was greater and diversification into new industry wider during World War II. In one sense, World War II was far more stressful. It led to a massive scarcity of food, the main wage good, and was thus a bad time for labour and labour-intensive occupations. The plantation sector suffered because of this effect. Possibly industry did too to a smaller extent.

Throughout these four periods, two conditions faced by large-scale industry changed only slowly. First, it continued to depend on the import of capital goods and manufactured inputs such as electrical machinery, transport equipment, and heavy and fine chemicals. Second, it continued to depend on foreign technicians. They were paid about twice the salary of an Indian available for the same job. This dependence weakened over time. But it weakened at different speeds across the major industries. Significant changes in both these conditions came only after Independence. Protection for the capital goods industry and larger government funding of higher and technical education weakened the dependence.

TYPES OF INDUSTRY DEFINED

Standard histories of Indian industrialization deal mainly with a type of firms described as modern industry or large-scale industry. 'Large-scale industry' can be defined by three basic characteristics, relating to technology, organization, and government regulation. First, it uses machinery and steam-powered technology, or it is the relatively more capital-intensive sector in manufacturing. Second, it is organized in large factories, sometimes employing several thousand persons, rather than in small factories or in 'households'. 'Households' are defined as units where members of the owner's family were the main workers. Third, these large factories satisfy the official definition of a factory. This definition has changed over time. Today it applies to any unit employing 10 or more workers and using electricity or employing 20 or more workers and not using electricity. Once such a unit is registered officially as a 'factory', it becomes subject to government regulations under the Factories Act concerning the wages and working conditions of the workers. A unit officially registered as a factory can sometimes escape implementing these regulations. But overall, the Factories Act has quite strongly influenced employer–employee contracts in large factories in India.

By contrast with large-scale industry, in numerous industrial firms in India, neither machinery, nor large factory, nor government regulation play significant roles. These form the relatively more labour-intensive component in manufacturing. We call this sector 'small-scale industry'. The family firm or the household is the standard type of industrial organization in this sphere. The present chapter will deal with small-scale industry. Large-scale industry will be dealt with in Chapter 7.

Large-scale industry was a product of the Industrial Revolution and its growth in India was partly a result of colonial India's economic relationship with Britain. For the majority of the firms in small-scale industry, on the other hand, the products and technologies dated before the colonial period. This set can be called 'traditional' small-scale industry. Important examples of traditional small-scale industry or handicrafts are handloom weaving, leather manufacture, and a variety of industries using metals, wood, and minerals. There were, however, a few small-scale firms that were modern in origin. Compared to large-scale industry, these were units of smaller scale, usually unregulated. And compared to traditional industry, these were usually of recent vintage, used machinery to a greater extent, and had a higher average scale. We can call this type 'modern small-scale industry'. In the inter-war period, a significant growth of modern small-scale industry took place, examples being foundries, cotton gins, jute presses, presses for extraction of edible oil, rice mills, and flour mills. Table 1 summarizes the main characteristics of the three types of industry.

The dividing line between traditional and modern small-scale industries was not a sharp one. Most types of modern small-scale industry, in fact, supplied old products. Thus grain milled by machinery and that milled by hand both supplied the same consumers, but by different technologies. Sometimes, however, new technology led to a new product altogether—for example, machine-milled rice was often seen as a distinct product from hand-pounded rice. In many cases, money made in a traditional small-scale industry was invested in starting firms that were bigger in scale, technologically more developed, and more capitalized. These would tend to be classified as 'modern small-scale industry' by our definition, even though the distance between modern and traditional in this case would be rather narrow. The example of handloom weavers who set up small factories equipped with power-driven looms is perhaps the most appropriate one.

The dividing line between small-scale and large-scale was probably a little sharper. But these too had close relationships. Large-scale industry supplied raw materials to small-scale industry. Workers often moved between them. And workers and entrepreneurs in small-scale industry sometimes learnt their skills and

Table 1 Different Types of Industry

	Large-scale industry	Small-scale industry	
		Modern	*Traditional*
Organization	Factories with several hundred workers and supervisory staff	Factories with usually less than a hundred workers	Household and small factories
Technology	Modern machinery, use of steam power, electricity	Ranging from hand tools to limited use of machinery	Usually hand tools
Regulation	Regulated by the Factories Act and other acts governing employment and management	Some regulated, some not	Usually not regulated
Vintage	Colonial	Colonial	Precolonial
Examples	Cotton mills, jute mills, steel, sugar, paper, etc.	Foundries, rice and flour mills, oil mills, weaving factories with power-driven looms	Handloom weaving

acquired new ideas by working in large-scale industry. The former could even buy second-hand machinery from the latter. Textiles supply examples of all three.

LONG-TERM PATTERN OF INDUSTRIALIZATION

A sketch of the long-term pattern of industrialization can be offered based on the employment statistics of the censuses. This dataset has problems, however. Occupational statistics in India began to be collected and reported from 1881, but the level of detail and the definition of work and workers changed so significantly between the early censuses that it is not easy to create reliable series by using the censuses before 1911. Having to start from the 1911 census is a major limitation in the case of traditional and modern small-scale industry, which saw important changes in the nineteenth century. But it is not a major limitation if we look at large-scale industry, which was a small sector until the inter-war period. There is another problem with employment data. Industrial units can differ in terms of the productivity of labour, so that the share of any one type of industry in employment can be different from its share in the income generated by industry. Income data by sector, however, is not as detailed as employment data.

Industrial employment data are available from two main sources: the census, which gives total employment in industry, and the statistics on officially registered factories, which gives employment for these registered factories. Large-scale industry dominated employment in registered factories. On the other hand, employment outside the registered factories was located mainly in traditional small-scale industry. The problematic category is modern small-scale industry, which straddled both factory and non-factory. It is fair to assume that most firms in modern small-scale industry did not register themselves. In the analysis that follows, employment in registered factories will be treated as employment in large-scale industry. Employment outside the registered factories will be treated as employment in small-scale industry.

Table 2 presents an overview of industrial employment in India since 1911. It shows that

Table 2 Total Employment and Industrial Employment, 1911–91

	Industrial employment (millions)	Total employment (millions)	Share of industry in total employment (%)
British India and the Princely States			
1911	17.5	148.9	11.8
1921	15.7	146.4	10.7
1931	15.6	153.9	10.2
Indian Union			
1961	20.0	188.7	10.6
1971	17.1	180.7	9.5
1981	25.1	242.0	10.4
1991	28.7	306.0	9.4
Annual rate of growth, log (%):			
1911–31	−0.6		
1961–91	1.2		

while both industrial and total employment have grown, the growth in the former has been rather slow and fluctuating. Measured in terms of the share of industry in total employment, India is not a significantly more industrialized country today than a century ago. But this conclusion needs to be qualified. The share of industry in the national income has grown steadily, despite the stagnation in employment share. An important conclusion from Table 2 is that industrial employment declined during 1911–31. This decline derived mainly from a decline in employment in small-scale industry. We shall return to this finding.

Table 3 shows that large-scale industry was, and remains a relatively small segment in employment. The overwhelming majority of Indian industrial workers functioned and continue to function in small-scale industry. Today, the share of large-scale industry in the real income from industry is about half. The share increased from 15 per cent in 1900 to about 40 per cent in 1947. The share of large-scale industry in employment grew slowly in the colonial period, rather rapidly between 1951 and 1971, and has been declining after 1971. The trend derived from a number of factors, one important factor being the scale of growth in public-sector enterprises.

Employment in small-scale industry fell before Independence. It grew at a small rate after Independence. After Independence, the censuses collect data separately for household industry and non-household industry. If we exclude employment in registered factories from non-household employment, we get employment in those units that are not officially recognized as factories and yet employ wage labour. We then have a distinction between two types of small-scale firms: households and unofficial or informal factories. In the period 1961–91, there has been a shift in employment from households to informal factories, or a conversion of the former to the latter. In short, the low rate of growth in employment does not mean an overall stagnation, but a

Table 3 Industrial Organization, 1911–91

(employment in millions, % of industrial employment in brackets)

	Large-scale industry	Small-scale industry	
		In family labour-oriented units	In wage labour-oriented units
1911	0.88 (5)	n.a.	n.a.
1921	1.57(10)	n.a.	n.a.
1931	1.57(10)	n.a.	n.a.
1961	3.00(15)	12.00(60)	5.00 (25)
1971	5.47 (32)	6.33 (37)	5.31 (31)
1981	7.78(31)	7.78(31)	9.54 (38)
1991	8.32 (29)	6.89 (24)	13.78(48)
Annual rate of growth, log (%):			
1911–31	2.9	–	–
1961–91	3.4	−1.8	3.4
1981–91	0.7	−1.2	3.7

Source: Census of India, various years; India, *Statistical Abstracts for British India,* Calcutta, various years; *Statistical Abstracts for India,* Delhi, various years.

shift from firms that use less productive and less specialized labour to firms that use more productive and more specialized labour. For the majority of workers in household industry work only part-time. Clearly, such a shift can reduce total employment and yet raise the productivity of labour by increasing the average hours contributed by workers.

Originally published as Tirthankar Roy, *The Economic History of India 1857–1947* (New Delhi, Oxford University Press, 2000), pp. 227–31, 183–7.

NOTE

1. Readings on this and the next two sections: A.K. Bagchi, *Private Investment in India, 1900–1939*, Cambridge, 1970; Rajat K. Ray, *Industrialization in India. Growth and Conflict in the Private Corporate Sector, 1914–1947*, Delhi: Oxford University Press, 1982 (paperback); Morris D. Morris, 'The Growth of Large-scale Industry to 1947' in *CEHI2*, pp. 553–676. Of these three works, the most convenient length is Morris D. Morris' which also covers the pre-1900 developments.

25

From Bazaar to Industry

*Omkar Goswami***

As we have seen in the theme essay of this section, the years of World War I marked an especially significant landmark in the rise of Indian-owned industry. The post-War increase in opportunities propelled enterprising bazaar firms to make the transition to industry.* As Tirthankar Roy points out, the newly rising industry was 'built on trading profits and the enterprise of the communities which dominated free trade'. The story of how bazaar groups broke into the hallowed precincts of modern industry, earlier largely a preserve of Europeans, is best recounted through the narrative of eastern India where the challenges were far more severe than in other parts of the subcontinent because of the dominant presence of European managing agency houses.†

In this article, Omkar Goswami, economist and business journalist, unravels these dramatic developments through the fortunes of four major actors, namely, the 'old sahibs of the expatriate managing agencies, the new Marwari banias, the new sahibs of the multinationals, and the Bengali babus'.‡ He examines the tensions, contradictions,

* See Section I: Bazaar, this volume.

† The story of eastern India is quite different from that of western India, where industry was also developing at the same time. In the east, industry was almost the exclusive preserve of European businessmen and dominated by British managing agencies, which monopolized shipping, transport, and banking. Thus breaking into industry proved to be especially challenging and many hurdles were placed in the way of any Indian enterprise that attempted to break this monopoly. See A.K. Bagchi, *Private Investment in India, 1930–1939* (Cambridge, Cambridge University Press, 1989). On the jute industry, see Tara Sethia, 'The Rise of the Jute Manufacturing Industry in Colonial India: A Global Perspective', *Journal of World History*, Vol. 7, No. 1, 1996.

‡ Also see his 'Collaboration and Conflict: European and Indian Capitalists and the Jute Economy of Bengal, 1919–1939', *Indian Economic and Social History Review*, Vol. 19, No. 2, 1982, and 'Then Came the Marwaris: Some

and changes that accompanied the rise of Indian industry from the nineteenth century onwards. He highlights the substantial increase in Indian enterprise in eastern India with Marwari and Gujarati merchants, traditionally traders and moneylenders, making an entry into the jute and coal industries after World War I.[§] While the Marwaris were rising in European-controlled industries, British managing agencies faced massive cash flow problems. Goswami notes that the decline of the European firm had little to do with the withdrawal of the Raj, but more with 'their own inefficiencies and their clinging on to an out-dated nineteenth century mercantile view in a world that had become more complex'. Much like the European firms, the case of the Bengali babus is not one of celebration. The babus focused their entrepreneurial energies on 'relatively advanced units' such as chemicals, pharmaceuticals, and publishing which, by the late 1930s, had 'either collapsed, been taken over by non-Bengalis, or fallen deeply into debt' due to the inability of raising sufficient funds and faced 'unforeseen competition in the product market'. This 'unforeseen competition' came primarily from large multinationals such as Unilever, General Electric Company, and Colgate Palmolive.[¶] Of the four actors, Goswami tells us, it was the Marwari entrepreneurs who emerged triumphant having been able to integrate their bazaar networks with the modern factory sector.

The history of industrialization of many developing countries in Asia is related to conflicts between foreigners and a growing local bourgeosie over industrial ownership and control. This article analyses one such country—India—from the end of World War I until a few years beyond independence.

At the time of independence in 1947, India's manufacturing sector accounted for a mere 17 per cent of the national income (Sivasubramonian 1965) and employed barely 10 per cent of the country's work force (Krishnamurthy 1983). The modern factory sector was even smaller in size. Concentrated largely around Calcutta, Bombay, and to a lesser extent Ahmedabad, Kanpur and Madras, it accounted for 9 per cent of net domestic product.[1]

Aspects of the Changes in the Pattern of Industrial Control in Eastern India', *Indian Economic and Social History Review*, Vol. 22, No. 3, 1985.

§ As such, in the inter-war years, the Marwaris began to move from trade to industry in primarily two ways: first, by setting up their own mills and collieries and, second, by purchasing shares in or lending money to companies controlled by Europeans.

¶ There is considerable research on multinationals in India such as Stuart Muirhead, *Crisis Banking in the East: The History of the Chartered Mercantile Bank of India, London and China, 1853–93* (Aldershot, Scolar Press, 1996); Compton Mackenzie, *Realms of Silver: One Hundred Years of Banking in the East* (London, Routledge & Kegan Paul, 1954); Hans Modig, *Swedish Match Interests in British India during the Interwar Years* (Stockholm, Liber Forlag, 1979); B.R. Tomlinson, 'British Business in India 1860–1970', in R.P.T. Davenport-Hines and Geoffrey Jones (eds), *British Business in Asia since 1860* (Cambridge, Cambridge University Press, 1989), pp. 101–5; Howard Cox, *The Global Cigarette: Origins and Evolution of British American Tobacco, 1880–1945* (Oxford, Oxford University Press, 2000); *Andrew Yule & Co. Ltd, 1863–1963* (Edinburgh, Printed by T. and A. Constable, 1963); and Lionel Carter, *Chronicles of British Business in Asia, 1850–1960: A Bibliography of Printed Company Histories with Short Accounts of the Concerns* (New Delhi, Manohar, 2002).

In spite of its relative smallness, the factory sector witnessed impressive growth, especially after World War I until 1947. Between 1900–1 and 1918–19, its real value added grew at a compound rate of around 1.7 per cent per year. After World War I the growth was more rapid: between 1919–20 and 1916–47, output from factories grew at 5.3 per cent per annum (Sivasubramonian 1965 and Heston 1983). Arguably the base was low. In 1900–1 modern factories accounted for merely Rs 298 million at constant 1938–9 prices (Sivasubramonian 1965: 256). Nevertheless, an overall annual growth of 3.4 per cent per year over forty-seven years was impressive enough, for it contributed to a more than sevenfold increase in output.

This growth in the factory sector induced a boom in research on India's industrial development and systems of industrial organization. In the 1930s, P.S. Lokanathan published his classic work, *Industrial Organisation in India*, which demonstrated the immense power, prestige, and influence of European managing agency houses (similar to holding companies) in India's commerce and industry. Since then successive works on business history—such as Buchanan 1934, Gadgil 1944, Hazari 1966, Bagchi 1972, and Ray 1979—have concentrated on explaining the wide-ranging power and presence of managing agencies throughout the first half of this century.

It would be foolhardy to deny the important role of colonial managing agencies in shaping the process of industrialization in Eastern India. However, this emphasis on the managing agency system in general and Anglo–Saxon colonial firms in particular has obscured our understanding of the evolution of other important corporate entities. Thus we know relatively little about the growth of native Marwari entrepreneurs in eastern India after World War I. We know still less about British and American multinational companies (MNCs), which entered in the late 1920s, 1930s and early 1940s. And we know even less about many nationalistic, *swadeshi* forays into manufacturing—notably Bengali enterprises that rose in the first few decades of the century but were out-competed by the 1950s.

At the risk of oversimplification, the extant strands of colonial business history may be summarized as follows. Eastern India was a British business enclave with colonial managing agencies exercising total control over the three major industries of the region—jute mills, collieries and tea plantations. In western India things were rather different: here the entrepreneurial abilities of Parsis, Gujaratis, Cutchi Memons, and Sindhis came into being by the late nineteenth century. Consequently, they occupied the commanding heights of Bombay and Ahmedabad's corporate sector. In the north and the south, too, Indian enterprise tended to dominate, especially after World War I.

Why was there such an obvious spatial diversity? Conventional discourse attempts to explain this in terms of the differential entrepreneurial abilities of various groups as well as the characteristics of different industries. Europeans prospered in eastern India because Bengalis, Biharis, Assamese, and Oriyas were indigent, feckless, and devoid of entrepreneurial drive. Moreover, most industries in the eastern religion were export-oriented where the British, with their more advanced knowledge of and contacts in foreign markets, had a clear comparative advantage. Analogously, almost all industrial activity in other parts of India was geared to supplying the domestic market. Because Indians there possessed a superior knowledge of markets and trade, they dominated. Finally, Indian entry into industry in the colonial era is explained in residual terms:

'As the importance of exports and imports in the commerce of India decreased, the scope of Indian entrepreneurs who were primarily oriented towards supplying the domestic market expanded' (Bagchi 1972: 195). Implicit in this statement is the belief that Indians could not and therefore did not expand otherwise.

Elegant at first blush, this schematization has several problems. If entry and dominance are to be explained in terms of market knowledge, we would be unequipped to explain the growth of MNCs, which catered exclusively to the domestic market and had no prior knowledge about the intricacies of marketing in the Indian subcontinent. This approach also overlooks the significant Indian entry that occurred after World War I in two industries that were hitherto dominated and controlled by British managing agencies: jute (which was an exportable) and coal (which was not).

In addition, the argument tends to make 1947 a much greater divide in business history than it was in reality. The standard argument runs as follows. By erecting formidable barriers to the entry of 'natives', colonial firms maintained an oligopolistic position in eastern India right up to 1947. These barriers were created and efficiently maintained because of a milieu that allowed Anglo-Saxon businessmen to reap the benefits of their bonds of racial affinity with the rulers of the land. With the snapping of such bonds in 1947, the colonial firms fell from grace and made a hasty retreat from India.

Unfortunately, this argument has factual problems. Although some British managing agencies packed up after 1947, many others remained. Even in 1960 Calcutta had Bird and Company, Andrew Yule, the Inchcape group, Shaw Wallace, Gillanders, and others that were still under British control, and the expatriate community continued to enjoy the privilege of sunbathing in exclusive whites-only swimming clubs,[2] even preventing Indian entry into the hallowed premises of the Bengal Club right up to the late 1960s. More important, this hypothesis cannot explain the growth and proliferation of the 'new sahibs'—those who ran wholly British-owned MNCs such as Lever Brothers, the Imperial Tobacco Company, Britannia Biscuits, Brooke Bond, Guest, Keen, Williams, and many others.

The fact is that after World War I there was a substantial influx of Indian entrepreneurship in eastern India, starting in the 1920s and intensifying in the 1930s and 1940s. This occurred not merely in, virgin areas but also in some industries where Europeans had hitherto held the upper hand, notably jute mills and collieries. Much of this entry was due to the Marwaris, who set up new units and steadily bought up shares of many European companies to a point where they were poised to take over such firms. Second, since the 1930s there was an enormous growth of MNCs—popularly known as India Limited Companies—which were wholly or largely owned by British and American parent companies. Very much a part of a global trend, these transnational firms catered entirely to the domestic market, had little to do with the older expatriate colonial agencies, and introduced new products as well as novel marketing methods. Finally, there were firms that prospered and then failed, notably some important swadeshi (nationalist) Bengali companies. They catered to the domestic market but in course of time were out-competed by the MNCs.

This article looks at these four interrelated themes: the problems of the old expatriate managing agencies, the rise of Marwari entrepreneurship, the growth of MNCs, and the rise and fall of a few nationalistic Bengali firms. Our focus is on eastern India for a simple reason: this region has been depicted as a classic European enclave with an unrelenting hegemony of British managing agencies throughout the colonial era. Is this a correct description of industrial development across forty-odd years? This article explores the changes in the fortunes of the four major actors: the old sahibs of the expatriate managing agencies, the new Marwari banias, the new sahibs of the MNCs, and the Bengali babus who ran the swadeshi firms.[3] In the process I hope to present a richer and more realistic view of the tensions, contradictions, and changes that accompanied the process of industrialization.

THE DECLINE OF EUROPEAN MANAGING AGENCIES AND THE GROWTH OF MARWARI FIRMS, 1918–57

The British mercantile presence in eastern India on the eve of World War I was truly staggering. Of 849 tea plantations, 729 (86 per cent) were managed by Britons. The larger of these were organized along joint-stock lines, and 96 per cent of 682 such companies had boards that were exclusively British (*Census of India*, 1911, 1, part 1: 446). All fifty jute mills were under the control of European managing agencies, and 97 per cent of the directorial positions were held by Britons (*Investor's India Year Book* [henceforth *IIYB*] 1918). At first glance, matters seemed somewhat different in the coal industry: only 47 per cent of the firms were managed by non-Indians. However, as in the tea plantations, the major collieries—commanding greater capital and larger mining rights—were joint-stock firms, and 89 per cent of these were controlled by European, mostly British, managing agencies (*IIYB* 1918).

In spite of such obvious British dominance, an environment had been created that helped Indian entry in the jute and coal industries in the interwar years. The Marwaris were very closely involved in raw jute procurement, trade, and export. They owned most of the baling houses and commission agencies in major up-country raw jute markets such as Sirajganj, Narainganj, Madaripur, and Goalundo and were the largest traders in the terminal markets of Calcutta. By 1903 the Calcutta Baled Jute Association—a body affiliated with the allegedly anti-Indian, European-controlled Bengal Chamber of Commerce—had 45 Marwari firms among its 133 members (Calcutta Baled Jute Association (hereafter, CBJA), *Report of the Committee 1903–4*). By the end of World War I, the Marwaris accounted for 63 per cent of the association's membership. Among its members were personalities like Ghansham Das Birla, Sarupchand Hukumchand, Surajmull Nagarmull, and Badridas Goenka—people who played important roles during the interwar years (CBJA, *Report of the Committee*, 1918–19). Perhaps the most significant evidence of Marwari dominance was the meteoric growth of fatka, or futures trading and hedge transactions in raw jute. Introduced by six Marwaris in 1905, *fatka* allowed Indian traders to make profitable futures trades and hedge contracts and undercut trading competition from European firms. For a long time fatka was considered illegal; however, such legalities could not prevent its growth, and by 1911 futures trade and hedging had come to stay.[4] In jute, therefore, Indians were extremely familiar with the nuances of trade.

In coal too, much of the internal trade from pitheads to the consuming centres was carried out by Marwari and Gujarati traders. There was already an Indian presence in mining. At the end of World War I, N.C. Sircar, a Bengali, managed seven collieries that accounted for more than three million rupees in paid-up capital (*IIYB* 1918: Section on coal; Simmons 1976: 189–90). In addition there were the proprietary or partnership firms of R.N. Bagchi, N.M.

Choudhuri, S.B. Raha, B.K. Roy, Kumar Roy, R.B. Sircar, K.B. Seal, and others—all Bengalis who, although occupying a subordinate position vis-à-vis the European managing agencies, still accounted for roughly a fifth of pithead output (Simmons 1976: 193–5).

Thus, well before World War I Indians had become familiar with the workings of two major European-controlled industries. There were hardly any technological barriers to entry. The process of converting raw jute to gunny was extremely simple, almost rudimentary. The technology of strip mining was cruder still: all it needed was shovels, pails, and gangs of low-paid tribal labourers. The point is best illustrated by a quotation from the Annual Report of the Chief Inspector of Mines: 'The richness of the deposits on the surface in Bengal has made it possible for mining to commence without much scientific knowledge, with total lack of experience, and yet with a considerable amount of financial success' (Simmons 1976: 204).

For Marwaris, who were traditionally involved in trade and moneylending, there was also no shortage of funds either for setting up industries or for working-capital requirements. In the period 1901–14 and during World War I, people such as Birla, Hukumchand, Mungeeram Bangur, Nagamull, Goenka, Baldeodas Bajoria, and Onkarmull Jatia had made fortunes in raw jute trade, share trading, and fatka—fortunes that were now available for investing in industries. For example, in the decade 1910–20 the average annual value of raw jute arrivals in Calcutta and Chittagong was Rs 5.86 billion (computed from data on IJMA, *Report of the Committee 1949*: 98–9, 116–7). Conservatively assuming that the Marwaris accounted for half this trade and that the trading profit was 15 per cent, profits accruing to Marwaris on account of raw jute trade alone were around Rs 440 million per year. This estimate excludes profits from fatka and from trade in jute bags and cloth.

Quite simply, as far as the Marwaris were concerned there were no barriers to entry in two major colonial industries, jute and coal. They were familiar with the trade, manufacturing techniques were rudimentary, there was no dearth of funds, and setting-up costs were not all that high. What remained was proof that manufacturing profits could be at least as much as those from trade, commerce, and moneylending.

Such proof came in abundance during the second half of the war. In the coal industry, purchases rose by 36 per cent between 1909–13 (average) and 1914–18, leading to a 30 per cent hike in prices. High colliery profits were made all around: the average net-profit rate, as a share of paid-up capital, was around 65 per cent; for many firms it surpassed 100 per cent (*IIYB* 1938–9; *IIYB* 1918). For jute mills the situation was spectacular. In 1918, for instance, thirty out of thirty-five joint-stock public limited companies declared net profits that were greater than 100 per cent of paid-up capital; of these, ten earned upward of 200 per cent; the modal dividend rose to 150 per cent of the face value of ordinary shares, and shares were quoted at ten times their par values (Goswami 1982: 147–8; Goswami 1985: 231).

In these bullish years Marwaris started moving from trade to industry in two ways. The first was fairly straightforward and has been noted by all business historians of the period: the establishment of new jute mills and collieries. What has been overlooked by researchers is the second form of entry: steady purchases of shares in companies controlled by European managing agencies, to a point where Marwaris could first force their way into boardrooms and then take over the firms. To understand how this came about, one needs to start with a brief outline of how firms were set up by European managing agencies.

A managing agency was either a privately held joint-stock company or, more frequently, a partnership firm. On the strength of its past managerial performance, the agency would float the shares of a new jute mill or a colliery company in the Calcutta Stock Exchange. Given the 'imprimatur' of the managing agency,[5] the stock was invariably oversubscribed within a day or two of the prospectus issue. Oversubscription and the existing share-market regulations made it simple for a managing agency to split up shares in such a way that it could control the company in spite of owning as little as 10 per cent of the stock. All it had to ensure was a large percentage of relatively small stockholders, friends or otherwise, who would gladly give their voting rights to the managing agency for an assured annual dividend.

The success of this *modus operandi* is brought out by Lokanathan's data for 1927–30. In seven of the ten jute mill companies controlled and managed by the Bird and Heilgers group, the parent companies held less than 25 per cent of the ordinary shares—a matter that vexed the chairman, Edward Benthall, to a point where he later ruled that a minimum of 25 per cent had to be held to prevent takeover bids (Lokanathan 1935: 187; the data are for 1927). For many other managing agencies control was achieved through a smaller ownership base. In three of the four jute mills managed by Jardine, Skinner and Company, the managing agency's holdings were between 6 per cent and 20 per cent of equity; McLeod controlled five jute mills owning 1 per cent and 18 per cent of the Stock; and Begg, Dunlop controlled four with an ownership that ranged between 10 per cent and 13 per cent of equity (Lokanathan 1935: 187).

Assured of a majority, the new company would have its first annual general meeting where it would (1) declare a board of directors constituted largely, if not entirely, of the partners of the managing agency; (2) appoint the managing agency to look after the managerial functions of the company; and (3) decide the annual payments to the managing agency for managing the company—usually a cut in the profits and a commission on sales. In short, the managing agencies had perfected a way of controlling companies and reaping benefits with minimal outlay.

There was a snag. With such narrow ownership bases, support through proxies was an essential for control. Everything hinged on the dividends. In the best of times, dividend is a poor instrument to maintain control over the small shareholders. If a concern declares low dividends, share prices tend to dip, and the uncommitted middle often chooses to sell out instead of taking further anticipated losses. On the other hand, if a company does exceptionally well and declares greater than expected dividends, share prices shoot up and many sell in order to make large capital gains. Corporate control requires a policy of declaring the expected dividend year after year and simultaneously minimizing variance: dividends must be just enough that shareholders do not sell either out of fear or greed.

It is easy to appreciate that such a strategy is extremely difficult to follow in theory and virtually impossible to sustain in practice. Proxy votes are advantageous in attaining control with minimal ownership, but they are also Damoclean swords, ready to drop whenever there are sharp oscillations in share prices. In the tumultuous interwar years it would have been a superhuman task to control share prices through dividends, and the failure to do so led to a growing presence of Marwaris on the boards of hitherto 'whites-only' companies.

The extent to which Marwaris entered the industry through stock market trading is best appreciated by a detailed examination of the records of jute-mill and colliery companies from 1920 to 1955. In 1918 only 3 out of 114 directorships of jute companies were held by Marwaris (*IIYB* 1918 : Section on jute). Six years later 16 out of the 46 jute mill companies controlled by expatriate managing agencies (41 per cent of the European firms) had at least one Marwari on their boards, and 5 had two Marwari directors (*IIYB* 1926: Section on jute).

Two factors explain this sudden influx of dhoti-clad, turbaned, 'unsophisticated' Marwaris into the rarefied atmosphere of European boardrooms. First, Marwaris rapidly purchased enough equity through the Stock Exchange to demand seats. The sellers were clearly smaller shareholders, more Europeans than Indians, who sold for windfall profits. During the last few years of the war and the period 1918–21, the industry made phenomenal profits, declared massive dividends, and saw share prices shoot to as much as ten times their par value. European officers in these companies were often given small lots of shares in the company they managed. In these halcyon years many sold their shares at the Stock Exchange for high profits.[6] The buyers were Marwaris.

The other method of boardroom entry is even more revealing, for it shows how strong the Marwaris were vis-à-vis colonial firms in spite of the seemingly subservient postures of the former in the presence of the latter. Starting with the late nineteenth century, certain Marwari families had developed close commercial links with expatriate managing agencies. The Jatias were the banias of Andrew Yule and Company (and their patriarch, Onkarmull, was a close friend of David Yule), the Kanorias of McLeod and Company, Rameshwar Nathany of Jardine, and the quartet of Baldeodas Bajoria, Mungeeram Bangur, Sohanlall Doodwawalla, and Badridas Goenka did business for Bird and Heilgers. During the inflationary years of the early 1920s many European-managed companies found themselves undercapitalized, strapped for funds, and needing cash to expand capacity in their jute mills. Marwari banias offered them loans at interest rates a point or two lower than the going rate of return on company debentures. As collateral they took blocks of jute mill shares. Through the 1920s most managing agencies had cash shortages, and the Marwaris continued to refinance these companies, held on to the shares, and got themselves onto boards.[7]

Trends were somewhat different in the case of collieries. The 1920s were years of relative prosperity for the jute industry: the real value of burlap export rose 44 per cent during the decade, and average gross profits were in the region of 55 per cent of paid up capital. Jute attracted funds in the 1920s. Coal did not. From 1924 on, this industry started experiencing a nasty downswing that went right into the depression. Railway budgets were cut and demand fell sharply, leading to a fall in prices. In 1925–9, the average pithead price was Rs 6.25 per ton, 52 per cent lower than the 1920–4 average (*IIYB* 1938–9: Review of the coal industry). The slump spelled bankruptcy for many small Indian-owned proprietary collieries. By 1928, three hundred small mines and leased collieries in the Jharia–Raniganj belt had closed down 'never to open again' (*IIYB* 1928–9: 71). As many as thirty of the forty-five new joint-stock companies floated by Europeans as well as Indians during the bullish 1918–24 period had to be liquidated. N. C. Sircar, the largest Indian coal baron, failed to raise the funds needed to meet his losses and working-capital requirements, was forced to transfer all his assets to H.V. Low and Company, and then spent the rest of his life as a repentant mendicant in the holy city of Banaras (for details on Sircar, see Simmons 1976: 194–5). In such a climate most Marwaris stayed away from coal.[8]

The coal industry saw far fewer shares of European-controlled companies change hands during the 1920s, in part because most of the collieries that collapsed were proprietary firms having no tradeable shares. More important, European managing agencies always owned a much larger proportion of colliery stocks compared to jute mills, which made takeover bids more difficult. In collieries, managing agencies generally owned 35 per cent or more of the equity. The two largest colliery interests were Andrew Yule and the Bird and Heilgers group. The former owned more than 35 per cent of the share capital in 75 per cent of its concerns, whereas the latter owned more than 30 per cent of equity in all its collieries (Lokanathan 1935: 187).

Why did the ownership pattern in the jute and coal industries differ so strikingly? In all probability the answer lies in the differences in initial capital requirements. At Rs 600,000, the equity needs of an average-sized colliery was about a fifth of what was required to set up a jute mill (*IIYB* 1919). With the same absolute outlay—say, Rs 200,000—a managing agency could own a safe 33 per cent of colliery stock but only 6.6 per cent of the shares of a jute mill, which made the latter more prone to takeover bids.

In addition to getting elected to boards through share purchases, Marwaris also opted for direct entry in jute and coal. In 1922 G.D. Birla and Sarupchand Hukumchand used a part of their World War I speculative profits to set up two wholly Indian-owned and Indian-controlled jute mills. Because of the profits in jute and by Birla's encouragement, seven Indian mills appeared in the 1920s—six near Calcutta and one in Kanpur, set up by Juggilal Kamlapat Singhania. These mills accounted for just a little more than 10 per cent of the total capacity, but their existence and growth in what had heretofore been a European preserve gave them both numerical strength and confidence in handling the sahibs (see Goswami 1982: 152–5).

Although the economic outlook of the coal industry was bleak, new collieries were set up, largely by Gujarati and Marwari traders. By 1925 there were at least thirty such proprietors in the Jharia–Raniganj belt, their combined output amounting to 400,000 tons per year (Simmons 1976: 197). The most important were the Agarwalla brothers and Sukhlall Karnani, who had bought the collieries under H.V. Low and Company. Among the Gujarati-Cutchi contingent were K.D. Vohra, Narayan Chowra, the Patel brothers, and Amritlal and N.H. Ojha, who formed several public limited companies in the 1930s (Simmons 1976: 198). Whereas Indian entry in jute was structured entirely around joint-stock, publicly held, limited-liability companies, in coal it took the form of proprietary or partnership firms. The move from the latter to the former occurred only in the 1930s. Moreover, as shown in Table 1, changes in ownership and control during the 1920s were far more modest in coal than in jute.

It is clear that even before the 1930s Indians had a reasonable presence in two major 'colonial' industries. Were these directorships mere window-dressing, doled out here and there by Europeans to appease nationalistic sentiments? If so, one would not expect the European mercantile community to be paranoiac about Marwaris and make them subjects of nasty racial epithets—which the Europeans did in abundance during the interwar years. As soon as Marwaris smarted entering Anglo–Saxon

Table 1 Directorships in the Coal and Jute Industries, December 1930

Indices	Jute	Coal
Number of IIYB-listed companies	50	73
Companies managed by Europeans	44 (88%)	62 (85%)
European companies having Marwari directors	26 (59%)	12 (19%)
European companies with equality of Marwari directors on board	12 (27%)	1 (2%)
Companies managed by Indians	5[a] (10%)	11[b] (15%)
Companies having Marwari directors	30 (60%)	33 (45%)

Source: *IIYB* 1931–2.
Notes: [a]One non-European company, Agarpara, was managed by an Armenian agency, B.N. Elias and Company.
[b]All under H.V. Low, which was by then owned by Sukhlall Karnani.

controlled industries, they were referred to as 'mugs with money'; when they entered they were invariably described as 'upto some dirty work'; they were regularly referred to as 'pirates', 'outsiders', 'corner boys of our great trade', and, most politely, 'short-sighted industrialists' (Goswami 1982, 1985). Because of his drive and his prestige in a wide section of the Marwari community, G.D. Birla was singled out as the villain. 'He has done more to encourage new mills than anyone,' commented 'Monty' Thomas of Bird and Company. 'If he can't get us out by kicking us out, he will get us out by unfair competition' (BP, Box I, Thomas Benthall, 12 Dec. 1928). Even Benthall, who was less anti-Indian than his colleagues, was so exasperated that he longed 'to see one of the upstart (Marwari) mills going into liquidation . . . and coming back to British management, whoever it may be' (BP, Edward Benthall to Paul Benthall, 8 Nov. 1937). Given such attitudes, it is unlikely that Marwaris were cordially invited to be puppet directors in European firms.[9] They were in boardrooms by virtue of having bulldozed their way in.

The growing strength of Indian entrepreneurs during the interwar era can also be inferred from the formation of several Indian trade associations. The Marwaris set up rival organizations such as the Bengal Jute Dealers' Association, the Jute Balers' Association, and the East Indian Jute and Hessian Exchange (through which they attempted to legitimize fatka). As early as 1912–13 Bengali mine owners had formed the Indian Mining Federation to counter the European-dominated Indian Mining Association. With the demise of Bengali entrepreneurs in the 1920s, the Marwaris and Gujaratis formed yet another body, the Indian Colliery Owners' Association, which clashed as frequently with the Bengalis as with the Europeans (Simmons 1976: 198–200).

Perhaps the most important index of the emergence of Indian entrepreneurship—not merely in jute and coal but in other industries—was the founding of the Indian Chamber of Commerce (ICC). Under Birla's initiative, the Indian Chamber of Commerce was set up in 1926 to 'speak for Indian business and political interests'; Birla was the first president. Dominated and energized by Birla, the ICC soon started orchestrating Marwari opposition to the Bengal Chamber of Commerce, which was controlled by the European managing agencies. Soon, an All-India Federation of Indian Chambers of Commerce and Industry (FICCI) was formed with entrepreneurs such as Birla, Purshottamdas Thakurdas, Dinshaw

Petit, Walchand Hirachand, Lala Shri Ram, Juggilal Singhania, M.C.T. Muthia Chettiar, and others (Ray 1979: 306–7). The establishment of the FICCI came as a rude shock to the expatriate mercantile community. In the late 1920s and early 1930s strenuous efforts were made by Europeans to dissolve the FICCI and incorporate Indians in their chamber of commerce. By then the rift was far too wide to be healed; and years of racial slander had taken their toll.[10] When the secretary of the Bengal Chamber of Commerce approached Debi Prasad Khaitan, a Marwari industrialist, to help forge an alliance among the various partners in the Empire, he was told that 'that was not to be, as the political convictions of Indians and Britishers (in their present mentality) are quite wide apart' (TP, D.P. Khaitan to Thakurdas, 9 Sep. 1927). With the passage of time, the old expatriate firms grew increasingly nervous about Indian entry. When in October 1935 both Birla and Hukumchand threatened to resign from the European-dominated Indian Jute Mill Association (IJMA), their grievances were immediately attended to. Benthall wrote: 'If we get into a position of two Jute Mill Associations, like the Chamber of Commerce, it will be one further nail in the coffin of our industry' (BP, Box IX, Benthall to Mackerrow, 29 Oct. 1935).

While Marwaris were in the ascendancy in European-controlled industries, the British managing agencies were going through all manner of crises, mostly linked to cash flow problems. In burlap and gunny manufacturing, raw jute accounted for 45 to 50 per cent of manufacturing costs, more in short crop years. Cash flow was maximized not so much by technical efficiency (which was conspicuously absent) but by control over raw jute supply and prices. By the late 1920s Marwaris had taken over virtually every aspect of the jute trade. Single families had interests in upcountry raw jute procurement, fibre trade in Calcutta, raw jute exports, futures markets in jute and burlap, fatka, shipping, and manufacturing. The surplus generated for each family through all these interlinked market activities—most of which were part of a huge 'bazaar' economy, outside the purview of audits and taxation—yielded cash flows substantially greater than those available to most European firms.

Not only were the colonial firms comparatively worse off in their funds position, but matters were made worse by a series of wrong investments during the bullish years immediately after World War I. The experience of the Bird and Heilgers group is quite revealing. Encouraged by phenomenal wartime profits, the company invested in all types of enterprise, often without any knowledge of the new product lines or its marketing channels. In the process, the firm overextended itself, and many of these 'war baby' companies died in infancy. Bird's venture into tanneries and shoe manufacturing collapsed in the 1920s; the graphite quarries set up in Orissa died by 1925; the Surma Valley Saw Mill in Assam shut shop in 1921, as did the Assam Saw and Timber Company. The failure of these and other post-World War I concerns cost Bird 9 million rupees plus 1.25 million pounds sterling, no small sum in the 1920s (Ray 1979: 269–70). The losses created severe liquidity problems. But more important, they injected into a nineteenth-century organizational system a further dose of commercial conservatism. Realizing that the 'firm had bitten off more than it could chew', the partners of Bird decided against further ventures in activities that were 'beyond the firm's normal experience' and agreed to stick to well-known, time-honoured 'sound business' (Harrison 1964: 134–6).

Concentrating on 'sound business', that is, jute and coal, might have been feasible in the 1920s.

In the depression of 1930–5, it was tantamount to sticking with losers. The depression led to an unprecedented crisis in the jute industry. The value of exports slumped from an average of Rs 549 million in 1925–9 to a low of Rs 215 million in 1934–5, a fall of 57 per cent; the price of burlap and jute bags dropped 46 per cent and 45 per cent respectively over the same period; and profits fell dramatically into the red (Goswami 1982). Things were just as bad in the coal industry. The average pithead price of steam-grade coal fell from a low of Rs 6.25 per ton in 1925–9 to a rock-bottom of Rs 4.25 per ton; gross profits, if any, were rarely above 5 per cent of paid-up capital (*IIYB, 1938–9*).

In such a situation there was an obvious cash shortage. Ideally the jute mills ought to have used reserves built up during the war and 1920s to meet working-capital needs and defray losses. However, they did something totally different. During 1930–4 the managing agencies drew down thirty million rupees from reserves to declare very high dividends that had no relationship whatsoever with true profits; when a second slump occurred in 1937–8, whatever was left in reserve—approximately eighteen million rupees—was totally exhausted to make exceptionally high dividend payments.[11]

The clue to this apparently senseless act relates to controlling proxy votes. With the depression, share prices started falling, and by 1932 stocks were being quoted at less than 50 per cent of their 1928 values (Goswami 1985: 240, chart A). The Marwari banias who held stock as collateral started demanding greater margins or larger stockholding; moreover, many small shareholders started selling out. Both these actions led to further Marwari entry and additional erosion of the control of European managing agencies over 'their' companies. The declaration of extremely high dividends in spite of taking losses was a desperate effort to stave off Indian entry.

This strategy did not pay off. Share prices fell in the mid 1930s and again in 1937–9, and cash positions simultaneously worsened. A few managing agencies, notably Andrew Yule and Bird, were quick to realize that they could not continue for long on the rump of jute, coal and tea, three classic nineteenth-century primary-product industries. However, diversifying during a depression with serious cash shortages is a difficult task, especially for companies as conventional and ossified as the Anglo–Saxon managing agencies. In 1935 Bird seriously attempted to move into steel-making and tried to set up a joint venture with two other firms, Tata Iron and Steel and Martin Burn. Tata, a Parsi enterprise, offered to put up 50 per cent of the capital as long as the other two put up the rest. But Martin Burn dropped out, and Bird's share rose from 25 per cent to 40 per cent, or Rs 8.25 million. Cash positions had become so bad that the largest European managing agency in Calcutta in the 1930s could not raise this sum of money, the proposal came to naught, and Bird remained with jute and coal.[12]

This event more than any other shows how things had changed for the older expatriate managing agencies. Most of them were in dire straits. Revenue from their staple products—jute, coal, and tea—had disappeared. They were acutely strapped for cash and working capital. Their seemingly impregnable trade associations were being outdone. They could not establish any cartel—like control over prices output, or entry. And they were being buffeted not only by unprecedented global events that were beyond their comprehension and reactive ability but also by Indians who were determined to enter their domain directly or via the bourse. Companies like Bird and some ventures of Andrew Yule managed to weather the storm. But other famous firms such as McLeod, Kettlewell Bullen, Begg Dunlop, Gillanders Arbuthnot, Duncan, and Anderson Wright faced serious takeover threats in many of their concerns.

The decline of the archetypal colonial firm and the growth of Marwaris in the 1930s is well illustrated by an almost masochistic cartoon in *Capital*, a European business weekly published in Calcutta. During the depression, many Marwari mills using second-hand equipment were selling cheaper, but substandard, burlap to America—the largest importer of jute cloth. An irate Uncle Sam finds this out and confronts a kilted Scottish partner of a managing agency:

> UNCLE SAM: (Holding a piece of burlap and roaring) Who did this?
>
> SCOT: (Trembling) Please, sir, it was not I. It was my boss. {Points at a pot-bellied, short, obese, dhoti-clad, betel-nut-chewing Marwari standing at the side}
> UNCLE SAM: (Incredulously) Is that your boss?
> SCOT: (Still trembling) Yes, sir. I can't do any business without asking his blessings.
> UNCLE SAM: (Forthwith whipping the Scot on his kilted posterior) Serves you right, then, you stupid fool, for having such a boss!
>
> (*Capital*, 16 Nov. 1933, p. 797)

In the 1930s there was also a substantial influx of Indians into collieries, and many partnership or proprietary firms were transformed into joint-stock companies. Among the Marwaris, the major entrants were the Jatias, Anandilal Poddar, the Karnanis, and later the Shethias, Beriwallas, Jhunjhunwallas, Bhuwalkas, and Jaipurias. Within the Gujarati community Amritlal Ojha not only bought up collieries but also transformed many into jointstock companies with Anandilal Poddar as the other major stockholder (*IIYB, 1938–9* and *1942–3*; Sections on coal). Punjabi entrepreneurs too entered the industry, notably Waliram Taneja and Karamchand Thapar, the latter setting up and acquiring six collieries in the mid-1930s (*IIYB, 1938–9*; Simmons 1976: 199). Others continued buying out shares of European collieries when prices were being quoted well below par and thereby got themselves onto the boards.

After 1935 many Marwari, Gujarati and Punjabi entrepreneurs in eastern India diversified into hitherto unknown and unfamiliar industries, activities in which they had little previous interest but which were also outside the ambit of European managing agencies. With the advent of substantial protection to the sugar industry, seven major refined sugar companies were set up by Indians in the eastern region. By 1939 the Marwaris accounted for 43 per cent of the total cane-crushing capacity in eastern India, and the largest sugar mill in the subcontinent, Rothas, was jointly owned by the Dalmia—Sahu Jain families (*IIYB* 1945–7: Section on sugar). Although the Thapar family kept collieries as its main activity, it rapidly branched out into the manufacture of sugar, paper and textiles. Bhartia pioneered entry into the engineering industry as early as in 1928, an effort that was later replicated by Birla when he set up the Textile Machinery Corporation (TEXMACO) and CIMMCO during the 1940s and by Lala Shri Ram when he took over the Jay Engineering Works in Calcutta in 1938. After making money in jute and textiles, the Singhanias of Kanpur branched out into engineering and insurance and then into paper, chemicals, and further acquisition of insurance companies. And Birla as well as Thapar reinvested profits from jute and coal by setting up major Indian banking and insurance companies (*IIYB* 1928–48, Ray 1979, Bagchi 1972).

The growth of Indian enterprise in areas outside the purview of European managing agencies is fairly well documented and need not be repeated. But how pervasive was Marwari entry into 'European industries', namely jute and coal? This is best seen from Table 2. One should note that during the mid 1940s Indian families generally opted for one of two strategies: either control by stock purchase or by direct entry. In jute the Bajorias, Bangurs, Goenkas, Kanorias, Kedias, and Jalans slowly acquired stocks until they could effectively control a European firm. On the other hand, Birla, Hukumchand, Surajmull Nagarmull, and Singhania concentrated on direct entry and founded their own concern. Similarly, in coal Ojha, Thapar, and Agarwalla were builders, whereas Karnani, Jaipuria, Shethia, and Sonthalia were acquirers.

Certain important conclusions emerge from Table 2. First, it seems that major changes in the ownership and control patterns occurred in the period 1942–5 and not immediately, or even a decade, after independence. In jute in 1942–5 there was a 14 percentage-point fall in the proportion of truly European-controlled companies; the size of this fall was not repeated for the next decade. The sell out of joint-stock collieries was more significant: the proportion of European-controlled coal companies fell by 24 per cent between 1942 and 1945. This conclusion differs radically from those of other business historians of the period.

Second, a close look at Table 2 shows that there were really no cataclysmic changes with independence. If we are to accept the hypothesis that the fortunes of colonial firms overwhelmingly depended on the rise and fall of Pax Britannica, we should then expect a massive retreat of European mercantile forces immediately after independence. Nothing of the sort occurred, at least on a scale worth considering. The companies that survived the 1930s and 1940s and fought off Indian intrusion (such as Bird, some units of Yule, companies under Macneill and Barry, Shaw Wallace, some units of Jardine, and Thomas Duff) remained after 1947 and were reasonably prosperous until the mid 1960s, when they were finally sold to Marwaris. The ones that packed up did not do so because the Raj had come to an end. They were inefficient, cash-strapped managing agencies that had lost the battle in the 1930s and early 1940s in the economic, not the political, arena. Deeply in debt, these companies were bought up by their old banias: Kettlewell Bullen was bought up by Bangur, Anderson Wright by Kedia, Begg Dunlop by Bajoria, Duncan by Keshav Prasad Goenka, and McLeod by Radha Kissen Kanoria.

It would be incorrect to ignore the role of independence or to eliminate the importance of colonialism in examining the fate of colonial firms. Nevertheless, it is necessary to recognize that the phrase 'forces of colonialism' has its occasional dangers, especially when it is used as a catch-all to explain everything that occurred between 1857 and 1947. In the limited arena of managing agencies in eastern India, the impact of decolonization on European business was not discontinuous and centred on 1947. For many colonial firms the rot had set in much earlier, beginning with the 1920s through the 1930s and 1940s; usually the decline had less to do with the empire and more with their own inefficiencies and their clinging to an outdated nineteenth-century mercantile view in a world that had become more complex.

THE GROWTH OF MULTINATIONAL AND THE RISE AND FALL OF BABUS

In spite of the Bengali's traditional aversion to business, during the first two decades of the twentieth century several Bengali-owned

Table 2 Changes in Directorial Positions in Coal and Jute, 1942–7 (percentage)

Companies	Jute					Coal				
	1942	1945	1948	1951	1957	1942	1945	1948	1951	1957
Indian Companies	20	24	24	25	29	24	41	47	46	47
European companies with Marwari directors	62	82	89	89	86	23	47	61	70	58
European companies de facto under Marwaris[a]	5	15	15	17	17	0	8	10	10	12
Companies controlled by Europeans	75	61	61	58	54	76	51	43	44	41
Companies with Marwari directors	63	80	85	86	89	37	61	82	88	83

Source: *IIYB* 1942–43, 1945–7, 1949, 1952, 1958.

Note: [a]I define European companies as de facto under Marwaris if the majority of the board members are Marwaris. These companies were now controlled by Marwaris, but they maintained their old names and registration. Thus, the percentage of companies controlled by Europeans would be 100 per cent less percentage of Indian companies less percentage of de facto Indian companies. It should be recognized that these percentages actually understate the Indian presence, especially in coal, because the data used here only take into account publicly held, limited-liability, joint-stock companies whose shares were quoted in the Calcutta Stock Exchange. In coal there were still numerous partnership and proprietary firms that were controlled entirely by Indians but do not appear here.

and managed firms were established. This was largely a result of the nationalistic swadeshi agitation that followed Curzon's partition of Bengal in 1905 but also a response to the slogans of economic nationalism of Jagdish Chandra Bose and Prafulla Chandra Ray. Many of these firms prospered in the 1910s, 1920s, and even the early 1930s but then went downhill. What caused this decline? What were their areas of specialization? These are some of the relatively unresearched areas in the business history of eastern India. Although very detailed company-level research is needed to arrive at definitive answers, one can still give a logically consistent analysis of the rise and fall of such firms.

By the beginning of World War I, quite a few Bengali firms were in operation in eastern India. Two cotton mills had been established: Banga Luxmi by the Nandi family and Mohini Mills, in Kushtia, by a Bengali Brahmin called Mohini Mohan Chakravarty. Like all swadeshi firms, these mills were exclusively under Bengali management, ownership and control. However, in comparison to the three major cotton mills in the region—Bowreah, Dunbar, and New Ring, all controlled by Kettlewell Bullen and Company—the Bengali firms were small, accounting for only 19 per cent of the total spindleage in 1918 (*IIYB, 1918*: Section on cotton mills). These two cotton mills were probably the only swadeshi units that opted for a 'traditional' nineteenth-century industry. Enthused by science and the strident technocratic nationalism of Prafulla Ray, other ventures went into relatively more advanced lines of manufacture. Calcutta saw the establishment of Bengal Chemicals and Pharmaceuticals (specializing in drugs and pharmacy products), Calcutta Chemicals (producing soap, toothpaste and herbal cosmetics), Bengal Lamps (electric bulbs), and Bengal Immunity (vaccines and other preventive medicines). Bengal Chemicals was founded by

Jagdish Bose and P.C. Ray and, in its period of growth, was managed by an almost-renaissance personality, Rajsekhar Bose. Calcutta Chemicals owed its existence to two Bengali families, the Mitras and the Dasguptas, who brought with them the latest techniques in cosmetic and soap manufacture from England, the United States and Germany. Kiran Shankar Roy, a wealthy Oxford-educated zamindar, set up Bengal Lamps. At the margin, there was also the Bengal Pottery Works owned by Manindra Chandra Nundy, the Maharajah of Kasimbazar.

In addition to these new, relatively-advanced units, there were several Bengali-owned collieries and also tea gardens in Assam and the Dooars. The Bengalis had also made a modest beginning in banking when the Dutt family founded the Comilla Bank in East Bengal. Moreover, there was another activity that Bengalis had entered in a big way: newspaper publishing. By 1910 the Ananda Bazar Group (owned by the Sarkars) and the Amrita Bazar–Jugantar–Basumati Group (owned by the Ghosh family) not only commanded a large circulation among the intelligentsia but were also considered by the British as fountain-heads of radical political thought.

Most of these enterprises did well right up to the late 1920s and even into the mid 1930s. These industries were supplying products in markets where there was very little competition from the biggest firms of the region, the European managing agents. Goods such as toothpaste, herbal soap, tooth powder, talc, antiflatulents, antipyretics, analgesics, vaccines and electric bulbs were not yet manufactured in India and were not imported in bulk by European managing agencies. These were slowly becoming necessities among the growing middle class, and the companies appealed to the patriotic, indeed regionalistic and chauvinistic, feelings of consumers. For instance, advertisements of Banga Luxmi cloth heralded the fact that it was Bengali cloth woven in Bengali mills by Bengali weavers and sold through Bengali retail stores.[13]

Yet by the late 1930s and 1940s most of these enterprises had either collapsed, been taken over by non-Bengalis, or fallen deeply into debt. To an extent the fall can be attributed to the Bengalis' almost innate inability to run a business. Partners quarrelled with each other and sold shares in a huff (a classic example being the Mitra–Dasgupta divide that almost ruined Calcutta Chemicals); close relatives who were given prominent positions turned out to be grossly inept managers; sons squabbled and squandered the spoils in protracted, expensive litigations. Such traits made Marwaris and Britons alike brand Bengalis as hot-headed, litigious, and inept businessmen. However, I suspect there were more fundamental economic reasons for their collapse, related to constraints in raising funds on the one hand and unforeseen competition in the product market on the other.

With rare exceptions, Bengali firms were closely held, private limited companies with relatively narrow equity bases. They were closely held in order to maintain their Bengali characteristics; they had low paid-up capitals because in the 1900s and 1910s funds were hard to come by for non-Europeans unless they were involved in trade, which Bengalis were not. Clearly corporate growth, measured in terms of sales volume, can be financed either through retained profits and loans or by raising fresh equity. Ploughing back retained profits year after year meant that shareholders had to live without dividends, a disagreeable prospect for most shareholders. A close examination of the records of most of the swadeshi companies would show that the shareholders were very reluctant to give up their dividends. Yet most of these firms specialized in relatively technologically-intensive product lines that demanded constant upgrading modernization, and diversification. The other option—issuing fresh equity to the general public—was rarely used out of a fear that outsiders would control the company and out of a desire to exclude Marwaris at all cost.[14] Thus, a Bengali firm could grow only as fast as its rate of profit; in fact, it grew at a slower pace because virtually all profits were declared as dividends.

There had to be financially-imposed limits on such growth. If profits were distributed as dividends and the equity base remained low, then expansion could only be financed by bank loans and debentures. However, every successive loan raised the debt-equity ratio until a point was reached where banks refused further advances. This is what seems to have happened to most swadeshi firms in the mid 1930s. When the depression led to an across-the-board fall in equity values, banks started calling for more cover and finally cut off credit lines. Bengal Chemicals, Banga Luxmi and Mohini Mills, the Bengal Pottery Works, Bengal Lamps, and many collieries suffered cash shortages. Some takeovers also occurred. Quite a few locked-out collieries were bought by non-Bengalis; Mohini Mills had to sell a part of its stock to a Gujarati trading agent; and the Bengal Pottery Works was bought by Lala Shri Ram (Ray 1979: 282).

Cash shortage was only one of the problems faced by many Bengali firms. An equally serious one was the emergence of multinational corporations (MNCs), many of which opted for precisely the products that were the lifeblood of swadeshi firms: soap, pharmaceuticals, electric appliances, vaccines, toothpaste, and so forth. In December 1937 Hari Shankar Paul of the Indian Soaps Manufacturers' Association bemoaned the fact that powerful, wholly foreign-owned companies with high-scale economies, low-cost technologies, greater capital, and large market-development outlays were driving small patriotic Indian firms from the market (*Hindusthan Standard*, 1 Jan. 1938). Paul was right. Unilevers set up Lever Brothers in Bombay in 1931. By the end of the 1930s, Lever Brothers had captured a sizable segment of the Indian soap market and was gearing for further expansion. In the field of electric bulbs, Bengal Lamp was being swamped, first by General Electric Company (GEC) and then by the Dutch-based Philips (India) Limited. Local biscuit manufacturers like Kolay and Sons had to compete with Britannia Biscuits, a wholly-owned subsidiary of the Associated Biscuit Manufacturers of the United Kingdom. And Colgate Palmolive was competing with Calcutta Chemicals in the market for toothpaste. We need more research to quantify the scale of such competition, but all indicators point to severe market losses, and by the mid 1940s most swadeshi firms were in serious trouble in the product market.

It is possible to present a tentative hypothesis about Bengali firms. In the early years of the century, these firms had taken the correct decision to introduce new products for the domestic market. The decision helped them in two ways. First, they catered to a hitherto untapped market, the growing eastern-Indian middle class. Second, in doing so, they stayed out of activities that were dominated by European managing agencies. From the 1930s on, they were caught in a pincer. One arm of the pincer was of their own making. Their shortage of funds and their failure to plough back sufficiently for modernization reflect their myopic view of business. But the other arm—entry of MNCs into their areas of operation—was exogenous to the system and beyond their control. Since MNC entry occurred during the 1930s, when Bengali firms were in acute financial trouble, the swadeshis were in no position to make appropriate counter-moves and were soon swept by the forces of 'the visible hand'.[15] Squeezed in the credit market and facing intense competition in product markets, the swadeshi firms gradually became moribund.

This hypothesis need to be closely tested and, regardless of outcome, promises to be an exciting area of research. One might even pose a stronger hypothesis. If Bengali firms had a degree of freedom either in the credit or in the product market, then they might have survived the 1930s and 1940s. Why, for instance, did Bengali newspapers remain unscathed through the period, even though all publishing was carried out by closely-held firms? An answer may be that the newspaper owners enjoyed a critical extra degree of freedom—the lack of MNC competition in the product market.

This brings us to the fourth and final development in the industrial arena—the entry and subsequent growth of MNCs. Table 3 shows how important they were by the 1950s.

Table 3 An Illustrative List of Multinationals in India, 1950

Parent Company	Subsidiary Company	Date	PUC[a]	Activity
AEI	AEI (India) Ltd.	1924	25	Elec. Engineering
	AEI Manf. Co. Ltd.	1939	25	Elec. Engineering
Alfred Herbert	A; Herbert (India)	1919	25	Machine Tools
Babcock & Wilcox	Babcock & Wilcox	1947	25	Boilers
Braithwaite	Braithwaite (India) Ltd.	1930	39	Mech. Engineering
British Oxygen	Indian Oxygen	1935	93	Industrial Gas
Cadbury Fry	Cadbury (India) Ltd.	1948	13	Cocoa products
Chloride	Chloride and Exide	1947	15	Batteries
Crompton Parkinson	Crompton Greaves	1937	50	Elec. Equipment
	Greaves Cotton	1937	25	Elec. Equipment
Dunlop Rubber	Dunlop (India) Ltd.	1926	170	Tyres
GEC	GEC (India) Ltd.	1911	50	Elec. Equipment
GKN	Guest Keen Williams	1931	141	Rly. Equipment
Godfrey Philips	Godfrey Philips (India)	1936	70	Tobacco
Goodlass Wall	Goodlass Wall Ltd.	1933	25	Paints
ICI	Alkali & Chemical Corp.	1937	93	Chemicals
Imperial Tobacco	Imperial Tobacco	1908	461	Tobacco
J. Stone	J Stone & Co. Ltd.	1931	27	Engineering
Jensen & Nicholson	Jensen & Nicholson Ltd.	1922	33	Paints
Metal Box	Metal Box (India) Ltd.	1933	105	Containers
Philips	Philips (India) Ltd.	1931	35	Elec. Equipment
Tuner Newall	Asbestos Cement Co.	1934	60	Asbestos
Westinghouse Brake	Saxby & Farmer	1923	25	Rly. Equipment
Unilever	Lever Brothers	1931	88	Soap
	Hindusthan Vanaspati	1934	105	Vegetable Oil
Union Carbide	Union Carbide (India)	1934	101	Batteries

Source: Tomlinson (1978: 676–7).
Note: [a]PUC refers to paid-up capital, in units of Rs 100,000.

This list is by no means exhaustive. For instance, there is no mention of the two largest tea-selling companies, Brooke Bond and Lipton, which entered in the interwar years and introduced a revolutionary concept in consumer-goods marketing: packaged, blended, standardized tea. Nor is there any mention of the major multinational oil companies, Burmah Shell, Caltex, and Stan-Vac (Esso), which soon came to control and cartelize the Indian market (Dasgupta 1971, especially chapters 2 and 3). In spite of these omissions, the list is impressive. The firms in Table 3 accounted for Rs 200 million of paid-up capital. The Imperial Tobacco Company alone had equity that could have bought at least eleven medium-sized jute mills. By 1950 the MNCs listed in Table 3 accounted for more than 15 per cent of the rupee capital invested in all types of industries; if we take the major omissions into account, the share would be upward of 20 per cent (computed from data given in Ray 1979: 45).

What prompted these firms to move to India? The first thing to note is that, in sharp contrast to the older colonial firms, all these MNCs catered exclusively to the domestic market. Several explanations have been offered regarding MNC entry. It has been argued that the emergence of high tariffs coupled with changes in the government's and railways' stores and purchase policy were the critical factors. Starting with the late 1920s the Indian government and railways moved away from global tenders toward first preference for the Indian companies. The entry of British MNCs like Guest Keen Nettlefold and the Westinghouse Brake and Signal Company was induced by these changes (Tomlinson 1982: 9). Jumping the ever-increasing tariff wall is stated as the other explanation. The Swedish Match Company set up the Western Indian Match Company (WIMCO) to avoid tariffs on safety matches and by 1945 accounted for 80 per cent of the market (Ray 1979: 151–61).

In trying to explain the entry of the MNCs, one needs to recognize that they were engaged in a wide variety of activities from making matches to electric bulbs, drugs, heavy engineering, cigarettes and toothpaste. Their entry occurred according to different imperatives. Moreover, jumping tariff walls can only be a necessary, not a sufficient, reason for entry. In the final analysis, entry is contingent on demand; if there is to be a unifying explanation, it must come from the demand side.

Here, standard explanations seem to fail. India was an abysmally poor country that could hardly sustain demand for essential wage-goods, let alone packaged tea, toothpaste, and good-quality cigarettes. At the turn of the century, India's per-capita national income in real terms was a paltry Rs 49.63; in 1946–7, it had crawled up to a mere Rs 59.57, a growth rate of merely about 1 per cent per annum (Sivasubramonian 1965: 337–8). To cater to the domestic market, the MNCs would have had to survive largely on the rate of population growth; this alone cannot justify such massive investments in the interwar years and in the 1940s.

The explanation lies in the distribution of national income. From 1900–1 until 1939–40, the urban sector enjoyed a steady increase in income terms of trade, which grew at a compound rate of a little under 3 per cent per year. By World War II the purchasing power of the urban populace had almost doubled in real terms compared to the 1900–1 level.[16] In fact, the depression resulted in a sharp fall in agricultural prices and the general price level and further increased the purchasing power in the urban areas. Moreover, the urban population grew very rapidly, especially during 1920–50. The net result was that in spite of an overall stagnation in per capita income, there was a growing urban populace that had become fairly prosperous and constituted a large market for consumer goods. A rapidly expanding population in cities and towns now demanded new products: packaged instead of loose tea, cigarettes instead of bidis,[17] biscuits, cement and asbestos for housing starts, sugar, soap, toothpaste, and hydrogenated vegetable oil. This growth in wage goods demand among roughly 15 per cent of the large subcontinental population triggered demands for other capital goods.

A notable feature of the MNCs was that the new non-Indian firms had few if any commercial links with the older colonial ones. Early entrants had tried tentative marketing tie-ups with managing agencies that were supposed to know more about the intricacies of the subcontinent's markets. But invariably such relations soured rapidly. A good example is Lever's experience in the 1920s with Boulton Brothers to market its soap and toiletries. Boulton turned out to be exceptionally inept, and eventually Lever had to write off large inventories, which convinced the management of the need for in-house marketing (Tomlinson 1982: 10). Like Chandlerian firms, the MNCs in India gradually created their own marketing network. Brooke Bond had a marketing structure that kept in touch with retailers in remote towns; by the mid 1930s ICI built up 1,500 depots, 15,000 distributors, and an in-house staff of 2,500 (Tomlinson 1982: 10). The MNCs also tended to interact with one another without the mediation of colonial firms. ICI helped Metal Box in its initial marketing; Metal Box supplied containers to the three petroleum companies; and Caltex, Shell, and Stan-Vac placed roofing orders for their depots with Asbestos Cement. Close interconnections plus the fact that the market expanded after World War II and during the 1950s helped to increase MNC presence as well as profitability in India. In fact, the three oil companies made enough profits to set up massive refineries in the 1950s, Shell and Esso at Trombay in 1954 and Caltex at Visakhapatnam in 1957 (Dasgupta 1971: 108–9).

By the mid 1950s MNCs had entered almost all major industries: chemicals, pharmaceuticals (which they effectively controlled), baby food, toothpaste, soap, cosmetics, cooking mediums, cigarettes, tea, coffee, petroleum and its by-products, chemicals, gases, engineering, and the like. Such entry not only shows the profitability of these ventures but also strengthens our view that independence per se had little effect on foreign business in India. If anything, MNC presence grew after independence in medium—as well as low—technology areas. And the new sahibs did very well in independent India: the profits of British MNCs in India were 120 per cent of the world average (Reddaway 1968: Table IV.5).

CONCLUDING REMARKS

There is an important unanswered question. Tea plantations were dominated by European companies up to the 1960s. Since the Marwaris were so adept at buying the stock of jute and coal companies, why did they ignore tea plantations? Unlike jute and coal, all major tea plantations were sterling companies registered in the London Stock Exchange. By the 1920s the Marwaris were very important players in the Calcutta Stock Exchange and accounted for the majority in every successive managing committee. But whatever their endowments, they were still nonentities in London. In the late-colonial era Marwaris were able to take over European-controlled rupee companies in

Calcutta, but it would have been impossible for them to carry out similar takeover bids in London.[18]

Our knowledge about different kinds of entrepreneurial activity in eastern India still has major gaps. We need to know quite a bit more about Bengali entrepreneurs and the managerial hierarchies that operated among MNCs. We also need to know more about the financial transactions of Marwari firms, how funds moved from one activity to another, and the manner in which cash flows were controlled. It will certainly take a while before one can produce a Chandlerian piece on business practices in eastern India, let alone India as a whole.

Nevertheless, it is clear that entrepreneurial activity was far more complex than has been recorded in the past. These were often different in strategy, in design, in the instruments used, and in implementation. The Marwaris integrated transactions from a massive, geographically-wide network of trade, commerce, moneylending, speculation, underwriting, and other constituents of a 'bazaar' economy with the modem factory sector—first jute mills and collieries and then activities that were far removed from the bazaar. Non-Indian managing agencies, so successful until the end of World War I, failed to come to grips with the complex postwar era. Bengalis attempted to start out as technocrats and succeeded briefly before being out-competed by better professionals. And the MNCs continued their expansion in India, as elsewhere, by introducing novel marketing methods and standardized products; they soon overcame their unfamiliarity with the terrain and became major players in India.

Given such a rich diversity of facts, the time has come for economic historians to eschew discourse that speaks only of colonial firms to the exclusion of all else. This article is a modest attempt at such a revision. Such revisionism does not imply that the colonial epoch should be explained without reference to colonialism. Ideally, it should do just the opposite: enrich our understanding of the dynamics of capitalist development in the imperial era.

Originally published as Omkar Goswami, '*Sahibs, Babus*, and *Banias*: Changes in Industrial Control in Eastern India, 1918–50', in Rajat Ray (ed.), *Entrepreneurship and Industry in India, 1800–1947* (Delhi, Oxford University Press, 1992), pp. 228–59.

NOTES

** The author is indebted to the Fulbright Program for giving him time off to spend a term at Harvard and Tufts in 1986, when the first draft was written and presented at seminars. He is also grateful to three anonymous referees of the journal for their comments. Rajat Ray, Amiya Bagchi, Sabhyasachi Bhattacharya, Dharma Kumar, Tom Tomlinson, Shanti Tangri, Eugene White, Ira Gang, and Morris D. Morris made helpful suggestions. The usual disclaimers apply.

1. At constant 1938–9 prices, the factory sector produced an average value added of Rs 2.33 billion per year between 1940–1 and 1946–7. Over the same period, national income was Rs 34.78 billion per annum (Sivasubramonian 1965: 256, 338).

2. In the late 1960s, it needed a maverick Marxist minister called Ram Chatterjee to put an end to the whites-only rule at the Calcutta Swimming Club. He walked in with four dozen loin-clothed tribals carrying bows and arrows, who promptly jumped into the pool. Thereafter, he demanded equal entry failing which he threatened an encore. A significant point worth nothing is that the club could maintain this apartheid in spite of being located less than a mile away from Writers' Building, the seat of power of the Government of West Bengal.

3. Sahibs are the white men, often meant for the bosses of companies. The most correct translation of banias would be traders, people of commercial caste groups, or moneylenders, and compradors of European

managing agencies. Babus mean the upper-caste Bengali gentry, often used by sahibs in a derogatory way.

4. The correct translation of fatka is a cross between 'speculation' and 'gambling'. For details on how fatka came into being, see *Capital*, a Calcutta weekly, 16 January 1930, pp. 139–40. For initial reactions of the European-controlled Jute Mills' Association, see Indian Jute Mills' Association (IJMA), *Report of the Committee 1911*, pp. 19–22.

5. This phrase is taken from Lokanathan (1935: 23): 'The imprimatur of a managing agency . . . was essential for the successful flotation of any public limited company in India.'

6. This is best illustrated in Edward Benthall's diary. In 1920, a senior Scottish technical manager at a jute mill advised a younger officer thus: 'Don't worry about your pay, son. Any time you want to make money, cross the street (to the stock exchange) and you can double your income in an hour' (Harrison 1964: 133–4).

7. This was noticed at the time by an astute civil servant called R.N. Gilchrist, who, unlike other mandarins, had little sympathy for European commercial houses. For Gilchrist's detailed noting, see Government of Bengal, West Bengal State Archives, Commerce Department, Commerce Branch, File 2-J-1, September 1932, Proceedings 87–134B; and also Goswami (1982).

8. Simmons (1976) has argued that the slump in the coal industry from 1925 and the depression thereafter 'irredeemably scared off a great deal of Bengali capital and entrepreneurial talent' (p. 196). However, there were cases of Indian entry, although in far smaller numbers than in jute. For instance, during the financial crisis of 1925–8, N.C. Sircar first took massive loans from a Marwari trader called Sukhlall Karnani. Subsequently, Karnani applied the screw and Sircar was forced to sell to H.V. Low, which also could not meet its debts to Karnani and had to sell all its interests to the Marwari for a song (Simmons 1976: 194–5). The Jatias also bought enough shares to be on the board of four collieries controlled by Andrew Yule and Company.

9. Many Bengalis, on the other hand, were dummy directors. They were invariably landlords (zamindars and self-styled rajas), who wore tweed, smoked pipes, knew all about thoroughbreds, and even went to Ascot as guests of carls, counts and lords. Prominent among these western-educated babus were Manindra Chandra Nundy (the zamindar of Kasimbazar), Bhupendra Narayan Sinha, Bejoy Prasad Singh-Roy, Lord Sinha of Raipur, the Maharajah of Santosh, and the Maharaja of Burdwan (the last better known as a celebrated party-giver, racehorse owner, and dipsomaniac than as a director). Of these directors, one never hears anything abusive—only high praise. That is to be expected. After all, the Bengali gentry knew what 'correctness' was all about and never threatened to take over firms run by Britons.

10. The racial slurs were manifold. Birla, for instance, was banned from entering the Sale Room of the London Jute Association and had to employ English brokers—any 'Tom, Jack or Ragstraw', to quote Birla—to conduct business on his behalf (TP, Birla to Thakurdas 19 Nov. 1928). At a lower level, colonialism sometimes meant poking canes at natives who stood in the way of Britons promenading down the Chowringhee in Calcutta. This practice was fondly recalled by J.A Mackerrow, a partner of Bird and Company, as an example of the idyllic life Englishmen had before World War I (BP. Box XIV).

11. Computed from the profit and loss data given for each jute mill in the *IIYB, 1930–1* to *1938–9*.

12. All it could raise was Rs 3 million and even this, if deployed, meant sacrificing the partners' profits for seven to ten years. For details, see Tomlinson (1981: 474–7).

13. These advertisements were bi-weekly, often daily, features in newspapers such as *Ananda Bazar Patrika*, *Jugantar*, *Amrita Bazar Patrika* and the *Dainik Basumati*.

14. The racial abuse that Bengalis reserved for Marwaris was (and still is) far worse than what the British had to say.

15. This phrase is from Chandler (1977).

16. In 1900–1 real per capita income of the urban sector stood at Rs 139 whereas that of the rural sector was Rs 40. In 1940–1, the per capita income of the rural sector had fallen to Rs 38, whereas that of the urban sector had increased to Rs 226. Computed from Sivasubramonian (1965).

17. *Bidis* are the poor man's smoke—something like cheap, tiny-sized cigarillos—and far cheaper and more humble.

18. In a sense, when the British created not one but three stock markets in Bombay, Calcutta and Madras, they reduced transactions costs and therefore unwittingly eliminated yet another barrier to Indian entry. Sterling companies, on the other hand, enjoyed

the advantages of this barrier to Indian entry until independence.

REFERENCES

Bagchi, Amiya K. 1972. *Private Investment in India, 1900–1939*. Cambridge: Cambridge University Press.

B.P. Benthall Papers. *Papers of Sir Edward Benthall*. Centre for South Asian Studies, Cambridge, England.

Buchanan, Daniel H. 1934. *The Development of Capitalistic Enterprise in India*. New York: Macmillan.

Capital. Calcutta weekly.

CBJA (Calcutta Baled Jute Association). 1903/04–1918/19. *Reports of the Committee*. Calcutta.

Dasgupta, Biplab. 1971. *The Oil Industry in India: Some Economic Aspects*. London: Frank Cass.

Gadgil, Dhananjaya R. 1944. *The Industrial Evolution of India in Recent Times*. Bombay: Asia.

Goswami, Omkar. 1982. 'Collaboration and Conflict: European and Indian Capitalists and the Jute Economy of Bengal, 1919–1939', *Indian Economic and Social History Review*, Vol. 19, No. 2, pp. 141–79.

——. 1985. 'Then Came the Marwaris: Some Aspects of the Changes in the Pattern of Industrial Control in Eastern India', *Indian Economic and Social History Review*, Vol. 22, No. 3, pp. 225–49.

Harrison, Godfrey. 1964. *Bird and Company of Calcutta: A History Produced to Mark the Firm's Centenary, 1864–1964*. Calcutta.

Hazari, R.K., 1966. *The Structure of the Corporate Private Sector: A Study of Concentration, Ownership, and Control*. Bombay: Asia.

Heston, Alan. 1983. 'National Income', in *The Cambridge Economic History of India*, ed. Dharma Kumar, Vol. 2. Cambridge: Cambridge University Press.

Hindusthan Standard. Calcutta daily.

IIYB-Investor's India Year Book, 1918–1960. Calcutta: Place, Siddon, and Gough.

IJMA-Indian Jute Mills Association. *Reports of the Committee*. Calcutta.

Krishnamurthy, J. 1983. 'The Occupation Structure', in *The Cambridge Economic History of India*, ed. Dharma Kumar, Vol. 2. Cambridge: Cambridge University Press.

Lokanathan, P.S. 1935. *Industrial Organisation in India*. London: Macmillan.

Ray, Rajat K. 1979. *Industrialization in India: Growth and Conflict in the Private Corporate Sector, 1914–47*. Delhi: Oxford University Press.

Simmons, Colin P. 1976. 'Indigenous Enterprise in the Indian Coal Mining Industry, c. 1835–1939', *Indian Economic and Social History Review*, Vol. 13, No. 2, pp. 189–218.

Sivasubramonian, S. 1965. 'National Income of India, 1900–1 to 1946–47', Ph.D. diss, Delhi School of Economics, Delhi.

——. 1977. 'Income from the Secondary Sector in India, 1900–47', *Indian Economic and Social History Review*, Vol. 14, No. 4.

Tomlinson, Brian R. 1978. 'Foreign Private Investment in India, 1920–1960.' *Modern Asian Studies 12*, no. 4: 655–77.

——. 1981. 'Colonial Firms and the Decline of Colonialism in Eastern India', *Modern Asian Studies*, Vol. 15, No. 3, pp. 455–86.

——. 1982. 'British Firms in India, 1900–1960', Mimeo.

T.P. Thakurdas Papers. *Papers of Sir Purshottamdas Thakurdas*. New Delhi: Nehru Memorial Museum and Library.

26

'Modern Ideas' and Industrial Initiatives
The Tatas of Bombay

Dwijendra Tripathi and Makrand Mehta

In contrast to eastern India, entrepreneurs in western India did not face such competitive antagonism. There were perhaps many reasons for this. Western India was conquered at a later stage by the British. European managing agencies were not as deeply embedded here and depended on indigenous merchants to act as middlemen and brokers, who arose from the mercantile communities of Parsis, Gujaratis, Sindhis, and Cutchi Memons which were well entrenched in the region by the late nineteenth century. Further, the worlds of the bazaar and modern industry remained more isolated elsewhere in the subcontinent but were more closely integrated in centres such as Bombay, thus allowing indigenous enterprise a more generous share in economic life.* The close connections between indigenous merchants and European business had led to a 'remarkably close-knit oligarchy which governed both the island and its overseas trade'.†

* See Tirthankar Roy, *The Economic History of India 1857–1947* (New Delhi, Oxford University Press, 2006), p. 255. There is considerable literature on the different patterns of industrialization in eastern and western India. See, for instance, Rajat Kanta Ray (ed.), *Entrepreneurship and Industry in India, 1800–1947* (New Delhi, Oxford University Press, 1992), 'Introduction'.

† Asiya Siddiqi, 'The Business World of Jamsetjee Jejeebhoy', *Indian Economic and Social History Review*, Vol. 19, 1982, pp. 301–24. Thus the Bombay Chamber of Commerce which was established in 1836 comprised both European and Indian firms. This would not have been possible in eastern India. On Bombay, also see Dick Kooiman, 'Bombay: From Fishing Village to Colonial Port City (1662–1947)', in Robert J. Ross and Gerald J. Telkamp (eds), *Colonial Cities* (Netherlands, Martinus Nijhoff Publishers, 1985), pp. 207–30. Also see Lakshmi Subramanian (ed.), *Ports, Towns, Cities* (Marg Publications, Mumbai, 2009), especially the articles by Jonathan Roy Barlow and Mariam Dossal.

In an enthralling chapter titled 'The Tatas', historians Dwijendra Tripathi and Makrand Mehta present an insight into the workings of the foremost business house of western India. Jamsetji Tata, from a priestly background, trained in India and China was inducted into the family business to work alongside his father.[‡] Despite early disappointments, Jamsetji continued to aspire and think innovatively. With the World Wars came the opportunity to expand and consolidate. The Tatas entered several businesses ranging from hydroelectric power generation to steel manufacturing to pharmaceuticals on a massive scale with the perspective to compete internationally; this helped them become the largest business house in the country by Independence. The family was deeply influenced by the West and its 'sense of enterprise', and Jamsetji perceived the Parsis as 'a bridge' between the colonizers and the colonized. Given their openness to Western ideas as well as their minority status, much like the rest of the Parsi community, the Tatas were able to construct for themselves an identity that enabled them to gain an 'insider status' in the British establishment.[§] This liminal position in Indian society, Tripathi and Mehta show, enabled the Tatas to symbolize bold entrepreneurship and national aspirations in the post-colonial era.

Bombay in the middle of the nineteenth century was more susceptible to new ideas and influences than an upcountry town like Ahmedabad. Founded by the British in the latter half of the seventeenth century, the city had virtually grown in the cradle of European influences. Although it was yet to acquire an aura of splendour and majesty, Bombay in the 1850s was already a principal business centre where native and English merchants freely interacted with one another. Having a number of educational institutions, it was one of the most developed centres for English education in the country. These factors were bringing about a 'social revolution' as a result of which the native customs and attitudes were 'in a fair way ... being swept away'.[1] More obviously, Bombay had replaced Surat as the principal port in the country. Largely because of its location, the city could experience the impact of the English industrial revolution much more directly than any other urban centre in India. In short, the conditions necessary for a transition from commercial capitalism to industrial capitalism prevailed in a much greater degree in Bombay than anywhere else in the British dependency.[2]

Those who heralded this transition were Parsees. Concentrated in the major urban centres of the Bombay presidency and thus denied the opportunity for agricultural pursuits, most Parsees depended for their livelihood either on trade and commerce or administrative jobs. Some of the principal traders and shipbuilders were Parsees; many were engaged

‡ There are a number of interesting writings on the Tatas. For instance, see F.R. Harris, *Jamsetji Nusserwanji Tata: A Chronicle of His Life* (Bombay, Blackie & Son, 1958); S.K. Sen, *The House of Tatas, 1839–1939* (Calcutta, Progressive Publishers, 1975); and R.M. Lala, *The Creation of Wealth: The Tatas from the 19th to the 21st Century* (New Delhi, Viking, 2004) and his *Beyond the Last Blue Mountain: A Life of J.R.D. Tata* (New Delhi, Penguin, 1992), *The Heartbeat of a Trust: The Story of the Sir Dorabji Tata Trust* (New Delhi, Tata McGraw-Hall, 1998), and *The Joy of Achievement: Conversations with JRD Tata* (New Delhi, Penguin, 1997).

§ See excerpt on Parsis in Section II: Mercantile Communities, this volume.

in commerce with foreign countries. But what set the Parsees apart from other groups and communities was that they uninhibitedly opened themselves to new influences and values. They had always displayed this basic trait ever since they migrated to India from Persia in the eighth century. This attitude, coupled with the fact that a large number of the Parsees were engaged in commercial and trading pursuits, brought them close to the European traders who needed their services as middlemen to deal with the native population. This enabled the Parsees to assimilate the ethos and attitudes of their masters.[3] Some Parsees had already accumulated sufficient capital through their commercial activities; their direct contact with British merchants in India—and through them the British industrial-technological set-up—pointed to new avenues of investment.

It is not surprising, therefore, that the pioneers of the textile industry in Bombay were Parsee traders, shippers, or bankers who had close business links with the British.[4] The family of Jamsetji Nusserwanji Tata, the founder of the illustrious business house that bears his name, was not among the earliest promoters of textile ventures but his success in exploiting opportunities in other fields was largely due to similar forces which had led some of his clansmen into textile manufacturing. An account of the stages through which J N Tata achieved a well-deserved position of eminence in Indian entrepreneurial history would justify this assertion.

I

The son of Nusserwanji Ratanji, J N Tata belonged to a family of priests who had remained in this profession for well over twenty-five generations. But since the Parsee religion does not envisage any conflict between priestly duties and business profession, Nusserwanji began to take interest in business and later moved from Navsari, his hometown in south Gujarat, to Bombay where a number of Parsees from his hometown had already gone in search of business opportunities. In Bombay Nusserwanji gradually emerged as a trader of some means. He was a shipper, China trader, exporter of cotton and opium, and importer of camphor, cinnamon, copper, brass, and gold. For a brief period he also served as a contractor for the British commissariat. Jamsetji grew up while his family and country both were passing through transition. The family was by no means rich when he was born in 1839, and India had no modern industries then. However, by the time he attained manhood his father could boast of a degree of prosperity, and the country had already entered the industrial era.

Nusserwanji took advantage not only of the business opportunity that the city of his adoption offered but also of its educational facilities. Jamsetji was sent to the Elphinstone College, one of the best institutions for western learning in the country, from where he passed out in 1858 as a 'green scholar', symbolising a degree holder. By then Nusserwanji's business operations had expanded considerably and he needed help. Young Jamsetji was inducted into his father's business under these conditions. He took little time to gain insight into the intricacies of markets and commodities. In 1859 he was despatched to China where he stayed for four years, acquiring an intimate knowledge of the eastern markets. After laying the foundation of the China House in Hong Kong and opening a branch of his firm in Shanghai, he returned to India in 1863. Bombay then was in the throes of a cotton export boom, the American civil war having interrupted imports of raw cotton into Great Britain from the cotton belt of America.[5]

The firm of Nusserwanji could not have possibly escaped the speculation mania which gripped Bombay in the wake of the cotton famine in Britain. In the then prevailing atmosphere only the most cautious could control their temptation. An additional factor induced the involvement of the Tatas in these activities: Premchand Roychand, virtually the king of the Bombay stock market, was a partner in their trading firm.[6] How much money the Tatas made during this period cannot be ascertained, but it was sufficient to encourage them to decide to open an agency in London.

Jamsetji was selected to supervise the new branch. He left for London with a number of securities including a large number of bills on the China market. Hardly had he reached England, when the cotton market crashed following the end of the American civil war. The house of Premchand Roychand collapsed, causing such dismay as Bombay had never witnessed before. The securities and the bills which Jamsetji had carried to London were rendered worthless. In this hour of crisis, it was his tact and perseverance that stood him in good stead. He explained to his creditors with a great deal of success that the crisis that his firm was facing was due to an abnormal situation. So impressed were his creditors with him that they appointed him his own liquidator. The way he weathered the storm increased his self-confidence. The trip proved beneficial to him in one more respect. He used the opportunity to study the working of the textile industry in Britain and various aspects of the cotton trade.

Unlike many other Bombay houses, the Tatas took much less time to recover from the shock largely because they had been less deeply involved in the mad rush than people like Premchand Roychand. By 1867, the damage to their position had been considerably repaired. The British invasion of Abyssinia at this time also facilitated their rehabilitation.[7] The Tatas in association with a few other merchants were given the contract for the new commissariat. This proved highly profitable, and by the end of the war they were richer by at least Rs 4 million. With renewed confidence, Nusserwanji re-established his China branches which the crash had forced to close down.

By the end of 1860s thus, Nusserwanji and his son were persons of some means. They also had had some meaningful interaction with the world of business beyond the borders of India; the younger man had personally observed and was impressed by the working of industrial units in England. By this time the Bombay textile industry had sufficiently recovered from the setback caused by the crash. Recovery was slow but steady, and new chimneys began to appear on the Bombay skyline.[8] The Tatas were now in a position to launch into a direction which would have been inconceivable just a decade earlier. J N Tata, with the blessings of his father and the support of a few partners, purchased an old and crumbling oil-pressing factory in 1869, converted it into a textile unit, and called it the Alexandra Mill. This marked his debut in the industrial field. He had no cause to regret it for only two years later he sold off the renovated unit for a handsome profit.

It is not clear why J N Tata decided to dispose of his company. Did he feel inadequately equipped to manage a cotton mill? Whatever the reason, soon after selling off the Alexandra Mill, he visited England with the object of gaining a first-hand knowledge of textile manufacturing in what was then the most developed country in the world. Having inspected a number of cotton mills at Manchester he returned home in 1874, determined to launch textile production in a big way. The most natural site for his proposed factory should have been Bombay, the city he had known and which most textile producers generally preferred for their manufacturing operations. But to Jamsetji these considerations appeared irrelevant; proximity to the sources of raw material and power weighed more heavily in his calculations. After a great deal of search, he finally selected Nagpur, located in the then Central Provinces. The city was the terminus of the Great Indian Peninsula Railway and was within easy reach of the cotton-growing tracts in Central India and coal deposits in eastern India.

The Central India Spinning Weaving and Manufacturing Company, founded in 1874, was the first industrial unit established by a Bombay businessman outside his city. The factory was named the Empress Mills for it started functioning on 1 January 1877, the day Queen Victoria was proclaimed the empress of India. The new venture had a few teething troubles and the company's performance was far from satisfactory initially. Consequently, the value of the shares began to fall. This, however, was a passing phase and Jamsetji, assisted by a group of trusted and competent managers, enabled the mill to turn the corner.[9]

The success of the Empress Mills encouraged Jamsetji to expand his textile operations. In 1886 he registered his second company, the Swadeshi Mills, for the production of finer varieties of yarn and cloth—an almost novel phenomenon in Bombay where most of the mills produced only coarse materials. Less than two decades later in 1903, he opened his third and last cotton company, the Advance Mills, at Ahmedabad. Both these units were acquired from their previous owners in extremely poor condition. Tata and his men, some of whom had been trained in his Nagpur company, converted them into profitable and progressive concerns within a short time.[10]

Some aspects of the working of these mills manifested Jamsetji's innovative spirit. In the Empress Mills, he introduced ring spindles when the device was yet to come in general use even in the United States where it had been invented, and Manchester was still lukewarm to it. The new spinning equipment was less complicated and its labour requirements were less exacting. It was, therefore, more suited to Indian conditions. According to the historian of the Indian cotton mills, its use 'gave to the mills in India an advantage against Lancashire which contemporary and later discussions have normally neglected'.[11] Jamsetji also introduced several labour welfare measures and incentive schemes which were yet to become common. His decision to acquire the two sick units displayed a streak of boldness, and the scheme to produce cloth of finer counts in the face of stiff competition from Manchester indicated his risk-bearing attitude. He even experimented with a new form of management in the Empress Mills. Instead of adopting the managing agency framework, very popular with Indian textile producers, he, for a number of years, looked after its affairs as its managing director, reporting to a board of directors and drawing a nominal salary. This, however, was too revolutionary an innovation under the conditions prevailing in India then and Jamsetji eventually had to embrace the managing agency structure. But he refused to follow the common practice of calculating the managing agents' remuneration on the basis of sales, and introduced the system of charging commission on profits[12] which in due course gained general acceptance in Indian business.

Jamsetji's innovative spirit was reflected in some other ventures which he tried to promote with varying success. These included his attempts to promote export of mangoes to Europe in cold storage steamers and preservation of perishable food items, such as fish, fruit and meat in an ice house. He also toyed with the idea of developing sericulture in Mysore. Poor public response killed the first two projects, and the apathy of the princely state proved fatal to the sericulture scheme. His effort to launch a shipping line between Bombay and Japan was motivated 'not only for the good and benefit of our family, but for that of our community, who have lost an old business of theirs; for our mill industry in which we are so heavily interested and on which the prosperity of Bombay so depends'.[13] But he could not cope with the challenge of the English shipping companies. With their monopoly position in the eastern waters, they reduced their freight to a ridiculously low level and drove Tata's nascent venture out of market before it had a chance to flourish.[14] The most successful among the minor ventures of Jamsetji was the establishment of the Taj Mahal Hotel in Bombay in 1901 which aimed at exploiting the growing tourist business.

Jamsetji's reputation as an entrepreneur does not rest on his textile companies, minor ventures, or even managerial experimentations. These undeniably contained some elements of entrepreneurship, but in launching his cotton companies, he was essentially a follower rather than a pacesetter; the early pioneers of the industry had made his task much less risky and arduous. And most of his minor ventures were almost stillborn. What really secured for him a towering position among the Indian captains of industry was his initiative to promote steel production in India—a goal he pursued with dogged tenacity till the end of his life.

The task was not simple. Even though the country was reputed to have large iron and coal deposits, and technology could be easily imported from England, all efforts to promote steel manufacturing in India in the eighteenth and nineteenth centuries had failed.[15] The industry required high finance and a skilled workforce. Even if these could be obtained, it was by no means easy to allay the fear in official circles that 'the establishment of the iron and steel industry would be viewed with disfavour by the persons interested in the manufacture of those articles in England'.[16] Reinforcing these difficulties were the ludicrous prospecting laws then in force which, as we have seen, had thwarted Ranchhodlal's mining plans. People were unwilling to make a large investment in exploration without being certain that they would be able to exploit the deposits discovered in the process.

Jamsetji must have been aware of these hurdles when he accidentally came across a copy of 'Report on the Financial Prospects of Iron-working in the Chanda District' prepared by Ritter von Schwartz, a German expert, who had a great deal of experience in exploring iron and coal deposits in India. By then, Jamsetji's Empress Mills had come out of the woods and he had earned considerable reputation for his managerial prowess and risk-taking attitude. He had also developed close acquaintance with a large number of British officers and businessmen in India and England. Schwartz had indicated that the Chanda deposits could yield ore suitable for conversion into iron and steel, with charcoal being used for smelting. The Parsee entrepreneur approached the chief commissioner of the Central Provinces for mining concessions but achieved nothing in the face of the prevailing legal provisions. Tata had no alternative but to wait for more favourable times.[17]

And he waited for nearly twenty years. Although the need to exploit the iron resources of India was realised as early as the 1850s when railway construction began, nothing concrete could be done for fear of the British steelmakers who would resent the loss of the rich Indian market. In the 1890s the fear began to recede largely because of the mounting challenge from Germany and the United States to the British monopoly in the Indian markets. Officials, therefore, began to see the positive side of an indigenous steel industry. Under these conditions it became necessary to relax the archaic regulations. The new rules, adopted in 1899, granted much greater security to the prospectors to reap the fruits of their labour. Viceroy Lord Curzon was much less dogmatic about *laissez faire* than many of his predecessors and believed that an industrialized India would be an asset to the Empire. Lord George Hamilton, the Secretary of State for India, was also favourably disposed towards Indian industrialization.

Both Hamilton and Curzon must have thought that the abolition of the irksome prospecting laws would induce English entrepreneurs to set up steel plants in India.[18] However, only one Englishman made a feeble attempt to enter the field. Jamsetji took the fullest advantage of the changed situation to revive his project. He met the Secretary of State in London ostensibly to discuss his plan to set up an institute for scientific learning. He used this opportunity to enlist Hamilton's support for his steel scheme as well. On his return Tata applied for and was granted prospecting licence for Lohara and Peepulgaon areas of Chanda district.

In the meantime Jamsetji had left for the United States in search of technical know-how. On his way he met Hamilton once again. He was assured every kind of assistance in the United States by the London branch of the famous American firm of J. Pierpont Morgan. Tata also visited Germany and familiarized himself with the steel industry in that country. Thus, when he reached the United States, he had already acquired a fair knowledge of the working of steel mills in the major steel-producing countries in Europe. In America, he visited a number of places known for steel production and met a well-known geologist, Charles Page Perin, in New York. Impressed by Tata's determination and convinced by his persuasion, Perin agreed to help in sun-eying the area. His associate, C M Weld, arrived in Bombay in 1903 and the exploration of Chanda began in full swing. It soon became clear that the Chanda deposits were hardly as rich as they were reputed to be and the coal found there was unsuitable for smelting. The steel project appeared to be in the doldrums once again.[19]

Jamsetji had already returned from his American tour when the disturbing news came. With his health failing, he entrusted the responsibility for the project to his forty-four-year old son Dorabji. Dorabji had grown in the shadow of his father whose values and dreams he admired and shared. Educated at Bombay and Cambridge and having come in close contact with prominent businessmen through his father, he fully appreciated the importance of industrial enterprise. He had been inducted into the management of the Empress Mills as early as 1884, and had been associated with the steel project from its very inception. He had also accompanied Weld in the fruitless Chanda explorations. Jamsetji's withdrawal from active supervision, thus, had no adverse effect on the progress of the project. The second line of leadership was as much committed to the idea as the older man himself.

The failure of the Chanda exploration was a serious setback to Jamsetji's plans. Fortunately, in this hour of despondency Dorabji came across a report by an Indian geologist, P N Bose, indicating that the areas in the neighbourhood of Durg district of the present-day Madhya Pradesh were rich in iron ore deposits. Dorabji, accompanied by Weld, rushed to the spot, completed the preliminary survey quickly, and secured the requisite prospecting licence. The explorations of the area was in full swing when Jamsetji passed away in 1904 in Germany.[20]

Another project that Jamsetji left unfinished was a scheme to generate hydroelectric power. The idea, like the steel plan, germinated in his mind during the early years of his career, but it took concrete shape only during the last years of his life. While searching for a site for his Empress Mills, Jamsetji had been struck by the sight of the famous Dhuandhar Falls near Jabalpur on the River Narmada. It was then that he first thought of the development of hydroelectric energy. However, he did nothing to give a practical shape to the idea until 1897 when Robert Miller of a well-known Bombay firm came forward with the proposal to generate energy from the Doodhsagar Falls lying in the Portuguese territory, a short distance away from the British boundary. An English engineer David Gostling, however, thought that the Lonavla region, midway between Bombay and Pune, would be more suitable for the purpose. Tata and the two Englishmen formed a syndicate to translate the idea into reality. The use of electric power was still not very common in the Indian mills, and coal was both expensive and polluting. The need for a better source of power, thus, was undeniable and the monsoon rains on the hills near Bombay seemed to provide more than sufficient water to generate as much power as the Bombay cotton industry could use.

Many preliminary tasks including the acquisition of land and repelling the threat from a rival syndicate were successfully completed, thanks to Tata's ability to win support from the key British officials including the Secretary of State. But nothing concrete had been achieved when Jamsetji died, leaving the scheme to the care of Dorabji who had been already inducted into the syndicate.[21]

II

Jamsetji's death caused no vacuum in the leadership. His two sons, Dorabji and Ratanji, were grown up and had been inducted into the business during his lifetime. R D Tata, his cousin, had been closely associated with the management of various enterprises in his capacity as a partner in Tata and Sons, the family managing agency firm, ever since its birth in 1887.[22] In addition, the pioneer left behind a number of near relatives and trusted employees who had contributed in varying degrees to the growth of the Tata business. They had been exposed to the British industrial environment and values either through education or contact, and all of them had glimpsed the vision of the founder, having worked with him closely for a number of years.

The subsequent development of the house, therefore, proceeded on the lines charted by Jamsetji. The plan to start steel production was pursued with great vigour. The swadeshi wave in the opening years of the twentieth century inspired enthusiastic public participation in the venture, and the Tatas faced no difficulty in raising finance for the company which was formally registered in 1907. The factories were erected under the supervision of Perin who headed a team of American technicians as consulting engineer. Within, three years, the quiet and tiny village of Sakchi (which was later named Jamshedpur) in Bihar was converted into a steel township. The Tata Iron and Steel Company (TISCO) with a plant capacity of 100,000 tons ingots went into operation in 1911.[23] To ensure an uninterrupted flow of fuel for the company, the house also acquired collieries in the nearby regions.

The hydroelectric scheme was also pursued with equal enthusiasm and the Tata Hydro-Electric Power Supply Company was registered as a public limited concern in 1910. The money market was tight then and the Tatas had some difficulty in raising finances. For some time it appeared that the company would have no alternative but to depend on British financiers. But thanks to the support of Lord Sydenham, the Governor of Bombay, and the untiring efforts of Dorabji, Indian princes and other investors came forward. Construction of dams and erection of machinery, supervised by British engineers, took five years, and power generation started in 1915.

It was then realized that Bombay needed more energy than the company could produce. As a part of a well-thought out expansion scheme, therefore, two more companies came in quick succession. The Andhra Valley Power Supply Company, launched in 1916, was to exploit the water power of the area about twelve miles north of Lonavla, and the Tata Power Company Limited which came into being in 1919, was to generate power from the resources in the regions west of Pune. By the end of the First World War, the Tata hydroelectric system, complete in all respects, was capable of satisfying the entire power needs of the Bombay region.[24] The war period also witnessed the consolidation of the TISCO largely because of government dependence on it for steel while the imports remained disrupted. The Viceroy had no hesitation in confessing: 'I can hardly imagine what we should have done during these four years if the Tata company had not been able to give us steel rails.'[25]

Jamsetji's successors, in the meantime, had moved into cement, another basic industry. The Tatas were not the first to conceive of a cement manufacturing project in India. Some attempts in this direction had been made as early as 1903, but they had failed. The India Cement Company, set up by the house in 1912, was the first successful venture which inspired many industrialists to enter the field. The Tatas themselves established another company, the Shahabad Cement Company, shortly after the outbreak of the war.[26] Other enterprises which wer added to the growing Tata empire between 1913 and 1919 included an engineering company, an electrochemical concern, a textile mill, a construction firm, a sugar corporation and a unit to manufacture vegetable oil and allied products like soap.[27] Dorabji and his associates also promoted an industrial bank—the first of its kind in India—and the New India Assurance Company which was to develop into one of the largest enterprises in the field.

The proliferation of the Tata companies, covering a variety of fields, was inspired by the buoyant business conditions during the war and all of them performed very well as long as the hostilities continued. The boom continued for a couple of years after the war. The fact of the matter, however, was that the Tatas, like many other business houses, had launched most of these concerns with an eye on the short-term gain and without adequate preparation.[28] This became clear when recessionary trends set in around 1922. Most of these 'war babies' began experiencing trouble and could not hold their own for a long time. Consequently, the Tata Engineering, the Tata Electro Chemicals, and the Sugar Corporation could not survive. The Tata Industrial Bank merged with the Central Bank of India; and Walchand Hirachand, who was a director in the Tata Construction, acquired this concern. If the Tata Mills—the textile firm set up during the war—and the Tata Oil Mills could maintain a precarious existence it was only due to. The support from the sister companies in the group and the managing agency firm. The cement companies came under extreme pressure because of cut-throat competition from a large number of new entrants. They were eventually merged with the Associated Cement Companies which came into being in 1936 with the amalgamation of practically all companies in the field.

The postwar plight of the new companies in the group was understandable, but even the older concerns could not withstand the postwar ordeal. If the Tatas' textile mills had to contend with a long period of slump, the TISCO suffered due to a more intractable factor. Encouraged by the progress during the war years, the production capacity of the company had been increased to 500,000 tons ingots between 1917 and 1921. While the TISCO now could produce more steel, its sales declined due to the resumption of import of cheap goods from the continent. As an anxious R D Tata, the chairman of the company, candidly told his shareholders in 1924: 'We are rapidly becoming once more the dumping ground of the whole world'.[29] The result was that the profits of the company dwindled considerably and its cash balance touched rockbottom.

It was, however, unthinkable for the Tatas to let the founder's most prized legacy languish. R D Tata declared that the company would not be allowed to die so long as he was alive. In concrete terms, he and his associates took three major steps. At the first stage, Dorabji pledged his personal fortunes to obtain a loan of Rs 10 million from the Imperial Bank of India which would not oblige the company without this additional security. Secondly, an additional loan of Rs 10 million was raised from the princely state of Gwalior through the good offices of F E Dinshaw, a prominent businessman of Bombay. And thirdly, the management stepped up its efforts to secure protection for the steel industry. In this task, it had the support of the nationalist elements in the Central Legislative Assembly. Initially, the government granted a substantial bounty on steel rails in 1924; three years later protective duties were imposed on imported steel.[30]

The loans helped the TISCO management to implement another scheme of expansion which was completed just before the Great Depression began in 1929. Government orders and protection also helped the company to stabilize its position. The TISCO was now in a position to compete with imported steel in the internal market; it also succeeded in building up an export market for pig iron. The onset of the depression disrupted the process of recovery, but the management continued with the programme of modernization. A steep rise in the price of machinery and consequently of steel helped the process considerably. As a result of the capital expenditure incurred during this period the company was in a position to increase its sales and diversify production. By 1934, the TISCO was in such good shape that the Steel Industry (Protection) Act of 1934, which removed some of the disincentives to imports imposed under the 1927 Act, caused no anxiety to the management. The company launched another modernization programme to bring the capacity of the plant to one million tons shortly before the Second World War began with the result that the TISCO was now in a position to meet 73 per cent of the nation's requirement for steel.[31]

While the Tatas displayed patience and a rare sense of courage in handling the affairs of the TISCO during the crisis following the First World War, they took recourse to a rather soft option in meeting the challenge faced by the hydroelectric companies. The Tata electric system had emerged from the war much less consolidated than the steel company; the condition became still worse after the war. One of the companies was not in a position to pay dividends even to the preference shareholders. Under these conditions the Tatas decided to sell 50 per cent of their holdings in the managing agency firm to an American syndicate in 1930. Consequently, between this date and 1951 when the control reverted back to the parent agency, the hydroelectric system was under the management of a joint firm. The decision was severely criticised in the Indian business circles and the nationalist press and somewhat tarnished the image of the house.[32]

Soon after the joint Indo-American agency took over the management of the hydroelectric companies, the second–generation leadership came to an end with the death of Dorabji Tata in 1932. Ratan Tata had already died in 1918, and R D Tata in 1925. Neither of Jamsetji's sons left any issue. So the leadership of the house came into the hands of J R D Tata. The son of R D Tata and his French wife, J R D had received his education in France. He had also lived in Japan for two years during the First World War where he attended a school run by the American Catholic mission. J R D had thoroughly imbibed the European ethos and values when he returned to India in 1924 at the age of 21.[33] During the next eight years he worked in the steel company as an apprentice and learnt a great deal about the business. N B Saklatvala and S D Saklatvala, Jamsetji's two nephews who had closely worked with the founder as well as with his immediate successors, were still actively connected with the management. In fact, for six years after Dorabji's death it was N B Saklatvala who was the formal head of the Tata empire. It was only after his death in 1938 that J R D was formally elected chairman of the Tata and Sons.[34]

Leading the house into air transport was J R D's first major contribution. Civil aviation had already developed into an industry in the western countries, but even as late as 1932 India had no air services. While a student in France, J R D had been fascinated by the flying device because of his friendship with the son of Louis Bleriot, the first man to fly across the English Channel. On returning to India he obtained a pilot's licence in 1929 from the Flying Club of Bombay which had been established only a year earlier. A year later he completed a solo flight between Bombay and Karachi and then persuaded Dorabji to start an airmail service between the two cities. This was the beginning of air transport in India and also of Air India which started as a division of the Tata and Sons. The introduction, of the Empire Mail Service in 1936, under which first class mail could be carried by air without surcharge, benefited the aviation venture of the Tatas immensely.[35]

The Tatas initiated two other ventures of rather unconventional nature during the years of depression. The Indian Standard Metal Company was established in 1936 to produce non-ferrous alloys and castings. Three years later the Tata Chemicals, then 'the biggest chemical works in the country', was floated.[36] This company owed its birth to a suggestion made in a Tariff Commission report of 1929. There was virtually no production of industrial chemicals in India then, and the country had to depend on imports for even basic inputs such as caustic soda, soda ash, and other soda compounds which textiles, glass, paper, soap, and a larger number of other industries required. The Tata management accepted a proposal of the government of the princely state of Baroda to set up the chemical factory at Mithapur, located in the Gaikwad territories on the Arabian Sea. The site selected augured well for the company because salt, the basic raw material, was available in plenty at Mithapur which literally means 'the city of salt'. But hardly had the first move towards launching production been made when the outbreak of the Second World War thwarted the calculations of the promoters.[37]

During the war all the enterprises in the Tata group prospered except the Tata Airlines and the Tata Chemicals, the former had to halt operations because all air services were commandeered by the government. The chemical firm could not start production until 1944 because of the difficulties in importing plant and equipment.

The commencement of the Mithapur operation has been deservedly hailed as 'a decisive phase in the development of the Indian chemical industry' and the beginning of 'the foundations of a heavy chemical industry in western India'.[38] But the result of the initial operations was disastrous. Some well-meaning friends even advised J R D to abandon the project, but he chose to persevere.[39] The disruption of the airlines and the frustration caused by the delay in commencing the Mithapur operations did not cause too much alarm in the management circles because the TISCO, the textile companies, and the Tata Oil harvested handsome profits, thanks to the demand generated by the war and dislocation of imports. Even the Tata Mills, tottering since 1924, turned the corner.

The Tatas emerged bigger and stronger from the war. They were now in a position to reorganize their activities and expand in new directions. Their first venture after the war was the Tata Engineering and Locomotive Company (TELCO), launched in 1945. It was the biggest Tata company to date. Initially it produced wagons and other components for the railways. Nine years after its inception, the company decided to manufacture commercial vehicles such as trucks and buses. For this purpose, it entered into collaboration with the famous firm of Daimler-Benz AB of West Germany. The first vehicle rolled down the assembly line within a year and the Tatas were all set to dominate the field.[40]

The birth of the TELCO was followed by the registration of the Air India as a public limited company in 1946. This was the realization of a dream the war had interrupted. In fact during the war, the Tatas had toyed with the idea of manufacturing aeroplanes and even set up a company, the Tata Aircrafts Limited, to produce invasion gliders. But the project had to be abandoned because the government did not possess aircrafts which could tow gliders. The Air India was not intended to revive the aircraft manufacturing project; its objective was to develop domestic passenger service. It is a measure of the Tatas' enthusiasm to promote air transport that within two years of the birth of the Air India, they decided to launch an international airline. However, by then India had become free and the government was not prepared to leave civil aviation entirely in the hands of the private sector. J R D's suggestion that the government of India should hold 49 per cent of share capital in the company resolved the matter; the Tatas were to hold 20 per cent, leaving the rest for public participation. Thus was born the Air India International which after the nationalization of air transport in 1953 came to be known as Air India. The Tata's domestic line, was merged with the Indian Airlines after nationalization. J R D, in recognition of his pioneering role in the field, was made the chairman of Air India and was given a seat on the board of India's domestic airline.[41]

The house promoted three more companies before the end of the First Plan period. The Lakme Limited (1952) which was to take up the manufacture of cosmetics was a subsidiary of the Tata Oil Mills. This was the only company for consumer goods the house established after the unhappy experience of the interwar years in this sphere. The other two undertakings, the Indian Tube Company and the Voltas Limited, were established in 1954. While the former was a manufacturing venture, the latter essentially was a trading company, resulting from the takeover of a Swiss firm, the Volkart Brothers, which specialized in distributing imported dyes and pharmaceuticals in India. The Tatas planned to convert it into a major engineering venture with special competence in large-scale air-conditioning and the supply of machinery for agriculture as well as industry.[42]

The above account presents only a partial view of the Tatas' business power. For, in addition to the companies mentioned above, the house controlled at least four companies[43] through two investment firms—the Investment Corporation of India and the Investa Industrial—set up in 1937 and 1941 respectively. After independence, the Tatas took over the Forbes, Forbes and Campbell, a leading British firm of managing agents, and thus acquired controlling interests in four companies: the Auto Accessories, the Bombay Safe Deposit, the Gokak Mills, and the Indian Vegetable Products. The house also acquired minority interests in a large number of concerns most of which were vertically related to the product lines of its major industrial units. As a result of its promotional activities and direct or indirect interests in a large number of companies, it dominated India's industrial life ever since the birth of its steel venture. Not only did it attain and retain the status of the largest business house in the country but also a number of companies controlled by it were the largest in their respective fields.[44]

III

Protesting against the imposition of excise duties on goods produced by Indian mills, Jamsetji Tata had written in 1894:

> Our small community is, to my thinking, peculiarly suited as interpreters and intermediaries between the rulers and the ruled in this country. Through their peculiar position, they have benefited more than any other class by English rule, and I am sure their gratitude to that rule is, as it ought to be, in due proportion to the advantage derived from it.... Pure natives of this country, whenever they venture to criticise the action of individuals in authority, are liable to have their motives questioned; but in the case of the Parsees such doubtful motives must be regarded as non-existent.[45]

The statement offers a clue to the understanding of a dominant element in the constellation of forces that guided Jamsetji's entrepreneurial urges and actions. In his judgement, the Parsees as a group were far apart from other Indians, whom he called 'pure natives'. Unlike other Indians, the Parsees, according to Jamsetji, had derived immense benefit from the British rule. Because of their proximity to and interaction with the British, they had become a bridge between the ruling masters and their non-Parsee Indian subjects. They identified so closely with the ruling class that they could attack the actions of the authorities without being accused of bias or ulterior motives. In other words, they were insiders rather than outsiders to the British establishment.

This characterization of the Parsees may not apply to the whole community but it represented, without question, Jamsetji's own view of himself. He admired the British sense of enterprise and looked upon himself as a representative of a class of Indians who were more eminently suited than their compatriots to emulate the British business experience. Perhaps he believed, as many Parsees of his age did, that the members of his community were 'not a whit behind ... Englishmen ... and the Europeans wherever the spirit of noble enterprise and great undertakings was concerned'.[46] With this kind of self–assessment, he measured his own business performance with reference to the British entrepreneurial class rather than the Indian business world.

It will be naive to suggest that this assessment of himself was innate to Jamsetji or simply because of his ethnic background. His education, his early business experiences, his interaction with the British businessmen, and his exposure to the outside world gave him an insight into profitable opportunities which most of his contemporaries, including those of his own community could hardly perceive. The financial strength that came to the family through the initial commercial and industrial ventures reinforced his will and ability to exploit the opportunities that he perceived; the contacts that he developed with influential circles facilitated his tasks. This explains why he always thought and acted big, be it the steel project, or the hydroelectric scheme, or the plan to establish an institute for scientific learning.[47]

In all his major projects, his basic inspiration came from the West, and he depended almost wholly on western technicians. Even the management structure adopted by him initially was patterned after the British. But the managing agency system was too deeply entrenched in Indian business to permit his experiment to succeed. Jamsetji's faith in the managerial acumen of his own clansmen was so great that all key positions in his enterprises were occupied by the Parsees.

Though Jamsetji did not live to bring his cherished schemes to fruition, his successors did not let the projects dissipate. This was because R D Tata, Dorabji, and others, who had worked closely with the founder and had been sufficiently exposed to the values and ethos that shaped his own thinking, shared his vision. They looked upon themselves as heirs to a heritage and the representatives of a house which symbolized not only bold entrepreneurship but also national aspirations to some extent. This was the major motive force behind the actions of the later generations of leaders. It is significant that during the 1920s when the circumstances conspired against the survival of some of their enterprises, they did everything in their power to save the principal legacies of the pioneer from ruin.

The entrepreneurial continuum of J R D Tata and his associates conformed to the personality of the Tata House. Having imbibed the spirit of his predecessors and interacted with the business world in developed countries, he promoted entrepreneurial ventures of unconventional nature. His entrepreneurial urges and inspiration behind them were similar to those of his forbears.

There is no denying the fact that the entrepreneurial achievement of the house was partly due to the help it received from the economic and political environment of the country. But the basic inspiration behind the activities of the successive generations of leaders was the spirit of enterprise that Jamsetji had bequeathed. And Jamsetji's own inspiration was essentially western in origin.

Originally published as Dwijendra Tripathi and Makrand Mehta 'The Tatas', in *Business Houses in Western India: A Study in Entrepreneurial Response, 1850–1956* (Delhi, Manohar, 1990), pp. 55–72.

NOTES

1. Dadabhai Naoroji, quoted in S.K. Sen, *The House of Tatas* (Calcutta, 1975), p. 7.

2. For the growth of Bombay as a commercial centre see Samuel T. Sheppard, *Bombay* (Bombay, 1932), pp. 154–8; Government of Bombay, *Gazetteer of Bombay City and Islands* (Bombay, 1909), Vol. II, pp. 168–71; James M Maclean, *Guide to Bombay: Historical, Statistical, and Descriptive* (Bombay, 1875), pp. 50–120.

3. Ashok V. Desai, 'The Origins of the Parsee Enterprise', *Indian Economic and Social History Review*, Vol. V, No. 4 (December 1968), pp. 310–11; D.F. Karaka, *History of the Parsis* (London, 1884), Vol. II, pp. 1–145; Amalendu Guha, 'The Comprador Role of Parsi Seths, 1750–1850', *Economic and Political Weekly*, Vol. V, No. 48 (28 November 1970), pp. 1933–6.

4. S.D. Mehta, *Cotton Mills of India, 1854–1954* (Bombay, 1954), pp. 3–25.

5. For the early career of J.N. Tata, see F.R. Harris, *Jamsetji Nusserwanji Tata* (Bombay, 1958), pp. 1–22. The effect of the American Civil War has been discussed in Dwijendra Tripathi, 'An Echo Beyond the Horizon: The Effect of the American Civil War on India', *Journal of Indian History*, Golden Jubilee Volume (Trivandrum, 1973), pp. 635–65.

6. See D.E. Wacha, *Premchand Roychand: His Early Life and Career* (Bombay, 1913); idem., *Shells from the Sands of Bombay: My Recollections and Reminiscences, 1860–1875* (Bombay, 1920) for Premchand's career; also Harris, *Jamsetji*, p. 5. Also see *Friend of India*, 29 June 29 1865; House of Commons, *Report of the Commissioners Appointed to Enquire into the Failure of the Bank of Bombay* (London, 1869), Vol. II, pp. 14–23.

7. The British invaded Abyssinia in 1867 to punish its king who had allegedly ill-treated some British citizens. The Tatas were the contractors to supply commissariat to the Indian troops employed in the campaign (Harris, *Jamsetji*, p. 11).

8. S.D. Mehta, *Cotton Mills of India*, pp. 40–63.

9. Central India Spinning, Weaving and Manufacturing Co., *Annual Reports* for the years 1875 to 1888; also Harris, *Jamsetji*, pp. 27–40.

10. Swadeshi Mills, *Annual Reports* for the years 1887 to 1900; Advance Mills, *Annual Reports* for the years 1904–1910. For the progress of the latter also see Natwarlal N. Desai, *Directory of Ahmedabad Mills Industry, 1929–1955* (Ahmedabad, 1958), p. 349.

11. S.D. Mehta, *Cotton Mills of India*, p. 44.

12. Harris, *Jamsetji*, pp. 32–5.

13. Quoted in *ibid.*, p. 94.

14. Ashok Mehta, *Indian Shipping* (Bombay, 1940), pp. 42–3; Commander K. Sridharan, *A Maritime History of India* (Delhi, 1965), pp. 136–7.

15. M.R. Chaudhuri, *The Iron and Steel Industry of India* (Calcutta, 1964), pp. 64–70.

16. Lord Ripon's Despatch of January 23, 1883, quoted in Sen, *Tatas*, p. 30.

17. Lovat Fraser, *Iron and Steel in India* (Bombay, 1919), pp. 11–13.

18. In a letter to the Indian Viceroy, the Secretary of State had written: 'I want to associate increased investment of British capital with a simultaneous action on the part of the government in developing industrial enterprise.' Hamilton to Curzon, 12 December 1900, *Curzon Papers*, 1899–1905, India Office Library, London.

19. John Keenan, *A Steelman in India* (New York, 1943), pp. 29–30; Harris, *Jamsetji*, pp. 169–72.

20. Harris, *ibid.*, pp. 173, 187.

21. *Ibid.*, pp. 218–24.

22. *Ibid.*, pp. 36–7, 50; R.M. Lala, *The Creation of Wealth: A Tata Story* (Bombay, 1981), p. 98.

23. Verrier Elwin, *The Story of Tata Steel* (privately printed, 1958), p. 40. Also a pamphlet 'The Tata Iron and Steel Company' published by TISCO on the occasion of Indian Productivity Year 1966, p. 1.

24. Lala, *The Creation of Wealth*, pp. 42–3.

25. Tata Iron and Steel Company, *Annual Reports* for the years 1914–15 to 1917–18. Also, Indian Tariff Board, *Report on Steel* (Delhi, 1924). The Viceroy's statement is quoted in Elwin, *The Story of Tata Steel*, p. 45.

26. *Investor's Encyclopaedia* for the year 1952–1953, 961; Associated Cement Companies, *The Story of the ACC* (Bombay, 1954), pp. 5–15.

27. Lala, *The Creation of Wealth*, pp. 53–4.

28. For the experience of a Calcutta-based English firm during the war years, see Godfrey Harrison, *Bird and Company of Calcutta* (Calcutta, 1964), pp. 110–13, 121–4.

29. Tata Iron and Steel Company, *Annual Report* for 1924–25.

30. Lala, *The Creation of Wealth*, p. 27; Elwin, *The Story of Tata Steel* , pp. 56–7; Indian Tariff Board, *Report on Steel* (Delhi, 1927).

31. Indian Tariff Board, *Report on Steel* (Delhi, 1934).

32. G.D. Birla referred to it as 'perturbing news'. Purushotam Thakurdas also admitted in a public speech on 29 August 1929 that 'the press and the public will not look upon the introduction of Americans in the Agency with favour'. Thakurdas to Birla, 16 August 1929 and Birla to Thakurdas, 20 August 1929 in *Thakurdas Papers*, File 68, Nehru Memorial Museum and Library, New Delhi.

33. J.R.D. Tata's interview with Leela Naidu and Binoy Thomas in *Society* (July 1981), pp. 22–29.

34. Lala, *The Creation of Wealth*, pp. 191–202.

35. *Ibid.*, pp. 59–67.

36. J.P. DeSouza, *History of the Chemical Industry in India* (Bombay, 1961), p. 57; Lala, *The Creation of Wealth*, pp. 69–73.

37. DeSouza, *History*, pp. 33–4.

38. *Ibid.*, p. 57.

39. Lala, *The Creation of Wealth*, p. 70.

40. Tata Engineering and Locomotive Company, *Annual Reports* for the years 1946 to 1955.

41. Lala, *The Creation of Wealth*, pp. 64–5.

42. *Ibid.*, pp. 86–9.

43. R.K. Hazari, *The Structure of the Private Corporate Sector: A Study of Concentration, Ownership, and Control* (London, 1966), pp. 49–50.

44. *Ibid.*, p. 44.

45. *Times of India*, 12 April 1894.

46. Dwijendra Tripathi, 'Parsees and the United States through some Unused Documents', *Indian Archives*, Vol. XXX, No. 1 (January–June 1981), pp. 52–68.

47. Harris, *Jamsetji*, pp. 118–45.

27

Challenging European Monopolies

The Story of Scindia Shipping

N.G. Jog

The formidable challenges faced by Indian entrepreneurs when trying to enter European preserves is best illustrated in the story of shipping, a sector that remained monopolized by British companies from the mid-nineteenth century till the inter-war years. Much of eastern shipping was controlled by the powerful British India Steam Navigation Company (BI), which had become the largest British shipping group after its merger with Pacific and Orient (P&O) Steamship Company. By 1914, the combined fleet of BI and P&O, under the control of James Lyle Mackay (Lord Inchcape), accounted for 10 per cent of the world's entire shipping tonnage.* Such was the dominance of British shipping that even in 1918 no more than 10 per cent of India's coastal trade and just about 2 per cent of its foreign trade was under Indian shipping companies.† Attempts in the early twentieth century by entrepreneurs such as Jamsetji Tata to enter the sector had been foiled due to the fierce rate cutting and ruthless competition to which they

* For a history of the company, see Lionel Carter, *Chronicles of British Business in Asia, 1850–1960: A Bibliography of Printed Company Histories with Short Accounts of the Concerns* (New Delhi, Manohar, 2002), pp. 17–20. On the Inchcape empire, see Stephanie Jones, *Trade and Shipping, Lord Inchcape, 1852–1932* (Manchester, Manchester University Press, 1989). On the vast empire of William Mackinnon which was the 'world's largest maritime conglomerate' in the nineteenth century, see Forbes Munro, *Maritime Enterprise and Empire: Sir William Mackinnon and His Business Network* (Suffolk, Boydell & Brewer, 2003). On the history of Indian shipping, see Radhakumud Mookerji, *Indian Shipping: A History of the Sea-borne Trade and Maritime Activity of the Indians from the Earliest Times 1884–1964* (Bombay, Orient Longman, 1957) and K. Sridharan, *A Maritime History of India* (Delhi, Publications Division, 1965).

† Daniel R. Headrick, *The Tentacles of Progress: Technology Transfer in the Age of Imperialism, 1850–1940* (New York, Oxford University Press, 1988), p. 368.

were subjected. Thus even at the end of World War I, shipping was a fiercely guarded European preserve.

Only in the inter-war years was this monopoly challenged. This story is recounted in this excerpt written by N.G. Jog and published by Scindia Steam Navigation Company in celebration of its golden jubilee in 1969. It looks at two 'nationalist entrepreneurs' and their ship named *Loyalty*. The first of the two was Walchand Hirachand, who discovered that the Maharajah of Gwalior was selling his ship for 25 lakh rupees in 1919. The second was Narrotam Morarjee, a leading textile magnate of Bombay. Both were 'primarily businessmen' who consciously decided to 'hitch the Scindia wagon on the star of nationalism'. In their nationalism-inspired scurry to establish the first Indian-owned steam shipping company, the biggest ambivalences surrounded the naming of the ship itself. The name chosen was *Loyalty* but the vital question was: 'to whom'? The British government? The national cause? Or the company's own interests? Thereafter, the maiden voyage is described as one which raised 'an emotional upsurge' not only for the passengers but also for the hundreds of people who had thronged the docks just to catch a glimpse of the first 'Indian' ship voyage to the metropole. However, it was not always fair sailing for *Loyalty*, especially since various British shipping interests were exerting subtle and/or overt measures to counter its success. Nonetheless, *Loyalty* heralded a new era in Indian shipping and marked a milestone in the entry of Indians into this mercantile sector.

The Arabian Sea and the Bay of Bengal had become a vast graveyard of Swadeshi shipping enterprises when the Scindia Steam Navigation Company Ltd. was founded in 1919. During the previous decade no Indian concern had dared to throw the gage to the powerful B.I. and P. & O. combine which, since 1914, was ruled by Lord Inchcape. During the war years (1914–18) no shipping company could be started for obvious reasons, though they proved a boom period for Indian industry. Vast fortunes were made and were seeking new avenues of investment. Indian capital and enterprise had established themselves in jute and textile, iron and steel, even mining and plantations. Only shipping had remained a close preserve of British interests and bade fair to do so permanently.

Since the war, the patriotic fervour of the country had developed a strong economic flavour. Impressed by the generous contribution of the people to the war effort and especially by the bravery of Indian soldiers, the Government of India also was inclined to modify a little its imperialist policy. Even before the Montford political reforms were introduced, the Industrial Commission had recommended in its report (1918) that the Government should initiate "a policy of energetic intervention in industrial affairs." Though its implementation was far away, it was no small gain that the Government had recognised the need to assist the industrialisation of the country. It provided just the incentive needed by Indian entrepreneurs.

The year 1919 provided a suitable setting for the entry of the Scindias on the Indian maritime scene. It cannot be said that the establishment of the company was the outcome of conscious planning or concerted thought, let alone feasibility studies by experts, which are the fashion nowadays. They would surely have disfavoured the formation of any Indian shipping venture. Scindias owe their birth to a stroke of inspiration, a moment of illumination, almost to an accident of history. No shadow was allowed to fall between the thought and the action, between the idea and its implementation. It was a veriest chance meeting between Walchand Hirachand and one Watson, a British engineer, during the former's railway journey from Delhi to Bombay on February 16, 1919, that disclosed to him that a passenger ship was for sale in Bombay. It was the s.s. "Loyalty" owned by the Maharaja Madhavrao Scindia of Gwalior. He had purchased it during the war from the Canadian Pacific Line; he transformed it into a hospital ship and put it into service of the Army at his own cost. When the war ended, the Government of India allowed the Maharaja to dispose of the ship as he liked. He was prepared to sell it for Rs. 25 lakhs (half of it as down payment) to the first bidder.

Why not make a bid for it?—it suddenly struck Walchand. After getting down in Bombay he proceeded straight from the Victoria Terminus station to the dock to have a look at the "Loyalty". His knowledge as a valuer of ships was nil. But he had native horse sense and a flair for business. After inspecting the ship, he drove to the office of Narottam Morarjee, the leading textile magnate of Bombay, who alone had the means, vision and daring to support such an ambitious proposition in those days. Narottam and Walchand decided to form a syndicate forthwith to buy the "Loyalty" and to establish a limited company to run it. Sir (then Mr.) Lalubhai Samaldas and Kilachand Devchand joined the Syndicate and the "Loyalty" changed ownership before February was over. Rarely before or after have Indian entrepreneurs shown such speedy execution of a project. Within another month, on March 27, 1919, the Scindia Steam Navigation Company Ltd. was registered with an authorised capital of Rs. 4.5 crores. The Managing Agency of Scindias was in the hand of Narottam Morarjee and Company, a new concern constituted of Narottam and two members of the Morarjee Goculdas family. The three other members of the Syndicate had also a share in the profits of the Managing Agency, though they were not its members. On the ninth day thereafter, on April 5, 1919, the s.s. "Loyalty" sailed from Bombay as an Indian passenger ship bound for Europe and the U.K. It was a historic day in India's maritime annals, the day on which our national shipping was reborn! Appropriately, since 1964, April 5, is celebrated annually as India's National Maritime Day.

Let us pause here and have a look at the two men who, almost unwittingly, ushered in a great national enterprise. We cannot say of Scindia what Seeley has said of the British Empire, that it was founded in a fit of absent-mindedness. For whatever Narottam and Walchand were, they could never be accused of ever being absentminded. Alertness and the instinct to seize an opportunity by the forelock was bred in their bones. Narottam Morarjee, the first chairman of Scindias, was the son of the illustrious Morarjee Goculdas, whose family firm owned textile mills in Bombay and Sholapur, and was well-known for its philanthropy. Narottam's greatgrandfather once owned sailing vessels which operated between Porbandar and other Gujarat ports. In a sense, therefore, Narottam was resuming his ancestral avocation. Owing to Morarjee's premature death, young Narottam was entrusted to the care of tutors and guardians of the standing of Sir Narayan Chandavarkar and Gopal Krishna Gokhale, Guru of Mahatma Gandhi. His contact with them broadened his mind and implanted in him a national outlook.

After he left college, Narottam joined his father's firm, Messrs. Morarjee Goculdas and Company, Merchants and Mill Agents. Under his management the firm attained high prestige and prosperity. Narottam's standing in the commercial and industrial world was evident from the fact that he became one of the founder directors of the Tata Iron and Steel Company. Soft-spoken and cultured, Narottam was one of nature's own gentlemen. Fortune and fame smiled on him, but he always remained the same unassuming person.

No greater contrast to Narottam could be imagined than Walchand Hirachand. Unlike the former, he was a self-made man. His family originally hailed from Saurashtra, but it had settled for two generations in Sholapur in Maharashtra. Walchand was thus an unusual combination of Gujarati and Maharashtrian traits. His Gujarati instinct for business was blended with Maratha vigour. He won his first fortunes as a military and railway contractor. Though he was a layman, he executed huge projects like the Bhore Ghat tunnelling on the Bombay-Poona railway line and the Bombay Reclamation.

He was a man with vision and drive and the ambition of industrialising his motherland possessed him early in his life. Quick of wit and sharp of tongue, Walchand brooked no opposition where the national interests were concerned.

These two men—each in many ways complemented the other—made a capital team. It was joined by Lalubhai Samaldas, who was a pioneer in the field of co-operation and served for a period as an Executive Councillor to the Governor of Bombay, and Kilachand Devchand who was known as the "Rice King" of Bombay. The Members of the Syndicate along with Ratansi D. Morarjee formed Scindia's first Board of Directors, which was later joined by F. E. Dinshaw, partner of Messrs. Payne and Co., Solicitors, C. E. Randle of the Bank of Baroda and A. J. Raymond of Messrs. E. D. Sassoon & Co. Narottam, with an unerring knack of finding the right man for the right job, appointed Mansukhlal A. Master as General Manager of the Company. Though trained for the law, Master devoted his knowledge, talent and energies to the services of Scindias and the advancement of Indian shipping.

Narottam and Walchand were primarily businessmen and they never dabbled in politics. But their sympathies were entirely with the Indian National Congress and they were not afraid of openly evincing them whenever the occasion arose. Though it was the fashion—and the safe course—then for any new concern to seek the patronage of British rulers and high officials, Narottam and Walchand made a firm decision to hitch the Scindia wagon to the star of nationalism. They must have been fully aware of the risks they were running, but they despised the slavish mentality then prevalent among businessmen. In the words of Dr. Rajendra Prasad, they were "prepared to suffer the disappointments and temporary setbacks and failures with the vicissitudes of the national movement until the day of liberation."

This identification with nationalism was not confined to business. It extended to the personal relations of Narottam and Walchand with Congress leaders. Gandhiji had always a soft corner for Narottam Morarjee, whose family, like his, hailed from Porbandar. Even after Narottam's death, he occasionally stayed in Bombay as a guest of Shantikumar and Sumati—the son and daughter-in-law of Narottam—and Directors of Scindias—in their Juhu house. His personal effects are still preserved with veneration by them. They courageously gave refuge to underground workers during the Quit India movement. Walchand, on his part, had established a rapport with Sardar Patel who was always a good friend of Scindias.

This association of Scindias with national leaders may seem a great asset today. But it

BALANCE SHEET AND **PROFIT AND LOSS ACCOUNT**

WITH

DIRECTOR'S REPORT

OF THE

Scindia Steam Navigation Co., Ltd.

TO BE LAID BEFORE THE

FIRST ORDINARY GENERAL MEETING OF THE SHAREHOLDERS

To be held on Saturday 30th October 1920.

BOARD OF DIRECTORS:

NAROTTAM MORARJEE Esq. *(Chairman.)*
The Hon. Mr. LALUBHAI SAMALDAS C. I. E.
KILLACHAND DEVCHAND Esq.
WALCHAND HIRACHAND Esq.
RATANSI D. MORARJEE Esq.
Sir D. E. WACH A Kt.
S. R. BOMANJI Esq.
C. E. RANDLE Esq.
C. A. LATIF Esq.

Managing Agents:
Messrs. NAROTTAM MORARJEE & Co.

Secretary:
Mr. MANSUKHLALA MASTER B. A., L. L. B.

Auditors:
Messrs. K. S. AIYAR & Co.
S. B. BILLIMORIA & Co.

Solicitors:
Messrs. PAYNE & Co.

BANKERS:
The TATA INDUSTRIAL BANK Ltd.
The BANK OF BARODA Ltd.
The EASTERN BANK Ltd.
The COMPTOIR NATIONAL DESCOMPTE DE PARIS.

Registered Office:
ISMAIL BUILDINGS, HORNBY ROAD, FORT, BOMBAY.

PRINTED AT THE "FORT GUNJA" PRESS, FORT.

FIRST ANNUAL REPORT
"...The Managing Agents, in view of the initial operations of the Company, decided to forego, as a special case, their full commission".

called for sterling patriotism and undaunted courage in the first thirty years of their existence. But then were they not out and out a national enterprise?

It was no surprise that with such a galaxy of able men at their helm and backed by Narottam's immense prestige in the business world, Scindia's capital was subscribed in no time at all, though Rs. 4.5 crores was till then the biggest amount raised by public subscription by any limited company—Tata Iron not excluded. Actually there was a scramble for purchasing Scindia's shares. The authorised capital was divided into 600,000 shares of Rs. 75 each (of which only Rs. 30 was called), 16,666 shares being issued as fully paid to the vendors.

Although the Gwalior Maharaja retained no interest—financial or otherwise—in the company, his name somehow came to be permanently associated with it. It is a curious association which has intrigued many, since Gwalior State was entirely land-locked and it had no maritime traditions or connections at all except perhaps a far-fetched one that a descendant of Kanhoji Angria, the famous Maratha naval Commander-in-Chief, had settled down in Gwalior. But if land-locked Switzerland or Austria could boast of a navy of its own, why should not the leading Indian shipping company sail the high seas under the appellation of Scindia? It is at any rate a designation which imprints itself on one's mind by its very unlikeliness. With half a century of stirring history behind them, Scindias may well ask today with Shakespeare: "What is in a name?"

Similar is the case with the name of Scindia's first ship, the s.s. "Loyalty", which was called the "Empress of India" by its first owners, the Canadian Pacific Line. It is customary to change the names of ships when they pass under new ownership. Why did not Scindias then change her name as they did of all their subsequent acquisitions? Incidentally, whoever later decided to attach the prefix "Jala" (meaning water) to Scindia's ships surely had a touch of inspiration. Today these "Jala-Kanyas" (water-maidens) sail the oceans proudly carrying the Indian Republic's flag to distant shores. Scindia's own house flag has a red Swastika in a white circle on a blue background. (The Swastika is an ancient Hindu emblem of luck.) "Loyalty" was an ambivalent name for the ship of an avowedly nationalist line. Loyalty to whom?—The British Government?—The Maharaja Scindia?—The national cause?—To the Scindia Company's own interests? Any inference could be possible according to the individual's inclination or fancy and perhaps it was best left as it was.

Before the s.s. "Loyalty" (g.r.t. 5,934) could sail, she had to be first transformed from a hospital into a passenger ship and certain other essential repairs and alterations had to be carried out. This was done expeditiously and the booking list opened. The announcement of her proposed sailing brought an immediate response. During the previous four war years civilians had great difficulty in securing passage and there was a long queue of British officials and their families and Indian businessmen and holiday-makers anxiously awaiting a berth on a ship sailing for the U.K. Scindias had therefore soon to close their booking. For Indian passengers the "Loyalty" had a special attraction but a number of Europeans too travelled by the ship, among them being the then Chief Justice of the Bombay High Court and his wife. Among the passengers were several princes—the Maharajah of Kashmir, the Maharajah of Kapurthala, the Thakore Sahebs of Limdi and Bhavnagar. Among the other distinguished passengers were Sir Chunilal V. Mehta, Mr. M. C. Chagla, Mr. Bhulabhai Desai, Sir Manilal

Nanavati and Mr. Mohan Amersey. Narottam Morarjee and Walchand Hirachand, of course, were on board, the former being accompanied by his son Shantikumar, a present director and then a boy of 17, going to Harrow for his studies. On the return journey the "Loyalty" had Dr. Jivraj Mehta as her medical officer.

Apart from those who had come to see off their friends and relatives, there were hundreds of people who had thronged the wharf simply to wish *bon voyage* to the first Indian passenger ship sailing to Europe. An emotional upsurge overtook passengers and onlookers alike as the s.s. "Loyalty" sounded the last siren, pulled up her anchor and left the shore of India. The minor inevitable shortcomings of the "Loyalty's" maiden voyage did not mar the enthusiasm of the passengers, who took occasion during the voyage to present a silver clock with a suitable inscription to the chairman. It is a treasured memento of the Morarjee family. Marseilles, the ship's first port of call, was reached on the eighteenth day and most passengers disembarked there. Certain urgent repairs had to be carried out at Marseilles which necessitated her detention there till May 7. She eventually reached Tilbury Docks in London on May 14, thus completing an historic voyage.

So far it was more or less fair sailing for the "Loyalty" as well as the Scindias. But both were soon confronted with problems and difficulties which it took all the ingenuity and resourcefulness of Narottam and Walchand to overcome. The ship itself had to undergo a thorough overhaul to secure Lloyd's "100 AI" certificate as a passenger steamer. This posed the first hurdle since no reputable ship-yard was prepared to undertake the job at a reasonable price and within a stipulated period. British shipping interests were none too-happy at this encroachment on their preserve. They exerted subtle pressures to dissuade ship-repairers from undertaking the job. Scindias had begun to experience the sullen lack of cooperation of Britishers from the very outset of the voyage. Even the British crew of the "Loyalty" had failed to display the requisite discipline and loyalty to their masters. Somehow, through the good offices of Kennedy, a former colleague of Lord Inchcape in his humble days, a firm was persuaded to undertake the repairs; but the estimate it gave was prohibitive. Scindia's technical advisers in Bombay had thought that the repairs in London would take six weeks and the cost would be about £10,000. The actuals were four times as much, thereby saddling Scindias with a huge liability and freezing their earnings, apart from dissipating a large part of the one-year exemption from the control of passenger fares and freight which the British Government had granted in respect of the "Loyalty".

Then there was the question of finding clearing agents to attend to the booking of passengers and freight. Once again Kennedy was prepared to assist Scindias, but a warning from Lord Inchcape to his principals, Messrs. Gellatley Hankey & Co., made him helpless. Narottam and Walchand had to become their own clearing agents in an alien land. These two men were not to be easily daunted. They rented another room at their hotel and opened a booking office. Passengers trickled in, but cargo was a different matter altogether and without sufficient cargo the "Loyalty" could not take to the sea. She needed a minimum ballast of 1,500 tons. Even those firms which had made tentative offers of cargo withdrew them under threats of established British shippers, who were determined to nip in the bud the incipient Indian challenge. The intrepid duo of Scindia directors rose to the occasion. They purchased 500 tons of pig iron and 1,000 tons of cement, loaded the ship with their own cargo and gave it the green signal. At last, the s.s. "Loyalty" sailed from London on her return voyage on November 1, 1919, with 352 passengers and a ballast-cum-cargo of 1,500 tons.

Scindias had made a daring debut in international shipping although at a heavy cost. They had bearded the lion in its own den. They had won the praise of their patrons and the plaudits of fellowcountrymen. They had served notice on all concerned that they had arrived. But as one swallow does not make a summer, one voyage does not establish a service.

The "Loyalty" managed to do a couple of more round voyages to Marseilles and Genoa but in view of the steeply rising cost of bunker coal and the depression in the shipping trade, Scindias were constrained to lay up "Loyalty" as it was more economic to do so. As a matter of fact, long before then, the Board of Directors had decided to sell the ship.

In the depression then prevailing it was not possible to find a purchaser for the "Loyalty" and she was laid up in Mazagaon basin under a caretaker. Her fast deteriorating condition made it inevitable that she would have to be sold for scrap. This was done on February 23, 1923, realising a measly amount of Rs. 1,35,250! The "Loyalty" met with a sad end, but her name is enshrined in India's mercantile annals.

Originally published as N.G. Jog, *Saga of Scindia: Struggle for the Survival of Indian Shipping and Ship-building* (Bombay, The Scindia Steam Navigation Co., Ltd., 1969), pp. 17–24.

28

Premier Industrial Centres
Bombay and Calcutta

Claude Markovits

Much of these industrial stirrings of the nineteenth and twentieth centuries occurred in the twin cities of Bombay and Calcutta where large-scale industry first emerged.* In the mid-eighteenth century, the colonial economy had three main centres—Madras, Bombay, and Calcutta—but by the end of the century, Madras lost out in status despite having been the oldest British settlement while Bombay and Calcutta were increasingly regarded as the premier ports and hubs of both political and commercial activity.

Historian Claude Markovits examines the unfolding of these two cities as business centres in the colonial period. The parallel saga is divided into three periods. In the first phase, from 1830 to 1860, Bombay rose to parity with Calcutta and witnessed an upswing in the trade cycle mainly due to a rise in the Chinese demand for opium and the export of cotton. The second phase between 1860 and 1920 is described by the author as the 'heyday of dual dominance' as Bombay's potential to rival Calcutta was severed because of the sudden end of the cotton boom and the differential impact of famines. Calcutta, however, had other advantages as it was the seat of the colonial government till 1911, hosted an overwhelming European business community, and was home to the economic prowess of the Marwaris. Both cities enjoyed dual dominance because of their control over jute and cotton and their dominance in rupee joint-stock and sterling companies. The inter-war period was a difficult one and this 'dual dominance came under fire', with a decline in foreign trade and high finance. Both Bombay and Calcutta were

* Of course, Ahmedabad also emerged at the same time as the centre of cotton spinning and weaving. On Ahmedabad, see Kenneth L. Gillion, *Ahmedabad: A Study in India Urban History* (Berkeley, University of California Press, 1968).

challenged by inland centres such as Coimbatore and Ahmedabad but managed to hold on to their 'corporate power' as groups based in them controlled companies in the newly industrializing interiors too. Markovits points out that it was the combination of World War II, colonial withdrawal, and the Partition that finally spelt doom for Calcutta, although it continued to maintain a slight advantage over Bombay in terms of corporate power until the 1950s.[†]

The twentieth century has seen a steady decline in the economic pre-eminence of the colonial cities of Calcutta and Bombay, though Bombay remains the country's commercial capital. Even though both Bombay and Calcutta have been included in the five cities selected by the Government of India in its Mega City project of the Eighth Five Year, they are being slowly overtaken in economic eminence.[‡] Cities such as Bangalore and Hyderabad, synonymous with the information technology revolution that has lately transformed India's economy, are being reinvented as the country's leading high-tech hubs and emerging 'informational cities'.[§]

Comparisons between Bombay and Calcutta as cities are a fairly hackneyed topic. However, a systematic comparison between those two metropolises, focusing on their role as command centres, has, to my knowledge, never been done. This paper is a very preliminary attempt at such an exercise. It draws attention, firstly, to the existence of a pattern of dual dominance in the Indian colonial economy, which is generally taken for granted but actually calls for some explaining. Possible counterfactuals existed. By the middle of the 18th century, the emerging colonial economy of India had three major foci, Bombay, Calcutta and Madras, and a tripolar structure was a distinctly possible outcome. Why Madras, which was the oldest British colonial foundation in India, could not maintain its rank, in spite of the consolidation of its hinterland brought about by the annexation of the Carnatic in 1801, need not detain us here. But we should keep in mind the fate of Madras, for, had not certain chance factors intervened, it could very well have been Bombay's: to become a backwater of Empire. Leaving aside the question of possible counterfactuals, the paper will focus on an analysis of the dominant couple formed by Bombay and Calcutta and of the changes it underwent over time.

In the first part of this paper I shall therefore examine the unfolding of what I call 'dual dominance'. The story clearly falls into three periods: from 1830 to 1860 Bombay rose to parity with Calcutta; then, from 1860 to 1920 we have the heyday of dual dominance, with

† On Bombay, also see other articles in Sujata Patel and Alice Thorner (eds), *Bombay: Metaphor for Modern India* (Bombay, Oxford University Press, 1996) and Mariam Dossal, *Imperial Designs and Indian Realities: The Planning of Bombay City, 1845–1875* (Bombay, Oxford University Press, 1991).

‡ The cities which have been earmarked for the Project are Mumbai (Bombay), Calcutta (Kolkata), Chennai (Madras), Bangalore (Bengaluru), and Hyderabad.

§ For the fascinating story of Bangalore, see Janaki Nair, *The Promise of the Metropolis: Bangalore's Twentieth Century* (New Delhi, Oxford University Press, 2005). On Hyderabad see Ratna Naidu, *Old Cities, New Predicaments: A Study of Hyderabad* (Delhi, Sage Publications, 1990) and C. Ramachandraiah and V.K. Bawa, 'Hyderabad in the Changing Political Economy', *Journal of Contemporary Asia*, Vol. 30, No. 4, 2000, pp. 562–74.

Calcutta as Number One, but Bombay as a close second; after 1920, as both cities went through the difficult interwar period, dual dominance, without being really challenged, found itself somehow eroded.

In the second part of the paper, I shall look for possible interpretations, focusing particularly on entrepreneurial responses. My hypothesis is that the better 'communal mix' of Bombay business, and in particular the lack of the kind of total European domination witnessed in Calcutta, was a major factor in Bombay's success, firstly at reaching parity with Calcutta, and then at maintaining it against heavy odds.

THE UNFOLDING OF 'DUAL DOMINANCE'

Even once it had securely displaced Surat as the main centre of colonial maritime trade on the western seaboard of India, by the middle of the 18th century, Bombay was nevertheless not in a position to compete on equal terms with Calcutta as a trading and financial centre. Its commercial fortune was largely linked, since the 1770s, to the China trade, with all the political and economic uncertainties this entailed, and it suffered from the absence of a rich and easily accessible agrarian hinterland, which was one of Calcutta's major assets. The successive annexations of Gujarat in 1800–03 and of the Maratha Empire in 1818 did not give it the boost which could have been expected, for they coincided with depressed conditions in the China trade and left unsolved the problem of better communications with the interior.

By 1820, even after the spate of annexations of the previous 20 years which had given it at last a proper hinterland, Bombay was still a fairly insignificant trading centre compared to Calcutta. In 1820/21 its merchandise export trade amounted in value to little more than a quarter of Calcutta's and its imports were valued at less than half Calcutta's.[1] The surplus of exports over imports was worth only a small fraction of Calcutta's surplus. Exports consisted mainly of cotton and opium[2] for the China market, which was then depressed. This depression persisted until the late 1820s. However, from 1830 onwards Bombay's trade entered a period of rapid growth and, by the late 1850s, the commercial importance of the city was comparable to that of Calcutta.

Bombay's Rise to Parity with Calcutta: 1830–1860

It is generally acknowledged that, prior to the railway age, there was no such thing as an 'Indian' economy; it was, rather, a congeries of regional economies loosely linked together, the major unifying factor being their growing subjection to British capital and to the needs of the metropolitan economy. In this context, 'dual dominance' is obviously not a relevant concept. We have to consider Western and Eastern India as two more or less separate economic entities within a nascent 'imperial world-system' of which the 'commanding heights' were situated in London, Liverpool, Manchester and Glasgow. Within this global system both Bombay and Calcutta can be seen as second-rank imperial cities, each having its own sphere of influence, with a limited amount of overlapping. Having very little industrial production prior to the mid-1850s, they functioned primarily as commercial emporia, draining the agricultural produce of their hinterlands and dispatching to the interior a growing but still limited quantity of imported manufactures in the fashion of the classical colonial port-cities. The only way to evaluate their respective importance is through a look at the statistics of the foreign seaborne trade.

It is therefore not surprising to find that a lasting upswing in the trade cycle was largely responsible for Bombay's surge of prosperity which allowed it to catch up with Calcutta and even, for a short while, to overtake it.

The upswing was mainly due to a rise in the Chinese demand for opium as well as to a growing tendency to ship the opium of Malwa through Bombay rather than through the ports of Portuguese India. The abolition of the Company monopoly of the China trade in 1833 stimulated that trade further. With the 'opening' of China by British guns in 1842, a huge market was securely offered to the enterprising Bombay merchants, the 'drug barons' of the 19th century. Before becoming the 'Manchester' of India, Bombay thus became its 'Medellin'. It also benefited from a renewed interest of the (original) Manchester in Indian cotton as the textile industry of Lancashire went through a period of quick expansion and found American cotton prices too high.

Between 1830/31 and 1860/61, the value of merchandise exports from Bombay increased sixfold and the value of opium sales alone increased more than tenfold.[3] The share of opium in the export trade rose from 25 per cent in 1830/31 to 42 per cent in 1860/61, that of cotton from an already high 36 per cent to 44 per cent.[4] The growing dependence of the Bombay export trade on those two commodities is striking. Although Bombay's exports in 1860 were 40 per cent higher than Calcutta's, the latter offered a more varied range with, besides opium and cotton, indigo and sugar being also significant staples. Bombay's imports increased only fourfold during the same interval, the major increases being in cotton piecegoods (which accounted for 37 per cent of all imports in 1860/61) and metals, while a new item, railway plant, accounted for over 6 per cent of imports, signalling the beginning of the railway era.[5] Thus Bombay had a considerable surplus of exports over imports, the magnitude of which clearly surpassed Calcutta's. The western-Indian city seemed to be not only catching up with the capital of Bengal, but appeared on its way to displacing it as the 'Urbs Prima in Indis'. At some point in the 1840s, its population overtook that of its rival and the Census taken in 1864, at the height of the cotton boom, revealed a population of more than 800,000, a fourfold increase since 1818 (Kosambi, 1986, 36). Most of them were recent migrants from the Konkan area of Maharashtra; there was also a considerable influx of traders from Gujarat.

However, the foundations of this new-found prosperity were fragile. Both the opium and the cotton trade were very speculative in nature and closely dependent on the state of the Chinese and British markets, and Bombay's communications with its opium and cotton-growing hinterland were still, in spite of some improvements in the state of the roads, both costly and subject to seasonal interruptions when the monsoon rains raged over the Western Ghats. In the absence of good communications with the interior, Bombay could not fully exploit its advantages as the natural 'Gateway of India' for European commerce, although a regular shipping service with England via Suez and Alexandria had been established in 1858.

The most promising development in the 1850s was actually the establishment of the first modern cotton-textile mills, but in 1860 their future was still far from assured as they struggled to carve for themselves a share of the Indian market in the face of fierce competition from Lancashire's mills. The beginning of the cotton textile industry in Bombay in 1854 preceded only by one year the starting of the first jute mill in Calcutta, and this synchronism in the use of modern machinery was eloquent testimony to the emergence of a structure of 'dual dominance' in the Indian colonial economy.

The Era of 'Dual Dominance': 1860–1920

In his compendium of the Indian Empire written in the early 1880s, W. W. Hunter remarked that, 'Calcutta and Bombay form the two central depôts for collection and distribution, to a degree without a parallel in other countries' (Hunter, 1886, 560), thus nicely articulating the thesis of 'dual dominance'. However, the reversal of the trend after 1865 must be noticed. While, from the mid-1850s, Bombay seemed on the way to displace Calcutta as the major centre, after 1865 it was never able again to clearly challenge the primacy of the capital of Bengal. The reasons for the re-establishment of Calcutta's supremacy have mainly to do with the political economy of colonial India, but conjunctural factors, such as the differential impact of famines and the financial collapse in Bombay consecutive to the sudden end of the cotton boom in 1865, have also to be taken into account.

But firstly it must be noticed that the last third of the 19th century saw some amount of real direct competition between the two cities. In the previous period, in the absence of an 'Indian' economy, there were very few opportunities for direct clashes of interests. With the advent of the railway age, it is generally acknowledged that the concept of an 'Indian' economy became more meaningful. Not that one should exaggerate the degree of unification of markets brought about by the construction of the railway network; in many ways both capital and labour markets remained segmented in colonial India; however, the railways eliminated the most glaring price differentials and stimulated the circulation of goods as well as men across the country (Hurd, in Kumar (ed.), 1983, 737–61). For three or four decades there was a certain amount of fluidity as the spheres of influence of the various centres underwent some redefinition at the margins. The birth of Indian nationalism during the same period also stimulated inter-city competition as the elites of both cities started to think in terms of the role of their own city in an all-India context and anxiously surveyed the progress of the rival city.

In the ongoing contest for supremacy between the two metropolitan cities of India, Calcutta's advantages were many. It was the seat of the colonial government till 1911, a not unimportant consideration since, in spite of its adherence to the Manchester school economics, the Government of India played a big role in allocating resources between regions, especially through the way it gave concessions to railway companies, and was particularly susceptible to pressures from Calcutta's overwhelmingly European business community. Calcutta had the largest concentration of European population and European capital in India; its European firms enjoyed particularly close links with the City of London, the financial hub of the world till at least 1914, and it drained Indian entrepreneurial talent and capital from as far afield as Marwar. It had easy communications with a vast agrarian hinterland extending from Eastern United Province to Assam, which produced most of the two major export crops grown in India, tea and jute, cotton having for its part never regained its shine of the boom years; and it had access to an abundant supply of labour attracted from this hinterland and even from as far as the Madras Presidency. It was close to the major energy source used in the 'modern' sector of the Indian economy, coal, which Bombay had to import from far afield. On the other hand, Bombay's area of labour recruitment was largely limited to Maharashtra (in particular the Konkan) and its indigenous entrepreneurial class came almost exclusively from Gujarat. As far as its European firms were concerned, they were less capitalized than their Calcutta counterparts, having more tenuous links to the City. The major advantages of Bombay over Calcutta were its better harbour and the shorter distance to Europe once the Suez route started being extensively used, which happened only in the 1880s.

A look at the statistics of the foreign seaborne trade reveals that over the 1871–1939 period Bombay on the whole trailed behind Calcutta but maintained a lead in the import trade. Table 1 gives five-yearly averages of exports and imports from Bombay and Bengal for 1871–1931 and 1934–1939.

On the basis of the data presented in Table 1, two major points need to be emphasized:

Table 1 Five-yearly Averages of Merchandise Exports and Imports from Bengal and Bombay (Rupees, million)

Period	Bengal		Bombay	
	Exports	Imports	Exports	Imports
1871–76	242	168	221	119
1876–81	302	192	225	154
1881–86	341	222	320	210
1886–91	375	257	370	275
1891–96	433	277	385	282
1896–1901	484	318	326	348
1901–06	589	375	438	332
1906–11	771	498	510	428
1911–16	924	621	580	522
1916–21	1,291	1,015	880	839
1921–26	1,302	902	1,027	908
1926–31	1,305	802	705	805
1934–39	735	427	332	583

Sources: Annual Statements of the Trade and Navigation of British India, Annual Statements of the Seaborne Trade of British India, for relevant years.

(a) that, with the exception of the quinquennial period 1886–91, Calcutta's foreign merchandise trade was always larger than Bombay's, though not by a very big margin. The situation prevailing in the 1860s had clearly been exceptional.

(b) that while, in the case of Bengal the curves of exports and imports were broadly similar, in the case of Bombay a certain disjunction is noticeable at various points in time, particularly in the 1890s when imports surpassed exports during one quinquennial period and after 1926 when the fall in imports was much slower than the fall in exports.

It seems useful, for the purpose of more detailed analysis, to distinguish between the trends in the export and in the import trade. In the export trade Calcutta's supremacy over Bombay was never challenged after 1870, a trend which reflected the increasingly crucial role played in India's export trade by tea and jute (both raw and manufactured) which were largely or exclusively grown in Calcutta's hinterland. On the other hand, Bombay's export trade suffered from the gradual disappearance of opium as an export commodity, from a fall in foreign demand for the short-fibre cotton grown in the Deccan, and from an increasing diversion of the export trade of Sind and the Punjab to Karachi. The most successful new item in Bombay's export trade was cotton twist and yarn which started being shipped to China in 1873 and by 1900/01 accounted for 16 per cent of Bombay's exports in value, overtaking opium and equalling oilseeds (raw cotton accounted for 28 per cent).[6] However, after 1905 this export trade petered out and the relatively good performance of Bombay's exports in the 1916–26 decade is largely to be attributed to high prices for raw cotton and a good market for it in Japan. The value of wheat exports also increased in the late 19th century.

The trend in the import trade is more puzzling and therefore deserves careful analysis. What accounts for the fact that, at various points in time, and particularly in the 1886–1901 period and after 1921, Bombay's import trade surpassed Calcutta's in value? Moreover, how are we to explain that its overall share in India's import trade remained more or less constant during the period under study while that of Karachi increased mainly at its expense, without supposing that this loss, which could not have been compensated in its entirety by a gain at the expense of Madras, must have somewhat been made up for at the expense of Calcutta?

Very detailed mapping of the hinterlands of the various ports in India at different points in time has to my knowledge never been done (see however Banga, 1992, for a recent attempt), which is of course a limiting factor. Networks for the redistribution of imported goods are much more difficult to analyse than those through which agricultural produce is exported; the latter are, so to speak, visible 'on the ground' and have also attracted a lot of attention from colonial officials. The former, which distribute a great variety of goods often in limited quantities, operate in a less obvious manner. For reasons of space, I shall limit myself to general remarks which are in the nature of informed guesses.

At a somewhat theoretical level, Bombay's capacity to increase over time its share of the import trade of India to the detriment of Calcutta has to be explained by having recourse to one of the following hypotheses: either an increase in the size of its hinterland at the expense of Calcutta's, or, if hinterlands were relatively fixed, growing income disparities between Bombay's and Calcutta's respective hinterlands making for greater consumption of imported items in the area supplied by Bombay (supposing an equal propensity to import in all regions, a supposition we shall make for convenience' sake and which is in any case not entirely unsubstantiated by available evidence), or widely divergent investment patterns reflecting much more rapid industrial growth in Western than in Eastern India. Let us examine each of these hypotheses in turn.

Change in the size of hinterlands could be either the result of the spatial expansion of Bombay's sphere of influence at the expense of Calcutta's or of a quicker pace of demographic growth in its existing sphere of influence. The latter hypothesis can be immediately rejected. Evidence from the population Censuses between 1872 and 1941 tends to show that the rate of growth of the population living in the zone served by Calcutta was marginally higher than that of the population living in Bombay's sphere of influence.[7] There remains therefore the possibility that Bombay's sphere of influence increased spatially at the expense of Calcutta's. Actually there is some evidence that, during the first phase of the railway era, c. 1860–1900, there occurred a certain redefinition in the hinterlands of the various ports and Bombay managed, thanks to the railway, to capture trade flows which were previously channeled through Calcutta. Given the fact that Bombay was closer to British and European ports than Calcutta, it could have made sense for an importer operating in interior areas which were more or less equidistant from both ports to reroute some imports to the Western Indian port. One has also to take into consideration the fact that, in the 1880–1916 period, there was a sort of rate war between railway companies serving the three ports of Karachi, Bombay and Calcutta (Hurd, op. cit., 753–4). Although its outcome is not very clear, railway statistics indicate that Bombay increased its share of the trade of the

United Provinces and Hyderabad State, two areas which in the pre-railway age were largely included in Calcutta's sphere.[8] So the pattern of railway development seems to have somehow favoured Bombay at the expense of Calcutta, and it had a greater impact on imports than on exports because the former were not subject to the kind of physical constraints which largely influenced the location of export crops. A change in the size of their respective hinterlands may therefore be the major explanation for Bombay's success in enlarging its share of India's import trade at the expense of Calcutta in the 1871–1901 period. Imports of cotton-textile machinery through Bombay also appear to have been always higher than imports of jute machinery through Calcutta, but the evidence of trade statistics is not enough to suggest widely divergent investment patterns in the areas respectively served by Bombay and by Calcutta.

During the following 20 years, while India's overall imports increased at a very quick pace, there was a reversal of trend as Calcutta regained some of the ground lost during the previous period and saw its import trade regularly surpass that of Bombay. It may be that this reversal was due to the changing fortunes in the rate war between railway companies, but I have not been able to test that hypothesis empirically. This was in any case a period of great commercial prosperity for India's two major cities, in spite of a certain amount of disruption created by the First World War.

However, since the middle of the 19th century, the economy of both cities had undergone some diversification as a sector of modern industry had developed and foreign trade can therefore no longer serve as the only gauge of their respective rankings. Bombay's cotton textile industry and Calcutta's jute mill industry were by 1914 largely comparable in terms of capital and output value while the labour force employed was much larger in the Calcutta jute mills than in the Bombay cotton mills (216,000 as against 110,000), reflecting the more labour-intensive character of the jute industry (Morris, in Kumar, 1983, 553–676). The two big cities then accounted for more than 50 per cent of total large-scale factory output in India.[9] In spite of the rapid development of the cotton-textile industry in a certain number of inland centres (Ahmedabad, Sholapur, Cawnpore) and of the location of the steel industry in Jamshedpur, the 'dual dominance' of Bombay and Calcutta over the large-scale factory sector remained basically unchallenged, especially if one takes into consideration that some of the largest factories situated outside Bombay and Calcutta had been set up and were controlled by Bombay or Calcutta-based firms (for example Tata Iron and Steel).

In the financial sector also, Bombay and Calcutta reigned supreme. They were the seats of the two major Presidency banks (the Bank of Madras operating on a much smaller scale) as well as of the exchange banks and most of the large Indian banks. By 1918, 83 per cent of the capital of all rupee joint-stock companies in India and 92 per cent of the capital of Sterling companies operating in India was controlled from Bombay and Calcutta (Goswami, in Chaudhuri, 1990, vol. II, 88). The respective shares of Bengal and Bombay were 43 and 40 per cent for rupee companies, 73 and 19 per cent for Sterling companies, the difference being largely due to tea companies which were almost all Sterling. Calcutta's largely European firms then controlled resources which were larger than those controlled by Bombay's mostly Indian firms, a fact which is not surprising, given the overall domination of British capital over the 'modern' sector of the Indian economy.

But it does not invalidate the thesis of 'dual dominance'.

'Dual Dominance' under Fire: 1920–1947

In the post-1920 period the dual dominance of Bombay and Calcutta over foreign trade, high finance and large-scale industry began to be somewhat eroded. At the political level, there was some shift in power and influence from coastal to interior areas, as exemplified by the rise of New Delhi as the effective capital of India in the 1920s and the emergence of the United Provinces as the main stronghold of the Indian nationalist movement. There were parallel trends in the economic domain: in a globally stagnant agricultural economy, the only region which continued to experience a significant growth in output was 'Greater Punjab' (Blyn, 1966). In large-scale industry, most of the growth of output occurred outside Bombay and Calcutta. After 1922, the Bombay cotton-textile industry ceased to grow and the 1920s and 1930s saw the rise of inland centres such as Ahmedabad and Coimbatore. Between 1920 and 1939 Bombay's share in India's cotton-textile industry fell from 43.9 to 28.3 per cent in spindles, and from 51 to 33.2 per cent for looms.[10] While Calcutta's jute industry continued to grow in the 1920s, although at a reduced rate, in the 1930s it actually contracted. The share of Bombay and Calcutta in global large-scale factory output had fallen to 30–35 per cent on the eve of World War II.[11] In the 1920s Calcutta did marginally better than Bombay but it was then more directly hit by the world depression which deeply affected the tea and jute sectors working almost exclusively for the export markets. In the late 1930s, however, Calcutta benefited from some investment in industry by large international firms, mainly British (Dunlop, Imperial Chemical Industries, BAT, etc.) and its industrial base started diversifying away from jute, while no comparable move was noticeable in Bombay. Calcutta's mostly Marwari firms also played an important role in the development of two of the 'growth' industries in India, sugar and paper (Bagchi, 1973).

In foreign trade, the most striking development was, within a much reduced volume of business, the relative buoyancy of Bombay's import trade as contrasted to its collapse in Calcutta. If one agrees with Bagchi that, from 1914 onwards, there was 'relative stability of the outlines of the hinterlands of major ports' (Bagchi, 1976, 253), how to then account for post-1921 developments? In the 1921–26 period, while Calcutta's import trade contracted, Bombay's imports continued to increase, though at a rate which was much slower than during the previous 20 years. Part of the explanation seems to lie in the exceptional figures for imports of cotton-textile machinery during that quinquennial period: they accounted for 5.9 per cent of all imports (as against 2.2 per cent in 1916–21 and 2.4 per cent in 1926–31). During the same period imports of jute machinery accounted for 2 per cent of imports through Calcutta.[12] Most of the machinery imported through Bombay was destined for Ahmedabad and other inland centres. In the following period, the contrast between Bombay and Calcutta is partly explained in terms of the unequal pace of development of import substitution in cotton textiles: by 1930, Eastern India was by far the greatest consumer of imported British piecegoods, while in the rest of India the market had been largely captured by domestic producers. Between 1930 and 1939, Lancashire lost most of its remaining Indian market, mostly situated in the Eastern Region, and by 1939 piecegoods represented only 7 per cent of all Calcutta imports.[13]

In 1939, although inland cities such as Ahmedabad, Cawnpore and Coimbatore had emerged as important industrial centres and were the seat of some fairly large business groups (Kasturbhai and Sarabhai in Ahmedabad, J. K. Singhania in Cawnpore), while Karachi and Madras had somewhat enlarged their share of India's foreign seaborne trade (in 1938/39 the two ports accounted for one-quarter of total imports and one-third of total exports) the overall dominance of Bombay and Calcutta over industry, finance and long-distance trade remained, in a reduced degree. The two cities were then more or less evenly matched in terms of corporate power. A survey of the largest 57 business groups operating in India in 1939 (Markovits, 1985, 192–3) shows that 24 Calcutta-based groups controlled 645 joint-stock companies with a total paid-up capital of over Rs 100 crores, while 16 Bombay-based groups controlled 131 companies with a paid-up capital of almost 60 crores. In terms of actual economic power, the two cities were more evenly matched than the figures suggest, for many companies in Bombay were undercapitalized and had very large fixed assets.

The Second World War spelt doom for Calcutta's economy which suffered from the proximity of military operations and the impact of the Bengal famine. Partition was the decisive blow from which the city never really recovered. However it retained its slight lead over Bombay in terms of corporate power till some time in the 1950s. In that decade, the government's decision to equalize freight rates on coal took away its last advantage over Bombay. The political troubles of the late 1960s led to Calcutta's final demotion from its status as one of the two major centres of business activity in India. Bombay has clearly emerged as the winner in the two-century-long fight for supremacy. Calcutta is today struggling to maintain its second place in the face of the rapid rise of both Delhi and Bangalore.

IN SEARCH OF AN EXPLANATION: BUSINESS CYCLES AND ENTREPRENEURIAL RESPONSE

The economic history of India between 1830 and 1950 has been characterized by large-scale fluctuations in the business cycle, some directly linked to international conditions, others more locally determined. Between 1830 and 1865, Bombay was the great beneficiary of the upswing in the opium and cotton markets, but in the next phase, lasting till the depression of 1930, Calcutta benefited by its proximity to the major producing zones of jute, tea and coal, which were the three major 'growth' commodities in the Indian economy. It would thus seem that Bombay's capacity to maintain global parity in the post-1865 phase was 'counter-cyclical' in nature. Why was Bombay over the long-term more successful than Calcutta at capitalizing on the upswings in the trade cycle? In the absence of a clearly interventionist policy by the colonial government aimed at redressing regional imbalances, the answer has to be found in differences in the behaviour of the business communities of the two cities.

Entrepreneurial Responses in Bombay and Calcutta: A Global Comparison

Measured by most conventional standards (capitalization, profits, value of output), the performance of business enterprise in Bombay and Calcutta does not seem to reveal major differences before the end of the colonial era. Calcutta business would even appear to have done slightly better. However, on closer examination, the achievements of Bombay businessmen over more than a century appear more impressive than those of their Calcutta colleagues, if one recalls the many advantages enjoyed by the capital of Bengal within the political economy of colonial India.

Bombay's ability to maximize its few advantages and minimize its many handicaps has obviously to do with the specific way in which its business community responded to opportunities and challenges. A very general comparison between business behaviour in Bombay and Calcutta would bring out a greater flexibility and a greater capacity for innovation on the part of Bombay businessmen.

They seem to have been better at adapting to changing trade conditions. Thus, although opium had been the mainstay of the fortunes of so many businessmen, the decline of the opium trade in the 1860–1910 period does not seem to have had a very negative impact on Bombay business. Most firms which had been prominent in the opium trade managed a successful reconversion towards the cotton trade or the cotton-textile industry; the number of casualties does not appear to have been very high. By contrast, in Calcutta the collapse of the indigo market in 1833 led to the demise of the major Agency firms which never went back into business.

The story of the cotton textile industry shows the same kind of flexibility. At first the Bombay millowners tried to gain a share of the domestic market in yarn and cloth but, faced with fierce competition from Lancashire and, increasingly from other centres in India, from 1873 onwards they turned to the Chinese market in a big way. In the 1880s, 80 per cent of Bombay yarn production went to China (Buchanan, 1934). However, faced with growing competition from Chinese and Japanese mills, they turned gradually again to the domestic market and, taking advantage of the Swadeshi movement of 1904–07, they reoriented their mills towards the production of cloth for the Indian consumer (Mehta, 1954). On the other hand in Calcutta the jute industry did not manage to carve a secure market for its products before the 1890s and, after a period of exceptional prosperity up to the First World War, was faced with a diminishing market due to the progress of jute substitutes (Chakrabarty, 1989). While the Bombay industry constantly introduced changes in layout and organization to adapt itself to changes in market conditions, Calcutta's jute barons remained faithful to fixed methods and refused to see the writing on the wall.

More generally, Calcutta business was less successful than Bombay's at shifting its activities to the domestic market, once external trade went through a prolonged depression from 1926 onwards. Of the major industries working for the internal market and, from 1930 onwards, benefiting from a varying degree of customs protection, only two, sugar and paper, owed part of their development to Calcutta's entrepreneurs, while cotton, iron and steel and cement were all three dominated by Bombay firms.

Apart from greater flexibility, Bombay businessmen also showed greater capacities for innovation. Most of the 'firsts' in the history of Indian finance and large-scale industry originated in Bombay: the first successful modern factory was Cowasji Davar's Oriental Spinning floated in 1854. Modern methods of financial promotion were introduced by the extraordinary financial genius, Premchand Roychand, who towered over the Bombay financial scene for 15 years (Rungta, 1970, 81–3). The first Stock Exchange, however rudimentary, was started in Bombay in 1875, while in Calcutta the Stock Exchange was formally constituted only in 1908. Bombay entrepreneurs were responsible for most of the technological innovations in Indian industry: thus the ring spindle was first introduced and adapted to Indian conditions at Tata's Empress Mills in Nagpur, a Bombay-financed and controlled company; Portland cement production was started by the Bombay firm of Khatau; modern steel production started in 1913 in the works of Tisco at Jamshedpur, another Tata company; the first large-scale hydroelectric schemes were promoted by the Tatas in the Western Ghats; the automobile and aeronautics industries were started by the great Bombay-based pioneer, Walchand Hirachand. The contributions of Calcutta entrepreneurs were less numerous and less remarkable: George Acland started the first jute mill in 1855, using an extremely rudimentary technology; Sir P. C. Ray pioneered the chemical and pharmaceutical industries at the time of the Swadeshi movement.

Although one should beware of exaggerating the contrast between the two cities and of romanticizing Bombay entrepreneurs, among whom were included the usual contingent of crooks and failures, the fact remains that over a long period Bombay business showed more dynamism than Calcutta's.

Race, Community and Enterprise: The Contrast between Bombay and Calcutta

Since Bagchi's pioneering study of 1970 (Bagchi, in Leach and Mukherjee, 1970, 223–56) drew attention to the contrast between the situation in Western India and in the rest of India, not much work has been done on the impact of race and community on business. However, I think it is in that direction that lies the most plausible explanation of the contrast between Bombay and Calcutta.

It has been often remarked that in Bombay relations between Indian and European businessmen were marked by less discrimination and less mutual antagonism than in Calcutta. To account for the difference, scholars have put forward two main explanations: firstly the fact that Western India was conquered by the British at a later stage than Eastern India, thus escaping the period of unabashed exploitation which cost so dearly to indigenous merchants in Bengal, and secondly the exceptional role played in Bombay by the Parsi community which was Indian but had a special relationship with the British. We need not go in detail into this problem here, but the situation in Bombay in the first quarter of the century is aptly characterized by Asiya Siddiqi who writes:

> there was, on the whole, little conflict between Indian merchants on the one hand and, on the other, European merchants and the Bombay Government. The Indian merchants, along with the members of a small group of European agency houses, with whom they were often intimately connected as brokers and business partners, formed a remarkably close-knit oligarchy which governed both the island and its overseas trade (Siddiqi, 1982, 305).

The close relationship between the great Parsi entrepreneur, Jamsetji Jejeebhoy and the British China-merchant, William Jardine, exemplifies that situation. During the same period in Calcutta, the dominance of the European Agency Houses was well established and their Indian collaborators were never treated as equals. When the Agency Houses collapsed in 1833, it was precisely the group of Indian collaborators who paid the heaviest price (Bagchi, 1987, 147–9) and the story repeated itself at the time of the crisis of the Union Bank 'which shook whatever confidence wealthy Indians in Calcutta had in their ability to collaborate with Europeans on profitable terms' (ibid., 223). The contrasting fates of Dwarkanath Tagore and Jamsetji Jejeebhoy, who were near-contemporaries, highlight the different way in which partnerships between Indians and Europeans worked in Calcutta and in Bombay.

By the middle of the 19th century, the contrast between Bombay and Calcutta was clear: in Calcutta Indian businessmen were excluded from the upper ranks of the business hierarchy and operated only as brokers, not as partners, while in Bombay partnerships between Europeans and Indians, mostly but not exclusively Parsis, were a common feature of business life, in the opium as well as in the cotton trade. In the promotion of banks as well, between 1840 and 1860 Indians were as much involved as Europeans (Bagchi, op. cit., 357).

In the post-1865 period, indigenous business in Bombay suffered in its turn from the increasing European domination of international shipping and trading networks, but it nevertheless managed to retain strong positions in some fields of foreign trade (in particular, China, the Middle East and East Africa) as well as in the cotton-textile industry. In spite of losing ground to Europeans (and Japanese) in the cotton trade, Indian businessmen in Bombay maintained an overall position of equality with the Europeans. In no sector of the economy was European business in Bombay capable of establishing the kind of oligopolistic control that a few managing agencies exercised in Calcutta over jute, tea and coal. On the eve of Second World War, the largest business firm in Bombay was an Indian firm, Tatas, with assets which were larger than those of the major European managing agencies such as Killick, Nixon & Co; Forbes, Forbes, Campbell; Wallace Bros.; and James Finlay & Co. Out of 16 business groups included in the above-mentioned survey, ten were exclusively under Indian control, four were British-controlled, but with Indian partners, one was Indian-controlled with a British partner (Associated Cement Companies) and one was controlled by a Baghdadi Jewish family (E. D. Sassoon & Co). By contrast, in Calcutta, out of 24 groups, 20 were under exclusive British control, one under American control (A. Yule), one under joint British and Indian control (Martin Burn), one British-managed but financially controlled by a big zamindar, the Maharajah of Darbhanga (O. Steel), and only one under exclusive Indian control (Birla).

Although most indigenous businessmen hailed from only one region. Gujarat, the ethnic and communal diversity of Bombay's business world was striking: it included merchants belonging to many communities of Gujarat, including the Parsis, the Hindu Vanis and Bhatias, the Muslim Bohras, Khojas and Memons, as well as businessmen from other provinces of India (Sind, Marwar), Baghdadi Jews (the different branches of the famous Sassoon family), non-British Europeans (the Swiss firm of Volkarts), Japanese (Toyo Menka Kaisha) and Britishers of various origins. The contrast was clear with the increasingly polarized and oligopolistic world of Calcutta where only two communities mattered: the Scots and the Marwaris. By 1914, merchants belonging to other communities (Bengalis, North Indian Muslims, Armenians, Jews) played only a minor role.

The polarization in Calcutta between the Scots and the Marwaris, the result of a symbiotic relationship which turned more and more antagonistic in the post-1914 period, had damaging effects on the fortunes of the city. The Calcutta Scots had become, in the second half of the 19th century, such an entrenched business community that they had taken complete control of trade in the three commodities which were the mainstay of Calcutta's prosperity: tea, jute and coal. During the same period, the Marwaris gradually replaced the Bengalis as brokers to the big European business houses in Calcutta (Timberg, 1978). The Scots behaved very arrogantly with their Marwari brokers who, in the jute trade, were an indispensable link to the rural areas, and did not form partnerships with them. The only way for the Marwaris to make a real breakthrough in the trade was therefore to resort to *fatka* (speculation) which they started doing around 1905 with a devastating effect on the spot prices of jute (Goswami, 1982, 143). As the Marwaris advanced from jute trading to jute baling, from there to shipping jute directly abroad and, after 1918, to setting up jute mills, the whole sector suffered from constant price wars which led to a very unhealthy situation. The racial arrogance of the Scots, signalled by their refusal to seek a compromise with the Marwaris, was partly responsible for the long-term decline of the industry in the post-1914 period. In the complex process of collaboration-cum-competition between those two business communities, they were both transformed. To fight European domination, the Marwaris were led to maximizing their existing assets, of which the major one was their skill at speculating. On the other hand, to prevent the growing inroads of the Marwaris into what they perceived as their preserve, the Scots increasingly relied on their political clout, which was however diminishing in a time of growing Indian nationalism. In the bargain they largely lost whatever entrepreneurial drive they ever had. Although the Marwaris emerged as the eventual winners, since by 1950 they controlled practically the whole of the jute sector and part of the tea sector, their victory was costly: they bought at highly inflated prices mills which were full of obsolete machinery, had a bad record of industrial relations and faced the problem of diminishing markets. They had wasted a lot of energy and money to control a declining business and in the process the whole of Calcutta's economy suffered since Marwari capitalists, too busy buying jute mills (and tea gardens) invested little in the more promising fields. There are many causes to Calcutta's post-1940 economic decline but the racial polarization of its business world is not the least of them.

Of course Bombay's business world was not the picture of harmony either. There were conflicts galore, especially in the difficult decades of the 1920s and 1930s. Racial exclusiveness and arrogance on the part of British businessmen was not unknown either, but the racial conflict did not dominate everything as in Calcutta. The conflict between the 'industrialists' and the 'marketeers' on the Bombay cotton market (Gordon, 1978) was not primarily along racial lines. If the 'marketeers' were all Indians, the industrialists were also in their majority Indians. Relations between Hindu and Muslim businessmen also appear to have been better in Bombay than in Calcutta. Bombay's active Gujarati Muslim business communities fully participated in the life of the various business associations, such as the Indian Merchants' Chamber, and a separate Muslim association was not created before the mid-1940s. In Calcutta, on the other hand, where Muslim participation in business was probably on the whole less important than in Bombay, but where there were a few powerful Muslim business groups (Adamji, Ispahani), a separate Muslim Chamber of Commerce was created as early as in 1932.

Less racial and communal strife in the business world meant a more rational use of capital resources. Businessmen belonging to various communities more easily formed partnerships in Bombay than elsewhere in India. Shareholding in joint-stock companies was more cross-communal in character there than in Calcutta.[14]

The conclusions I draw from this rapid study are mainly two: firstly that, within the common framework of a colonial economy, significantly different regional sub-systems can develop, depending on the specific curve of the trade cycle in different commodity markets and on the varying capacity of the local business communities to capitalize on the upswings; secondly, that over the long-term the particular ethos and 'communal mix' of the local business community can be more decisive than factor endowment in explaining the rise of a city. Thus, while Calcutta suffered a lot from being the sterile battleground of a racial war dividing its business community, Bombay benefited by a more dynamic atmosphere of emulation and competition. This is not to say that the kind of capitalistic development that Bombay has come to exemplify is morally appealing; it is after all the city of the scam. But, in terms of efficiency, it clearly emerged as the winner.

Originally published Claude Markovits, 'Bombay as a Business Centre in the Colonial Period: A Comparison with Calcutta', in Sujata Patel and Alice Thorner (eds), *Bombay: Metaphor for Modern India* (Bombay, Oxford University Press, 1996), pp. 26–46.

NOTES

1. The exact figures for Bengal were: exports, Rs 56,800,000; imports, Rs 22,500,000. See K. N. Chaudhuri, 'Foreign Trade and Balance of Payments (1757–1947)', in D. Kumar (ed.), *The Cambridge Economic History of India*, Vol. 2, Cambridge, 1983, Table 10.4, p. 828. For Bombay, they were: exports, Rs 15,500,000; imports, Rs 11,000,000. See *The Gazetteer of Bombay City and Island*, Vol. I, Bombay, 1909, Appendix IV, pp. 514–15. and Vol. V, pp. 518–19.

2. Raw cotton exports were worth Rs 5,200,000 and exports of opium amounted to Rs 3,200,000. *Gazetteer*, ibid.

3. In 1830/31, opium exports were worth Rs 6,300,000; in 1860/61 they reached Rs 66,000,000. Ibid.

4. Calculated from figures in ibid.

5. Total imports of metals were over Rs 12,000,000, some 13 per cent of the total value of imports. Calculated from ibid.

6. Calculated from ibid.

7. During the 1871–1921 period, the east zone, which largely corresponded with Calcutta's hinterland had an average annual growth rate of 0.52 per cent, which was higher than the rates of the west zone (0.14 per cent) and of the central zone (0.47 per cent), which formed the bulk of Bombay's hinterland. See L. and P. Visaria, 'Population (1757–1947)', in *Cambridge Economic History of India*, Vol. 2, Table 5.8, p. 490.

8. In 1888/89, railborne exports from Bombay to the United Provinces represented 6.5 per cent of total railborne exports from Bombay and those destined for the Nizam's territory accounted for 5 per cent of the total. In 1907/08, the respective shares of the United Provinces and of the Nizam's territory in Bombay's railborne export trade were 8 and 6 per cent. (Calculated from figures in *Gazetteer*, op. cit., p. 448.)

9. Calculated from M.D. Morris, 'The Growth of Large-scale Industry to 1947', in *Cambridge Economic History*, Vol. 2, Table 7.22, p. 641. Jute manufactures, entirely concentrated in Calcutta, represented 15 per cent of the net output of large-scale factory production, and cotton textiles 36 per cent, of which Bombay accounted for over 40 per cent. Assuming that the two cities accounted for approximately 50 per cent of the output of all other industries, i.e. around 25 per cent of total factory output, one reaches a total of 50–55 per cent.

10. See *Indian Textile Journal Jubilee Number*, 1940.

11. Calculated from Morris, *passim*. The share of jute manufactures in total output had fallen to 8 per cent, that of cotton textiles to 29 per cent (of which Bombay accounted only for one third).

12. Calculated from figures of textile machinery imports in A.K. Bagchi, *Private Investment in India, 1930–1939*, Cambridge, 1973, Table 7.10, p. 258 and Table 8.1, p. 273.

13. See *Annual Statement of the Seaborne Trade of British India, 1938–39*, Calcutta, 1940.

14. As comes out of perusing shareholders' lists included in P. Lovett, *The Mirror of Investment*, Calcutta, 1927.

BIBLIOGRAPHY

Annual Statement of the Seaborne Trade of British India 1938–39 (1940) Calcutta, CISD.

Bagchi, A.K. (1970) 'European and Indian Entrepreneurship in India, 1900–30', in E. Leach and S.N. Mukherjee (eds), *Elites in South Asia*, Cambridge, Cambridge University Press, pp. 223–56.

—— (1973) *Private Investment in India, 1900–1939*, Cambridge, Cambridge University Press.

—— (1976) 'Reflections on Patterns of Regional Growth in India During the Period of British Rule', *Bengal Past and Present*, Vol. XCV (I), No. 180, pp. 247–89.

—— (1987) *The Evolution of the State Bank of India. The Roots, 1806–1876. Part I: The Early Years, 1806–1860*, Bombay, Oxford University Press.

Banga, I. (ed.) (1992) *Ports and their Hinterlands in India (1700–1950)*, Delhi, Manohar.

Blyn, G. (1966) *Agricultural Trends in India 1891–1947: Output, Availability and Productivity*, Philadelphia, University of Pennsylvania Press.

Buchanan, D.H. (1934) *The Development of Capitalistic Enterprise in India*, New York, Macmillan.

Chakrabarty, D. (1989) *Rethinking Working-Class History, Bengal 1890–1940*, Princeton, Princeton University Press.

Chaudhuri, K.N. (1983) 'Foreign Trade and Balance of Payments (1757–1947)', in D. Kumar (ed.), *The Cambridge Economic History of India*, Vol. 2, pp. 804–77.

The Gazetteer of Bombay City and Island (1909) Vol. I, Bombay.

Gordon, A.D.D. (1978) *Businessmen and Politics: Rising Nationalism and a Modernising Economy in Bombay, 1918–1933*, Delhi, Manohar.

Goswami, O. (1982) 'Collaboration and Conflict: European and Indian Capitalists and the Jute Economy of Bengal, 1919–39', *Indian Economic and Social History Review*, Vol. XXI, No. 2, 1982, pp. 141–79.

—— (1990) 'Calcutta's Economy 1918–1970. The Fall from Grace', in S. Chaudhuri (ed.), *Calcutta, The Living City*, Vol. II, Calcutta, Oxford University Press, pp. 88–96.

Hunter, W.W. (1886) *The Indian Empire. Its People History and Products*, London, Trubner, (2nd edn).

Hurd, J.M. (1983) 'Railways', in D. Kumar (ed.), *The Cambridge Economic History of India*, Vol. 2, Cambridge, Cambridge University Press, pp. 737–61.

Kosambi, M. (1986) *Bombay in Transition: The Growth and Social Ecology of a Colonial City, 1880–1980*, Stockholm, Almqvist & Wiksell.

Lovett, P. (1927) *The Mirror of Investment*, Calcutta, Capital.

Markovits, C. (1985) *Indian Business and Nationalist Politics, 1931–39*, Cambridge, Cambridge University Press.

Mehta, S.D. (1954) *The Cotton Mills of India, 1854–1954*, Bombay, The Millowners' Association.

Morris, M.D. (1983) 'The Growth of Large-Scale Industry to 1947', in D. Kumar (ed.), *The Cambridge Economic History of India*, Vol. 2, Cambridge, Cambridge University Press, pp. 553–76.

Rungta, R.S. (1970) *Rise of Business Corporations in India, 1851–1900*, Cambridge, Cambridge University Press.

Siddiqi, A. (1982) 'The Business World of Jamsetjee Jejeebhoy', *Indian Economic and Social History Review*, Vol. XIX, Nos 3 & 4, pp. 301–24.

Timberg, T.A. (1978) *The Marwaris: From Traders to Industrialists*, Delhi, Vikas, 1978.

Visaria, L. and P. Visaria (1983) 'Population (1757–1947)', in D. Kumar (ed.), *The Cambridge Economic History of India*, Vol. 2, pp. 463–532.

29

'Towards Maturity'
Indian Business in the Inter-War Years

Dwijendra Tripathi

The inter-war years—stage three in Roy's periodization of the rise of Indian industry—were a time of expansion and diversification for Indian-owned industry. Indian enterprise increased its share of industry by challenging European monopolies in sectors such as jute and coal and by establishing industries in new sectors such as sugar, paper, shipping, engineering, chemicals, and air transport.* In this excerpt, Tripathi recounts the fascinating tale of some important business houses and charts their fortunes and trajectories during this critical period. He begins with the Tatas, who imbued with confidence because of wartime opportunities of World War I faced new challenges at the end of the war. Important 'turnarounds' had to be effected while the second-generation leadership of the Tatas ended with the death of Dorabji Tata in 1932, and the businesses were taken over by his nephew Nowroji B. Saklatwala and later Jehangir Ratanji Dadabhoy. Overcoming many challenges, the Tatas expanded to 14 major companies with combined sales of 280 crore rupees by the end of the inter-war period. Thereafter, Tripathi discusses the trials faced by the Birlas during the same period. He notes G.D. Birla's 'wait and watch' policy of the 1920s, and his initiatives to stir the group back to active investment in the 1930s. Despite not having as much investment capital as the Tatas, it was G.D. Birla who emerged as the most dominant voice representing Indian

* On this, see D. Tripathi, *The Oxford History of Indian Business*, p. 175. On the prosperity witnessed in Ahmedabad industry in these years, see Kenneth L. Gillion, *Ahmedabad: A Study in India Urban History* (Berkeley, University of California Press, 1968). On the jute industry, see Bishnupriya Gupta, 'Why did Collusion Fail? The Indian Jute Industry in the Inter-War Years', *Business History*, Vol. 47, No. 4, October 2005, pp. 532–52. Also see Gita Piramal, *Business Legends* (Colombia, South Asia Books, 1998) for the stories of Birla, Walchand Hirachand, Kasturbhai Lalbhai, and J.R.D. Tata.

business. Among other stories discussed in this excerpt is that of Lala Shri Ram who boosted his fortunes during World War I by supplying tents to the government and the army. After making massive profits, Shri Ram went on to acquire about 16 per cent in the Delhi Cotton Mills, a company in which his father Madan Mohan Lal worked as a secretary. Later diversifications were made into sugar, ceramics, light engineering, electric fans, pressure gauges, and railway signalling apparatuses along with sewing machines.† Amid stories of expansion and prosperity, there were also many which saw a steep decline in fortunes, especially in the textile manufacturing sector.

Others who are discussed in this excerpt are the Singhanias, Jamnalal Bajaj, Ramkrishna Dalmia, and Karamchand Thapar.‡ Despite many spectacular developments in both north and south India, Tripathi contemplates that even though the percentage of Indian-owned industry had risen, the structure and strategies of management remained virtually identical to those of the colonial masters.

EXPANSION OF OLDER HOUSES

The Tatas[1] unquestionably were at the top of them all when World War I ended. Imbued with confidence and hope, thanks to the wartime performance, the management of the house had to contend with new realities, coming in the wake of recessionary trends that set in after 1922. The textile companies in the group came under a great deal of strain in the face of shrinking profits, but they weathered the storm because of the vast domestic market for their products, coupled with the fact that they were among the best managed mills in the industry. Thanks to concern for minute details for equipment, labour welfare, and quality, all cotton companies in the group, with the exception of Tata Mills set up during the war, continued to pay reasonably good dividends during the 1920s—sometimes as high as 50 per cent—and set aside sufficient amount for reserve. The Tatas, however, had trouble with their 'war babies' which found it difficult to stand on their feet when the war-created crutches of demand crumbled down with the arrival of peace. Consequently, they were all wound up or otherwise disposed of one by one with the exception of Tata Oil Mills and Tata Mills, which maintained a precarious existence with the support from the sister concerns in the group and the managing agency firm. While Tata Industrial Bank was merged with Central Bank of India, Tata Construction was acquired by Walchand Hirachand. Tata's cement companies, launched slightly before the war, came under extreme pressure because of the emergence of a number of new units in north and central India, resulting in excess production

† For an interesting biography of Shri Ram, see Arun Joshi, *Lala Shri Ram: A Study in Entrepreneurship and Management* (New Delhi, Orient Longman, 1973). Also see Bharat Ram, *Reminiscences and Reflections* (New Delhi, Vikas, 1990).

‡ On Jamnalal Bajaj see B.R. Nanda, *In Gandhi's Footsteps: The Life and Times of Jamnalal Bajaj* (New Delhi, Oxford University Press, 1990); on Bajaj Auto see S. Budhiraja, G. Piramal, and S. Ghoshal, 'Bajaj Auto Limited: Transformation of a Giant', in Sumantra Ghoshal, Gita Piramal, and Sudeep Budhiraja (compiled), *World Class in India: A Casebook of Companies in Transformation* (New Delhi, Penguin, 2001), pp. 3–32.

and consequent fall in prices. The resumption of imports from Britain made the matter still worse. The cement manufacturers tried to solve the problem by setting up quasi-monopolistic, cartel-type agencies to regulate the production and distribution of their product. When all these devices failed, 10 out of 12 companies existing in 1936 decided to merge themselves to form Associated Cement Companies. The Tatas' cement companies were among these 10. The merger resulted from the tireless efforts of Framroze E. Dinshaw of Bombay, who himself controlled three cement units and was also responsible for the management of Gwalior Cement Company floated by the princely state of Gwalior, of which he was the financial advisor. He, however, did not live to see the fruit of his labour as the merger became effective a few months after his death.

The problem created by the post-war plight of the 'war babies' was nothing in comparison with the difficulties in which the Tatas' most prestigious undertaking, TISCO, found itself soon after the war. The genesis of the problem lay in an ambitious plan of expansion launched while the war was still in progress. Encouraged by the wartime performance, Dorabji and his associates decided to increase the production capacity from 100,000 tonnes of ingots to 420,000 tonnes of ingots—more than four times the original capacity. The wartime success obviously had an unrealistic impact on their planning or else their calculations could not have failed to take into account the impact of resumed imports on the post-war demand situation even if they could not foresee the impending recession. The 'Greater Expansion' scheme, should have been completed by 1921, but was delayed primarily because of the shortage of equipment, with the result that a large amount of capital remained locked up in facilities producing nothing. By the time the expanded plant became operational, the ground reality in the market had drastically changed because of the increased quantity of imports of steel products, cheaper in price and preferred by consumers. Consequently, while TISCO now produced more steel, it sold less of it. As an anxious R. D. Tata, Jamsetji's cousin and partner who was now the chairman of the company, candidly told his shareholders in 1924: 'We are rapidly becoming the dumping ground of the whole world.' The result was that the profits of the company plummeted considerably and its cash balance touched rockbottom.

It was, however, unthinkable for the Tatas to let the founder's most prized legacy languish or pass on to any other party. R. D. Tata declared that the company would not be allowed to die so long as he was alive. In concrete terms, he and his associates took three major steps. First, the company borrowed £2 million on the London market. This obviously was a desperate measure as the Tatas had never borrowed abroad, and would never do it again. Secondly, Dorabji pledged his personal fortunes to obtain a loan of Rs 100 lakh from Imperial Bank of India (set up by amalgamating the three Presidency banks in 1921). An additional loan of Rs 100 lakh was raised from the princely state of Gwalior through the good offices of F. E. Dinshaw, a prominent businessman of Bombay and the financial advisor to the Scindia durbar. And thirdly, the management stepped up its efforts to secure protection to the steel industry. The nationalist elements in the Central Legislative Assembly, constituted under the Reform Act of 1919, supported the Tatas with one voice, and the government perhaps still remembered the yeoman service rendered during the war by TISCO. Consequently, the company was granted a substantial bounty on steel rails in 1924; three years later, protective duties were levied on imported steel. Incidentally, steel was the first industry to benefit by the new industrial policy.

The loans helped the TISCO management implement another scheme of expansion, completed just before the Great Depression began in 1929. Government orders and protection also helped the company stabilize its position. Simultaneously, the company launched a vigorous drive to cut cost and increase efficiency through a series of technical improvements and better utilization of labour force. These included the increase in the blast furnace capacity, expansion of the size of open hearth furnaces, gradual substitution of foreign technicians by Indian hands costing the company roughly 50 per cent less, reduction in labour force, and better coordination between various departments.[2] As a result of these measures, TISCO succeeded in bringing down the cost of production substantially and thus compete with the imported steel. The onset of the Depression disrupted the process of recovery, but the management continued with the modernization, which helped augment output and diversify into new steel products. As TISCO had no real domestic competitor in the field[3] it was in a position to supply a substantial portion of demand for steel products in the country, raising its market share to as much as 68 per cent of the total quantity of steel sold in India. In addition, the company also captured a large market abroad for pig iron[4] which could be produced more cheaply in India. Buoyed by its success in placing its affairs on an even keel, the company launched another modernization programme to raise the capacity of the plant to one million tonnes shortly before World War II began. As the Indian steel industry continued to enjoy the benefits of protection, the risk involved in expanding the production capacity was much less than a similar exercise undertaken about two decades ago entailed.

While TISCO's fight for its own survival and growth during the inter-war period more than succeeded, the management's hope that their steel enterprises would induce the rise of firms engaged in ancillary industrial activities in and around Jamshedpur materialized only partially. Although several such firms were projected during the war or its immediate aftermath, only one actually came into being before TISCO ran into deep waters. This was Tinplate Company of India, floated as a joint venture with Burmah Oil company in 1922 to produce the basic material for manufacturing containers required for packaging petroleum and some other products. There was and remained for decades only a limited demand for tinplate in country and Burmah Oil Company consumed almost the total output of Tinplate Company. Tariff protection coupled with the installation of a capitalintensive plant, that required a relatively small number of foreign technicians to run, helped the company replace imports very substantially. Other steel-consuming ventures, projected or planned during this period, included companies to produce railway wagons, agricultural implements, steel wire products, cable, and enamelled ironware. Production of sulphuric acid from the TISCO by-products was also contemplated. Interlinked with product lines of TISCO, all these plans theoretically were in the right direction. But most of them were either stillborn or less than successful, because of the limited demand for their products.[5] Indian Standard Metal Company, established in 1936 to produce non-ferrous alloys and castings, had better luck. But by the time it came into being, TISCO had already come out of the woods. As a part of the strategy to create or help create a cluster of steel-using companies in the vicinity of Jamshedpur, the TISCO management also supported a Sikh entrepreneur, Indra Singh, in his industrial designs which, as we shall see later, would eventually catapult him into the group of twenty-largest business houses in the country.[6]

While the Tatas demonstrated exemplary patience and a great deal of fortitude in handling the affairs of their steel company during these years of crisis, they took recourse to a rather soft option to alleviate the post-war agonies of their electric companies which emerged from the war much less consolidated than TISCO. And the conditions became worse as the Depression hit the Bombay mill industry, the main users of power from the Tata electric system. One of the three companies was not in a position to pay dividend even to the holders of preference shares. Unable to reverse the process, the Tatas sold 50 per cent of their holdings in the managing agency firm to American & Foreign Power, a syndicate based in the United States, in 1930. The decision was severely criticized in the Indian business circles. G. D. Birla, who was slowly emerging as a rival centre of power felt 'perturbed' because the people looked upon the Tatas as a 'national house' while his friend and a director of Tata and Sons, Purshotam Thakurdas, conceded that the press and the public did not view the 'introduction of Americans with favour'.[7] The decision obviously tarnished the image of the Tatas, but preoccupied with their efforts to turn TISCO around, they thought it best to avoid another major battle. Consequently, their hydroelectric system would remain under a joint control until 1951, when the management reverted back to the parent agency, as stipulated in the original agreement with the American syndicate.

Soon after the joint Indo-American agency took over the management of the hydroelectric system, the second-generation leadership of the house came to an end with the death of Dorabji Tata in 1932. His younger brother, Ratan, had already died as early as 1918, and R. D. Tata in 1925. Jamsetji's sons left no issues. Jamsetji's nephew, Nowroji B. Saklatvala, who had closely worked with the founder, succeeded Dorabji as the head of the Tata empire and remained in this position until his death. The reversal of the TISCO fortunes and many other developments took place under his leadership. A part of the credit, however, must go to his key associates, among whom were his brother, Sohrab D. Saklatvala, and a much younger man, Jehangir Ratanji Dadabhoy (JRD) Tata. Son of R. D. Tata and his French wife, JRD had his education in France and had thoroughly imbibed European values and ethos before returning to India in 1924 at the age of 21. An eight-year-long apprenticeship with the steel company provided him with a great deal of insights into the intricacies of business. During the post-Dorab regime, he was treated as a critical partner in most of the decision making and thus was fully prepared to take over the leadership of the group when Saklatvala suddenly passed away in 1938. JRD was 35 years old then. His fellow directors elected him as the chairman of the group, in a fit of absentmindedness he often jocularly used to say.

Leading the house into air transport was JRD's major contribution. Civil aviation had already developed into an industry in the Western countries, but even as late as 1932, India had no air services. While a student in France, JRD had been fascinated by the flying device partly because of his friendship with the son of Louis Bleriot, the first individual to fly across the English Channel. Returning to India, he secured a pilot's licence, and undertook successfully a solo flight between Bombay and Karachi to demonstrate his capabilities. He then persuaded Dorabji to start an airmail service between these two major cities of the Presidency. This marked the beginning of the age of air transport in the country and also of

Air-India, which started as a division of Tata and Sons. The introduction of the Empire Mail Service by the government in 1936, under which first-class mails could be carried by air without surcharge, came as a boon to the young Air-India.

The Tatas' aviation venture, however, was yet to stabilize itself when World War II broke out. So was the case with another ambitious project launched by them after JRD came to the helm. This was Tata Chemicals, reputed to be the biggest chemical works in the country[8] at the time of its birth in 1939. The inspiration for forming the company was a suggestion made in a Tariff Commission report of 1929. India produced no industrial chemicals then; the country consequently was wholly dependent on imports for even basic inputs such as caustic soda, soda ash, and other soda compounds that textiles, glass, paper, soap, and many other industries required. Searching for an appropriate location, the Tata management accepted a proposal from the Maharaja of Baroda to set up their chemical factory at Mithapur situated near Dwarka on the seacoast in his state. The site selected was ideal because salt, the basic raw material was available in plenty at Mithapur, which literally means 'the city of salt'. But hardly had the first move towards launching the project been made, when the outbreak of World War II disrupted all the calculations of the promoters.

By this time, the Tatas had as many as 14 major companies under their control with combined sales of Rs 280 crore.[9] None in the Indian industry was anywhere close to it. A still more impressive testimony to the quality of their entrepreneurship was the fact that most of their companies were engaged in basic industries, requiring large investment and involving long gestation. The Tatas, without question, had become the 'first family' of Indian business by the end of the 1930s.

The Birlas who would later emerge as the Tatas' most formidable rival for supremacy in the Indian business world were still far behind. Late entry into the industries was only one of the reasons; the post-war environment was another and perhaps more important. The jute mill they had projected soon after the war faced a series of difficulties, partly because of the impediments created by the expatriates. At one stage an exasperated Ghanshyam Das Birla (GD) was even ready to sell the unit to Andrew Yule and Company. Things did not come to this pass and Birla Jute finally became operational in 1922. However, given the fluctuating fortunes of the industry after 1923—and the situation became worse during the Great Depression[10]—there was no question of the Birlas setting up another jute mill, even though seven mills under Indian control came into being during the 1920s—six near Calcutta and one in Kanpur—under the inspiration of the lead given by the Birlas and Sarupchand Hukumchand. The Birlas' cotton projects experienced somewhat similar problems. The mill he had acquired in Delhi soon after the war (named Birla Mills) had more teething troubles than GD had anticipated at the time of acquisition. However, the prospects of the textile industry in 1921—when the Birlas decided to set up a brand new cotton mill in Gwalior, lured by the offer of important concessions by Maharaja Scindia of the princely state—were still promising. Jiyajirao Cotton Mills, floated that year, was the result. Production started a year later. The post-war boom was still continuing, which encouraged the Birlas to add one more cotton mill to their expanding empire. This was the old Kesoram Mills, founded in 1877, which the Birlas acquired from Andrew Yule and Company.[11]

The economic environment was already showing signs of turning hostile at the time of the Kesoram acquisition. It became worse subsequently because of, among other things, the rising imports from England and Japan. But there were some favourable signs in the wind as well for the Indian cotton manufacturer. The universally despised excise duty on the production of Indian mills had been finally abolished in 1924. Bowing to the Indian pressure, the government gave some relief to the industry by imposing import duty on textile products, first on yarn and later on piece-goods. More importantly, the government finally conceded the principle of protection for specific varieties of cotton goods by imposing 5 per cent protective duty on imports from countries other than England in 1930. Subsequently, the duty was increased to 25 per cent on British goods and 33.5 per cent on non-British goods under the system of Imperial Preference introduced as a result of the Ottawa Agreement.[12] The wave of *swadeshi* too that swept the nation once again in 1930–1 in response to Gandhi's renewed call to boycott foreign goods served to prop up the sagging morale of the Indian cotton producer. Unlike the *swadeshi* movement of 1904–5, that had remained confined only to the urban areas, the message of the new agitation reached the rural masses as well who were the major consumers of the products of Indian mills. The rising preference in consequence for homemade products could not have failed to influence the demand situation.

The overall economic environment after 1923, however, was confusing and remained so until the outbreak of World War II. It was by no means easy to assess with any degree of certainty the meaning of these factors for the industry. Different entrepreneurs responded to the situation differently. While some, frightened by the uneven demand pattern, decided to reduce their operations or postpone their expansion plans waiting for better days to return, a few daring spirits expanded their production facilities in their bid to reduce the cost of production and thus the price of the final product. A substantial number of textile mills changed hands because their original owners thought it safer to concede defeat to the negative forces in the environment than to challenge them. Consequently, the industry had many new entrants, drawn particularly from the trading sector. There were others who intensified their sales drive. Nobody probably knew what strategy would mitigate, if not altogether eliminate, the rigours of uncertainty affecting the industry.

With short and limited experience in the industry, and with all their companies being still relatively young and not in a very healthy state, the Birlas must have felt it imprudent to risk expansion of their industrial net under these conditions. An attitude of calculating caution, that a long association with commercial pursuits normally generates, probably had a preponderant influence on their investment decisions. Whatever the case, there were no new Birla floatations for almost a decade after 1922, and Kesoram Mills was the sole acquisition.[13] Trading and speculation were the preferred preoccupation of the house until 1931, when a statutory change in the government policy stirred them once again into organizing new industrial concerns. This was the tariff protection granted to the Indian sugar industry in 1931. There was nothing like a sugar industry in India until then. Parry's sugar factories were all that the south had and Begg Sutherland and Co. with a few factories in the United Provinces and Bihar had a near monopoly on the production of white sugar in the north before World War I. Imports were free and the demand for white sugar in India was rather limited because of the Indians preferring the traditional variety produced in small *karkhanas*. Whatever quantity of white sugar India could consume was imported—the bulk being from Java. The number of factories went up during the war years when the imports virtually stopped, but most of them were small in size and functioned rather inefficiently. This is clear from the fact that in 1919–20, out of 22 sugar factories in the country, the total output of 18 was only 23,100 tonnes—a quantity roughly equal to the production of only three average-size factories.[14] Some half-hearted attempts made by the government to improve the competitiveness of the Indian sugar industry during the 1920s bore little fruit. The decision to grant tariff protection to the industry was a reluctant concession to the need for a more positive approach. In no time, new mills sprang up. New floatations came so fast that within a span of seven years between 1929–30 and 1936–7 the number of factories increased from 27 to 150, and by 1938–9 the industry was third in the Indian organized sector in terms of total capital and fourth in terms of fixed capital employed. In terms of the value of output, it ranked fourth behind cotton textile, jute, and iron and steel.[15]

The Birlas were among the first to seize the opportunity provided by the new policy. As if to make up for their industrial inactivity during the better part of the 1920s, they set up, one after the other, as many as five sugar plants within a short period of just two years between 1931 and 1933 in eastern UP and western Bihar where sugar cane was grown in abundance. Machinery prices had crashed in the wake of the deepening Depression the world over, which facilitated the task of the promoters of the sugar companies. The result was a very rapid increase in production, causing a mild glut in the market. To attract customers, the Birlas resorted to appealing to the nationalist sentiments of the consumers by emphasizing on the *swadeshi* character of their enterprise and quality of their product: 'Pure and Refined Swadeshi Sugar' and 'a sure rival to Java Sugar', proclaimed an advertisement issued by one of the mills. The strategy paid off as by the close of the 1930s, the Birlas were the third largest producer of sugar in the country. Only Begg Sutherland (nine plants, and crushing capacity of 6251 tonnes) and the Delhi-based Punjabi house of Gokulchand Narang (eight plants and 6900 tonne crushing capacity) were ahead of the Birlas whose five plants had a crushing capacity of 5400 tonnes.[16]

Their rising sugar fortune seems to have whetted the Birlas' appetite for industrial floatations. Sutlej Cotton Mills in Lahore set up in 1934 was one of these. But the most ambitious Birla venture of the decade was Orient Paper Mill, the brainchild of Braj Mohan, the youngest of the four Birla brothers. Registered in 1936, the company breached what until then was a European monopoly for, both of the two existing paper companies in the country, Titaghur Paper and Bengal Paper Mills, were under European control, the first under Andrew Yule and the other under Balmer Lawrie. Despite the fact that the industry had been granted protection as early as 1925, not many new paper-making units had come into being simply because *sabai* grass, the basic raw material, was never available in plenty. As a result of strenuous efforts of the European agency houses engaged in paper manufacturing such as Andrew Yule, Heilgers, and Balmer Lawrie, it became possible by the mid-1930s to produce bamboo pulp as a substitute for *sabai* grass pulp for making paper. A few Indian houses now seized the opportunity to take to paper production. The Birlas were among the earliest three of these (the others being Thapars and Bajorias) to enter the field. However, the production capacity targeted by the Birlas was much higher (about 11,000 tonnes as against about 8500 tonnes by Thapars and 3500 tonnes by Bajorias), next only to the largest paper makers in the country, namely Titaghur (31,000 tonnes), and equal to Bengal Paper (11,000 tonnes). Although the Birlas' paper company was yet to start production when the outbreak of World War II changed the entire business scene, the machinery from Germany had already arrived, which would stand the company in good stead during the war. A far more important initiative taken by the Birlas on the eve of the war was the launching of Textile Machinery Corporation (TEXMACO). This was the first step ever taken by an industrial group to reduce India's total dependence on Britain for textile machinery.[17] However, the Birlas' plant in Calcutta was requisitioned by the government for war purposes shortly after it became operational. The commencement of textile machinery manufacturing, therefore, would wait until after the end of the war.

With the exception of TEXMACO, all the other companies of the Birlas were in consumer goods industries that required relatively low investment. So, even though they were not far behind the Tatas in respect of the total number of companies under their management on the eve of the war (11), in terms of capital invested in these companies, they still had a long way to go. And yet it was G. D. Birla, and not anyone from the Tatas, who emerged as the most dominant voice of the Indian business during this period. This was largely due to his efforts to organize the disparate indigenous elements under a common platform and the close links he had forged with the leaders of the freedom movement, especially Gandhi. He, however, pursued a very balanced course, as we shall see later, to make sure that he did not unduly offend the expatriates or alienate the government. His contemporary Walchand Hirachand's nationalism had little regard for such sophistication. Belonging to a Gujarati Jain family, Walchand had grown up in Sholapur where his ancestors[18] were engaged in trading and moneylending, far away from the place of their origin in the princely state of Idar (now a part of Gujarat). His father, Hirachand, had selling agencies of a few textile mills at Sholapur, including the units set up by the famous Bhatia millowners of Bombay, Morarjee Gokuldas. During his youth as student at Bombay and Poona, Walchand had come under the influence of nationalist propaganda; the speeches and writings of leaders like Dadabhai Naoroji and Mahadeo Govind Ranade, the torchbearers of Indian nationalism then, had left a great impression on him. Intense nationalism was thus ingrained in Walchand's character from a very early stage of his life.

Hirachand would have expected his son to join him in the trade and agency business, but Walchand decided to explore other possibilities. In the process, he first took up a contract to supply fuel material to a Sholapur mill, but soon moved on to railway construction in partnership with one Laxman Phatak who, as a former railway employee, had some idea of the railways' requirements. So successfully did the partners complete their very first project, undertaken in 1903, that they did not have to worry about future assignments. By 1912 the Walchand-Phatak partnership had become a well-established and prosperous firm. World War I created more jobs for them and brought greater prosperity. By the time the war ended, Walchand in his own right had become a man of some means, developed a great deal of confidence in himself, and built up a sizeable business that his father and small traders in Sholapur had never dreamt of. With the new experience and self-made capital, he was now ready to exploit new opportunities.

[...]

Though Scindia received Walchand's best attention during the inter-war years, he never neglected his original business of construction nor shut his eyes to other possibilities. Soon after the end of World War I, he joined hands with the Tatas to float Tata Construction Company, with which his construction firm, Walchand Phatak and Co. was merged. Though he held only a minority interest in Tata Construction, Walchand emerged as the most dominant figure in its management because of his understanding of this line of business. Tata Construction took over the business of Marshland Price and Company in 1920 and acquired a Calcutta-based firm which manufactured cement pipes under a process developed by an Australian, Walter Reginald Hume. This became the precursor of what eventually emerged as Indian Hume Pipe Company in 1926—a subsidiary of Tata Construction. Two more subsidiaries were formed the same year—Hindustan Construction Company, to build dams, tunnels, bridges, canals, airfields, ports, factory buildings, etc., and All India Construction Company, to undertake projects in Sind and the North-West Frontier Province. By this time, Walchand himself had become the managing director of Tata Construction. The Tatas in the meantime were losing interest in the construction line, preoccupied as they were with the affairs of their more prestigious concerns like Tata Steel and Tata Hydroelectric System, and sold off their interest to Walchand. The company was now renamed Premier Construction Company with its headquarter in the imposing Construction House that Walchand built in the Ballard Estate area of Bombay.

Walchand, in the meantime, had diversified into sugar production, taking advantage of the protection granted to the industry in 1932. His Ravalgaon Sugar Farm Limited had its factories in a village of the same name situated near Girna Canal in Nasik district where Walchand had bought a huge piece of land at a throwaway price several years ago. For a decade after its acquisition, the property had been used for sundry purposes like cultivating commercial crops, such as cotton, sugarcane, and groundnut, or ginning cotton and making jaggery. After launching into sugar production, Walchand and his two brothers, Lalchand and Gulabchand, developed it into 'one of the best equipped and most efficient sugar farm in India'. Named as Walchandnagar by Lalchand, the Ravalgaon complex grew its own sugarcane under the supervision of competent agricultural experts trained in Java and Australia, the-then leading sugar-producing countries. The sugar produced at the farm was transported to the distribution centres by means of the most modern infrastructural facilities, including a 40-kilometre-long light railway track connecting the factory site with the nearest railway station. Apart from sugar production, Walchandnagar became a home for a number of ancillary industries by 1939.

Walchand was a dreamer and he initiated, during the 1930s, projects to manufacture cars and aircraft and launched an airline—projects that to less daring spirits must have appeared as foolhardiness. However, effective steps to operationalize them were taken only after the outbreak of World War II. We would, therefore, deal with these projects in a later chapter. Perhaps the prosperity of his construction companies and the Walchandnagar industries made it possible for him to dream wild dreams, even if his shipping ventures continued to fight for existence. Laxmanrao Kirloskar,[19] his contemporary and like him, imbued with nationalist pride, though less flamboyant in its expression, had no such cushion. Although

Kirloskarwadi—a well-integrated and modern factory complex at a site gifted by his erstwhile classmate and later the head of the princely state of Aundh (which now forms a part of Satara and Sangli districts of Maharashtra)—had already developed before World War I, his product lines still consisted of mainly two items, improved iron plough and shaft cutter, when the war came. In the wake of the rising demand for raw cotton, from the Indian textile industry, demand for Kirloskars ploughs also went up, but so did the cost of inputs such as steel, colour, and oil. Kirloskar Brothers, therefore, could make only modest profit during the war. Neverthless, they were in a much better shape at the end of the war, by which time the total capital invested at Kirloskarwadi had gone up to a figure of Rs 5 lakh. With a view to generating more capital to finance their expansion plans, Kirloskar Brothers, a partnership firm until then, was converted into a public limited company in 1920. Kirloskar Sons and Co., consisting of Laxmanrao, his brothers, relatives, and son Shantanu, would be the managing agents of the company.

With their improved financial position, the Kirloskars launched a vigorous programme of expansion and diversification soon after peace returned. New products such as a drilling machine, windlasses, draw pulleys (to facilitate drawing of water from wells for irrigation), a groundnut decorticator, and a vastly improved plough were put into the market. However, the most impressive additions to the product lines in the 1920s were a diesel engine and a centrifugal pump which would reduce the farmer's dependence on the slow, traditional methods for drawing well water for irrigation. Most of these products were developed by Laxmanrao himself—a self-trained engineer. But their quality was such that an American engineer, who happened to see Kirloskars' engines and pumps at an agricultural exhibition in Poona, could hardly believe that such sophisticated equipment could be produced by Indians. After 1926, Laxmanrao had his eldest son, Shantanu, to help him in technical as well as managerial aspects of the business. Shantanu had an engineering degree from the prestigious Massachusetts Institute of Technology (MIT) in the United States. He used his knowledge and skill to develop a new and improved model of the diesel engine. He also developed a special type of sugarcane crusher under the brand name 'Kamal'. In the meantime, the production system was thoroughly streamlined with a view to making it more effective and efficient. These measures, along with a vigorous publicity programme, brought about a much needed stability in the Kirloskar operations during the 1920s.

The Depression, however, destabilized the Kirloskars once again. There were less and less buyers, and less and less things to produce. Their customers were farmers whose purchasing power the Depression had particularly curbed. As a result, the production of ploughs had to be stopped, stocks of 'Kamal' remained unsold, and a substantial part of the production capacity had to be kept idle. To meet the situation, the Kirloskars set up facilities for producing nuts and bolts, but could not compete with the imported products. They then experimented with sundry goods such as lathes, looms, and gas plants and steel furniture. They also undertook the production of body-building materials for commercial vehicles. These products had some demand among urban consumers whose buying capacity had been impaired much less. To meet the challenge of the buyers' market the firm also launched a vigorous marketing campaign led by Shantanu who traversed, at great personal discomfort, through a large part of the country to convince the farmers to buy the iron ploughs and cane crushers, offering, among other things, after-sales service as an incentive. These measures, however, were sufficient to just keep the house afloat during those difficult years.

The Kirloskar's problems during the depressed state of the 1930s stemmed partly from the fact that their product portfolio was much too limited. Companies operating mainly in the engineering sector were at any rate the hardest hit. However, even the business groups that had their fingers in a variety of industrial pies, such as the one headed by Lala Shri Ram, also found it difficult to weather the storm. Though his ancestors, Punjabi Banias by caste, were among the original promoters of the Delhi Cloth Mills (DCM), founded roughly around the same time when Laxmanrao Kirloskar started his industrial journey, the Lala was still a backbencher in the Indian business world until much after the end of World War I.[20] This was so because the family holdings in the company were too small to give them even a semblance of control over its management, and they had no other business of their own. Shri Ram's father, Madan Mohan Lal, was the paid secretary of DCM whose job was to maintain accounts and share registers, arrange for the board meetings, and carry on correspondence on behalf of the company. The executive powers were vested in the managing director, as the company had no managing agents. Shri Ram never became a full-fledged secretary. Having tried his hand at a variety of minor commercial ventures, in none of which he particularly distinguished himself, he became, shortly before World War I to broke out, a sort of joint secretary, with the concurrence of the board, to assist his father. Shri Ram was 25 years old then and Delhi Cloth Mills, producing both yarn and cloth, had already achieved some measure of security, thanks largely to the impact of the *swadeshi* movement.

World War I boosted the fortunes of DCM still further—not so much through the sales of cloth and yarn but through the supply of tents that the army and the government needed in large numbers. The civil servants too needed tents, as their offices in Delhi, where the capital had been shifted from Calcutta recently, were still to be completed. To meet this demand, Shri Ram adopted a strategy that added to his personal solvency, while proving beneficial to DCM at the same time. He organized a separate 'tent company' in which the DCM had a 50 per cent stake; the remaining 50 per cent was shared between himself and a contractor, who had very close links with the government, on 20:30 per cent basis. The tent contract enabled the partners to reap great benefits. DCM's profits swelled to several times its normal earnings and Shri Ram emerged from the war as a man of some means and great reputation for his business acumen. More importantly, with the money earned through the army contract, Shri Ram and his father increased their holdings in DCM to 16 per cent by 1921 which was sufficient to give them the control of the company.[21] Thirty-two years after its birth, DCM thus became a fiefdom of its paid secretaries. The production facilities were expanded before the post-war boom ended, which along with the fact that DCM was the only textile producer in the Delhi-Punjab region, enabled the company to increase its sales more than three times between 1923 and 1929. After the Great Depression set in, DCM, like other companies, did feel the brunt. Still, both sales and profits of the company registered a net rise between 1931 and 1939 because of three factors: accent on production of coarser and cheaper varieties of cloth; Gandhi's call for boycotting foreign goods during the early 1930s; and a number of incentives, including bonus on sales given to the sales agents, the virtual lynchpin in the distribution system of the products of Indian cotton mills.

Encouraged by these results, the DCM management decided to set up another textile mill away from Delhi in western Punjab where cotton was grown in abundance but no textile mill existed. With steep fall in the machinery prices during the Depression, it was much less costly to put up a factory. The company known as Lyallpur Cotton Mills went into production in 1935. It was one of the most modern factories of its times in India, as C. D. Deshmukh, then the Governor of Reserve Bank of India, noted a few years later: 'I have yet to see an industrial unit of such importance so thoughtfully conceived, so thoroughly organized, and so considerably operated.'[22] The Lyallpur Cotton Mills, however, could never come up to the expectations and on many occasions the management had to allot shares in lieu of dividends. It was a rather unusual method to raise the capital, but it at least helped the company to retain its credit.

DCM, in the meantime, had diversified into another industry—sugar. This was mainly in response to the protection granted to the industry that had drawn Birla, Walchand, and a host of others into the field. Even though the company did better in its textile operations than many cotton mills in Bombay and Ahmedabad during the 1930s, the DCM directors were not too sanguine about the fate of the industry when the Depression set in as the annual report of 1932–3 candidly conceded: 'The future of the textile industry is very dark indeed.' Branching out into sugar would help balance off the possible decline in the earnings from the textile operations, Shri Ram and his associates reasoned, and decided barely within three days of the passing of the Sugar Industry Protection Act of 1932, to add a sugar unit to DCM. A site was quickly selected at village Daurala in Meerut district near Delhi and a factory, erected under the personal supervision of the Lala, was ready for production within a year. The result of the first year of working seemed to confirm the management's calculations when Daurala Sugar Works contributed as much as 42 per cent of the total profit that DCM earned. However, mushroom growth of sugar companies, many in the vicinity of Meerut itself, in the wake of the tariff protection caused a virtual glut in the market, resulting in a declining profit from DCM's sugar division. The management tried to save the situation by acquiring a farm near the factory to grow sugar cane, changing over to a process of production that yielded a higher recovery and produced better quality of sugar, and adding new items to its product lines such as coffee crystals, sweets, syrups, and squashes. And yet Daurala's contribution to DCM's coffers remained limited to less than 10 per cent of the total during most part of the 1930s. There was some improvement in the situation after the company joined the Indian Sugar Syndicate, a kind of central marketing organization set up by 92 sugar firms in the country in 1937. Still Daurala Sugar Works remained saddled with excess stocks.

Sugar, being a processing industry like cotton textiles, was not far removed from DCM's main business. Diversifying into pottery definitely was, and but for the patient persuasion from a long-time friend and a brilliant ceramic expert, Shri Ram perhaps would have never gone into the line. The friend was Madan Lal Bhagat, originally from Rawalpindi, whose father had had an unsuccessful stint with pottery production. Keen on reviving the family business, he learnt of Bengal Pottery Works of Calcutta, founded under the influence of the *swadeshi* spirit at the turn of the century. The company had remained beset with problems ever since its birth, because of the poor quality of its products and inefficient management. The Great Depression made its position still worse and a tired management was ready to dispose of the sick baby. Confident of his own ability to turn the company around, Bhagat wanted to acquire it but did not have sufficient funds. After a great deal of thought, Shri Ram, known for taking quick decisions, agreed to join Bhagat to form a managing agency, S. Lall Bhagat and Co., to take over Bengal Potteries. (S. Lall stood for Shankar Lal, Shri Ram's younger brother.) The acquisition formalities were completed in 1934. Bhagat, besides being a member of the new board, also became the general manager of the company. The association of the Lala with the pottery firm raised its public image and prominent business figures like Purshotamdas Thakurdas and Padampat Singhania acquired a substantial number of shares. Bhagat made strenuous efforts to reorganize the whole system, improve the quality of goods, and introduce new products. At the time of the takeover, ceramic insulators were the main item the company produced, which made it heavily dependent on government orders. Bhagat tried to change over to bazaar goods, but with rising competition from Japan and the obsolete machinery the company had, he could achieve but little. Although the company made some profits almost every year after it changed hands, there was only a marginal improvement in its general health under the new management. Just before the outbreak of World War II, however, a new and up-to-date plant had been installed which would stand the company in good stead to meet the augmented demand for its goods in the near future.

Light engineering was another industry sector that Shri Ram entered during the 1930s. Entry into this line too, as in the case of potteries, was through acquisition. Jay Engineering Works (JEW), set up in Calcutta by an engineer Bishan Das Basil with the financial backing of some Marwari traders in 1935, was only two years old when it became a part of the DCM Group. The company had been doing badly ever since its inception and Shri Ram and his associates had no illusion about their own ability to turn it around easily and quickly. India did not have much of a light engineering industry, and products like electric fan and sewing machine were freely imported. Basil had hoped that he would be able to beat the foreign competition by offering his products at a much lower price. But the sewing machine developed by him, the only item the company produced at the time of the takeover, attracted few customers despite a vigorous sales campaign. Shri Ram, however, believed that Indians were capable of competing with foreign producers of light engineering goods. This conviction was the only basis for the takeover. Madan Mohan Lal Shri Ram and Co., controlling 70 per cent of the capital jointly with friends and relatives, became the managing agents after the company changed hands. Basil was retained as the chief engineer. The new management planned to manufacture, besides sewing machines, electric fans, cooking ranges, pressure gauges, railway signalling apparatuses, and water meters. The factories were planned and machinery installed, keeping in view the need of these product lines. But the company was still running in loss when it had to divert its resources to produce goods required by the government to meet the exigencies of World War II.

Diversification did not help DCM in the short run. In fact, it is the earnings from the textile operations that seem to have fed the diversification programme to an extent. However, the production infrastructure developed in the course of diversification would contribute in no small measure to the prosperity of the group later. In contrast, the textile manufacturers in western India by and large showed little enthusiasm for diversification. This was particularly true of Ahmedabad where the industry had made phenomenal progress since the beginning of the century—growing from merely 29 mills in 1900 to 72 by 1929. During this period, the old leaders like Ranchhodlal Chhotalal and Mansukhbhai Bhagubhai families had been relegated to insignificance mainly because of the incompetence of the founders' successors, and new ones like Mangaldas Girdhardas Parekh and Amratlal Shodhan had come to the forefront, both rising from the position of small traders. Also, companies having only spinning operations had virtually disappeared from the scene. The Depression did not change the overall situation very radically. Only a few weaklings closed down, but since as many as eight new companies had been established just before the Depression began to really bite, the number of mills remained almost the same. The relative position of the families controlling the industry, however, changed drastically. The Shodhan family, the leader of the industry in 1929, could not withstand the pressure because of infighting and mismanagement and had to dispose of most of their companies to others. The Parekhs somehow held on to their own, but remained more or less stagnant waiting for the better days to return. And Ambalal Sarabhai, who controlled only one mill, but had a high status among the Ahmedabad mill owners refused to expand even though his Ahmedabad Manufacturing and Calico Printing Company (Calico Mills)—the largest single unit in the industry—made handsome profits. The company produced only higher-count goods that were not severely hit by the Depression. In contrast, the Lalbhais, who had only a token presence on the Ahmedabad industrial horizon attempted their major expansion between 1929 and 1931—just before the Great Depression set in—so as to emerge as the leader of the industry by the middle of the decade.[23]

Kasturbhai Lalbhai had only one mill, with about 26,900 spindles and 400 looms, under his control in 1920. By 1936, the number of his units had gone up to seven with a total of 235,062 spindles and 11,425 looms, including Arvind Mills, the only other company in the city besides Calico to produce finer counts. These companies together represented more than 12 per cent and more than 24 per cent of the total spinning and weaving capacities respectively in Ahmedabad. The product mix of these mills, manufacturing between them a variety of goods targeting different consumer groups, was a major factor in the Lalbhais' success in meeting the challenge of the Depression. In fact, it was only Arvind Mills, catering to the higher income groups that was less affected by the Depression, that showed consistently good performance during these difficult years, which compensated to some extent for the uneven fortunes of the other mills in the group. Unmindful of the uncertainties of the present, the Lalbhais did something during the Depression years that few in the industry did: they expanded and modernized the production apparatus of their companies. Taking advantage of the lower movement of prices in the machinery market, they added processing facilities of various descriptions, such as bleaching, dyeing, and finishing plants, to all their mills, and wherever necessary, the spinning and weaving machinery were replaced or overhauled.

While expanding his textile empire, Kasturbhai, like the other Ahmedabad industrialists, gave little thought to diversification. With their trading and moneylending background and nurtured in a city that had a long and entrenched commercial tradition, they probably felt more secure sticking to a familiar sector than to risk branching out into unknown areas. These elements, we may recall, had entered even the textile industry only after its profitability was firmly established. Even though Kasturbhai had come to the conclusion by the mid-1930s that there were 'many other industries where the profit margin is much better',[24] in concrete terms he did little to lead his house into other fields. Just before the outbreak of World War II, however, he was preparing to mount a company to produce starch, a basic material for processing textile goods. None in India produced starch then and the rising imports of it indicated a sure demand. The company, however, became operational after the war began. At any rate it was a minor venture requiring little technological sophistication, Ahmedabad, by and large, remained a one-industry city, earning the sobriquet 'the Manchester of India'.

Though, by and large, conservative and cautious in the matter of diversification, the Ahmedabad mill owners as a group helped, though unwittingly, launch a unique experiment in the area of industrial relations. Its genesis lay in the rise in the wages of the mill workers during the war. At the end of the war they were earning as much as 90 per cent more than the rates prevailing earlier. Apart from the rise in the cost of living, the increase was due to a special bonus, constituting about 70 per cent of the additions the workers had been given to dissuade them from leaving the city when a plague epidemic struck Ahmedabad in July 1917. In a period of high profits, the mill owners could not afford any disruption in their operations. By the beginning of 1918, however, the plague menace was virtually over, while the demand for textile products demonstrated a slackening trend. The Ahmedabad Millowners Association, led by Ambalal Sarabhai, therefore, decided to withdraw the plague bonus. The workers protested against the move and appealed to Gandhi, staying then at his Sabarmati Ashram in Ahmedabad, for help. Gandhi's intervention, however, failed and the workers led by Gandhi himself and his disciples, Anusuyaben (Ambalal's sister) and Shankerlal Banker, went on a strike that lasted several weeks.[25] The stalemate ended only when the mill owners agreed to Gandhi's suggestion to refer the matter to a mutually acceptable board of arbitrators whose judgment would be binding on both the parties. Gandhi organized the workers into the Textile Labour Association (Majoor Mahajan in Gujarati) which entered into an agreement with the Ahmedabad Millowners Association to settle all disputes through arbitration. Though occasional difficulties between the labour and capital still arose, Ahmedabad by and large enjoyed henceforward a great deal of industrial peace, thanks largely to this arrangement. In the absence of such a machinery, the operations of the Bombay mills, in contrast, continued to be plagued by a series of labour strikes during the 1920s and the 1930s.

The Ahmedabad mill owners remained confined not only to a single industry, but also to a single city. For some inexplicable reasons,[26] they exhibited practically no interest in setting up industrial firms elsewhere in the country or even at other places in the Gujarat region. Perhaps the only exception was Mafatlal, who had, as we have seen earlier, entered the industry with the establishment of a cotton mill at Ahmedabad during the *swadeshi* movement of 1904–5. However, his next two mills were set up away from the principal textile centre of Gujarat—at Nadiad, about 50 kilometres to the south of Ahmedabad—in 1912, and at Surat, nearer to Bombay, in 1916. These expansions took place through the acquisition of existing companies, which were restructured, reorganized, and renamed.[27] By the end of World War I, he had come to the definite conclusion that Ahmedabad was too narrow a place to operate from. Bombay now became his virtual headquarters.

By the time Mafatlal moved to Bombay, the textile industry in the metropolis had already entered into a crisis situation, which was aggravated still further during the next two decades because of a conjunction of factors—shrinking foreign markets, in the wake of the post-war slump and Depression, for coarser varieties of cotton goods that the Bombay mills had all along concentrated on producing; rising competition in the domestic coarse goods markets consequent upon the spread of cotton mill industry to other cities and regions and increasing imports from Japan; higher cost of labour and land in Bombay than elsewhere; and the consolidation of a militant trade unionism. A large number of Bombay mills—as many as 30 out of 80—had changed hands during the boom years between 1917 and 1922, leading to the inflation in capital value. Bombay proportionately had more factories with obsolete machinery and the cost of replacement was much higher than elsewhere. The result was that despite a series of tariff measures and trade agreements to check the Japanese threat and limit imports from Britain to certain specific categories of goods that posed no serious competition to the Indian mills, the Bombay industry continued to reel under the weight of the Depression almost until the end of the 1930s. It is no surprise that the number of Bombay mills that stopped working was far larger than elsewhere—22 out of 75. The most distinguished casualty was the Currimbhoy group, the second largest managing agents in the city controlling as many as 12 companies, and the only Muslim among the prominent industrialists of the city. Most other houses somehow escaped such a cruel fate, but few, if any, remained unaffected by the blasts of Depression.[28] The depressed state of the business gave an opportunity to some trading families to enter industry by acquiring cheaply the mill companies in distress. These included the Marwari firms of Ramnarain Ramnivas Ruia and Chaturbhuj Piramal. The former took over the managing agency of Bradbury and Phoenix Mills and the latter of Morarjee Gokuldas Mills. The Morarjee Gokuldas family also lost their mill at Sholapur, Sholapur Spinning and Weaving Company to another Marwari, the Jhajharias, and was practically out of the cotton textile industry.

Mafatlal's response to the business climate prevailing during the two World Wars was quite different from that of textile manufacturers in Ahmedabad as well as Bombay. On the one hand, he continued to consolidate his textile operations by acquiring and floating new companies, keeping in view the shift in the demand pattern; on the other, a number of enterprises, both in related and unrelated areas were set up with a view to reducing undue dependence on a single industry. As mentioned before, he already had three mills in three different cities of Gujarat. Using a part of the profits from these companies, he acquired one more in Bombay—China Mill, founded by a Parsee family in 1887 but now in distress—at a bargain price. The mill soon turned the corner under the Mafatlal management. However, it was becoming clear to him that with the rise of new centres of textile production, the market for coarse and medium count goods that his mills produced was going to be increasingly crowded. The solution to the problem lay in producing finer counts. A decision of the government in 1929, to give some concessions to the producers of finer counts also fortified Mafatlal's resolve to diversify into such products. The result was the birth of Mafatlal Fine Spinning and Manufacturing Company in 1930 with up-to-date machinery and allied facilities for large-scale production. Factories were set up at Navsari in the princely state of Baroda to take advantage of the attractive tax concessions the Gaikwad rulers gave to industrialists to lure them to set up enterprises in their kingdom. Three years later, the Gujarati millowners took over the management of the Indian Bleaching, Dyeing, and Printing Works at Bombay with a view to providing for the processing facilities for his growing textile empire.

This clearly was a step, howsoever feeble, towards forward integration, which was still uncommon in the Indian textile industry, where much of the processing was carried out in the informal sector without much use of machinery. Integration, both forward and backward, had always been a part of Mafatlal's strategy to strengthen his textile operations. Much before the birth of his Navsari company, he had established a number of ginneries in the cotton-growing regions of Gujarat to supply clean cotton to his as well as others' mills, and also set up a trading firm in Bombay to coordinate the sale of the ginned product. He had also set up a few ginneries in Uganda in partnership with the Gujarati settlers in that British colony; he now took control of Bombay Uganda Company at Bombay from the Bradburys, who were badly hit by the Great Depression, to market the output of his African ginneries. To complete the integrated circle, as it were, his cotton companies, while selling most of their output through commission agents as the Indian mills did in general, also had a few retail shops of their own in Bombay, Calcutta, Bangalore, and Amritsar which also dealt in the products of other mills. DCM of Lala Shri Ram was the only other textile producer that sold a small portion of its output through the company-owned outlets.

These initiatives of the Mafatlal group, though not very common among the textile magnates of western India, were still in the realm of an industry that was closely identified with that region and with native Indian entrepreneurship. The establishment of Gagalbhai Jute Mills, named after Mafatlal's father, in Calcutta in 1929 was a clear manifestation of Mafatlal's desire to explore other possibilities. But why he selected jute is not clear, as this industry was not in a very happy state during the 1920s. Moreover, Mafatlal was not unaware of the tight European hold on this industry despite the success of Birla and Sarupchand Hukumchand to breach their monopoly. His step, thus, was a bold challenge to the firmly entrenched, formidable foreign interests. What was even bolder was that the Kanbi Sheth refused to submit to the dictates of the Indian Jute Mills Association (IJMA) and kept his company out of it instead. The mill soon established a reputation for the quality of its products and proved the wisdom of Mafatlal's move that must have seemed rash to many in the beginning. Sugar and shipping were other non-textile lines that claimed Mafatlal's attention during the 1930s. However, he neither took over an existing firm nor floated a new company in these fields but remained content with acquiring limited interests in concerns controlled by others—in Phaltan Sugar Works of Africa and Ratnagar Steam Navigation Company. The former served the east African markets, while the latter was promoted by Walchand Hirachand and some other businessmen of Bombay, to operate on Bombay-Panjim route in competition with the Bombay

Steam Navigation Company. Operating on the Bombay-Panjim route, this British monopoly charged exorbitant rates.

NEW ENTRANTS

What the above discussion brings out is that the interwar period proved to be one of opportunities as well as of challenges for many Indian entrepreneurs who had already established a fairly stable position in the world of Indian industry before World War I. The period also brought new entrants into the industrial field. Juggilal Singhania of Kanpur, who had set up a small cotton mill in 1921, and his son Kamlapat added several new enterprises during the 1920s and the 1930s, including a jute mill, two cotton mills, two sugar mills, and a small light engineering firm under the name of J. K. Iron and Steel Company.[29] Another Marwari trader who branched out into industry during this period was Jamnalal Bajaj of Wardha who founded Hindustan Sugar Mills at Golgokarannath in the United Provinces in 1932 and acquired a steel rolling mill, Mukund Iron and Steel Works Ltd. at Lahore in 1937, jointly with Jeewanlal Motichand, a Gujarati friend of his, then based in Calcutta. The credit for nursing these companies to health, however, goes to Rameshwar Prasad Nevatia, Bajaj's son-in-law, as the founder had wholly dedicated his life to the causes dear to Gandhi, and had practically disassociated himself from the management of his business.[30] Ramkrishna Dalmia, a Marwari from Rohtak, in Punjab, who would have a meteoric rise in the Indian industry during and after World War II, made his debut in industry shortly before the war broke out with the establishment of five sugar mills in Bihar. He later set up Dalmia Cement Company with factories in Bihar, Punjab, Sind, and Madras, all functioning as a part of a diversified group known as Rohtas Industries. Having made his money in speculation and trade, this highly individualistic Marwari refused to join the selling syndicates formed to meet the problem of overproduction in sugar and cement. He kept his company out of the Indian Sugar Syndicate and refused to merge his cement enterprise with ACC, to which he gave a stiff competition. He was also among the first Indians to start manufacturing paper.[31]

Another Punjabi, who entered the industrial field during the inter-war years and would rise to great heights later, was Karamchand Thapar of Ludhiana.[32] Though claiming descent from the ancient Kshatriyas in the Hindu caste hierarchy, most Punjabi Khatris had taken to trading by the beginning of the middle of the nineteenth century. Civil service was another attractive occupational choice for them. Karamchand, with a smattering of college education, had a preference for police service, but instead joined his relatives who carried on business as coal dealers, merchants, and real estate agents in Calcutta. Having gained considerable experience in this field and made some money, he founded his own trading firm, Karamchand Thapar & Brothers, in 1929. The Thapars, however, soon entered the industrial field and registered their presence in three different sectors in which they would develop dominant interest later. The first in point of time was sugar manufacturing. The acquisition in 1932, soon after the industry was granted tariff protection, of a tottering concern located at Baitalpur in Gorakhpur district of the United Provinces marked the Thapars' entry into this sector. This was followed by the birth of Deoria Sugar Mills three years later with its factories located in the neighbourhood of Shri Sita Ram Sugar Company, the Thapars had acquired at Baitalpur. Both the mills continued to feel the brunt of glut in the market until the establishment of Indian Sugar Syndicate, which brought out some order in an otherwise chaotic situation, but the real improvement came only after the outbreak of World War II.

Coal mining was another sector the Thapars entered during the 1930s. Though still a European preserve, the field had been attracting many Indians, particularly Marwaris, Gujaratis, and Punjabis since the beginning of the twentieth century. In fact in 1933, when Karamchand Thapar floated his first colliery concern, four or five of his fellow Punjabis had already entered the field. Another company under his management, Oriental Coal, was set up in 1936 to operate two collieries in Manbhum and Burdwan districts of Bengal. Three more companies in this field came into being within the next three years—the biggest being Eastern Syndicate Limited with the authorized capital of more than Rs 2.10 crore. The third major sector the young industrialist (Karamchand was just 36 years old then) entered in the 1930s was paper manufacturing with the setting up of Shree Gopal Mills in 1936 after taking over Punjab Pulp and Paper Mills, then under liquidation, at Jamuna Nagar in Ambala district of Punjab. We may recall that the Birlas had set up their Orient Paper the same year that also witnessed the birth of Star Paper Mills, set up by another Marwari family, the Bajorias, who had made a fortune in jute trade. These, along with Dalmias' Rohtas Industries, were the earliest paper manufacturing units founded and controlled by the Indians.

Gujarmal Modi, whose trading family had a long tradition of supplying provisions to the army, was another Punjabi Hindu to take to manufacturing, defying the opposition from his conservative father. Originally from Patiala, he first organized a sugar mill in 1933 at Begamabad near Delhi. The town was a part of the United Provinces where the business climate in his judgment was more favourable than in his native princely state. Modi Sugar Mills suffered from similar vicissitudes as the other companies during the Depression. An undeterred Modi, however, promoted a vegetable oil producing concern, Modi Vanaspati Manufacturing Company, just before the war broke out. These two units would later develop into the highly diversified Modi Industries Ltd., with its headquarters at the sprawling industrial township of Modinagar near Delhi.[33]

The inter-war years, thus, witnessed the emergence of industrial enterprises at places far removed from the narrow confines of western and eastern India, and the expansion of such enterprises to many parts in the north and north-west which had remained hitherto unaffected by industrial stirrings. These resulted from the initiatives and accomplishments of new entrants into industry and also of those who were still at the periphery of the industrial life of the country when World War I ended. A few cotton mills of modest sizes, most of them promoted by Marwari traders, also sprang up in central India.[34] But perhaps the most spectacular development took place in south India, that had virtually no Indian on its industrial horizon well until after World War I. Coimbatore in the Madras Presidency, which developed into a major centre of textile industry during the inter-war years, had no cotton company at all until the beginning of the 1920s. The first steps towards transition were taken not by those families or communities which had a long tradition of trading, such as the Chettiers, but the Naidu or Kamma entrepreneurs, belonging to the landholding classes. They started off by setting up, like many entrepreneurs in the west and the north, ginning factories and then went on to promote a number of cotton mills in the immediate post-war period. The major role in this development was played by three Naidu families—G. Kuppuswami Naidu, V. Rangaswami Naidu, and P. S. G. Naidu. They were all large landholders cultivating cotton who took to cotton trading around the turn of the century. The profits made during the war years enabled them to promote cotton companies, which were all spinning units of modest sizes. Among the factors that contributed to the success of their enterprises were the ready access to raw materials produced in the nearby regions, the presence of a large number of handloom weavers in Madras, and availability of cheap electric power.[35] The Chettiers, the counterparts of Marwaris in the South, remained practically aloof from the modern sector, though two or three Chettier-promoted mills did come into existence between 1921 and 1925. Not until after 1930 did the Chettiers begin to look seriously upon modern industry as an avenue of prudent investment. A number of Chettier moneylenders in Burma suffered colossal losses around this time, as the bulk of their money loaned against the security of agricultural land became unrecoverable during the depression. This was among the most important reasons that induced them to turn to the textile industry at home. On the eve of World War II, however, their presence on the industrial horizon of the South was still very limited.

In fact, families belonging to the social collectivities, not commonly associated with business-type occupations, were much more visible in the industrial field of the South at this time. The emergence of one of the most prominent industrial houses in the region during the inter-war years was the outcome of the enterprising initiatives of Seshasayee Brothers. Brahman by caste, and trained as electrical engineers, R. Seshasayee and his brother-in-law, V. Seshasayee, started off with a road transport service around Trichinopoly in the Madras Presidency. They later moved into servicing and sale of buses, cars, and motor cycles and then into design, supply, and erection of electrical installations in south Madras during the 1920s, in which field the partners established an enviable reputation. This helped them form three public limited companies between 1924 and 1937 to cater to the need of three different regions of the Presidency. The investing public subscribed to the capital with great enthusiasm largely because of the reputation the partners had already earned, so that they had to arrange for only a small fraction of the capital from their own resources. On the eve of World War II, thus, Seshasayee Brothers had already laid a strong foundation for future expansion and growth.[36] Another Brahman business house in the South also began to take shape during the 1930s. Its origin lay in a commercial concern, India Trading Company Limited, which traded in steel. Founded by C. Rajan Iyer around the beginning of World War I, the company earned handsome profits during the war. With his improved financial position and some valuable experience gained in this line, he made a debut in industry with the promotion of Indian Steel Rolling Mills Limited in 1934. This was the first enterprise in this field in south India.

STRUCTURE AND STRATEGIES

While the industrial enterprises under the Indian control and management on the eve of World War II encompassed, as the above discussion brings out, a much larger territory in terms of both scope and scale than was the case just two decades ago, no significant change took place in the realm of structure and strategies. The management of practically all industrial firms continued to revolve around the managing agency system to which the Company Law enacted in 1936 accorded a statutory legitimacy. This, however, was nothing more than the recognition of an obvious reality, as only very few industrial companies had developed under private proprietorship even before the passage of the 1936 legislation, and these were all as a rule small undertakings.[37] DCM of Lala Shri Ram was perhaps the only major undertaking which had no managing agents for several years, and all executive powers were vested in the managing director who functioned under the general supervision of a functional board. However, as the company's operations expanded, the DCM board decided to entrust the management to the partnership firm of Shankarlall Bharat Ram and Co., named after Shri Ram's younger brother and younger son, with effect from January 1937.[38] As there were no legal restrictions on the number of companies a managing agency firm could have under its care,[39] most of the managing agencies had management responsibilities for several undertakings. Lala Shri Ram, however, preferred to place all his major companies under separate managing agencies. His friend Kasturbhai Lalbhai in Ahmedabad did likewise. However, the various managing agencies constituted by them were interlinked through some family members being common to all of them, and through interlocked holdings.

As the structure remained unchanged, so did the strategies. Private funds still remained the main sources of industrial finance, as the Indian banking system never became entirely free from the crisis that had overtaken it after 1913. Despite the amalgamation in 1921 of three Presidency Banks into a single institution, Imperial Bank of India, functioning under tight government supervision and the creation in 1934 of a central banking institution, Reserve Bank of India, to regulate the operations of private banking companies, banks continued to fail in large numbers at regular intervals in the absence of adequate legal safeguards. Though most of the institutions that had survived the crisis during the years of World War I continued to gain in strength, and those that failed during the inter-war years were small and weak institutions, the Indian banking system still addressed by and large limited and short term needs of individuals. So underdeveloped was the system that not until 1936 was a banking firm given a legal definition.[40] Even though there were occasions when a bank extended temporary accommodation to an industrial firm controlled by an influential family—Lala Shri Ram, for instance, arranged a loan of Rs 3,00,000 for his Bengal Potteries in 1938 from Punjab National Bank[41]—the banking system was yet to become an effective instrument of industrialization. And the stock markets remained as weak and disorganized as ever though many cities, apart from Bombay and Calcutta, had stock exchanges by 1939, and the government tried to bring about some order in their working through legislation. That the nominal value of a typical company share was still Rs 100, a substantial amount, was a positive proof that nobody expected to raise much capital from persons of modest means through stock market operations. Under these conditions, the joint family system, buttressed by community linkages, proved to be the most valuable social institution to provide funds for promoting industrial concerns. And these industrial concerns, in turn, helped promote future companies by investing in them. In other words, companies floated by a family became an extension of it for raising industrial finance.

In this fashion, it was not necessary for a family to control a company through direct investment; it could be done through investments made by companies already under the control of the family concerned. Apart from this, a family having direct control over a number of companies may also have substantial, but short of controlling, interest—often referred to as minority interest—in the enterprises under the control of some other family. Thus evolved the concept of business groups or business houses consisting of companies controlled directly by a family—the 'inner circle' firms to use R. K. Hazari's terminology—and those controlled through other companies already under its control or in which the family had a significant minority interest—Hazari's outer circle.[42] The few Indian houses that had set up insurance companies—Tatas, Birlas, and Mafatlals, to mention the most prominent among them—had at their disposal a convenient source of investible funds. Many used charitable trusts created by them to control their companies. None did better in this respect than the Tatas whose direct holdings in the companies under their management have always been very low, the bulk of the shares being held by the trusts under their control.

The Tatas were also somewhat more imaginative and innovative in building up funds through reserve and depreciation. The company law in force laid down no fixed norms in these respects and most managements considered it more important to offer higher dividends, with an eye on quick returns, than to provide for future improvements. The Tatas, in contrast, raised a substantial amount through depreciation that was used for plant extension and improvement of machinery in their steel company.[43] Kasturbhai Lalbhai, using a similar financial strategy, gave a whole company to the shareholders of one of his cotton mills free of cost. His most ambitious undertaking until then, Arvind Mills, was financed wholly by capitalizing Rs 225 lakh from the reserve of Raipur Mills, the only concern he had inherited from his father. Arvind, thus, was Raipur's gift to its shareholders.[44] Such innovative strategies, however, were rare. The Indian industrialists in general pursued financial strategies that were not very different from those followed by trading concerns—a reminder of the source most of them sprang from.

The situation with regard to strategies in other areas was more or less similar. The era of an efficient management control system had not yet arrived even in the West; the question of having anything like this in India did not arise. The Marwari firms, such as Birlas, used the so-called *partha* system[45] to keep track of the state of business on a day-to-day basis. A sophisticated variant of a widespread practice among the traders and indigenous bankers, it entailed a simple exercise in preparing daily statements of expenditure, production, and sales, which gave on a regular basis an idea of the state of business to the top management. Others probably kept track of their operations through more informal rule-of-thumb means. With regard to welfare measures for the workers, most industrialists, barring a few distinguished exceptions like the Tatas and Lala Shri Ram, acted either under pressure from the labour unions, which became fairly strong during the inter-war years, or from legislations. They dealt with the shareholders of their companies in a similar fashion. Few, if any, managements voluntarily included such data and information in their annual balance sheets that the shareholders might need to come to an independent, intelligent judgment about the health of the companies in which they had interests. In fact, no Indian firm had developed anything like a policy of social accountability to enable the shareholders to make an informed assessment of the state of business. Balance sheets, which could have been an instrument of such a policy, were more in the nature of a routine document to satisfy the legal requirements than a source of relevant data and education to the shareholders.[46] And as the managing agents had a tight control over the voting powers in their firms, the shareholders could do little to bring about a change.

Developments in the realm of marketing were not impressive either. Commission agents were the most favoured channel for the distribution of industrial goods. In many cases, the services of the same agents were used to distribute a variety of goods. Apart from selling the products for which they had agencies, these agents also provided valuable inputs to the companies concerned about the changing requirement of the consumers, i.e. taste, quality, price, etc. In other words, they also became market researchers of sorts for companies whose goods they distributed. Although some industrialists like Lala Shri Ram and Mafatlal had a few company-owned retail stores to distribute the products of their undertakings,[47] they too depended on commission agents to sell the bulk of their products.

The Lalbhais were probably the only house that made a conscious and determined bid to attempt some innovation in this area. They too like others sold their goods through commission agents until the beginning of the 1930s. However, after the birth of Arvind Mills, the second producer of superior variety textiles in Ahmedabad, the management of Calico Mills, the only manufacturer of fine and superfine goods in the city until then, did not countenance with equanimity the emergence of a competitor. Warned by Ambalal Sarabhai, who controlled Calico, that they had to choose between Calico and Arvind, Maskati Mahajan, the organization of the local cloth distributors, opted to stay with the latter. Under these conditions, the Arvind management decided to sell the Arvind products through a system that centred around a network of indenting agents appointed by the company in different parts of the country. The indenting agents canvassed orders and identified suitable retailers. The consignments were sent directly to the selected merchants who took delivery after depositing the payments in banks specified by the management. This system of marketing was quite popular in Britain, but the Lalbhais were among the first to introduce it in India.[48] The Binnys were the only group in the country that used this system of marketing with a great deal of profit.

TRADE–INDUSTRY NEXUS

It was hardly surprising that the structures and strategies of industrial undertakings seemed to be an extension of the ways the Indian trading organizations functioned. For, there continued to exist, despite the progress of industrialization, a very close nexus between the traders and industrialists. Most of the industrial houses still kept their family *pedhis* and trading establishments intact, and the number of traders serving on the boards of industrial firms was by no means small. In many groups, transition from trade to industry was not yet complete; so, trading and industrial operations were not fully divorced from each other. Besides, there were people among traders whose position in the Indian business world was no less important than some of the prominent industrialists. Purshotamdas Thakurdas in Bombay, Badridas Goenka in Calcutta, and T. V. Sundaram Iyengar in Madras wielded the kind of influence in their respective regions and even at the national levels that many industrialists might have envied. Known as the 'cotton king' because of his dominant position in cotton trade, Thakurdas[49] served on as many as 21 industrial companies without having a controlling interest in any. A director in many Tatas' companies and a close confidant of Dorabji Tata, he was in constant personal contact with G. D. Birla. One of the key founders of the Indian Merchants' Chamber and East India Cotton Association, that regulated cotton trade at the national level, he played, as we shall see later, a critical role in the creation of the Federation of Indian Chambers of Commerce and Industry (FICCI). Goenka enjoyed a similar position in eastern India. Though a graduate—few Marwari boys of his generation could claim such a distinction—he was the leader of the conservative section of the Marwari community in Calcutta, confronting the reformist group led by G. D. Birla. He too, like Purshotamdas, served on the boards of many companies, including Imperial Bank of India (he became its chairman in 1933, being the first Indian to hold this position) and Reserve Bank of India.[50]

Originally published as Dwijendra Tripathi, 'Towards Maturity', in Dwijendra Tripathi, *The Oxford History of Indian Business* (New Delhi, Oxford University Press, 2004), pp. 176–82 and 185–99.

NOTES

1. Unless otherwise indicated, this account of the Tatas is largely based on Dwijendra Tripathi and M. Mehta, *Business Houses in Western India: A Study in Entrepreneurial Response, 1850–1956*, New Delhi: Manohar, 1990, pp. 65–8.

2. Based on the reports of Indian Tariff Board for various years. A.K. Bagchi, *Private Investment in India, 1900–1939*, Cambridge: Cambridge University Press, 1972, has discussed this in greater detail, pp. 316–19.

3. Indian iron and Steel Company floated in 1918 by Burn and Co. produced only pig iron. It did not have a plan to manufacture steel but did not implement it because of uncertainty about demand. An enterprise projected by Bird and Co. of Calcutta jointly with a Sheffield-based British firm to produce steel in India had to be dropped because of fear of inadequate returns. As will be discussed in Chapter XII, another attempt by Bird and Company to organize a steel mill in 1934—this time jointly with the Tatas and Martin Burn and Co.—failed too. The only other company making steel in India, other than TISCO, was Mysore Iron and Steel Works, promoted by the princely state of Mysore, which started producing a small quantity of pig iron in 1923, but steel production had to wait until 1936, and the quantity produced was too small to offer any competition to TISCO. It was not until 1937, when Steel Corporation of Bengal promoted by Martin Burn was registered, that India had its second integrated iron and steel company. However, it started producing steel only at the end of 1939.TISCO and Steel Corporation entered into an agreement for joint distribution of their product. Dharma Kumar (ed.), *The Cambridge Economic History of India*, Vol. II, Cambridge: Cambridge University Press, 1982, p. 627.

4. As a result of the Ottawa Agreement of 1932, Britain began taking a larger quantity of pig iron from India—as much as 87 per cent of the total. Ibid., p. 628n.

5. Ibid., pp. 630–1.

6. Gita Piramal, *Business Legends*, New Delhi: Penguin, 1998, p. 456.

7. G.D. Birla to Purshotam Thakurdas, 20 August 1929; Thakurdas to Birla, 16 August 1929, Thakurdas Papers, File No. 68, Nehru Memorial Museum and Library, New Delhi.

8. J.P. Desouza, *History of the Chemical Industry in India*, Bombay: Technical Press, 1961, p. 57.

9. Piramal, *Business Legends*, p. 465.

10. Bagchi, *Private Investment in India*, pp. 275–90.

11. Piramal, *Business Legends*, pp. 30–7.

12. This agreement was the outcome of the Imperial Economic Conference held at Ottawa in 1932 which worked out preferential tariffs for trade in the British Empire and the Dominions and between Britain and India. For details see, B.N. Adarkar, 'The Ottawa Pact', in *Economic Problems of Modern India*, R.K. Mukherjee (ed.), London: Macmillan, 1939, pp. 378–95.

13. G.D. Birla's purchase of *Hindustan Times* (founded in 1924) in 1927 was essentially due to his concern to provide for a mouthpiece of the national movement. He never looked upon it as a business venture. See Ram Nivas Jaju, *G.D. Birla: A Biography*, New Delhi: Vikas, 1986, p. 98. Birla also helped the publication of two other nationalist papers—*The Searchlight* from Patna and *The Leader* from Allahabad.

14. Bagchi, *Private Investment in India*, pp. 362–81.

15. Kumar (ed.), *The Cambridge Economic History of India*, Vol. II, pp. 635–7.

16. Piramal, *Business Legends*, pp. 56–8; Rajat K. Ray, *Industrialization in India*, Delhi: Oxford University Press, 1979, pp. 143–4.

17. Ray, *Industrialization in India*, pp. 133–7, 193–5.

18. This account is mainly based on Tripathi and Mehta, *Business Houses*, pp. 147–63.

19. For a more elaborate account of the Kirloskars, see ibid., pp. 137–41.

20. This account of Lala Shri Ram and his business exploits is based primarily on Arun Joshi, *Lala Shri Ram: A Study in Entrepreneurship and Industrial Management*, New Delhi: Orient Longman, 1973, pp. 236–98.

21. In April 1921, DCM along with a large inventory of goods was gutted in a fire. It was widely believed that the fire was deliberately caused to depress the stocks and thus enable Lala Madan Mohan Lal to gain control of the company. Joshi, *Lala Shri Ram*, pp. 197–201 has argued against this belief.

22. Quoted in ibid., p. 235.

23. For details, see Dwijendra Tripathi, 'Birth, Growth and Death of Firms in a Proto-Industrial Economy: The Experience of the Ahmedabad Textile Industry', *Indian Historical Review*, Vol. 16, Nos 1–2, 1989–1990; also N.N. Desai, *Directory of Ahmedabad Mill Industry, 1923–1933*, Ahmedabad: N.N. Desai, 1935, and ibid., *1929–1956*, Ahmedabad: N.N. Desai, 1957, *passim*. Desai's Directories provide brief biographical sketches of the Ahmedabad millowners along with the description of their companies.

24. For a comprehensive account of Kasturbhai Lalbhai's career, see Dwijendra Tripathi, *Dynamics of a Tradition: Kasturbhai Lalbhai and His Entrepreneurship*, New Delhi: Manohar, 1981. Kasturbhai's statement about the profit margin being higher in other industries is on p. 79.

25. Mahadeo Desai, *The Righteous Struggle*, Ahmedabad: Nav Jivan, 1951 is a first-hand account of the strike and the events that followed. For a more detailed and analytical view, see Sujata Dalal, *The Making of Industrial Relations: The Ahmedabad Textile Industry, 1918–1939*, Delhi: Oxford University press, 1987.

26. This has been attributed to the '*gaddi* concept of management' based on a belief that an undertaking to be well managed must be within the range of the personal supervision of the top leadership. Belonging to the families of erstwhile traders and moneylenders, who were used to managing their operations from their '*gaddis*' or the seats, most of the Ahmedabad industrialists had inherited this belief from their forefathers. For details, see Tripathi, *Dynamics of Tradition*, pp. 210–11.

27. For a more detailed account of Mafatlal's career, see Tripathi and Mehta, *Business Houses in Western India*, pp. 108–10.

28. Bagchi, *Private Investment in India*, pp. 247–53; Kumar (ed.), *The Cambridge Economic History of India*, pp. 616–24; and Thomas A. Timberg, *The Marwaris: From Traders to Industrialists*, New Delhi: Vikas, 1978, pp. 226–7.

29. P. Chentasal Rao, *Lakshmipat Singhania: His Concepts and Creations*, New Delhi: Vikas, 1986, pp. 13–20.

30. B.R. Nanda, *In Gandhi's Footstep: The Life and Times of Jamnalal Bajaj*, Delhi: Oxford University Press, 1990, pp. 307–17; also Gita Piramal and M. Herdeck, *India's Industrialists*, Bombay: India Book Distributors, 1986, pp. 31–7.

31. Two books of autobiographical nature written by Ramkrishna Dalmia are the main sources of our information on him. These are *A Short Sketch of the Beginning of My Life* and *Some Notes and Reminiscences* (both privately published in 1959). *The Indian Yearbook* for 1939–40 (Vol. 26) gives some details about his early life (p. 1218). Also see *Silver Jubilee Souvenir*, 1934–64, published by Dalmia Cement Company.

32. This account of the Thapars is based on a number of interviews the author had with some officials of the Thapar Group of Companies in 1974, supplemented by the annual reports of the relevant companies.

33. For details, see P.P.S. Chauhan, *A Vision of Karmayogi Gujarmal Modi*, Modinagar: Allied Publicity Bureau, 1977.

34. For a ready list, see Timberg, *The Marwaris*, pp. 226–7.

35. Raman Mahadevan, 'Entrepreneurship and Business Communities in Colonial Madras, 1900–1929', in *Business Communities of India: A Historical Perspective*, D. Tripathi (ed.), New Delhi: Manohar, 1984, pp. 230–2.

36. This account is pieced together on the basis of information and material furnished by Seshsayee Brothers Ltd. Also see R.K. Hazari, *The Structure of*

the Corporate Private Sector: A Study of Concentration, Ownership and Control, London: Asia Publishing House, 1966, pp. 250–3.

37. F.W. Brimmer, 'The Setting of Entrepreneurship in India', *Quarterly Journal of Economics*, Vol. 69, No. 3, November 1955, pp. 551–76.

38. Joshi, *Lala Shri Ram*, pp. 272–4.

39. The Company Law adopted in 1936 (technically an amendment to the Company Law of 1913) for the first time attempted to enforce some measure of government control over business organizations. Managing agency as an institution received legal recognition for the first time and the role and functions of managing agents were defined. The act, however, did not curtail the freedom of managing agents in any significant manner.

40. The Company Law of 1936 for the first time defined a banking company.

41. Joshi, *Lala Shri Ram*, p. 261.

42. Hazari, *The Structure of the Corporate Private Sector*, p. 7.

43. Indian Tariff Board Report on Iron and Steel, New Delhi, 1934.

44. Tripathi, *The Dynamics of Tradition*, p. 69.

45. No systematic study of the indigenous system of accounting exists. For a brief description of the *partha* system, see D.K. Taknet, *Marwari Samaj* in Hindi, Jaipur: Kumar Prakashan, 1989, pp. 95–6; Jaju, *G.D. Birla*, pp. 218–23. Both Taknet and Jaju seem to present a highly exaggerated, romantic notion of the *partha* system.

46. For a detailed account, see Dwijendra Tripathi and J. Ramchandran, 'Corporate Management and Social Accountability in India: A Historical Survey', presented at the seminar on Strategy and Structure in Indian Business: Historical Evolution , at the Indian Institute of Management. Ahmedabad, during 6–8 April 1987.

47. Joshi, *Lala Shri Ram*, p. 320; Tripathi and Mehta, *Business Houses in Western India*, p. 108.

48. Tripathi, *Dynamics of a Tradition*, pp. 168–9.

49. Frank Moraes, *Sir Purshotamdas Thakurdas*, Bombay: Asia, 1957, *passim*.

50. B.D. Goenka, *Mere Sansmaran* in Hindi, Delhi: Prabhat Prakashan, *passim*.

30

Imperialism and Capitalism

Aditya Mukherjee and Mridula Mukherjee

Historians Aditya Mukherjee and Mridula Mukherjee begin by discussing the rise of Indian capitalism, arguing that the growth of Indian industry in colonial India did not occur entirely because of colonialism but in spite of or in opposition to it. Highlighting the structural changes that the Indian economy underwent during the British era, they argue that on the eve of Independence, the Indian capitalist class was better placed than capitalists in comparable situations. The authors believe that capitalists were able to organize themselves as a coherent class and subordinate all inter-class conflicts. Given this solidarity, the capitalist class influenced the nationalist movement and was able to influence the emergence of a post-colonial bourgeois order.*

Thereafter, the authors discuss the post-1947 economic trends and highlight the uniqueness of the Indian experience which, they argue, cannot be wholly subsumed under any major theory. From the outset, the new Indian state relied very little on foreign trade. For instance, total foreign trade in 1953–77 as a proportion of the country's gross domestic product was only at about 13 per cent. Although India did register moderate economic growth of about 5 to 6 per cent per annum, both authors argue (by showing the case of foreign capital and its restricted role in the Indian economy) that the Indian economy underwent intense economic restructuring, typically an attempt to disarticulate the colonial or peripheral structure it had inherited from the British.

* Also see Aditya Mukherjee, *Imperialism, Nationalism, and the Making of the Indian Capitalist Class, 1920–1947* (New Delhi, Sage Publications, 2002).

India has received far less attention than it deserves in the field of political economy of development of post-colonial societies of the third world. Much of the vast body of recent literature on the development strategies followed by newly industrialising countries (NICs) focuses almost exclusively on Latin America, East Asia and Africa. It either does not take into account the qualitatively different experience of India or relegates her experience to an almost embarrassed footnote. This may be because the Indian experience does not fit into the neat models put forward by a wide range of 'dependency theorists', neo-Marxist world system analysts or the current 'liberal' reincarnation of the post Second World War 'modernisation' theorists. Or is it because of India's failure to be spectacular, either as a success (in terms of rate of growth) like East Asia or as a disaster like several countries of Africa and Latin America?

In this essay we propose to discuss the Indian experience of development since independence in 1947. Our framework for discussion will not be the usual one of assessing the relative merits or demerits of certain policy options or strategies such as export-oriented industrialisation (EOI) or import substituting industrialisation (ISI). We believe that these options cannot be evaluated in a historical vacuum as their success or failure is inextricably linked up with a large number of historically specific conditions. Instead, our emphasis will be on trying to relate the specific path followed by India to the historico-structural conditions in which it was placed.

The first two parts of the paper will highlight the nature of the political, economic and ideological development of the Indian bourgeoisie in the colonial period as well as certain trends in the colonial economy before 1947.[1] These two aspects were extremely important in determining the nature of the state and economy at and after independence. In the third part we will outline the actual trends that have emerged in the Indian economy since independence as a result of the specific path of development that was followed. In part four we will discuss certain other factors which were crucial to the path of development followed by India, viz, the nature of hegemonic ideology in the Indian national movement as well as in Indian society after independence, the role of political democracy, the balance of class forces in India since independence, the role of the state and the public sector and the size of the Indian home market. In part five we conclude with a discussion of some of the political implications of post-independence Indian development.

ECONOMIC BASIS BEFORE INDEPENDENCE

Recent writings of radical left scholars like Samir Amin (1974a: 33ff), A K Bagchi (1973), Hamza Alavi (1975, 1982), Ernest Mandel (1962: 480), etc, implicitly assume that colonial economies, or even post-colonial peripheral economies after achieving political independence, necessarily developed in a fashion which led to the further structuring in a dependent fashion of these economies and their bourgeoisies, making it impossible for them to break out of this dependent status without opting out of the world capitalist system altogether. This task naturally could not be performed by the dependent bourgeoisies of colonial and neo-colonial countries.[2] This formulation is generally made on the basis of the experience of certain colonies and neo-colonies of Latin America, Africa, etc, which exhibit certain specific growth patterns, and is then sought to be generalised, almost as a kind of law of development, for all colonies and ex-colonies.

The study of the actual historical evolution of the colonial economy and colonial bourgeoisie (in the case of the latter particularly its political and ideological evolution) of a country such as India, which demonstrates a different tendency, is not even attempted. A significant body of Indian communist thinking since as early as the 1920s also more or less fell into the same pattern and made similar assumptions, and therefore, naturally diagnosed the inevitability of the bourgeoisie's 'sell out' to imperialism and argued that the struggle for national liberation could, in such a situation, only be led by the working class [A Mukherjee, 1981].

However, when we actually examine the developments in colonial India, especially since the First World. War, we find that there were significant changes occurring in the Indian economy and a certain measure of economic development was taking place, albeit *in spite of and in opposition to colonialism*, which enabled the Indian capitalist class to grow and establish a considerably large independent economic base for capital accumulation even in the colonial period, and on a *qualitatively bigger scale* since independence. The economic position at least, therefore, did not appear to preclude the possibility of the emergence of a national bourgeoisie and independent national development: in fact, on the contrary, it facilitated the process.

Let us take a very brief and schematic look at some of the economic trends that emerged in India during the colonial period.

First, a major and generally undisputed development in the Indian colonial economy in the twentieth century was the initiation of a rapid phase of import substitution in most of the major consumer goods industries and certain intermediate and capital goods industries like textiles, sugar, matches, cement, paper, iron and steel, etc, [Subramanian and Homfray, 1946: 48–50]. This process began in the early twentieth century, picked up by the First World War and the 1920s, got a major push in the 1930s and the Second World War period, and took a quantum leap in the years following independence. In any case, by 1939, India was more or less self-sufficient in her major consumer goods requirements. Significantly, the bulk of this process was occurring under the aegis of independent indigenous capital.

Second, apart from import substitution, there was a growing tendency towards inward orientation, with indigenous producers, who were earlier producing for export, shifting towards the home market, a good example being the cotton textile industry [Bagchi, 1972: Ch 3 and 7].

Third, while India's total volume of international trade since the First World War was showing a general decline, her internal trade in many basic items like cotton manufacture, sugar, iron and steel and cement, increased about two to three times [Subrarnanian and Homfray, 1946: 45, 51].

Fourth, there was in this period, for a multiplicity of reasons, a rapid shift of traditional 'pre-capitalist' accumulations in trade, usury, landlordism, etc, to industry. While many of the princes financed big industry, a lot of trading-usury capital went into smaller enterprises [Levkovsky, 1966: 233 ff, 319].

Fifth, as compared to the pre-First World War period, in the post-war period upto 1945 there was a gradual and more consistent shift in the pattern of foreign trade. The proportion of manufactured goods in total exports showed a significant increase, and in total imports showed an even more significant decrease. Conversely, the proportion of raw materials in total exports showed a definite decrease and the proportion of raw materials and capital goods (as distinct from consumer goods) in total imports showed a comparative increase [R L Varshney, 1965; Subramanian and Homfray, 1946; 47]. This tendency towards a reversal of India's traditional colonial pattern of foreign trade suggested a considerable amount of indigenous industrial growth. However, if a static view is taken at any point of time, the structure of foreign trade was still clearly colonial.

Sixth, contrary to traditional belief,[3] the actual net inflow of foreign capital to India was never very large and was particularly insignificant in the area of industrial investment. Most foreign capital in the twentieth century came in the form of loans to meet the balance of payments deficits caused not in a small measure by the unilateral transfers made to the metropolis in the form of home-charges and by interest charges and dividends accruing due to earlier foreign loans and investments. In fact, if one pitted the outflows on current account due to interest, dividends and home charges against the net inflow due to foreign borrowing on the capital account, one would find that there was an outflow of capital from India virtually throughout the colonial period and certainly since the First World War [Bagchi, 1972: 160; Bannerji, 1963: 195, 200]. However, even if one considers only the flows in the capital account, then also it is clear that foreign capital flow fell off after the brief spurt of the early 1920s, and, by the early 1930s, Indian repayments and repatriation of foreign debt and earlier foreign investments exceeded fresh investments, i e, there was a net outflow of foreign capital [Bannerji, 1963: 195, 200]. The process of repatriation which began in the early 1930s picked up after 1935, and, with the onset of the Second World War, both repatriation of sterling public debt and retirement of private foreign loans and investments increased rapidly [Kidron, 1965: 53ff; Bannerji, 1963: 195, 200]. It was in fact during the Second World War, when Britain made large war purchases in India, that India ceased to be a debtor country and by the end of the war had accumulated as credit against Britain a whopping sterling balance of nearly 15,000 million.[4] Not only did the growing dependence on the London money market cease, the economy had in fact acquired a major bargaining position.

Further, for a variety of reasons, areas where traditional foreign capital dominated, e g, plantations, jute, foreign trade underwent a relative stagnation after the First World War. Also, a dual process of repatriation and Indianisation of this traditional foreign capital set in. On the other hand, compared to the rapid growth of indigenous enterprise in this period, the intrusion of the new type of foreign capital in the form of direct investments by multi-national corporations, which began in the early 1930s and 1940s, remained very small till independence. And, as we shall discuss later in the essay, though such investments did increase considerably post-independence, they were kept under strict control and never allowed to acquire a dominant position in the country.

Last, between 1914 and 1947, the Indian capitalist class, through a process of economic and political struggle, and taking advantage of the two wars and the Great Depression [Chandra, 1970] as well as the specific crisis faced by British imperialism during those years, was able to significantly increase its hold over the Indian economy vis-à-vis foreign capital. This was achieved chiefly through the following three processes: (a) by entering new areas and accounting for the overwhelming proportion of the new investments made since the 1920s, e g, in sugar, cement, paper, heavy chemicals, iron and steel [Bagchi, 1972: 83ff, 192ff; Ray, 1979: Ch 3]; (b) by edging out or encroaching upon in greater or smaller degree the various traditional areas of European influence and dominance, eg, banking, life insurance, jute, textiles, shipping, foreign trade, coal, tea [Kidron, 1965: Ch 2; Bagchi, 1972]; (c) through a faster growth, in terms of investment and output, of areas where Indian capital dominated, as opposed to those where European interests were dominant, eg, cotton vs jute, Bombay and other interior regions vs Bengal and the metropolitan centres, home market-oriented industries vs export-oriented industries like jute and plantations, internal trade vs foreign trade and so on [Bagchi, 1972: 83ff, 433ff].

A study done by the Gokhale Institute in 1951 clearly shows that the control of Indian capital in the large industries in India extended rapidly in comparison with European control between 1915–16 and 1943–44. By 1944, Indian private capital controlled about 62 per cent of the large industrial units employing 1,000 or more workers, and about 58 per cent of the labour force in such factories. The corresponding figures for British private capital were 27 per cent and 32 per cent. Indian capital thus controlled more than twice the number of the larger units controlled by British capital and slightly less than twice the labour force employed in such factories [Gokhale Institute, 1951; and Roy, 1953: 18–20].

However, while private British capital still had a significant share of the larger establishments, these constituted only 4.7 per cent of the total factory units and employed 57 per cent of the labour force [Roy, 1953: 2]. In the rest of the factories, representing 95.3 per cent of the total units and employing 43 per cent of the labour force, Indian control was absolute.[5] This made the total Indian share in modern factory industry including small scale industry very high indeed.[6]

One may point out here that the political and economic significance of total Indian control over the small scale sector has been generally ignored, and bears a lot of emphasis. Recent works show that despite a much faster rate of growth of large scale manufacturing compared to the small scale sector, the income generated from the small scale sector was larger than that generated in large scale manufacturing till as late as 1941 [Sivasubramaniam, 1977]. Besides, the fixed investments and total capital employed in certain sectors like flour mills (rarely noticed and entirely Indian) was far greater than that employed in areas such as woollens, soap, glass, matches, basic chemicals, etc [Levkovsky, 1966: 287]. Politically, too, the fact that the entire small sector in India was Indian-owned, as contrasted to other colonies like Egypt and Indonesia, where it was Greek, Syrian, and Chinese, would have interesting connotations regarding the size, strength and politics of the indigenous national bourgeoisie, and the potential of imperial divisive tactics.

Estimates of the rough share of Indian capital in the domestic market have also been made. On the eve of independence, the share of foreign enterprises in the total gross output of Indian industry was only 25 per cent. Since roughly half of it was for export, one can say that about 12.5 per cent of the internal market was covered by foreign enterprises in India. It we add to this the share of the market that was supplied by imports, it emerges that foreign capital both from within and outside the country controlled not more than 27 or 28 per cent of the domestic market [Shirokov, 1973: 48–49]. This left about 72–73 per cent of the domestic market for indigenous enterprise even before independence.

In the financial sphere too, where earlier European capital was supreme, the Indian bourgeoisie made massive inroads. While in 1914 foreign banks held 70 per cent of the deposits, by 1937 they held 57 per cent, and by 1947 a mere 17 per cent [Kidron, 1965: 42; Gokhale Institute, 1951]. In the 1940s, Indian companies showed rapid growth in the insurance business as well, especially in life insurance. Also, the assets and paid up capital of the larger Indian companies expanded rapidly in the 1940s leaving the top European houses far behind.[7]

The various factors listed above suggest that what are considered to be some of the typical disarticulating features of an extroverted colonial economy [see Alavi, 1979; Amin, 1974a: 15ff] were, to an extent, however hesitatingly, getting reversed, even within the over-arching colonial structure. First, there was a growing tendency towards surplus value being appropriated through extended reproduction in the colony, and it was being accumulated and invested by an independent indigenous bourgeoisie though within the constraints of a colonial economy. We emphasise this because it is very different from extended reproduction not taking place in the colony or extended reproduction occurring in the colony but surplus value being appropriated by a metropolitan bourgeoisie and invested in the metropolitan countries. Second, there was a growing tendency towards indigenous industry being articulated with the indigenous agriculture and the home market. The typical colonial feature of colonial agriculture being articulated with metropolitan industry and the home market with metropolitan industry was showing a decline. Third, the hold of foreign capital was declining and the indigenous bourgeoisie had gradually acquired a dominating position in the indigenous production sphere, as well as the home market. Last, the Indian economy, like the indigenous bourgeoisie, had acquired a minimal strength and bargaining position vis-à-vis the metropolitan centre. Good examples of this change were the shift from being weighed down by huge debts to accumulation of large foreign exchange balances, and the colonial bourgeoisie's ability to bargain effectively while associating with foreign capital in setting up enterprises [see A Mukherjee, 1979: 140ff] or while negotiating trade agreements with Britain.[8]

Thus the Indian economy and the Indian bourgeoisie were in a much stronger position compared to most other colonies on the eve of independence. In any case, India at that moment did not appear to be in the most opportune phase for the 'ushering in of dependent capitalism' or neo-colonialism as some would put it.

Having said all this, it is absolutely necessary to clarify that all the developments we have listed above, suggesting the growth of a certain level of independent capitalism within the colonial structure, did not occur as a result of colonialism. They were not produced by colonialism itself but were a product of the space wrenched from it. It is easily demonstrable that all the developments listed above occurred, to list some of the causes, either (a) in struggle, political and economic, against imperialism, whether through the national movement, legislative assemblies, business chambers or directly by entrepreneurs, as in shipping, or (b) when the grip of imperialism weakened or loosened due to world factors autonomous of the logic of the colonial system, such as the world wars and the depression, or (c) when the principal metropolis lost out in competition to other metropolitan centres and preferred to permit indigenous enterprise in the colony to grow rather than allow other foreign powers to capture the colonial market, e g, protection to cotton, iron and steel, matches and sugar being related to competition from Japan, Belgium, Germany, Sweden and Java (a Dutch colony), or (d) due to the inner contradictions of colonialism itself, e g, when the increasing need for revenue from the colony to enable remittance or drain could no more be met from a stagnating or even declining agricultural sector but had to be met through import tariffs, thus providing indigenous manufacture a certain amount of protection. In other words, the specific non-colonial type of developments in the twentieth century occurred *not as a result of colonial contact but in spite of or in opposition to it.*

This clarification is necessary in order to counter the crude notions of 'decolonisation' popular both in right wing and left wing interpretations.[9] The notion of decolonisation has implications such as that imperialism was pulling out, of its own volition, as the colony ceased to pay, or that imperialism now continued in an altered form, and it was encouraging industrialisation and therefore, the colonial bourgeoisie had no basic contradictions with it. The reality was very different. Though the Indian capitalist class increased its strength, imperialist exploitation and the consequent underdevelopment did not cease, and the colony, far from ceasing to pay, was subjected to a greater and more blatant direct appropriation of surplus through currency manipulations, forced loans, large military expenditures and numerous other unilateral transfers.[10] Also, though India's importance as a market for British goods, in terms of volume of imports, had declined, she remained nevertheless one of Britain's most important markets [Tomlinson, 1979; Chatterjee, 1981]. The Indian economy till 1947 remained essentially backward and structurally colonial. In 1947, India was still a basically agricultural country with a very small secondary sector both in terms of output and employment. Imperialism continued to put major fetters on industrialisation. Foreign capital continued its hold in certain sectors and the dependence on the world capitalist system for capital goods and technology remained—a dependence which the Indian capitalist class and later the independent Indian state made efforts to break, not without considerable success.

The reason we have emphasised the specific non-colonial type of developments occurring in India in the twentieth century is to suggest that the economic situation in India had become one where it was by no means impossible for an independent national bourgeoisie to develop. In fact, the strength of the Indian bourgeoisie and the Indian economy at independence was far greater than was the case in most other post-colonial societies at a comparable stage, and this had important implications for post-independence development.

INDIAN BOURGEOISIE BEFORE INDEPENDENCE: POLITICO-IDEOLOGICAL DIMENSION

Let me state at the outset that a colonial capitalist class cannot be characterised or its position derived as being either national or comprador, anti-imperialist or collaborationist, simply on the basis of its economic position and that of the colonial economy vis-à-vis the metropolitan bourgeoisie and the world capitalist system, respectively. The position of the class is equally importantly determined on the basis of its specific historical evolution at the levels of its political and ideological consciousness and practice.[11] There is, in fact, the possibility, as appears to be the case for the Indian bourgeoisie, as well as perhaps the Indian national movement, of the class and the movement being politically and ideologically very advanced, in a sense 'over-developed' or 'over-determined' as compared to their 'objective' economic bases. To put it in other words, the process of the formation of the 'class for itself' could push far ahead of the process of the growth of 'the class in itself'—though both the processes were dialectically interlinked to each other. Also, the former process by pushing ahead could have important consequences in terms of quickening the pace of the latter process.

All this is not to deny the crucial importance of the economic position of the class vis-à-vis foreign capital and the metropolitan economy, but merely to put it in a broader perspective. One of the most striking features of post-First. World War colonial India was the extent to which the Indian capitalist class constituted itself as a class. It not only emerged as an economic category with a growing independent base for capital accumulation but was also able to organise itself on an all-India basis, successfully subordinating various intra-class conflicts as well as its short-term class interests to the long–term interests of the class as a whole, getting constituted politically as a 'class for itself' and developing a hegemonic ideology vis-à-vis other classes and the nation. The fact that the capitalist class was ahead of any other class in India in almost all the above aspects played an important part in determining the nature and course of the anti-imperialist movement in India, which significantly ended with the establishment of an independent bourgeois order.

We shall now trace the political and ideological development of the Indian capitalist class and also its organisational strength during colonial rule. Since the early 1920s, efforts were being made by leading capitalists like G D Birla and Purshottamdas Thakurdas to establish a national level organisation of Indian commercial, industrial and financial interests. The initial objective was to create the capacity to effectively lobby with the colonial government [P T Papers, 1923, Fl 42, Pt 3]. This effort culminated in the formation of the Federation of Indian Chambers of Commerce and Industry (hereafter federation or FICCI) in 1927, with a large and rapidly increasing representation from all parts of India. The FICCI was soon recognised by the British government as well as the Indian people as representing the dominant opinion as well as the consensus within the Indian capitalist class. By the end of the 1920s, the Indian capitalist class had succeeded in creating a class organisation on a national basis which effectively subsumed or subordinated various existing divisions within the class, in the long-term interest of the class as a whole.

The federation was treated as a platform from which redressal could be sought from the government for the immediate grievances of various sections of the capitalist class, and also as a forum for organising public opinion, both within the class and outside, on larger issues which affected not only the Indian capitalists but the Indian economy as a whole [FICCI, AR, 1941: 22–24; 1946: 71]. In the process the Indian capitalists, with some of the most astute minds of the period in their ranks, developed a comprehensive economic critique of imperialism in all its manifestations, whether it be direct appropriation through home charges, or exploitation through trade, finance, currency manipulations or foreign investments, including in their sweep the now fashionable concept of unequal exchange occurring in trade between countries with widely divergent productivity levels.[12] They kept a watchful eye on the complex national and international developments, especially those related to imperialism and which had a bearing on Indian economic development, and forcefully argued the national position.[13] The leaders of the Indian national movement often saw their assistance as invaluable and treated their opinions and expertise on many national economic issues with respect [PT Papers, Fl 42, Pt 2: 104]. The leaders of the capitalist class also clearly saw the role of the FICCI as being that of 'national guardians of trade, commerce and industry', pertaining in the economic sphere in colonial India the functions of a national government [FICCI, AR, 1943:150; 1944: 203].

However, the FICCI was not to remain merely a sort of trade union organisation of the capitalist class fighting for its economic demands and doing ideological propaganda to achieve the same. The leaders of the capitalist class clearly saw the necessity of the class effectively intervening in politics. As Purshottamdas, president of FICCI, declared at its second annual meeting in 1928: 'We can no more separate our politics from our economics'. Further, the intervention of the class in politics was to be on the side of Indian nationalism. 'Indian commerce and industry are intimately associated with and are, indeed, an integral part of the national movement—growing with its growth and strengthening with its strength' [FICCI, AR, 1928: 4]. G D Birla was to confess a little later that, contrary to what was earlier anticipated, it was now clear that 'It is impossible in the present... political condition of our country to convert the government to our views... the only solution... lies in every Indian businessman strengthening the hands of those who are fighting for the freedom of our country'. [FICCI, AR, 1930: 264].

On the basis of the above understanding, the Indian capitalist class constantly reacted to the existing national movement and evolved a complex strategy towards both its mass civil disobedience and constitutional struggle phases.[14]

A few more comments about the politico-ideological stance of the Indian capitalist class vis-à-vis imperialism and other social classes in India, such as the landlords and the working class, are in order. The position taken by the capitalist class on these issues had an important impact on the nature of post-independence developments.

One of the most persistent themes regarding the Indian bourgeoisie has been that (a) its dependence on foreign capital and interest in trade especially in imported goods, (b) its links with feudal land-owning interests and (c) its fear of the left or popular movements from below led it either to surrender or to repeatedly compromise and collaborate with imperialism. This argument was first put forward by the communists nearly 60 years ago in the 1920s, applying mechanically the experience of countries like China to India, and has been repeated in its substance ever since.[15] Surprisingly, the same view continues to be held, with even less justification, for the post–colonial Indian bourgeoisie, not only by the different streams of the Indian communist movement, though with certain variations [see Chandra, 1981], but even in Marxist academic writing [Patnaik, 1975: 77–78].

Let us take a look at these generalisations. First, as we have shown above, and discussed in detail elsewhere, the Indian capitalist class grew independently and in opposition to foreign capital and maintained a consistent opposition to domination by foreign capital. It somewhat softened its attitude towards foreign capital (even going in for collaborations with it) only when it had grown sufficiently in strength and was convinced of being able, with the help of an imminent independent national state, to utilise foreign capital for its own economic development without succumbing to foreign domination [A Mukherjee, 1979]. However, the capitalists were quite clear that entry of foreign capital in *crucial* areas would not only wipe out Indian (national) concerns but also 'fetter the hands of the future popular government of the country towards industrialisation on national lines' [FICCI, Proc of EC, 1934: 21]. Further, Indian capital was never dependent on foreign finance for resources for investment but only on foreign capital equipment and technology. This dependence did not lead to the acceptance of a subservient position but on the contrary to a concerted effort, first by the capitalist class and later by the national state, to overcome it with the help of a multipronged strategy [see A Mukherjee, 1976, 1978, 1979].

As regards the capitalist class's links with trade, particularly in imported goods, the overall strategy of the Indian capitalist class appeared to remain unaffected by it. The FICCI, in its entire history, not once argued for the expansion of these importing interests but on the contrary consistently agitated for reduction in imports through protection and other measures. In any case, the tendency to link trading interests, as distinct from industrial interests, with elements of compradorism [Sarkar, 1976: 120; Markovits, 1978: 47–50] flies in the face of the fact that in India the trading groups participated in the anti-imperialist agitations in a much more militant and active manner than the industrialists [Gordon, 1978]. This approach not only ignores the existence of considerable overlap between trading and industrial interests but also adopts a completely static view, missing the fact that these two interests were in fact parts of a continuum on which the former shifted to the latter over time. Besides, this reductionist tendency to mechanically link sections of the class with any one political position totally denies any role to ideology. And the Indian capitalist class had consciously adopted in broad terms the ideology of an 'industrial national bourgeoisie'.

It may be pertinent here to also deal with the shibboleth that the big bourgeoisie or, as some would have it, its monopoly crust [Levkovsky, 1966: 323] was more prone to collaborate with foreign capital and faced 'no major conflict' with it [Bagchi, 1973; Roy, 1953: 89ff]. Our research, however, suggests that it was Indian big business, trying to enter areas like shipping, automobiles, locomotives, chemicals, banking and insurance, which felt most strongly the constraints created by imperialism and faced stiff competition from foreign capital. It is not accidental that in the leadership of FICCI Indian big business was very well represented.

In fact, the cause and the role of the very early crystallisation of tendencies towards concentration and monopoly among indigenous capital have not been fully appreciated. This phenomenon was an aspect of a backward[16] and late[17] capitalism trying to emerge in a hostile colonial context where great concentration of resources with control over diverse areas with considerable vertical and horizontal integration[18] was perhaps the only way of effectively counteracting the 'collective monopoly'[19] of the alien interests.

Second, the Indian capitalists class's 'links' with feudal interests have been greatly exaggerated and the role of these links in its being pro-feudal and in blunting its anti-imperialism has been assumed and never actually demonstrated. None of the major business houses had 'significant semi-feudal land holding' though 'several of them' had 'large-scale capitalist farms' [Chandra, 1972a: 141–169]. More importantly, the comprehensive reforms in agriculture suggested by the dominant section of the Indian capitalist class were geared precisely towards the undermining of the existing feudal and semi-feudal tendencies in Indian agriculture.[20] They wanted land reforms which would abolish tenancy and rentier landlordism in favour of peasant proprietorship. The state was to, over time, 'extinguish' the claims of the landlords over their lands by making a lump sum payment, and establish a class of peasant proprietors in direct contact with the state. Till this was achieved, security of tenure for tenants was to be assured and rents were to be controlled to prevent speculative investment in land. Further, co-operativisation was to be introduced on a wide scale in the spheres of marketing to circumvent the hold of rural merchant usurers and secure remunerative prices for the direct cultivator, of finance, to 'liquidate the burden of agricultural indebtedness' and of production, using compulsion if necessary, to meet the problem of small uneconomic holdings.[21] Also, minimum agricultural wages were to be fixed and agricultural income tax was to be introduced on a graduated scale and if possible with an exemption limit. Last, productivity was to be increased by commencing a comprehensive programme of irrigation, fertilisers and modern agricultural research, the results of which were to be popularised by introducing 'model farms' on the scale of one such farm for every ten villages. Clearly, the Indian capitalists were proposing a programme of agrarian reforms which would free Indian agriculture of its semi-feudal constraints and usher in modern capitalist and peasant farming. That they did not support 'radical agrarian programmes' in the sense of outright expropriation of landlords without compensation, or that they sought agrarian reform which was oriented not in favour of the landless labourers and poor peasants but that of rich and middle peasants and improving capitalist landlords, was not a result of their ' "feudal" connections', as Sarkar [1976: 121] would argue, but of their being a bourgeois precapitalist class. [22]

Much has also been made of the big landlords and 'feudal' princes[23] investing liberally in large business enterprises set up by Indian capitalists [Roy, 1953: Ch 8]. To our mind, this is no proof of Indian capitalists having 'feudal links' which forced them to compromise with feudalism. On the contrary, this phenomenon is quite common in the transitional phase to industrial capitalism when traditional pre-capitalist accumulations (both from landlordism and rural trading-usury) are sought to be utilised in the new emerging system. Marx's notion of the second path, of capitalism from above, is relevant here. The crucial question is one of determining the *direction* in which the society and economy was moving, which in this case certainly was not that of feudalism. The continuing of elements of the old order does not necessarily indicate a capitulation to it.

What bears emphasis, however, is the fact that whatever, if any, be the 'links' of the Indian capitalist class with 'feudal' interests, these links did not lead to its adopting a pro-feudal and therefore, pro-imperialist stance. While, as we have seen, their economic programme undermined feudalism, politically, too, the Indian capitalists throughout kept their distance from the pro-imperialist landlords and princes, whether it be in legislative assemblies or at the round table conferences or in any other forum.

Third in India the 'fear of organised labour' or, to use the phrase of the 1920s, the 'menace of the red spectre' never became, for a variety of reasons, strong enough to push the Indian bourgeoisie into the 'lap' of imperialism [see Chandra, 1972a; 1972b]. Whenever the left threat was seen to be becoming important, the extremely self-conscious Indian capitalists responded not by seeking help from imperialism but by attempting *inter-alia* to strengthen the right wing of the nationalist stream. In fact, the Indian capitalists evolved a subtle, many sided strategy to contain the left, no part of which involved a sell out to imperialism. For example, when in 1929 certain capitalists, to meet the high pitch of communist activity among the working class trade unions, attempted to form a class party where European and Indian capitalists would combine, the leaders of the Indian capitalist class firmly opposed this move. As G D Birla put it in 1929, 'The salvation of the capitalists does not lie in joining hands with reactionary elements' (pro-imperialist European interests in India) but in 'co-operat(ing) with those who through constitutional means want to change the government for a national one' [PT Papers, Fl 42, Pt V]. Purshottamdas was to reiterate the clearly perceived primacy of the national over the social contradiction, '. . . we are Indians first and merchants and industrialists afterwards. . .'[24]

Further, the capitalists were careful not to attempt to 'kill Bolshevism and communism with such frail weapons' as frontally attacking the left with class organisations of the capitalists, which would carry no weight with 'the masses' or even the 'middle classes'. As G D Birla clearly put it, 'I have not the least doubt in my mind that a purely capitalist organisation is the last body to put up an effective fight against communism' [PT Papers 1929; Fl 42, Pt V]. A much superior method, as Birla was to clarify later in 1936 when Jawaharlal Nehru's leftism was seen as posing a danger, was to 'let those who have given up property to say what you want to say'.[25] The correct strategy was to 'strengthen the hands' of the right wing nationalists such as 'Vallabhbhai and Bhulabhai who are fighting against socialism'.[26] The government was also urged to give concessions to the right wing nationalists otherwise it would be 'helping the socialists indirectly' [Birla, 1953: 194].

Further, the capialists were to encourage extensive ideological work through their 'political and ideological representatives' to fight socialism [see A Mukherjee, 1976; 1978]. Simultaneously, the 'root cause' or "raison d'etre of communism' was to be studied and steps taken to 'alleviate poverty and discontent' and adopt a 'sympathetic attitude' towards labour [G D Birla in PT Papers, 1929, Fl 42, Pt V]. It is with this perspective that the post-war economic development committee set up by the capitalists in 1942, which eventually drafted the Bombay Plan, was to function. The committee was to recognise 'the inevitability of a change in the direction of a socialist economy' and be 'prepared to make such adjustments as may meet all reasonable demands before the socialist movement assume (d) the form of a full-fledged revolution'. The attempt was to incorporate 'whatever is sound and feasible in the socialist movement' and see 'how far socialist demands could be accommodated without capitalism surrendering any of its essential features'. The eventual plan (Bombay Plan) was to therefore seriously take up the questions of equitable distribution, partial nationalisation, etc, with this objective clearly in mind [PT Papers, 1942, Fl 291, Pt 1]. 'A consistent. . . programme of reforms' was the 'most effective remedy against violent social upheavals' [FICCI, AR, 1943: 31].

The Indian capitalist class's response to the threat from the left was thus not one of panic, making it go over to the side of imperialism, but was a mature one. While remaining on the side of nationalism, it evolved a subtle strategy of combating the left—in certain respects pre-empting the worldwide successful attempts by post-war reformist welfare capitalist states to save capitalism as a system.

In other words, while the Indian capitalist class's strategy was definitely anti-socialist and bourgeois, it was not pro-imperialist. One may add here that the bourgeoisie's understandable inclination to remain within a bourgeois framework is often misinterpreted as its accepting or attempting to grow within the imperial framework. For example, Bagchi sees the capitalists' arguing for '... a capitalist order of society, international collaboration between capitalists of all countries, avoidance of drastic social change and respect for the fundamental rights of property' as proof of their 'remain(ing) imprisioned by some of the basic presuppositions of the British imperial system...' [Bagchi, 1972: 428], while all that it actually demonstrates is their desire to maintain the capitalist system. This confusion arises because of the basic assumption made since the early 1920s, and which lasts till today, that colonial countries could not break the hold of imperialism so long as they remained within the parameters of capitalism; only shooting out of the capitalist orbit into socialism could achieve this task.[27] Given this understanding, being bourgeois by definition meant being pro-imperialist. Consequently, quite often a political strategy of anti-imperialism which was at best bourgeois was seen as being pro-imperialist, or, at times, the non-pursuance of a revolutionary socialist strategy against imperialism was seen as compromising with imperialism. In reality, however, the Indian bourgeoisie, rather than attempt to remain and grow within the imperialist framework, built up a multi-pronged strategy precisely to undermine it; and the Indian national movement did succeed in overthrowing imperialism, though remaining, despite contending forces, under bourgeois ideological hegemony, and in establishing an essentially independent capitalist society, however weak and prone to dangers of potential neo-colonialism.[28]

We have argued extensively elsewhere [A Mukherjee, 1982: 264–284] that the Indian bourgeoisie did not create, lead or even crucially determine or influence the course of the Indian national movement. It is nevertheless important to identify the bourgeois role in facilitating the maintenance of bourgeoisie ideological hegemony over the Indian national movement.

Most important in this connection was the fact that the bourgeoisie at no point abandoned the side of nationalism whatever the fear or provocation due to the radicalisation of the national movement or the temptations offered by imperialism [A Mukherjee, 1982]. If the bourgeoisie had gone over to the side of imperialism, it would have greatly facilitated the growth of the forces which argued for a simultaneous overthrow of imperialism and capitalism or at least for working class hegemony over the national movement. If, on the other hand, it did not, then eroding the hegemony of an ally in the task of overthrowing imperialism—the principal contradiction for all classes in colonial Indian society—would not be so simple. It would require a complex understanding of the concrete Indian reality and the evolution of equally complex strategy and tactics, a task the left failed to perform [A Mukherjee, 1981].

Second, the Indian bourgeoisie was aware that bourgeois hegemony in the anti-imperialist struggle was to be maintained not by simply buying up, manipulating or pressurising the nationalist leaders [as argued by Sarkar, 1976, Gordon, 1978] but by successfully projecting its own class needs or interests as representing the societal interest or the interest of the nation; in Marx's words, by '... represent(ing) its interests as the common interest of all members of society'.[29] It was extremely conscious that it should not appear to be pushing its own narrow class interest or putting class before nation, but as speaking in the interest of the Indian nation [see A Mukherjee, 1976]. Further, this projecting of a class interest as the rational interest is not achieved through manipulation, but in certain conjunctures by establishing a genuine coalescence of the two. In a colonial society, for example, there was, up to a point, a genuine unity of interest between the national bourgeoisie and the rest of society, as all of them were oppressed by imperialism.[30]

Third, a major index of the maturity of a class is its ability to identify its broad long-term interest (i e, maintenance of its overall hegemony over the rest of society) and willingness to subordinate its narrow short-term interest, sometimes at considerable cost, for the sake of the former. This perspective is necessary not only for sections within the class vis-à-vis the class as a whole, but also for the class vis-à-vis the rest of sociey. The Indian capitalist class, particularly its leadership, demonstrated remarkable maturity in this respect. Further, the Indian capitalists recognised the fact that a popular movement (and after independence a popular government) had to, to a certain extent, balance conflicting class interests [see A Mukherjee, 1978]. Each class, being aware that it could not directly claim sole hegemony over it, would have to act in a subtle way, essentially trying to ensure that the movement, despite contending hegemonies, remained in substance within the broad parameters of its class perspective.

Last, the failure or weakness of the left, which lagged far behind the bourgeoisie in its understanding of some of the aspects mentioned above, especially the subtle relationship between the class, the party and the nation, partially facilitated the continuance of bourgeois ideological hegemony over the Indian national movement. The left in its understanding of Indian society constantly tended to collapse the categories of class, party and nation, seeing a direct instrumental linkage between them. It failed to see the relative autonomy of the Indian national movement from all classes including the bourgeoisie and resorted to crude class reductionism [see Josh, 1981; Joshi, 1977; A Mukherjee, 1981, 1982].

Further, it was not enough, as the left has consistently tended to do, with some exceptions, to crudely attribute all possible socially reactionary roles to the bourgeoisie and hope that this would 'expose' the bourgeoisie, leading to a diminution of its influence or even its overthrow. When untrue, and sometimes blatantly so, such assertions carried little weight with the people. For example, the communist argument that the Indian bourgeoisie was comprador or essentially pro-imperialist and pro-feudal, and so was the Congress under bourgeois pressure, and that independence achieved by such a bourgeoisie or party was not real independence at all, but was a sell out, contributed in no small degree to their alienation from the Indian people, who even in their common sense wisdom could see the falsity of these charges. What was necessary was to identify and recognise all the socially positive aspects of the Indian bourgeoisie, and then undertake the difficult task of demonstrating effectively why, despite these positive aspects, the bourgeois class perspective was inhibiting or preventing social progress along the most desirable lines. Again, a task the left failed to perform, even after independence. This led to the left remaining relatively weak and permanently 'small and growing', never posing a serious enough threat to bourgeois hegemony.

ECONOMIC TRENDS SINCE 1947

At independence India had certain advantages compared to most other post-colonial societies. We have already discussed some of these, viz, the size, strength and independent character of the indigenous bourgeoisie and certain trends in the economy as a whole in the colonial period.

However, despite the incipient trends in the reverse direction towards the end of the colonial period, the Indian economy in 1947 was still basically structurally colonial; an externally oriented, internally disarticulated economy, with a very weak infrastructural and industrial base especially in capital goods; and a stagnant if not declining agriculture still dominated the economy.

In the years following independence a major effort was made to 'unstructure' the inherited colonial structure. We will now briefly outline the nature of development in post-independence India, particularly the aspects which reflect as well as determine the Indian economy's linkages with the external world. In doing so, we will examine some of the indices used by 'dependency theorists' and neo-Marxist world system analysts, etc, in determining the issue of peripheral or dependent development and self-reliant independent development. The attempt will be to highlight the sharp contrast between the paths followed by India and those taken by most of the developing countries of Latin America, Africa and East Asia.

Foreign Trade

One of the striking features of the Indian economy since independence has been its extremely low dependence on foreign trade. The total foreign trade as a proportion of the country's GNP remained around 10–13 per cent only between 1953 and 1977. Unlike most of the post-colonial third world countries, especially the NICs, the export sector in India has not been crucial, accounting for only five to six per cent of the GNP over this period [Kelkar, 1980: 23]. The Indian economy was thus no longer typically extroverted as it had become under the impact of colonialism which had destroyed the traditional balance between agriculture and industry, turning the country into an exporter of raw materials and food and importer of manufactured goods. Indian production since independence has been primarily dependent on the home market and inter-sectoral exchanges within the economy. The Indian economy is thus to an extent not crucially conditioned by or dependent upon the changes occurring in the metropolitan economies. (For example, India's performance in the 1970s when there was a world depression was much better than that of the other Low Income Countries on the whole [Varshney, 1984: 1512].

Further, the commodity and geographical concentration of Indian exports has been declining significantly since independence. In other words, dependence on one or a limited number of products and a few, set trading partners for exports, so typical of most underdeveloped countries, declined visibly in India. A similar diversification was achieved in imports. Further, the dependence on western metropolitan countries for foreign trade declined substantially, being compensated by increase in trade with socialist and developing countries [Kelkar, 1980: 6–8].

Moreover, the composition of Indian exports was undergoing a further change along the lines of the trends which had started to an extent even before independence. Not only were exports any longer predominantly of primary products but even in manufacturing exports there was a shift away from traditional simple products, like textiles. For example, by 1977–78 nearly 60 per cent of Indian exports were of manufactured goods, a large part of which was accounted for by technologically intensive products like engineering goods, electronics, consultancy, computer software, etc. A very significant aspect of India's export sector was that it was developed preponderantly by indigenous capital. In the 1970s, transnational corporations did not contribute even five per cent of India's exports [Kelkar, 1980: 7, 15]. There did not emerge an 'export oligarchy' as in Latin America, with important influence over the state and state policy.

Role of Foreign Capital

We have already noted the trend towards the declining influence of foreign capital in the Indian economy in the colonial period, especially since the 1930s. Immediately after independence, India, with plans for rapid industrialisation, needed and allowed direct foreign investments, though under strict controls laid down by the independent national state. Foreign capital was severely curtailed in the traditional areas preferred by it during colonial rule i e, extractive and other export industries, plantations, foreign trade, banking, insurance and consumer goods industries for the home market (Areas relatively easily substituted by indigenous private and state enterprise). It was on the other hand encouraged to come into high technology areas, especially capital goods industries producing for the home market. Here too, restrictions were placed on the exporting of the multiplier effects of foreign investments through the use of foreign raw materials and intermediate goods and the attempt was to encourage the progressive use of indigenous materials. The new foreign capital that came after independence in fact did go into modern technologically advanced sectors of industry and that too increasingly not in branches of European companies but in subsidiaries or more frequently in ventures involving minority foreign participation [Patnaik, 1975: 61]. As Arun Bose, in his excellent study, concluded: the 'slogan' at independence was 'foreign capital must either flow into manufacture for the home market using indigenous materials or "dry up"'. [1965: 525].

There are some other very significant aspects of the role of foreign capital in post-independence India (whose importance is often not seen), all of which were geared to ensuring that foreign capital did not acquire a dominating position in the national economy.

First, the total volume of foreign capital as a proportion of the aggregate national economy was always kept fairly low. Figures showing that the share of foreign capital in total *private* investment in India increased in the first three plans (i e, 1951–56, 1956–61 and 1961–66), from 13 per cent to 23 per cent to 24 per cent, are often quoted to show increasing domination of foreign capital in India [see Meghnad Desai, 1975: 23]. What is ignored is that the share of private investment itself in total investments had been declining sharply, from 53.6 per cent to 45.4 per cent to 39 per cent, over the first three plans [Mundle, 1974: 5]. Though in absolute terms foreign investment increased quite rapidly, its relative share in the economy in fact declined between 1948 and 1974—public sector investment and private Indian investment grew much more rapidly, especially towards the end of the period [Martinussen, 1980a: 18]. An indication of the rapid growth of the public sector can be got from a look at the statistics of joint stock companies. The total paid up capital in government companies represented 75 per cent of the entire corporate sector's paid up capital in 1978, having risen from 3.4 per cent in 1951 to 30 per cent in 1961 and to about 50 per cent in the early 1970s [Martinussen, 1980b: 24–25]. In terms of total volume, too, foreign capital in the Indian economy was very small—the total accumulated foreign private investment in India (split up among an increasingly larger number of nations) upto 1974 being a meagre Rs 19,430 million [Martinussen, 1980a: 18].

This amounted to less than three per cent of the GNP of just the year 1974 and about 20 per cent of the net domestic capital formation of again only that year, at current prices [Basic Statistics, 1981: 15]. In fact, the foreign exchange reserves India has held more or less continuously since 1977 were themselves about two-and-a-half to three times higher than the entire foreign private investments till 1974 [Basic Statistics, 1981: 121]. (Hypothetically just the foreign exchange reserves could buy out several times over the entire foreign private investments in India).

The size of foreign aid including concessional and grant aid was fairly low as well. Further, it was declining in importance over time, despite the crisis due to the hikes in oil prices. The net aid between 1956 and 1968–69 averaged at about 3.2 per cent of the NNP while between 1969–70 and 1971–78 it averaged about 1 per cent of NNP [from Kelkar, 1980: Table iv]. This certainly is not a classic example of an economy dominated by foreign capital or TNCs.

Second, contrary to popular notions, the outflow due to foreign private investments, ie, remittance of profits, dividends, royalties, technical fees and interest payments, was not too large, being Rs 5,240 million for the years 1964 to 1972 which amounted to merely five per cent of the export earning of that period [Kelkar, 1980: 14]. As a percentage of gross capital formation the outflows would be smaller and as a percentage of GDP these would be insignificant. Another estimate which includes outflows on account of both foreign aid and foreign capital (i e, interest on debt and total remittance by foreign companies) shows that the outflows, excluding amortisation, in 1976–77, as a proportion of exports were about seven per cent and as a proportion of GNP a meagre 0.4 per cent; including amortisation the outflows came to 16.9 per cent of exports and one per cent of the GNP. The total remittance by foreign companies came to only 2.2 per cent of exports. [Basic Statistics, 1981: 15; *Handbook of Statistics*, 1979: 37]. Besides, the proportion of outflows due to external debt to total exports have shown a secular decline between 1970–71 and 1979–80, falling by over half [Johnson, 1983: 184]. In fact, the eminent Indian economist, K N Raj, has argued that, given the sharp rise in internal savings since the mid-1970s, the economy should be able to maintain a rate of growth of 4 to 4 $^1/_4$ per cent per annum, and even raise it further without any foreign aid [1979: 16]. A far cry from the situation in several Latin American countries where the debt service burden in recent years (by 1983, 80 per cent of disbursed debt was owed to private creditors) has been about 30 to 50 per cent of export earnings and about six to seven per cent of the GNP, i e, between one-third to half the current rate of capital formation, severely affecting the rate of growth of the economy [Sunkel, 1986].

Third, while it is true that foreign capital tended to come into the most profitable areas of the economy [Patnaik, 1975: 68], it was not allowed to attain control over or to dominate, to use a key phrase of the Nehruvian era, the 'commanding heights' of the economy. Even as early as 1956 the percentage share of foreign private capital in the total capital investment in certain key industries like cement, general engineering and electrical engineering, chemicals and iron and steel was only 2.25, 2.82, 1.27 and 10.03 respectively [Kurien, 1966: 250]. The large mass consumer durables industries like cycles, fans, sewing machines and radios also had a remarkably low foreign capital participation. The same is true of the non-mass consumer durables sector such as scooters, automobiles and refrigerators. In the mass consumption non-durables sector such as textiles, Indian industries have completely dominated since independence. Foreign capital, however, was very important in non-core though highly profitable industries like soap, toothpaste and cosmetics.

The key areas where foreign capital domination continued for a very long time was oil, drugs and pharmaceuticals and rubber goods. Here, too, over time foreign influence was severely curtailed. The spectacular success was in the field-of oil where a prolonged confrontation between the government and the major foreign oil companies ended in 'an almost complete elimination of the major foreign oil companies', with the taking over by the government of the assets of these companies in 1976 [Martinussen, 1980b: 75]. In rubber goods and household consumer goods like soap, indigenous private enterprises have emerged as major competitors in recent years, though in the drugs and pharmaceutical industry, despite the setting up of the public sector Indian Drugs and Pharmaceuticals Ltd, foreign domination has been considerable. However, even in the pharmaceutical industry, the market share of total sales that domestic firms held in India in 1975 was 25 per cent, while in countries like Belgium, Canada and Australia the domestic share was only 10, 15, and 15 per cent respectively. Even countries like UK, Italy and Netherlands had a domestic share of only 40 per cent, not too far ahead of India. In 1977, the domestic share in India went upto 30 per cent [Gereffi, 1983: Table 6.6 and 7.2].

Foreign banks have historically played a crucial role in the penetration of foreign capital into the indigenous economy. In India, however, in the financial sphere too, foreign participation has been kept minimal. By 1970, public sector banks controlled 84.7 per cent of the total deposits in scheduled commercial banks while other Indian banks controlled 6.4 per cent, leaving only 8.9 per cent of the total deposits with foreign banks [Mundle, 1974: 12]. Again, between 1969 and 1981 the total branch expansion of all commercial banks in India was 27,445, increasing from 5,262 to 35,707 (significantly about half of this increase was in rural areas), while branches of foreign banks increased by only two, from 130 to 132 [*Economic Survey*, 1981–82: 114]. The picture was more or less the same in the other financial institutions like insurance companies etc.

Fourth, the items of foreign collaborations. A few years prior to independence, Indian capitalists westing to enter new high technology and capital intensive areas like automobiles, aircraft manufacture, heavy chemicals, ship building, electrical engineering and textile machinery went into a series of collaboration agreements with foreign companies. What is distinctive about these agreements is that while the Indian capitalists were willing to pay out large sums in royalty, or for outright purchase of technology, they refused to allow the foreign company to get a controlling position in the company floated. Foreign equity participation was haggled down to a very low proportion or totally refused and foreign representation on the company board was also kept very low. The major motive for these collaborations was the Indian capitalists' need to acquire capital goods and technology, given the Indian economy's weak industrial and technological base at that time. The collaborations did not reflect compradorism or willingness of Indian capitalists to become junior partners to foreign corporations [see A Mukherjee, 1979: 140ff].

After independence, the preponderant majority of foreign collaborations were 'pure' technical collaborations, i e, with no financial participation by the foreign collaborator. In very limited instances were foreign participants allowed to retain controlling shares. In fact, as the industrial base of the Indian economy widened with impressive gains in the capital goods sector (more on this below), the effective restrictions on TNCs with interests in India became more and more stringent [Martinussen, 1980a: 14–15]. However, dependence on foreign collaborations for technical know-how, especially in high-technology areas, has continued. This is today perhaps the key area of Indian dependence on the advanced sector of the world system.

However, it was in the direction of developing an indigenous scientific and technological base that India under Nehru's leadership took major strides. From virtually an insignificant beginning, India has today raised a stock of human capital trained in the field of science and technology which at least in quantitative terms is third in the world, behind only the US and the Soviet Union. The stock of scientific and technical personnel increased in India from 0.19 million to 2.32 million between 1950–1977. The national expenditure on scientific research and development also grew rapidly from Rs 10 million in 1948–49 to Rs 4,500 million in 1976–77, amounting to 0.65 per cent of the GNP of that year [Kelkar, 1980: 17]. Despite this spectacular growth, India continues to lag far behind in the field of science and technology because of a number of factors including the dismal record of the private sector in research and development (most of the R and D effort being state initiated and funded), the reticence, to put it mildly, of the TNCs in transferring up-to-date technology [Bagchi, 1986], an over emphasis on technology at the cost of basic science, a considerable 'brain-drain' to the advanced countries, etc.

A brief look at certain other trends in the Indian economy may be in order. India's tremendous advance in agriculture is now common knowledge. From virtual stagnation if not deceleration in agricultural growth in the last half century of colonial rule [Blyn, 1966], Indian agricultural output increased in the 1950s at the annual rate of 3.5 per cent [Patnaik, 1975: 63]. The average annual rate of growth of value added in agriculture between 1960 and 1984 has been about 2.6 per cent at factor cost and constant prices [Raj, 1984]. In Punjab, the supposedly most advanced region in the colonial period, all crop agricultural yield increased at the rate of only 0.36 per cent per year between 1901 and 1941. The contrast since independence is spectacular. Between 1950–51 and 1969–70 the productivity of eleven major crops in Punjab increased at an average rate of 12.5 per cent per year—a spectacular transformation by any standards [M Mukherjee, 1985: 72]. The Punjab pattern has been gradually spreading to other parts of the country. Indian food imports, consequently, have declined dramatically over the last decade, barring edible oils [Economic Survey, 1981–82: 85, 129], and India now has an impressive buffer stock in foodgrains amounting to nearly 30 million tons.

The annual rate of growth of GDP has been about 3.75 per cent from 1952 to 1976 and about 4.25 per cent in the recent past. Value added in manufacture grew at the average annual rate of about 5.2 per cent from 1952 till 1984 [Raj, 1984]. The gross domestic savings and gross domestic capital formation have averaged over 22 per cent since the mid-1970s [Economic Survey, 1981–82: 73] with the rate of gross fixed capital formation being about 18 per cent of GDP in the closing years of the 1970s; [Raj, 1984]. These rates of growth do not compare unfavourably with the rates of growth seen in most advanced industrial countries at the time of their 'take off'.

We believe that an assessment of the developments in India since independence cannot be based on indices such as the absolute level and rates of increase of per capita income, national income, per capita consumption of steel, etc. Indices such as these, so popular with the UN agencies, tell us little about the structure or the long term internal dynamic of an economy. Going by one such index, that of per capita income, Kuwait in 1960 ranked higher than the United States though the societies were poles apart in terms of structural strength [see Amin, 1974a].

A superior method of assessment or comparison of economic development especially in the context of domination and dependence is to look at the structure of the overall economy, viz, nature of intersectoral exchanges within the economy, nature of its external linkages in trade, capital movements, technology, etc, potential of generating growth without external dependence, nature of the home market, etc [see Amin, 1974a]. The crucial feature of the Indian economy since independence has been its movement in the direction of structural reorientation—the slow and steady dismantling of a typically disarticulated colonial or peripheral economic structure in an attempt to generate an inward oriented, self-centred development.

Going by the basic criteria used by a wide range of 'dependency theorists' to measure dependence or autonomy, viz, the extent to which an economy is able to have self-centred capital accumulation or the extent to which capital accumulation in an economy is not dominated by or subject to developments in another economy [see Evans, 1979: 26–27], India's record is quite impressive. In the post Second World War years and immediately after independence, the chief bottleneck for industrial development in India was the non-availability of capital goods, almost all of which had to be imported [A Mukherjee, 1979: 131ff]. Over the years the dependence on the outside world, especially TNCs, for capital goods to maintain a certain rate of capital formation declined rapidly. For example, between 1960–61 and 1973–74 the share of imported equipment in total fixed investment in the form of equipment declined from 43 per cent to only nine per cent, even though the total investment increased by nearly $2^1/_2$ times [Kelkar, 1980: 8].[31] Table 1 shows the rapid growth of the intermediate and capital goods sector between 1951 and 1979. In other words India's dependence on the external world for capital goods had become relatively small and it was able to make more than 90 per cent of its fixed investments without recourse to imports.

This does suggest a fairly comprehensive spread in India's economic capabilities over time especially in the capital goods sector. This became possible largely because of the planned emphasis on building an indigenous capital goods sector, especially since the Second Plan, and the predominant role played by the public sector in creating the necessary physical, financial and human infrastructure, facilitated considerably by assistance from the socialist bloc [Patnaik, 1975: 60].

Thus, unlike in several countries of Latin America [Gereffi, 1983: 33, Gereffi and Wyman, 1985: 10, Chart 3], in India the attempt to advance import substitution first to the consumer durables industries (e g, automobiles and consumer electronics) and then the capital goods sector (having already largely achieved the 'easy' import substitution in mass consumer goods industries like textiles) did not lead to increasing dependence on foreign investments and imports. On the contrary, the extension of horizontal ISI and the launching of vertical ISI in India instead of leading to 'internationalisation of the domestic market' through large-scale entry of TNCs [Evans, 1979: 31], as happened in Latin American countries, achieved what it was meant to: an expansion of the indigenous industrial base and a decline in external dependence.

Going by certain similar criteria identified succinctly by Samir Amin [see 1974b] to show the basic structural differences between the core and the periphery in the world system, India appears to be a backward but independent capitalist country at the edges of the core (i e, structurally closer to the core), rather than a typical dependency of the peripheral type. As suggested by the basic post-independence trends discussed above, Indian development was not internally disarticulated, i e, based primarily on an export sector and a luxury consumption sector both articulated to the centre in terms of markets, import of capital goods and foreign investment. In fact, Indian development was increasingly in the direction of what Amin [1974b] calls a 'central determining relationship' where an indigenous mass consumption goods sector is articulated with an indigenous capital goods sector. Even the luxury goods sector, kept relatively small in the total economy; was basically articulated with the indigenous capital goods sector. Similarly, the colonial situation where both Indian agriculture and industry were articulated with the metropolis [Alavi, 1975] was now reversed; the two sectors being basically articulated with each other.

It is necessary to clarify here that one is talking of overall structure and trends and not attempting to minimise the continuing Indian dependence on the core for high technology, basic science research and partially on what Marx calls department IA goods, i e, machines to produce machines. But though in the Indian case this dependence is greater, this kind of dependence exists even among backward countries of the core vis-à-vis the advanced core countries, though in broad structural terms they remain within the core. India's dependence is also that of a backward capitalist country on advanced capitalist countries, it is not the dependence of a neo-colony on the metropolis, or of a 'dependency' of periphery on the core.

Some Canadian scholars have argued [see Nelles, 1983: 38] that Canada, despite very high income rates, has a strong tinge of structural dependency similar to that prevailing in some of the smaller European economies and in Brazil, Mexico, Argentina, etc [see also Wallerstein, 1979: 83–84]. Similarly, it can be argued that India, despite very low income rates, lower than several countries of the periphery, demonstrates significant structural similarities with core countries, especially the backward ones among them.

ROLE OF POLITICAL INSTITUTIONS AND IDEOLOGY

Apart from the size, strength and nature of the Indian bourgeoisie and the Indian economy at independence, there were certain other important historico-structural factors which go towards explaining the specific developments India has seen since independence.

First, and probably the most important in this respect, was the legacy of the Indian national movement. The founding fathers of the Indian national movement had already by the last quarter of the nineteenth century developed a comprehensive and sophisticated critique of imperialism and the colonial structure [Chandra, 1966]. They were perhaps among the first in the world to do so. They made the shift in the understanding that modern imperialism was underdeveloping the colonies rather than deepening or creating the conditions for the development of capitalism roughly at the same time as did Marx and worked out a detailed economic critique of colonialism even before Hobson and Lenin [see Chandra, 1980, 1985]. A sophisticated anti-imperialist ideology thus permeated the national movement over a very long historical period and gave it firm roots in anti-colonialism which could not be easily swayed, diluted or compromised, as it was in the case of many other national liberation struggles [see Chandra, 1985: 4]. In the twentieth century, with the rise of the left and its strong influence in the national movement, this commitment to anti-imperialism got further strengthened. The left influence was felt through individual socialists or Marxists within the leadership of the Indian National Congress (the basic *platform* of the anti-imperialist movement in India) like Nehru, or through the Congress Socialist Party which was a strong and growing influence within the Congress in the 1930s and 1940s, or through the Communist Party which flitted in and out of the Congress, as well as through the radical revolutionary terrorists. It would not be wrong to say that the dominant section of the educated youth of the 1930s, and especially the 1940s, those who were to constitute the first generation intelligentsia after independence, were influenced by left radicalism of one variety or other. The left, despite its poor record since independence, still continues to be a significant ideological current in Indian society today.

Further, the fact that the Indian national movement was perhaps the greatest mass movement (as distinct from a cadre-based revolutionary movement) history has seen in modern times had certain important implications. One of its crucial features was that as a mass movement it took, through its struggle and ideological work, the two basic ideas of democracy and anti-imperialism down to very deep layers of Indian society. These ideas spread first among the intelligentsia and then gradually to the middle and lower middle classes and the capitalist class and with the emergence of Gandhi among the peasant masses.[32] The rise of the left helped spread them further among the workers and the peasants.

The deep ingraining of these two ideas among the people of India has had a lot to do with the maintenance, till today, despite extremely adverse conditions, of both political democracy (except a brief two year aberration from 1975–77) and political and economic independence.[33] It has prevented any serious threat in India of the formation of a typical third

Table 1 India: Indices of Industrial Production 1951–1979

Industrial Group	1960 = 100			1970 = 100
	1951	1961	1971	1978–79
General	55	109	153	186
Textiles	80	103	106	110
Basic metals	47	119	209	144
Machinery	22	121	373	208
Electrical machinery	26	110	405	162

Source: Government of India, 'India: A Reference Annual', New Delhi, 1980: 312, quoted in Johnson [1983: 136].

world type of comprador or semi-comprador military-bureaucratic puppet government which would toe the imperialist line in return for a guarantee of the maintenance of its power and of the narrow interests it represents. It has so far successfully stalled the ideological onslaught unleashed by a narrow section (though growing in recent times) which has been arguing for the World Bank–IMF model of 'liberal' policies favoured by international capital.

Political democracy has been seen to be not conducive to capitalist accumulation in the NICs of Latin America and East Asia which all have authoritarian regimes of one variety or another [Evans, 1979: 47–48, Gereffi and Wyman, 1985: 23ff]. In India, however, political democracy (along with the long anti-imperialist ideological tradition) has been greatly responsible for the country remaining on the path of self-reliant, independent capitalist accumulation. It has been a guarantee against the selling out of national economic and political interests by small elite groups or authoritarian regimes. Also, political democracy has given the India state far greater political and economic bargaining power vis-à-vis the advanced nations and international capital because it. It has also forced a relatively greater sharing (though by no means equitable) of the fruits of economic growth with the less privileged sections of the Indian people. Here too, the legacy of the pro-poor and egalitarian (though not necessarily socialist) orientation of the national movement has been important [Chandra, 1985].

Second, the balance of class forces in India since independence enabled (as well as reflected) the nature of the developmental path followed by India. The emergence of a ruling coalition consisting of a 'triple alliance' between international capital, state and local capital is seen as central to dependent capitalist development in Latin America [see Evans, 1979: 31–34, 52]. A similar alliance has been argued for even the East Asian NICs though here the role of international capital in the alliance is relatively minor [Gereffi and Wyman, 1985: 25]. In India, however, a foreign bourgeoisie or international capital did not constitute a part of the state or the ruling class coalition after independence. The bargaining with international capital was not occurring within the state or the ruling class coalition of which international capital was a part, as in Latin America and East Asia, but between an independent state reflecting an entirely indigenous ruling class coalition and international capital—an important difference in terms of autonomy.

The autonomy of the Indian state vis-à-vis the advanced countries is most clearly seen in its foreign relations. India's foreign policy has been independent to a degree rarely seen in any other third world country and it has consistently supported anti-imperialism all over the world. India has also refused to become a puppet in the hands of either of the superpowers and has in fact been a major motive force behind the nonaligned movement comprising about a hundred countries. In recent years, India has tried to spearhead a movement for economic and political co-operation among the third world countries to resist unitedly the domination of the advanced countries.

Indian variants of the 'triple alliance' model, i e that the Indian state after independence is dominated by the bourgeoisie/big bourgeoisie and landlords[34] who are increasingly collaborating with foreign finance capital/imperialism/TNCs, have been argued for a long time and continue to be argued today by the Marxist orthodoxy [see, e g, Bagchi, 1982: 93–4; Namboodiripad, 1973; Alavi, 1975: 1260; 1966: 79–80; Kurien, 1975; Dasgupta, 1975: 115–117; Patnaik, 1975: 78]—admittedly increasingly more or less as a token salute to the party line, as the overwhelming evidence has begun to point in another direction. Less doctrinaire studies have increasingly questioned this view in recent times [e g, Raj, 1973; Mundle, 1974: 11, 17; Roy, 1975; Chandra, 1972a, 1972b, 1981].

As we argued in section I, Indian capital even in the colonial period remained independent of the metropolitan bourgeoisie. After independence, with the backing of the national state, which Indian capital had seen as a crucial factor in its favour against foreign capital [A Mukherjee, 1979: 144], it had even less reason to accept the hegemony of foreign capital. However, over time, given the backing of the national state and the considerable increase in its own strength Indian capital became relatively less xenophobic about foreign capital. Still, as seen in section III, foreign capital was greatly restricted and was not allowed to acquire a significant hold over the Indian bourgeoisie as a whole,[35] or the Indian economy, and certainly not over Indian politics.

As for the feudal landlords, they were increasingly politically isolated and marginalised even in the colonial period, being the only class outside the anti-imperialist class coalition. After independence the land reforms, however slow and oriented in favour of the upper sections of the peasantry, broke the political and economic might of this class. Rich peasants and to a small extent Junker type capitalist landlords rather than feudal landlords dominate the rural scene of India today, exercising significant political and economic clout even at the national level.

The working class in India has been unionised on a large scale in the organised sector and has a long valiant tradition of trade union struggles. However, the left as an alternative national political current has been suffering a secular decline over time, even among the working class. Even on the purely trade union question, the left no longer has the bulk of the working class behind it. This is partly because of the economism pervading the Indian left [see M Mukherjee, 1983] and partially because of its inability to correctly characterise the Indian reality—consistently fighting false battles based on a false reading of Indian reality and outdated dogma [see Chandra, 1974, 1981; A Mukherjee, 1981]. Organisation of poor peasants and agricultural labour has remained rudimentary in most parts of the country. Also, the maintenance of a certain minimum amount of indigenous national development has prevented a situation of popular upsurge, whether under left wing or right wing hegemony, which could not be absorbed by the state and the existing institutions.[36] Thus on the whole, the threat from the left or 'popular pressure from below' never acquired serious enough proportions for the creation of the classic situation where the bourgeoisie would go over to imperialism or seek external help for its very survival.

Further, in India the size of an elite which is tied to the advanced capitalist 'centre' in its ideology and consumption styles has not been so large as to become a significant factor in her developmental strategy, as is the case in Latin America [Sunkel, 1986]. Again, partially because of political democracy and the existing hegemonic ideology in the country, sections of society like the large bureaucracy, military personnel, public sector employees, and professionals in universities and technical and scientific institutions have not been able to distance themselves in income, consumption pattern, lifestyle and political influence from the rest of society to the degree they have been able to in many of the developing countries of Latin America and Africa. As a result, the state has been able to severely restrict the import of luxury consumer durables, saving scarce foreign exchange which could be used to import crucial intermediate and capital goods. Also, the restriction of the process of 'internationalisation of consumption' through luxury demands of a large and powerful elite, before indigenous industry could on its own produce these goods, helped prevent the 'internationalisation of the domestic market' through large-scale entry of TNCs.

The dominant classes which have emerged in India since independence are the industrial bourgeoisie and the rich peasantry. The ruling bloc consists of these two classes and a broad section of the middle classes. The popular democratic government mediates the interests of the ruling bloc and the less privileged sections of Indian society though it essentially functions with the ideology of a reformist, welfare capitalism; this despite the popular rhetoric since Nehru's times of building a 'socialistic pattern of society'. Though the bourgeoisie in India as in other third world countries has been unable to exercise exclusive political domination or economic hegemony over the society, the Indian state and civil society has remained largely under bourgeois ideological hegemony despite the existence of contending trends including that of the left. So far the balance of class forces has not tilted in a direction that could pose a serious threat to the pursuing of the path of independent capitalist development.[37]

Third, the role of the state is central to any analysis of India's development and her position vis-à-vis the world capitalist system. The weight that can be exercised by the state of a country like India, given its sub-continental proportions and huge population, is very different from that of most of the small countries of the third world.

The state's role in India was not confined to planning and the use of the instruments of government policy but it actively intervened in the production process on a massive scale. Almost a decade before independence, the Indian National Congress through the National Planning Committee worked out a comprehensive multi-pronged plan of how India after independence was to telescope developments that normally span an entire historical epoch into a few years. The issue was how to bring about modern industrial development in a backward and still essentially colonial economy, without becoming dependent on foreign capital or imperialism. Planning and the public sector were seen to be crucial for such an effort.

The Indian capitalists too saw the necessity of the public sector and partial nationalisation and were among the first to argue for it. They saw the public sector as particularly necessary for developing basic heavy industries which require large investments and involve a time lag in returns. Also, the state was to be the preferred channel for bringing in the necessary foreign credits, loans, aid, etc, as it would be in a better position than private capitalists to deal with foreign capital without being swamped by it. The choice as the capitalists saw it was between the public sector playing a key role in developing basic industries, defence industries, public utilities, mobilising financial resources, etc, and dependent growth under foreign domination. They opted for the former.[38]

The course followed by planning and the public sector after independence was basically in line with the strategy worked out before independence. Since the Second Plan the public sector entered heavy industry in a big way. Over time the public sector has created a strong intermediate and capital goods base in the country, having started or played a major role in the fields of steel, heavy engineering, heavy electricals, heavy chemicals, machine tools, agricultural machinery, fertiliser, ship building, aircraft manufacture, railway locomotives and wagons, oil exploration and refineries, coal, electric power, nuclear power, defence industries, etc. It has, through the nationalisation of banks and insurance and the consequent tremendous expansion in these sectors, greatly increased the financial resource base of the country. The state has also as pointed out earlier, played a crucial role in considerably decreasing India's dependence on advanced countries in the fields of science and technology.

However, the public sector—contrary to what its early left nationalist protagonists (in the 1930s and 1940s) hoped and what certain radical trends argue even today—did not lead to socialism nor did it take the country a step in that direction [A Mukherjee, 1978]. The issue was not simply the establishing of institutions like the public sector. The crucial question was which government in what existing balance of class forces was introducing these institutions. In fact, as several studies now show [e g, Mundle, 1974], the public sector in the specific Indian context ended up strengthening the industrial and rural bourgeoisie. At the same time, in an alternate scenario where the balance of class forces shifts in favour of the left, the public sector has been correctly seen as an institution that could be turned to the advantage of the forces seeking the transition to socialism.[39] What the public sector has been able to achieve given the nature of Indian society and politics is that it has considerably diversified and expanded the economic base of the country, reducing foreign dependence on creating

Table 2 Index of Growth with 1950–51 as Base = 100 Except Where Indicated

	1950–51	1960–61	1973–74	1978–79
Industrial production		100 (1960 as base)	200.8	150.1 (with 1970 as base = 100)
Joint stock companies: Paid up capital (Base 1954–55)	100 (1954–55)	187.6		1225.0
Electricity generated	100	306.1		1675.0
Shipping: gross registered tonnage (150 GRT and above)	100	230.4		1439.6
Rado receivers	100	389.9		3591.7
Bank deposits of scheduled and non-scheduled banks (base 1951–52)	100 (1951–52)	204.5		3089.2
Motor vehicles on road (based on taxed vehicles only for 1950–51, thereafter includes vehicles exempted from tax)	100	216.9		1206.7
Agricultural production (base triennium ending 1969–70 = 100)	58.5	86.7		121.1
Per-capita income (at 1970–71 prices)	73.6	88.3		115.0

Source: Basic Statistics [1981: 1–5].

some of the crucial necessary conditions for a continued struggle against potential foreign domination.[40]

Last, the size of the Indian market has been a crucial factor in enabling India to pursue an inward oriented self-centred path of development. This option is not open to most of the third world countries especially the smaller ones amongst them. India's population of over 700 million is more than double that of all the Latin American countries put together. Also, political democracy and civil rights have prevented the increasing immiserisation of too large a proportion of the population. Besides, even if a fraction of the total population lives considerably above the subsistence level (and in India a substantial proportion does), the aggregate demand for industrial goods would be large enough to sustain a reasonable rate of industrialisation in a protected environment. Also, the tremendous stepping up of public investment since independence has played a major role in expanding the domestic market. A large captive domestic market has made possible the growth of indigenous industry, however inefficient and technologically obsolescent it might be: Tables 1–3 and the statistics elsewhere give an idea of the growth potential in certain areas.

In other words, unlike so many other NICs which face, for various reasons, an internal market constraint [see Wallerstein, 1979: 79], India was not inexorably pushed towards a strategy of export-led growth, which requires competitiveness in the world market and consequently engenders domination by TNCs.

CONCLUDING REMARKS

First, the Indian attempt at independent industrialisation in the twentieth century is not comparable with the transition to capitalism made by the present advanced capitalist countries in an entirely different historical context, nor with the tremendous industrial development seen in the Soviet Union. India is trying to industrialise with political democracy and civil rights including powerful trade union rights. India cannot industrialise on the backs of the working class and/or the peasantry by extracting surplus from these sections for industrial investment to the degree that all the advanced countries of today had done. Nor does it have colonial possessions. The paths of the enclosure movements, forced collectivisation, high land tax (as in Japan), total suppression of trade union rights, colonial surplus extraction, etc, are not open to India today.

Political democracy and adult franchise have meant for India that it cannot heavily tax agriculture (the preponderant majority of the population still live in rural areas), which contributes about 40 per cent of the GDP [Varshney, 1984]. Neither has it been politically possible to turn the terms of trade against agriculture or use other instruments of state policy to extract surplus from agriculture for industrial investment. In fact, since independence there has been a net inflow of resources from the non-agricultural sector to the agricultural sector [see Mundle; 1974: 13–16]. Similarly, the working class, especially in the organised sector, is strongly unionised and has won significant economic concessions, often including the pegging of wages to the price index. One example of its growing bargaining power is the increase in the index number of man days lost through collective bargaining from 100 in 1961 (base year) to 891.6 in 1980 [Basic Statistics, 1981: 2]. Clearly there is a limit to how far the working class can be exploited.

Also, the strength of the TNCs and the economic and technological distance between the advanced countries and the backward countries is far greater today than it was a hundred or even 50 years ago. Consequently, the minimum capital intensity and initial resources required to enter any industry and be competitive is infinitely larger today than what it was when most countries industrialised. The days of the yeoman farmer shifting to industry are essentially over. It is in these new and extremely difficult conditions that India is attempting an independent capitalist development.

Basic to the Indian strategy of development so far has been the emphasis on structure, both political and economic, rather than simply rapid growth. India has so far resisted the trade-off between economic independence and a faster rate of growth. It has also resisted a trade-off between political democracy and faster growth. Such trade-offs, made by most of the NICs, have some very obvious and serious shortcomings. While it is possible to have a faster rate of growth in the short run with massive inputs of foreign capital and free entry of TNCs, in the long run such a policy negates and original basic objective of independent self-centred development which would ensure continued growth. Similarly, trading political democracy and civil rights for growth not only involves tremendous human welfare costs unacceptable to any civilised society, it also militates against the building and maintenance of an independent political and economic structure, as we have argued above.

Second, a common confusion arises when the flexibility of the Indian developmental strategy is mistaken for a strategy of compromise with imperialism or even as a 'sell out' to it. India has since independence often seen swings[41] in its broad economic policy. Within a few years after independence India adopted a policy of protectionism vis-à-vis the outside world, then in the 1960s it liberalised its economy considerably; but this was followed by a reversion to economic nationalism and increase in restrictions in the 1970s; and again in recent years, it has opened up certain selected areas of the economy. In the 1960s the opening up was largely due to the weak position of India caused by the costly wars with China and Pakistan and a series of droughts, all leading to a major balance of payments crisis. The change in economic policy in that period was partially a result of external pressure, particularly of the United States and the World Bank, in return for help. The recent opening up in the 1980s is to be understood in a more complex manner. A rigidly autarchic ISI strategy in the long run tends to produce inefficiencies in the economy, increasing the distance in productivity levels vis-à-vis the advanced countries. A partial opening up would force the economy, especially its monopoly sector, to update itself in the face of world competition. One reason why India has to be competitive in the world market at least in certain areas is that it must maintain a minimum level of exports necessary to finance her requirements of key capital goods and technology which it has not been able to indigenise as yet.[42] Also the Indian state and the Indian bourgeoisie are in a better position today than they were at independence to withstand limited world competition. Collaboration agreements necessary for acquiring advanced technology can now be negotiated, in a carefully controlled manner, without necessarily being swamped by foreign capital. An opening up at an earlier stage could have been disastrous while a controlled opening up today may be necessary if the country is not to be left behind completely in terms of efficiency and technological capability. However, there is no reason to believe, as developments in the last few months confirm, that even this selective liberalisation or opening up is going to be a permanent one. A reversion to restrictionism is likely as soon as threats to the system as a whole, or to important sectors within it, emerge due to the opening up.

Further, one cannot take a static view and argue that a particular policy at all times involves an unequal relationship vis-à-vis the advanced countries. What is crucial is the direction in which the economy is moving. A country may enter into a phase of short term tactical dependence and import foreign capital and technology and it may even pay for it through highly subsidised exports (thus transferring surplus), but it may use this temporarily unequal situation for the strategic objective of strengthening its economy and reducing its long term external dependence; (China in recent years seems to be attempting just such a strategy). The converse can also be true where the nature of contact with the advanced world leads to further dependence in the long run. The crucial question therefore is: which state, with what balance of class forces, ideology and strategic objective, adopts certain policy options. The policy options by themselves only tell us part of the story.

The point one is making is that each swing or change in policy has to be empirically evaluated and critiqued in a specific manner. It cannot automatically be characterised as a basic shift, providing the 'final' proof of the bourgeoisie's or the bourgeois state's inherent tendency to sell out.[43] This kind of repeated crying wolf tends to have predictable diminishing returns especially in terms of decline in credibility of the left among the intelligentsia and the mass of the people. It thus reduces the ability of the left to intervene decisively if and when such a shift comes. More importantly, it leaves the left totally impotent in terms of working out a strategy for transforming or overthrowing the existing bourgeois structure which might not undergo a basic shift in the direction of neo-colonialism in the concretely relevant or predictable long run. It keeps the Left perpetually chasing the elusive chimera of the final crisis, in this case the sell-out to imperialism.

Third, our analysis above shows that Indian development so far has led to the

Table 3 Industrial Production, 1950–51, 1979–80 and Planned for 1984–85

	1950–51	1979–80	1984–85
Man-made fibres (thousand tons)	2.1	168	246
Steel, saleable (million tons)	1.1	6.0	11.5
Bicycles (thousand)	99	3,840	3,700
Machine tools (Rs million)	2.7	1,652	2.500
Sewing machines (thousand)	33	206	431
Cement (million tons)	2.7	17.6	34.5
Rubber tyres, motor (million)	0.6	6.2	9.2
Aluminium (thousand tons)	3.9	192	300
Iron ore (million tons)	3.6	39	60
Fertiliser, nitrogenous and phosphatic (million tons)	0.02	2.99	5.6
Sugar (million tons)	1.1	3.9	7.6
Sulphuric acid (million tons)	0.01	2.2	3.6

Source: Johnson [1983: 136].

reversing of most of the elements of a colonial or peripheral structure rather than leading to her getting sucked into a process of further peripheralisation, or being turned into a neo-colony. Further, India has managed to achieve this while remaining within the capitalist system. When we state this we are not at all arguing for the adoption of such a path by other third world countries or the continuance of this path by India.[44] The fragility and the dangers involved in this path, of getting reintegrated into an imperial structure, are fully recognised. Also, there is no doubt that this path pushes the cost of development as far as possible on the weaker sections of society. The grinding poverty that continues in India is enough proof of that. We must nevertheless recognise the empirical reality that India, in the specific historical conditions faced by her, has managed to develop independently along this path. This reality is ignored by radical trends which argue that unless countries in the periphery break put of the capitalist system (into socialism) they would necessarily be pushed into a position of further dependence.

An important reason why we emphasise our view of the Indian reality is that from it emerges a set of political implications which are vastly different from the positions traditionally argued by the left. If the Indian state today is an independent state under bourgeois hegemony, i e, it is neither a 'triple alliance' nor a 'bourgeois landlord state increasingly collaborating with imperialism', if the Indian economy today is an independent though backward capitalist one rather than a neo-colonial dependency, then the central contradiction in India today is capitalism and not imperialism, or feudalism and imperialism. What is on the agenda therefore, for those who seek a basic transformation of Indian society, is not the completion of the bourgeois democratic revolution (basically the strategic goal of all the major Communist Parties in India), but the creating of the conditions for a socialist transformation. The present system needs to be overthrown or transformed because it has the inequities and constraints of the bourgeois path of development, and not because it is integrated with imperialism. Undoubtedly, the struggle for a socialist transformation would involve a simultaneous struggle against imperialism. As Bipan Chandra, one of the first to systematically question the traditional left paradigm, has argued, the task in India after 1947 is an anti-capitalist socialist revolution of which anti-imperialism is an integral part and not an anti-imperialist, anti-feudal revolution of which anti-capitalism is an integral part [1972a: 168; 1983: 387ff]—a formulation which has crucial implications regarding the strategic and tactical class alliances necessary for social transformation.

We do not move closer to socialism by denying or refusing to recognise all actual capitalist development and repeatedly predicting a crisis or a 'sell-out' to imperialism. An alternate strategy to combat the actually existing and growing capitalism has to be devised. Indeed it is a complex and difficult task to move towards a socialist transformation by struggling against strong *indigenous* classes with a sophisticated array of political, economic and especially ideological weapons ranged in their favour. It may be easier to organise agitation against an easily identifiable foreign exploiter, when one is available. It is also easier to talk in terms of an utopian goal of uniting all socialist forces of the world against world capitalism to form a socialist world government [see Wallerstein, 1979: 35, 91, 101, 118], rather than pursue the real task of building socialist forces against indigenous bourgeois structures (on national planes) wherever that is the chief contradiction, whether in the advanced or backward sectors of the world economy. But then the easier solutions, if they do not reflect reality, are no solutions at all.

Similarly, one is a bit uncomfortable with the tendency in some radical circles to locate future class struggle in the world as between the 'peripheral' and 'advanced' nations or between the 'peripheral proletariat' and the 'metropolitan bourgeoisie'. Organising socialist opposition in the advanced countries has undoubtedly become very difficult but the burden of bringing about a socialist transformation is one burden that the centre cannot so easily transmit to the periphery.

Originally published as Aditya Mukherjee and Mridula Mukherjee, 'Imperialism and Growth of Indian Capitalism in Twentieth Century', *Economic and Political Weekly*, Vol. XXIII, No. 11, 12 March 1988, pp. 531–46.

NOTES

1. The first two parts of this paper are based heavily on A. Mukherjee (1982).

2. Samir Amin would see the emerging class struggle to be between the peripheral proletariat and the metropolitan bourgeoisie. The possibility of a long-term conflict between the colonial bourgeoisie and the metropolitan bourgeoisie is thus ignored, the former being seen as an adjunct of the latter (1974a: 25ff, 33ff).

3. Marxist orthodoxy assumed that the imperialism of the third stage necessarily meant massive foreign investment in the colonies.

4. Statement of Sterling Balances of Reserve Bank of India, *Purshottamdas Thakurdas Papers* (PT Papers), Fl 381, Nehru Memorial Museum and Library, New Delhi. Purshottamdas Thakurdas was one of the major leaders and ideologues of the Indian bourgeoisie in the colonial period.

5. In a rather generous estimate for 1947, Shirokov calculated that foreign enterprises owned 8.4 per cent of all enterprises and employed 24.3 per cent of the total labour force in organised industry, and in the bigger enterprises (employing more than 1,000 workers) the corresponding foreign shares were 30.2 per cent and 38.2 per cent. Also, by 1948, foreign companies controlled at best about 25 per cent of the total investments in private industry, leaving a rather large share for Indian investment (1973: 47–48).

6. In fact exclusion of the small sector, as well as dependence on sources relating to metropolitan areas where foreign capital dominated, often gives a misleading picture of the overall control and influence of foreign capital (see, e g, Ray, 1979: 43ff).

7. In 1946, total assets of the Indian business houses of Tata, Dalmia-Jain and Birla were Rs 6,000 million while the combined assets of the three largest European Companies, Andrew Yule, Bird Heilgers and Martin Burn (Indo-British), were only Rs 740 million. Similarly, between 1939 and 1948, the paid up capital of Tata and Birla increased from Rs 21 million and Rs 11.5 million to Rs 364 million and Rs 206.1 million respectively. While two other Indian companies had crossed the 100 million mark by 1948, there was only one European company, Bird Heilgers, with Rs 116.7 million, which had managed to do so (Shirokov, 1973: 49; Tomlinson, 1978).

8. The early twentieth century when the Indian capitalist class was dependent on the British umbrella to protect its foreign markets (e g, in China) contrasts sharply with the 1930s when the Indian capitalists with their inward orientation and greater control over the home market could reject the Ottawa Trade Agreement and partially the Modi-Lees Pact and bargain strongly in the Indo-British Trade Agreement of 1937–39, which also they ultimately rejected (see Kannangara, 1968; Chatterjee, 1981; Markovits, 1978).

9. The right-wing interpretations are be seen in the works of Dewey (1978) and Drummond (1972) where it is even argued that after First World War it was India which was in many respects exploiting Britain, rather than otherwise. For an interesting variation of the decolonisation thesis, see Tomlinson (1979). The left wing view originated among communists in the 1920s with overtones of it remaining till today (see A. Mukherjee, 1981: 28).

10. See Matthen (1980) and Bannerji (1963). The apparent paradox of a simultaneous growth of the indigenous capitalist class and an increase in imperialist exploitation is explained by the fact that the brunt of the impact of the latter was borne by the less privileged sections of the Indian people and that part of the growth of the Indian capitalist class was not by adding new capacity but by the taking over of British firms.

11. '. . .Class defines itself as in fact, it eventuates' (E.P. Thompson, 1978). See also seen in the case of the Indian capitalist class which in the 1920s and 1930s, when its position was relatively weak, remained totally opposed to any foreign capital, but in the 1940s, having somewhat consolidated its Nicos Poulantzas (1975: 70–71), for a similar view. We have argued elsewhere that an objective situation of economic weakness of a colonial bourgeoisie may not necessarily produce a class which accepts a dependent status but, on the contrary, may produce a class which makes spirited attempts politically and otherwise to break out of its dependent status and to develop independently. The reverse may also be true where a relatively economically strong class may remain backward ideologically and politically and therefore accept a relatively greater dependent status than would a politically advanced but economically weak class. Further, if only a one to one relationship is seen, where the economic base reflects only its own image (which is in a sense pre-determined) at the politico-ideological level, then there would be little possibility of socio-economic change on the basis of political and ideological intervention. This would be crude economic determinism. An example of how a simple link cannot be made between a weak economic position and surrender to imperialism is economic strength and being certain of being able to use the *weight of the imminent independent national state* against foreign domination, became willing to make concessions to and enter into agreements with foreign capital (see A. Mukherjee, 1979: 106, 143–44).

12. The speeches in FICCI, press communiques issued by their leaders and pamphlets produced by them, often products of the labours of the Research Committee of the Federation which investigated questions like rural debt, foreign capital, etc, and, later, journals like the *Eastern Economist* brought out by capitalists are some of the sources where their views can be seen. For an interesting awareness of 'unequal exchange', see G.D. Birla in FICCI, AR (1934: 173), S.P. Jain and B.M. Birla in FICCI, AR (1943: 129; 1946: 104–05).

13. For example, since the early 1920s, Purshottamdas put up a major battle against the British policy of currency manipulation and fiscal deflation which had wide repercussions for the Indian economy. In the 1940s, he, G.D. Birla and others led a significant agitation to obtain for India her hard earned sterling balances with Britain and made energetic attempts to secure India her rightful position in the post-war international monetary negotiations leading to the formation of the IMF. See particularly, FICCI, AR and FICCI, Correspondence (1944 to 1946).

14. See A. Mukherjee (1982) for a detailed discussion of the relationship of the Indian capitalist class with the Indian national movement.

15. For Communist characterisation in the 1920s, see A. Mukerjee (1981). For an example of a recent academic reiteration of the same view, see Sarkar (1976: 120–21, 146).

16. First, the limited market in a backward economy (e.g., for automobiles) quite often necessitated a virtual monopoly of the entire market to enter production profitably. Second, in a backward economy, to enter a new sophisticated area, the business house would have to manufacture the entire range of ancillary products itself and sometimes even provide basic infrastructure like power and roads. The textile machinery industry in India had to produce as many as 17,944 component parts itself, requiring huge financial resources which only a large house like Birlas could raise. See Ray (1979: 194) for this figure.

17. One aspect of late capitalism is that developments here do not go through the same stages as the early capitalist economies; certain intermediate stages of capitalist development are skipped. To begin manufacture under conditions of virtual free trade, a late entrant would have to achieve almost the same degree of capital intensity and scale as already achieved elsewhere to be competitive.

18. The example of the Dalmia-Jain group is an extreme one though by no means exceptional. By 1946 this group had controlling interests in chemical plants, paper mills, plywood, spare parts factories, railways, electriciy, vegetable *ghee*, soap, research laboratories, number of presses and publications, banks, insurance companies, investment companies, sugar mills, jute mills, cotton mills, flour mills, airlines, cement, coal, foodstuffs and collieries (Gokhale Institute, 1951: 47–50).

19. How the 'collective monopoly' of European (finance, trade, banking, industry, etc) interests prevented indigenous investment in industry is superbly brought out by A.K. Bagchi in his major work (1972). Perhaps another reason why Indian houses diversified into so many areas was that, since state support in any one area was never assured, they needed to spread their risks.

20. We are summarising below the views put

forward by a wide cross-section of the Indian capitalist class in what was popularly known as the Bombay Plan (the signatories to which were Purshottamdas Thakurdas, J.R.D. Tata, G.D. Birla, Ardeshir Dalal, Sri Ram, Kasturbhai Lalbhai, A.D. Shroff and John Mathai) or in the FICCI. (See Purshottamdas Thakurdas et al., 1945: 36–40, 73–83; FICCI, AR, 1943: p. 61, 1945: 7–8, 1947: 8–9). The views of the capitalists in the rest of the para are taken from the above sources except where otherwise indicated.

21. The FICCI president in 1945, J.C. Setalvad, went to the extent of suggesting that the government should experiment with not only cooperative but even collective farming on the Russian model, for which Soviet experts should be called for consultation (FICCI, AR, 1945: 7–8). However, this was by no means the general view among the capitalists who were very clear in rejecting the Soviet model, opting for co-operative farming.

22. The experience of India since 1947 and of various other countries like Germany, Japan England etc. suggests that this was a feasible model of agrarian reform from above which overthrew feudalism in agriculture.

23. One cannot perhaps lump all Indian princes, especially the progressive ones among them who were committed to fairly wide-ranging modernisation along capitalist lines, as feudal; they were more like the Meiji oligarchs and Bismarckian Junkers. It is significant that in the inter-war period, a substantial part of industrial investment in India occurred in the princely states (Bagchi, 1972: 210, 214–15).

24. Purshottamdas to N.M. Mazumdar, June 7, 1929 (PT Papers, Fl 42, Pt II). Also support was not given to the imperialist government to extend its existing powers in the name of suppressing communists as was attempted through the Public Safety Bill (FICCI, AR, 1928).

25. G.D. Birla to Walchand, May 26, 1936 (PT Papers, Fl 177). Similarly *Indian Finance* of March 11, 1944 warned against the class speaking 'with too obvious a concern for its own class interest... condemn(ing) itself in the eyes of the public'.

26. G.D. Birla to Walchand, May 26, 1936 (PT Papers, 1936, Fl 177). 'The right wing Congressmen are... fighting two forces—the government and the Socialists' (G.D. Birla, 1953: 193).

27. M.N. Roy, e g, argued in 1927 that the 'overthrow of imperialist domination cannot be a bourgeois revolution' (A. Mukherjee, 1981). See also Bagchi (1972: 426–28) for a similar perspective.

28. Perry Anderson recognises this and argues that the establishment of a bourgeois democracy in India in 1947 and its more or less successful practice over the last thirty years demonstrates the falsity of Trotsky's notion, declared after 1924, that henceforth there could be no successful bourgeois democratic revolution in any of the colonial countries (1976: 118).

29. Marx and Engels in 1846, referring to the bourgeoisie's struggle against feudalism, made the following comment which is relevant to the colonial situation in India as well: 'For each new class which puts itself in the place of one ruling before it, is compelled, merely in order to carry through its aim, to represent its interests as the common interest of all the members of society, that is, expressed in ideal form: it has to give its ideas the form of universality, and represent them as the only rational, universally valid ones. The class making a revolution appears from the very start, if only because it is opposed to a class, not as a class, but as the representative of the whole of society, it appears as the whole mass of society confronting the one ruling class' (1964: 61–62).

30. As Poulantzas also notes, 'The national bourgeoisie is capable of adopting, in certain specific conjunctures of the anti-imperialist and national liberation struggle, class positions which make it part of the people, it can therefore be brought into a certain type of alliance with the popular masses' (1975: 71).

31. Another estimate shows that the imported supplies of the following products as a percentage of total available in India declined sharply between 1960–61 and 1977–78; textile machinery from 69 to 11, iron and steel from 36 to 1.1, and aluminium from 58 to 2 (Johnson, 1983: 138).

32. Our interviews with hundreds of grassroots level participants in the national movement throughout the country has confirmed the view that the people at the lowest level did understand and absorb fairly sophisticated nationalist ideas (see Chandra, 1985: 3ff).

33. Democracy came to India not as a gift or legacy of colonial rule by an advanced democracy, as is often argued, but as a result of nearly three quarters of a century of struggle by the national movement against a rule which initially denied India the most elementary levels of democracy and then conceded a measure of civil liberties and democratic rights under severe pressure.

34. The term landlord is often not clearly defined but the implication is clearly feudal landlords or 'remnants of feudalism' (Patnaik, 1975: 78).

35. The Indian bourgeoisie's relationship with the TNCs does not demonstrate what Wallerstein (1979: 102) calls the 'defining structural characteristics' of a non-socialist semi-peripheral country, where the 'indigenous bourgeoisie is structurally linked to corporations located in the core countries' to a degree 'far larger than is true of the bourgeoisie within any core country'. We also find it difficult to agree with Wallerstein's formulation (1979: 105) that the national bourgeoisie is nationalist only in the narrow sense that it is *always* ready to 'brandish the flag' as a 'negotiating instrument with the rest of the capitalist world economy' for its 'blackmail effect' and puts the 'flag in cold storage for a price'. This formulation is uncharacteristically instrumentalist, and fails to take account of the fact that the 'flag' is crucial to the independent *survival* of the bourgeoisie. The national bourgeoisie would sell out only if there was a compelling reason to do so, such as a threat to its existence from popular movements. Otherwise it is in the long term *class interest* of the national bourgeoisie to stick to the 'flag' and identify its interests with the nation. The Indian bourgeoisie has as yet not had a reason for committing *hara-kiri* for a 'price'.

36. Charles Bergquist (1986) shows the inverse correlation between indigenous national development and strength of left labour movement in Latin America.

37. The growing political strength of the rich peasantry however has had some implications regarding the availability of surplus for industrial investment as we will see later.

38. The whole issue of planning and the public sector prior to independence has been discussed in A. Mukherjee (1976, 1978).

39. A similar argument has been made by 'A Student of Political Economy' (1982) and Paresh Chattopadhyay, quoted in S Habib (1975).

40. Samir Amin's contention (1974b: 16) that in the countries of the periphery, the public sector only strengthens or reinforces the peripheral structure is not valid for India. Here the public sector has played a major role in undermining the colonial structure.

41. We are using the expression 'swing' as a contrast to 'shift'. 'Swing' connoting a movement back and forth from basically the same position, while a shift involves a basic altering, of the position.

42. This is by no means to be seen as a shift to an export-led growth strategy which has very different implications. At best one may call it an 'export dependent' growth strategy (A Student of Political Economy, 1982: 32).

43. The most recent example at hand is the IMF loan taken by India in the early 1980s, the largest ever given by the Fund. A wide spectrum of the Indian Left immediately raised an outcry that India had finally mortgaged her economic and political sovereignty. Today, almost everybody agrees that India has been able to absorb the loan and no serious threat to her basic economic and political structure is predicted on this count.

44. We would like to clearly demarcate our position from that of the neo-corporatists in Latin America (see Bergquist, 1986).

REFERENCES

A Student of Political Economy, 1982, 'Indian Development: Option and Choices', *Mainstream*, Vol. 22, No. 29 (March 20).

Alavi, Hamza, 1966, 'Indian Capitalism and Foreign Imperialism', *New Left Review*, No. 37 (May–June).

——, 1975, 'India and the Colonial Mode of Production', *Economic and Political Weekly*, Vol. 10, Nos 33–35 (August).

——, 1979, 'The Structure of Colonial Social Formations', mimeo.

—— et al., 1982, *Capitalism and Colonial Production*, London and Canberra, Croom Helm.

Amin, Samir, 1974a, *Accumulation on a World Scale*, 2 Vols, New York, Monthly Review Press.

——, 1974b, 'Accumulation and Development: A Theoretical Model', *Review of African Political Economy*, pp. 9–26.

Anderson, Perry, 1976, *Considerations on Western Marxism*, London, New Left Books.

Bagchi, A.K., 1972, *Private Investment in India, 1900–1939*, Cambridge, Cambridge University Press.

——, 1973, 'Foreign Capital and Economic Development in India, A Schematic View', in K. Gough and H. Sharma (eds), *Imperialism*

and Revolution in South Asia, Monthly Review Press.
——, 1982, *The Political Economy of Underdevelopment*, Cambridge, Cambridge University Press.
——, 1986, 'Foreign Collaboration in Indian Industry', *Economic and Political Weekly*, Vol. 21, No. 21 (May), pp. 915–918.
Bannerji, A.K., 1963; *India's Balance of Payments*, Bombay, Asia Publishing House.
Bergquist, Charles, 1986.
Birla, G.D., 1953, *In the Shadow of the Mahatma*, Bombay, Orient Longman.
Blyn, George, 1966, *Agricultural Trends in India, 1891–1947: Output, Availability, and Productivity*, Philadelphia, University of Pennsylvania Press.
Bose, Arun, 1965, 'Foreign Capital', in V.B. Singh (ed.), *The Economic History of India: 1857–1956*, Bombay, Allied, pp. 485–527.
Central Statistical Organisation, Government of India, 1981, *Basic Statistics Relating to the Indian Economy*.
Chandra, Bipan, 1966, *The Rise and Growth of Economic Nationalism in India*, New Delhi, People's Publishing House.
——, 1970, 'Colonialism and Modernisation', Presidential Address, Indian History Congress, Jabalpur. Also in Chandra, 1979, pp. 1–37.
——, 1972a, 'The Indian Capitalist Class and Imperialism before 1947', Paper read at the International Seminar on Imperialism, Independence and Social Transformation in the Contemporary World, New Delhi. Also in Chandra, 1979, pp. 144–170.
——, 1972b, 'Modern India and Imperialism', Paper read at Bertrand Russel Centenary Symposium on Spheres of Influence in the Age of Imperialism, Linz, Austria. Also in Chandra, 1979, pp. 204–22.
——, 1974, 'Marxism in India, A Total Rectification', *Seminar*, No. 178, (June).
——, 1979, *Nationalism and Colonialism in Modern India*, New Delhi, Orient Longman.
——, 1980, 'Karl Marx, His Theories of Asian Societies, and Colonial Rule', in *Sociological Theories: Race and Colonialism*, UNESCO. An abbreviated version in *Review*, Vol. 1, Summer, 1981, pp. 13–19.
——, 1981, 'A Strategy in Crisis—The CPI Debate 1955–1956', *Studies in History*, Vol. 3, Nos 1 and 3, pp. 259–400. Also in Chandra, 1983.
——, (ed.) 1983, *The Indian Left: Critical Appraisals*, New Delhi, Vikas.
——, 1985, 'The Long-Term Dynamics of the Indian National Congress', Presidential Address, Indian History Congress, Amritsar.
Chatterjee, B., 1981, 'Business and Politics in the 1930s, Lancashire and the Making of the Indo-British Trade Agreement', *Modern Asian Studies*, Vol. 15, No. 3, pp. 527–573.
Communist Party of India (Marxist), 1979, *Handbook of Statistics*, New Delhi.
Dasgupta, Biplab, 1975, 'Class Character of the Ruling Class in India', in Kurien, 1975, pp. 115–128.
Desai, Meghnad, 1975, 'India: Emerging Contradictions of Slow Capitalist Development', in Robin Blackburn (ed.), *Explosion in a Subcontinent: India, Pakistan, Bangladesh and Ceylon*, Penguin, pp. 11–51.
Dewey, C., 1978, 'The End of Imperialism of Free Trade: The Eclipse of the Lancashire Lobby and the Concession of Fiscal Autonomy to India', in Dewey and Hopkins (eds), *Imperial Impact: Studies in the Economic History of Africa and India*, London.
Drummond, I. M., 1972, *British Economic Policy and the Empire*, London.
Evans, Peter, 1979, *Dependent Development: The Alliance of Multinational, State, and Local Capital in Brazil*, Princeton, NJ, Princeton University Press.
Federation of Indian Chambers of Commerce and Industry (FICCI), *Annual Reports* (AR), 1927–47.
——, *Correspondence Volumes* (Corresp), 1927–47.
——, *Proceedings of the Executive Committee* (Proc of EC), 1927–47.

Gereffi, Gary, 1983, *The Pharmaceutical Industry and Dependency in the Third World*, Princeton, NJ, Princeton University Press.

——, and Wyman, Donald 1985, Development Strategies in Latin America and East Asia, mimeo.

Gokhale Institute, 1951, *Notes on the Rise of Business Communities in India*, New York.

Gordon, A.D.D., 1978, *Business and Politics, Rising Nationalism and Modernising Economy in Bombay*, 1918–1933, New Delhi: Manohar.

Government of India, *Economic Survey*, Delhi, 1981–82.

Habib, Sayera, 1975, 'The State Sector of the Indian Economy', in Kurien, 1975, pp. 166–71.

Johnson, B.L.C., 1983, *Development in South Asia*, Penguin.

Josh, Bhagwan, 1981, 'Nationalism, Third International and Indian Communists: Communist Party and the United National Front, 1934–39', *Studies in History*, Vol. 3, Nos 1 and 2, pp. 147–200. Also in Chandra, 1983.

Joshi, Sashi, 1977, 'The Ideological Origins of the Communist Party of India, 1920–25', Unpublished M. Phil dissertation, Jawaharlal Nehru University, New Delhi.

Kannangara, A.P., 1968, 'Indian Millowners and Indian Nationalism before 1914', *Past and Present*, No. 40 (July).

Kelkar, Vijay, 1980, 'India and the World Economy: A Search for Self-Reliance', Paper read at Seminar on Jawaharlal Nehru and Planned Development, New Delhi.

Kidron, M., 1965, *Foreign Investments in India*, London: Oxford University Press.

Kurien, Mathew, 1966, *Impact of Foreign Capital on Indian Economy*, New Delhi: People's Publishing House.

——, 1975, 'Class Character of the Indian State', in Mathew Kurien (ed.), *India—State and Society*, Bombay: Orient Longman.

Levkovsky, A.I., 1966, *Capitalism in India*, Delhi: People's Publishing House.

Mandel, Ernest, 1962, *Marxist Economic Theory*, 2 Vols, Calcutta: Rupa.

Markovits, C., 1978, 'Indian Business and Nationalist Politics from 1931–1939', Unpublished D. Phil dissertation, Cambridge University.

Martinussen, John, 1980a, 'National Legislation and Regulations Relating to the Activities of Transnational Corporations in India', Paper prepared for the Seminar on the Relationship between Governments and Transnational Corporations in Third World Development, Copenhagen.

——, 1980b, *The Public Sector in India*, Denmark: University of Aarhus.

——, 1980c, *The State in Peripheral and Post-Colonial Societies: India and Pakistan*, Aarhus: Politica.

Marx, K. and F. Engels [1846] 1964, *German Ideology*, Moscow: Progress Publishers.

Matthen, Ousep, 1980, 'Monetary Aspects of the Inter-War Economy of India', Unpublished D. Phil Dissertation, Jawaharlal Nehru University, New Delhi.

Mukherjee, Aditya, 1976, 'Indian Capitalist Class and the Public Sector', *Economic and Political Weekly*, Vol. 11, No. 3 (17 January), pp. 67–73.

——, 1978, 'Indian Capitalist Class and Congress on National Planning and Public Sector 1930–47', *Economic and Political Weekly*, Vol. 13, No. 35 (2 September), pp. 1516–28: Reprinted in K.N. Panikkar (ed.), 1980, *National and Left Movements in India*, New Delhi, Vikas.

——, 1979, 'Indian Capitalist Class and Foreign Capital', *Studies in History*, Vol. 1, No. 1 (January–June), pp. 105–48.

——, 1981, 'The Workers' and Peasants' Parties 1926–30: An Aspect of Communism in India', *Studies in History*, Vol. 3, Nos 1 and 2, pp. 1–44. Also in Chandra, 1983.

——, 1981a, 'Business and Politics in Bombay', *Indian Historical Review*, Vol. 9, Nos 1–2, pp. 214–22.

——, [1982] 1986, 'The Indian Capitalist Class: Aspects of Its Economic, Political and Ideological Development in the Colonial Period, 1927–47', Paper read at Indian

History Congress, Kurukshetra. Reprinted in S Bhattacharya and Romila Thapar (eds), *Situating Indian History*, Delhi, Oxford University Press, pp. 239–87.

Mukherjee, Mridula, 1983, 'Communists and Peasants in Punjab: A Focus on the Muzara Movement in Patiala, 1937–53', in Chandra, 1983, pp. 401–46.

——, 1985, 'Commercialisation and Agrarian Change in Pre-Independence Punjab', in K.N. Raj et al. (ed.), *Essays on the Commercialisation of Indian Agriculture*, Delhi, Oxford University Press, pp. 51–104.

Mundle, Sudipto, 1974, 'State Character and Economic Policy', *Social Scientists*, Vol. 2, No. 10 (May), pp. 3–19.

Namboodiripad, E.M.S., 1973, 'On Intermediate Regimes', *Economic and Political Weekly* (1 December).

Nelles, H.V., 1983, 'Interpreting Canadian Economic Development', Paper for the Shastri Indo-Canadian Institute Workshop on Canadian History, New Delhi.

Patnaik, P., 1975, 'Imperialism and the Growth of Indian Capitalism', in Robin Blackburn (ed.), *Explosion in a Subcontinent: India, Pakistan, Bangladesh and Ceylon*, Penguin, pp. 51–78.

Poulantzas, Nicos, 1975, *Classes in Contemporary Capitalism*, London, New Left Books.

Purshottamdas Thakurdas Papers, Nehru Memorial Museum and Library.

Purshottamdas Thakurdas et al., 1945, *A Plan of Economic Development for India*, Part I and II, Penguin.

Raj, K.N., 1973, 'The Politics and Economics of 'Intermediate Regimes', *Economic and Political Weekly* (7 July).

——, 1979, 'Prospective Changes', *Seminar*, No. 244 (December), pp. 12–16.

——, 1984, 'Some Observations on Economic Growth in India over the Period 1952–53 to 1982–83', *Economic and Political Weekly*, Vol. 19, No. 41 (October), pp. 1801–04.

Ray, Rajat, 1979, *Industrialisation in India, Growth and Conflict in the Private Corporate Sector, 1914–47*, New Delhi: Oxford University Press.

Roy, Ajit, 1953, *Indian Monopoly Capital*, Calcutta.

——, 1975, 'Sharers in Indian State Power', in Kurien, 1975, pp. 129–43.

Sarkar, S., 1976, 'Logic of Gandhian Nationalism: Civil Disobedience and the Gandhi Irwin Pact: 1930–1931', *Indian Historical Review*, Vol. 3, No. 1 (July).

Shirokov, G.K., 1973, *Industrialisation in India*, Moscow, Progress Publishers.

Sivasubramaniam, S., 1977, 'Income from the Secondary Sector in India', *Indian Economic and Social History Review*, (October–December).

Subramanian and Homfray, 1946, *Recent Social and Economic Trends in India*, Delhi, Government of India.

Sunkel, Oswaldo, 1986, 'Debt Crisis in Latin America', Series of Four Lectures at Duke University, USA (March–April).

Thompson, E.P., 1978, 'Eighteenth Century English Society', *Social History*, Vol. 3, No. 2 (May).

Tomlinson, B.R., 1978, 'Foreign Private Investment in India, 1920–50', *Modern Asian Studies*, Vol. 12, Pt 4 (October).

——, 1979, *The Political Economy of the Raj, 1914–47*, London, Macmillan.

Varshney, A., 1984, 'Political Economy of Slow Industrial Growth in India', *Economic and Political Weekly* (1 September), pp. 1511–17.

Varshney, R.L., 1965, 'Foreign Trade', in V.B. Singh (ed.), *Economic History of India: 1857–1956*, Bombay, Allied, pp. 444–84.

Wallerstein, Immanuel, 1979, *The Capitalist World-Economy*, Cambridge, Cambridge University Press.

31

Industry after Independence
Initial Challenges and Dilemmas

Ashok S. Ganguly

The years following India's Independence were marked by both apprehension as well as anticipation of opportunity for private enterprise. Within business circles, there was much uncertainty about the kind of economic policies the independent government would follow and the role the private sector would be called upon to play. Business leaders had, in 1944, authored the Bombay Plan, putting forth their views about national economic reconstruction and envisaging a prominent role for the private sector in independent India. However, Leftist pronouncements by leading nationalist figures, especially Nehru, in the lead-up to Independence and declarations by the Congress of its economic programme soon after Independence (such as the report of the Economic Programme Committee in 1948) caused much uncertainty and apprehension.* Some of these fears were allayed with the Industrial Policy Resolution in April 1949 and then with the inauguration of the First Five-Year Plan which, in many ways, was similar to the Bombay Plan, and assured a significant role for the private sector.† Of the total investment of 3500 crore rupees, 2000 crore rupees were to be in public sector and 1500

* In January 1948, the Economic Programme Committee of the ruling Congress put forth its vision and declared nationalization of public utilities and key industries, public ownership of monopolies, and early abolition of managing agencies as the party's goals. It also recommended that the process of transfer of assets from private to public ownership for industries should commence within five years.

† The Industrial Policy Resolution of 1948 was the first official policy framework for the national economy. It declared that public ownership of assets would only be confined to three industries (munitions, atomic energy, railways); in six others (coal, iron and steel, aircraft manufacturing, shipbuilding, telegraphic and telephone materials, minerals), the government reserved the right to start new ventures. However, existing firms in these areas were to remain free from government control and no redistribution of assets was to take place for at least 10 years.

crore rupees in the private sector, while a large field was left open to the private sector. These were signs that the future of the private sector was secure.

Yet, by the late 1950s, especially after the Avadi session of the Congress when the party adopted the 'socialist pattern of society' as its declared objective, the socialist rhetoric became more pronounced, making private enterprise feel somewhat restricted. This was followed by the Second Five-Year Plan, which emphasized the creation of a large capital goods industry, favoured the public sector, and advocated a tightening of licenses and a consolidation of the license permit raj.[‡] However, private enterprise did enjoy a protected market and also gained from the opportunities that came with the increased pace of industrial development to which the leadership was committed.

Ashok Ganguly, chairperson of Hindustan Lever Limited (Unilever's Indian subsidiary) in the 1980s, recounts the company's evolution in the 1950s. A British company, Lever Brothers had entered India as early as 1913 and after its merger with the Dutch Margarine Union and the formation of Unilever, it started local manufacture of vegetable ghee in 1932 and soap in 1933. In the mid-1930s, it entered new lines such as milk products and dried vegetables. At the end of the War, it entered the realm of health care products including its popular toothpaste. The story of Hindustan Lever (now Hindustan Unilever) is an especially interesting one since, like other multinationals in the immediate post-Independence period, it faced the challenge of going 'local' by allowing for larger local shareholding and appointing Indians as managers.[§] It was in keeping with this that the three businesses of Hindustan Vanaspati Manufacturing Limited, Lever Brothers India Limited, and United Traders Limited were merged to create Hindustan Lever in 1956, and 10 per cent of the equity was sold to the public.[¶] Between 1956 and 1963, the company achieved average profits of 9.3 per cent, higher

‡ On these developments, see Francine R. Frankel, *India's Political Economy, 1947–1977: The Gradual Revolution* (Princeton, Princeton University Press, 1978); Arvind Panagariya, *India: The Emerging Giant* (New Delhi, Oxford University Press, 2007); Hiranmay Karlekar (ed.), *Independent India: The First Fifty Years* (Delhi, Oxford University Press, 1998); and Lloyd I. Rudolph and Susanne Hoeber Rudolph, *In Pursuit of Lakshmi: The Political Economy of the Indian State* (Chicago, University of Chicago Press, 1987). For an understanding of industrial stagnation, see Isher Judge Ahluwalia, *Industrial Growth in India. Stagnation since the Mid-sixties* (Delhi, Oxford University Press, 1985).

§ On this theme, also see Stephanie Jones, *Merchants of the Raj: British Managing Agency Houses in Calcutta Yesterday and Today* (Basingstoke, Macmillan, 1992). There is interesting literature on British businesses such as B.R. Tomlinson, 'British Business in India, 1860–1947', in R.P.T. Davenport-Hines and Geoffrey Jones (eds), *British Business in Asia since 1860* (Cambridge, Cambridge University Press, 1989) and Anna Maria Misra, *Business, Race and politics in British India, 1850–1960* (Oxford, Clarendon Press, 1999).

¶ In 1931, Unilever set up its first Indian subsidiary, Hindustan Vanaspati Manufacturing Company, followed by Lever Brothers India Limited (1933) and United Traders Limited (1935). See G. Jones, 'Managing Governments: Unilever in India and Turkey, 1950–1980', Harvard Business School Working Paper, 2006, available online at http://www.hbs.edu/research/pdf/06-061.pdf, last accessed on 14 January 2010. Also see G. Jones, *Renewing Unilever: Transformation and Tradition* (Oxford, Oxford University Press, 2005); Charles Wilson, *The History of Unilever: A Study in Economic Growth and Social Change* (London, Cassell, 1954); D.K. Fieldhouse, *Unilever Overseas: The Anatomy of a Multinational 1895–1965* (London, Hoover Institution Publication, 1978); and Lionel Carter, *Chronicles of British Business in Asia, 1850–1960: A Bibliography of Printed Company Histories with Short Accounts of the Concerns* (New Delhi, Manohar, 2002), pp. 196–200.

than in other areas such as Europe (9 per cent).** Ganguly recalls the company's strategy which enabled it reach 'commanding heights'. The two key areas were 'management' and 'research and development'. The former was a dynamic institution of the company where new managers were groomed in line with the ever changing socio-historical circumstances and the latter was started in 1958 as a different department, enabling the company to make breakthroughs in developing innovations which relieved reliance on foreign capital and consumer goods imports.††

DEVELOPMENTS AT HLL

Change is seldom apparent immediately. It would be wrong to try to correlate change quantitatively in order to comprehend its impact. Although qualitative, the effects of planned change are substantive as they cover a longer time span and leave their indelible mark on societies, organisations and individuals. Shorter-term changes are generally reactive responses to immediate environmental stimuli as contrasted with proactive and planned change. In this section of Hindustan Lever we are not concerned with short-range reactive changes, but with broad trends and signals of long-term developments.

Hindustan Lever, as it is today, is a product of managing change over several decades. Management of change is a tradition in the company which is reinforced and refined by successive generations of managers. Whereas there are several examples of change spread over the years, in order to illustrate the point, it may be sufficient to describe only a few significant events. Some of these have been referred to in earlier speeches but do bear repeating in order to place them in the historical perspective. The purpose is to refocus on and reinforce for the future those qualities which have permitted Hindustan Lever to grow, diversify and become a significant part of the Indian private sector.

Management

The growth and development of what we now recognise as modern Indian professional management in Hindustan Lever is the result of a long-term plan for managing the Indian business. The progression of this plan eventually led to the appointment of the first Indian Chairman, Mr. Prakash Tandon in 1961, to be succeeded in later years by Mr. Vasant Rajadhyaksha followed by Mr. T. Thomas. Much of the company's managerial strengths today are a consequence of the developments which flowed out of this perspective programme. The programme has progressively matured to a point when Indian managers are valued internationally, with Mr. Thomas joining the Unilever Board in 1979 and several managers occupying senior, including Board, positions in a number of Unilever companies outside India.

Within Hindustan Lever the process of change continues to keep pace with the rapidly evolving industrial and social environment.

** Lionel Carter, Ibid., pp. 196–97.

†† Also see Charlotte Butler and Sumantra Ghoshal, 'Hindustan Lever Limited: Levers for Change', in Sumantra Ghoshal, Gita Piramal, and Sudeep Budhiraja (compiled), *World Class in India: A Casebook of Companies in Transformation* (New Delhi, Penguin, 2001), pp. 33–67.

Training and development have played a critical role in preparing all sections of employees and helped foster a climate for improved productivity and meaningful human relations. While many modern management tools from the West as well as Japan have obviously been useful, it is now increasingly apparent that our own social values have a predominant influence in order to successfully manage an industrial enterprise in India.

It is this interweaving of social values along with appropriate management practices which will become more crucial for successful future developments. Successful management ultimately combines a concern for those who are employed in the company, the shareholders, the consumers as well as society at large.

Research and Development

Another landmark event in the process of change was the decision to invest in scientific research and development in India by Hindustan Lever in 1958. At a time when the country's balance of trade was very adverse and raw material shortages and other growth constraints were developing, the establishment of a modern Research & Development centre was an act of wisdom and foresight. In retrospect much of Hindustan Lever's market leadership in consumer products, its diversification into chemicals, agribusiness and exports and a deep-rooted company-wide innovative work ethic can be traced back to the confidence generated by the Research & Development set-up, over the years.

In addition to the recognised eminence of the work of Hindustan Lever's research scientists in India and abroad as well as an impressive number of patents and publications from its research centre, it may be useful to recall a few specific examples of achievements in the industrial sphere. The successful Research & Development undertaken on minor and unconventional oils in the sixties virtually ended the dependence of the soap industry on imported raw materials and indigenous edible oils. The use of minor and unconventional oils has generated a major local industry and is a prime example of the impact of import substitution. People tend to forget that some simple end products are the result of some very complex innovation and scientific research. This work is a classic example of one such case.

Organic synthesis of fine chemicals and fundamental work on catalysts led to the rapid development of Hindustan Lever's chemicals business, which has grown further with the investment in STPP and DAP fertilisers in later years. Similarly, the significant discoveries in plant physiology, photosynthesis and bacterial genetics laid the foundation of an agribusiness which has exciting growth potential. The understanding of the endocrinology of prawns has helped us to enhance aquaculture and this is the basis of a new fish-farming opportunity. The first commercial Chromatographic fractionation technology has permitted significant value addition to sal fat exports. There are several other examples but these are illustrative. The research laboratory's work is of international standard as indeed all research work ought to be and is today an important constituent of Unilever Research along with two research establishments in UK, and one each in Holland and the USA.

Scientific discoveries and innovation today are an integral part of Hindustan Lever's strategic plans for the future. The single most valuable lesson of undertaking frontier area scientific research in our company was the learning process of transfer of technology. It is now clear, following more than twenty years of experience, that the ability to transform discovery into a commercially viable end product or new knowledge with frequent iterations of what works in the laboratory with what is required in the market-place is the single most important difference between viable and non-productive research. The Research & Development effort being an integral part of the main business in Hindustan Lever was imperative for whatever success we have achieved in this respect. It provided a workable framework for accountability without unduly interfering with the pursuit of science. The other was the ability of the business to be patient with what is invariably a slow process of converting discovery into technology.

Originally published as Ashok S. Ganguly, *Industry and Liberalization* (Bombay, Allied Publishers, 1994), pp. 173–6.

32

The Restrictive 1960s and 1970s

Critiquing Government Policies

Aditya Vikram Birla

The late 1960s and 1970s were, yet again, a restive time for the private sector as it faced an increasingly regulated atmosphere. There was some improvement in the industrial climate during the Shastri years when the leadership tried to bring about a radical change in the economic paradigm, compelled by an environment of stagnating agriculture, slow industrial growth, shrinking foreign exchange reserves, increased unemployment, acute commodity shortages, and national income growth at half the expected rate. The leadership signalled a move away from the old Nehruvian controls to a framework based on incentives, a move towards economic decentralization, and more openness to foreign capital. Among the changes were the removal of controls from sectors such as steel and cement. However, these measures could not be implemented fully because of the sudden demise of Shastri. It proved to be too brief an interregnum.

Thereafter, the new leadership under Mrs Gandhi withdrew support to growth-oriented economic policies to a Leftist position with a populist appeal. In came pervasive controls, nationalization of private sector banks and coal, increased government regulations through state lending in various commodities, a string of enquiries aimed at restricting private enterprise (Monopolies and Restrictive Trade Practices Commission, 1964; R.K. Hazari Committee on Industrial Planning and Licensing Policy, 1967; Administrative Reforms Commission, 1968; S. Dutt Industrial Licensing Committee, 1969), a political rhetoric of the dangers of concentration of economic power in the hands of private enterprise, and a leadership bent on restricting the growth of 'monopoly houses'.*

* See Arvind Panagariya, *India: The Emerging Giant* (New Delhi, Oxford University Press, 2008), chapter 3, pp. 47–77 and Francine R. Frankel, *India's Political Economy, 1947–1977: The Gradual Revolution* (Princeton, Princeton University Press, 1978).

These two speeches by Aditya Birla, then head of the Aditya Vikram Birla Group, are outspoken indictments of government policies and the restrictions faced by private enterprise. The first, an address delivered on receiving the Madras Management Association's 'Business Leadership Award', spells out the challenges that business faced in the economic environment of the 1970s. Birla frankly expresses frustration at the restrictive state policies that business encounters. He is especially critical because of problems faced in raising industrial capital and rues the state's dominance of financial institutions, banks, and mutual funds. To Birla, this was a case of 'stifling the privateness of the private sector' and he appeals to management associations to take up the grievances of private enterprise.†

The second speech, delivered to the Indo-American Society named 'Indian Joint Ventures Abroad', highlights the oeuvre of not just a businessman but also a Third World businessman. Birla begins by contextualizing the idea of the joint venture which, in the 1970s, had evolved into a mode of doing business to which the Third World had adapted, given the global economic climate of increasing interdependence of economies. For Birla, the Indian contribution was instrumental given the knowledge that Indian entrepreneurs took with them, from their own experience which made them particularly attuned to conditions in other Third World states. Thereafter, Birla discusses his own experiences in Southeast Asia and confesses that the biggest hurdle he faced was within India because of the government's inflexibility, its discouragement of foreign ventures and the license permit system.

I

Ladies and Gentlemen.

It is a great honour and privilege for me, to be chosen for the "Business Leadership Award for 1990", by your Association. I accept the same with happiness and humility. I however, fully realise that the award, in reality, is a tribute to all my colleagues, who have worked with commitment, sincerity and loyalty to the organisation. I also resolve that I will strive harder to truly justify the honour that has been bestowed on me.

On this occasion, I consider it my duty to pay homage to the late Thiru Anantharamakrishnan, a leader of men and a pioneer in the field of engineering industries. The Amalgamations Group, created by this legendary industrialist, has made far-reaching contribution to the industrial growth of our country. And now, his able grand-daughter, the very distinguished chairperson Ms. Mallika Srinivasan is carrying forward the great tradition.

Friends, the Madras Management Association is fulfilling a very important role in the Indian Management scenario. Today, if you see the world over, the most important single factor that contributes to progress, prosperity and economic health is 'good management' Whether it is the management of the industry or agriculture or administration, the basic input of the health of all these sectors, is sound and efficient management. It is in this

† On Aditya Birla see Gita Piramal, *Business Maharajas* (New Delhi, Penguin, 1997) and Minhaz Merchant, *Aditya Vikram Birla: A Biography* (New Delhi, Viking, 1997).

context that the development of managers and the development of the art and culture of management is of prime importance in India to ensure a healthy corporate sector and a prosperous nation.

The subject for today's talk is "My Experience of Indian Management and the Present Business Environment" Let me first share my experiences in the field of Corporate Management with all of you.

You must have heard the best exponents of management and their theories. I am, however, handicapped, because I am not a management graduate. I am a technocrat—a Chemical Engineer—and I have no knowledge of the basic text book principles of management. What I have learnt is perhaps through practice. Therefore, if I talk on management, it is more from the experiences gained, from the mistakes made, and not from the text-books that I may have read.

If I narrate my experiences, it is only to substantiate what I have to say. Perhaps these actual happenings would make what I wish to say more relevant, meaningful and purposeful.

Friends, in the management of corporations, there are a gamut of activities that have to be taken care of and I would like to touch briefly on those aspects which are important.

MEN

To start with, I think the most important lesson in management that I have learnt from my grandfather is that major investments should be made in the selection, training and building up of people. He also taught me to repose full trust and confidence in people. Your men will be as loyal to you, as you are to them. He taught me that even ordinary people can give extraordinary results, given an opportunity. You have to train people by delegating authority to them. When you delegate, people will make mistakes, but it is through the making of these mistakes, that you build up people. You must have the forbearance, fortitude, patience and a large heart to bear the losses in the training of people. Opportunity must be given to people to perform. Don't hesitate in giving authority. When I came back from USA, my father gave to me an industrial licence, and told me to put up a textile mill, all by myself, with no help from the group. He had the vision and the guts to delegate responsibility. I must have made innumerable mistakes, but the training was worth all the mistakes I made.

My second perception, about creation of men, is that in-house creation of men is far superior to the bringing in of people through head hunters or transplanting people from other organisations into your organisation. Each organisation has its own culture, its own theories, its own environment, its own method of doing work and the best method of training people, is in-house training and in-house promotions. Of course, people have to be taken from outside, if your expansion is faster than creation of people. One has to resort to this. But the basic thrust and the basic core has to be from the strength, generated from your very own people.

I would like to share with you, that most of the presidents working today in our organisation, were either accounts assistants or management trainees or those who rose from the very low levels of the managerial ladder. They have made the best leaders, having risen from the ranks.

In the training of personnel, we have relied not so much on a formal training programme system, as we have trained people by actually putting them on the job, and thrusting and delegating responsibility to them and at the same time, keeping full checks through various reports to ensure accountability. This has given us tremendous results. This is the way, we create committed manpower.

LEADERSHIP

We now come to leadership. Whilst, as I have stated, numerous factors make good management, one cannot escape the fact that good leadership is one of the very important factors for success. Friends, gone are the days, when the boss was automatically the leader, and the cardinal rules, while dealing with the boss were: Rule No. 1—The Boss is always right and Rule No. 2—If the boss is wrong, refer to Rule No. 1!

I have found times without number, when good leadership has made all the difference. Loss making units have been turned into profit spinners by a mere change of leadership.

I have tried to analyse what goes into the making of a good leader. Why do some men become good leaders? Here again, there are several qualities and several routes to attain excellence in leadership. Some people attain leadership through financial management, some through good management of labour and good human relations. Again, some attain leadership through marketing—Lee Iacoca is a fine example. Some go through the route of administrative controls and some through quality control and technical management of production, like the chairman of Honda. So, there are several routes that people take to leadership, but there is one thing common in all these, and that is, hard work and commitment. There can be no substitute for hard work and commitment.

When talking of commitment, I am reminded of the story of a shop owner, who on his deathbed, enquired about the whereabouts of his wife and three sons. When he was assured that all four were at his bedside, he yelled in alarm, "Then, who the hell is minding the shop?" Friends, this is commitment for you!

A leader again always leads by:

1. Personal example
2. By creating a team
3. By delegating responsibility
4. By choosing the right man for the right job
5. Perseverance and
6. By giving two positive inputs to the corporations, Direction and Motion—Direction, that is a goal and Motion, that is positive activity for achieving the goal.

Good leadership can make all the difference between success and failure. There are several Lee Iacocas who are proving it all the time. Many of you here are leaders and many will become leaders. Leaders can sometimes be lonely. With you, I share one though. Sometimes in adversities, when all efforts are made and you don't find results, one loses heart and in such times, the famous verse from Bhagvad Gita

> Thy business is with the action only, never with its fruits.

has given me great solace.

Then again when times are uncertain, gloom looms large, the doha from Ramayana

> Gain or loss, life or death, credit or discredit they are all in the hands of God

This gives me equanimity and strength in times of distress. I hope you as leaders will also derive strength from this thought.

INNOVATION

Friends, from men and leaders, I now come to an exciting subject—innovation. This is both challenging and rewarding and essential for excellence in management. I have learnt that a corporation has to face new challenges all the time. We have to keep changing strategies, goals, and our approach to meet the changing scenario constantly. For instance, environment and ecology were unknown words till a decade back. Today, they are all encompassing. A new factor has been thrown in. Similarly, constantly new challenges come up. To face up to these challenges, one has to innovate to survive and excel.

Friends, I must stress however that innovation, also, faces impediments from the inertia of status quo, which inhibits people from making innovations. Yet, corporations need to break status quo all the time. Established norms and methods of doing business must be questioned, if we want to progress. Innovation is questioning and challenging the existing for something better, more exciting and more rewarding.

I cite one example. When the first oil crisis hit the industry, we as the largest manufacturers of Viscose Staple Fibre in the world, faced a severe profit crunch. Oil and energy are major inputs, for producing Viscose Staple Fibre. We used to consume 16.4 tonnes of steam per tonne of fibre produced. With innovation, which brought with it better monitoring and management, additional equipments, new technology, new energy saving devices, process changes and debottlenecking, we could reduce the consumption from 16.4 tonnes to barely 5.6 tonnes per tonne of fibre, over a period of two years. We saved Rs. 34 crores per year for the whole Group.

Another striking example is our palm oil plant in Malaysia. We started as the smallest plant, but by innovation, cut down on our cost of production substantially. In an industry, where the profit margins are 2 to 3%, the cost cutting gave us a tremendous edge in our marketing. By offering finer rates, we could expand our market share and today we have emerged, as the largest manufacturers of palm oil in the world. All through innovation. Innovation in cutting costs.

PRODUCTIVITY—MEN

Let us now talk of productivity. Constant efforts have to be put in for improving productivity of men and machines, all the time. We have to improve on our existing systems, however good they may be. The norms that are excellent today, will become outdated tomorrow. What seems unachieveable today, becomes a matter of fact tomorrow and the day-after, becomes obsolete. A corporation cannot remain static. It cannot maintain its position. It either improves or deteriorates. Therefore, if you do not constantly strive to remain a step ahead of competition, by improving productivity all the time, you will be left behind.

Those who have succeeded in maximising productivity of men and machines, would have found various rewards. I will cite one of my experiences. In a spinning mill in India, the normal workload for 30s count is one workman attending to three Ring Frame machines, whereas in our mill in Philippines, the same worker attends to 10 RFs. This is a quantum jump in output. How was it achieved? By two methods—1) The breakage rate of yarn was reduced from four to nearly one, by better equipment and conditioning. 2) Even with this, we found that while the worker could piece the yarn breakages of 10 machines, he could not physically walk the distance involved. We innovated. You will be surprised, we provided roller skates to the worker and trained him in skating! Finally, he could succeed in covering the distances involved in tending to 10 RFs. We did both—innovate as well as improve worker productivity.

The world is fast changing. It is a dynamic, ruthless and constantly changing environment.

Those who innovate, those who constantly strive for higher productivity, will survive and prosper. Those who do not, will fade into oblivion. Don't forget, friends, that there is also tremendous fulfilment and job satisfaction if you achieve something.

If you are successful in your efforts, the corporate world is full of dreams, full of joy and pleasure. But if you do not keep progressing, industry can be a nightmare. You have to strive constantly for survival and progress.

My grandfather used to say: "Industry is a jealous mistress! She requires constant wooing."

PRODUCTIVITY—MACHINES

In productivity of machines, I have found that there is always room for improvement. What is lacking is the will, the vision and the commitment to exploit the machines to get the best out of them. We build most of the times our own mental barriers, which are most difficult to overcome, than the actual problem of increasing productivity.

As Eric Hoffer, the great American philosopher, said: "In a time of change, it is the learners who inherit the future. The learned find themselves equipped to live only in a world that no longer exists."

With marginal extra investment, by removing bottlenecks, with a few balancing equipments, with the throwing in of better technology, we can achieve remarkable progress and results. In one of my plants, supplied by the largest manufacturer of Sodium Tri Poly Phosphate in the world, the machine productivity was increased over a period of two years by 100%. From the guaranteed 80 tpd by the manufacturers to 170 tpd—a quantum jump in productivity by the above methods, with a mere 10% increase in capital cost. I can give you several such personal experiences. Several examples are known to you also. In textiles, production of 20s count has increased from a mere 8 ozs per spindle in 1968 to 16 ozs per spindle in 1990 in India itself!

What I wish to emphasise, is, that we must have an open mind, we must be open to new ideas, to new perspectives and to new technology and should not create our own mental barriers and limitations.

It was thought that the four minute mile record could not be broken. It was.

There is nothing, which cannot be achieved, provided you have an open mind, the will, the devotion, determination, enthusiasm and vision to achieve the seemingly impossible.

Talking of openmindness, the Rigveda says:

Let noble thoughts come to us from all over the universe

QUALITY

Friends, from productivity we now talk of quality. Though from my experience, actually we should have talked of quality first, because good quality leads to higher productivity. Quality is extremely important in the competitive environment of a shrinking world. Myopic managers not conscious of quality will lose in a world without frontiers.

As you are aware, the world is becoming a small place to live in. I will give you one example. We produce staple fibre in Thailand, for which we buy pulp from Canada. This fibre made in Thailand, is sent to Indonesia for converting to yarn, in our unit there. This yarn, is then exported from Indonesia to Belgium, where it is made into carpets and finally, the carpet is exported to Canada! From Canada to Canada around the world!

When you see all this, you instantly realise that with fast communications through satellites, fax machines, supersonic transport, the world is fast shrinking into one big well-knit market, where national barriers are fast fading out. In this environment, the most single important factor that management must apply its mind to is quality and timely deliveries. The importance of quality cannot be overemphasised. In the early 80s, in our various spinning mills in South East Asia, we went for extremely high productivity, but the quality suffered. Our production was 7% higher than even those of the Japanese. We were proud of this achievement. We were selling yarn, as the market was good. We thought we had mastered the art of marketing and management. However, to our chagrin, in mid eighties, there was an over-supply of yarn. The market took a dip. We ran into serious difficulties in marketing because of quality problems.

What was acceptable in a good market, became unacceptable in a competitive environment. We realised that we could not market our products to good quality conscious customers and had to sell to weak customers, whose credit rating was poor. At great cost, we learnt that quality consciousness is a must for survival. We changed our policy, and today, we are proud that we have one of the finest qualities of yarn, produced anywhere in the world, and we are exporting to Europe, Australia and lo and behold, even to Japan, the citadel of quality.

We also learnt a further lesson, which may come as a total surprise to you and that is, that if you are quality conscious, you actually cut down, on your cost of production and marketing. The notion that to maintain your quality, your costs go up is totally wrong. The natural question that arises is, how do your costs go down if your emphasis is on quality. The answer is (1) the wear and tear of your machines comes down, (2) machine productivity improves, (3) you save on costs of maintenance, (4) you achieve higher productivity of labour, (5) you get a better realisation for your product, (6) there are no claims from customers, (7) selling to the best customers whose credit rating is good, results in reduction of bad debts. All in all, the costs savings are incalculable because of quality. Therefore, I would strongly advocate that any and every enterprise must keep quality as its foremost goal. We have done so, and we have benefited from this. Dr. J.M. Juram voices similar views, packaged differently. He says, "While quality costs, poor quality costs more."

PROJECT MANAGEMENT

Friends, for any enterprise, the foundation should be solid. For this, when putting up projects, three very important areas need to be fully taken care of: firstly, to adopt the best know-how that is available in the world; secondly, buy the best equipment. Do not compromise on the quality of the equipment for marginal extra costs. The cheaper machine normally turns out to be the most expensive ultimately. I have experienced this several times. Thirdly, whilst putting up the plant, the minimum economic world sized plant should always be borne in mind. One should not compromise on these three basic criteria. This ensures a strong foundation.

SUGGESTED MANAGEMENT SYSTEM

Friends, I have spoken a lot. You may now be tempted to ask me, what kind of management style do you propose. I would like to share with you the management system, which I feel is effective. We follow a style, which I term as "Participative management by consensus".

In this system, reviews and decisions are taken in groups. A group of people get together, to review the working of the company periodically. They go into the various aspects and problems and prepare action plans. In the taking of a decision, instead of one man taking a decision, it is done as a consensus decision, which emerges out of the discussions in the group.

A course of action is suggested by one of them, others pick holes in it, corrections or alternatives are explored, and when finally a decision is reached, it is mature, balanced and well thought out. It represents the wisdom and commitment of many heads. The chances of the correctness of such a decision, are far greater than if one person were to have taken it in isolation.

I am reminded of Alfred Sloan, former chairman of General Motors, who once adjourned a meeting, when everybody quickly agreed with his proposal. He remarked "Gentlemen, I do not think you have studied the proposals in depth. Let us meet again, when I can hear some negative points about my proposal."

This suggested style of management also has the added advantage, which is extremely relevant, that whilst taking a decision, a group of people feel and know that they have participated in the actual decision-making process and that the decision is theirs. They feel elevated and perceive themselves as a part of the management team, with the result, that they get committed to the decision. The implementation of this decision, therefore, carries the mark of commitment of each team member. The implementation is much smoother and quicker, with each member contributing his full mite.

MANAGEMENT—A SCIENCE OR AN ART?

Friends, before I end I would mention that I have often been asked whether management is a science or an art. I do not know what the text books say. My own perception is that at the basic roots, management is a science. If one is inducted as an accounts assistant, one does not have to practise any art. He has to follow a science. The science of the double entry book keeping. But, as you climb up the ladder, you move into a realm, where the science gradually turns into an art, where there are no clearly defined action plans or basic theories.

There is no set method of taking a decision. Sometimes, the intuitive faculty takes precedence over the analytical mind.

At the top, one of the foremost things is to deal with people. How do you deal with people? This is not a science. Each person has to be dealt with in a different manner. It is an art. You have to develop your own art of dealing with each situation. This art is something which is peculiar to each individual and one has to develop his own trait.

BUSINESS ENVIRONMENT

I have talked a lot on management, but our subject is 'My experience of Indian Management and the present Business Environment'. Let me make just one point, which is a burning issue in our business environment. Friends, Indian industry has come of age. This has been possible because of its entrepreneurs.

I have the experience of working in eight countries and I find, that as far as entrepreneurship goes, we Indians, are second to none—in number or in quality. This is something that India can really be proud of. However, we have to nuture this, we have to create a business environment, where entrepreneurship can flourish.

An entrepreneur is one, who takes risks and exercises the constructive freedom of private ownership. Unfortunately, today the very privateness of the private sector is at stake.

Government Financial Institutions, Banks and Mutual Funds on an average hold 35 to 40% of the equity of blue chip companies. In some, they even hold a majority. Their control over the private sector is increasing day-by-day. Their holding percentage is increasing at an alarming rate, and if projections are made, within the next 3 to 4 years, in most of the blue-chip companies, the government institutions will control, more than 50% of the equity. It is indeed ominous and fearsome. It is an irony that private funds, routed through the Mutual Funds, controlled by the government, are stifling the privateness of the private sector.

Private Funds Stifling the Privateness of the Private Sector

We must unite and raise our voice against this. Management Associations, such as yours, must take up and highlight this fact, this problem, in Delhi and suggest ways and means to the government to correct this grave situation. A ceiling on the combined holdings as also individual holdings by the institutions and mutual funds must be enforced by the Government to safeguard the freedom of the private sector. Then again, the concept of a non-voting equity share should be thought of. Lending institutions should be asked to disinvest in favour of mutual funds, to keep a balance between supply and demand for shares, within the overall ceiling. Lending and developmental Institutions' role, is to promote and develop industry and not to control it in perpetuity. It is an irony that the poor, genuine investor, for whose benefit all this is being done, is starved of blue chips at affordable prices, due to the high prices of shares, as a result of mutual funds and institutional operations. Friends, a solution has to be found, sooner than later. This is a challenge which MMA must take up and probe this problem for solutions.

Need for More Executives

One last observation—while we have no dearth of entrepreneurs, we have to develop further on managerial cadres. We have excellent managerial talent, but it is not available in the numbers that is required. This is an area where we have to concentrate and work on. We have seen times without number that enterprising Indians, have put up industries, yet come to grief because of lack of managerial acumen. We have to create, more professional managers and we also need, more executive entrepreneurs, those who combine the talent of an executive and an entrepreneur. Entrepreneurs can dream, but of what use is a dream, if there is no manager or executive, to convert those dreams into reality. We need both. We need the vision of the entrepreneurs as well as the good management of the Executives. I am reminded of Shri Krishna and Arjuna.

Wherever there is Krishna, the Yogeshwar, the thinker, the visionary and Arjuna, the Archer, the executor, there you have happiness, victory, and prosperity.

Entrepreneurs are born. Executives are made.

The Madras Management Association, must strive and create managers and executives for our country. Good Management is the key word to success in industry, in agriculture and for that matter, in any sphere of activity. You are, therefore, in your association, playing a very important national role in a key area.

Take up the challenge of creating managers with a missionary zeal and God be with you. Posterity will thank you for your efforts.

Thank you.

This is the text of the S. Anantharamkrishnan Memorial Lecture by Aditya Vikram Birla, 'My Experience of Indian Management and Present Business Environment', October 1990, *Aditya Vikram Birla Papers*, Mumbai.

II

Friends,

I am thankful to Mr Chitalia and the Indo-American Society for inviting me here this evening to speak on "Indian Joint Ventures Abroad". I am very impressed by the constructive and useful activities of the society. I find that an Exhibition has also been arranged by the American Consulate on multinationals which is timely and enlightening.

Coming to to-day's subject from time immemorial nations have traded for mutual benefits. However, as rapid industrialisation took place the concept shifted from only trade to trade and joint ventures. In the beginning setting up of joint ventures was mainly done by developed countries. However, in the last quater century we find that a lot of joint ventures have been put up by developing countries between themselves.

One of India's first joint ventures was by our group in Ethiopia which did exceedingly well—so well that Emperor Haile Salasee bestowed the rare honour of decorating my Father with the highest honour of the country—Order of Menelick the second. Since then India has gone a long way, and to give you the present statistics the total number of joint ventures sanctioned by the Govt of India are 310, of which projects in production are 83, and projects under implementation are 105. The rest are still to materialise or have been dropped. The total Indian Investment is approved projects is 83.99 crores, of which 69.08 crores is in effective projects, which are in production or under implementation. The total earnings repatriated till date are 5.25 crores of which 2 crores are in the form of dividends and 3.25 crores are by way of technical know how, managerial fees, royalties etc. The total exports due to these joint ventures are to the tune of 50 crores which is no mean achievement. Most of these ventures are in developing countries. There is also great scope for joint–ventures in third countries, to be set up in collaboration with developed countries. After our Prime Minister's recent visit to the U.S.A. President Curter is sending a special emissary to India to explore the possibilities of Indo-American Joint ventures in third countries.

The concept of joint ventures is to be viewed against the new pattern of global economic inter dependence. Developing countries can reap mutual benefits by inter dependence and complementing the skills of each other by putting up joint ventures. These act as a cementing link between developing countries. The orthodox argument of competing resource endowment, among the developing countries, as against the complementarity between the developed and developing world has been negatived by the experience of last two decades. In fact joint ventures between developing countries is in some case more suited than between the advanced and the developing countries. I will come to this later on. Joint ventures are a natural consequence of the outcome of the emerging international division of labour, requiring developed countries to go more for sophisticated, highly technical and capital intensive areas, while leaving less complex and labour intensive fields to the developing nations. This has changed the complexion of the economic relations between developing and developed countries. Thus to make the optimal use of the new international division of labour joint ventures can play an effective role. In the contemporary context, joint ventures and other forms of collaborations are not merely instruments of trade transactions but have wider implications. They act as catalysts to foster and promote the commercial fraternity among the developing countries.

Another important factor that is helping the development of joint ventures is the tariff barrier that each country is putting up, thereby shutting out its market to outside countries, and thus encouraging manufacture of number of items in the country itself.

Joint ventures promoted by India are designed mainly to foster closer and lasting economic ties with other countries. India shares its wealth of experience and expertise which it has developed with other developing nations. After all we must remember we are the tenth largest industrialised nation and the third largest in terms of technical and managerial man power. I may mention that the expertise that India has developed is more suited and relevant to the developing countries in areas such as textiles, chemicals, and other labour intensive and smaller industries because our technology can be adopted more easily.

The maximum number of Indian joint ventures is in South East Asia. My own experience also is of this area where we have put up more than a dozen joint ventures and therefore I will share my experiences with you. Rather than talking in terms of generalities, which tend to become boring and do not carry home the point, please give me the liberty to talk to you about my own experiences which probably would be more meaningful.

Government's restriction on expansion of large houses in India could be one of the reasons for our rapid expansion in South East Asia. It may be amusing to you if I were to tell you that the Govt did not permit Gwalior Rayon, one of our large concerns, to add to its capacity of Viscose fibre in India, but we were permitted to set up a joint venture in Thailand where we are today manufacturing 40 tons of Staple Fibre per day and to top it all, India, which cannot meet its viscose demand by local production is today importing from our own joint venture plant. Strange indeed are the ways of the Government, where foreign imports from Indian joint ventures are considered favourably, but not expansion in India.

We started our first joint venture in Thailand with 12000 spindles in 1968, which has now been expanded to 30,000 spindles. Our second factory in Thailand was the Rayon plant that we started with 24 tons and have now expanded to 40 tons per day. We were handed over the management of a sick textile mill because of the reputation and goodwill that we had built up and this unit is now the premier trend setter in fabrics. You will be surprised that our textile mill was the only mill in Thailand which made a profit last year when most of the Japanese and American mills made substantial losses. I give this example to substantiate my point that I made earlier that in certain areas Indian technology is more suited to developing countries. The reason for making profits was that we diversified our product mix. The Japanese would normally have a smaller product range of say 3 to 4 varities run in mass production, whilst we run about 10 to 12 varieties in the game capacity mill, This to the Japanese is probably unscientific. But then because of the market being smaller, our strategy of marketing smaller quantities of various products paid us rich dividends and gave us an edge over others.

Similarly in Philippines we have started a joint venture for textiles and President

Marcos during my last visit complimented us by stating that our unit had the best profit to sales ratio in the entire textile industry in Philippines. My Grand Father was invited as the personal guest of the President, The King of Thailand invited us for dinner. They paid handsome tributes and this is shown clearly in the booklet I have distributed. This is an honour not to Mr. Birla but to the entire business community of India.

Similarly in Indonesia and Malaysia our joint ventures are doing well and we are able to compete against international giants without any difficulty. Please do not misunderstand me that I am blowing my own trumpet. This is just to illustrate to you that Indian Technology and Management in certain circumstances is better suited to developing countries.

I may mention our joint ventures in these countries are not confined to industrial ventures alone as some of our staff members have gone a step further in fostering good relations between the two countries and have actually married local maidens.

Let me dwell on some of the advantages and disadvantages that we face in putting up joint ventures. The satisfaction of earning a good name for our country is tremendous. You will find that wherever we have put up joint ventures, tremendous good will has been generated. Whilst in the first venture we had difficulty in selling equity shares of Rs 50 lacs, in our subsequent venture we did not have difficulty even in selling shares of Rs 3 ½ crores.

This shows the confidence that has been generated amongst investors in these countries. Then again the earnings to India by way of remittances of royalty, know how fees, dividends and free exports from these joint ventures have been substantial. The biggest attraction is the recognition the credit, the appreciation and encouragement that you get from your efforts from Government officials and others.

I may mention an interesting experience that I had in Singapore. The Singapore Government invited us to put up a joint venture and the Industries Minister asked me if I needed any help. When I enquiried how long it would take to get the licence cleared, he was a little amazed and asked his officer what I meant by this. They were quite perlexed and he said, well Mr. Birla as far as we are concerned there are no permissions to be given by us. We will be very happy if you start the industry tomorrow.

Putting up industries, once you have a reputation, is easier in these countries for the following reasons: We first come to financing. As far as banks are concerned, there are no lengthy forms and formats of the kind that we have in India. Permissions are given very easily and quickly once the banks are satisfied about the capability and honesty of the enterpreneurs. You will be surprised that we applied for a loan of Rs 5 crores to Bangkok Bank, one of the leading banks in Bangkok. The proposal was cleared in three weeks. Of course they knew of our performance in our first textile plant and they were highly impressed, but still I was a little stunned because I am an Indian and used to Indian conditions. I asked the Chairman how he had approved a loan of Rs 5 crores without even asking any questions. His answer was very simple. He said, number one we have trust in you and number two we have seen your performance in India and since you are proposing to manufacture 40 tons of an item against 250 tons that you are present manufacturing in India, I for one see no reason why a party which is competent to product 250 tons cannot produce 40 tons. This is the kind of reception that one gets in case you can gain their confidence. Then let us come to getting clearances for your projects from the Govt. Depending on country to country, the clearance can take as little as 4 months and a maximum of 8 months. One of the remarkable thing about the clearances is that all the processing is done by a centralised agency normally called the Board of Investment. This agency gives you all the necessary clearances. You do not have to go from pillar to post and through a maze of Govt red tapism. I wish our Govt could also emulate these good practices.

In all these countries, there is no company law of the kind that we have in India. Three or four pages is all that they have thought of to regulate the companies. They are more interested in promoting the companies and production rather than regulating production and or controlling the industries.

Then we come to labour. I have found that labour in general is disciplined and conscientious. Though the labour is not as skilled as that in India and not industrially oriented, they are willing to learn. There are few strikes and the Govt do not favour strikes since it hampers production. This naturally helps industrial growth.

Tax laws again are simple and various tax incentives are given to promote industries. You will be surprised to know the kind of incentives that have been given for our latest joint venture in Carbon Black in Thailand. They are so keen to industrialise the country that they asked us what kind of incentives we require for putting up the plant. Being an Indian, I had no dearth of suggestions to make. A list of 32 points were given to them. To my utter surprise, on some of the points on which I had never dreamt of getting approvals, they agreed. I would like to mention some of the incentives just to enlighten you of the attitude that they have. They gave a 8 year tax holiday, 8 year duty free import of raw materials, 8 year holiday for business tax, which is a kind of sales tax, 8 year tax holiday for all remittances of royalties, technical know how fees, which normally would attract a tax of 20%. A guarantee by the Govt not to promote any industry for the Carbon Black for the next 5 years after we go into production. A guarantee by the Govt that the import duties on Carbon Black would be enhanced to 30% from the present level of 10%. 6 months before we go into production. Believe me, I could not have asked for more. They are practically guaranteeing your profits. I am giving you these illustrations so that you realise fully the impact on industrial development that these helpful policies of these Governments have.

These are some of the advantages, but it is not a bed of roses. There are many difficulties also. The biggest difficulty which an Indian businessman faces is the question of marketing. Here Indian businessmen accustomed to a large market feel that anything produced under the sun will be sold without any difficulty.

However, in these countries the market is small and before any work is started the first pre-requisite is to do a thorough and complete market survey. Most of the Indian joint ventures have come to grief because of inadequate market knowledge. Some of the other difficulties concern the attitude of the Govt of India. I may mention them in short. The permission from the Govt should be expedited so as to facilitate early implementation. The Govt before giving permission insists on getting a letter from the foreign Govt that they have given us necessary permissions to start the joint venture. This is indeed paradoxical. When we are going to set up joint ventures in other countries, the permission should be given first from our Govt rather than insist on the permission from the host Govt. I wish we realise such simple matters. The second point is that the Govt is very stingy about permitting expenses for exploratory trips for doing the market study and for visiting the countries to get Govt clearances. I do not for one see how we can do all these jobs without adequate expenses being sanctioned from the Reserve Bank. It is, I think, only due to the ingenuity of the Indian businessmen that so many joint ventures have come up in spite of the Govt's not too helpful attitude, I feel that if a person can set up an industrial venture in India, he can be successful anywhere in the world. Then again, normally cash participation is not allowed is joint ventures abroad. I feel this should be liberalised further in view of the comfortable foreign exchange position of the country. By telling our joint venture partners that we are not bringing in any cash and instead are exporting machineries, we unnecessarily create doubts.

There are other areas where the Govt would be wise to look into. Any investment guarantee would be most welcome. All the assets of joint ventures in Ethiopia were nationalised, not even a cent has been received as compensation. Double taxation is prevalent among all these countries. The Govt would do well to enter into tax treaties so that this unnecessary burden is removed. For those joint ventures which come into financial difficulties, the Govt should allow the promoters to remit cash remittances to solve their cash liquidity problems. These steps would go a long way towards enduring the success and strengthening further the present and future joint ventures.

I have dealt with some of the aspects of joint ventures and illustrated them with my personal experiences. Now if you have any questions I would be only too pleased to answer them.

Thank you again for having given me this opportunity to be here with you this evening.

This is the text of Aditya Vikram Birla's speech, 27 June 1978, at the Indo-American Society, *Aditya Birla Papers*, Mumbai.

33

The Beginnings of Overseas Expansion

Minhaz Merchant

In the restrictive atmosphere that private enterprise faced in the 1970s, groups were forced to find innovative ways to expand. In the face of such challenges, some looked for investment opportunities outside the country, especially in the developing world. This led to the emergence of Indian companies as multinationals, heralding yet another phase in their dramatic history. The Aditya Vikram Birla Group also reacted to the restrictive policies by expanding overseas. Between 1970 and 1985, the Birla group established plants in Thailand, Malaysia, the Philippines, Indonesia, and Egypt. So rapid was the expansion that within a few years, overseas activity accounted for one-third of its overall business. The group emerged as India's first genuine multinational. It became the world's leading producer of viscose staple fiber, palm oil, and insulators, and the world's sixth largest producer of carbon black.*

This story is vividly reconstructed in the excerpt that follows by Minhaz Merchant, well-known editor and columnist. Examining Aditya Birla's first foreign venture in the 1960s into Southeast Asia, Merchant notes the role played by trusted managers and loyalists of the Birla family, but the key figure that stands out is Aditya Birla himself. In the context of the sixties, there were huge impediments to raising finances internally; thus, Birla ventured abroad by raising capital primarily from non-resident Indians and persons of Indian origin living in Thailand. Merchant recounts the establishment of Indo-Thai Synthetics, a yarn manufacturing company which symbolized the beginnings of a global empire. The success of this venture encouraged Birla to launch an expansion programme across Southeast Asia, especially Indonesia, Malaysia, and the Philippines. Although communist victory in Vietnam seemed imminent and the region was in the grip of much

* Also see Gita Piramal, *Business Maharajas* (New Delhi, Penguin, 1997).

tension, Birla continued to establish factories. All this expansion led to the emergence of the group as an important Indian multinational which, by 1997, boasted of factories and offices across 23 countries with an annual turnover of about 3 billion US dollars.

... That same sense of fierce independence made Aditya, a mere four years after beginning his business career in India with Eastern Spinning and Hindustan Gas, turn his attention to Southeast Asia. The choice was curious not merely because the region was economically backward. More than that, it was 1969, and the Vietnam war raged ferociously. Thailand, not far from Vietnam or the killing fields of Cambodia and Laos, hardly seemed the ideal country for an orthodox Indian business family to invest in.

But Aditya, even in the formative years of his business career, had developed a keen sense of the world. He knew that the Vietnam war would end one day and the economies of the region would devour foreign investment as reconstruction began. Thailand had already opened up its economy to foreign investment. It had an underdeveloped infrastructure, few industries and a business-friendly government. Aditya realized instinctively that Thailand could give him precisely those opportunities for growth that socialist India could not and would not.

There remained one seemingly intractable problem: foreign exchange. Indian laws forbade businessmen acquiring hard currency. The only way to invest in Thailand was by being financially inventive. But even then initial capital abroad was required. At this stage one of Aditya's closest friends stepped in. Ashwin Kothari had studied chemical engineering at MIT with Aditya and was a director in Eastern Spinning. His cousin, Vijay Mehta, was a diamond merchant with operations in Antwerp and Bangkok. 'I asked Vijaybhai whether he would like to invest in Adity's proposed Thai project,' recalls Kothari. 'He told me he would. I then offered to introduce him to Aditya and B.K. babu.'

A meeting was set up in Basant Vihar, B.K. Birla's sprawling estate in Calcutta. Mehta flew in specially from Antwerp for the meeting. 'Vijaybhai Mehta met Aditya and mvself in earlv 1969, right there,' recounts B.K. Birla, pointing towards the family's large dining room. 'Mr Mehta wished to invest Rs. 12.50 lakh—in those days that was around $300,000. I tried to dissuade him. "You may lose your money," I told him. But he was adamant. He said to me, "I have full faith in the Birla family. I will invest at least Rs. 12.50 lakh."'

That, along with contributions from other NRI partners and several Thai businessmen, would take care of the foreign component of the new company's equity. But what of the Birla family's contribution which would necessarily have to be made in foreign exchange? This is where the family's legendary ingenuity and resourcefulness came into full play. A group company was asked to supply steel fabrication materials and ancillary machinery to the Thai plant. The dollar value of the machinery was counted as the Birla family's equity contribution.

With the help of NRI investors and transplanted Indian machinery, Aditya Birla thus launched a global presence that would, in 1997, comprise dozens of factories and trading offices in twenty-three countries outside India with a combined annual turnover of $3 billion (Rs. 11,000 crore).

The driving ambition of a young MIT engineer, laced with the characteristic Birla quality of taking large, calculated risks to secure large financial rewards, had taken the Thai venture from drawing board to factory construction in a few short months. The key aide who would play a major role in executing Aditya's global ambitions over the next twenty-five years—and who had driven Aditya in the rented Toyota to the critical Board of Investment meeting in Bangkok on June 10, 1969—was S.S. Mahansaria. Sitting today in his elegant downtown Bangkok office, Mahansaria presents the picture of the archetypal senior Birla executive: utterly loyal, dedicated and committed to relentless growth. Recalls Nirbhay Jain, senior president of Century Rayon, a part of B.K. Birla's diversified Rs. 6,000 crore group: 'One day, several years ago, Aditya babu had come to our house for dinner. Mr B.K. Birla was there as well. We got to talking about Aditya babu's Thailand-based companies and especially Mr Mahansaria. "Mahansariaji has a very good lifestyle and spends more money every month than I do," joked Aditya babu over dinner. "I like that. I want my executives to project a powerful image of the Birla group abroad."'

A greying, swarthy man now in his late fifties, Mahansaria has lived and worked out of Bangkok for the past twenty-eight years. 'I first met Aditya babu in 1964 when he was given charge of Hindustan Gas and Co. Ltd.,' he recalls. 'I had joined the company in December 1963 and he returned from MIT seven months after that, in July 1964. I worked under him at Hindustan Gas for the next five years till he asked me to go to Bangkok in April 1969.'

Aditya had begun to toy with the idea of expanding abroad as early as 1966. 'After a few years in Calcutta,' says Mahansaria, 'Aditya babu felt that since there were a lot of problems in India at the time—licences, red tape, quotas—we should look at business opportunities overseas. In 1966, it was decided in principle that the Birla group should explore the possibility of setting up an industrial unit outside India. And then the name of Thailand came up. We sent an executive from Calcutta to investigate. He remained in Bangkok for five months and reported back that there was potential for putting up a small textile spinning plant. But nothing much was done at the time.'

Over a year later, in 1968, a delegation of the Indo-Thai Chamber of Commerce arrived in Calcutta. The delegation was led by Suryan Raiva, a Thai national, and comprised several top Thai and non-resident Indian business leaders. The objective: to attract Indian industry to Thailand which had just launched a global campaign to draw foreign investment. Aditya met Raiva who formally invited the Birlas to invest in Thailand. He promised them all help with government clearances and project finance. Aditya was enthused. He despatched another executive, K.K. Agarwal, to Bangkok with the specific assignment that he should apply for a spinning plant licence. Agarwal stayed in Bangkok for nearly six months. Towards the end of his visit, he submitted a proposal to the Thailand Board of Investment requesting it to issue the Birlas a licence for a small textile spinning plant to be located just outside Bangkok. To his utter astonishment, the request was granted within weeks. Delighted, Agarwal returned to Calcutta and submitted a detailed report to Aditya. The question now was: should the spinning plant be put up in a country where the Birlas had no previous business experience?

Another trusted Birla executive, G.L. Mundhra, was sent to Bangkok to conduct a final market study. A profitability statement was made. Mundhra reported to Aditya that the profit potential of a Thailand-based spinning plant was around Rs. 18 lakh a year. The total investment required was estimated at Rs. 1.05 crore (then around $3 million). These were significant amounts in the late 1960s even for an asset-rich group like the Birlas.

Aditya pondered Mundhra's report. The profitability figures seemed promising but he wanted them vetted before plunging into his first foreign venture. Aditya turned to Mahansaria. The instructions he gave the family loyalist were terse and precise: go to Bangkok and report back on whether or not the group should go ahead with the construction of the spinning plant. Mahansaria was reluctant to go at first. 'I had never handled outside affairs before and had no experience,' he recalls. 'Moreover, we still did not have very strong references in Bangkok. But Aditya babu and the president of Hindustan Gas, G.R. Hadda, convinced me to go.'

Mahansaria had by then been promoted to vice-president, commercial, of Hindustan Gas. He was regarded as one of the rising stars in the Birla firmament and had caught Aditya's eye. Before leaving for Bangkok, Mahansaria asked Mundhra to give him all the relevant papers. After studying them carefully, Mahansaria reduced the profit projections of the proposed spinning mill in Thailand from Rs. 18 lakh to Rs. 14 lakh. He told Aditya that, before sending him to Bangkok for further investigations, a basic decision should be made on whether the family really wished to invest in a country on the periphery of the Vietnam war. Once they went ahead, he warned Aditya, there could be no turning back.

Aditya received Mahansaria's revised projections in March 1969. He consulted with his father and senior group executives but the decision to go ahead, he knew, would now have to be his alone. Within days, Aditya had decided. Project Bangkok was on.

Mahansaria was asked to pack his bags and leave immediately for the Thai capital. He arrived in Bangkok on April 10 without his family (they would join him only three months later). In Bangkok, the first thing he did was to phone Suryan Raiva who had led the Thai business delegation to India a year ago. Raiva was a wealthy hotelier. 'I stayed only at his hotel,' says Mahansaria. 'He gave me a suite at a very cheap price.'

During his first month in Bangkok Mahansaria had nothing more than Mundhra's project report to go on. 'I had to borrow a typewriter from someone to type my letters,' he recalls. 'I used to go myself to the post office to send telexes. There was no fax in those days. It was very difficult to get through to India even on telex. But somehow the work was done and the necessary papers submitted to the Bank of America. The Thai banks did not really entertain us. They said, we don't know you.'

Then, in May 1969, Mahansaria made an important breakthrough. He met Amarnath Sachdev, the powerful and influential president of the Indo-Thai Chamber of Commerce, with whom he discussed the spinning mill project. 'After a few more meetings,' says Mahansaria, 'Sachdev agreed to invest Rs. 12–15 lakh. I then approached other investors, mostly Thai nationals of Indian origin. I managed to arrange one lakh from one investor, then Rs. 50,000 from another, Rs. 75,000 from a third. It was almost like raising venture capital. Ultimately, within a few months, I got the new company registered. The necessary capital was now in place. Bank financing was also organized, and we started looking for a plant site. By that time I had developed a good rapport with the Indo-Thai Chamber of Commerce. It was decided that a function should be organized by the chamber at which Aditya babu would be invited to give a short speech. A lot would depend on how Thai and Indian investors in Bangkok reacted to that speech. Our future depended on Aditya babu making a good impression.'

Back home in Calcutta, Aditya pored over a growing pile of telexes and reports from Mahansaria. His vice-president had now been in Bangkok for nearly two months. It was early June and Calcutta continued to swelter after a particularly long and hot summer. On June 3, 1969, Aditya received a telex from Bangkok that brought a smile to his face and set in motion a chain of events that would culminate in the construction of the biggest overseas empire by a resident Indian industrialist. The telex crackled with optimism: things in Bangkok, Mahansaria reported, were finally beginning to take shape; financial commitments from several local investors were pouring in and setting up a greenfield textile spinning plant in Thailand now seemed an increasingly viable proposition.

Aditya was delighted. At twenty-five, he was brimming with confidence and convinced that a great business opportunity lay buried on the periphery of war-torn Southeast Asia. He telexed Mahansaria that he would arrive in Bangkok on June 10. Meanwhile, Aditya again discussed the Thai project threadbare with his father. Basant Kumar was quietly encouraging but advised Aditya to proceed with caution. Days before son Kumar Mangalam's second birthday, Aditya boarded an early morning flight to Bangkok. He had previously travelled to Thailand as a student but this was his first visit there on business.

Mahansaria received Aditya at Bangkok airport in a hired Toyota car. The two men drove straight to the Hotel Siam Intercontinental where Aditya would stay for the next four days before returning to Calcutta in time to celebrate Kumar's birthday. Plunging into a hectic schedule, Aditya met senior Thai and Indian businessmen to assess the strength of financial support for the spinning plant. He visited the Thailand Board of Investment and delivered a speech to the Indo-Thai Chamber of Commerce which received a standing ovation. It was his first major public address abroad. Over the next few days Aditya examined the financing that had been firmed up for the project. A Rs. 25 lakh loan was arranged from the Bank of America and another Rs. 25 lakh from Indian Overseas Bank. Just over Rs. 50 lakh had been committed by local investors and NRIs. The Birlas' equity contribution was to be Rs. 12.50 lakh by way of the dollar value of auxiliary equipment and steel fabrications sent to Thailand from India by Birla group companies. The spinning machines, it was decided, would be bought from Japan.

Aditya told a group of investors on the last day of his trip that he would return soon; meanwhile, he asked Mahansaria and his aides to proceed with the project with all speed. For the next two months, Birla executives deputed from Calcutta fanned out looking for suitable land to build the spinning mill. The sites Mahansaria had initially selected were examined again. One that lay 50 km from Bangkok was finally chosen. Construction work at the site began on November 12, 1969. By happy coincidence, Aditya turned twenty-six the same week.

... In 1967, Aditya started a small readymade garments factory in Liluwa, near Howrah, which ran into early teething problems. Aditya again consulted Bagrodia. 'It was a very small unit,' remembers Bagrodia, 'and I suggested that we shift the entire factory into the Kesoram Rayon complex. We had a cellophane paper unit which was lying idle and this was used to house Aditya babu's readymade garments factory.' Once Bagrodia officially joined the Aditya Birla group in September 1969—after eleven years with Basant Kumar—he became a key pivot of Aditya's ambitious Southeast Asian strategy.

During his second visit to Bangkok in December 1969, Aditya inspected and approved the new plant site on the outskirts of the Thai capital. He made a detailed survey of the machinery to be imported from Japan, the ancillary equipment to be sent by Birla companies in India and the number of spindles the plant should commence operations with. His experience of running Eastern Spinning in Calcutta over the past five years had given him an in-depth knowledge of textile plants. Aditya and his Thai investor-partners named the company Indo-Thai Synthetics Ltd. and decided to install just over 12,000 spindles to begin with. By September 1970, Indo-Thai Synthetics Ltd. was up and running and already had 300 workers, including Birla executives in key managerial and technical positions.

Not everything, however, was proceeding smoothly. The Birla team in Bangkok soon realized that Mundhra's earlier projections were erroneous and based on a defective market study. 'We had planned on producing a particular type of yarn and then discovered that the demand for that yarn was simply not there,' says Mahansaria. 'So there we were in a foreign country where our resources were practically zero and faced with the prospect of our main product not finding a market. If the company lost money, the matter could become serious. We realized that our yarn could not be sold locally unless we had doubling machines to convert it into double yarn.'

An SOS went out to Birla headquarters in Calcutta. Aditya immediately swung into action. He arranged for yarn doubling machines to be airlifted to Bangkok from an old plant belonging to his father's company, Jayashree Textiles. 'Around four very old doubling machines were sent to Thailand,' recalls a Birla executive. 'That really saved the Bangkok project. We then started converting our yarn into double yarn which was sold in the export market and that helped us bring the company on an even keel within the next few months.'

In Indo-Thai Synthetic's first year of commercial operation, 1970–71, the company miraculously broke even. The Mahansaria-Mundhra profitability target of Rs. 14 lakh was reached by 1972–73 and then, as one senior Calcutta-based Birla executive says, 'it just kept on going up and up'. The ownership pattern of Indo-Thai Synthetics closely paralleled that of future Aditya Birla group joint ventures in Southeast Asia. The Birla's typically held 20–25 per cent of the equity through group crossholdings and the rest was placed with local investors, NRIs and the public. Management control, however, lay—by tacit agreement but no formal MOUs—with the Aditya Birla group, an arrangement that suited everybody. The key to it was that the Birla's would continue to give shareholders handsome dividends (routinely 50–100 per cent a year) and the majority equity holders would not interfere managerially.

... With his first overseas company, Indo-Thai Synthetics, doing well, Aditya's confidence had grown. Throughout the 1970s, he used his Bangkok base to launch a rapid but strategically thought-out expansion drive in Southeast Asia. Indo-Thai Synthetics started exporting to Indonesia and several other neighbouring countries in 1972. Mahansaria himself now began to make regular visits to Indonesia. To begin with the purpose was selling Indo-Thai Synthetics' production. Then, after a year, he says, 'We thought of putting up a spinning plant in Indonesia itself since we were already exporting there. So without even the knowledge of Aditya babu, I applied for a licence for which Mr. B.K. Birla's Century Textiles—and I was unaware of this—had also applied. Century's executives came to know that Mr. Mahansaria of Thailand has applied for the licence. B.K.

babu called me up to ask if this were true. I said, "Yes, because there is a demand I thought let me apply for the licence and then we can take the decision to go ahead or not subsequently." B.K. babu later told Aditya babu, "I will give you my licence and you can implement the project in Indonesia." This was in 1972–73.'

A year later, another opportunity presented itself. Amarnath Sachdev, a large investor in Indo-Thai Synthetics, owned 50 per cent of a weaving and processing textile plant. He had set up the factory with a relative in Thailand. It was a new plant and Sachdev lost heavily on it. 'Amarnath Sachdev requested us to help him,' says Mahansaria. 'We thought it was our moral duty to help as he had also assisted us with funding when we were starting Indo-Thai Synthetics in 1969. So I went to the plant, studied it and then told him that he should sell Birla's 50 per cent of his share. I took the proposal to Aditya babu and convinced him to buy the 50 per cent share, not with the intention to make money but to achieve some integration in terms of manufacturing yarn and earn goodwill from our investors. Aditya babu agreed to buy, Amarnath Sachdev agreed to sell and that is how we began our weaving operations in Thailand and also started the process of vertical integration in our various factories.'

Well-settled now in Thailand and with a toe-hold in Indonesia, Aditya instructed his men to explore newer product categories. The group had expertise in rayon fibre in India and decided to put the skill to use in Thailand. It was 1973–74. The Vietnam war had reached a bloody climax. A communist victory was imminent; Southeast Asia quaked at the prospect. Undeterred, Aditya asked his men to prepare a project report on a new rayon plant. The report arrived on Aditya's table in Bombay in early 1974. Within days he had okayed it. A loan application was filed with leading Thai banks and other funding solicited. Shares were offered to private investors. Then disaster struck. The communist victory in the Vietnam war and a Japanese report criticizing a market survey conducted by the Birla's on the demand for rayon in the region scared off potential investors. For the first time, it appeared that the famous Birla touch had failed. A worried Mahansaria turned to Amarnath Sachdev and asked him: 'Are you going to take a few shares?' Sachdev replied that he could at the most buy 5 per cent to 6 per cent of the equity. The total cost of the rayon project was $10 million—equivalent to Rs. 8 crore at 1974 conversion rates. Sachdev was himself financially overstretched and could invest only a token amount, perhaps $250,000 (Rs. 20 lakh).

Once again, the Birlas used their ingenuity. They told Sachdev that even if he did not invest a significant amount, he should announce that he was doing so. Once he did that, other Thailand-based Indians would follow suit. That is exactly what happened. But the funding problem was not over. Local banks insisted on a strict 1:1 debt-equity ratio. That meant putting in $5 million of equity or Rs. 4 crore at the then prevailing exchange rates—a significant sum in 1974. Aditya was, however, determined to go ahead with the rayon plant and arranged the funding of the enlarged equity through Grasim in India. Grasim exported machinery worth a dollar value of Rs. 72 lakh, giving it 18 per cent of the new company's Rs. 4 crore equity. The company, Thai Rayon Co. Ltd., would go on to become the Aditya Birla group's flagship in Southeast Asia. Construction of the plant began in 1975 and production commenced in September 1976.

By 1976, therefore, the Aditya Birla group already had four major ventures up and running in Southeast Asia: Indo-Thai Synthetics, Century Textiles and Thai Rayon in Thailand and P.T. Elegant Textile Industry in Indonesia. For P.T. Elegant the spinning machines had been imported from Texmaco, a K.K. Birla group company, underscoring how the complex web of ties helped the Birlas expand and consolidate overseas.

Finance was no longer a problem. Those NRIs who had invested in Aditya's earlier ventures and been rewarded with high dividends gladly invested in the new projects. Ashwin Kothari's cousin Vijay Mehta bought equity in Indo-Thai Synthetics and P.T. Elegant while another NRI, Haru Mahtani, also invested a significant amount in the Indonesian venture. Enthused by the Thai and Indonesian successes, Aditya deputed Mahesh Bagrodia to explore business opportunities in Malaysia and the Philippines, two other still-emerging economies in the mid-1970s. Though Aditya himself spent less than a month in Southeast Asia every year, virtually nothing escaped his attention. In 1976, with ventures in the Philippines and Malaysia slated to take off, Aditya began to revamp his overseas command structure. Mahansaria was put in overall charge of Thailand and Indonesia from his Bangkok base. S.C. Sacheti was asked to monitor the Philippines and Malaysia came under R.S. Bathwal, a Birla loyalist from Calcutta, and R.L. Parikh. The various companies in each country reported to their respective country heads, who in turn kept Aditya informed with daily profit and loss *parta* statements and detailed monthly reviews of operations. It was decentralized management at its best and an early lesson on how to run an incipient multinational operation.

Any variations in production or profit and loss figures were immediately spotted and ruthlessly put right. Aditya had developed a mental toughness that would see him through many crises. Mahansaria describes how Aditya reacted to one in 1976: 'We were setting up Thai Carbon Black Co. Ltd. Phillips Petroleum, a world leader in carbon black technology, had promised to invest with us but suddenly, at the last moment, it decided to withdraw and we had no alternative but to go 100 per cent on our own. I was in Calcutta when the fax came from Phillips Petroleum. I was upset and feeling very sorry about it all. Aditya babu told me not to worry. He gave me the confidence to go ahead on our own without Phillips Petroleum even though it involved a complete financial recalculation. The company is today one of our flagships and though Phillips Petroleum withdrew financial support, it stayed on as our technological collaborator.'

Mahesh Bagrodia had by now become one of Aditya's closest aides. He had impressed Aditya by setting up his first caustic soda plant in Nagda within budget and on time. 'In July 1971 I promised Aditya babu that the plant would be commissioned by October 1, 1972,' recalls Bagrodia. 'He felt it was impossible. So did G.D. babu. But the deadline was met.' G.D. visited the plant and phoned Aditya to congratulate him. Delighted, Aditya gave increasing responsibility—and power—to Bagrodia. In 1974 Aditya obtained a licence to set up a spinning mill in the Philippines. Bagrodia was put in charge of the project. 'I went to Manila, arranged the funding and identified prospective investors,' says Bagrodia. 'Before this project, any spinning mill took at least one year to set up. I told Aditya babu that I would put up the Philippines spinning plant in six months. He informed Mahansariaji in Thailand, who told him over the phone that it would take a minimum of twelve months. I stopped over in Bangkok en route to Manila and met Mahansariaji; he told me the same thing.'

Bagrodia proved everyone wrong. The Philippines plant was commissioned in 5 months and 29 days.

Aditya expanded his overseas empire rapidly after 1976, spurred by friendly government policies in Southeast Asia and burgeoning post-Vietnam war reconstruction. A new carbon black plant was set up in Thailand in 1979–80. A viscose rayon staple fibre plant, P.T. Indo Bharat Rayon, was built in Indonesia in 1980. Though he travelled to his overseas plants only three or four times a year, Aditya's involvement during those visits was total. He would discuss operational and financial matters with his senior executives, often till three in the morning. 'Once when we were sitting in the Thai Rayon factory,' says Mahansaria, 'the Thai Carbon factory, just across the road, had a severe explosion in the boiler. But the accident did not upset Aditya babu at all and we carried on with our discussions as if nothing had happened. He was always composed and in control of the situation.'

Aditya used every overseas trip to meet the presidents of local and foreign banks as well as prominent government officials. The Birlas' high-level diplomatic contacts also helped. Romesh Bhandari was ambassador to Thailand in 1972–74 and introduced Aditya to a large Korean company. The meeting resulted in Grasim executing a Rs. 6 crore turnkey fibre project in Korea. When G.D. Birla and Aditya visited Thailand in 1974, they were among the few industrialists invited to dine with the King. Aditya and G.D. were feted by the Thai Chamber of Commerce and stayed at the hotel Disut Thani. It was a hotel that would become Aditya's favourite and he stayed there virtually every time he visited Bangkok.

It was during his business trips to Southeast Asia that Aditya let his natural reserve slip. In 1977, Aditya and Rajashree were on a routine visit to their Indonesian factories. Aditya, accompanied by Mahansaria, was driving from the plant site to Jakarta, 160 km away. Rajashree awaited them in a downtown Jakarta hotel. Aditya was at the wheel of a rented Toyota Crown. Darkness had fallen and he was driving fast, making Mahansaria decidedly nervous. 'I told him, please stop the car,' says Mahansaria. 'But when he stopped the car momentarily, it would not start up again. Unfortunately, we did not have any money with us. Suddenly I saw a bus coming. So I said, "Aditya babu, let's go by bus." What was worrying me was that if we did not reach the hotel on time, people would start getting anxious and start hunting for us—it was already 10.00 p.m. I had only a dollar with me and even if we went by bus it would take a lot of time. So we dropped the idea of taking the bus. We both started pushing the car. Finally, we reached a petrol pump, got the car repaired and reached our hotel in Jakarta by midnight. A very anxious Mrs. Rajashree Birla was at the hotel waiting for us. Later, Aditya babu often joked about the time he pushed a rented Toyota car in the Indonesian countryside at nearly midnight.'

Meanwhile, Aditya's Southeast Asian companies continued to prosper and, in 1982–83, Thai Rayon declared the highest dividend in its history—175 per cent. 'No wonder,' says one Thailand-based Birla executive, 'that there was a virtual stampede every time we offered shares to the public.' S.K. Saboo, executive president of Grasim and a loyalist from the G.D. era, adds: 'When Thai Rayon started production in 1976, Aditya babu was in Thailand and he was so excited that he brought the first sample of the fibre to Bombay on the morning of the day his grandfather was to fly to Europe. He made sure to tell him at the airport lobby, "Look, grandfather, you have been here manufacturing this since 1954, now I have also done it in Thailand." And G.D. was very proud of him.'

The Thai Rayon plant, with its landscaped gardens, spotless machine rooms and computer-controlled process systems, is one of the most technologically advanced in Asia. It set the standard for future AVB joint venture projects in Southeast Asia. Aditya insisted on sourcing the best technology worldwide for his plants. Pan Century Edible Oils, set up in Malaysia in 1977 and now the world's largest palm oil refinery, processes over 15 per cent of Malaysia's palm oil production. Its gleaming high-tech orange and silver hydrogen gas plant is set amidst landscaped grounds and its R&D laboratory is one of the world's most sophisticated.

Apart from importing the best global technology, the AVB group's plants in Southeast Asia stand out for their aesthetic, sometimes stunning architecture. Thai Polyphosphate and Chemicals Co. Ltd., set up in 1984 in collaboration with Albright and Wilson Ltd., UK (a wholly-owned subsidiary of Tenneco Inc., USA, the leading manufacturer of phosphates in the world), has a spotlessly clean, freshly painted yellow, red and white interior that belies its huge daily production of corrosive phosphate chemicals. Thai Acrylic Fibre Company Ltd., established in 1987 in technical collaboration with Japan Exlan Co. Ltd., is surrounded by lush green gardens and is a recipient of the Thai government's award for environmental excellence. Its sprawling, cream-coloured building houses computerized process-control systems that produce 32,000 tonnes of acrylic fibre every year on completely automated machines.

By the early 1980s, Aditya Birla and his men—especially Mahansaria and Bagrodia—had built a Southeast Asian group with global-sized plants and large product synergies with the family's Indian companies. Aditya's growing business responsibilities, however, did not lead him to alter his well-set routine. The family led a quiet but busy life.

Originally published as Minhaz Merchant, *Aditya Vikram Birla: A Biography* (Delhi, Viking, 1997), pp. 4–11, 13–14, 153–9.

34

Harnessing the Capital Market
The Ambani Story

T.N. Ninan and Jagannath Dubashi

At the same time as business houses like the Aditya Vikram Birla Group moved overseas in an attempt to bypass the restrictive atmosphere at home, industrialist Dhirubhai Ambani exploited the stock exchange innovatively to counter state domination of financial institutions and to capitalize on an undeveloped financial market.

Among the business persons of the 1970s who transformed the landscape of Indian business history, Dhirubhai Ambani is eminent. Born to an ordinary Modh bania family of a village schoolteacher, Ambani manipulated the license quota regime of the 1980s to emerge as the most successful entrepreneur of his time. Starting out with Reliance Commercial Corporation, a small trading firm in Bombay, Ambani moved on to dealing in imported nylon and then set up his own industry, Reliance Textiles, in 1966. He overcame the highly regulated industrial environment, the licensing system, and the red tape by cultivating close relations with the political establishment. Alongside, he raised industrial finance by issuing convertible debentures.*

Soon after the first initial public offering in 1977 of 28 lakh shares, to which more than 58,000 investors subscribed, Reliance became a 'darling of the stock exchange'. In 1992, it became the first Indian company to tap the global depository receipt market and the only one to raise 50- and 100-year bonds in the US debt markets. From a non-entity, Reliance emerged as the third largest industrial group in the 1980s, after the Tatas

* Essentially, convertible debentures were issued which guaranteed returns in the form of interest and could be converted into shares in the future thus offering prospective capital appreciation. Investor interest was sustained by the high dividends the company offered and the bonus shares it gave out. Ambani used the stock exchange to raise finance and created the 'equity cult' in the Indian capital market. This caught the imagination of the Indian middle class which started investing in equity in a market dominated by state-owned financial institutions.

and the Birlas—and all this during the heyday of the license permit raj. Ambani was unstoppable—a media report described the growth of the group as a juggernaut—and Reliance became one of the few Indian companies to be listed on the *Forbes* list of the world's wealthy and *Fortune's* list of the leading 500 companies in the developing world. By 2002, Reliance had a gross annual turnover of close to 15 billion dollars with interests ranging from synthetic fibers, textiles, petrochemicals, oil and gas exploration, and telecommunications, to financial services.†

This article by noted journalists T.N. Ninan and Jagannath Dubashi provides a succinct account of the rise, successes, and setbacks of the Ambani empire from its origins in the 1960s up till the 1980s. It includes a candid 1985 interview in which Ambani confesses his willingness to curry favour with politicians to pursue business ends, asserting that he would '*salaam* anyone in the government'.

"I am the bubble that burst," says Dhirubhai Hirachand Ambani with a wicked gleam—recalling media forecasts a few years ago that his company, Reliance Textile Industries, was a "bubble that could burst". But the press has been wrong, his numerous critics have been wrong, and the doomsayers have finally fallen silent. For the facts now stare them in the face.

Today, Reliance is barely 18 years old, but it already has the largest net worth among all private companies in India. It made more profits last year than any private company in the country, and it ranks third in both sales and total assets among the country's corporate giants.

Reliance has just paid out more money as share dividends than any company in Indian history. It has more investors than anyone else: 1.2 million. And Ambani talks of taking that figure to five million in the next two or three years. That is equivalent to the head of every household in Bombay, Calcutta and Delhi becoming an investor in Reliance.

The company last month had the largest ever attendance at any annual shareholders' meeting: 12,000. No hall in the city of Bombay could hold that number, so the meeting had to be finally held in a football ground.

The list of 'firsts' continues. Reliance produces more cloth every day than any other textile company, and does it more profitably than any other company. It is the country's largest importer of synthetic yarn. The company already produces more polyester filament yarn than any other rival in the business (10,000 tonnes), and is more than doubling its capacity. Soon, it will also be the country's largest if not its only producer of polyester staple fibre, purified terephtalic acid and mono-ethylene glycol—both these being raw materials for polyester fibre—and of linear alkyl benzene, which is used to make synthetic detergents.

Reliance is investing more money every day than any other private corporate entity. The projects currently under way involve a total investment of Rs 675 crore, and all the projects will be completed in two years, which makes for an investment of almost Rs 1 crore every day. Already, Reliance holds what is probably a world record in setting up a 10,000 tonne

† On Ambani, see Paranjoy Guha Thakurta, 'The two faces of Dhirubhai Ambani', *Seminar*, January 2003. For a biography of Ambani see Hamish McDonald's *The Polyster Prince: The Rise of Dhirubhai Ambani* (Australia, Allen & Unwin, 1998). Also see his recent *Ambani and Sons* (Roli, 2010).

polyester yarn plant in 14 months, and the plant reached full capacity production in four days. Ambani now plans to break that record: his 45,000-tonne polyester fibre project may be completed in 12 months.

It goes without saying, of course, that Reliance has proved to be the finest investment proposition ever seen by the Indian investor. Anyone who invested Rs 1,000 in Reliance when the company first offered shares to the public less than eight years ago, in late 1977, has so far got Rs 3,937 in dividends alone, while the market value of his investment is more than Rs 50,000.

Dhirubhai Ambani himself started his first venture, the Reliance Commercial Corporation, 25 years ago with a total capital of Rs 15,000. In 1967, he then floated Reliance Textiles with Rs 15 lakh in the kitty. Today, the market value of Reliance shares totals—hold your breath—more than Rs 10,000 crore. And Ambani estimates his personal net worth at Rs 150 crore.

The village schoolteacher's son has certainly made good. His company will soon be the single largest contributor to tax revenues, with excise and other duties payable estimated for 1987 at Rs 600 crore, which is roughly 5 per cent of the Central Government's total excise collection. By then, Reliance will almost certainly be the country's largest private company in terms of both sales and assets (it currently ranks third, behind the two Tata giants Tata Steel and Tata Engineering—both many decades old). And it will in all probability be the first private Indian company to figure in *Fortune* magazine's list of the 500 largest corporations outside the United States.

Indeed, when everyone thinks that Ambani has finally arrived, he himself thinks that he has only begun. Everything that the company has achieved over the last 18 years will be achieved all over again in the next three years. The company's turnover is billed to go up from Rs 604 crore last year to Rs 1,400 crore in 1987, its net worth is expected to climb from Rs 246 crore to Rs 550 crore, and its fixed assets from Rs 520 crore to Rs 1,200 crore. As if that weren't enough, gross profit as a percentage of sales is expected to climb from 19.6 per cent to an unbelievable 29 per cent.

The most incredible part of this story is that even after investing Rs 675 crore in the next two years, the company will still not be fully stretched financially. Right now, Reliance does not owe a paisa to any of the Government-owned financial institutions, on whom virtually every other company depends for finance. And even when the current projects are completed, the ratio of its loans to share capital will leave room for more loans to finance fresh investment of between Rs 800 crore and Rs 1,000 crore. And though Ambani is not saying so, he is already working on new projects to venture into as soon as he is ready for them. The growth, it seems, will continue. And the bubble does not seem about to burst.

No one, least of all Dhirubhai himself, could have foreseen all this. At school in Junagadh in Gujarat, from where the young tycoon-to-be matriculated while staying in a local hostel, his ambitions were limited to possessing a car or a jeep. Later, he went to Aden as a clerk in A. Beesse and Company, a French firm that acted as agents for Shell Oil. Dhirubhai was soon put in charge of retail marketing, his work taking him to such out of the way places as Eritrea, Djibouti, Somaliland, Kenya and Uganda. "*Mazaa aathi thi*" (I used to have fun), he now says of his past with a laugh.

Soon enough, the entrepreneurial bug bit him, and he returned to Bombay to start his first venture, the Reliance Commercial Corporation, with a total capital of Rs 15,000 and a shared office in Bombay's Bhaat Bazaar. He exported ginger, cardamom, turmeric and other spices to the west Asian market where he had established links during his Aden stint, and then branched out into textiles and yarn in the early 1960s. His most unusual export, however, was the good earth: a sheikh in Saudi Arabia was keen on cultivating a rose garden and needed a good soil mixture, which Ambani supplied, ready as always to seize a commercial opportunity.

In the years that followed, Ambani specialised in hawking imported yarn. A Bombay businessman recalls the Ambani of those days as being a "pucca Gujarati bania", stalking the city's yarn market, living off tea-shop snacks and endlessly chewing paan. Dhirubhai's younger son. Anil, recalls that through much of the 1960s the family lived in a one-room chawl, with Anil and elder brother Mukesh growing up in the neighbourhood bylanes.

By 1967, Dhirubhai was ready to start Reliance Textile Industries as a private limited company with a share capital of Rs 15 lakh. He didn't have all the money he needed, so he asked the people he knew for help. This included Viren Shah of Mukand Iron and Steel Company, who came from Ambani's seaside village of Chorwad (now a tourist spot) and whose family was the biggest landowner in the village. Shah told a friend later that he was asked by Dhirubhai for Rs 4 lakh, but that he turned down the request on the ground that "this project will not fly". He couldn't have been more wrong.

Somehow, Ambani has always attracted scepticism. Even in 1977, when Reliance was changing to a public limited company and its shares were being offered to the general public, numerous investors didn't want a slice of the still untested cake. D.N. Shroff, then president of the Silk and Art Silk Mills Association and a long-time friend of the man he calls Dhiru, remembers trying to persuade friends in government to buy Reliance shares worth Rs 1 lakh, but with practically no luck.

If few people saw then that this was going to be a goldmine, and that Ambani had the fabled Midas touch, the critics kept pace with Ambani through his early successes. Throughout the 1970s, Ambani made most of his money importing and exporting rayon and nylon yarn and fabrics, on which the profit margins were stupendous because of their domestic scarcity. Grabbing scarce import licences, often hawking them at a premium, Ambani was quicker off the mark than everyone else in the biggest money-spinning operation of the decade. Critics have charged then and ever since that there was more to this initial success than is publicly known.

RECORD GAINS

An investor who has invested Rs 1,000 in 100 equity shares of Reliance in 1977 has gained 50-fold in eight years.

Investment in 1977 + 100 Shares	Rs 1,000
Dividend for 1977–78	Rs 275
Dividend for 1979	Rs 250
Bonus at the rate of 3:5 + 60 shares	
Dividend for 1980	Rs 400
Dividend for 1981	Rs 560
Dividend for 1982	Rs 660
Bonus at the rate of 3:5 + 96 Shares	
Dividend for 1983	Rs 768
Dividend for 1984	Rs 1,024
Total dividends earned + Total shares in 1984 = 256	Rs 3,937
The market value of 1 equity share today is around Rs 210 × 256 =	Rs 210 Rs 53,760
Total dividend received	Rs 3,937
Total gains on Rs 1,000	Rs 57,697

THE TOP THREE			
	Net Worth	Net Sales	Gross Profit
Reliance	246	604	95
TISCO	233	781	64
TELCO	195	755	62

Shroff recalls criticism at the time from a host of rival industrialists, who charged that Ambani was indulging in black marketing. He informed Dhirubhai of the criticism, and the man's response was typical. He asked Shroff to summon a meeting of his executive committee, comprising the biggest industrialists in the synthetics business Dhirubhai was then invited to face his critics, but he had them silent with one question: "You accuse me of black marketing, but which one of you has not slept with me?" Since all of them had at one stage or another bought yarn from or sold yarn to Ambani at the going rate, none of them had an answer. Dhirubhai had made his point: no one in the business could act holier than Ambani.

Other criticisms have been voiced over the years: that Ambani has used friends in high places to get his way and to put down rivals, that Ambani has mysteriously managed to always get the licences he wants, and to get the Government to announce duty rates that help him while putting own his rivals. Dhirubhai himself affects impatience with such carping, but there may well be a point to what the critics say.

In 1982, for instance, Reliance was getting ready to manufacture polyester yarn from imported dimethy terephthalate DMT. while the rival Orkay Silk Mills planned to use polyester chips as raw material. But in the budget of that year, the Government raised the import duty on polyester chips so that the Orkay project now faced a price handicap in the market. Then, in November 1982, almost immediately after the Reliance polyester yarn factory went into production, the import duty on the yarn was raised by the Government—giving Ambani a price protection that helped his profit margins.

Such cases can be multiplied. And Ambani's denials and explanations are not entirely convincing. He argues, for instance, that his friendship or acquaintance with people like former prime minister Indira Gandhi and her special assistant, R.K. Dhawan, were not helpful to him in his business: "One bureaucrat low down the ladder can say no to something which no one can then overrule."

Nevertheless, the fact remains that in 1980 he joined hands with some Congress (I) members of Parliament from Gujarat to host a party in a New Delhi hotel immediately after the Lok Sabha elections, a party that Mrs Gandhi attended as almost her first public engagenent after being sworn in. Also, a liaison manager in an industry quite unconnected with Ambani's recalls sitting in the office of a joint secretary in the Industry Ministry when the joint secretary got a telephone call from Dhawan asking why Ambani's licence application had not been cleared. A short while later, Dhawan was on the line again, asking about progress, and the joint secretary was reduced to stammered explanations about the cyclostyling machine taking too much time.

It would be a mistake, however, to attribute more importance to all this than is warranted. As a friend of Ambani explains. "Any poor man who has made his money quickly and become wealthy has used a ladder that is not clean. But anyone who thinks that Ambani is successful only or largely because of this is living in a fool's paradise. The fact is that Ambani is a consummate businessman."

Naroda & Patalganga

OLD AND NEW

In a dark corner of a huge shed stands the machine which began it all: a warp knitting machine, one of four which Dhirubhai Ambani had installed less than two decades ago at Naroda, a few kilometres from the textile city of Ahmedabad. Today, Reliance's Naroda Textile Complex houses over a thousand machines in 110 acres of land, employs 8,400 workers, uses up electricity to the tune of Rs 3 lakh and turns out 2 lakh metres of fabric daily. Says Susheel Kothari, chief executive: "No one else could have done what we have in such a short time."

Kothari belongs to the old guard—he was with Dhirubhai in his first venture, the Reliance Commercial Corporation—and it is perhaps a measure of the company's overpowering work ethos that he has had no difficulty adjusting to the new guard: represented by none other than Anil Ambani, 26, the younger of Dhirubhai's two sons and the boss of what is the most modern mill in the country. "Our greatest advantage," says Anil, "is that we adjust very quickly to change. The other mills are decades old, so are the people who work there. It's much easier for us to institute newer procedures."

Anil explains that they are constantly modernising: last year, 280 state-of-the-art water-jet looms—where the yarn is flung across the threads by a jet of water—were installed. The textile industry in general still uses machines that are many decades old, but at Reliance, the average life of a machine is five to seven years. This makes sense, because as the licensed capacity is linked to the loom, putting in faster and faster loom means more production. Already, a loom today produces five times as much cloth as the ones 10 years ago did.

The pride of the plant is its unique computerised information system installed early this year at a cost of Rs 1 crore. Tapping keys on a terminal in his office. Anil can get information on each and every loom's functioning—production, stoppages, efficiency and so on. "We know what is happening at any given minute. The grasp that this gives us of every day working is tremendous." M.P. Gupta, manager, weaving, says, "Anil plans to link the system to the head office in Bombay, so that his father can have the same kind of access."

The lack of paper on managers' desks is another refreshing aspect of corporate life at Naroda. Says H.N. Arora, general manager, personnel and administration: "We try to take all decisions as quickly as possible, without going through the hassles of intrays and out-trays. Anilbhai is very accessible." Anil himself recounts how he sometimes comes in early and drops little pieces of paper on everybody's desk, saying, "Why isn't this file cleared? Why is there so much paper lying about?" "It seems to work," he says impishly.

Modern and immensely functional as it is, Naroda is already the past for Reliance. The future is closer to Bombay, on a sprawling 300-acre site, 71 km from the great metropolis where Dhirubhai's drive to become a petrochemicals potentate is taking shape at a frenetic pace. The Reliance complex at Patalganga takes up almost half of the entire industrial estate, dwarfing other plants like Orkay's Polyester and Bombay Dyeing's DMT factory. The core of the complex is of course, the 10,000 tonnes a year PFY (polyester filament yarn) plant, designed by Du Pont, set up in a record time of 14 months. The expansion to 25,000 tonnes is going ahead rapidly and all around can be seen the skeletons of structures which will house the other petrochemical operations. According to Mukesh Ambani, 28, Dhirubhai's elder son who is incharge of the crucial petrochemicals drive, the company started thinking about backward integration in the late '70s. "We were already in textiles so from there to production of the basic chemicals was a logical step backward."

In about 10 years, therefore, Reliance will have conceived of, planned and implemented a series of projects which should see it producing, beside 25,000 tonnes of polyester yarn, 45,000 tonnes of polyester staple fibre (PSF), 75,000 tonnes of purified terephthalic acid (PTA), 40,000 tonnes of mono ethylene glycol (MEG) and 50,000 tonnes of linear alkyl benzene (LAB). "Diligence is the main reason for our speedy success," says Mukesh.

The man who has fuelled this enormous drive sits miles away in Bombay, leaving his sons and other colleagues to carry on the job. Dhirubhai Ambani visits Naroda twice a year, and Patalganga once in three months. His confidence in his people is not surprising, really, for it is only a function of his tremendous confidence in himself.

—Jagannath Dubashi
in Naroda and Patalganga

That point should be well taken. For one thing, Ambani uses the same techniques and strategies that others do to influence government decisions and to run his business. The difference is that he is better at the game than they are. And as he himself says. "You have to sell your idea to the Government, and show how the company's plans fit in with national priorities. For instance, we import edible oils worth Rs 1,400 crore every year, so Reliance is looking at the possibility of going in for commercial plantations. The Government says it does not have money for projects, and I point out that Reliance can finance the project from its own resources."

The more important point, of course, is that Ambani has numerous strengths as a businessman, combining a talent for everything from marketing to finance and choice of technology. If he excelled in his early years in spotting a quick-money commercial opportunity, latching on first to a high-profit area of exports and imports, fixing on synthetic textiles as the growth-cum-profit area with maximum potential and later in knowing how to get his way with the Government, he has other strengths as well: spotting the right technology to adopt, working out innovative ways of marketing his yarn and financial wizardry with the hallmark of genius that has not been seen in Indian industry for some decades.

While other businessmen were thinking of going in for DMT plants that would feed polyester fibre units, Ambani spotted a worldwide shift in favour of a cheaper substitute, purified terephthalic acid (PTA), and went ahead with a PTA project.

While most yarn producing companies sold their product wholesale, Ambani and cousin Rasiklal Meswani, executive director in charge of yarn sales, set up a complicated retail selling system under which yarn is sold directly to small-scale weavers who then sell their grey fabric back to Reliance, which processes and finishes this before unloading it on to the market as Reliance cloth with its Vimal brand name. In the process, Ambani has been able to get around the licence capacity limitations of his own weaving section and turn out far more cloth than he would otherwise have been able to. Says a contented Meswani: "As many as 25,000 units convert yarn into fabric for Reliance, and 30 to 40 per cent of our fabric comes this way. In the process, we have also earned the support of large numbers of customers for our yarn, because we guarantee them a market for their cloth."

If that speaks of Ambani's capacity for innovation, there are numerous other examples, especially in the field of finance, that underline the same point. Back in 1979, it was Ambani who first pushed through a forgotten idea in corporate finance, the convertible debenture. He had the devil of a time convincing the

DHIRUBHAI AMBANI

"I will salaam anyone in the Government"

A QUARTER century ago, Dhirubhai Hirachand Ambani put up his first commercial name-plate, that of the Reliance Commercial Corporation, in a corner of a borrowed office in an unpretentious part of Bombay. He couldn't afford his own office then.

Today, the 52-year-old tycoon has a 'Chairman's office' that takes up 8,000 square feet of plush carpeting in downtown Nariman Point. Ambani himself sits in a personal office embellished almost wholly in white, including white telephones. Four floors below is parked a white Cadillac, which Ambani used to use until he switched recently to a gold Mercedes 500. And on most days he prefers to dress in white safari suits that have almost become his sartorial trade mark.

The man himself is a bundle of energy, pacing in and out of his office, hitching up his trousers on an increasingly weighty torso, then sitting for a while to answer questions, and reaching out for a handshake after a wisecrack.

He obviously enjoys his increasing financial muscle, but has a problem with keeping his physical weight down. "I take a walk every morning, and go to the Oberoi health club in the evening. On week-ends, I try to go hiking in the Khandala hills." Although he still checks in at 76 kg, he has lost 14 kg in recent weeks. But even when he exercises or goes through his health club work-outs, his razor-sharp mind is never off business. Share brokers and yarn traders crowd round him constantly at the Oberoi health club.

He is not religious and does no regular pujas, but believes in God. He clearly has less faith in journalists, for he is constantly on his guard during interviews, watching which way the questions are headed, promising confidential information off the record and then delivering some innocuous titbit.

Last fortnight in Bombay, he spoke at length to Senior Editor T.N. Ninan and Senior Correspondent Jagannath Dubashi. Excerpts:

Q. ***We'd like to start at the beginning. How did you start in life?***

A. I had a very humble beginning. My father was a village schoolteacher. I started at the age of 17 as a clerk in a French firm in Aden. Please mention this, because I am proud of it and people should get inspiration from this.

Q. ***What were you paid?***

A. Rs 300 a month. But I rose quickly, and when I left after eight years, I was in charge of retail marketing, getting Rs 1,100 a month.

Q. ***Why did you go to Aden?***

A. I got the opportunity. I would have gone to South Africa if I had got a job there. *Roti ka sawal tha* (It was a question of bread).

Q. ***Did you finish school?***

A. I did my matriculation, with only pass marks (laughs).

Q. ***What was your ambition when you were young?***

A. I wanted to buy a car, an old jeep perhaps. I was a member of the Civil Guards, something like today's NCC. We had to salute our officers who went around in jeeps. So I thought: one day I will also ride in a jeep and somebody else will salute me.

Q. ***Did you think then of starting any industry?***

A. Not at all. At 17 you can't expect much, and that too in a small village.

Q. ***What is the main reason for the success of Reliance Textiles?***

A. I have seen over the past 15 years that people with savings do not have the correct avenues for investment. This is particularly true of the salaried and the middle class. They have to invest in bank deposits or units, which do not give very good returns. So more and more middle class people are attracted to my shares, and this is the success of Reliance.

Q. ***Would you call this Reliance's biggest contribution to industry?***

A. What was the situation 15 years ago? Suppose I wanted to start a company: 60 per cent shares I would buy, 20 per cent would go to relatives, and the rest the brokers would get. Now Reliance has created a revolution in the corporate sector. I have 12 lakh investors in Reliance, and this will become five million. Middle class people are joining hands to build something big. In the process, the country benefits.

In 1980, the total resources mobilised in the capital market was Rs 100 crore. Last year, it was Rs 2,500 crore. That shows we had the water but no pumping station. Everybody is now installing pumping stations. Just look at the number of people who have issued debentures.

Q. ***Do you think your financial strategy could be applied on a broader scale in India?***

A. Yes, of course. For our seventh plan we don't have money for power projects, bridges, railways. There is no money with the Government, that is true, but there is money with the public. We can pump that money to a hundred Reliances and build a strong country.

Q. ***One reason for your success is your ability to manage the external environment. How do you do this?***

A. The most important external environment is the Government of India. You have to sell your ideas to the Government. Selling the idea is the most important thing, and for that I'd meet anybody in the Government, I am willing to *salaam* anyone. One thing you won't find in me and that is an ego.

Q. ***But if three companies are trying to get the same licence, why does the Government favour you?***

A. I tell them that I am putting in my own company's resources, and that the others will have to borrow from the financial institutions. My main edge is that we mobilise our own resources.

Q. ***Pranab Mukherjee is supposed to have helped get your last four licences.***

A. People who wanted to criticise Pranab Mukherjee used me as gunpowder. Pranab was in the Finance Ministry, which does not issue licences. Also, how many people have got licences in India, and how many of them have implemented these licences? The country should salute people who implement projects quickly.

Q. You say the Finance Ministry does not issue licences, but it does decide duty levels, and these have often been structured to help you.

A. I don't think this is true.

Q. The new Government is said to be less friendly towards you, and the report is that they did not allow you to issue a convertible debenture issue, so that you had to go in for a non-convertible debenture issue.

A. We asked for a non-convertible issue and we got it. We don't require more equity, so we don't need to convert the new debentures into equity.

Q. What do you think of Rajiv Gandhi, and of the policies that he is trying to implement?

A. He is a first-class person, very honest, very sincere. And his policies will work. He is not just helping industry, he is helping the country to move faster.

Q. What new projects do you have in mind for Reliance? There is talk of oil exploration, computers, plantations and so on.

A. We will seize every opportunity we get. We continuously monitor every area, but that does not mean we will go into all of them. After all, if I see 100 girls, it doesn't mean I will marry all of them. But I must see all of them before I make my choice, mustn't I?

Q. How do you see your basic role in the company, now that it has grown to such a size?

A. Supervising everything and everybody, seeing that everything runs to schedule, solving problems.

Q. Have you set yourself a goal, like making Reliance the largest company in the country?

A. I would not like to say what I want to do before I do it.

Government of its attractiveness as an investment proposition, arguing that it offered investors a guaranteed return as interest while simultaneously offering the prospect of capital appreciation when a part of the debenture was converted into shares.

The idea clicked, Reliance has issued six series of debentures in as many years for raising a record Rs 268 crore from the market, and other companies have jumped onto the bandwagon. As a result, the share market in the country has got its biggest boost in recent years because of the advent of the debenture. In the process, of course, Ambani has become the ordinary investor's stock market deity.

More daredevil ideas were to follow, some of them breathtaking in their originality. Ever since 1977–78, for instance, Reliance had not paid a rupee as tax on the substantial profits it earned, essentially because of outstanding tax planning by Ambani. But in 1983, the Government announced in the budget that companies would have to compulsorily pay tax on at least 30 per cent of their profits. Almost everyone thought then that this would slow down Reliance's frenetic expansion as some of the company's profits would be mopped up by the Government. But Ambani would have none of it. He announced shortly afterwards that the company was capitalising Rs 93 crore interest charges on its project loans, an unheard of stratagem that converted on-going expenditure into assets on which Reliance could now claim a higher depreciation write-off from its profits. Result: Reliance has stayed a zero tax company.

The purists have demurred, of course. Reliance's own auditors have noted in the company's annual report that the capitalisation of interest is not a practice recommended by the Institute of Chartered Accountants. But Ambani is undeterred, and he has got what he wants.

Still more breathtaking financial legerdemain was to follow. Last year, Ambani was getting ready to launch on his latest clutch of projects. But the company was financially stretched, with little elbow room to increase its borrowings. The solution: the non-convertible part of the company's debentures were also converted into shares.

This seemingly simple gimmick killed several birds with one stone. First, it reduced the company's debt while increasing its equity capital, so that the debt-equity ratio now provided room for more borrowings. Second, the debentures with a face value of Rs 100 were exchanged for 1.2 equity shares of Rs 10 each. This would seem unattractive for the investor, except for the fact that the Rs 10 share was then selling at Rs 115, while the market value of the Rs 100 debenture was only Rs 84. So the investor handed in an asset worth Rs 84 and got back another asset worth Rs 138 on the market.

The element of genius showed through this because while the investor gained, Reliance did too. The company had liquidated debt worth Rs 100 in the books and given out assets worth Rs 12 in the books. The balance went into the reserves fund, which swelled overnight by a whopping Rs 63.2 crore, while the 13.5 per cent interest burden on the debenture was replaced by a smaller dividend burden. Dhirubhai demurs modestly when asked who thought of this absolutely brilliant stratagem, attributing it to teamwork, but son Anil says the real brain was none other than Dhirubhai himself.

So the list of Ambani's strengths grows longer: commercial skill, technical understanding, financial wizardry, managing the Government, marketing innovation. But even this is not a complete list, for there is still more to the man who is now reckoned by everyone as the brightest star on the corporate firmament. Two additional strengths are revolutionary project management techniques that compress construction and erection time and the constant drive to modernise plant and machinery so that his own company escapes the fate of much of the textile industry.

Ambani takes an obvious pride in the speed with which he implements his industrial licences. His worsted spinning plant at Naroda, near Ahmedabad, was installed in eight months of getting the licence. In 1981, when he got the Government's permission to instal the latest draw texturing machines, he had the equipment flown in and installed in next to no time. This may partly have been because of criticism from his rivals that he had been allowed to get the machines when others had not, and he may have wanted to instal the equipment before the Government changed its mind. Nevertheless, the lightning reflexes of the man clearly stood out from the episode.

In 1982, he outdid E.I.Du Pont de Nemours, his collaborators for the polyester filament yarn project at Patalganga in Maharashtra, by getting the plant ready in 14 months, something that Du Pont itself had never managed to do in other countries. The real hero behind this achievement is Dhirubhai's elder son. Mukesh, an unassuming youngster of 28 years who wears his Stanford MBA lightly but who clearly has his father's genius in his veins. Mukesh attributes the record pace of project implementation very matter-of-factly to "diligence", and to the fact that he had no prior experience, "so I did not see the problems, only the solutions". But it takes S.P. Chakravorty, chief executive at Patalganga, to point out that whereas other companies would wait for equipment on order to land before linking its various pieces through the long arrays of pipes that are integral to a petrochemical complex, Reliance has done the opposite: at Patalganga, scores of kilometres of pipes were laid in readiness for the equipment, which was installed as soon as it landed. The magnitude of this achievement can be judged from the fact that one of Reliance's new projects has 220 km of pipes.

Modernisation is another key to Reliance's success. The Naroda plant was first started in the early 1970s with four warp knitting machines, but these are already museum pieces. As Dhirubhai's younger son Anil, who completed his own MBA from the Wharton School in 14 months before taking charge of the Naroda complex, points out, the average life of the machines at Naroda is only five to seven years. Last year, the company spent Rs 50 crore for importing 280 state-of-the-art waterjet looms and 16 projectile jacquard weaving machines. Investment of an even higher order is now planned for further modernization and expansion.

When all is said and done, however, Ambani's greatest strength is probably his ability to keep changing to the situation in which he finds himself. He started out as an operator in international trade; when he shifted to manufacturing, the vast bulk of his sales continued to go out as exports—because that is where the profits lay, given the premium-fetching import replenishment licences that he got on his exports. He then shifted from knitting to weaving, switching focus to the domestic market. And just when everyone thought that Ambani's profile was getting fixed, he did the chameleon act yet again by starting a petrochemical operation that has now resulted in the logical culmination: Reliance Textile Industries is changing its name to Reliance Industries.

The bulk of the company's investment will soon be in polyester filament yarn and staple fibre, and then in PTA, mono-ethylene glycol (MEG) and linear alkyl benzene (LAB). And future investment could well be in a Rs 500 crore aromatics plant in Uttar Pradesh that will use four lakh tonnes of naphtha turned out every year by the Mathura oil refinery. Aromatics is the upstream raw material for synthetic fabrics, and will mark for Ambani the culmination of his drive for backward integration. So from being the country's most high-profile textile magnate, Ambani is about to transform himself into a petrochemicals giant. But he might change yet again, moving into oilseed plantations and oil exploration. As he himself says, "I will go in whatever direction that suits me."

Through these transformations, he has managed change in other ways as well. When he started out, his business forced him to footslog it through Bombay's teeming yarn market, and to wait outside the doors of the very textile tycoons who now envy him his success, because at that time they were his valued clients. Today, he can sit through half-day long sessions with journalists without a telephone call to disturb him: he has passed responsibilities down the line, and people take decisions at their levels.

He puts in no more than an eight-hour day, clocking in at 10.15 every morning when a 50-to

60-page report is always waiting for him, giving every detail that matters on the previous day's operations: production, marketing, finance. His role now is confined to supervising the functioning of his senior executives, making sure things are running to schedule and that problems are solved. And there is a mildly puzzled incomprehension when asked how he managed the shift from a one-man yarn hawker to the rarefied atmosphere of an 8,000 square feet 'Chairman's office'. "Decentralisation is the answer," he says simply.

If that is indeed the case, the two people he relies on most of all are his sons. For while he scoffs at their American degrees, touting instead the homegrown virtues of native entrepreneurship, he clearly relies on Mukesh to see the company through its Rs 675 crore expansion spree and on Anil, the more outgoing and articulate son, for running the textile complex and looking after the company's total marketing.

Meswani is another key figure: paunchy, and wise in the ways of the yarn market, Meswani has been with cousin Dhirubhai for the last quarter century. "He has taught me everything," Meswani says, and Dhirubhai clearly trusts his cousin to look after the company's complex yarn marketing operations.

Chakravorty is another key executive, pulled out of J.K. Synthetics by Dhirubhai and asked to help Mukesh with the Patalganga operation. There are others like these, but Ambani now says he does not even bother with the recruitment of most of his personnel. He gives candidates the once over only if they are going to join in the key slots at the top. Everything else is decided lower down. And asked us to what kind of people he looks for, Ambani answers simply: "Engineers with talent."

All this decentralisation notwithstanding, Ambani's interests range far and wide. He is probably the best informed man in the country on the ups and downs of the smuggling business, because synthetic textiles are one of the most prominent items on the smugglers' list and these smuggled supplies his main competition.

Ambani's men estimate that a staggering Rs 3,000 crore worth of textiles are smuggled into India every year, a figure compiled by referring to the supplies reaching the United Arab Emirates from such sources as Japan, Korea, Taiwan, Hong Kong and Singapore.

Ambani also keeps a close check on the activities of his rivals. Last year, the excise authorities mounted a major raid on Orkay Silk Mills. The result reported in the newspapers last month was a Rs 10-crore fine on the company and a Rs 50-lakh personal fine on its chairman, Kapal Mehra.

It is widely believed in Bombay's business circles that Ambani had a hand in the initial tip-off to the authorities, who then mounted the raid. Whether this is true or not the fact remains that there is no one to beat Dhirubhai when it comes to close-range fighting. Four years ago, when Ambani was trying to get a licence from the Government to manufacture polyester filament yarn, all the existing producers under the banner of the Association of Synthetic Fibre Industry ganged up to prevent Ambani from getting the Government's go-ahead.

But they reckoned without the trick up Ambani's sleeve. Knowing that the best way to break a cartel is to get one or two of its members on your side with the promise of goodies. Ambani seems to have driven a wedge through the ranks of the opposition, which quickly fell apart for his own licence to come through. It may be purely coincidental that around the same time J.K. Synthetics got the Government's clearance for expanding its own plant, but there are few in the industry who do not believe that the two events are connected.

But such successes in the teeth of opposition inevitably generate more opposition, and some of this surfaced on the Bombay stock exchange in 1982. Ambani was just then readying for the single biggest capital issue in Indian corporate history (convertible debentures worth Rs 50 crore), and it was important that Reliance shares maintained a good price on the market so that investor confidence in the company was boosted.

But barely six weeks before the debenture issue was due to open in May, mysterious forces began hammering down the price of the Reliance share, which dropped from Rs 131 to Rs 121 in 25 minutes of unprecedented trading and near panic. But Ambani reacted with lightning speed and his men were quickly on the floor of the stock exchange, picking up every share that was offered. By the end of the day, the price had recovered to Rs 125, and a quickly formed "Friends of Reliance Association" took the battle into the opponents' corner. They kept buying for the next few weeks, driving the share price up.

In most share market transactions, sellers do not have shares ready for delivery because they intend to buy back later at a lower price. This game was now thwarted because Ambani's men had driven the price so high. So the very sellers who were trying to beat down the price earlier now started buying because Ambani's men insisted on delivery, and this took the share price still higher, to a record level of Rs 175 and more. The sellers eventually lost an estimated Rs 3.5 crore for their pains.

Ambani's men had turned the knife with a vengeance after getting in deep, and the forces who had mounted the attack in the first place—presumably Dhirubhai's rivals in business—learnt a lesson that they will never forget: do not meddle with Reliance shares. In fact, Ambani is suspected to have tried to pay Orkay in the same coin last year, when it was Orkay's turn to float a share issue.

If Ambani emerged triumphant from some of these financial skirmishes, he got his fingers slightly burnt in 1983 when some non-resident Indian companies with such unlikely names as Fiasco Investments and Crocodile Investments bought Reliance shares. It turned out on investigation that some of the people whose names were listed as the directors of these companies had not even heard of Reliance, casting some doubt on who the real investors were. Ambani himself explains this away by saying that "non-resident Indian investors will never reveal their true identity", but most observers believe that this particular episode has not yet been fully explained.

But such controversies appear to be nothing more than occasional hiccups even as Reliance continues to digest one project after another and to gain weight rapidly. So even Ambani's contemporaries in business are now forced to pay tribute. Says Kapal Mehra of Orkay: "His track record shows that he is a go-getter. There has been a lot of controversy about the method he has adopted, but he has been successful, and I wish there were more people like Dhirubhai in India." And Virenchee Sagar, managing director of Nirlon, says: "He has this enormous, extraordinary ambition which should see him go far."

Such accolades, some of them grudgingly delivered, come on top of the adulation that is already Ambani's because of the unprecedented returns that he has given his investors. And the question inevitably crops up: what next?

There are clear signs that some leading lights of the Rajiv Gandhi government are not fond of Ambani, and one minister has a dossier ready on his past activities. But it is doubtful if even this can now come in Dhirubhai's way: Reliance is too big, and its creator still has a lot of creativity left in him.

Persistent rumour suggests that Ambani might get into the media game. His Mudra advertising agency, launched initially for in-house work, has already become one of the largest agencies in the business, with billings last year of Rs 8 crore. Mudra's offshoot is now investing Rs 4 crore in new video equipment that will launch Ambani into the growing field of TV and video film production. Bombay has also been buzzing with talk of an offer he made to R.K. Karanjia, editor of the local tabloid *The Daily*, and journalists have been approached with job offers by people claiming to be speaking on behalf of Ambani.

But Ambani denies emphatically that he wants to get into the media business. If one takes him at his word, he still has numerous fields beckoning him. Quite apart from the various projects that he has already on hand, he has a stake in a new private oil exploration company floated with other investors by H.T. Parekh. And as he points out, he has the ability to "pump money out of the people." In a capital starved economy, anyone who can get the capital together will clearly have no shortage of work to get done whether it is in edible oilseed plantations, oil related projects or computers, which too Dhirubhai is looking at.

One thing is certain. As he takes his morning constitutional on the Worli seaface, or has his standard breakfast of a papaya. Ambani is still thinking of the future, not the past. At 52, he has a good decade of work still ahead of him: and if his dreams come true, at the end of that period Reliance Industries could well be four or five times the size it is today. No one, of course, will be surprised.

Originally published as T.N. Ninan and Jagannath Dubashi, 'Dhirubhai Ambani: The Super Tycoon', *India Today*, 30 June 1985, pp. 72–80.

BUSINESS IN THE POST-REFORMS ERA

SECTION V

35

'From Regulation to Liberalization'
Post-1985 Indian Economy

Tarun Das

In June 1991, there occurred a dramatic shift in India's economic paradigm when far-reaching reforms were enacted under the stewardship of Dr Manmohan Singh as finance minister. It heralded a new stage in the story of Indian capital. The new direction taken since then has emphasized free enterprise, removal of licensing and control, and gradual opening up of the economy. Among the seminal changes that impacted on the fortunes of the private sector were the reduction of industrial licensing, devaluation of the rupee and its convertibility on the trade account, opening of equity markets, encouragement of foreign direct investment, permission to companies to raise capital on international markets, and reduction of import tariffs.* All these were harbingers of a new phase in India's industrial history, the impact of which has been dramatic.

Bringing the story of Indian industry into the 1990s, Tarun Das, chief mentor of the Confederation of Indian Industry and Padma Bhushan awardee in 2006 for his contribution to trade and industry, succinctly summarizes the evolution of the Indian economy from its post-Independence phase of 'regulation' to its current state of 'liberalization'. Das begins by noting the landmark year of 1956 when the Industrial

*For an insightful view of the reforms unleashed in what Gurcharan Das has called the 'golden summer' see his *India Unbound: From Independence to the Global Information Age* (New Delhi, Penguin, 2002). For an understanding of the economic policies and growth trajectories of the Indian economy since 1950, see Arvind Panagariya, *India: The Emerging Giant* (New Delhi, Oxford University Press, 2008). On the reforms, also see Amit Bhaduri and Deepak Nayyar, *The Intelligent Person's Guide to Liberalization* (New Delhi, Penguin, 1996); Pranab K. Bardhan, *The Political Economy of Development in India* (Oxford, Blackwell, 1984); and Jagdish N. Bhagwati, *India in Transition: Freeing the Economy* (Oxford, Clarendon, 1993). Also see *Oxford Review of Economic Policy*, Vol. 23, No. 2, 2007, especially Kaushik Basu and Annemie Mertens, 'The Patterns and Causes of Economic Growth in India'.

Policy Resolution declared that the commanding heights of the Indian economy would be taken by the public sector in the hope of progressing towards a mixed economy. Thereafter, he examines what he considers 'the most difficult period' from 1969 through 1974, difficult because politics came to be dictated by populism and economic policies were influenced by powerful forces which used them as tools to win elections. Das notes that even though the Indian state made good on its initial aims of enforcing a fair regulation regime in the first 15 years of its Independence, by the 1980s, the Indian economy was crippled to a state of stagnation mainly due to high incidence of duties and levies, bureaucratic delays, and fragmented industrial structures. Winds of change blew in 1974, when the need for liberalization was felt due to the worsening balance of payments situation. This led to the slight slackening of duty-free imports, in the hope of promoting export-oriented production facilities. Yet it was only in 1985 that the leadership began to formulate plans for economic liberalization and, from 1991, the process was hastened. It was decided that the public sector would not be expanded and that the new engine of growth would be the private sector, especially with the aid of foreign direct investment and small-scale industry, which would enable the Indian economy to integrate better with the global regime of capitalism.

Das ends on a rather positive note by noting that the economy now not only encourages, but indeed demands, firms to be competitive with inbuilt flexibility and adjustment mechanisms. He laments, however, that bureaucratic and administrative reforms are far from complete and urges the government to expedite matters if India is to emerge as a major player in global economic affairs and developmental processes.

Nineteen forty-seven to 1997, a fifty-year period, is an appropriate time frame for review and stocktaking of India's industrial development process. In India's case, it also happens to be the first fifty years of national development after Independence. At the time of Independence, India was among the few colonial economies that had an industrial and manufacturing sector. There were, in existence, industries such as steel, cement, textiles, sugar, paper board, light consumer goods and a range of engineering industries. Compared to other newly-independent countries, urban India was also better off in terms of industrial infrastructure, institutional facilities and networks, facilities for higher learning and scientific and technological research. There was also a network of financial systems, consisting of commercial banks and a capital market.

However, both industrial activity and urban centres were limited and concentrated. The overall industrial economy was not large enough to meet the needs of the economy as a whole. Infrastructure was inadequate and lacking in most areas. The base did exist, but was not strong enough for the superstructure that was needed in the future. Besides, there was the huge task of achieving faster growth of an economy with high incidences of underdevelopment and poverty. Rapid industrialization was naturally the need of the day to generate economic growth and employment.

An industry-driven development strategy was, therefore, considered appropriate for rapid economic development and, accordingly, from the early 1950s, strategies for industrialization received considerable attention. Beginning with Independence in 1947, and up to the end of the

First Five Year Plan in 1955–6, the focus was on consolidation, while framing the broad contours of policy and regulation. The need was felt for putting in place some regulatory mechanism for planned development and to establish supporting institutions.

Towards this objective certain important initiatives were taken during the period 1947–55, namely the enactment of Capital Control (Issues) Act 1947, Factories Act 1948, Minimum Wages Act 1947, and so on. With a view to augmenting capital resources for investment, and particularly developments in finance, at the all-India level, the Industrial Finance Corporation was set up in 1948 and, at the state level, the State Financial Corporation Act was enacted to enable state governments to set up their own financial institutions.

One of the principal goals of development strategy was to promote the growth of indigenous industries through import substitution measures. Besides, a shortage of foreign exchange resources had also necessitated stricter import trade control. At the same time, the need for export promotion through a diversification of the export basket was realized. In order to meet these objectives, the Import Trade Control Act was passed in 1947, and the Export Trade (Control) Order 1955 was introduced. However, the basic philosophy of that industrialization that was to come was spelt out in the Industrial Policy Resolution of 1948 (IPR'48), that specified the role of government in future industrial development and earmarked the scope for private sector investment.

After the IPR'48 came the Industries (Development & Regulation) (IDR) Act 1951 with a view to imposing licensing control on investment and production. The objectives behind this act were threefold, namely:

(i) to ensure efficient allocation of available resources,

(ii) to channelize investment in the desired directions, and

(iii) to curb the concentration of economic power in the hands of a few.

As a promotional measure, the Office of the Director General of Technical Development (DGTD) was set up to encourage technology upgradation and channelize the induction of appropriate technology. Under the DGTD, several industry-specific Development Councils were created to monitor the growth of those industries.

Nineteen hundred and fifty-six was a landmark year in the history of post-Independence industrialization strategy. The Industrial Policy Resolution of 1956 was announced with clearcut guidelines on the role of different sectors in India's industrialization drive, with the commanding height occupied by the public sector. While establishment of a mixed economy and 'growth with equity' were the primary objectives, there was a major assumption about the efficacy of the private sector. It was assumed that the private sector had limited skills and resources to invest in infrastructure and basic industries that constituted the backbone of an industrial economy. Accordingly, the sphere of large private sector units was restricted to a limited list of areas which were specified in Appendix I of the IDR Act 1951. The Second Five Year Plan set the tone of industrialization strategy with its focus on the rapid development of infrastructure and heavy industries. While the public sector had to focus on the development of infrastructure and core industries, the private sector could concentrate on the development of consumer goods industries, for which an elaborate scheme was worked out through a mix of trade and fiscal policies.

The government, however, did not stop at that. Having given the leading role of guiding

India's future industrialization to the public sector, it had also felt concerned about the concentration of economic power. Various studies and committees were instituted to examine the effectiveness of the IDR Act, and it was established that the licensing regime did not result in diffusion of economic power. Following this, several amendments were introduced to the IDR act with a view to tightening licensing control. The Secretariat for Industrial Approvals was set up to scrutinize investment proposals. Most important was the enactment of the Monopolies and Restrictive Trade Practices (MRTP) Act in 1969 with the sole objective of controlling monopolies and large industrial houses, who were denied expansion/ extension of capacity and even additional investment required for modernization.

THE MOST DIFFICULT PERIOD

Nineteen hundred and sixty-nine to 1974 was the most difficult period for India's private sector. Besides the MRTP Act 1969, the Foreign Exchange Regulation Act (FERA) was introduced in 1973. The objective was to ensure the effective and desired allocation of scarce foreign exchange and prevent misuse and draining out. It was also used to curb the growth opportunities of foreign companies, who were asked to dilute their equities to 40 per cent or less. It was following this that some of the erstwhile multinationals chose to wind up their Indian operations. Those who did not, had diluted their equities to 40 per cent or less to become Indian companies.

Beginning 1970, the government had also initiated the nationalization of many private companies, irrespective of the sectors they belonged to. In addition, coal, some heavy engineering industries, banking and insurance and several consumer goods industries such as textiles, bicycles, and so on were nationalized. Following this, the government also sought to restrict the scope of the private sector by making direct investment in the consumer goods industry. Some of the nationalization flowed from government policy and some from the objective of a revival of sick industries.

The Second Five Year Plan as well as the Third led to a huge balance-of-payment crisis. There was a major economic crisis in the 1960s as a result. The political environment also had considerable effect on future economic policies. As populism became the order of the day in politics, central investment policies came to be influenced by this trend, and the public sector was found a convenient tool for propagating a spirit of economic populism.

The political process seriously affected not only economic policies but even the implementation of Plan projects where implementation was delayed. All this had its impact on the performance of the industrial sector since the mid 1960s. It was, therefore, not surprising that there was a long period of industrial stagnation (1965–80). Providential and circumstantial forces were not kind either. There was a major drought in the mid 1960s, and a food crisis subsequent to that. Two wars with Pakistan and then the oil crisis also dealt a severe blow, with a debilitating impact on the fundamentals of the macro economy. There was an acute resource crisis throughout. Tax rates were raised to such high levels that no further increase was possible.

To sum up the situation till 1980, one can say that India had made a good beginning toward industrialization. The conceptual and theoretical backdrops to the various regulatory measures were almost perfect. But down the years, these perspectives were lost. Within less than two decades from the beginning, the industrial economy was bogged in a severe state of stagnation. Instead of reaching the take-off stage, Indian development was restricted to low rates of growth in the national economy and industry. All the ailments of Indian industry that we are concerned about today have their origin in this period, to be precise during 1965–74. These include high cost, high incidence of duties and levies, uncompetitive private and public sectors, delay in project implementation, bureaucratic delays, fragmented industrial structure and so on.

There was yet another significant development that took place during the period on policy with respect to the small-scale sector. The policy of reservation for exclusive production in the small-scale sector was introduced in 1967 when only eight items were reserved, and subsequently the items reserved for the small-scale sector were significantly increased. Again, the stated objectives were laudable. One of these was to encourage the growth of entrepreneurship and motivate people toward self-sufficiency on the entrepreneurial route. Another was to ensure the spread of industrial activities across the states and regions, so that there was a geographical balance in industrialization. Also, it was thought that this would help in the development of ancillarization and sub-contracting, leading to interdependence among large, medium and small-scale sectors on the one hand and between the public and private sectors on the other. But the implementation of the policy was directed in a different way and most often this policy was used to curb the growth of large industrial enterprises. In fact, this was one of the major reasons for the neglect of modernization and technology upgradation in the large-scale private sector, where no capacity expansion and no new investment were allowed on the grounds that the products concerned were reserved for the small-scale sector.

WINDS OF CHANGE

There was a welcome shift in the thought processes of policy-makers during 1974–84. The need for liberalization was felt in 1974, when some minor steps were taken to allow large enterprises to undertake some modernization. In 1977, the first non-Congress government at the centre introduced an Industrial Policy Statement that did talk about further strengthening the role of the public sector but also underlined the need for improving the efficiency of such units. At the same time, it had also recognized the need for giving greater freedom of operation to small-scale enterprises and underlined the need for a larger industrial spread through the development of a nucleus of enterprises at the village level. But this was short-lived. It was also at that time—in the late 1970s—that the thought of liberalizing the trade policy with the objective of facilitating technology upgradation and the creation of export capacity came up for debate.

On coming back to power, the Congress government came out with its own Industrial Policy Statement of 1980. Like the earlier policy statement of 1977, this new statement also re-emphasized the role of the public sector, but for the first time the negative attitude towards large private-sector units was in the process of dilution, following a number of industrial policy notifications giving more freedom to large enterprises.

In view of the severe balance-of-payments crisis of the late 1970s, there was a remarkable shift in the thrust of industrial policy toward the creation of export production facilities. Export production was practically delicensed and several export processing zones were set up to create exclusive enclaves for export production. Alongside this, import policies were subjected to phased liberalization, the key feature of which was a gradual expansion of the list of items under OGL imports and duty-free import facility for export production.

The measures introduced during the period (1974–84) were not significant enough, but went a long way in increasing industrial production and also changing the composition of exports in favour of manufactured items. It did help the industrial economy to come out of the prolonged stagnation it was subjected to. Also, during this period one could see the emergence of certain new industries, adding further depth and dimension to India's diversified manufacturing base. Among others, this period witnessed the emergence of petro-chemical sectors and its downstream industries, the electronics industry, and the automobile industry to some extent.

The beginning of the current industrial and economic policy could be seen with the launching of the Seventh Five Year Plan in 1985 when the prime minister urged the country to look forward to the twenty-first century and underlined the imperative of building a globally competitive industrial economy. The government also encouraged the growth of new technology-intensive industries with a view to bridging the technology gap that was allowed to widen all these years. The period from 1985 to 1988 was extremely significant from the point of view of the liberalization of industrial policy. A series of policy measures were taken to deregulate and decontrol investment and production. The measures were aimed at creating new capacities as well as expanding the existing ones through modernization. Unfortunately, the process of liberalization could not be continued. Political turmoil had engulfed the country while the economy was sliding dangerously into a crisis of unprecedented dimensions. The severe macro-economic difficulties which overtook it by the end of the 1980s culminated in a major crisis in 1991.

At least for the industrial economy, however, this crisis had little to do with liberalization. The need for liberalizing the industrial policy and giving private enterprises a leading role in shaping the economic destiny of the country was felt earlier than the 1991 reform. There was little disagreement on this issue. There was also hardly any disagreement that the public sector was in need of reform and, by the end of the 1980s, there was a general agreement that it could not continue to be given the position of the commanding height, though it need not be dispensed with. The disagreement, if at all, had pertained to the role of foreign capital and the extent to which foreign enterprises should be allowed to participate. Even here, there was an agreement on the need to look afresh at the Foreign Direct Investment (FDI) policy and adopting a more flexible approach. In other words, the following changes took place with respect to our understanding about the future direction of industrialization:

- the public sector could not be the sole engine of growth
- the private sector had to take this responsibility as well
- FDI had a positive role to play in shaping the future of India's industrial economy, and
- Indian industry must be made competitive in the domestic as well as the international markets.

Beginning 1991, the process of liberalization started in 1985 has been hastened. There is hardly any licensing control on investment and production. Foreign investment policy has been liberalized to fit into an internationally comparable framework. The sphere of the public sector has not been expanded, and a disinvestment process has been initiated as a step toward privatization. More pragmatic policies have been introduced with respect to the small-scale sector so as to ensure that investment limits do not come in the way of building linkages and technology upgradation. Trade policy, which is an integral supporting policy for industrialization, has been liberalized with a view to inducting external competition and facilitate competitiveness. The private sector has been invited to play a role in infrastructure development, and policy measures have been introduced to enable Indian industry to operate globally and invest overseas.

A NEW CLIMATE

All this has brought about a new climate of growth and competitiveness in India's industrial economy. Currently, Indian industry is undergoing a major restructuring exercise faced with a competitive environment. But the fact is that Indian industry has a lot of ground to cover. It is, therefore, imperative that the transition phase is adequately managed and guided to ensure that the basic objectives of liberalization, namely globalization and competitiveness of Indian industry, are realized. This calls for careful policy planning, efficient economic administration at all levels of governance and the creation of an enabling environment.

Indian industry will have to respond to the challenges of competition at home and also face greater competition in the global marketplace. Internal reorganization, the induction of professionalism in management practices, the development and utilization of manpower, technology upgradation, the effective management of industrial relations and, overall, a new paradigm of corporate management are some of the hitherto neglected areas that need attention. At the same time, in order to facilitate efficiency at the micro-level of operations, there is a need for broadening as well as deepening economic reform, penetrating all layers of administration. Given this, India can enter a new era of industrialization that will place it firmly as a major industrial power in the twenty-first century world economy.

To conclude, a successful globalization of Indian industry will much depend on how the future industrial policy is directed. The contours of industrial policy have changed. Industrial development, and particularly competitiveness, is no longer a matter of a typical industrial policy that relates to investment, production, distribution and pricing. It has to be viewed in the overall context of macro-economic policy in all its dimensions. An effective macro-economic policy, with in-built flexibility and an adjustment mechanism, has a great bearing on industrial competitiveness. There is, accordingly, a need for a more comprehensive and flexible policy approach.

Economic administration also has an equally important role to play. It has to be responsive, flexible and forward-looking. This underlines the need for reforms at various levels of the administration. Another imperative is building efficient infrastructure, and this is an area where the role of government is still considered very important while the private sector provides supplementary initiatives. Infrastructure must be supportive not only of production but also consumption. Last but not the least, there is an urgent need to improve the law-and-order situation in the country. A law and order situation conducive to efficiency and competitiveness is too obvious to need any elaboration.

India has now emerged, after fifty years, as a nation with the potential to be a major economic power of the world, thanks to its human and natural resources. Indian industry is already at a globally competitive standard in a number of sectors, such as textiles, software, gems and jewellery, and automotive components. It is therefore transiting from a highly sheltered, protected environment to a globally competitive industrial scenario, based on interdependence and uncertainty. Inspite of the many difficulties experienced in the last fifty years, India's industrialization process has the capability to now stand on a near-equal footing in the global village. The twenty-first century will witness many changes and restructuring but industry in India will continue to play a major part in the development process.

Originally published as Tarun Das, 'Industry: From Regulation to Liberalization', in Hiranmay Karlekar (ed.), *Independent India: The First Fifty Years* (Delhi, Oxford University Press, 1998), pp. 169–75.

36

Post-Liberalization Business Successes

Dwijendra Tripathi and Jyoti Jumani

The private sector has responded to the measures outlined in the previous selection with enthusiasm. Tremendous energies have been unleashed. These are recounted here by Dwijendra Tripathi who notes that not only have new industries emerged but older sectors too have demonstrated increased productivity and competitiveness. He highlights developments in four types of industries: information technology and allied industries (with the phenomenal rise in older initiatives such as Tata Consultancy Services as well as newer companies such as Infosys and Wipro); those previously held back from expansion because of supply constraints such as automobiles and telecommunications; those that could not fulfil their potential due to public sector priority such as civil aviation and electronic media; and finally those which had large domestic demand but were curtailed because of inadequate technology and infrastructure such as health care. Tripathi also examines the impact of liberalization on trade, acquisitions and mergers, and the financial sectors, all of which have responded positively to the new environment. Finally, the author comments on new entrepreneurs from the 'knowledge-based category' and women entrepreneurs who have recently come to the fore. He makes a convincing case that a new outward-looking, optimistic worldview has emerged in business.

...The Rao government introduced some other reforms during its tenure. The most important among these were allowing private participation in power generation, giving a statutory status to Securities and Exchange Board of India (SEBI), determining the price of new issues based on market forces, and permitting private sector participation in the road sector. These changes, with the exception of the last mentioned, were introduced during the first two years of the Rao regime. By 1994 the pace of reform unfortunately slowed down under pressure from vested political interests. This prevented Manmohan Singh from attending to some other items on his agenda that included full convertibility of the rupee, overhaul of tax structure, and reining in the subsidy regime. He had, nevertheless, set in motion a process that proved irreversible.

Rao's government failed to win another mandate in the parliamentary elections of May 1996, largely because of its mishandling of the Hindu-Muslim imbroglio centred around the Babri Mosque—Ram Janmabhumi temple at Ayodhya in Uttar Pradesh and other failings on the political front. But even the governments that followed at the centre (there were three between 1996 and the general elections of 2004) continued with the tempo of change, despite having different political persuasions. The appointment of a Disinvestment Commission in August 1996 to decide the public sector enterprises to be privatized, massive cuts in income tax and tariff rates in 1998, the disinvestment or strategic sale of government holdings to the tune of Rs 44,882 crore in government-owned companies by March 2004, and opening up of the insurance business to private enterprise in 2000, amply bear this out. Admittedly, the post-Rao governments could not provide the same kind of dynamism to the agenda for reform largely because of their own internal contradictions. But none tried to put the clock back. The Rao—Singh initiative thus not only achieved a much-needed breakthrough in what had become a static economic scenario, but also helped evolve a national consensus in favour of change. The left parties were the only political formation that still continued to voice reservation, although many people believed that the approach of their own government in West Bengal to matters relating to economy and business was closer to the reform agenda than to the official party line.

The abolition of stifling restrictions and introduction of salutary changes in what may be termed as 'confiscatory' taxation policies unleashed the creative energies of the Indian private sector that had been kept under tight control during the licence-permit raj. All impediments to expansion, experimentation, and even innovation suddenly vanished as if by the waving of a magical wand. Business confidence, never too high during the licence-permit raj, became all pervasive. The will to partake of the emerging opportunities, not only in the country but also in other parts of the world, received a great spurt. Global competition became the buzz word in the Indian business circles. Old established business houses entered new lines of business that had earlier been out of bounds for them and a host of new entrepreneurs came to the fore to mount undertakings in areas they would not have earlier thought of. Banks and financial institutions came out with generous schemes to support business initiatives, and venture capitalists, almost an unknown tribe in the age of restrictions, emerged on the scene with vigour. Foreign investment, looked upon with suspicion if not downright hostility under the old regime, was now eagerly sought after, and for the multinational enterprises India with its 300 million strong middle class emerged as too attractive a market to be ignored. A small but influential group of industrialists, the so called Bombay Club led by Ratan Tata, would have liked the government to create what they called a 'level playing field', a euphemism for differential treatment to Indian-controlled enterprises vis-à-vis the Indian operations of multinationals. But few followed their lead. The consumer, who had earlier been at the shortest end of the priorities of the producer, was the greatest beneficiary of these developments. For as the competition for providing goods and services increased, he became a force to reckon with in the total scheme of things.

Admittedly, these steps taken to dismantle the licence-permit raj severally or individually did not amount to a revolution—much more needs to be done to deserve that description—but no other word can signify the change more appropriately. It is neither possible nor even necessary for the purpose of this volume to recount and analyse the impact of this 'mini revolution' on the Indian private sector. The developments at any rate are still too close to our own times to admit of a proper historical assessment. The best we can do is to point to the major business trends that have come to the surface in the wake of liberalization.

IMPACT ON PRIVATE ENTERPRISE—INDUSTRY AND TRADE

The most visible effect has been on the general industrial scene. New industries not existing before liberalization have come to the fore and existing industries have become more productive and competitive. These can be classified, though at the cost of some arbitrariness and overlapping, in the following four categories.

The first category includes industries now producing goods and services that had virtually no domestic demand earlier. Of these, information technology and allied industries have demonstrated the most spectacular rise. The birth of this industry can be traced back to as early as 1968 when Tata Consultancy Services (TCS) was set up at the initiative of J.R.D. Tata. The first software company in the country, it somehow kept its head above water until Rajiv Gandhi's technology-friendly team opened up new opportunities for enterprises like TCS. Demand for the services offered by the company, both in India and abroad, multiplied by leaps and bounds as liberalization gained momentum, and TCS's turnover touched almost the Rs 5000 crore mark by 2002. There has been no turning back since.

Most of the software companies formed during the 1970s and 1980s experienced similar spectacular growth. Infosys Technologies, Bangalore, offers the best illustration. Led by N.R. Narayana Murthy, its founders had neither the money to mount a business enterprise nor the experience to run it. Belonging to a south Indian Brahman family and the son of a schoolteacher, the leader of the group, an electrical engineer by training, had started his career as a systems analyst at the Indian Institute of Management, Ahmedabad (IIM-A)—a pretty low position in the Institute's academic hierarchy. His co-promoters, all young software professionals, also came from families with modest resources. To launch their company, they borrowed small amounts from various sources, including their wives. Their real struggle, however, started after the company was launched in 1982 when the licence-permit raj still held sway. Financial limitations apart, it was not easy to import necessary equipment because of a high tariff wall and many other constraints. Things began to improve only with the opening of the economy. The ever-growing demand for software services in the developed world catapulted Infosys to frontline position in the Indian business world. With its shares being traded at prices several times their face value, the market value of the company that had started with barely Rs 5000 touched dizzy heights by the turn of the century. In March 1999, Infosys Technologies became the first Indian company to be listed on an American stock exchange.

The rising fortunes of the IT industry attracted many others already engaged in some other lines. One of these was Azim Hasham Premji. His Wipro Corporation, like

TCS, was a small concern when its present head assumed its leadership in 1966 after the death of his father M.H. Hasham Premji. At that time the family was in the business of processing vegetable oil. This appeared to be too restricted a field to young Azim who diversified first into medical systems and later computer hardware when IBM closed its Indian operations in 1977. What, however, gave a real boost to his business was his entry into software development in the early 1990s. Providing software services to several top companies in the world, some of which were in the Fortune 500 list, Wipro became a household name by the turn of the century with its net worth amounting to several billion rupees, and Azim Premji the richest Indian, according to Forbes rating. Like Wipro, technocrat Shiv Nadar's Hindustan Computers Ltd. (HCL), struggling with computer hardware manufacturing since its inception in the mid-1970s, developed into a respectable enterprise only after a liberalized economy provided it the necessary space to diversify into software services. These success stories encouraged others to launch IT-related enterprises. One of these was B. Ramalinga Raju who moved away from the family business of cotton spinning and construction to set up Satyam Computers in 1992 and propel it on to the global stage through a high-capacity satellite link.

These examples are illustrative of how liberalization transformed the atmosphere for software companies. This is eloquently reflected in the turnover of the Indian software industry that jumped from a mere Rs 430 crore in 1991 to Rs 28,350 crore by 2001. The progress of the software industry has resulted in the rise of another industry, Business Process Outsourcing (BPO), in the last few years. In fact, little was heard of it in India until 1999. BPO is basically a cost-cutting device involving transfer of mundane white-collar jobs—such as preparing routine reports, processing voluminous financial data, and compiling statutory reports for governments—by large companies to specialized firms, thus obviating the need for maintaining in-house staff for the purpose. India's BPO industry started with large foreign companies opening their own captive organizations in the country for this purpose. This inspired the rise of call centres owned and managed by Indians which could offer the required services at much cheaper rates because of the lower labour cost. The ability to handle the English language along with computer technology has given a great deal of competitive advantage to India vis-à-vis many other countries with lower labour costs. The result has been the mushrooming of BPO centres in India. So successful have the Indian call centres been that the developed West has started feeling the pinch of the outflow of jobs that in ordinary course of things would have been handled by their own nationals. As for India, IT or IT-related industries have been the fastest growing sector with almost 90 per cent of the sales coming from abroad.

The second category consists of industries that had large domestic demand for their product but could not develop before liberalization because of supply-side constraints. The automobile industry is the best example. Well until the beginning of the 1990s the Indian consumer had to put up with a long waiting period for acquiring a car and commercial vehicles and had to remain content with shoddy products (with the exception of Maruti), for nothing better was available. With the facility for making foreign direct investment (FDI) available to them after liberalization, multinational automobile manufacturers entered the Indian market in a big way. Almost all the major international auto firms have set up their manufacturing facilities in India. These companies have brought with them the manufacturing and technical skills as also the management systems required for making quality products. The result is that Maruti 800, which was seen as the ultimate status symbol for an average middle class Indian well up to the end of the 1980s, has now been reduced to the position of a basic model!

Significantly, foreign models or models based on borrowed technology are not the only quality vehicles available in India. For Indica, designed and produced by Tata Motors (TELCO renamed), is successfully competing with the products of multinational companies both in India and abroad. Just a few years ago it would have been inconceivable for an Indian company to produce a passenger car based on designs and technical know-how developed indigenously. The entry of the multinationals and the rise of the Indian automobile industry have also given fillip to the auto components industry. For, the automobile industry could not have developed without the development of a supplier industry. Spurred by companies like Bharat Forge and Sundaram Clayton, the Indian auto ancillary industry has by now become globally competitive at least for low-value components.

Apart from the auto industry, the opening of the Indian market has attracted multinationals to some other sectors as well. Their Indian operations, carried on alone or jointly with Indian companies, are now producing a variety of goods for which Indians earlier visiting the developed countries would flock to the stores: Kelloggs cereals, McDonald's fast food, Arrow shirts, Levis jeans, Gillette toiletries, Rexona deodorants, beauty care products, wines, spirits, and a host of other articles. These are now available, made or processed in India itself, under licence from the parent company. It is difficult to think of any prominent multinational—whether American, European, British, Japanese, or Korean—that has not yet entered the Indian manufacturing industry either through setting up its own independent operation or through collaboration and franchise arrangements. Multinationals have also entered the service industry in a big way, alone wherever possible and jointly with Indian firms wherever necessary. A good example is the insurance sector. Even though the FDI participation in this line cannot exceed 26 per cent, a number of foreign concerns have joined hands with well-known Indian business groups to promote at least twelve insurance companies in the last few years. These young concerns have not only broken the monopoly of the government-controlled Life Insurance Corporation of India, but also brought about a much-needed modernization of this sector to the immense relief of harried consumers.

How attractive a market India has become for the foreign investors is clear from the fact that whereas the total FDI investment in India in 1991 stood at merely US \$ 234 million, the average yearly investment between 1998 and 2003 has been around US \$ 2.5 billion. Foreign institutional investors (FII) have played a critical role in this development. Their principal route to participation in the Indian business has been through buying equity shares in the Indian companies. The cumulative FII investment since the equity market was opened up in 1992 until the end of 2003 was US \$ 21 billion. The rate of growth can be measured by the fact that within a single year from 2002, FII investment increased by almost ten times—from US \$ 739 million to US \$ 7.59 billion. There are at present over 620 FIIs registered in India for participating in the equity market. Dwelling upon the value of the Indian market for foreign investors, an American TV commentator recently observed: 'For American CEOs [Chief Executive Officers] trying to grow their companies, the issue is whether they embrace globalization. If they do, they must have a presence in India.'

Significantly, the emerging climate for business in India has also inspired some Indians who have made a name for themselves in business abroad, to seek investment opportunities in their home country. These include the Hinduja Brothers occupying a prominent place in the British business and Lakshmi N. Mittal, the largest steel producer in the world, also based in the UK. Before liberalization they had limited presence in India, and showed little inclination to expand it.

The vigour of the multinational invasion and growing FDI have caused some alarm among assorted groups of politicians, intellectuals, and economists. But the Indian middle class, fed up with shoddy, unattractive, and inefficient products and services offered by the Indian firms for more than four decades after Independence, is happy with these developments, unmindful of the political and economic costs to the nation—real or imaginary. For the entry of the foreign firms and the resultant competition have led to the much-needed improvement in the products and services of indigenous firms as well.

Apart from the auto industry and others discussed in the foregoing pages, telecommunications is another example of industries in the second category. Despite its large population, India still had a small telephone network until as late as 1990. The government-controlled Posts and Telegraph Department could not meet the enormous demand for phone connections in urban centres simply because the state-owned Indian Telephone Industries (ITI) could not produce instruments in sufficient number. A long waiting list was the inevitable consequence. With the opening of the telecommunications sector for private participation, a number of manufacturers, including established business groups such as the Tatas, Godrej, and BPL, took to producing telephones. Short supply of instruments thus became a thing of the past. By the end of the 1990s, in most Indian cities one could get telephone connections almost for the asking. In more recent years, the telephone network has expanded to the villages as well. No pre-liberalization observer could have foreseen this development.

The telecommunications revolution is also reflected in the spectacular growth of cellular phone services. No sooner was the telecom sector open for public participation, than a number of established business houses branched out into mobile phone services. The beginning was made by the Aditya Birla group; others such as Reliance, Tatas, and Essar followed soon. Collaboration with foreign operators in the field greatly aided this development. The foreign companies were prevented from establishing telecom services on their own because the government did not permit more than 49 per cent foreign investment in this sector.

While the big houses were competing for their share of the cake, a young Punjabi was slowly but surely emerging on the centre stage of Indian business through this line of business. This was Sunil Bharti Mittal. A graduate of the Harvard Business School, this Ludhiana-based entrepreneur was still confined to small businesses such as producing bicycle parts and telephone equipment until 1993 when the telecom sector was opened for private participation. Making a cautious beginning with a cellular service for Delhi under the brand name of Airtel, the first in the nation's capital city, he soon consolidated his position in this field by expanding his operations to Himachal Pradesh, Madhya Pradesh, Andhra Pradesh, Karnataka, Tamil Nadu, and Gujarat. In the process his company, Bharti Enterprises, acquired J.T. Mobiles in Andhra Pradesh and Sky Cell in Chennai to emerge as the largest cellular operator in the country by the end of the century. Within a brief span of five years after entering the telecom line, Bharti Enterprises increased its turnover from Rs 30 crore to Rs 500 crore—almost seventeen times—and it is still steadily increasing. As a result of enormous expansion of the cellular phone services, a facility that was limited to the rich alone until just a few years back has become a common convenience at grassroots level.

Industries that could not realize their full potential before liberalization owing to the stranglehold of the public sector constitute our third category. Civil aviation is a case in point. With monopolistic control on air transport in the country the state-owned Indian Airlines had become an apology of a flying organization by the end of the 1980s because of callous inefficiency and mismanagement. The announcement of the open air policy in 1990 followed by the repeal of the Air Transport Act (that had reserved air transport for the public sector) in 1994 opened up a new business opportunity for private enterprise. Beginning with 1993, a host of private carriers, most of them promoted by well-established business houses, sprang up within no time. All of them except two exited the scene as fast as they had emerged because of mismanagement and conflict among the promoters. The exceptions were Jet Airways and Sahara Airlines. The promoters in both cases were upstart businessmen and both started their operations in 1993. Jet Airways was founded by a group of non-resident Indians led by Naresh Goyal with 40 per cent participation of two West Asian airlines, while Sahara was an initiative of the Sahara group of companies headed by Subroto Roy about whom little had been heard before 1990.

We still know precious little about Roy's family background and the strategies that helped him carve out a distinct niche for himself in the Indian business world within a very short time. Air transport occupies a rather modest part of his total operation that includes IT-related businesses such as e-commerce, e-learning, and video conferencing, and life insurance, housing finance, urban housing, media, and entertainment. He launched his business, shortly before the onset of liberalization, with parabanking—collecting small deposits, sometimes as small as Re 1 a day or Rs 5 a month, and offering unusually high rates of interest on them—which still remains an important lifeline of his operations. Rising from a small town in the backward eastern Uttar Pradesh to become one of the most powerful business figures in north India, Subroto Roy is an entirely post-liberalization phenomenon.

Jet and Sahara, both went from strength to strength during the 1990s—Jet much more so than Sahara—and both are now flying on international routes. In the meantime more private airlines have come on the scene, offering a variety of fare structures and, in the process, expanding the base of the air travelling class. The quality of services offered by the private airlines has forced Indian Airlines to wake up to its responsibilities to its passengers. The efficiency now visible in the operations of the state-owned company is wholly due to the competition offered by the private airlines. And now with their flexible fare structure, these new airlines are likely to put pressure on Indian Railways also to improve its services.

Electronic media is another example of the industries that have made great strides in recent years because of the receding shadow of the public sector. During the pre-liberalization days, television mogul Rupert Murdoch's Star TV, beaming special programmes for Indian viewers from Hong Kong, was the only private channel to break the monotony of the government-controlled Doordarshan's offerings. A quiet entrepreneurial initiative of an unknown Indian gave to the country its first satellite channel. Coming from a family of small traders and with modest education, Subhash Chandra had shown some feeble signs of entrepreneurial ability and also made some money through a couple of innovative but small ventures when the electronic media was thrown open for private participation. Joining hands with Star TV, he first launched Zee TV, a Hindi news and entertainment channel, to gauge the market. As the channel became immensely popular with the Hindi-speaking viewers, both in India and abroad, he bought out Star TV's holdings in the enterprise to bring Zee TV under his sole control and launched several subsidiary channels, each specializing in specific kind of programmes. His example was emulated later by many others including Prannoy Roy, the promoter of New Delhi Television, but the fact that Subhash Chandra was the first to enter the line, challenging the might of Murdoch, makes his case somewhat special.

Our fourth category consists of industries that had large, though latent, domestic demand for their products and services but remained grossly underdeveloped during the age of control because of difficulties in assembling requisite technology, equipment, and infrastructure. Health care is perhaps the best example; it remained in a pitiable state all through the licence-permit raj because state and urban governments and a few charitable institutions, apart from private practitioners, were the only providers of these services. Barring a few distinguished exceptions, the Indian corporate system remained aloof from the field. When Dr Prathap Reddy pioneered the idea of corporate hospitals with the launching of the Apollo Group of Hospitals in 1983, few in the Indian business world followed his lead. The result was that secondary and tertiary health-care facilities, by and large unavailable in the country, were out of reach for ordinary citizens. Post-liberalization, a number of hospitals with state-of-the-art facilities have come up at the initiative and under the management of private enterprise. These have proved to be a boon to Indians in the middle income groups. Patients from the United Kingdom and some other developed countries are also trickling in to these facilities because the cost these patients have to incur for treatment in India is a fraction of what they would pay for similar services at home. If this trend continues, the kind of medical infrastructure that is developing in the country may give a great boost to what is generally called health tourism.

Liberalization has impacted not only industries but also the trade sector. The most visible impact is on retailing which never realized its full potential in the past. As big companies never showed any interest in this branch—shops owned by some companies to sell their own products is not what is meant by retailing here—it remained synonymous with small operators until very recently. A fast-developing educated middle class in urban India coupled with growing contact with the West and a modern lifestyle has changed this and a number of new enterprises operating a chain of retail stores and supermarkets have come up in recent years. Kishore Biyani showed the way by launching Pantaloon Retail (India) in 1992; a host of others followed such as Lifestyle, Shoppers' Stop, and Piramyd. Some of the established houses, including the Tatas, have also moved into retailing in a big way. Because of their initiative, big shopping malls and departmental stores on western lines have now started dotting the streets of major urban centers in the country. The success of these early ventures has attracted many more large players to the field such as Reliance, Wipro, Hero, K.K. Modi, and Godrej who are planning to set up stores or shopping malls in various cities. No one would have imagined just a few years ago that retailing, always a poor relation in Indian business, would emerge as such a promising area of investment for corporate India. A number of global retailing giants like Wal-mart, Tesco, and Correfour are ready to expand into the vast Indian market the moment the government clears FDI in this sector.

All this is indicative of growing dynamism in Indian business. This is also reflected in another area, acquisition and merger (A&M) activity, which is usually considered to be a necessary concomitant of a dynamic business environment. The statistics are revealing. Whereas the five years antedating 1991 witnessed a total of only 160 attempts of A&M, of which 120 were successful, the figure for just 1999–2000 was 205. The industry areas that account for the largest number of cases include telecommunications, chemicals, and the financial sector. The most celebrated examples of acquisitions, though not of merger, have been the taking over of Videsh Sanchar Nigam Limited (VSNL) by the Tatas, and of Indian Petrochemical Corporation Limited (IPCL), Baroda, by the Reliance group. The Tatas acquired VSNL, a public sector company providing transnational telephony that was divested in 1996. The IPCL too was a public sector company that came into the Reliance fold in 2002 through the process of disinvestment.

While the Tatas' acquisition consolidated their position in the telecommunications sector, the taking over of IPCL by Reliance seems to have been in continuation of a plan on the part of the group to diversify into petroleum and allied sectors. For, soon after the liberalization process was under way, the group had started developing a petrochemicals complex at Hazira near Surat and an oil refinery at Jamnagar. It later moved into some other areas such as electric power generation and supply, industrial finance, and oil and natural gas exploration. The aggressiveness with which the Reliance group pursued its goal of expansion through acquisition and diversification is reflected in the fact that by the end of the century it beat the Tatas to the number one position in Indian business—fulfilling a cherished dream of its founder, Dhirubhai Ambani.

Some other important acquisitions in recent years pertain to areas other than those listed above. These include Hindustan Lever's acquisition of Tata Oil Mills and Brooke Bond Tea Company, Aditya Birla's group taking over Larsen & Toubro's cement operation, the acquisition of Ahmedabad Electricity Company by Torrent—primarily a pharmaceutical company—brewery firm Shaw Wallace exiting from Manu Chhabria's fold into Vijay Mallya's United Breweries, and the B.M. Khaitan group acquiring Williamson Tea Assam Ltd from the Magor family of Britain. While Mallya has now emerged as the second largest producer of alcoholic drinks in the world, the Williamson acquisition has made Khaitan's McLeod Russel India Ltd (MRIL) the world's largest integrated tea company. Ajay Piramal built up a whole new line of business through acquisitions and mergers. He had, after completing his education, joined the textile mill that the

Piramal family controlled. He, however, branched out into the pharmaceutical industry in 1988 by acquiring an old company. This marked the beginning of a series of acquisitions and mergers that made his enterprise, Nicholas Piramal, the fourth largest pharmaceutical company in the country by the turn of the century.

All said and done, however, there have been more acquisitions than mergers, and most of the acquisitions have resulted from mutually agreed arrangements. Hostile takeovers have been few and far between. This is partly due to legal safeguards created by the Government of India which has always disfavoured hostile takeover. As for the mergers, most of these have been intra-group in nature effected with a view to restructuring the existing businesses for better performance. The recent merger of three companies belonging to the Aditya Birla group into a single enterprise, Aditya Birla Nuvo, is a case in point. On the basis of the available examples it is hard to indicate the direction in which Indian business will move in this respect, but in all likelihood consolidation through merger will gain momentum. It may be recalled in this context that in the post-Civil War America, merger and acquisition went hand-in-hand with an unusually accelerated pace of development of business that put that country on the road to becoming the most industrialized society in the world. The recent European experience suggests the same thing.

THE FINANCIAL SECTOR

Like the industrial sector, commercial banking too has undergone significant changes. Before liberalization, public financial institutions, created soon after Independence to support large industrial projects, and nationalized banks dominated the banking sector in the country with a sprinkling of a small number of branches of a few foreign banks. The public sector banks and financial institutions may have been well-equipped to meet the demands of banking services in the age of economic restrictions, but they were hardly capable of coping up with the needs of the more dynamic times that liberalization brought in. The emergence of new banks with a modern outlook in consonance with the temper of the times was a natural consequence. As it was far easier now for private parties to float new banking firms, as many as eight institutions in this genre emerged within barely eight years of Reserve Bank of India (RBI) issuing new guidelines for setting up new private sector banks in 1993. Of these HDFC Bank, in the setting up of which the Housing Development Finance Corporation played a critical role, and ICICI Bank, an offshoot of Industrial Credit and Investment Corporation of India (which would later merge with the Bank) were the most important. Emulating these examples, Industrial Development Bank of India (IDBI), another financial institution set up in the early years of the republic, also floated a commercial bank of its own. Fresh opportunities in the field also attracted private players of which Kotak Mahindra Bank, promoted recently by Uday Kotak of an old trading family in association with Mahindra & Mahindra, is a good example. That the new private banks accounted for 6 per cent of the total assets and 10 per cent of the total profits of the banking industry by the turn of the century (2001) tells us something about the position they have carved out for themselves.

The new private banks, when they appeared on the Indian business horizon, were very different from their public sector counterparts in terms of the range of services offered and customer care. Their most distinguishing feature, however, has been the use of computer technology to cut transaction costs and the introduction of modern-day services such as the automated teller machine (ATM) and credit card. The origin of such services can be traced to a pilot project known as 'Suvidh' launched by the Indian subsidiary of the multinational Citibank at Bangalore under which customers were encouraged to conduct transactions by telephone, over the net, or through ATM. How far Citibank's experiment inspired the new private banks to introduce these devices is difficult to ascertain. But the fact is that they, particularly HDFC Bank and ICICI Bank, have managed to leverage technology to centralize the backends, reduce the number of employees, cut transaction costs, and add to their services. Such has been the impact of the new banks on the Indian business scene that even the nationalized banks have been forced or inspired to emulate their younger counterparts to leverage technology to modernize their operations. Significantly, banks now provide not only working capital loans to industry but also 'consumer loans', which they seldom did before liberalization. Consequently, the housing industry and consumer-durables industry have gained because the consumer can get loans at low cost.

All this indicates that the Indian banking sector has entered a more competitive phase than at any time before in its history, making it almost imperative for the weaklings to merge with more solvent entities. Significantly, the banking industry has witnessed eleven cases of mergers since 1993, when RBI made it obligatory for Indian commercial banks, both in public and private sectors, to have a minimum of Rs 100 crore as the capital base. These developments suggest that the Indian banking sector is going to gather enough strength to become a more effective engine of business growth than has been the case so far.

The venture capitalist is another engine of business growth that has emerged after liberalization. Venture capitalists usually provide the start-up capital through equity participation to operationalize a promising business idea but have neither the inclination nor perhaps the ability to run the venture. They proactively scout for competent individuals, preferably with some evidence of proven ability and experience in the field, to launch and run the company as a joint enterprise. This route to entrepreneurial initiative, very much established in the West, did not exist in India at all until the mid-1990s. The beginning in this respect was made by the entry of some of the world's leading venture capital players such as Warburg Pincus and the Carlyle group. But not more than Rs 90 crore of venture capital had been invested in India until as late as 1997. By the end of the century, however, the figure had jumped to Rs 4800 crore with more than fifty venture capital firms operating in the field. Most of them are American and European. But a few Indian institutions of this kind have also emerged as a sort of multiplier effect. The most important of them all is ICICI Venture Funds Management Company, which has emerged as the second largest venture capital firm in the country, Warburg Pincus being the first.

The areas in which the venture capitalists have been active so far are IT or IT-related businesses, but other fields may also attract them in the future. For venture capital investments have been consistently rising and India is likely to absorb close to Rs 50,000 crore before long, according to an authoritative estimate. The figure is still a drop in the ocean but it is a potent pointer to the shape of things to come.

These developments in the Indian financial sector, though important, are almost dwarfed into insignificance in comparison with what has happened to the stock markets. Some crude statistics will bear this out. While the number of companies listed on the Bombay Stock Exchange (BSE), then the most important capital market in the country, in March 1992 was just 2601, it had jumped to 5937 by December 2000 despite the establishment of the National Stock Exchange (NSE) in 1992 to which some of the companies, that would have otherwise turned to the BSE, were diverted. In 1991–2, the highest level to which the sensitivity index (sensex) of stock values reached was 4285; by the end of 2005 it had crossed the 9000 mark. And the end of the upward spiral was nowhere in sight. Another indicator is that whereas the sensex showed merely 2 per cent average appreciation between Independence and the mid-1980s, the average annual increase between March 1992 and November 2005 has been more than 14.5 per cent. Although the Indian stock markets had started gaining momentum since the mid-1970s, thanks largely to Dhirubhai Ambani's successful experiment of using this medium to raise finance for his ventures, it was only after the relaxation of controls that they began to be seen as an important source of business finance.

The process began in May 1992 with the abolition of the Capital Issue Control Act of 1947. A few months later, foreign institutional investors (FIIs) were permitted to invest in the Indian securities market. The birth of the NSE in November 1992 was a milestone in strengthening the institutional base. The significance of this development is clear from the fact that within less than three years after its birth the NSE overtook the BSE as the largest stock exchange in terms of the volume of trading.

The revitalization of the stock market has not been an unmixed evil. Persons like Harshad Mehta who manipulated the system to cause a major scam in May 1992, and Ketan Parekh who was responsible for repeating Mehta's mischief in March 2001, are cases in point. Despite the statutory powers granted to Securities and Exchange Board of India (SEBI) as early as January 1992 to regulate the stock markets, the agency has not been very effective in its mission, and unscrupulous individuals still somehow find ways to beat the system. This drawback notwithstanding, the rise of stock markets as a major source of business finance must be considered a significant development in liberalized India.

ENTREPRENEURS AND ENTREPRENEURSHIP

The new climate for enterprise, emerging in the wake of liberalization has shown, to quote Shitin Desai the managing director of DSP Merrill Lynch, an American venture capital firm operating in India, that 'there are huge local and global opportunities in India'. It is natural under these conditions for new enterprise creators to emerge. The exploits of some of these have already been referred to in the section on industry and trade in this chapter. A few more names may be added to the list. Significantly, a large majority of the businesses launched by new entrepreneurs belong to the knowledge-based category, and most of them have taken the venture capital route.

One of the most successful of such businesses has been Dr Anji Reddy's, Dr Reddy's Laboratories, a health care and pharmaceutical company at Hyderabad. With a degree in Medical Chemistry from a prestigious American University, he started his career with Indian Drugs and Pharmaceutical Corporation (IDPL), a public sector enterprise, but later set up his own company to produce drugs based on his own formulations. The products of his company found a market in the United States too where he had to face a court case on the charge of patent violation which he won. With his confidence boosted, he turned global and set up a production base in China's special trading zone near Shanghai, his being the first Indian enterprise to do so. Although Anji Reddy had launched his venture a few years before the onset of liberalization, the real consolidation of his operations occurred only during the 1990s when his Laboratories transformed from a small bulk drug manufacturer into a fully integrated drug research company. By listing his firm on New York Stock Exchange in 2001, he has also measured up to global benchmarks of performance and evaluation. Like Dr Reddy's Laboratories, Habil Khorakiwala's biotechnology and pharmaceutical company Wockhardt, though formed as early as the 1960s, came to life only after liberalization. Almost unheard of before 1990, it now boasts of an annual turnover of more than Rs 1280 crore.

Ashok Soota is another example of a salaried man turned entrepreneur, thanks to the new business climate. Working as vice president in the IT giant Wipro, he decided to become his own employer, and to that end set up Mindtree Consulting in Bangalore in association with a colleague, Subroto Bagchi, and with the help of a venture capital firm that provided the startup capital. Srini Rajan, the country head of Texas Instruments, and Suresh Rajpal, the CEO of a joint venture promoted by Hindustan Computer Ltd (HCL) and Hewlett-Packard (HP), did likewise, setting up their IT firms—Ittiam Systems and Trigyu Technologies respectively. Both are now respected names in their fields of operation. Many more examples of this kind can be cited.

While knowledge-based enterprises have been the most distinguishing feature of the post-liberalization entrepreneurship, traditional businesses too have thrown up new entrepreneurs with visible impact on the national scene. Ahmedabad-based Gautam Adani is perhaps the best example. Born in a trading family of modest means, he started his business career as an importer of plastics, but later switched over to exports in 1989 when the Government of India announced a policy of granting 100 per cent tax exemption for export items. Thus was born Adani Exports Limited (AEL). The progress was swift, and by 2004 the company was trading in almost sixty commodities spread over fifty countries with a turnover of US $ 1.6 billion. The Adanis in the meantime also diversified into vegetable oils, natural gas distribution, retailing, and the BPO business. But what has given the group a distinctive identity is their involvement in port development following the Gujarat government's decision, announced in 1995, to invite private sector participation for updating facilities at the port sites on the Gujarat coast. Responding to this policy the Adanis joined the state government to launch Gujarat Adani Port Limited (GAPL) in 1998 for the development of Mundra port. The infrastructure that has been developed at this port by the company is rated amongst the best in the country. It is a measure of the Adanis' entrepreneurial quality that within the short period of a decade and a half their group has acquired a national status and developed into a Rs 11,000 crore empire.

The post-liberalization period has also witnessed an upsurge of entrepreneurship among women. Although a few women did play critical managerial roles in family-owned enterprises—such as Sumati Morarjee and Anu Agha who assumed leadership of their family concerns, Scindia Steam Navigation Company and Thermax Limited respectively, after the death of their husbands—and some small-scale undertakings came up at the initiative of women, few women, except perhaps Kiran Mazumdar with her Biocon, were visible on the contours of Indian business before the liberalization process set in. Things began to change as the business climate improved. As per the reports of Federation of Indian Chambers of Commerce and Industry's (FICCI's) ladies organization, there was a 100 per cent growth in its ranks between 1996 and 2001. Federation of Women Entrepreneurs has estimated the increase in the number of women entrepreneurs in the country during this period to be in the order of 35 per cent. Although their entrepreneurial exploits in all cases may not be directly attributable to the opportunities created by liberalization, the new environment has had something to do with the inspiration behind their initiatives. Some of the noteworthy names among the women who have emerged on the business scene in the post-liberalization era are Ishita Swarup and Tina Sapra who set up a flourishing call centre in Delhi; Revathi Kasturi who launched Tarang Software in 2000 jointly with her brother at Bangalore; Shahnaz Hussain whose herbal empire is now estimated to be worth Rs 300 crore; Suhag Khemlani who has chosen sky-scraper cleaning for her business; and Ekta Kapoor, whose Balaji Telefilms is well regarded for its quality entertainment.

The achievements of none of these, however, come anywhere close to Kiran Mazumdar's. Though her Biocon's pre-liberalization record was by no means unimpressive, the company achieved its full potential only in the post-liberalization period. Well until the beginning of the 1990s, it was still a single product company. With the launching of a number of subsidiaries in 1993 and 1994, Biocon India developed into an integrated business group, producing a variety of biopharmaceutical products. Noted for the excellence of its products, the company was awarded the coveted ISO 9001 certification from RWTUC, Germany, in 1993, much before any other enterprise in the world claimed this recognition. Progress during the 1990s was so fast that by the end of the century Biocon's annual sales touched Rs 100 crore, enabling Mazumdar to buy off her Irish partner. If Mazumdar was simply a successful woman entrepreneur up to the end of the 1980s, she won a place for herself among the nation's corporate leaders by the end of the 1990s, presiding over India's largest biotech company.

Like Mazumdar, the post-liberalization resurgence in Indian business has pushed a number of entrepreneurs and family groups, that were still struggling for recognition, into the mainstream of corporate India. According to a recent report in the *Economic Times*, at least eight such groups, all of which trace their origin to the mid-1980s, have registered 100 per cent growth in the last five years to storm into the Rs 1000 crore-plus turnover club. These include the JP group of Jaiprakash Gaur which boasts of a market value of about Rs. 6700 crore—50 per cent higher than the combined market value of Nusli Wadia's Bombay Dyeing and Britannia—and Rajesh Exports of Rajesh Mehta whose revenue is equal to that of the entire Godrej group.

A NEW WORLDVIEW

More important than all that has been said above is the fact that there has been a radical change in the worldview of Indian business since the liberalization process went under way. A basically inward-looking attitude—the result of a long period of colonial subjugation supplemented by severe curbs on the freedom of enterprise continuing for almost forty years after Independence—has yielded place to an outward-looking attitude characterized by confidence and optimism. There is no denying the fact that Aditya Birla and a few other corporate leaders did, in the past, attempt to transcend the physical boundaries of the country while conceiving and implementing their business plans, but an overwhelming majority remained content with exploiting opportunities in the vast domestic market rendered safe by a protective web. As liberalization gradually opened the Indian economy to the world, and the forces of globalization gained momentum, Indian business houses began to look for gainful opportunities in other parts of the world including the developed countries. Interestingly enough Oil and Natural Gas Corporation (ONGC—Oil and Natural Gas Commission until 1996), a public sector company, has become the largest investor abroad. Its wholly owned subsidiary ONGC Videsh Limited (OVL) has operations in Russia, Iran, Iraq, Sudan, Libya, Myanmar, and Vietnam. Indian Oil Corporation operates in Sri Lanka and plans to expand in other Asian countries. Another public-sector giant, Gail (India) Ltd engaged in the exploration, processing, and distribution of natural gas, too has emerged as an important international player in its field of operation in recent years. The liberalized environment, it seems, has generated a competitive worldview among public-sector undertakings as well.

Among private sector firms, Reliance, which claims to be India's first global company, has oil blocks in Yemen and has recently acquired Flag Telecom, an international bandwidth provider, and Treviara, a Hoechst company based in Germany. The Tatas, another private sector giant, have acquired Daewoo's truck operations in Korea, Natsteel in Singapore, and Tyco Global Network with 60,000 kms of undersea cable network in North America, Europe, and Asia. The house has also registered its presence in the United States and a number of countries of Europe and Asia. And the Aditya Birla group, the first to make forays out of India way back in the late 1960s, has expanded its operations in several countries of South East Asia, Egypt, Canada, Australia, and China. Mahindra & Mahindra, Bajaj Auto, and TVS are among other notable Indian groups with global ambitions. While the Mahindras have tractor operations in the United States and China, Bajaj and TVS are planning to set up local operations abroad—the former in Indonesia and the latter in Iran.

It is not only the big houses, but also some of the smaller companies that have been acquiring stakes in businesses abroad. The chemicals major Atul Products Ltd for instance, has wholly owned subsidiaries in the United States, Europe, and China, and Zee TV is planning to launch a global news network. Perhaps the most aggressive about expanding abroad have been the Indian drug manufacturers, who before the liberalization were like second-class citizens in their own country in comparison with the Indian subsidiaries of multinationals. Practically all of them—Dr Reddy's Laboratories, Zydus Cadila (Cadila Laboratories formed in 1951 split in 1992 between the two founders, the name of the other offshoot being Cadila Pharmaceuticals), Nicholas Piramal, and Ranbaxy to name the most important ones—have carved varying degrees of presence for themselves in other countries including the developed West. The most common route to expansion abroad has been the setting up of joint ventures with reputed drug manufacturers to gauge the market at the first stage and then to acquire, after a few years, the foreign partner's holdings in the company. As most of the Indian drug companies have installed manufacturing plants approved by the United States Food and Drug Administration (USFDA) at their home bases—India has the largest number of such plants in the world outside the United States—it is easy for them to penetrate the world market through the production of generic drugs of world standards that their subsidiaries, joint ventures, or strategic partners abroad distribute. Ranbaxy, the most aggressive of them all in this respect, has ground presence in forty-four countries including North American and European countries, and its products are sold in more than a hundred countries. Dr Reddy's Laboratories is not far behind. Significantly, around 50 per cent of the sales of most pharma companies come from their global operations.

Looking at these and other cases of foreign forays by Indian enterprises, it is safe to conclude that having missed out on the chance to partake of global opportunities during the licence-permit raj, the Indian business world is keen to make up for the time lost. The fact that more than twenty-five Indian companies were registered on the British and American stock exchanges by the beginning of the current century as compared to none in 1991 clearly indicates this trend. During the three years since 2001, Indian companies made an investment of about Rs 9000 crore in foreign acquisitions and acquired as many as 120 foreign firms, according to an authoritative estimate. Significantly enough, these acquisitions have been spread over a number of sectors; they have not been restricted to only a few areas, such as information technology, pharmaceuticals, and petroleum industries. And in so doing, at least some Indian companies have emerged as world leaders in their respective fields. Bharat Forge, which became the second largest forging company in the world after acquiring a German forging company in 2004, is a case in point. It has recently acquired another European firm, this time in Sweden. The much younger Infosys has acquired an Australian software company. Foreign acquisition in fact seems to have become a passion with Indian enterprises, both old and new, and hardly a week passes without some report to this effect appearing in the financial newspapers.

The new outward-looking attitude is reflected not only in the Indian companies setting up production facilities abroad but also in modifying their product lines in India with an eye on the world market. Arvind Mills belonging to the Lalbhai group is a case in point. Until almost the mid-1980s this Ahmedabad-based enterprise was still a regional or at best national player, producing cotton goods for the Indian market. Soon after the winds of economic reform began to sweep through India, the company revamped its production strategy to target foreign producers of denim garments. And in the process Arvind emerged as the largest denim manufacturer in the world, supplying the fabric to more than seventy countries. Although the management had to recently shut down the Mauritius subsidiary set up in 1992, this has had no effect on its position as a major textile player in the world. Interestingly, Arvind has carved out a niche for itself in what is usually counted among the so-called sunset industries.

The following statistics, published in a recent issue of the *Economic Times* (21 October 2005) may highlight the impact of liberalization on India's business landscape. The aggregate net sales of the top 100 companies have grown to Rs 976,419 crore in 2004–5 in comparison with Rs 130,448 crore in 1990–1; profits during the same period have leap-frogged to Rs 91,552 crore from a mere Rs 6885 crore;

and profit margins have doubled from 5 to 10 per cent—a reflection of the corporate sector's success in cutting costs, streamlining operations, and reducing the cost of capital. The last fifteen years have witnessed the entry of forty-three new companies in the top-hundred list, pushing back many erstwhile illustrious names. The new entrants include firms such as ICICI Bank, Hero Honda, Wipro, Infosys, Jet Airways, Ranbaxy, Satyam Computers, and HDFC Bank, while companies like Escorts, JK Synthetics, Mukund Iron, Premier Auto, Modi Rubber, and BPL have been left behind.

STRATEGIES AND STRUCTURES

In the midst of all these momentous developments, the strategies and structures in the Indian business world have obviously not remained insulated against the forces of change. Although departure from the old ways in these respects is by its very nature slow and not so easily perceptible, one can detect some feeble pointers to the emergence of new trends in the functional areas of management. Perhaps the most visible impact of liberalization is in the realm of marketing. A number of aggressive selling devices, almost absent from the scene or employed sparingly in the age of control, have come into play in recent years in the wake of growing competition. Tempting incentives, blistering publicity through eye-catching hoardings, imaginative advertisements in the print media, a spate of commercials on television channels, hire-purchase facilities, and an unending string of 'sales' offering goods and services at reduced rates—these and many other selling devices so common in the West have now made deep inroads in India. Never before in the business history of India was the Indian consumer an object of such wooing and pampering.

Financial strategies too have undergone some change, though not to the same degree as marketing. As banks, financial institutions, and venture capitalists have developed attractive schemes of business financing; private sources of finance, such as the family, have lost their importance. And a veritable equity cult has gained momentum, as raising capital through stock markets has become much more popular than ever before. This, among other things, is responsible for the increasingly larger number of business splits—there have been about twenty since 1990. Unlike before, when most of the breakups came after the third generation, splits are now taking place much earlier. The recent spilt in the Reliance group is a most obvious example.

How this would eventually affect the family-centric structure of the Indian business is hard to anticipate but there is no doubt that the value of management professionals even in family-controlled businesses has been going up as the environment has become more competitive. Not only has the demand for the business graduate gone up severalfold and is constantly growing, but also the salary and perks that he expects and is in fact offered have no resemblance with what his pre-liberalization counterpart received. This is because he is considered to be an indispensable resource to maximize the shareholders' wealth. Thus, even though the formal managerial structure has undergone little change since liberalization, a much-needed professionalism is being brought to bear on the operations of the Indian companies. And to make sure that the professionals give their best, many companies have introduced appropriate changes in their personnel policies. A few organizations such as the Murugappa group and Ranbaxy have even experimented with placing professionals at the top. There is no doubt that the professional manager has much greater autonomy today and the working environment in the corporate offices is much more relaxed, much more permissive, and much less authoritarian.

Liberalization has brought about some change in the attitude towards technology development also—an area that remained the weakest link in the Indian business all through the colonial period and to which Independence made little difference. The Tatas' success in producing a passenger car based on indigenously developed technology is the most visible example of change in this sphere. But there are other indicators too. Expenditure on research and development (R&D), a rather dispensable item for most Indian companies until the onset of liberalization, went up to US $ 19 billion, according to Organization of Economic Cooperation and Development (OECD), placing India among the top ten countries of the world in this respect. Indian companies filed in 2003 as many as 1700 patent applications (up from 1200 in 2002) with the US Patent and Trade Mark Office. The number filed in India that year was 15000. Admittedly, the R&D activity is still too modest for a country of India's size and pool of technical manpower at its disposal. But what is noteworthy is that a beginning has been made in an area that had almost totally been neglected before.

The liberalized India has experienced many other salutary developments in its business climate. Only the most important aspects have been dealt with here. These are sufficient to suggest that even the partial liberalization of the economy has released a massive pent-up urge to perceive and exploit new avenues of gain and offer new products and services. What would have happened if liberalization had come about earlier and with a more comprehensive coverage and less cautious speed can be anybody's guess.

Originally published as Dwijendra Tripathi and Jyoti Jumani, *The Concise Oxford History of Indian Business* (New Delhi, Oxford University Press, 2007), pp. 210–32.

37

Challenges and Opportunities of Economic Liberalization

Corporate Restructuring

Nirmalya Kumar, Pradipta K. Mohapatra, and Suj Chandrasekhar

The private sector's enthusiasm in response to the economic liberalization, as recounted in the previous excerpt, has been channellized into measures like corporate restructuring, which firms have implemented in the face of new challenges. Such significant changes in Indian companies after 1991, as they aspire to global status, are recounted in this selection from the recent work by scholars Nirmalya Kumar, Pradipta K. Mohapatra, and Suj Chandrasekhar.

This excerpt looks at measures that firms have taken, such as 'cleaning balance sheets', enhancing competitiveness, focusing on consumers and core competencies so they could benchmark themselves internationally, and implementing changes in management styles and practices. The authors make a convincing case that private sector firms are pursuing global ambitions and effectively transforming themselves into world class companies, ready to take on the opportunities which globalization presents.

Corporate Restructuring

The post-1991 reforms changed the environment for Indian business. Indian companies realized that the traditional Indian business model appropriate for "sheltered firms" had to be abandoned. First, the liberalization of industrial licensing meant that new domestic players could easily emerge in what were previously tightly controlled industrial sectors. As a result, companies went through a tough corporate restructuring program to enhance *domestic competitiveness* in the face of a more aggressive marketplace. Second, as import tariffs were cut and entry barriers for foreign companies were reduced, international players began to view India as a potential market. Subsequently, they brought to India their world-class products and services This forced even Indian firms with no global ambitions to become *globally competitive* to survive this foreign competition.

The transformation of Indian companies and business houses post-1991 was a crucial step in preparing Indian companies for the global marketplace. And, not surprisingly, some of them have become global players. The decade-long Indian corporate restructuring program had four essential elements: cleaning the balance sheet, improving competitiveness, focusing on core businesses, and strengthening management.

Cleaning the Balance Sheet

The balance sheets of most Indian companies in 1991 were poor. Established companies had the ability to raise money from banks, and many had done so at relatively favorable rates. These borrowed funds exceeded what the business itself could utilize. Instead the money was placed in an investment portfolio and invested in other group companies. As mentioned earlier, these cross-holdings allowed the ultimate promoters of these companies to control a vast network of group companies with very little of their own funds. The other shareholders in these companies disliked this arrangement, but could do almost nothing about it as the regulatory regime did not empower them or protect their interests.

As the Securities and Exchange Board of India (SEBI) began adopting reforms in corporate governance and empowering small shareholders along the lines of the American stock markets, companies were forced to shed these investments and cross-holdings. Given the complexity and ubiquity of corporate cross-holdings, their disentanglement was a time-consuming process. But every major Indian business group had to address it.

The balance sheets also suffered from substantial distortions in the valuation of assets. Many firms had assets with inflated values on their books. These needed to be recorded at their real market value. On the other hand, certain other assets on the books—usually property, cars, and art—were valued much below their market price. The logic here was that these undervalued assets would at some stage be sold to the promoters at book value. It was essentially a mechanism for transferring funds from the firm to the owners with the controlling interest, at the cost of the minority shareholders. Large Indian companies had to go through a painful process of cleaning up their balance sheets to bring the assets in line with market values. The boom in property and the resulting revaluation to reflect the rising prices helped companies write down the overvalued assets.

Strong balance sheets were essential for companies to attract new share capital from domestic and foreign sources. The infusion of capital helped reduce the historically high debt-to-equity ratios in Indian firms. More critically, it was needed to make the necessary capital investments to become competitive in the new deregulated marketplace. Finally, funds were also required to ramp up capacity to keep pace with the rapid domestic growth that followed the liberalization program.

Improving Competitiveness

Under the protection of the benign environment pre-1991 and without the discipline of a tough competitive marketplace, Indian companies had become bloated. Costs, productivity, and quality had all become victims as companies could simply pass on inefficiencies to the consumer. Companies had little choice but to seek dramatic improvements on these fronts if they were to survive in the new marketplace.

To reduce costs and improve productivity, companies became more demanding of their suppliers and employees. Traditionally, Indian firms, because of the high import duties, had relied exclusively on Indian suppliers, and frequently substituted the available cheap labor for sophisticated capital equipment. Baba Kalyani, who led the transformation of Bharat Forge from a labor-intensive to a technology-intensive manufacturing firm, observed the conditions that forced firms to make inappropriate choices: "You waited a year for an equipment-import license, got less than you wanted, then paid an 80 percent import duty."[1] Even computing the import duties was a nightmare. For example, a new Burroughs computer imported by TCS in 1974 attracted a tariff of 101 percent, including import duty, auxiliary duty, countervailing duty, and a levy to help pay for the war in Bangladesh![2]

In the 1980s, Maruti, through its partnership with Suzuki of Japan, brought to India the concepts of tight cost control and process engineering. At that time, there were no auto component manufacturers in India capable of producing to Japanese standards. Yet the Indian government required Indian-made parts in Maruti cars. Suzuki was responsible for the first wave of modern component technology in India with its concept of Indian entrepreneurs and Japanese companies together supplying Maruti plants. It launched a Japanese-backed supplier development program, where Japanese component manufacturers often took small stakes in the Indian auto component manufacturers, helping them achieve world-class quality and cost standards.

In family-controlled firms, suppliers were frequently relatives of the promoter. The promoter had set them up in business to allow them to make a decent living. The procurement managers were keenly aware of these relationships, and therefore did not lean too hard on the suppliers with respect to prices, quality standards, or delivery reliability. The new competitive environment forced, and liberalization allowed, firms to access the global supply chain and obtain inputs on a par with global standards at competitive prices.

Most Indian firms were overstaffed with strong, militant unions that protected the employees. In the new environment, companies began downsizing the workforce by providing incentives for workers to retire early. In addition, even unions began to be more flexible in the private negotiating rooms. Union bosses initially realized that layoffs were inevitable, and later that jobs were available elsewhere as the economy was rapidly expanding. For example, at Mahindra & Mahindra, in 1991 it took 1,230 workers to manufacture seventy engines a day; in 1994 productivity had improved to the point where 760 workers could produce 125 engines a day.[3]

Finally, India always had a very poor reputation for quality and customer focus. Pre-1991, the problem was for consumers to find products rather than for companies to find customers. Reflecting on this era, Baba Kalyani, chairman of Bharat Forge, remarked: "The concept of quality used to be that if it works somehow, it's okay, but it doesn't need to work all the time."[4] Clearly this had to change if Indian brands were going to compete not just with each other, but also against the multinational companies entering the country.

The IT sector in India was a beacon in demonstrating that India could achieve world-class standards. The Capability Maturity

Model (CMM) from the Software Engineering Institute at Carnegie Mellon University assesses software companies for quality. Level 5 is the highest level on the maturity scale; in 1994 Motorola's software center at Bangalore became the world's second CMM Level 5 unit (the first was at NASA). By 2003, there were eighty software centers in the world assessed at CMM Level 5, and of those, sixty were in India.

Focusing on Core Businesses

The highly diversified Indian business groups quickly realized that they needed to focus on a few industries where they could obtain leading domestic positions. Building these positions would require significant investments. Focusing the portfolio would not only free up resources from noncore companies but through their divestment would also generate additional capital for the core business. In the early 1990s, many large business groups in India went through an exercise of identifying their core businesses. For example, the RPG Group went from twenty to six areas. In 1998 even Tata reduced the number of group-affiliated companies from eighty to thirty by trimming its lines of business from twenty-five to a dozen.[5]

The focus on a few core areas allowed companies to consolidate their domestic positions and had a subtle impact on their aspirations. Firms were no longer satisfied by claiming that they were number one or two in India; instead they began touting their world ranking. For example, MRF started asserting it was among the top fifteen tire manufacturers in the world, while Ranbaxy emphasized its position among the top ten generic pharmaceutical producers in the world. Slowly but surely, Indian companies began benchmarking themselves against world competitors. It was a first step toward global ambitions for Indian firms.

Strengthening Management

In a populous country with relatively few opportunities in the corporate world, Indian companies never saw managerial talent as an important source of competitive advantage. Compensation levels were extremely low. In the 1980s, it was not surprising for top executives to earn as little as $5,000 per year! Relationships, loyalty, and trust were valued in professional managers more than talent and competence. This was especially true in family-owned firms where many critical positions were occupied by family members. This explains the common usage of the term *professional manager* in India to distinguish such a leader from the "owner manager" and family members.

Often these family firms were run on feudalistic norms whereby all important decisions had to flow through a powerful promoter. This frustrated competent professional managers, and their only options were the few Indian subsidiaries of multinational companies. Some of these multinational companies, like Unilever and Imperial Tobacco, recognized that managerial talent was available in India at a relatively low cost and raided their Indian subsidiaries for overseas operations.

Post-1991, Indian firms, especially the family business houses, realized that professional managers had value as they could take responsibility and deliver results. Not surprisingly, they began to scour the Indian subsidiaries of multinational companies for management talent and move away from "one-person" rule. In the ensuing war for talent, professional manager salaries shot up dramatically. In addition, variable pay and stock options were introduced. In addition to competing for the best talent, managers were empowered and firms began investing in their training. Today, Indian managers, relative to their peers in other countries, probably have the highest standard of living in the world. These managers brought the world-class practices and processes they had learned at multinational companies to Indian firms, thereby preparing Indian business to be globally competitive.

The Role of Owners

As would be expected, the general corporate restructuring program described here varied considerably in how business groups and companies implemented the corporate restructuring program. Some firms started the restructuring process even prior to 1991, while others are still struggling with it. There were substantial differences among the owners, and to a large extent, the owner's philosophy determined the degree to which the painful restructuring medicine was adopted by the group. Some of the heads of family business groups and companies were rather aggressive in changing the old ways. Other business groups suffered from poor leadership and family splits of assets. As a result, some renowned family business houses witnessed an unprecedented decline in the 1990s. The important point here is that owner-promoters in Indian companies, rather than the corporate resources available, played the major role in distinguishing between subsequent winners and losers.

The new regulations made it impossible to exercise control of companies with small equity stakes and helped spur consolidation within industries. Furthermore, the liberalization allowed new companies to emerge in sectors such as IT, media, pharmaceuticals, and property. Several of these relatively new companies and groups, like Dr. Reddy's, Subhas Chandra, and Wipro, had by 1999 entered the list of the top twenty Indian business groups. This was possible because with liberalization, unlike in the prereform era, groups with high product relatedness and low institutional relatedness were the relative top performers in the 1990s.[6] The ability to exploit institutional gaps became less critical than the ability to effectively manage a business. Instead, more traditional, textbook business success factors of articulating a clear vision and strategy, understanding customer needs, whilst focusing on core competencies, innovation, and implementation became most important.

UNLEASHED—HOW INDIAN COMPANIES ARE TAKING ON THE WORLD

The corporate restructuring brought confidence to Indian business. Indian companies transformed themselves from domestic players, scared of global competitors and constantly seeking government protection in domestic markets, into confident players capable of building Indian multinationals. As they have gone from being passive resisters to active promoters of globalization, Indian firms are continuing to force a change in government policies toward a more open Indian market and business environment.

As stated in the introduction, we conducted interviews with the leaders of global Indian companies in our sample. We supplemented these interviews with secondary research and follow-up telephone interviews to ascertain how Indian companies went global, what challenges they faced in doing so, and how these challenges were overcome. Two factors clearly emerged as drivers of globalization: overcoming the mind-set barrier and having a dominant lever.

Overcoming the Mind-set Barrier

"We asked ourselves: Why don't we become one of India's MNCs in manufacturing? By doing so we will have better access to the market, better access to knowledge, better access to new developments," explained Baba Kalyani of Bharat Forge, elaborating on the firm's incentive to go global.[7] Nevertheless, he added, it took Bharat Forge seven years to find its first customer because, coming from a so-called underdeveloped, low-cost country, the company had to battle all kinds of doubts regarding its capability and technology. The Bharat Forge experience raised three issues about overcoming the mind-set barrier that came up repeatedly in our interviews: making a leap of faith, persistence in the face of initial setbacks on the path to globalization, and overcoming the liabilities of "Made in India" origin.

Making a Leap of Faith

For an Indian company to go global requires, at some level, a leap of faith into the unknown. In the face of skepticism, the entrepreneur or owner made the decision to go for it despite what to unbiased observers may have seemed like long odds. Anand Mahindra, in his interview, mentioned that, while pursuing his MBA at Harvard Business School, he was disappointed that there were no case studies or examples of Indian global brands. It fired his ambition and led him to decide that when he took over the family business, Mahindra would be a global brand. Much later he did just that: "We decided that we weren't going to be in any business that wasn't global ... You're not safe if you're only at home. You can't compete in a small pool anymore."[8]

Similarly, Ranbaxy, a generic drug maker in India, had been exporting its products since 1975, but had never really made any money on these international sales.[9] In 1993, the then CEO, Parvinder Singh, challenged his organization to become an international research-based pharmaceutical firm. When his managers questioned whether it was possible to build such a firm in a country like India, he responded that Ranbaxy cannot change India but what it can be is a pocket of excellence. Ranbaxy, he argued, must be an island in India. Today it is one the world's top ten generic producers with presence in twenty-three of the twenty-five largest markets and manufacturing facilities in eleven countries.[10]

Persistence in the Face of Initial Setbacks

Becoming a global corporation is a learning game. In most of the companies that we researched, it was not a straight-line process. There were initial setbacks. For example, in Essel Propack's first attempt to acquire a piece of land for its operations in China, the vendor absconded with the money. Anand Mahindra described his firm's first international incursion into Greece as a chapter on "how not to do it!"[11] Staring at these initial setbacks, in light of a growing and profitable domestic business, it would have been easy for all of these companies to retreat from global markets. Yet they persevered, and learned from their mistakes.

The initial hotel properties acquired in the 1980s by the Taj Group in cities such as Chicago, New York, and London were "B" level properties. But they were what the Taj Group could afford given the foreign exchange limitations the government placed on Indian companies. These subpar properties were not consistent with the upscale Taj image. Taj executives were not motivated by these international properties, and as a consequence, these hotels soon deteriorated in terms of customer experience and became largely unprofitable. Taj realized that its competence was in running five-star hotels. Later, when Taj became serious about its international operations in the developed markets, it had to shed all of these initial acquisitions.

Learning from this experience, in the Taj Group's next sortie into developed markets, it acquired prestigious hotels—including the Ritz-Carlton in Boston, Campton Place in San Francisco, and Blue Sydney in Australia—at top dollar. What made Taj persevere was the realization that going global was an imperative. R. K. Krishna Kumar, vice chairman of Taj Hotels, said: "The Tata Group has always recognized that the world marketplace is not divisible... There's a strategic compulsion to go outside India for many of our businesses because we believe the global market is one marketplace."[12]

Overcoming the Liabilities of Indian Origin

Until the late 1990s, before the IT outsourcing boom, the image of India was detrimental to Indian business. At its worst, India was identified with abject poverty. Most images and stories of India in the international press reflected this with pictures of starving masses, natural disasters, and famines. At its best, India was seen as an old and mystical culture. The images most frequently associated with this view featured snake charmers, historical palaces, temples, and holy men. While both of these were, and still are, reflective of India's reality, they missed another India—an India populated by pockets of technological sophistication, an entrepreneurial private sector, and a well-educated workforce.

Given India's image, it was extremely difficult to convince global customers that an Indian supplier could be a reliable source of good-quality products made by a technologically sophisticated company. When Indian companies began knocking on the doors of large multinational firms, which had many choices within their global supply chains, it was difficult to close the sale. Imagine an Indian executive a decade ago, trying to convince the big three U.S. automakers to buy from Bharat Forge, or persuade Procter & Gamble that Essel Propack should be its supplier in the United States.

Indian entrepreneurs learned that, in competitive global markets, there was always another supplier willing to match the Indian firm's low prices. Therefore, Indian companies had to recognize that price as a weapon could take you only so far. To obtain the order required more than that: Indian firms had to demonstrate they had the world-class capabilities (assets, processes, and knowledge) to compete in international markets. Only then would global customers be reassured.

Dominant Lever

After conducting their research, the hope of academics is to discover some common patterns so as to group firms according to a few generic global strategies. For example, Ramamurti and Singh propose four generic international strategies that characterize India's emerging multinationals, with an illustrative example for each: local optimizer (Mahindra & Mahindra), low-cost partner (Infosys), global consolidator (ArcelorMittal), and global first mover (Suzlon).[13] We were unable to fit all our cases neatly into this typology, and in some categories, such as global first mover, were unable to identify any Indian company beyond Suzlon. Instead, we discovered that the companies in our sample chose very different strategies in their paths to having an international footprint. Moreover, they could not be faithfully arrayed in any simple typology. Each company in our sample had a dominant lever that they exploited to access international markets.

We were interested to see how these companies used their dominant lever to launch their globalization once they overcame the country-of-origin liability. While no company used a single dominant lever exclusively, our nine case studies demonstrate nine different dominant levers.

ArcelorMittal saw an opportunity in the fragmented steel industry, recognizing that national champions would lose to a global champion. Consolidating the fragmented steel industry created a truly global company with the ability to reduce risk and leverage capabilities across markets. Mittal's unique vision changed the industry.

Companies like Infosys and i-flex solutions were *born* global, because they understood that while there was a huge human capital advantage in India, the fulfillment had to be global. "Infosys started with no brand, no technology, no faith in marketing capability, and no access to foreign exchange," recalled Nandan Nilekani.[14] Infosys and, more generally, the IT sector (TCS, and Wipro in particular) were instrumental in sparking the imagination of Indian entrepreneurs to seek "born global" business models that exploit India's large pools of reasonably priced skilled workers. From Hollywood studios outsourcing animation to lawyers outsourcing preparation of briefs, the potential for India's skilled workers to be the world's workforce are substantial.

Bharat Forge employed reasonably priced engineering talent to transform itself from an 85 percent blue-collar workforce to an 85 percent professional workforce. Replacing unskilled workers with engineers on the plant floor led to a significant advantage in design capabilities. The product development time of two to three weeks (versus industry standards of six to twelve months) delivered the "wow" factor to prospective clients.

Essel Propack's induction into the global circle began once it convinced Procter & Gamble that it could be P&G's best supplier—a quality supplier and a process-oriented supplier. The company went out of its way to build a relationship with P&G, which subsequently allowed Essel Propack to enter Egypt, China, and finally the United States as a supplier.

A transformational merger is a frequently employed strategy to become a global firm. Hindalco did exactly that with its 2007 acquisition of Novelis, a world leader in aluminum rolling and can recycling. By combining its previous upstream focus with Novelis's dominance of downstream operations, Hindalco became an integrated global major in the industry. Several other Indian firms, such as Tata Tea and United Breweries, have also used acquisitions as a path to globalization.

Other companies, like Tata Motors, Godrej, and Marico, have utilized the specific product competencies developed for India to enter other emerging markets. Given India's size, domestic leadership often confers global scale, as seen at both Mahindra & Mahindra and VIP. As Anand Mahindra observed, "India is the largest tractor market in the world, and if you are the largest tractor maker in India, it is a disservice to India if you are not a global force."[15]

Ratan Tata, the group chairman, has been a transformational leader in making this relatively sleepy giant dance in the global markets, making bold acquisitions for individual group companies that leverage the combined financial muscle of the entire group. As in Suzlon and the other companies we examined, the role of the leader has been an important catalyst for those Indian firms that have made the transition to global.

CONCLUSION

The first seminal study of India's multinationals was done twenty-five years ago by Sanjaya Lall, who discussed the patterns of foreign direct investment by Indian companies in the 1970s.[16] We can contrast the global strategies of Indian companies today with those Lall identified. Four dramatic changes are evident in how Indian companies are pursuing global strategies in this decade vis-à-vis the 1970s.

First, in the 1970s the pattern of foreign direct investment was highly concentrated, with seven family business groups accounting for at least three-quarters of it. In contrast, the companies featured as case studies, except for Hindalco (Aditya Birla Group), Tata Group, and Mahindra & Mahindra, either did not exist or, if they did, were not included on the list of the largest twenty Indian business houses of 1980. What has really inspired Indian companies to go overseas, including the more aggressive internationalization of the Birla and Tata groups, is the success of the "born global" IT sector and Lakshmi Mittal. It is these latter two, rather than any of the old family business groups, that are responsible for waking up Indian business to seriously examine global opportunities. Today, the overseas footprint of corporate India is drawn from a much broader set of Indian firms.

Second, prior to 1980, 80 percent of Indian overseas activity was manufacturing based. The success of Indian outsourcing has instead tilted the nature of Indian global operations toward the service sector. It reflects the change in India's economy over the past three decades. Services now account for 50 percent of India's gross domestic product; industry and agriculture account for 25 percent each.[17] This is a very unusual profile for a developing country, where the economies, and especially exports, tend to be dominated by manufacturing (e.g., China), natural resources (e.g., Middle East), or agriculture (Latin America).

Third, observing the success of the IT sector in the United States, Indian companies are now focused on expansion opportunities in the developed markets of North America and Europe. This is in contrast to the 1970s, when most of the foreign investment of Indian firms flowed to other developing markets like Africa and Southeast Asia. Indian firms today have the confidence that they can succeed in the most demanding markets of the world.

Fourth, as they focus on the developed world, Indian companies recognize that they do not have the appropriate brands, product lines, or distribution networks. As many of them are impatient to go global, they have chosen to acquire these resources. Almost every Indian firm in our study has made some acquisition in the developed markets. And instead of taking minority positions in foreign joint ventures, as was the practice in the 1970s, Indian companies are now either setting up wholly owned subsidiaries or buying majority interests. They seem to have no interest in being a minority partner. Thus, the *relative* focus of Indian companies' globalization has shifted from favoring greenfield operations and minority stakes in developing countries to taking controlling positions through acquisitions in developed countries.

Indian companies are no longer the traditional low-price bidders for foreign assets and companies, slow to appoint international advisors. Instead, they have become self-assured and savvy investors, financing large deals and paying global prices. World-class management and improved earnings have given them the ability to access global liquidity and financial markets. Despite the global financial crisis of 2008 and the meltdown of markets worldwide, the future will no doubt bring financing of foreign acquisitions with their own stock. And, who knows, future rupee convertibility may lead to rupee acquisitions! All of this was unimaginable in 1991, even by the biggest of India bulls.

Originally published as Nirmalya Kumar, with Pradipta K. Mohapatra and Suj Chandrasekhar, *India's Global Powerhouses: How They Are Taking On the World* (Boston, Harvard Business Press, 2009), pp. 36–49. Reprinted by permission of Harvard Business Press.

NOTES

1. John Elliot, "Manufacturing Takes Off," *Fortune* (Europe edition), October 29, 2007, 80.

2. "Face Value: Ram Drive," *Economist*, August 23, 2008, 59.

3. Anuradha Raghunathan, "Anand Mahindra's Great Global Dreams," *Forbes*, April 19, 2006, http://www.rediff.com/money/2006/apr/19forbes.htm.

4. Elliot, "Manufacturing Takes Off."

5. S.D. Naik, "Decade of Corporate Churning and Change," *Hindu Business Line*, July 31, 2001, http://www.thehindubusinessline.com/businessline/2001/07/31/stories/043120ma.htm.

6. B.L. Kedia, D. Mukherjee, and S. Lahiri, "Indian Business Groups: Evolution and Transformation," *Asia Pacific Journal of Management*, Vol. 23, December 2006, 559–77.

7. Baba Kalyani of Bharat Forge, interview by authors, February 5, 2007.

8. Raghunathan, "Anand Mahindra's Great Global Dreams."

9. The Ranbaxy exmaple comes from Christopher Bartlett and Sumantra Ghoshal, "Going Global," *Harvard Business Review*, March 2000, 132–41.

10. http://www.ranbaxy.com/aboutus/aspx.aboutus.

11. Anand Mahindra of Mahindra & Mahindra, interview by authors, February 7, 2007.

12. Megha Bahree, "Palatial Pieces," *Forbes*, July 5, 2007, http://www.forbes.com/business/global/2007/0507/026.html

13. Ravi Ramamurti and Jitendra V. Singh, "Generic Strategies of India's Emerging Multinationals," in *Emerging Multinationals from Emerging Markets*, (eds) Ravi Ramamurti and Jitendra V. Singh (Cambridge, UK: Cambridge University Press, 2009).

14. Anand Mahindra of Mahindra & Mahindra, interview by authors, February 7, 2007.

15. Sanjaya Lall, "The Emergence of Third World Multinationals: Indian Joint Ventures Overseas," *World Development*, Vol. 10, No. 2, February 1982, 127–46.

16. Fareed Zakaria, *The Post-American World* (W.W. Norton & Company, 2009).

38

Challenges and Opportunities of Economic Liberalization

The Tata Group

R.M. Lala

The Tata Group is one of the oldest and most respected Asian conglomerates. Founded in 1868 by Jamsetji Tata, it is today a 63 billion dollar company (2008) and India's largest conglomerate of nearly 100 companies with 300 subsidiaries in 40 businesses.* It operates in 81 countries, employs an estimated 350,000 employees, and has interests ranging from steel to software, tea, fertilizers, insurance, automobiles, IT, wristwatches, and telecommunications. Given its long history, its adeptness at adjusting to different economic scenarios is not surprising. In the challenging era of economic liberalization, it responded proactively by putting in place many measures with a view to 'laying foundations for the future'.

These measures, taken under the stewardship of director Ratan Tata, are discussed here by R.M. Lala, biographer of Jamsetji Tata and J.R.D. Tata and himself a director of Tata Trust. Lala highlights the group's concern that reputation and 'high brand equity' should never, ever be compromised. He reveals some of the changes initiated in ways of dealing with companies managed by the group, the new code of ethics that was implemented, and the new 'brand equity Business Promotion agreement'. The excerpt also points out the new entries from 1992 to 2002 and major acquisitions carried out during this period.

*On the Tatas see 'Tata Group', in Nirmalya Kumar, Pratipta K. Mohapatra, and Suj Chandrasekhar, *India's Global Powerhouses: How They are Taking on the World* (Boston, Harvard Business Press, 2009), pp. 157–76.

LAYING FOUNDATIONS FOR THE FUTURE

When Ratan Tata became chairman of Tata Sons, the old order changed not only for the house of Tata but also for the nation. Far reaching liberalization of the Indian economy coupled with globalization heralded an era of new opportunities and challenges. To meet these challenges he took a number of measures, among them:

Increasing Tatas holdings in companies it managed. In the old days Tatas had such support and trust of the shareholders (including financial institutions) that they could manage a major company (Tata Electric) with a holding of only 2 per cent. Holdings of Tatas in some companies, in 1992 and in 2002 are noted hereunder:

(in per cent)

	1992	2002
Tata Steel	8	26
Telco	17	32
Tata Chemicals	30	30
Tata Tea	30	30
Voltas	22	25
Indian Hotels	41	37

In some of the newer companies the Tata stakes are:

(in per cent)

Tata Infotech	74
Trent Ltd.	26
Tata Infomedia	50

To consolidate and direct group policies the following steps were taken:

A Group Executive Office was established in 1998 comprising the group chairman and five members involved in group companies, group finance, group HR and new group projects. Later on, in 2002, a Tata Group Corporate Centre (GCC) was established which included the GEO members and comprised Mr R.N. Tata, Mr N.A. Soonawala, Dr J.J. Irani, Mr R.K. Krishna Kumar, Mr R. Gopalakrishnan, Mr Ishaat Hussain and Mr K.A. Chaukar.

A code of ethics was formulated to warrant the use of the name Tatas. If any company flagrantly defied it, the name of Tatas is to be withdrawn from it. While Tatas do not claim to be perfect, JRD often told me: 'But Tatas are different.' In official, as in personal life, people have their moments of frailty and may cross the ethical fence. Then they at least know that they have done so and can always return. When all the moral fences are down, there is no point of return.

The Tata Business Excellence Model was initiated in 1994. The Tata brand is immensely valuable. Recognizing this, the group leadership also realized that while many Tata companies take positive steps to enhance the brand there were also several companies which were not performing very well, and which were eroding the brand. In the mid-1990s a decision was taken to have a more formal relationship between Tata Sons and each Tata company. This saw the birth of the Brand Equity and Business Promotion (BEBP) agreement.

The philosophy is that every Tata company is an independent entity, but is also a member of the Tata family, for a number of reasons that include stake-holding, directorships, value systems, etc. It is essential for good corporate governance that before signing the BEBP agreement, the board of each company must independently decide to sign the agreement. The Tata Sons board takes its own view on this. Once both agree to proceed, the agreement is signed and the benefits of the use of the Tata group composite mark and the attendant brand promotion schemes flow to the company. A company that signs the agreement commits to two things:

It commits to adopting the Tata Business Excellence Model (TBEM) as a 'way of life'. The TBEM, which is a near clone of the Malcolm Baldrige Model used by the U.S. government to recognize high performing companies, is essentially a set of criteria distilled from high performing companies in the U.S. and converted into generic 'What do you do?' and 'How do you do it?' questions.

Companies that achieve a score of 500 are emerging industry leaders in the international context. Of the companies that signed the agreement Tata Steel was the first to surpass the 500 mark which is a recognition that they are amongst the best in the field by international standard. Tata Consultancy Services, Tata Engineering's Commercial Vehicle Business Unit, Titan Industries and the tube business of Tata Steel have all crossed the 500 mark level. They will cross 600 within a short time, as they continue to improve.

Now, nine years after the programme was initiated, forty companies have signed the BEBP agreement. Most (but not all) are progressing well. Of the companies twenty-eight meet the eligibility criteria (400 points) and are entering the External Assessment Programme.

A decade ago when some in the industry were still lobbying for protection for their industry, Tatas set about to make Tata companies—that so chose—to be globally competitive and to meet strict international criteria for their operations.

- The Tata name carries a high brand equity and the companies subscribing have to pay a small percentage of 0.10 to 0.25 per cent of their net profits for the use of the Tata name in the company and/or the product. A new Tata logo was also designed.
- Efficiency rather than the size of the group became the criteria. Unless the group had a leadership position or could attain it in the first three ranks, exit could be considered. The growth potential had also to be considered.
- A new look was taken at its portfolios.

The new specific entries of the decade 1992–2002 are in:

Automobile	
• Passenger Cars	- Tata Engineering
• Auto Components	- Tata Auto Components
Telecommunication	
• Service-Basic	- Tata Teleservices
• Cellular	- Birla-Tata-AT&T, now Idea
• International Long Distance	- VSNL (through acquisition)
Fertilizers	- Tata Chemicals
Global Tea	- Tetley Plc (through acquisition)
Insurance	- Tata AIG

The exit from companies brought into Tatas a sum of Rs 2,500 crore ($0.50 billion). Entries cost over Rs 10,000 crore ($2.2 billion).

The major acquisitions of Tatas since 1992 have been: Tetley, VSNL and CMC—Computer Maintenance Corporation—the latter two divested by the Government of India. Hindustan Lever Chemicals was acquired from HLL.

- Portfolio restructuring means rationalization. There seemed no point in Tata Steel running its own captive power plant. It was sold to Tata Power. The three Tata electric companies were merged into one and called 'Tata Power'.

Voltas, an engineering company, was also in agrochemicals which was hived off to Rallis India. In addition to Tata International (formerly Tata Exports), Tata Steel was also trading internationally. That function was handed over to Tata International.

When Ratan Tata came to to the top position, his first challenge was to put the companies in a framework where they would move in one direction. He got a firmer hold of the companies. 'We have endeavoured to leave much of the autonomy of the company to the company. If a company wants to enter a particular business—say, the armaments business—and the group feels that it should not, it will object to the move as a shareholder. If the company persists in pursuing that line we will sell our stake in the company.' (*India Today*, 24 February 2003)

Manufacturing accounts for about 65 per cent of Tatas turnover and services for 35 per cent.[1] However, services constitute a much larger percentage of the group's profits.

Tatas are a global player in I.T. and in tea, and to a lesser extent in hotels. Tata Consultancy Services is the largest I.T. company in Asia. The Tata Tea-Tetley combination makes it the world's second largest in tea company. Tata Tea has the largest acreage of any tea company in the world.

When Ratan Tata stepped down as executive chairman in December 2002, he could claim that Tatas were no more a loose confederation of companies but a tightly knit group streamlined to meet the challenges of the future. Some well-known names in Indian business who did not undertake this task in time have disintegrated. JRD with his stature and charisma had a personalized style of working. To hold the group together for the future the system of working needed to be institutionalized. Ratan Tata has accomplished this.

Originally published as R.M. Lala, *The Creation of Wealth: The Tatas from the 19th to the 21st Century* (New Delhi, Penguin, 2004), pp. 216–20.

NOTE

1. *Source*: Tata's Department of Economics and Statistics.

39

The Coming of Age of Indian Business
Global Aspirations

T.N. Ninan and P.G. Mathai

In the opening decade of the twenty-first century, a confident private sector has gone on a global acquisitions spree. Displaying fierce aggression, companies have bought even at the height of bull runs. This fast-changing scenario is apparent from the fact that outward deals which were a mere 0.7 billion dollars in 2000–1 rose to 4.3 billion dollars by 2005 and to 15 billion dollars by 2006.* The pace of acquisitions is increasing each year; cross-border deals in nine months of 2005 were 7.8 billion dollars and jumped to 23 billion dollars in a corresponding period in 2006, marking a two-fold increase.† Some of the larger acquisitions have been Tata–Corus Jaguar Land Rover (2008), Hindalco–Novelis (2007), Videocon–Daewoo Electronics Corp (2006), Dr Reddy's Labs–Betapharm (2006), Tata Steel–Natsteel (2005), and Suzlon Energy–Hansen (2006). The top 10 deals alone account for an estimated 21,500 million dollars.

The Tata Group has also embarked on an ambitious acquisitions binge since 2003 with the buying up of the truck unit of Daewoo, a stake in Indonesia's biggest coal mines, Tetley Tea, Incat International, steel mills in Singapore, Thailand, and Vietnam, the Corus group, Jaguar and Land Rover, and hotels in New York, Boston, and San Francisco among a host of other acquisitions. The takeover from Ford of Jaguar and Land Rover, a 1.15 billion pound deal, was not the most expensive but certainly the most symbolic as it

* See Arun Prabhudesai, 'Indian Mergers and Acquisitions: The Changing Face of Indian Business,' 16 August 2007, available online at http://trak.in/tags/business/2007/08/16/indian-mergers-acquisitions-changing-indian-business/, last accessed on 14 January 2010. Also see Gita Piramal, *Business Maharajas* (New Delhi, Viking, 1996), chapter on 'Ratan Tata', pp. 365–407.

† Kumara Mangalam Birla, 'New Frontiers, New Thinking', *Outlook*, 12 April 2007.

heralded the acquisition of a 'symbol of British style and engineering superiority' and 'the makers of James Bond's new wheels, Inspector Morse's classic and the workhorse of the British Army'.[‡] Scholars estimate that the Group's overall cross-border acquisitions have been 38, valued at 18 billion dollars. In 2008, the Group has generated 38 billion dollars in international revenues.[§]

In this two-part interview Ratan Tata, head of the Tata Group since 1991, sometimes called 'India's humble business king', talks with noted business journalists T.N. Ninan and P.G. Mathai with characteristic modesty.[¶] Tata candidly discusses his business empire, succession, overseas expansion, and future plans.

'WE NEVER COMPROMISED ON ETHICS'

Getting a diverse group of 80 companies into shape is never easy, and two years after stepping down as Executive Chairman **Ratan Tata** evaluates the group's performance and finds that while it is still a bit resistant to change, the top firms are doing well, and international operations are in much better shape, with new overseas acquisitions on the projected growth path.

Excerpts from the first part of a two-part interview with **T.N. Ninan** and **Palakunnathu G. Mathai.**

Looking back at what's happened in the last decade and more, how much of what you expected to achieve have you been able to accomplish so far?

This is somewhat difficult to respond to because some of what one wanted to do changed with the times and market conditions. On a scale of 10, it would probably be a six or seven—that's the kind of intuitive feel I have of where we are.

What stands out in that?

One is certainly the greater integration of the group and that has added an enormous strength to what we've done because we really were a disparate group of companies.

The second is the greater alignment, which is also part of the integration, an ability to integrate and converge on goals. The other has been the unified corporate visibility in terms of logos and signage.

Then we set some goals on sales and profits which we didn't meet per se in the time frame because we went through those three years of an economic downturn.

We were off by a year. All the companies, the major ones, are economic value added (EVA) positive today which has never happened before.

So you don't have any negative EVA now?

‡ See Dean Nelson, 'The Reverse Raj: Indian Businesses Turn Tables on Imperial Master', *Times*, 30 March 2008, available online at http://www.timesonline.co.uk/tol/news/world/asia/article3646320.ece, last accessed on 14 January 2010.

§ For a list of acquisitions, see Nirmalya Kumar, Pratipta K. Mohapatra, and Suj Chandrasekhar, *India's Global Powerhouses: How They Are Taking On the World* (Boston, Harvard Business Press, 2009), pp. 162–3.

¶ Also see Dominic O'Connell, 'Interview: Ratan Tata, India's Humble Business King', available online at http://business.timesonline.co.uk/tol/business/entrepreneur/article6256642.ece, last accessed on 14 January 2010.

We don't have any negative EVA now in the major 12–13 companies. Two years ago, we set ourselves the goal of going international. Things are coming together.

We haven't achieved as much on the portfolio restructuring side as we had hoped we would do. And on that front there have been more human problems than anything else. The shortfall has been much more in the area of taking the 80 companies and bringing them down to 30 or 40 in 10 or 12 different businesses.

Where do you see the return on capital employed, return on net worth, those kind of numbers, for the group?

Because we are using EVA, we're certainly better than the cost of money. For the top 12 companies, the return on net worth has risen from 16.7 per cent in 1994–95 to 26.6 per cent in 2003–04.

You weren't very keen on steel as an industry at one point. Has that changed?

No, that's not true. When McKinsey was involved, it was very negative on steel. I've always held a view that steel provided a return that was below the cost of money.

So I felt that we couldn't even think of exiting Tata Steel and that Tata Steel needed to look at another line of business that gave it a better return, that is, a second line of business, not in lieu of steel.

That has changed now. Per capita consumption of steel in India is so low that in India the steel business is going to grow and it's not a sunset business. But the returns have to be better.

Tata Steel has done a lot on cost cutting and so on. There's no doubt that the market and the prices have catapulted the steel industry into something totally different from what it was four years ago.

Do you feel that the group's traditional emphasis on doing business a certain kind of way, which was sometimes used as an argument for saying that we won't get the kind of numbers that other people get, is still a constraint?

You mean in terms of ethics and values? Yes, it's still a constraint. But we're very heartened that we've not compromised on those and have grown the way we have. Our topline has grown more than four times (to Rs 61,434 crore) from (what it was in) 1991 (Rs 13,290 crore).

Has the group been re-assessed by the public, because there are changes in rankings in surveys that people do on the most admired CEO, the most respected companies and so on?

First, I don't give too much weightage to that because you're the dog when you're doing badly. If Tata Motors is in a loss, we say, look the market shrunk but our market share didn't shrink. But nobody listens to you.

Suddenly when the market booms again, the same company under the same management producing the same products just goes through the roof and everybody calls it a turnaround.

Nobody wanted to listen to you and understand you. So I don't pay much credence to these. Part of it is also the fact that the group is more integrated today than what it was before.

Are you ready for another downturn, should it come? And since the more likely scenario is rapid growth—how do you see yourself in that context?

One of the major drivers of going international is to get out of the clutches of the single economy and to have the ability to spread yourself over greater geographies which are presumably not aligned in the same economic cycle.

We feel that this broader base is going to equip us better against a downturn. And we have, through that last downturn, taken off a lot of fat and a lot of cost out of many of our companies and we're better equipped to deal with a downturn than we were at that time.

And still be EVA positive?

Certainly we try to be. When there is a downturn, margins will fall but so long as you can cover your overheads and run full up as they did in the last downturn, Tata Steel will continue to be okay. A product company like Tata Motors will face initial change in product pricing but its product offering is more robust and more secure.

I've just come back from South Africa where the Indica has, in the first three months of launch, exceeded any other vehicle launch in South Africa. We are looking forward to selling 10,000 a year.

The two most successful product launches have been the Renault and Kia, but we've exceeded them in the first three months. I find it very heartening that people in South Africa are saying, "Oh, you're connected with the car?"

Other than the restructuring, what else is there that makes you give what you expected to achieve a six out of 10 and not a higher figure?

I don't think restructuring is unfinished, because it's going to be a continuous thing. In answer to your question, we are less risk averse than we were and we're less conservative, but we're still resistant to change and that's a human issue.

It reflects, perhaps, in the fact that we still have more traditional incumbents in our companies who are afraid of change and it reflects on our HR policy which doesn't adequately allow for mistakes to be made.

Looking forward, can you go into the details of the internationalisation issue you referred to?

Internationalisation will take two forms. One is the growth of our own companies abroad. The second is the important change we mandated 10 years ago which is, please don't look at organic growth alone but look at acquisitions as a means to grow.

Our willingness to look at companies that we can acquire has been another wave of international growth. In that we have tried to be different.

We have tried very hard and quite successfully to let some of the major acquisitions we have made—be it Tetley, Daewoo and now Hispano—be themselves with the face, touch and feel of a local company, just owned by an Indian company.

At the same time we have been able to integrate product plans and strategies. So Tetley has the same management as it had when we acquired it. Daewoo has the same management.

I intervened in Tata Motors when it was going to send 14–16 people to Korea and said, don't do that. Put one finance person and one integration person there to integrate the two operations. Don't just bombard the organisation with Indians and give everyone a feeling that this is an Indian takeover.

The same is true of Hispano where we have put just one or two people there. And it seems to work well because those people continue to have their visibility and in each case there's a great sense of belonging to the family.

Are the companies doing well after you took over?

Both Tetley and Daewoo are doing much better than they were doing before. Even VSNL is doing better. Though we lost the main business, we set ourselves the task of identifying a new line of business.

We looked at broadband as the way to go. We invested, I think very boldly, in undersea cable capacity, first on our own and then made a somewhat gutsy move to acquire Tyco's entire network.

We've now got the second network operator in South Africa. So we will actually be the VSNL of all of South Africa, including in fixed line. We will shortly be allowed to apply for a licence for cellular services.

We will be the second network operator, we'll be one of six or seven cellular operators, but we will be probably amongst the larger telephone providers with a network. Certainly in the data area we will be the largest.

As a group going into other markets, into these other cultures—does it function smoothly?

We've really not had too much of a problem. Korea perhaps has been one that's been culturally the most different. We've had surprisingly little trouble. We were welcomed in a very heartening manner, oddly enough for reasons unwarranted for us because we're the Tatas.

We were welcomed in Korea against the Americans because of the Buddhist connections. The first day I had lunch with the workers in the canteen through interpreters. This was the common thread, as against the company going to a US or Christian company.

But in South Africa and Bangladesh, where we weren't expecting an Indian company to receive a great deal, we've received a good response.

So there have been no adjustment issues?

Somehow an Indian company comes across as being neutral. If we can continue to not do the typical American style takeover deal and pepper the company with our executives and our systems [we'll be fine].

It takes a little more time to do due diligence on the company and make sure that the chemistry is right and the people are converted. Once you've done that, what you want to do is to basically leave that company alone.

In the case of Daewoo, we had 26 per cent of their market share in Korea and we got the use of the Daewoo name, too. The market share is now 33 per cent or so.

Do you have a team that's on the look out for acquisitions or is it just tactical, opportunistic?

We look for them. We don't have a big M&A group—we have one centre and the person who's focused on this is Arun Gandhi, who we brought on to the board of Tata Sons. He's been focused on mergers and acquisitions for many years and has been a very useful and worthwhile addition because he's been in the Tyco deal.

What percentage of business now is overseas, including exports from here, and where do you see that in five years?

A little more than 20 per cent.

And in five years?

Assuming that India has a promising future, I would see more than 30–35 per cent coming from overseas. I really don't want to see us 60:40.

'THE FORTUNE IS INDEED AT THE BOTTOM OF THE PYRAMID'

The fastest growth, Tata Group Chairman **Ratan Tata** says, does indeed lie at the bottom of the pyramid and discusses his group's plans to get to it, including a fundamental re-look at how products/services are produced.

He expresses a bit of disappointment over how the telecom/media ventures have done, explains Sivasankaran's role in the group as well as his plans to now look for a successor. Excerpts from the concluding part of an interview with **T.N. Ninan** and **Palakunnathu G. Mathai.**

You seem to have adopted C K Prahalad's thesis that fortune lies at the bottom of the pyramid. That's the trend that we see when you focus on the Rs 1 lakh car, IndiOne hotel and the sub-Rs 10,000 air conditioner. Do you want to attack the Indian market through a different way than earlier?

In the hotel and car areas, we're going where the fastest growth is going to be—reaching the masses. We're going to expand our base rather than merely look at the five-star brand or at the higher end of automobiles.

We're going to go after growth not just by expanding our existing products but by creating products that will reach out to the lower-end of the pyramid.

I would imagine that the fastest-growing segment in the hotel business is going to be down there somewhere, not on top. So the low-end hotel—not the stripped down hotel, but one that provides all the amenities with no frills—is going to be a model that will grow.

We have only a small window because we're not doing anything that is proprietary to us. We'll get lots of copycats coming in. So we have to move at a rate so that we can own that space.

What volumes would you look at for the Rs 1 lakh-plus car?

Let me first tell you what the potential is. Leave growth figures out, take the snapshot today—we sell 5 million two-wheelers and about 600,000 low-end cars.

You can position a product well below the conventional car, slightly below the used small car and into the motorcycle range, for families that ride three or four on a scooter—the 2CV Citroen or Deux Chevaux approach.

Today, the opportunity to do something like that by using plastics, smaller engines, superior packaging is far, far greater. We hope we can give the public the car that probably has 80–90 per cent of the inner space of the Indica, rear engine, not a stripped down car, not a motorcycle with four wheels.

The advantage is that you start from scratch. So you really look at what you can do. We wanted to be able to manufacture this on a low-cost assembly base and we'd like to develop the manufacturing modules along with the car.

We would produce all the high volume cars and kits ourselves. So, in effect only the assembly will be done outside. What we need is low-cost assembly akin to a CKD or an SKU kind of operation here.

This has not been done in the automobile industry anywhere.

The automobile industry has always looked at scale not only in components but also in assembly. So we've got to break that paradigm. You're amortising all that cost and all the robotics and everything else.

You do enough to ensure that you've got consistent quality and you can work that into the design. For instance, you have 80–90 robots welding a car. So maybe you can develop a process that doesn't require welding but uses adhesives and so on.

You said somewhere that you wish you were 10 years younger because the opportunities now are so exciting. Is there a temptation to stay on beyond your tenure?

That is a difficult question to answer. On the one hand, you obviously want to finish what you've started.

By finish I mean that you've just started thinking about a low-end car and you want to do it, and you're involved in seeing the hotel business grow and maybe a couple of other things, too.

At the same time, selfishly, I want to leave when I can still walk and play golf and do the things I want to do, rather than being semi-mobile. I've seen a little bit of that and I don't want to follow that. It is a bit of a dilemma.

Because you've made no apparent moves for a succession.

I will do that.

But you haven't done it yet. It's less than three years since you stepped down as executive chairman.

Two years.

Are you not leaving it late?

There are different views on that. You can anoint someone early and then have the organisation battle that person, or you can be watching and grooming [someone] and that happens all over the world.

People are even brought in from outside in several US companies overnight. So there will be a time period and I hope there will be a smooth transition.

You don't expect a change in the time frame?

That's not for me to say. I set the criteria at that time and I would like that to stay.

Regarding telecom, we're told you're not happy with how it's gone so far.

I don't know who told you that. Telecom takes a lot of investment. It takes in many ways a different mindset to what we have in many of our companies.

Let me elaborate because on the one hand, it's a hi-tech business in terms of technology and on the other, it is like soap in terms of distribution and sales and marketing.

It's almost like a fast-moving consumer goods company on the one side and a technically oriented company on the other. You've got to go through that transition, make the right decisions technologically, and transition that into an everyday product.

We have emerged as another all-India telecom company, but we have lost time and we have not gained that critical mass as fast as we might have.

Are you disappointed with the Star DTH venture. It hasn't really moved forward.

Yes, it has not moved. We are an open society and yet there are vested interests that don't want it open.

Is there an issue where effective control would be with your partner?

No. To say that we would have nothing to do with it would not be true because we have always been keen to have it be a company that in many ways is Indian. The way we saw it we would be developing Indian content.

Would you be getting into content itself?

Whether we farm out or do it ourselves (that is, through the joint venture), the fact is that it would be Indian content. It would not just be a grafting of what Sky or Star did abroad.

I thought you stayed away from the media as an industry.

From the print media, yes.

But not electronic?

This would be more on the lines of entertainment. DTH is more on the lines of entertainment.

But it doesn't stop you from doing news?

It doesn't stop us from doing news. In fact, I think you'd be crazy not to have a news element.

So this means a major move into the media, entertainment and news?

Yes. [Mr Tata later clarified that the group was not entering the media industry and that any group initiatives in this connection would be confined to the group's joint DTH venture with the Star group.]

So it's not just carriage and not just a tie-in with telecom at some stage?

No. It could have a tie-in with telecom in the sense that we are looking at somehow carrying video into the home. There are three ways to do it: wirelessly, through cable operators and through the telephone line.

Pallonji Mistry stepped down from the board of Tata Sons. There's been no replacement so far for him.

Mr Mistry has no right of nomination. If there were a member of the Mistry family that comes on the board, it would be to represent the shareholding—if we chose to make that happen.

Mr Mistry himself came on the board, we recognised him as the largest shareholder (of Tata Sons). We may take that view again in the future. So there is no issue of replacing him and there's no fixed number for the board. We may replace him or add more people who may not be from his family.

On Indian Hotels, there has been interest in acquiring the Raffles group. Have these talks fallen through?

Today there are no active talks.

There is no forward movement in hotels acquisitions overseas.

We are in dialogue in several cases. As you know, we have a management contract in Mauritius, we run an operation in the Seychelles, we are looking at South Africa, Europe and the US and we want to be in those countries. So we are scouting, we are exploring and we are in dialogue where opportunities exist.

The last time we met you, you had discussed the issue of integrating the group's IT companies. Now that the TCS IPO is over, does that intention remain?

The intention is still the same.

What is C Sivasankaran's role in the group?

He has been someone who has known the telecom industry and has helped us enormously in terms of defining some of the areas. We had a gap in terms of how we address the purchase of capital equipment.

He has saved us enormous amounts of money in that sense. In the process, he's been someone I've come to consider a friend and who I believe has helped us in terms of gross savings more than anyone else I have seen in the group.

Is he completely outside your corporate structure?

He would like to leave it that way and that's fine by me, too.

There's no intention of formalising the relationship with the group?

No, there has been no intention of doing that. Nor does he want that. We've had some convergence of views, he has been in the telecom business. Our gain from him has been quite substantial and I am quite happy to acknowledge that publicly.

Are you still shooting for a doubling of profits every three or four years?

No, we set that as a task and have achieved that. Whether we want to do it again or want to do something different is something we will decide. That's what I meant when I said that times have changed; you can't be doing the same thing again and again.

If you were to look five years into the future, what headline changes do you think will take place?

I would hope that some of our plans mature into bigger businesses. I would imagine that as a group we would be much more prominent in the IT and communications area than we are today, and that we have some international scale in some of our businesses and that we'd have the same value system and ethics as we do today.

I hope the fabric of the country allows us to do so.

Originally published as a two-part interview with Ratan Tata by T.N. Ninan and P.G. Mathai, 'We've Done Well without Compromising on Ethics', 14 March 2005, and 'The Fortune is Indeed at the Bottom of the Pyramid', 15 March 2005, *Business Standard*.

40

Taking India to the World
Acquiring Companies Overseas

Kumar Mangalam Birla

Another large group which epitomizes the new face of confidence of the private sector is the Aditya Vikram Birla (AVB) Group, led by Kumar Mangalam Birla since 1995. A US$ 29.2 billion conglomerate with global assets in excess of US$ 22 billion (2010), the AVB Group earns over 60 per cent of its revenue overseas, with operations in 25 countries, and employs a workforce of 130,000. While its core interest remains commodity business with its flagship companies, Hindalco, Grasim, Indian Rayon, and Indo-Gulf, it has recently forayed into information technology, information technology-enabled services, telecommunications, financial services (insurance, broking), apparel, and retail (supermarts, hypermarts). Birla has led a string of 12 acquisitions such as Novelis in Canada (which was the largest Indian investment in North America), Mount Gordon and Nifty copper mines in Australia, and Spice Communications, Ultra Tech, Indal, Madura Garments, and PSI Data Systems in India.* He has also professionalized the group, which for long placed loyalty over competence, thus leading it on to the path of managerial capitalism.

In a forthright manner, Birla comments on Indian business as it aspires to become a global superpower. He reflects on the reasons for this 'intense M&A activity', the benefits

* Also see Kumar Mangalam Birla, 'Bringing People Together', *Outlook Business*, 23 August 2008; 'The Birla Interview', *Economic Times*, Mumbai, 20 May 2009; 'The Kumar Birla Interview', *Economic Times*, Mumbai, 7 March 2008; and 'The Organization Man', *Business Today*, 17 July 2005. The group is an acknowledged world leader in viscose staple fiber, the world's ninth largest producer of cement and fifth largest of carbon black, Asia's largest integrated aluminum producer, and the world's fastest growing copper company. On one of the Group's key companies—Hindalco, see Nirmalya Kumar, Pradipta K. Mohapatra, and Suj Chandrasekhar, *India's Global Powerhouses: How They are Taking On the World* (Harvard, Harvard Business Press, 2009), pp. 107–10.

of such acquisitions, and the challenges companies face. He admits that though his own group has a global presence, encompassing Southeast Asia, Egypt, China, Canada, Australia, United States, United Kingdom, Germany, and Hungary, it has yet to emerge as a 'top of the mind brand'. Though the age of the Indian multinational may have arrived, Birla confesses that India Inc. still has a long way to go.

India Inc is already spreading its wings abroad. Now deals will happen across a broad spectrum of industries and in dispersed geographies. Even the profile of the companies will change—mid-size and small firms too will go global.

India today is in the mainstream of global consciousness. There is a new-found sense of self-assuredness. The entrepreneurship and dynamism its corporate houses have shown over the last five years have been and continue to be quite remarkable.

India has morphed well in the socio-economic dimensions and it boasts of a robust economic growth rate. Its demographic advantage is universally recognised. The rich-poor divide is narrowing. Many Indian companies are now globally benchmarkable. So there is every reason for us to be on a high. Small wonder then that India commands a new-found respect in the global arena.

The acquisitive appetite that companies have displayed signals the emergence of a new India. Until recently global multinationals had been planting their flags here. Now, the scenario is changing as increasingly domestic business houses have begun acquiring companies overseas. This has secured a niche for Indian business in the global economy and I believe it can only keep growing in significance. I believe the value of Indian cross-border deals between January and October 2006 is estimated at $23 billion, compared to $7.8 billion during the corresponding period of 2005—almost a two-fold rise. The average deal size also grew, from $32 million in 2005 to $47 million in the first half of 2006. A Grant Thornton India survey has very significant pointers. Of the 200 companies surveyed by it, 162 (that is nearly 81%) said they were exploring the M&A option to grow. Of these 162, only 60 had actually undertaken the M&A route in the past. This clearly signals intense M&A activity going forward.

Tata Steel, Infosys, Tata Consultancy Services, Wipro, Bharat Forge, Ranbaxy and, of course, we, at the Aditya Birla Group, have bought companies overseas or set up service organisations.

Undoubtedly, Indian companies are going to become much more global in the coming years. They seem all set to sign increasingly bigger deals, in India and overseas. More important, the deals will happen across a broader spectrum of industries and in more dispersed geographies. Significantly, the profile of players will also change—it won't be just the larger companies involved in M&As, but mid-size and small companies as well.

REFORMS PERFORM

The spurt in India's M&A is the outcome of a number of converging factors. We have been fortunate to have had a political system that backed the bold initiatives integral to change and reform. Successive governments have been equally committed to the continuity and consistency of reform policy. The government has made financing easier over the past few years so that Indian companies have the resources for acquisitions. The reforms to capital markets such as funding foreign direct investment through the external commercial borrowing route, and the removal of regulatory limits to debt that companies can raise, have facilitated bold acquisitions across sectors. Second, the far higher valuations of Indian stocks compared to the stocks of overseas companies—together with a stronger rupee—give Indian entrepreneurs a strong 'currency' to carry out acquisitions, even as acquisitions often are funded by cash and debt through offshore special purpose vehicles.

A larger global presence entails potentially huge benefits. Global market access, state-of-the-art technology, scale and size then become a given. Take, for instance, our proposed acquisition of Novelis. While a landmark deal for Hindalco and our group, it is in line with our long-term strategy of expanding the global presence across various businesses and is consistent with our vision of "Taking India to the World." This will establish a global, integrated aluminium producer with low-cost alumina and aluminium production facilities melded with high-end aluminium rolled product capabilities. The Novelis deal will give us immediate scale and a global footprint. We were attracted to Novelis by its sheer size, scale, and cutting-edge technology, which would have taken us over five years to build—a luxury we can ill-afford. In aluminium, one needs to invest in downstream to go up the value chain. India does not offer suitable downstream investment opportunities of a global scale.

INDIAN MULTINATIONALS

While the age of the Indian multinational is here, we in India Inc have a long way to go. We have to work constantly to open our organisation's windows to the winds of new ideas and a multi-ethnic workforce. It is relatively simpler to address cross-border issues pertaining to technology, finance, markets and products but extremely difficult to cope with challenges relating to the human dimension. Being a true-blue multinational is only partly about geographic spread. It is more about a mindset that wants to leverage resources seamlessly, across geographic boundaries. It is a mindset that is eager to build unique capabilities to transcend the barriers of language and cultures to create value. It's about being global in attitudes without letting go of your roots.

A major challenge relates to establishing brand equity. I believe Indian companies will take some time to move up the ladder of brand recognition. I say this based on our experience, where in some countries our group has a high brand equity. In the 1960s, when my father, fettered by the Licence Raj, looked beyond the Indian shores, it was truly a visionary act. We take great pride in the fact of our group being the first truly Indian MNC, having established major companies in the South East Asia. But in this region, it has taken us years of sustained performance—following best employment practices and being a good corporate citizen—to earn brand recognition.

Let me give you an example of how we built our brand in Canada. We acquired a pulp mill that had been closed. We had to convince diverse constituencies, ranging from the union to the provincial government and politicians. This took long, but our candour, sincerity and commitment paid off. Today, many employees in the mill feel that they are better off as part of an Indian MNC rather than with a local company that presided over its closure.

As I look ahead, I believe the war for talent will intensify and that could become a major speed-breaker. There is acute competition, rather, a scramble for inducting and retaining people with the competencies apposite for a globalising corporation. When a company goes global, its internal demography transforms into a socio-cultural potpourri. There is an inherent instability. Corporations that embark on this growth trajectory will face churn and uncertainty amidst change. On such a journey, success will come to those corporations in which the leadership is alchemical and values-driven.

Originally published as Kumar Mangalam Birla, 'New Frontiers, New Thinking', *Outlook Business*, 12 April 2007.

41

'India Inc'

The New Face of Business—Infosys

N.R. Narayana Murthy

One of the most spectacular success stories of the impact of economic reforms on the private sector is that of information technology (IT) and allied industries. An ignored sector with little domestic demand, hindered by the license-permit raj, difficulties of importing equipment (due to high tariffs), and financial limitations, the sector has undergone a huge transformation since liberalization. Although its origins go back to the formation of Tata Consultancy Services (TCS) in 1969, it is a success story of the 1990s when growth rates have averaged from 26 per cent to 106 per cent a year.* With increasing demand for software services from the developed world, a number of important players entered the field such as Wipro, founded by Azim Hashim Premji, Hindustan Computers Limited, and Tech Mahindra Limited, but TCS still remains the largest IT services exporter.† There has been no looking back since the 1990s. Low-end services have now been replaced by high-end outsourcing, ranging from R&D to business transformation services to developing software for next-generation cockpits, designing part of the wing of the double-decker A380 and Boeing's much awaited 787 Dreamliner and sophisticated pharmaceutical research including entire phases of drug development.‡

* 'India's High-end and Sheepish Capitalism', *New York Times*, 16 December 1999, available online at http://www.nytimes.com/1999/12/16/world/india-s-high-tech-and-sheepish-capitalism.html?scp=4&sq=narayana%20murthy%20&st=cse&pagewanted=1, last accessed on 14 January 2010.

† Some of these have been looked at in Dwijendra Tripathi and Jyoti Jumani, *Concise Oxford History of Indian Business* (New Delhi, Oxford University Press, 2007), pp. 210–32.

‡ Such has been the rise of the sector that companies are outsourcing lower-level outsourcing and opening offices in developing countries. On this, see 'Outsourcing Works, So India is Exporting Jobs', *New York Times*, 25 September

Perhaps the most engaging of these success sagas is that of N. R. Narayana Murthy and Infosys Technologies, Bangalore, the 'bellwether of Indian software services'. Founded in 1982 by seven professionals with an investment of merely US$ 1,000, Infosys grew by 2008 to a US$ 4 billion company.[§] Yet, its most important hallmark is not its financial success but the fact that it represents corporate India at its best via its pioneering practices like offering stock options to employees, opening books to independent auditors, moving away from personal/familial management practices, and contributing liberally to philanthropic causes, which represent a major change in Indian business culture. Murthy himself has become something of an iconic figure and an inspiration to professionals seeking an entrepreneurial path.[¶]

In this candid interview, Murthy talks about the milestones in his life and career, dreams as a student, experience at IIT Kanpur, first job as a systems analyst at the Indian Institute of Management Ahmedabad, leftist inclinations, the genesis of Infosys, its early challenges, impact of the 1991 reforms, and reflections on the software sector. He also explains his idea of 'compassionate capitalism' and, in characteristic Murthy approach, asserts that 'the power of money is the power to give'.

At 53, N.R. Narayana Murthy, chairman and CEO, Infosys Technologies (1998–99 sales: Rs 513 crore), heads India's most successful Silicon Valley style start-up. Established in 1981 by seven professionals who pooled in their savings of Rs 10,000 (borrowed from their wives), Infosys has set all kinds of records. It was the first company to institute a company-wide, performance-based Employee Stock Option Plan that cut right across the hierarchy. This year, it was the first India-registered company to list on an American stock exchange (NASDAQ).

2007, available online at http://www.nytimes.com/2007/09/25/business/worldbusiness/25outsource.html, last accessed on 14 January 2010. Also see 'In India: Outsourcing Moves to the Top Floor', *New York Times*, 3 April 2007, available online at http://www.nytimes.com/2007/04/03/business/worldbusiness/03iht-rupee.1.5125157.html?scp=17&sq=narayana%20murthy&st=cse, last accessed on 14 January 2010.

§ Two-thirds of its clients are in the US and includes corporates like Reebok, Visa, Boeing, Cisco Systems, and New York Life.

¶ Infosys initially focused on the demands of the international market. Its 'body shopping' strategy capitalized on India's huge repository of highly-trained English-speaking computer engineers. It entailed transferring Indian talent to client sites outside for software coding and development work. Exploiting the wage differentials between IT workers in India and their counterparts in the US, this was bound to be a successful financial strategy. Since 1987, however, offices have been set up in Boston and elsewhere to build the US client base. As multinationals began to move low-end maintenance and systems migration projects to India, and as high-end services were offered by Infosys, its client base has expanded to include 500 Forbes Global 2000 companies. On this, see Nirmalya Kumar, Pradipta K. Mohapatra, and Suj Chandrasekhar, *India's Global Powerhouses: How They are Taking On the World* (Harvard, Harvard Business Press, 2009), pp. 65–82. Also see Kavita Abraham and Sumantra Ghoshal, 'Infosys Technologies Limited: Going Global', in Sumantra Ghoshal, Gita Piramal, and Sudeep Budhiraja (compiled), *World Class in India: A Casebook of Companies in Transformation* (New Delhi, Penguin, 2001), pp. 618–39 and Tarun Khanna, *Billions of Entrepreneurs: How China and India are Reshaping Their Futures and Yours* (Boston, Mass, Harvard Business School Press, 2007), pp. 121–40.

On measures of transparency and corporate governance, Infosys is the epitome of the upright corporate citizen.

To Murthy goes the credit for first having the vision to see the opportunity in software, pick the right team and more significantly keep it together. The Infosys success is striking since all of its founders come from middle class backgrounds, had no backing of any business house but simply leveraged their brainpower and sweat equity. This is a model for the new generation of Indian enterprises in the coming millennium.

The fifth born of eight children, Murthy's father was a modest school teacher in Mysore who could not afford to send his son to IIT. Today, his 7.7% stake in Infosys makes Murthy a very wealthy man, with an estimated networth of Rs 2,500 crore. Yet he continues to cling to his roots, staying in a house in the middle class area of Jayanagar in Bangalore with his engineer wife Sudha and their two children, Akshata and Rohan. He was interviewed by Naazneen Karmali in Bangalore.

What made you initially choose engineering as a career?

My uncle was a civil servant and my father was very keen that I take that up as a career but somehow it didn't appeal to me. Those were the days when engineering was considered the in thing along with medicine. People didn't think that being an economist or a social scientist could be a productive career.

I had got admission to the IIT by passing the entrance exam with a fairly high rank and a scholarship. But the scholarship was to be disbursed at the end of the year. I remember talking to my father who said that there was no way he could afford to pay since he was earning Rs 250 per month. He said: If you're smart you can go to any college and be able to do something worthwhile. So I joined the local engineering college.

Did you have any role models who inspired you in your career?

Those days our role models were our teachers, both in school and university. They taught us to be inquisitive and articulate. You have to imagine a lower middle class family in a district headquarters in the '60s. My father used to tell us about the importance of putting public good before private good; mother would talk about sacrifice and truth. Beyond the basic values of life they didn't discuss too much about our careers.

My dream was to become a junior engineer in a hydroelectric power plant, Nehru's temples of modern India. What appealed to me was that they were non-polluting and set in pristine surroundings. Also, being an electrical engineer, there was this macho thing about building a big generator. But as a top-ranking student, people advised me to do my masters. It was not easy for people like us from a certain section of society that was considered already advantaged to get a job in Karnataka because of the reservation system and so I postponed the career decision for two years by doing my masters.

So you finally made it to IIT; what was that experience like?

IIT Kanpur was in its halcyon days. We had so many young professors who had done their Ph.Ds in the US and had come back to India. They were all in their 20s and 30s and full of energy and optimism. Also, under the Kanpur Indo-American programme, IIT had links with eight American universities like MIT, Berkeley, Purdue. What that meant was that when MIT got an IBM computer they sent one to Kanpur. We were introduced to computers—that wonder machine—and I was hooked.

What prompted you to opt for the unconventional job offer from IIM?

The phase I enjoyed the most was my time at IIM Ahmedabad where I took up a job as chief systems programmer. In those days there were few computer science graduates so we got five job offers each. I had offers from HMT, ECIL, TELCO, Air India. The salary in those places was much higher than at the IIM. But Prof. Krishnayya of IIM who came to IIT Kanpur talked to me for an hour about this great, modern mini-computer that he was going to install and that IIM would be the third business school in the world to install a time-sharing system after Harvard and Stanford. He also said that the atmosphere was collegial, we'd work 20 hours a day and learn a lot. Taking this job at a salary of Rs 800 a month was the best decision of my life.

I learnt so many things from Krishnayya. He is probably the person who influenced me the most. He taught us how important it is to aspire. We used to work 20 hours a day; go home at 3 a.m. sometimes and be back at 7 a.m. There was so much opportunity to learn. We designed and implemented a basic interpreter for ECIL. I learnt what it is to be an engineer. It isn't theory but application of the theory to solve problems and make a difference to society.

You worked overseas early in your career. What did you learn from your stint abroad?

My years in Paris were the most influential years of my life. I observed how in a western country even the socialists understood that wealth has to be first created before it can be distributed. That there could only be a few leaders to create wealth. And that it's the job of the government to create an environment where it's possible for people to create wealth. I realised that all this talk of socialism as practised in India was not meaningful. Our country treated communism as an 'ism' that was completely disassociated from the reality of the context. You cannot distribute poverty.

My father always told us that India had a lot to learn from the West. Also, he was a great fan of classical music. On Sundays, AIR used to play music for an hour. One day I asked him: why should I listen to this alien music? He said: What appeals to me is that in a symphony there are over 100 people, each of whom is a maestro, but they come together as a team to play according to a script under this conductor and produce something divine. They prove that one plus one can be more than two. It's a great example of teamwork.

What prompted your change of heart from being a staunch leftist?

After my Paris stay, I donated my earnings and with $450 in my pocket decided to return home overland. I came to Nis, a border town between the then Yugoslavia and Bulgaria, to take the Sofia Express. I struck up conversation with a girl in the compartment. After about 45 minutes the train stopped, the police took the girl away, ransacked my backpack, and put me in a room that had no mattress and a window 10 ft high. They kept me there for 60 hours after which they freed me saying that since I was from a friendly country they were letting me go. I felt that if this system treats friends this way then I did not want anything to do with it. This experience really shook me.

So the socialist in you became a committed capitalist?

I am a 100% free marketeer but I call myself a compassionate capitalist. While I'm very conservative in economic matters I'm very liberal about social matters. But I have no illusions about socialism. In a country like India, when we have to make capitalism an attractive alternative to people, it is extremely important for us to show tremendous compassion to the less fortunate. That doesn't mean that you should give jobs to people who don't deserve them or that you should make less profits but wherever you can show compassion you should.

What was the initial business plan of Infosys based on?

We were very clear that we wanted to be in India. There were many opportunities to settle outside but we wanted to create an institution in India. We knew there was hardly a market here, so we had to look at the export market from day one. At that time we had no idea how far it would go but our satisfaction comes mainly from working with bright, smart and hard-working young men and women.

Our first contract was from Databasics in New York. We had worked with them at Patni Computer Systems but they wanted to set up on their own software group in India. We convinced them that we could do as good a job. My colleagues left for the US to work on-site on the project. I stayed back to set up the infrastructure. We decided to import a computer so that we could add value from India.

How easy or difficult was it in those days to get a business like yours off the ground?

In those days it would take anywhere between 15 to 24 months to get a computer. We started in 1981 but our first computer was installed only in February 1984. Getting a loan was very difficult. We had worked out a time-sharing deal with MICO on the basis of which ANZ did a project report. But ANZ refused to give us the loan. Several other banks also turned us down. It was just by chance on a flight that I happened to be sitting next to K.S.N. Murthy of the Karnataka State Industrial Investment and Development Corporation, and we got our break. They redid the entire project report over 14 hours a day for a week and got it sanctioned in 15 days.

Right from day one our idea was to add value from India. To do that we needed certain factor conditions—computers, telephone lines. It took us a year to get a phone in Bangalore. There was a rule then that higher priority was to be given to retired government servants than businesses. We had a contract for $3,50,000; in addition we would get an IBM compatible machine on loan from our customer. All that they insisted was that we have a telephone so that they could contact us. The customer said: Look I understand that you are a group of competent people, but if you want to do it from India you must convince us that you can establish a line of communication. So, much against our desire, we had to ship the team out.

One has to go through all these experiences because it makes you understand your own frailties and also helps you develop respect for God. I've been extraordinarily lucky in life. I've received much more from society than I've given. I have many friends who are much smarter, much more accomplished, but somehow life has dealt me so many good cards that I can't ascribe it to anything other than God's grace.

Did you ever at any point feel like giving up?

There came a time in 1990 when we were floundering. We had offers to buy us out which my colleagues thought we should consider since we weren't making too much headway. We had a 4–5 hour discussion and I could feel the sense of despondency. So I pulled a fast one. I said guys don't worry, I'll buy you out. I know it's going to be tough in this country but I have no doubt that we'll see light. In minutes, they all said that we're with you. From now onwards we will never discuss the issue of closing down, getting tired or giving up. This marathon will be restarted.

Leadership is about making what seems impossible, possible; about changing the perception of what reality is. The reality in India is dirty roads, pollution, bad traffic, etc. Reality is what we make it; it is for us to change. If you give confidence to people they can achieve tremendous things. We have run this company as professionally as any other corporation in the world in terms of the principles of corporate governance, in not using corporate resources for personal conveniences, with respect for the professional.

What was the turning point for Infosys?

Chance favours the prepared mind. Just as we got determined to run the marathon with much greater gusto, liberalisation happened. If there is one company that symbolises all the good that came out of liberalisation, it is Infosys. It did four things for us: It enhanced the velocity of decision-making in government. It used to take 8 to 12 months to get a computer and the decision depended on the *babu* in Delhi. After 1991, it wasn't necessary to go to Delhi for approvals. We could walk across to the Software Technology Park here and get licenses in half a day for $1 million.

Second, equity became a viable financing option. Abolishing the Controller of Capital Issues had a multiplier effect on Indian enterprises. Prior to 1991, an officer was charged with the authority to decide at what premium a company went public and generally he always looked at the past. But capital markets are about the future. With low premiums, new entrepreneurs were reluctant to approach the capital markets. Once the company and lead manager were allowed to decide the premium, that set us free.

The government also liberalised the RBI rules for current account transactions. This meant that it was easy to travel abroad, establish offices and get consultants. Prior to 1991, we had to make an application to RBI which could take 5 to 10 days. Today I can travel in the next 6 hours. So it's a big change.

The most important thing is that government reversed the policy of foreign investment and allowed 100% ownership for MNCs. This is the main reason why Infosys came up. At the time many hi-tech companies came in and that created competition, not in the marketplace but for our human resources. People told me that Murthy your game is up, all your people will leave.

We could react in three ways: that this is our *karma*. We'll grow but not much—the Hindu philosophy. The second alternative was to lobby the government not to permit 100% ownership by MNCs. As president of NASSCOM, I could have kept all these guys out. But that was against my fundamental philosophy. The third was to find out why our youngsters would want to leave us and see if we could create those conditions in Infosys.

A successful corporation is one that introspects about internal transformation first before blaming the context, competition or external circumstances. Everyone bought into this philosophy and how we could bring about a fundamental transformation. We increased our salaries, we introduced a stock option plan so that our people would have much more money than any other Indian MNC. We also decided to make it a fun place to work because our assets walk out of the door every evening mentally and physically tired. We must make sure that they come back with a zest to work.

I am a firm believer that this country has a lot to learn from the West. We have to be open-minded, learn all the good things from them, and become stronger. For me a democracy is one where people put public good before private good; where responsibilities come before the rights.

What has kept the Infosys team together through all these years?

How do we stay together? We have unwritten rules. Everybody knows that if we want to work as a team we have to be transaction based. We start every transaction on a zero base. It is perfectly feasible for us to disagree on a transaction but we start the next transaction without any bias. Only an argument that has merit wins; it has nothing to do with hierarchy. Disagreeing is in the nature of things. When you bring a set of people who have respect for each others' competence in certain areas and you're transaction-oriented then it can work as it has in our case.

Our value system was like the British Constitution—it was all unwritten but extremely well practiced. If I were to have another opportunity to found another company, I would never ask for anyone else—these are truly remarkable people. Our value system is the true strength of Infosys. Besides, we have complementary skills. For example, I have an eye for detail and am comfortable with balance sheets and numbers. Then I can also get into the big picture. Nandan has a great ability to communicate and get himself connected to networks; his thinking is very strategic. Raghavan is a good people manager. Gopal is the best among us in technology. Shibulal and Dinesh are great on projects—so there's a complementarity of skills

What do you think was your best business decision?

Well, I think the best business decision was to introspect. We will press on the pedal. We will compete with the best of the multinationals in terms of retaining people, in terms of creating a brand equity. I think if you ask me what distinguishes Infosys from many other companies, it is the following: We have a very strong value system. In fact, when I address new hires the main thing I talk to them about is the value system. I tell them that even in the most fierce competitive situation they must never talk ill of customers. For heaven's sake don't short change anybody. Never ever violate any law of the land. It is better to lose a billion dollars than a good night's sleep. It is a true meritocracy. Raghavan's two children are engineers but they did not come here to ask for a job. They worked elsewhere before they went to the US to do their MBA. It is our responsibility to maintain the dignity of professionals here.

The second thing that's unique about Infosys is that we have accepted that speed and imagination are the only two context-invariant and time-invariant parameters for success. We don't think that we have any extraordinary legacy/strength that will carry us through the years. If we continue to innovate and to adapt then we will survive or else we'll disappear like dew on a summer morning. So there's a sense of paranoia and a certain fear that tomorrow we may not get food on the table if we don't satisfy our customers. We don't think anything is given to us. We're as good as our last quarterly result. If we don't do well in the next quarter, we'll be wiped out.

So far Infosys has grown organically. Are you looking at acquisitions as a future growth strategy?

Indeed. Adding 50% to $500 million is so much more difficult than adding 50% to $100 million. We are looking at acquisitions though we haven't identified any company yet. We want to look at a group/company that will add to the top line immediately but will also add to the bottomline in the medium term. Ideally it should be a small company, so that the cross-cultural issues can be handled more easily. Third, it must have an intellectual property right, either in the form of a methodology or a tool or processes which can be scaled up across Infosys for improving productivity in an emerging area like e-commerce, CRM etc. Finally, it could also be an aged technology product which has fallen on bad days but one that has a captive customer base. We can take that and enhance it technologically because we have the strength here to do that. And because there's a captive customer base it's much easier to sell. In any product, selling to the first 20 customers is the hardest.

Many feel that software companies are riding the boom in demand for y2k remedial work. What will be Infosys' life after y2k?

We will continue be a software services company because as technology changes rapidly, companies will want to leverage the internet for gaining competitive advantage. There will be tremendous opportunities for companies like Infosys to re-engineer existing systems, enhance functionality. But the fundamental strength will have to be learnability of experience. That is, how quickly you understand a new paradigm, a new technology and apply it to bring business benefit to customers. As long as learnability is alive and kicking at Infosys, we will have no problems about our future.

What are the big challenges facing you?

We have to put in systems, processes and tools to leverage technology to enhance the quality and productivity of our people. If today we take 100 hours to do something, then next year we should take 95 hours. Second, we must learn to manage growth. Inspite of recruiting larger numbers we should operate as a small, close knit, nimble company. That's the task of this management.

My vision is to make Infosys a globally respected software corporation, delivering best of breed solutions employing best in class professionals. That's different from an MNC which generally has subsidiaries in different countries, manufactures and sells there. As a corollary to that, I want it to be a place where people of different nationalities, religions and races will come together and compete in an environment of harmony and meritocracy. We believe that the local people are the best people in a given environment.

What are the challenges that the software sector faces in the new millennium?

One, we have to create corporate brand equity and product/services brand equity outside India. Indian industry's record of doing this has been pathetic. We have to become multicultural as local people are most effective in a local environment. And we have to learn to operate in a multicultural environment. We have few examples of Indian companies successfully doing so.

The most difficult challenge is recruiting, enabling, empowering and retaining the best and brightest talent. Enhancing per capita revenue productivity and moving up the value chain is the next big challenge because our costs are going up in India. Unless we do this, our success won't survive in the long run.

Will Infosys move up the value chain to become a product company in the future?

Our profitability and margins are the best in the services industry. Compare us with anybody on NASDAQ. The net income margin of Infosys is as good as any product company with the exception of Microsoft. It's not necessary to transform ourselves into a product company. In fact, in the Net economy it is services companies like Amazon.com, Priceline, eBay that have been growing. I'm not worried about traditional thinking that one must have a product. Infosys has enhanced its per capita productivity at least 10% in last five years. We are positioned to continue to be profitable.

Does government have a role to play in the IT sector? One view is that IT has grown because the government has been hands-off and now that an IT ministry has been set up it could pose a roadblock. What is your view?

The government has a role in creating a context for Indian entrepreneurs to succeed. They should concentrate on a policy regime and not a case-by-case syndrome. If decisions of corporations are not taken in boardrooms but in some government office then we won't go anywhere. Our company has been at the leading edge in pushing the policy regime. When we got listed on NASDAQ we required a policy regime. We need the cooperation of government as we move forward.

What opportunity does the growing power of the Internet pose for your company?

Internet is a great phenomenon particularly for a country like India because it has meant the death of distance. It has brought the anywhere, anytime paradigm. In a large resource scarce country like India, it is going to play a crucial role in ensuring that both business to business and business to customer benefits accrue much faster to both industry and consumers.

Thanks to the emergence of companies like Amazon, the traditional companies have realised that they have to shape up or ship out. So there's a tremendous emphasis on leveraging the power of the internet. We understand online transaction processing very well—we have done it for 18 years. E-commerce requires the ability to mount a robust and secure an online transaction processing engine, a certain application layer. The only difference is that you have to create a user-friendly web front end which skill we've developed in the last 2–3 years. We have a big advantage of over new e-commerce companies because the design and implementation of a high performance engine is something we've been doing for years. US corporations are in a hurry to get on to the e-commerce bandwagon and this is a clear opportunity for us.

The stockmarket seems to have discovered the worth of IT and Infotech stocks are seeing ever rising valuations. How do you react to this?

I tell my colleagues not to look at the stockmarket. What we should worry about day after day is to provide quality products on time, within budget to our customers. We must show transparency to investors, not violate any law of the land, and be in harmony with society. That's our main charter and we should stick to it. The stockmarket may or may not reward us even if we do that. This is ephemeral. We should not be too ecstatic about it today or get despondent if it falls tomorrow.

People say that the intellectual elite of India is now in Silicon Valley. What is your view?

Twenty years ago if someone had asked me whether Indians should go abroad, I would have said No. Today I have a completely different view. The need of the country today is to create a good brand equity of the country. That will be created by high quality Indians in some numbers establishing themselves abroad. I don't feel bad about it. If some people go we should cheer them, applaud them, make them feel welcome, and give them emotional support. Because they are doing a great job of enhancing the equity of India.

It's very easy to sit in India and say *Mera Bharat Mahaan*. Economic power is the only thing that counts in today's word. We have to create an image in the minds of foreigners that Indians can do it. In fact, that has already happened in the Valley. If an Indian is involved in a venture, then the venture capitalist will look positively at it. We have to convert this country so that we not only retain people here but also attract some of them back.

What advice would you give to the next generation of entrepreneurs?

Early to bed and early to rise and work like hell. Those people who have entrepreneurial strengths need to get a marketable idea and understand the window of opportunity for it. They have to bring together a team that has mutually exclusive, but collectively exhaustive skills and work out a value system. Entrepreneurship is about running a marathon, not a 100 metre dash.

What does money mean to you?

Beyond a certain level of comfort I think one's wealth should be seen as an opportunity to make a difference to society. My colleagues think so too. The power of money is the power to give. Obviously it will have to be done in a gradual manner over the years, but there's no doubt that a majority of what we have will be given to public causes.

What drives you then if not money?

There's a saying in America that the reward for winning a pinball game is to get a chance to play the next one. In most situations, the pleasure comes from the journey, not the destination.

Originally published as an interview with N.R. Narayana Murthy, 'Values First', *India 1999: A Symposium in the Year that Was, Seminar*, No. 485, 2000.

Contributors

C.V. Aiyar is an economist who has worked with Union Bank and EXIMBANK. His publications include with Thomas A. Timberg, 'Informal Credit Markets in India', in *Economic Development and Cultural Change* (1984).

C.A. Bayly is a historian and currently the Vere Harmsworth Professor of Imperial and Naval History at the University of Cambridge and the Director of the Centre of South Asian Studies, Cambridge. Some of his major works include *The Local Roots of Indian Politics: Allahabad, 1880–1920* (1975), *Rulers, Townsmen, and Bazaars: North Indian Society in the Age of British Expansion, 1770–1870* (1983), *Empire and Information: Intelligence Gathering and Social Communication in India, 1780–1870* (1996), *Origins of Nationality in South Asia: Patriotism and Ethical Government in the Making of Modern India* (2001), *The Birth of the Modern World, 1780–1914: Global Connections and Comparisons* (2004), and with Tim Harper, *Forgotten Wars: The End of Britain's Asian Empire* (2007).

Aditya Vikram Birla (1943–1995) was a well-known industrialist and founder of the Aditya Birla Group. He oversaw the diversification of his family's business into textiles, petrochemicals, and telecommunications, and expanded overseas to Thailand, Indonesia, Philippines, and Egypt. Under his leadership, the Birla group of companies became the largest producer of Viscose staple fibre and refiner of palm oil.

Basant Kumar Birla, industrialist, is Chairman of the B.K. Birla Group of Industries. His biography is entitled *A Rare Legacy: Memoirs of B.K. Birla* (1994).

Kumar Mangalam Birla is a well-known Indian industrialist and presently the Chairman of the Aditya Birla Group which includes companies like Grasim and Hindalco. He is also a member of the Prime Minister's Advisory Council on trade and industry. He has a publication entitled 'Power to the People', in Dinna Louise C. Dayao (ed.), *Asian Business Wisdom: Lessons from the Region's Best and Brightest Business Leaders* (2000).

Jaya Chaliha is a freelance writer. With Bunny Gupta she has published 'Barabazar', in Sukanta Chaudhuri (ed.), *Calcutta: The Living City*, Vol. II: The Present and Future (1990) and with Minakshie Das Gupta, they have co-authored *The Calcutta Cook Book: A Treasury of Over 200 Recipes from Pavement to Palace* (1995).

Suj Chandrasekhar is Principal at Strategic Insights Inc., a consulting firm in Washington, D.C. Together with Nirmalya Kumar and Pradipta K. Mohapatra, he has co-authored the book *India's Global Powerhouses: How They Are Taking On the World* (2009).

Ramkrishna Dalmia (1893–1978), an industrialist from Rohtak district, Punjab, belonged to a family of traders and started his career with trading and speculating. The profits made from speculative activity during the years of the world economic depression enabled Dalmia to break into industry in the 1930s. He had interests in cement, sugar, paper, and chemicals. He also controlled *The Times of India*. Dalmia wrote his reminiscences, *Some Notes and Reminiscences* (1948) and *A Short Sketch of the Beginnings of My Life and a Guide to Bliss* (1962).

Tarun Das served as Chief Mentor at the Confederation of Indian Industry (CII) till November 2009 and is now President of the Aspen Institute of India and on numerous company boards. In 2006 he was awarded the Padma Bhushan by the President of India. His writings include 'Industry: From Regulation to Liberalization', in Hiranmay Karlekar (ed.), *Independent India: The First Fifty Years* (1998), and with Colette Mathur and Frank-Jurgen Richter, *India Rising: Emergence of a New World Power* (2005).

Ashok V. Desai is an economist and Consultant Editor of the *Telegraph* and *Business Standard*. He has also served as Chief Consultant in India's Ministry of Finance during 1991–3. His publications include *Technology Absorption in Indian Industry* (1988), 'The Origins of Parsi Enterprise', in Rajat Kanta Ray (ed.), *Entrepreneurship and Industry in India, 1800–1947* (1992), *My Economic Affair* (1993), *The Economics and Politics of Transition to an Open Market Economy: India* (1999), and *India's Telecommunications Industry: History, Analysis, Diagnosis* (2006).

Christine Dobbin, historian, is presently a Visiting Fellow at the School of Culture, History & Language, College of Asia & the Pacific, Australian National University. Her interests lie in the Southeast Asian region and some of her notable publications include *Basic Documents in the Development of Modern India and Pakistan, 1835–1947* (1970), *Urban Leadership in Western India: Politics and Communities in Bombay City, 1840–1885* (1972), *Islamic Revivalism in a Changing Peasant Economy: Central Sumatra, 1784–1847* (1983), and *Asian Entrepreneurial Minorities: Conjoint Communities in the Making of the World Economy, 1570–1940* (1996).

Jagannath Dubashi is a business journalist and has co-authored (with T.N. Ninan) 'Dhirubhai Ambani: The Super Tycoon', *India Today*, 30 June 1985.

Sudipt Dutta, journalist, is the author of *Family Business in India* (1997).

Asghar Ali Engineer is a writer and activist, and presently heads the Institute of Islamic Studies and the Centre for Study of Society and Secularism, Mumbai. His writings include *The Bohras* (1980), an edited book *Bohras and Their Struggle for Reforms* (1986), 'Islam, Liberalism, Democracy', in S.M. Naseem and Khalid Nadvi (eds), *The Post-Colonial State and Social Transformation in India and Pakistan* (2002), and 'Islam and Secularism', in Ibrahim M. Abu Rabi (ed.), *The Blackwell Companion to Contemporary Islamic Thought* (2006).

Ashok S. Ganguly is an industry expert and currently the Chairman of Firstsource Solutions Ltd and ABP Pvt Ltd (Ananda Bazar Patrika Group). He currently serves as a member in the Prime Minister's Council on Trade and Industry and since 2009 is Member of Rajya Sabha. His publications include *Industry and Liberalization* (1994), with Prem K. Chadha and A. Lahiri (eds), *Strategic Manufacturing for Competitive Advantage* (1998), and *Business-Driven Research and Development: Managing Knowledge to Create Wealth* (1999).

Pieter Gorter is an independent researcher. His publications include *Small Industrialists, Big Ambitions: Economic and Political Networks on a Large Industrial Estate in West India* (1996) and 'Representation or Racket? Political Networks in an Industrial Estate in West India', in Philippe Cadène and Mark Holmström (eds), *Decentralized Production in India: Industrial Districts, Flexible Specialization, and Employment* (1998).

Omkar Goswami, an economist and business journalist, is Founder and Chairman of the Corporate and Economic Research Group (CERG) Advisory Private Limited and Editor of *Business India*. His publications include '*Sahibs*, *Babus*, and *Banias*: Changes in Industrial Control in Eastern India, 1918–50', in Rajat Kanta Ray (ed.), *Entrepreneurship and Industry in India, 1800–1947* (1992), 'Corporate Governance in India', in *Taking Action against Corruption in Asia and the Pacific: Proceedings of the Third Regional Anti-Corruption Conference* (2002), and 'Agriculture in Slump: The Peasant Economy of East and North Bengal in the 1930s', in G. Balachandran (ed.), *India and the World Economy, 1850–1950* (2003).

Maria Graham (1785–1842) was a British author and traveller. She was an influential figure in expanding the fields of women's writing in her time. Most recently in 2008, Graham was honoured by the Chilean government in recognition of her pioneering works depicting Chile as a young nation in the English language. Graham's travels are reflected in the following publications: *Journal of a Residence in India* (1813, 2nd edition), *Letters on India, with Etchings and a Map* (1814), *Three Months Passed in the Mountains East of Rome, during the Year 1819* (1820), *Journal of a Voyage to Brazil, and Residence there, during Part of the Years 1821, 1822, 1823* (1824), and *Journal of a Residence in Chile during the Year 1822, and a Voyage from Chile to Brazil in 1823* (1824).

Bunny Gupta is a freelance writer. Along with Jaya Chaliha, she has published 'Barabazar', in Sukanta Chaudhuri (ed.), *Calcutta: The Living City*, Vol. II: The Present and Future (1990) and with Minakshie Das Gupta, they have co-authored *The Calcutta Cook Book: A Treasury of Over 200 Recipes from Pavement to Palace* (1995).

R.K. Hazari, an industrial economist, headed the Hazari Committee under the Planning Commission, which investigated the nature of corporate governance of the 20 top business houses of the time. His publications include *The Structure of the Corporate Private Sector: A Study of Concentration, Ownership and Control* (1966), with Wolfgang Friedmann and S.D. Mehta, *Public International Development Financing in India: A Research Project of the Columbia University School of Law* (1968), and *Essays on Industrial Policy* (1986).

Jawaharilal Jain was a trader and writer based in Bara Bazaar, Calcutta. He published *Ramvilas Poddar: Jiwan Rekha aur Smritiyan* (1936).

L.C. Jain, economist, taught at the University of Allahabad and at the University of the Punjab, Lahore. He was also Secretary of the United Provinces Banking Inquiry Committee from 1929 to 1930. His publications include *Indigenous Banking in India* (1929) and *The Monetary Problems in India* (1933).

N.G. Jog is an author. His publications include *Churchill's Blind-Spot: India* (1944), with K.A. Abbas, *A Report to Gandhiji: A Survey of Indian and World Events during the 21 Months of Gandhiji's Incarceration* (1944), *Judge or Judas?* (1945), *In Freedom's Quest: A Biography of Netaji Subhas Chandra Bose* (1969), *Saga of Scindia: Struggle for the Revival of Indian Shipping and Shipbuilding [1919–1969]* (1969), *Lokamanya Bal Gangadhar Tilak* (1970), and with Sisir K. Bose, Alexander Werth, and S.A. Ayer (eds), *A Beacon across Asia: A Biography of Subhas Chandra Bose* (1973).

Jyoti Jumani is a freelance teacher, researcher, and writer. She has co-authored (with Dwijendra Tripathi) *The Concise Oxford History of Indian Business* (2007).

Medha M. Kudaisya, historian, is Associate Professor at the National University of Singapore. Her publications include *The Life and Times of G.D. Birla* (2003), co-edited with Ng Chin Keong, *Chinese and Indian Business: Historical Antecedents* (2009), and '"A Mighty Adventure": Institutionalising the Idea of Planning in Post-colonial India, 1947–60', in *Modern Asian Studies*, Vol. 43 (2009).

Nirmalya Kumar is presently Professor of Marketing and Co-Director of the Aditya Birla India Centre at London Business School. His publications include *Marketing as Strategy: Understanding the CEO's Agenda for Driving Growth and Innovation* (2004), with Jan-Benedict E.M. Steenkamp, *Private Label Strategy: How to Meet the Store Brand Challenge* (2007), and with James C. Anderson and James A. Narus, *Value Merchants: Demonstrating and Documenting Superior Value in Business*

Markets (2007). Together with Suj Chandrasekhar and Pradipta K. Mohapatra, he has co-authored the book, *India's Global Powerhouses: How They Are Taking On the World* (2009).

R.M. Lala is an author, editor, and publisher. He has served as the Director of Sir Dorabji Tata Trust and is Co-Founder and Chairman of the Centre for the Advancement of Philanthropy. His major publications include *Creation of Wealth: The Tata Story* (1981), *Beyond the Last Blue Mountain: A Life of J.R.D. Tata* (1992), *The Joy of Achievement: Conversations with J.R.D. Tata* (1995), and *The Creation of Wealth: The Tatas from the 19th to the 21st Century* (2004).

Claude Markovits, historian, is Director of Research at the National Centre for Scientific Research in Paris, France. His major publications include *Indian Business and Nationalist Politics, 1931–1939: The Indigenous Capitalist Class and the Rise of the Congress Party* (1985), *The Global World of Indian Merchants, 1750–1947: Traders of Sind from Bukhara to Panama* (2000), (ed.) *A History of Modern India, 1480–1950* (2002), with Jacques Pouchepadass and Sanjay Subrahmanyam (eds), *Society and Circulation: Mobile People and Itinerant Cultures in South Asia, 1750–1950* (2006), and *Merchants, Traders, Entrepreneurs: Indian Business in the Colonial Era* (2008).

P.G. Mathai is a writer and co-author (with T.N. Ninan) of 'We've Done Well without Compromising on Ethics', 14 March 2005, and 'The Fortune is Indeed at the Bottom of the Pyramid', 15 March 2005, *Business Standard*.

Makrand Mehta is a historian and Professor of History at Gujarat University, Ahmedabad. His publications include *The Ahmedabad Cotton Textile Industry: Genesis and Growth* (1982), (ed.) *Regional Roots of Indian Nationalism: Gujarat, Maharashtra, and Rajasthan* (1990), with Dwijendra Tripathi (eds), *Business Houses in Western India: A Study in Entrepreneurial Response, 1850–1956* (1990), *Indian Merchants and Entrepreneurs in Historical Perspective: With Special Reference to Shroffs of Gujarat, 17th to 19th Centuries* (1991), and most recently *History of International Trade and Custom Duties in Gujarat* (2009).

Minhaz Merchant is a biographer, editor, columnist, and publisher. He started his journalistic career with *The Times of India* and *India Today*. He has founded over a dozen magazines and is also the founder-managing editor of *Innovate*, a publication for U.S. policymakers and CEOs. His publications include the best-selling *Rajiv Gandhi: The End of a Dream* (1991) and *Aditya Vikram Birla: A Biography* (1997).

Balchand Modi, from Churu, was a Calcutta-based trader who was very active in community life. He wrote a number of books such as *Desh ke Itihas Main Marwari Jati ka Sthan* (1986), *Agarwal Itihas Parichay* (2006), and *Agarwal Jati ka Itihas* (2006).

Pradipta K. Mohapatra is the Co-Founder and Chairman of Executive & Business Coaching Foundation India Ltd. Together with Nirmalya Kumar and Suj Chandrasekhar, he has co-authored the book, *India's Global Powerhouses: How They Are Taking On the World* (2009).

Aditya Mukherjee, historian, is Professor of Contemporary Indian History at the Centre for Historical Studies, Jawaharlal Nehru University, New Delhi, and Director of the Jawaharlal Nehru Institute of Advanced Study. His publications include co-authored with Bipan Chandra et al., *India's Struggle for Independence* (1989), co-authored with Bipan Chandra et al., *India After Independence, 1947–2000* (2000), and *Imperialism, Nationalism and the Making of the Indian Capitalist Class 1927–1947* (2002).

Mridula Mukherjee, historian, is presently Professor of Modern History at the Centre for Historical Studies, Jawaharlal Nehru University, New Delhi, and Director of the Nehru Memorial Museum and Library. Her joint publications with Aditya Mukherjee include 'Imperialism and the Growth of Indian Capitalism in the Twentieth Century', *Economic and Political Weekly*, Vol. XXIII, No. 11 (1988) and 'Communalization of Education, The History Textbook Controversy: An Overview', *Mainstream*, Annual Number (2001), and with Bipan Chandra et al., *India After Independence, 1947–2000* (2000).

N.R. Narayana Murthy is a businessman, software engineer, and Founder of Infosys Technologies, India. He is presently the non-executive Chairman of Infosys and also serves on the boards of various organizations such as the DBS Bank of Singapore, the Reserve Bank of India, NDTV India, the European FMCG giant Unilever, and British Telecommunications. In 2000, he received the Padma Shri and in 2008, he became the recipient of the Padma Vibhushan as well as the Légion d'honneur—the highest civilian award by France. In 2009, his lectures were published in a book entitled *A Better India: A Better World* (2009).

Radhakrishna Nevatia was a trader based in Bara Bazaar, Calcutta. He was active in Marwari community life and was responsible for the establishment of a number of community organizations such as the Shri Barabazaar Kumarsabha Pustakalaya and the Barabazaar Yukak Sabha. He was also an important member of the Akhil Bharatvarshiya Agarwal Mahasabha and the Akhil Bharatvarshiya Marwari Sammelan. Alongside, he wrote a number of books such as *Bara Marwari Samaj ki Ahutiyan* (n.d.), (ed.) *Shri Ramdev Chokhany* (1950), and *Bazaar ke Karyakarta* (1982).

T.N. Ninan is a journalist and presently the Editorial Director and Chairman of Business Standard Ltd, which publishes *Business Standard*. He is former Editor of *The Economic Times* and had also been the Executive Editor of *India Today*. He is the recipient of the B.D. Goenka Award for excellence in journalism in 1992 and the Sachin Chaudhari Award for excellence in financial journalism in 1984. He is a well-known figure on national television as a commentator on current issues.

T. Postans (1808–1846) was a Captain in the Bombay Army who entered the Bombay Native Infantry from 1829 onwards and served in Sindh between 1839 and 1846. His two major publications reflect his personal experiences: *Hints to Cadets: With a Few Observations on the Military Service of the Honourable East-India Company* (1842) and *Personal Observations on Sindh: The Manners and Customs of Its Inhabitants, and Its Productive Capabilities* (1843).

Rajat Kanta Ray is a historian and presently the Vice-Chancellor of Visva Bharati University in West Bengal. His major recent publications include *Urban Roots of Indian Nationalism: Pressure Groups and Conflict of Interests in Calcutta City Politics, 1875–1939* (1979), *Industrialization in India: Growth and Conflict in the Private Corporate Sector, 1914–47* (1982), *Social Conflict and Political Unrest in Bengal 1875–1927* (1985), (ed.) *Mind, Body and Society: Life and Mentality in Colonial Bengal* (1996), *Exploring Emotional History: Gender, Mentality, and Literature in the Indian Awakening* (2001), and *The Felt Community: Commonality and Mentality before the Emergence of Indian Nationalism* (2007).

Tirthankar Roy, economic historian, is Reader in Economic History at the London School of Economics. His authored publications include *Artisans and Industrialization: Indian Weaving in the Twentieth Century* (1993), *Traditional Industry in the Economy of Colonial India* (1999), *The Economic History of India, 1857–1947* (2000), *Rethinking Economic Change in India: Labour and Livelihood* (2005), and *Company of Kinsmen: Community and Enterprise in South Asian History 1600–1950* (2010).

D.K. Taknet is a business historian based in Jaipur and presently Director of the Indian Institute of Marwari Entrepreneurship (IIME). His publications include *Industrial Entrepreneurship of Shekhawati Marwaris* (1986), *Marwari Samaj* (1989), *Marwari Samaj aur Brij Mohan Birla* (1993), *B.M. Birla: A Great Visionary* (1996), and *The Heritage of Indian Tea: The Past, the Present, and the Road Ahead* (2002).

Thomas A. Timberg is an economist who has published widely on South and Southeast Asia. Amongst his important works on India are 'A North Indian Firm as Seen through Its Business Records, 1860–1914: Tarachand Ghanshyamdas, a "Great" Marwari Firm', *Indian Economic and Social History Review*, Vol. I, No. 3 (1971), *The Marwaris: From Traders to Industrialists* (1978), 'Hiatus and Incubator: Indigenous Trade and Traders, 1837–1857', in Asiya Siddiqi (ed.), *Trade and Finance in Colonial India* (1995), 'Big and Free is Beautiful: India and China, the Past 40 Years and the Next', *Economic Development and Cultural Change* (1997), 'Two Discourses: Financial Liberalization Happened', *Economic and Political Weekly* (1997), and 'The Impact of Indian Economic Liberalization on U.S.–India Relations', *School of Advanced International Studies (SAIS) Review* (1998).

Dwijendra Tripathi is a business historian. He was the Kasturbhai Lalbhai Professor of Business History and Entrepreneurship at the Indian Institute of Management, Ahmedabad and is the founder Editor of *The Journal of Entrepreneurship*. His publications include *Dynamics of a Tradition: Kasturbhai Lalbhai and His Entrepreneurship* (1982), with Makrand Mehta, *Business Houses in Western India: A Study in Entrepreneurial Response, 1850–1956* (1990), an edited volume on *Business and Politics in India: A Historical Perspective* (1991), *The Oxford History of Indian Business* (2004), with Jyoti Jumani, *The Concise Oxford History of Indian Business* (2007), and 'Colonial Syndrome and Technology Choices in Indian Industry', in Medha M. Kudaisya and Ng Chin Keong (eds), *Chinese and Indian Business: Historical Antecedents* (2009).

Copyright Statement

Every effort has been made to trace the copyright holder of some of the pieces included in this volume. The publisher would be pleased to hear from the copyright owner so that proper acknowledgement can be made in future editions.

SECTION I: BAZAAR

- Chapter 1, Bazaar: 'Pulsating Heart' of the Indian Economy, Rajat Kanta Ray. Originally published in *The Indian Economic and Social History Review*, Vol. 25, No. 3, 1988, pp. 263–318. Copyright ©The Indian Economic and Social History Association, New Delhi, 1988. All rights reserved. Reproduced with the permission of the copyright holders and the publishers, Sage Publications India Pvt. Ltd, New Delhi.
- Chapter 3, Indigenous Credit Instruments and Systems, L.C. Jain. Originally published as *Indigenous Banking in India* (London, Macmillan and Co., Limited, 1929), pp. 70–92. Reproduced with permission of Palgrave Macmillan.
- Chapter 9, Speculative Profits during War Times, Ramkrishna Dalmia. Originally published as *Some Notes and Reminiscences* (Bombay, Times of India Press, 1948), pp. 11–17. Reproduced with permission of the author's family.
- Chapter 11, Contemporary Informal Credit Markets and Systems, Thomas A. Timberg and C.V. Aiyar. Originally published as 'Informal Credit Markets in India', *Economic Development and Cultural Change*, Vol. 33, No. 1, 1984, pp. 43–59. © 1984 by The University of Chicago. All rights reserved. Reproduced with permission of the University of Chicago Press.

SECTION II: MERCANTILE COMMUNITIES

- Chapter 12, Merchant Communities: Identities and Solidarities, C.A. Bayly. Originally published as 'Indian Merchants in a "Traditional" Setting: Benaras, 1780–1830', in Clive Dewey and A. Hopkins (eds), *The Imperial Impact : Studies in the Economic History of Africa and India* (London, The Athlone Press, University of London, 1978), pp. 171–93. Reproduced with permission of the author.

- Chapter 15, Marwaris: From 'Community' to 'Class', Dwijendra Tripathi. Originally published as 'From Community to Class: The Marwari in a Historical Perspective', in B.L. Bhadani and Dwijendra Tripathi (eds), *Facets of a Marwari Historian* (Jaipur, Publication Scheme, 1996), pp. 189–96. Reproduced with permission of the author.
- Chapter 16, Nattukottai Chettiars: Caste ad Business Organization, Christine Dobbin. Originally published as 'From Madras to Burma: The Nattukottai Chettiars and Development 1852–1939', in Christine Dobbin, *Asian Entrepreneurial Minorities: Conjoint Communities in the Making of the World Economy 1570–1940* (Surrey, Curzon Press, 1996), pp. 131–55. Reproduced with permission of the author.
- Chapter 17, The Bohras Today: Characteristics of Business Enterprise, Asghar Ali Engineer. Originally published as *The Bohras* (Delhi, Vikas Publishing House, 1980), pp. 145–7. Reproduced with permission of the author.

SECTION III: FAMILY AND FIRM

- Chapter 19, The Family Firm: A Microcosm, C.A. Bayly. Originally published as *Rulers, Townsmen and Bazaars: North Indian Society in the Age of British Expansion 1770–1870* (Cambridge, Cambridge University Press, 1983), pp. 375–93. Reproduced with permission of the author.
- Chapter 21, 'Family and Firm': Commercial Concerns and Social Mores, Basant Kumar Birla. Originally published as *A Rare Legacy: Memoirs of B.K. Birla* (Bombay, Image Incorporated, 1994), pp. 25–32. Reproduced with permission of the author.
- Chapter 23, Family Firms in Present-Day India, Sudipt Dutta. Originally published as *Family Business in India* (New Delhi, Response Books, 1997), pp. 124–37. Reproduced with permission of the publisher.

SECTION IV: RISE OF INDIAN INDUSTRY

- Chapter 26, 'Modern Ideas' and Industrial Initiatives: The Tatas of Bombay, Dwijendra Tripathi and Makrand Mehta. Originally published as 'The Tatas', in *Business Houses in Western India: A Study in Entrepreneurial History, 1850–1956* (Delhi, Manohar, 1990), pp. 55–72. Reproduced with permission of the author.
- Chapter 27, Challenging European Monopolies: The Story of Scindia Shipping, N.G. Jog. Originally published as *Saga of Scindia: Struggle for the Survival of Indian Shipping and Shipbuilding* (Bombay, The Scindia Steam Navigation Co., Ltd., 1969), pp. 17–24. Reproduced with permission of the publisher.
- Chapter 30, Imperialism and Capitalism, Aditya Mukherjee and Mridula Mukherjee. Originally published as 'Imperialism and Growth of Indian Capitalism in Twentieth Century', *Economic and*

Political Weekly, Vol. XXIII, No. 11, 12 March 1988, pp. 531–46. Reproduced with permission of the author.

- Chapter 31, Industry after Independence: Initial Challenges and Dilemmas, Ashok S. Ganguly. Originally published as *Industry and Liberalization* (Bombay, Allied Publishers, 1994), pp. 173–76. Reproduced with permission of the author.
- Chapter 32, The Restrictive 1960s and 1970s: Critiquing Government Policies, Aditya Vikram Birla. This chapter comprises of two speeches: (i) the S. Anantharamkrishnan Memorial Lecture, 'My Experience of Indian Management and Present Business Environment', October 1990, *Aditya Vikram Birla Papers*, Mumbai, and (ii) speech at the Indo-American Society, 27 June 1978, *Aditya Birla Papers*, Mumbai. Reproduced with permission of the author.
- Chapter 33, The Beginnings of Overseas Expansion, Minhaz Merchant. Originally published as *Aditya Vikram Birla: A Biography* (Delhi, Viking, 1997), pp. 4–11, 13–14, 153–9. Reproduced with permission of the author.
- Chapter 34, 'Harnessing the Capital Market: The Ambani Story, T.N. Ninan and Jagannath Dubashi. Originally published as 'Dhirubhai Ambani: The Super Tycoon', *India Today*, 30 June 1985, pp. 72–80. Reproduced with permission of T.N. Ninan.

SECTION V: BUSINESS IN THE POST-REFORMS ERA

- Chapter 37, Challenges and Opportunities of Economic Liberalization: Corporate Restructuring, Nirmalya Kumar, Pradipta K. Mohapatra, and Suj Chandrasekhar. Originally published as *India's Global Powerhouses: How They Are Taking On the World* (Boston, Harvard Business Press, 2009), pp. 36–49. © 2009 Nirmalya Kumar, Pradipta K. Mohapatra, and Suj Chandrasekhar. All rights reserved. Reproduced with permission of the author and publisher.
- Chapter 38, Challenges and Opportunities of Economic Liberalization: The Tata Group, R.M. Lala. Originally published as R.M. Lala, *The Creation of Wealth: The Tatas from the 19th to the 21st Century* (New Delhi, Penguin, 2004), pp. 216–20. Reproduced with permission of the author.
- Chapter 39, The Coming of Age of Indian Business: Global Aspirations, T.N. Ninan and P.G. Mathai. Originally published as a two-part interview with Ratan Tata, 'We've Done Well without Compromising on Ethics', 14 March 2005, and 'The Fortune is Indeed at the Bottom of the Pyramid', 15 March 2005, *Business Standard*. Reproduced with permission of T.N. Ninan.
- Chapter 40, Taking India to the World: Acquiring Companies Overseas, Kumar Mangalam Birla. Originally published as 'New Frontiers, New Thinking', *Outlook Business*, 12 April 2007. Reproduced with permission of the author.
- Chapter 41, 'India Inc': The New Face of Business—Infosys. Originally published as an interview with N.R. Narayana Murthy, 'Values First', *India 1999: A Symposium in the Year that Was, Seminar*, No. 485, 2000. Reproduced with permission of *Seminar*.

Index